Implementing SAP® Governance, Risk, and Compliance

SAP PRESS

SAP PRESS is a joint initiative of SAP and Galileo Press. The know-how offered by SAP specialists combined with the expertise of the Galileo Press publishing house offers the reader expert books in the field. SAP PRESS features first-hand information and expert advice, and provides useful skills for professional decision-making.

SAP PRESS offers a variety of books on technical and business-related topics for the SAP user. For further information, please visit our website: *www.sap-press.com*.

Asokkumar Christian, D. Rajen Iyer, and Atul Sudhalkar

Implementing SAP® Governance, Risk, and Compliance

Galileo Press

Bonn • Boston

Galileo Press is named after the Italian physicist, mathematician, and philosopher Galileo Galilei (1564—1642). He is known as one of the founders of modern science and an advocate of our contemporary, heliocentric worldview. His words *Eppur si muove* (And yet it moves) have become legendary. The Galileo Press logo depicts Jupiter orbited by the four Galilean moons, which were discovered by Galileo in 1610.

Editor Katy Spencer
Copyeditor Julie McNamee
Cover Design Graham Geary
Photo Credit iStockphoto.com/1028594/© tapuzina
Layout Design Vera Brauner
Production Kelly O'Callaghan
Typesetting SatzPro, Krefeld (Germany)
Printed and bound in the United States of America, on paper from sustainable sources

ISBN 978-1-59229-881-5

1st edition 2014

Library of Congress Cataloging-in-Publication Data
Christian, Asokkumar.
Implementing SAP governance, risk, and compliance / Asokkumar Christian, D. Rajen Iyer, and Atul Sudhalkar. -- 1st edition.
pages cm
ISBN 978-1-59229-881-5 (print) -- ISBN 1-59229-881-8 (print) -- ISBN 978-1-59229-882-2 (e-book) – ISBN 978-1-59229-883-9 (print and e-book) 1. SAP ERP. 2. Business--Computer programs.
3. Business--Data processing.
4. Management information systems. I. Iyer, Rajen. II. Sudhalkar, Atul. III. Title.
HF5548.4.R2.C47 2014
650.0285'53--dc23
2013040749

Contents at a Glance

Dear Reader,

Navigating the changing tides of corporate compliance and governance can be as temperamental as the wild waters of the ocean itself. Developing a comprehensive GRC strategy that is both reactive and adaptive to the changing market is hardly an easy course to plot. Set your course and get ready to explore the best approach to implementing the GRC suite.

Join our expert author team as they guide you through the implementation process of the SAP Governance, Risk, and Compliance module and its components—Access Control, Process Control, Global Trade Services, and Risk Management. Learn to develop effective business solutions, aggregate data, and save time with SAP's GRC tool. I'm confident that with these authors at the helm, you will find working with SAP's GRC suite to be smooth sailing. If swells or riptides start to shake your boat, you will benefit from the practical guidance contained within.

As always, we appreciate your business and welcome your feedback. What did you think about *Implementing SAP Governance, Risk and Compliance*? Your comments and suggestions are the most useful tools to help us improve our books for you, the reader. We encourage you to visit our website at *www.sap-press.com* and share your feedback.

Katy Spencer
Editor, SAP PRESS

Galileo Press
Boston, MA

katy.spencer@galileo-press.com
www.sap-press.com

Contents

Preface

Risk is ever changing for today's global companies, so an enterprise's risk management strategy needs to be adaptive and flexible but still meet strict regulatory requirements. Done properly, an effectively implemented governance, risk, and compliance (GRC) strategy creates a central nervous system for a company, quickly identifying not only risk but also competitive opportunities. GRC, as both a business process and the software that support it is hardly new, but its importance for corporations has been increasing as regulations are rewritten, compliance strictly enforced, and enterprise management turns a critical eye on corporate GRC strategies. The pain points for the implementation of a GRC software solution are challenging and certainly not limited to SAP. These pain points include the proper optimization of the GRC system, adaptability to frequent changing regulations, and the alignment of business processes and people to a corporate GRC strategy. With regulations changing, on an almost daily basis, companies are struggling to address compliance and risk management comprehensively. SAP offers a comprehensive GRC solution that promotes a thorough understanding of the implementation considerations and allows companies to be more adaptable to changing markets. This book comprehensively addresses how to fully implement and maximize the potential of the SAP GRC platform and work toward eliminating the pain points surrounding GRC implementations and move readers towards a holistic GRC system.

With SAP GRC 10, SAP has introduced a common platform for compliance for internal control with SAP Access Control and Business Process Management (BPM), trade compliance with SAP Global Trade Services (GTS), and enterprise risk with SAP Risk Management. Prior to SAP GRC 10, the different components of SAP GRC—SAP Access Control, SAP Process Control, SAP Global Trade Services (GTS) and SAP Risk Management—were separate applications. With SAP GRC 10.x, the common platform is able to use the cross-synergy between these applications.

SAP Access Control allows you to control access to your systems, SAP Process Control manages and monitors the end-to-end process and functional areas within the company, SAP GTS helps manage the international trade compliance and customs, and SAP Risk Management helps manage the enterprise risk.

Structure of This Book

The book starts with a general overview of the SAP GRC suite's common platform and then shifts to discuss each of the components (and their implementation): SAP Access Control, SAP Process Control, SAP GTS, and SAP Risk Management. After SAP GRC is appropriately configured, we look at the monitoring and assessment of the properly implemented SAP GRC system and how the system can be integrated to create an in-depth GRC process. Through the use of best practices, lessons learned, and sample scenarios, you'll thoroughly understand how to properly implement and use the facets of SAP GRC and the SAP Access Control, SAP Process Control, SAP GTS, and SAP Risk Management components. The concepts demonstrated will help you make the best of your investment in the comprehensive SAP GRC platform and provides a solution that covers the internal compliance and external trade and supply chain compliance.

Target Audience

This book is written for several different audiences based on their various needs in working with SAP GRC. This title is aimed at functional analysts, project managers, SAP security analysts, internal auditors, trade and compliance professionals, and program managers for systems implementation of SAP Access Control, SAP Process Control, SAP GTS, and SAP Risk Management.

This was a different task putting together a book that covered such a wide topics as GRC while at the same time covering the details of all the modules involved for this audience. The concept of GRC has been around since 2002 but has evolved over the years, and with the SAP GRC 10.x platform, a comprehensive solution is the result. We've created this book to be a reference guide for SAP users, consultants, and analysts from both the technical and functional sides. We've explained the concepts and the use case of these applications across your enterprise.

How to Use This Book

Given that the book appeals to many audiences, it has been designed so that sections are interconnected yet can be read independently. You can read from start to finish or simply progress straight to the chapters of specific interest. The objective is to demystify much of the mystique that surrounds GRC and describe it in a comprehensible manner. We start the book with the general overview of SAP GRC and than get into the specific modules.

Marginal note example

You will note that the book includes marginal notes where relevant. An example of a marginal note is located to the right in the margin. These notes will help you quickly identify additional topics within a section.

Conclusion

SAP GRC is a very wide subject to cover, and it includes four major applications: SAP Access Control, SAP Process Control, SAP GTS, and SAP Risk Management. Currently, there is no book in the market that covers all of the components of SAP GRC as one whole topic. We decided to write this book to address compliance as an umbrella that covers the internal and external aspects of an enterprise. You'll learn the application in individual and in relationship to the SAP GRC platform. The book has been written with step-by-step instructions so that you can understand the concepts easily. The concepts are also illustrated through numerous business examples throughout the book.

We hope that you enjoy this book and benefit from it as much as we enjoyed creating it. It's our ultimate goal that you are comfortable with your SAP GRC implementation. A properly implemented SAP GRC system can help ensure that your company is meeting strategic guidelines, your global operations are meeting regulations, and you aren't exposed to unnecessary risk. We hope our experience and expertise is of benefit to you as you start your implementation process.

Acknowledgments

D. Rajen Iyer

GRC is a very wide subject to cover, which has four major applications, like SAP GRC AC, PC, GTS and RM. As SAP decided to come up with the GRC 10.x platform, we saw customers had challenges making best use of the investment and synergy among the module. The platform provided the opportunity for implementation consultants to innovate and come up with solutions that cut across different GRC components. Currently there is no book in the market that covers all the component of SAP GRC as a one whole topic. We decided to write this book address compliance an umbrella that covers the internal and external aspect of an enterprise. The readers will learn the application in individual and in relationship to the Governance, Risk and Compliance platform.

I would like to express my gratitude towards my co-authors, Asok for his hard work and dedication, Satyen for helping us with his expertise in Risk Management to make this a comprehensive book, and finally Atul for his in-depth knowledge on the Process Control and new areas of GRC applications.

I would like to thank my wife, Padmaja providing me with the support and motivation, and my kids, Pranaav and Pranati for all the inspiration I needed.

I would like to thank Krypt, Inc. and the team in providing us with the GRC 10.x landscape and support in building use cases and proof of concept that helped build this book.

I would like to thank Katy Spencer personally for providing guidance throughout the process and, for most importantly being patient and persistent. I would also like to thank her and her editorial team in providing an excellent support and feedback in making this final product.

Asokkumar Christian

My foremost thanks go to Rajen for his motivation and for his being the driving force behind my writing this book. Thanks to the authors Atul and Satyen who extended their support in their expertise area to complement our work in order to cover the entirety of SAP GRC and newer technology, to make this book more beneficial to the target readers.

I would also like to extend my gratitude to Katy Spencer who guided us in bringing this book to greater heights. Thanks to my parents and friends those who have supported all these days in my learning path. Last but not least, thanks to my wife Chithra, and my kids, Abhi and Avoniko for their support and understanding during the writing process.

Atul Sudhalkar

I thank Rajen for proposing this book, and encouraging me to participate. Satyen was very gracious to agree to contribute his expertise in SAP Risk Management. My manager, Kevin McCollom was very supportive and encouraging, for which I owe him sincere thanks. Finally, our editor Katy Spencer has shown remarkable patience and skill in keeping all of us authors on track.

This chapter provides you with an overview of the SAP GRC suite, which is comprised of SAP Access Control, SAP Process Control, SAP Risk Management, and SAP Global Trade Services. You'll learn how to monitor risk, handle compliance with various regulations, and manage and govern the corporate IT landscape intelligently. The chapter also covers the newer SAP GRC 10 platform and its integration to core SAP ERP and satellite systems.

1 SAP Governance, Risk, and Compliance Overview

SAP Governance, Risk, and Compliance (SAP GRC) helps companies capture and comply with regulations and policies, as well as report on all compliance-related activities for internal/external auditors, C-level users, process owners, and the SAP security team. The unified SAP GRC platform addresses various compliance areas related to controls and risks across various business processes at a company level. SAP GRC can help customers address any regulatory requirements, for instance, to meet financial, environmental, health and safety, and sustainability regulations imposed by governments and regulatory bodies on companies and their business partners.

SAP GRC customers find it necessary to adjust their implementations rather more frequently than is typical for other enterprise applications for many reasons. As with so much else, customers implementing SAP GRC start small and expand their SAP GRC practices over time. Regulatory compliance is a fast-evolving challenge for companies, with a multitude of regulatory bodies and ever-changing laws. Furthermore, today's global companies face regulatory compliance pressures from multiple jurisdictions, and many regulations apply not just to activities carried out within their particular jurisdiction but also globally. SAP GRC implementations are more of a journey than a one-time effort.

In short, SAP GRC requires frequent adjustments to accommodate the following:

- Evolving regulations and changing laws
- Mergers, acquisitions, and splits
- Changing geographic scope as companies reach new markets or shift operations
- Evolving sophistication of SAP GRC usage and practice in the company

We recommend thinking about SAP GRC implementations as an iterative activity—you start well, but you start small. You then expand and fine-tune the usage on a regular basis to cope with all of the changes mentioned earlier.

As an example of evolving regulations, consider the US Sarbanes-Oxley (SOX) Act. Enacted in 2002, it was implemented in financial regulations by the Securities and Exchange Commission (SEC), which continued to fine-tune the regulations until 2010. SOX was mirrored over the years by similar Acts in Japan, Germany, and many other countries. Any company that conducted business in more than one of these countries over that period obviously saw an increasing thicket of sometimes overlapping regulations.

Documenting and testing key financial controls (manual or automated) requires enormous effort. But investment in SAP Access Control and SAP Process Control implementations, via automated internal controls and IT controls, yields increased efficiency of operations, better audit readiness, and reduced risk of penalties for noncompliance. SAP Risk Management helps to balance business opportunities with financial, legal, and operational risks to be identified in time to minimize the market penalties from high-impact events and monitor them continuously.

With release 10.0, SAP GRC integrated all four products (SAP Access Control, SAP Process Control, SAP Risk Management, SAP GTS) into a single software component, as illustrated in Figure 1.1. This platform provides seamless harmonization to maintain compliance across global SAP ERP landscape.

GRC Suite as a streamlined single software component

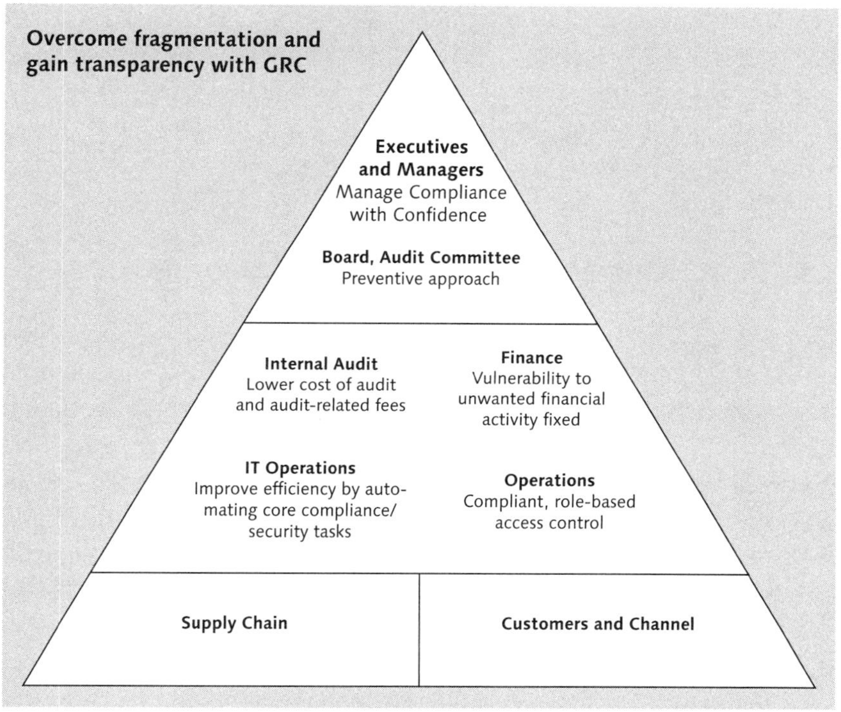

Figure 1.1 Integrated Governance, Risk, and Compliance

Ensuring compliance to regulations by documenting the regulatory requirements and corresponding control objectives, and measuring compliance to these is very expensive. It's also inescapable, and until a few years ago, most companies did this work manually, with minimal support from standard office software. Such mostly manual efforts don't scale well with increasingly tight regulatory requirements, nor do they yield any economies of scale.

An effective compliance monitoring program really requires good software support. This is what SAP GRC delivers for its customers. A good GRC implementation improves visibility by explicitly modeling all requirements and objectives. SAP GRC improves audit-readiness by keeping track of all compliance-related activities: testing, assessments, monitoring, and remediation. Both manual and automated control monitoring work better through SAP GRC because all such activities can occur on a schedule and can be tracked. Risk evaluations, mitigation measures, trends, and follow-up actions are all modeled and tracked.

In this chapter, we'll explore the various components of the SAP GRC suite to provide a very quick tour through the functionality. This chapter is intended to be a foundational chapter that we'll build upon throughout the rest of the book.

1.1 SAP GRC Suite Overview and Components

SAP GRC provides end-to-end automation for documenting, detecting, remediating, mitigating, and preventing risks enterprise-wide, resulting in proper segregation of duties (SoDs), proper operation of configuration and inherent controls, and oversight over transactions where necessary beyond proper configurations. SAP GRC does so at lower cost, at reduced risk, and with better business performance. The SAP GRC suite contains the following components to address compliance management.

SAP GRC Suite components

- SAP Access Control
- SAP Process Control
- SAP Risk Management
- SAP Global Trade Services (SAP GTS)
- SAP Nota Fiscal Electronica (SAP NFE)

Even though it's called the SAP GRC suite, each element can be individually implemented to suit an enterprise's need.

The SAP GRC suite components touch upon many areas of today's businesses and can have an impact enterprise-wide. Some of the common process areas addressed by SAP GRC include the following:

Common processes supported by SAP GRC

- Internal controls
- Corporate security

- Governance
- Compliance
- Risk management
- Legal
- Audit
- Finance
- Human resources
- Information technology
- Quality management
- Social responsibility and sustainability
- Import/export regulatory compliance

A properly implemented SAP GRC suite can be beneficial to a global business. However, before we get into the specifics of each component of the SAP GRC suite (Sections 1.1.3 through 1.1.6), we want to clarify the benefits of an integrated approach to the SAP GRC suite.

1.1.1 Value of the Suite as a Whole

An SAP GRC implementation affects how companies achieve and monitor compliance to regulations and how they monitor risk and controls. SAP GRC enables customers to proactively monitor key risks and controls, measure compliance, detect and fix problems, and maintain audit trails of all monitoring and remediation. Also the flexible rule engine provided with the SAP GRC system (described in Chapter 13) helps to easily define monitoring rules.

Shared master data

The common components and shared master data of SAP Access Control, SAP Process Control, and SAP Risk Management ensure that after you create systems and master data such as organizational structures, these are then used to list or report compliances and risks. As a part of SAP Access Control harmonization with SAP Process Control and SAP Risk Management, they use a common user interface (UI) layer and Data Dictionary. This provides a common look and feel to the UI and user navigation through shared work centers. SAP GRC 10.0 and 10.1 are based on the ABAP Application Server (ABAP AS), and so integrates with other SAP GRC products to leverage SAP's core strengths. SAP GRC 10.0 allows expanded functionality such as the following:

GRC 10.0 expanded functionality

- Customization (IMG) functions and transport management
- Object level security
- Archiving and audit tracking
- Using SAP standard workflow engine with flexible Multistage Multipath (MSMP) workflow
- Business Rules Framework Plus (BRF+) rule engine to make flexible decisions and approvals workflow much easier for the user community to modify according to their needs
- User maintenance and role-based authorizations
- Change management and auditable records
- Seamless access to end users to reach out with various functions in SAP GRC
- Increased visibility and easy reporting for any global organization made by integrated platform and common shared components
- Integration with SAP ERP systems using SAP NetWeaver Process Integration (PI) with contents such as SLL-LEG and SLL-NFE add-ons for SAP GTS and SAP NFE

1.1.2 Reasons to Implement SAP GRC

Let's consider some additional compelling reasons to implement SAP GRC. SAP has inherent controls built-in to protect master data, configuration data, and transactional data. Such inherent controls prevent major errors.

Built-in controls

For example:

- Duplicate checks through message control
- Sequential documents through number ranges
- Automatic integration and postings
- Online data analysis

- All transactions through unique documents
- History of transactions executed by users retained, including date, time, and user
- Logging and history of program changes

But sometimes, these controls are turned off or misconfigured. In other cases, due to some unique features of the business process in question, these controls may not be enough. That is, the controls offer to limit transactions in ways that are inadequate for your goals. Finally, particularly when multiple backend systems are involved in a business process (e.g., SAP ERP Financials processes an invoice payment to supplier for orders placed via a separate SAP SRM system, or when more than one SAP ERP instance is active in the production landscape), configurations in one system obviously don't directly control the execution of transactions in another system.

In such situations, you'll need to assure regulatory compliance via the SAP GRC Suite.

Throughout the next few sections, Sections 1.1.3 through 1.1.6, we will review the SAP GRC product suite. Naturally, we will have entire chapters dedicated to these components and their configuration but these sections will serve as a primer for our discussions.

1.1.3 SAP Access Control

Many companies ask themselves the following questions surrounding roles and security within their organization:

- Who are our users?
- What do they have access to?
- How did they get that access, who approved, and why?
- Are the extra access privileges provided to handle some extreme situations still available?
- Why is the active user ID available in the system even though the user left the company months ago?

These questions are raised with basic business challenges on access and authorization control either from the audit perspective or IT perspective. Without any proper control to the systems, there are chances of accidental or intentional activities due to additional access privileges, which can impact business directly or indirectly. Due to IT security and landscape complexity, at some point, manual controls over access may be too cumbersome to handle and that ends with unidentified access risks or segregation of duties (SoD) across an enterprise.

It's understood that good control is essential, but control should provide operational efficiency and restrain users from inadvertent data breaches due to those little extra privileges. Providing the right access to perform business functions without SoD issues are like a double-edged sword that impacts the business either way. SAP Access Control provides a good control over SoD and risk analysis. It provides all mechanisms to simplify and streamline access provisioning and keeps the IT environment clean and risk free.

Addressing Segregation of Duties

SAP Access Control is considered the foremost application to detect and address SoD issues. SoD issues are among the top audit issues reported by major auditing firms. SAP Access Control also governs risks on IT controls and provides options to mitigate if any of these SoD issues can't be isolated due to their business nature. Considering today's complicated IT landscape comprising various enterprise resource planning systems, it's obvious that flexibility and complexity are directly proportional. Implementing the SAP ERP system is extremely flexible to configure to suite business processes; at the same time, this increases the complexity of maintaining role-based access controls. SAP Access Control addresses this aptly and simply.

Despite these strengths, there are some challenges and assumptions made in providing an employee access using SAP Access Control:

Challenges and assumptions made in implementing SAP Access Control

- Little to no evaluation of risk prior to on-boarding and providing access
- Granting access to meet deadlines
- Employee turnover
- Forgotten access

- Complexity and time to review access levels
- Knowing when to reduce permission or remove permission
- Outsourcing

Let's take a look at a few scenarios detailing these challenges.

First, providing access to employees is assumed to be easy and straightforward, but many businesses assign access without valuating underlying risks to expedite the process and to enable their business to do so without much hassle during on-boarding or covering an absentee. The second challenge that businesses can face is that despite policies in place, some situations push IT teams and/or business teams to provide additional privileges to deal with some critical situations, such as meeting shipment deadlines or month-end closings. After some time, these additional privileges provided to the employee are forgotten, and the company is exposed to risks arising from this lapse in alertness.

Addressing changing business user roles and responsibilities

The business users' roles and responsibilities are keep changing to meet the needs of current dynamic and continuously evolving IT and business environment. To cope with these changes of privileges in IT landscape, companies practice either manual or automated processes. During this process removal of unwanted existing privileges were missed out. Mostly in such situations user provisioning are not analyzed for risks due to system complexity. Even some companies practicing to verify SoD manually and it's an extremely complex and time-consuming task to check SoD along with existing authorization and roles. Typically, when you go against time and business deadlines, this leads to relaxed security that allows the users with far more access to resources than required. Besides security issues, the same behavior drives up licensing costs, as more users end up having access to certain applications than strictly necessary. In this scenario, the focus lies on assigning permission rather than reducing them, for all of the correct reasons (allowing people to do their work) but with adverse results. According to the 2010 ACFE Report on Occupational Fraud and Abuse, the lack of internal controls and the SoD was cited as one of the most reported fraudulent activities.

Other risk factors that companies face include outsourcing to different countries where there are laws to reinstate neither security nor privacy, and, over time, companies can lose control of data because they have no input into third-party personnel selection or data monitoring. Third parties may have a contractual obligation to protect data but no statutory requirement. Let's think through how to handle these kinds of situations and what's required to safeguard the interests of investors, employees, shareholders, and the whole ecosystem around the company.

Audit or IT team personnel are the one who realize or identify any compliance issues or deficiencies on SAP IT General Controls (ITGC). In such cases, there is no guarantee that a 100% check is performed on a regular basis to identify compliance issues or deficiencies. You'll see how all of these challenges and issues are dealt with through the proper implementation of SAP Access Control. Figure 1.2 is a good starting place to understand the different SAP Access Control components and how each can be implemented with short-term and long-term benefits.

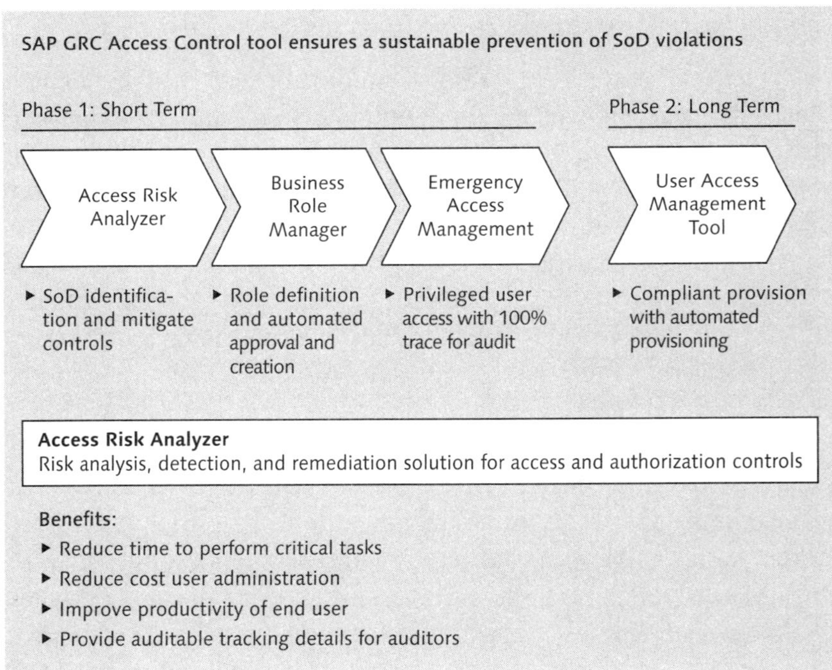

Figure 1.2 SAP Access Control Components

Let's discuss the different components shown in Figure 1.2 in detail. We'll start with a general overview of the SAP Access Control tools and their functions to put IT General Controls (ITGC) in place as a part of the

SAP GRC initiative and then shift to a more detailed discussion of these components after.

SAP Access Control has four major components:

- **Access Risk Analysis Tool**
  Supports real-time compliance to detect, remove, and prevent access and authorization risk by preventing security and control violations before they occur.
- **Business Role Manager (BRM) tool**
  Standardizes and centralizes role creation with automated workflow process and maintenance.
- **Emergency Access Management (EAM) tool**
  Enables users to perform emergency activities outside their roles as a "privileged user" in a controlled and auditable environment.
- **User Access Management tool**
  Automates provisioning, test for SoD risks, and streamlines approvals to the appropriate business approvers to move according to policy definition with the least manual work to IT staff and provide a complete history of user access. This is a part of the stay clean phase. In addition to this, web services enhance the integration with SAP NetWeaver Identity Management (SAP NetWeaver ID Management), which facilitates enterprise-wide compliant user provisioning.

SAP GRC solutions help companies comply with SOX and other regulatory mandates by enabling organizations to rapidly identify and remove authorization risks from IT systems. SAP Access Control allows preventive controls to be embedded into business processes to identify and prevent future SoD violations from being introduced without proper approval and mitigation. SAP Access Control also provides regular SoD and access review, which is a good maintenance exercise that makes tighter control across the enterprise. There are options such as monitoring total number of critical transaction codes/profiles accessed or generating alerts and sending emails to responsible control owners or monitors.

Access Risk Analysis Tool

This tool enables you to analyze IT system access for SoD and fully automated security audits. Given the prevalence of SoD issues, SAP has provided the Access Risk Analysis tool with a global rule set based on industry best practices to make a quick start toward security risk analysis. These risks are classified as High, Medium, and Low with the options of categorizing and customizing to meet any corporate audit team's needs.

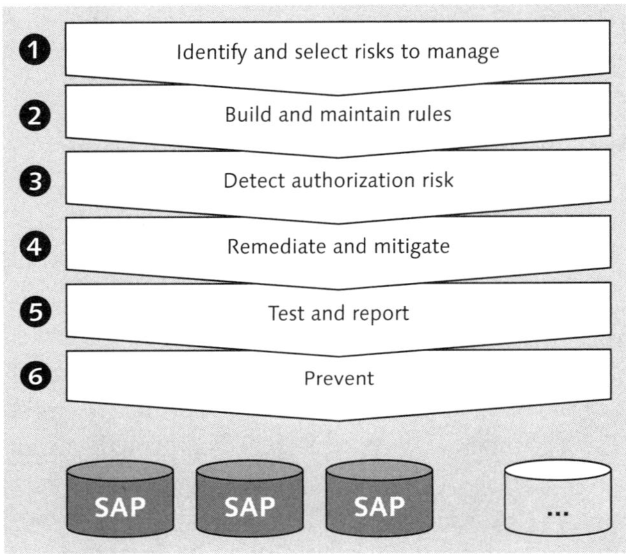

Figure 1.3 Access Risk Analysis

Access Risk Analysis tool performs risk analysis and reporting can be done with various options. SoD reporting or risk analysis can be completed in Access Risk Analysis tool against users, user groups, roles, and profiles. The SoD report details critical actions, critical permissions, critical roles, and profiles.

Risk terminator functionality can be implemented as an option, and this is activated on all systems that are connected to SAP Access Control. This indirectly helps to identify and prevent risks by stopping direct assignments in connected systems (backend).

Emergency Access Management tool

Emergency Access Management tool enables users to perform activities to solve the crisis of business access without compromising extra privileges by providing answers to the top open audit issue during some extraordinary or emergency situation. As shown in Figure 1.4, the Emergency Access Management tool allows for the automation of the SoD process from identifying risk to preventing risk.

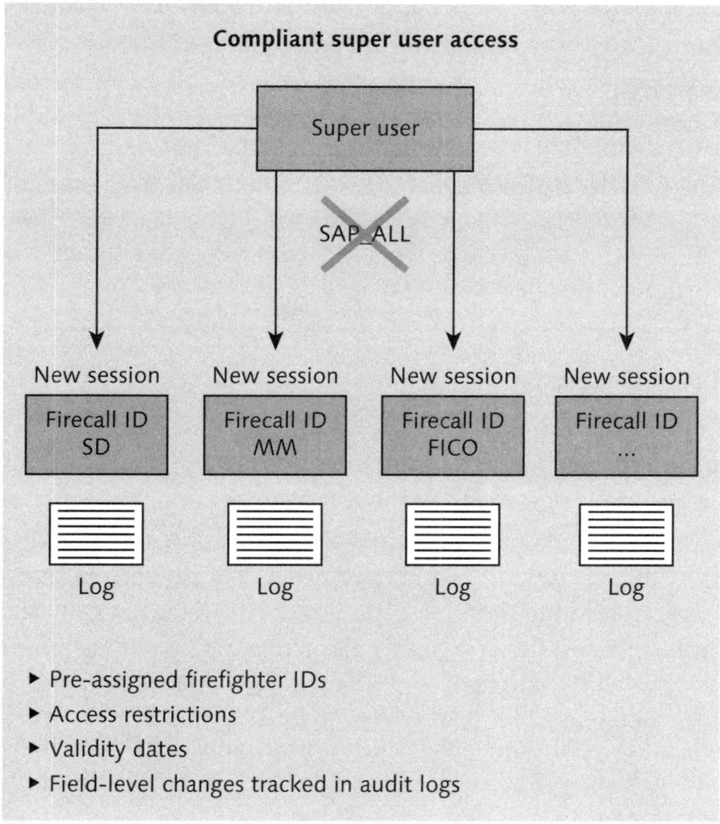

Figure 1.4 Emergency Access Management Tool

Those individuals who have access to EAM are able to track users, monitor and log the activities, and integrate multiple systems to reporting and logging from a single point. This tool handles some occasional extra IT privileges for a specified number of days for some extraordinary situations or access issues. This tool reports firefighter activities with filtering, sorting, and downloading options of various input values for auditing purposes. Some of the improved options of centralized Emergency Access Management include the following.

Emergency Access Management centralized functions

- Provides documented process to deal with emergency access
- Log reporting details, captures, and sends the details via workflow to make sure relevant persons are alerted with enough information about what an employee accessed using this privileged tool
- Defines and assigns firefighters, approvers, and controllers from single system
- Provides centralized firefighter ID to access different SAP ERP systems

These tools are parts of your ITGC start clean phase and Business Role Manager and User Access Management tools will help you to stay clean phase of ITGC. In the next section, we'll see the benefits of another SAP Access Control tool: Business Role Manager.

Business Role Manager Tool

Another element of SAP Access Control is the Business Role Manager tool. As mentioned earlier, this tool enforces the role for SoD during design time. From the perception to the complete creation, a role passes through an automated workflow with various stages and approval processes that involve role owners, auditors, and security persons. Business Role Manager makes long-term maintenance easier, reduces costs, and ensures compliance to meet corporate goals along with good documentation that is traceable. Whether you're starting a new role design or a role redesign, you may take advantage of these capabilities:

Business Role Manager tool capabilities

- Embedded risk analysis
- Configurable design methodology
- Documented approval

BRM ensures that role definition, role development without risk or with minimized risk, role testing, and role management are consistent across an enterprise. Figure 1.5 shows the schematic flow of the business role manager tool in an automated environment for approval, risk analysis, testing, and documenting.

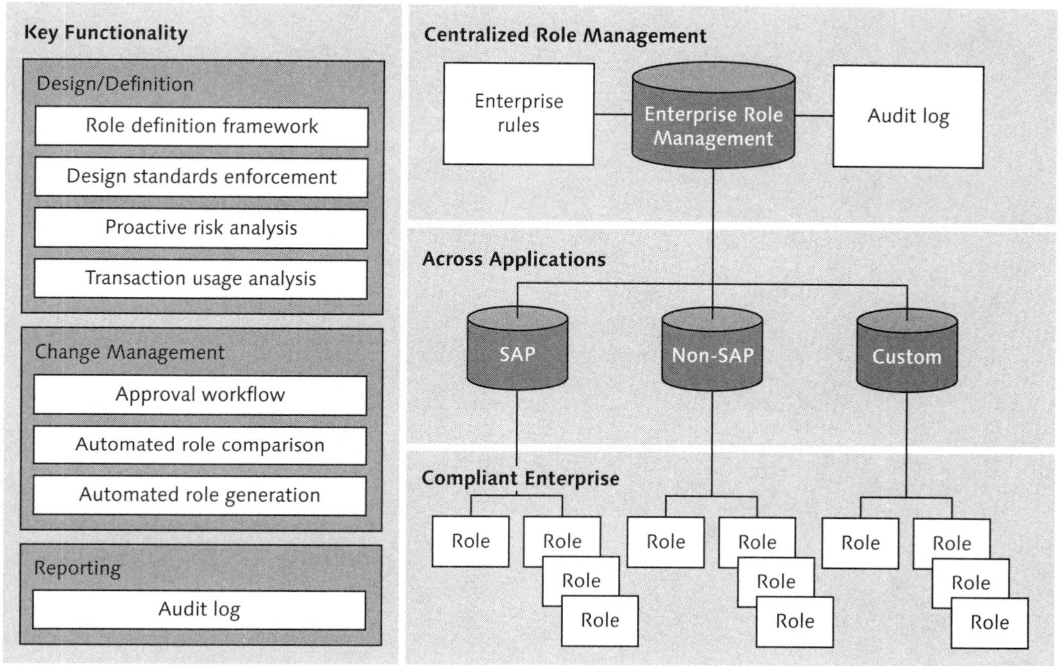

Figure 1.5 Schematic Diagram of Business Role Manager Tool

User Access Management Tool

The User Access Management tool automates the full hire to retire cycle business and audit requirements in the right proportion without jeopardizing any issues in the corporate environment. The hire to retire cycle of any employee runs through various roles and responsibilities that are set to provide sufficient authorization to perform a user's business activities, and changes automatically carried out by HR trigger their IT controls. Even if there is a manual access request creation process using the User Access Management tool, SoD risk analysis is simulated for users, and all of the risks shown to the approver and based on approver decision provisioning is done automatically as shown in Figure 1.6.

Getting a Better Return on Investment with SAP Access Control

Some SAP Access Control customers miss some of the basic concepts of SAP Access Control tools that can help them get a better return on investment (ROI) by leveraging the tool's maximum capacity. Understanding the available options and using them appropriately provides more manageable details over ITGC to IT, business, internal audit, and external audit teams. Figure 1.7 shows that most companies' use of SAP Access Control is in the preliminary stage, and, to improve ROI, it's important to know about all of the functions of the system. With the ABAP platform changes from SAP Access Control 10.0, the options to integrate with other systems become easier and more flexible.

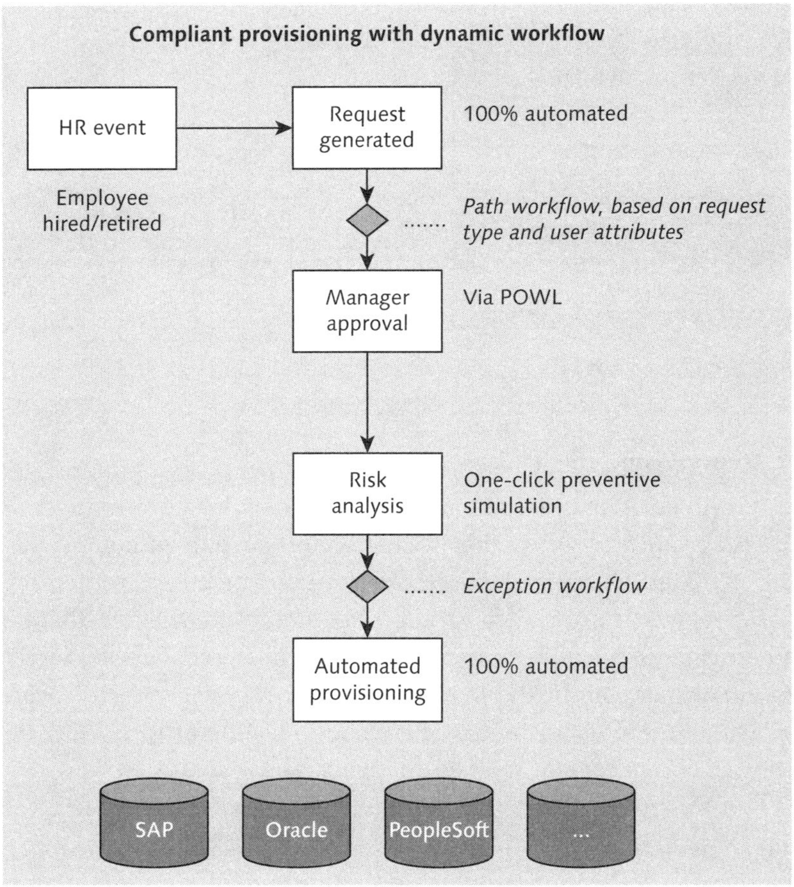

Figure 1.6 Schematic Flow Diagram Depicting the User Access Management Tool

SAP Access Control supports all target audiences with an unprecedented level of ease, effectiveness, and comprehensiveness. Auditing and management teams can leverage SAP Access Control for automating the periodic reviews on user access and SoD risks.

Task automation

Automating these tasks and other approvals, monitoring, and requesting processes in the background serves to trigger emails and sends the review details to respective owners or controllers who then verify the correctness of data to protect ITGC. Such automation on SAP ERP systems and extending these automation to other non-SAP systems give a better return on investments to the companies. Most of the companies that implemented SAP Access Control are still in preliminary stage as shown in Figure 1.7. SAP Access Control 10.x versions has the flexibility to extend more powerful expansion to compliance processes.

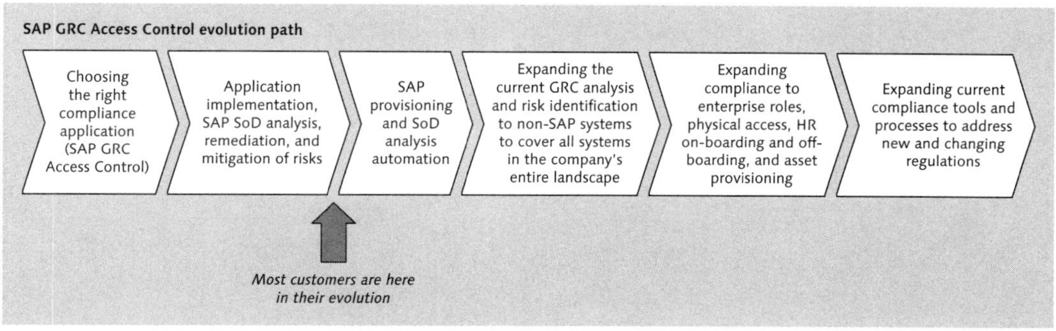

Figure 1.7 Add-On Functions to Increase ROI

Now that we've discussed SAP Access Control, let's shift our focus to the SAP Process Control component of the SAP GRC suite.

1.1.4 SAP Process Control

SAP Process Control helps customers capture their regulatory and policy compliance activities. SAP Process Control organizes regulatory compliance by regulation, business process, and organizational hierarchies. This helps clarify organizational roles by varying control objectives and strategies, and simplifies reporting.

Figure 1.8 shows the SAP GRC 10.0 Master Data tab. Note that what constitutes master data for SAP GRC is very different from traditional SAP ERP-centric views of master data.

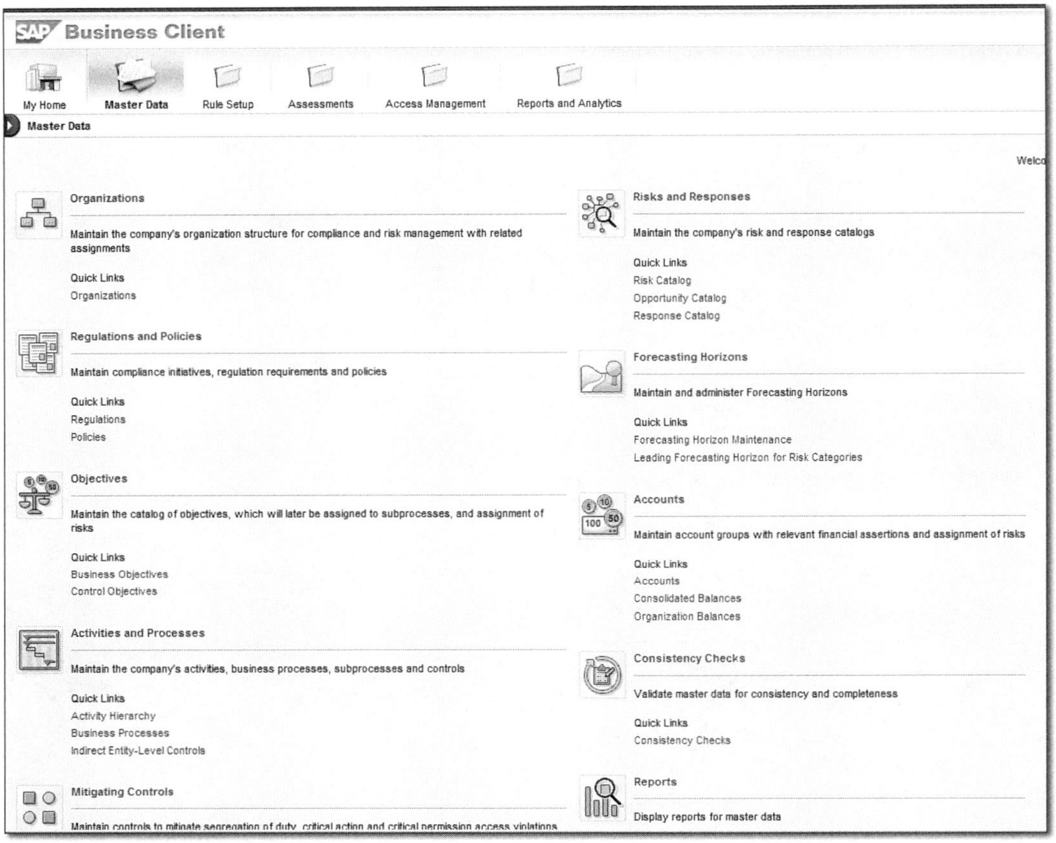

Figure 1.8 Master Data Tab with SAP Process Control with the SAP NetWeaver Business Client

A Note about SAP GRC Screenshots

The screenshots of SAP GRC applications lean heavily toward SAP NetWeaver Business Client (NWBC) installations of SAP GRC. SAP GRC under SAP Portal looks cosmetically different, although functionally it behaves exactly the same.

In taking these screenshots, we've used a privileged user with wide-ranging access to SAP GRC functionality. Your experience with more realistic user roles will likely be somewhat different: screens will appear less cluttered and more focused around the functionality you intend to use.

Finally, some of our earlier screenshots used SAP GRC 10.0 release installations, and some of the later screens used SAP GRC 10.1. Because release 10.1 is a minor release building on 10.0, the differences are very minor and should cause no confusion at all. SAP Process Control features SAP ERP integration and automated control testing and monitoring, which can help reduce audit cycles and cost of compliance, as well as provide a higher degree of reliability and integrity in financial statements.

SAP Process Control capabilities

SAP Process Control enables organizations to do the following:

- Document their control environments
- Test and assess controls
- Track issues for remediation
- Certify and report on the state and quality of process controls
- Manage policies
- Perform continuous controls monitoring using a combination of data forms, automated workflows, certification, and interactive reports

Using a combination of data forms, automated workflows, certification, and interactive reports, this solution enables members of internal control, audit, and business process teams to effectively manage compliance activities.

Compliance Management

You can capture your specific compliance management plans and intentions in SAP Process Control. Modeling of policies, regulations, business process and organizational hierarchies, risks, and controls are all core components of SAP Process Control. It also includes powerful and flexible continuous controls monitoring (CCM) capabilities. CCM can be used to measure the effectiveness of controls, to monitor compliance, and to ensure that configuration and master data settings are valid.

Policy Management

Policy management features cover the life cycle of policies: drafting, approval, implementation, revisions, and so on. Policy implementation can be tracked and audit trailed because policies can be communicated via email, and acknowledgements can be tracked. SAP Process Control integration with Adobe Interactive Forms (AIF) allows such communication to be offline—meaning that users don't have to be directly logged in to SAP Process Control for policies to be sent to them or for users to acknowledge the policies.

Figure 1.9 shows a previously created policy. Note that the policy life cycle mentioned earlier is shown in the different tables, as are the relationships between policies, risks, controls, and so on. In particular, note the different ways policies (and changes to these) can be communicated to employees in an effective and measurable way.

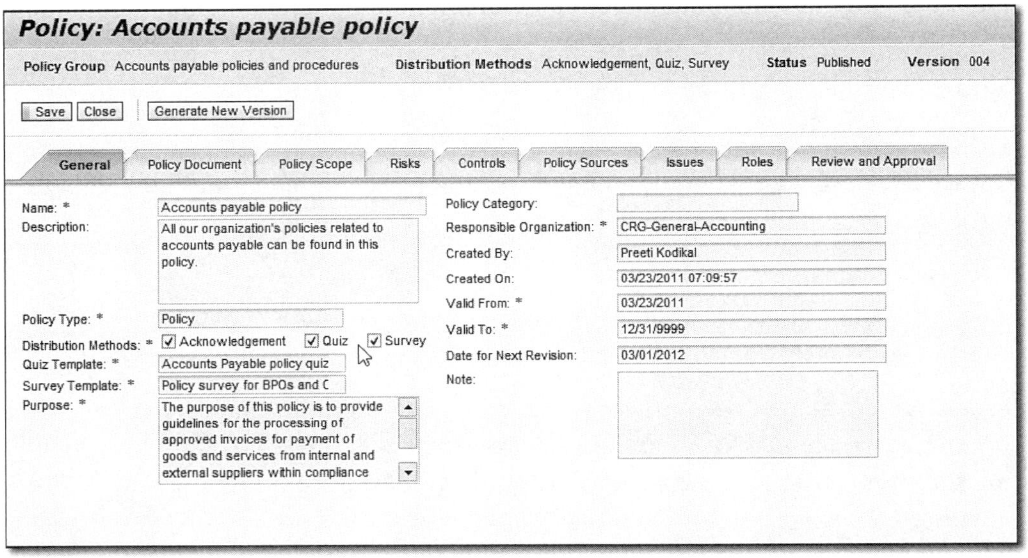

Figure 1.9 Accounts Payable Policy with SAP GRC 10 SAP Process Control

Planning and evaluation support includes risk-based scoping to focus attention and efforts where most needed. Surveys and assessments can be created, distributed, and tracked in SAP Process Control, and AIF support enables these activities to also be carried out offline and reliably communicated back asynchronously.

Figure 1.10 shows the ASSESSMENTS" tab, which includes links to various risk and control effectiveness testing and other planning activities.

Continuous Control Monitoring and SAP Process Control

SAP Process Control Continuous Control Monitoring supports customers' planning needs and also ongoing monitoring. SAP Process Control can monitor any backend system but is optimized for SAP ABAP applications, including SAP ERP, SAP NetWeaver Business Warehouse (SAP NetWeaver BW), SAP Customer Relationship Management (SAP CRM), and so on.

One key differentiator for Process Control Continuous Control Monitoring is enhanced capabilities around sensitive configuration and master data settings. SAP applications are highly configurable, and these settings can be fine-tuned to ensure that only compliant transactions are allowed through. This is one of SAP's key strengths and the heart of SAP's preventive control capabilities. But such controls are only as effective as the correctness of the configuration and master data settings. In this context, *correct* means accurately reflecting user intent. Businesses routinely need to adjust these settings to reflect a dynamic business environment; address and bank information updates, evolving markets, process optimization, changing contracts, and so on, all require continuous adjustment to these settings.

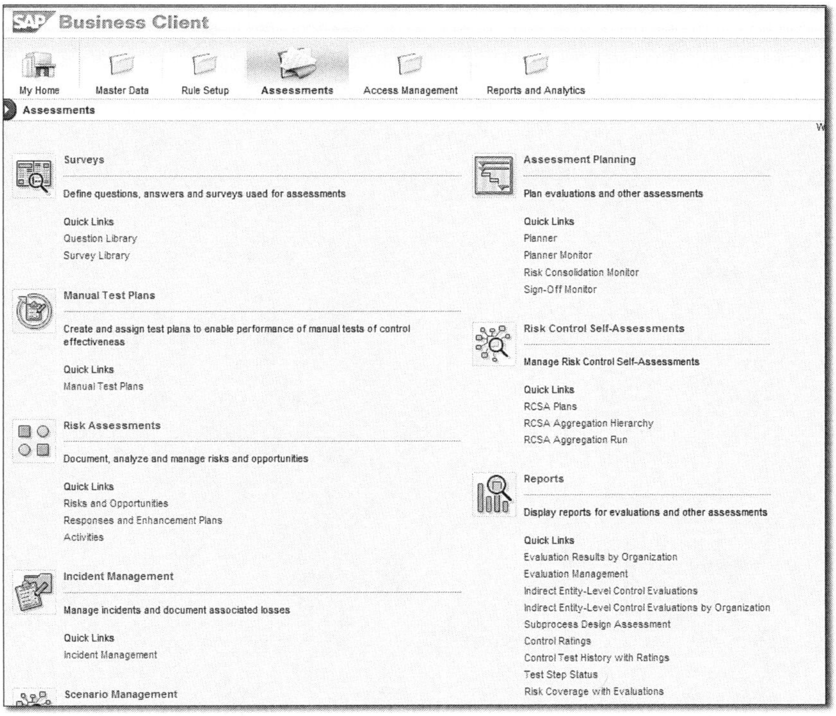

Figure 1.10 Assessment Tab

SAP Process Control can reconstruct past configuration and master data settings over a test time period (e.g., last quarter, last year, etc.). This guarantees that all sensitive settings can be reviewed and tested for correctness, which is a powerful feature unique to SAP Process Control.

Business Rule Framework Plus

A flexible rule engine marks a key advance in the SAP Process Control 10.0 release for monitoring. SAP Process Control 10.0 uses the SAP NetWeaver standard BRF+ rule engine, which gives customers great power, at relatively low cost in terms of required expertise.

Reporting and analytics are supported natively through the popular SAP Crystal Reports engine, and also via integration with SAP NetWeaver BW. Delivered reports can be extensively customized.

Figure 1.11 shows the RULE SETUP tab, which includes CONTINUOUS MONITORING links from which users can set up automated monitoring rules against backend systems.

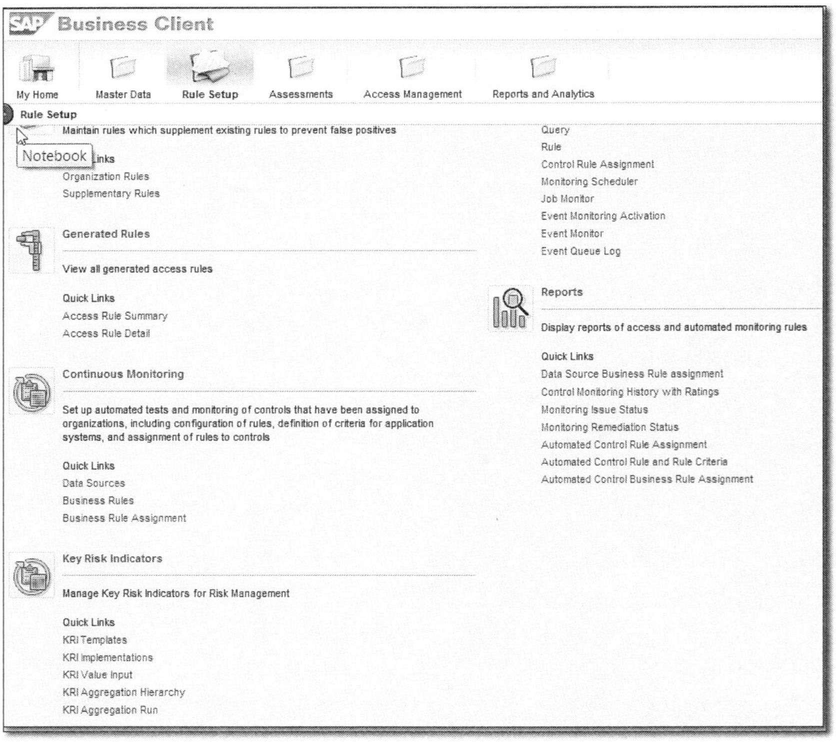

Figure 1.11 Rule Setup Tab

SAP Process Control uses the standard SAP business workflow (i.e., ABAP workflow) to route tasks to SAP Process Control users. The ABAP workflow is recognized as easy to understand, robust, and reliable, and for supporting extensive administrative needs for rerouting, escalating, and so on.

ABAP workflow

As noted earlier, with release 10.0, SAP has made great strides in harmonizing SAP Access Control, SAP Process Control, and SAP Risk Management. The user experience is greatly harmonized, and much of the master data that was previously separate in the SAP GRC suite is now shared. In particular, SAP Process Control is evolving within the suite as the master repository of compliance intent and context.

For example, segregation of duties is a compliance strategy; but the motivation for SoD can be a specific regulatory framework (e.g., SOX and related non-US regulations), good management practices, fraud management, or a combination of several such reasons. With release 10.0, SAP Access Control risk assessments can be linked to the specific SAP Process Control control, which mitigates a particular risk (e.g., invoice payment authority combined with vendor creation), that in turn is linked to one or more regulatory frameworks. This puts the organization's compliance-related activities in context, provides the right parameters for testing and monitoring, and also unifies reporting needs.

In fact, Figure 1.11 includes all of the UI links relevant to SAP Access Control and SAP Risk Management users as well. In general, the high configurability of SAP applications means that a customer ensures that only people with relevant roles see the individual application functionality links. A SAP Process Control control owner, for instance, sees the workflow inbox, some reports and analytics, the job monitor, and perhaps little else. (Remember that these screenshots used a particularly broad-based role profile just to capture all links in one place.)

User Interface for SAP GRC suite

SAP Process Control exhibits an internal audit mindset, in the sense that regulatory compliance is the theme or background for most SAP Process Control activities. But the policy management and Continuous Control Monitoring (CCM) features new in the 10.0 release take it well beyond a supplementary tool for internal audit. It still supports internal auditors, of course, for instance in the risk-based scoping activities. Further, there is ongoing and increasing integration with the SAP Audit Management product (which is included with every SAP NetWeaver license).

Risk–Based Process Controls

Through Risk-Based Process Controls, you can implement various compliance initiatives managed within your company. Each compliance initiative follows one or more of the following business processes:

Compliance initiatives integrated with business processes

- **Document compliance initiative**
  Define the compliance structure for your compliance initiative, including all relevant organizations, processes, risks, and controls.
- **Plan**
  Determine and establish your assessment and test strategy.
- **Perform assessments and tests**
  Monitor your state of compliance through the execution of assessments of various aspects of your internal controls environment and through the automated monitoring and manual testing of controls.
- **Remediate issues**
  Resolve identified issues to bring your state of checks and balances back into order.
- **Certify results**
  Obtain approval from the organization to certify that all planned assessments and tests have been performed and that all identified issues are known or remediated.

Process Control Scenario

This is a very high-level explanation with a sample scenario to address what SAP Process Control means to your enterprise; subsequent chapters flesh this out in more detail. This definitely reduces your cost of compliance and speeds up your auditing process.

Let's take the Order to Cash (OTC) process and consider that we want to do an audit check on the internal controls. Vendor master maintenance transaction can be deselected with the Blocked for Payment option for a certain period of time and reset back to its original condition. During this period of time, it's not 100% possible for an internal audit or external audit to detect such deficiencies unless the changes are tracked via table changes. Changes tracked via table changes will heavily impact

Online Transactional Processing (OLTP) of the SAP ERP system. With the help of defined SAP Process Control scenarios and hundreds of automated controls allows for the extension of control for customs and queries. This allows business to meet challenges and address all require internal control in a fully automated way. This allows users to monitor, track and escalate necessary risk situations.

This highlighted scenario talks about transactional controls, and similarly master data and configuration controls can be used as automated controls and detect any system malpractices. This increases everyone's confidence and trust over the company. Similarly ITGC from SAP Access Control can be integrated with SAP Process Control for monitoring.

We've reviewed the SAP Access Control and SAP Process Control components of the SAP GRC suite, so now let's turn our focus to the SAP Risk Management component.

1.1.5 SAP Risk Management

SAP Risk Management helps organizations automate and coordinate their Enterprise Risk Management (ERM) activities. Reliable and accurate risk information enables business users such as risk managers, line of business (LOB) owners, and executives to make better decisions and improve performance. SAP Risk Management helps organizations preserve and grow enterprise value by doing the following:

- Aligning risk management with business value drivers
- Creating continuous insight into the status of risk
- Acting on emerging risks and opportunities

SAP Risk Management solution capabilities are closely aligned with best practice industry ERM frameworks such as ISO 31000 and COSO II ERM.

Risk is typically a complex multidimensional topic impacting a variety of strategic, financial, and operational *key performance indicators* (KPIs) within an enterprise. SAP GRC 10.0 introduces a new analytical visualization for risks as shown in Figure 1.12. Such visualization is called the "bow-tie" risk view. While providing a complete transactional context, this visualization enables a powerful way to engage with the rest of the business and have value conversations.

SAP Risk Management views

Figure 1.12 shows the IDENTIFY RISK view of the bow-tie diagram. In the center, the INCONSISTENT FINANCIAL REPORTING risk is shown in red. On the left side of the risk, you can see the risk DRIVERS (or causes), along with the risk IMPACTS (or consequences) shown on the right hand side. On the top, you can see the context of the risk defined in terms of the applicable organizations, RISK CATEGORY, and business ACTIVITY. Users can update the risk definition with simple drag-and-drop techniques using the risk taxonomies available in the left panel.

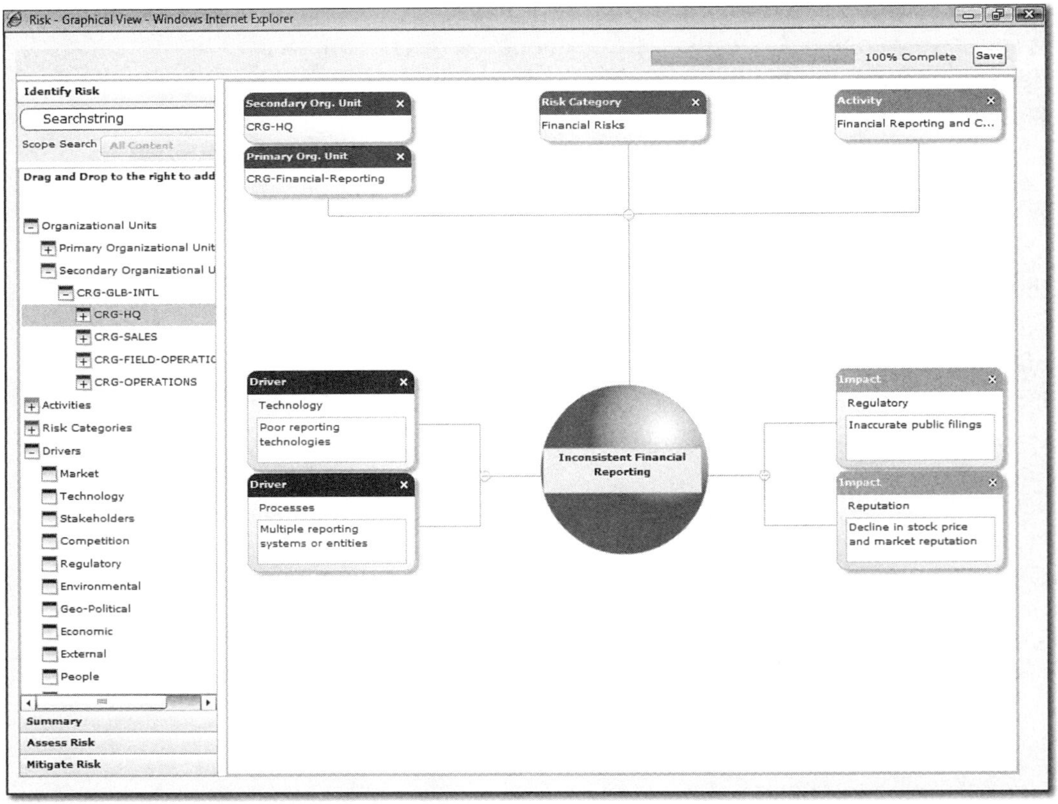

Figure 1.12 SAP Risk Management Bow-Tie Diagramm

Although not shown in Figure 1.12, the bow-tie visualization also includes SUMMARY, ASSESS RISK, and MITIGATE RISK views. The SUMMARY view shows the entire risk with all of the supporting details. The ASSESS RISK view allows users to perform risk assessments and also shows how the assessments have changed over time. The MITIGATE RISK view shows a catalog of all available risk responses and controls for mitigation. Using drag-and-drop techniques, users can add and remove mitigations for the risk and also perform residual risk assessments. The bow-tie risk visualization allows for an engaging business discussion about risk with multiple stakeholders within an enterprise.

Enterprise Risk Management components

Now let's look at the conceptual components of the Enterprise Risk Management (ERM) process in a little more detail:

- **Plan**
  ERM begins with planning. Planning enables organizations to focus risk management implementation on what is most relevant for their business. Planning ensures that the risk management initiative starts with a complete understanding of context, business value drivers, risk appetite, threshold levels, and business objectives to be achieved.
- **Link**
  Risks are identified, documented, and aligned with the business context, including drivers/causes, impacts/consequences, organizations, risk categories, activities, and objectives.
- **Analyze**
  Risks are analyzed using quantitative and qualitative methods for prioritization and developing effective treatment strategies.
- **Respond**
  Risk evaluation helps select the risks (and opportunities) for treatment by balancing the costs of implementing each option against the benefits derived from it.
- **Monitor and report**
  Monitoring of the effectiveness and completeness of the risk treatments, taking corrective actions, and communicating the status of risks occur in this phase. Key Risk Indicators (KRIs), which are leading indicators of risk, are also used in risk monitoring. KRIs can monitor information in SAP as well as non-SAP based transactional and analytical systems.

In addition to the standard ERM capabilities, the SAP Risk Management license also includes the Operational Risk Management (ORM) functionality applicable for financial institutions—banks, insurance companies, automotive companies with finance divisions, as well as energy and utility companies involved in commodities trading. The default solution installation has the ORM functionality turned off. Before we discuss how to enable this additional functionality, let's define ORM, the need for financial institutions to manage operational risk along with enterprise risk, and the benefits such customers can expect from the solution.

More than ever, financial institutions are investing in IT solutions to automate and optimize SAP GRC activities. Fraught with change, unpredictability, and risk, today's business environment demands an effective operational risk management strategy.

Regulatory requirements and SAP Risk Management

Additionally, regulatory requirements such as the Basel II Capital Accord (Basel II), the planned Basel III Capital Accord (Basel III), and Solvency II require comprehensive measurement of both internal and external risks. An organization must focus simultaneously on in-house process controls for fraud detection, employment practices, and workplace safety, as well as understand the impact of external factors on the business and have failovers in place in case of IT system failures.

In addition to obtaining reports from various LOBs, organizations must create an enterprise view of risk that reflects and measures potential threats to the institution. With the entire organization exposed to operational risk, decisions and recommendations to management must satisfy both existing and upcoming regulations and standards as well as align with the enterprise strategy.

Operational Risk Management as a Component of SAP Risk Management

Traditional operational risk management methods, where bits of information are rolled up from various lines of business, are no longer sufficient to achieve these goals. To create real value through an operational risk management process, an organization must evaluate the exposure of the whole institution in-line with its business strategy. While meeting these business challenges, you must also understand potential exposures of IT systems. Additionally, management and regulators expect financial institutions to integrate external risk factors into a holistic picture of the risks it faces.

Operational Risk Management capabilities

SAP Operational Risk Management enables customers to do the following:

- Measure, monitor, and control through KRIs.
- Improve profitability through more accurate and future-oriented risk measurement.
- Satisfy regulatory requirements such as Basel II, Basel III, and Solvency II.
- Integrate ORM processes with existing operational systems such as HR, credit processing, and transactional banking systems.
- Integrate ORM into enterprise risk reporting alongside credit risk, market, and liquidity risk management.
- Support loss and capital reduction.
- Increase rating agency confidence and profitability.
- Optimize risk mitigation through integration with the SAP Access Control application and the SAP Process Control solutions.

Note

Customers that want to use the ORM functionality can use SAP Note 1601962 (*https://service.sap.com/support/notes/1601962*) to turn on the additional features.

SAP Risk Management and GRC 10.0

With SAP GRC 10.0, SAP Risk Management is completely harmonized and integrated with SAP Process Control and SAP Access Control. The UI and master data components are also shared. Chapter 15 provides a detailed procedure for implementing SAP Risk Management for both the ERM and the ORM scenarios. Chapter 15 also provides a customer solution adoption model where customers can implement a specific set of solution capabilities based on the maturity of their risk management program.

Having covered the commonly known components of the SAP GRC suite (SAP Access Control, SAP Process Control, and SAP Risk Management), now we'll shift our focus to the other components of the SAP GRC suite: SAP Global Trade Services and SAP Nota Fiscal Electronica.

1.1.6 SAP Global Trade Services and SAP Nota Fiscal Electronica

With the rise of a global economy, international trade is increasing and becoming crucial as a major source of economic revenue to a large number of countries around the world. *Global trade* is the exchange of capital, goods, and services across international borders or territories.

Impact of globalization

Globalization is also driving the outsourcing of manufacturing, services, and intellectual property management. As part of that development, organizations are looking closely at the lowest-common denominator of global trade: import and export. Most world-class, multinational organizations across a wide variety of industries are building significant infrastructures and processes to support increased globalization.

Import, export, and ERP systems

There are generally four critical elements that make up an import/export transaction; from a global trade compliance perspective, these are the key aspects to check against before a transaction can be approved for import or export.

- **Business partner**
  A customer, individual, partner, or vendor.
- **Country**
  The product is either shipped from or received into this country.
- **Classification**
  The goods, services, or products classification under the Commerce Control List (CCL) or United State Munitions List.
- **License**
  Exception or no license required for product shipment export or import.

To begin, let's discuss the basics of exporting and importing. In a typical simple supply chain process, most companies have customers, vendors, financial institutions, and other partners. In most instances, when an organization sells a product to an international customer, it needs to cross borders to fulfill the order. The export laws of the country from which the goods are shipped are applied to this outbound movement. Similarly, when an organization sources goods and services from a vendor located in another country, the import laws of the receiving country are applied.

Key trade data touch points

The source system can be any enterprise resource planning system, where the key trade data touch points are identified as the following (see Figure 1.13):

- Materials are created or changed (in SAP GTS, these are identified as Product Create/Change).
- Customers are created or changed (in SAP GTS, these are identified as Business Partner Create/Change).
- A product is updated with a trade attribute, for example. The important fields are the export classifications and import tariff number.
- Business partner screening is against denied party list screening.
- Document compliance check or screening is used for sanctioned party lists, embargos, or license determination.
- Document Services provides the documents generation for customs declarations.

SAP Global Trade Services capabilities

The key functional elements in SAP GTS are the following:

- Content for classification, denied party list, duty, preferential rules
- Product classification, which provides the classification assignment from export and import processing
- Sanctioned party list screening of business partners against denied party list content
- Compliance checks consisting of sanctioned party list screening, embargos, and license determination for transactions
- Form printing and electronic communication for customs declaration
- Preferential processing, valuation, duty calculation/drawback

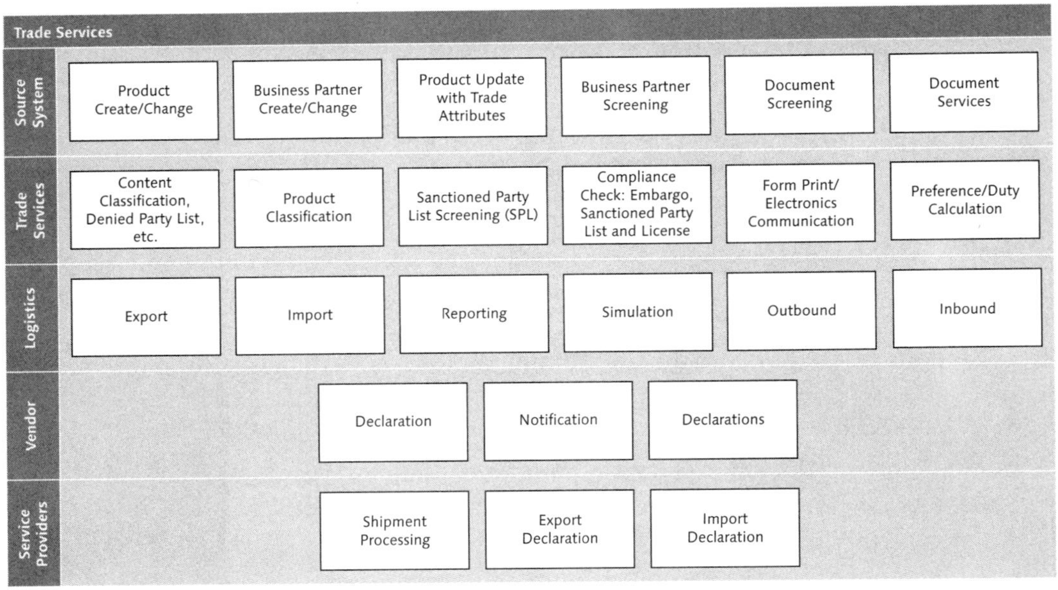

Figure 1.13 Trade Services

Logistics process integration with SAP Global Trade Services

Any Logistics process (see Figure 1.13) involves one of the trade services:

- **Outbound transactions**
  For example, sales order, delivery note, and so on.
- **Inbound transactions**
  For example, purchase order (POs), inbound delivery, and so on.
- **Export**
  The outbound transaction triggers the export process.
- **Import**
  The inbound process triggers the import process.
- **Reporting**
  Part of the trade process for Logistics transactions, for example, the Intrastat (Intra European Community Trade Statistics) and Extrastat (Extra European Community Trade Statistics) reports.
- **Simulations**
  Functions that allow you to do a mock-up run and check on business transactions.

Trade Checks and Services

When companies use an enterprise resource planning system to perform their supply chain transactions, they have to perform export or import checks based on the goods being sent out or received into the country. These trade checks can be performed using the SAP GTS application. Any transaction within the enterprise resource system has product and business partner information; from a global trade point of view, these products are identified for export or import classification and checked for license for permission to export or import. Additionally, business partners are screened for appearance on the denied party list.

When a customer requests a part or service, for example, the contract is acknowledged with an order, which is presented as a sales order in the enterprise resource planning system. If this part has to be shipped to a different country and crosses borders in the process, export regulation of the departing country apply. This supply chain process checks for trade compliance within an SAP GTS system. Similarly, if the company plans to purchase goods from a vendor located in a different country, it must comply with import regulations.

Components of SAP Global Trade Services

SAP GTS has four major components:

- SAP Compliance Management
- SAP Customs Management
- SAP Risk Management
- Electronic Compliance Reporting (ECR)

Business Processes supported with SAP Global Trade Services

The trade system business processes can be put into high-level functionality as follows (see Figure 1.14):

- Product classification
- Business partner
- Export management
- Import management
- Trade preference

Product classification starts with the transfer of a product or material from the enterprise resource planning system, either an SAP or non-SAP system, to SAP GTS. The content for classification can be uploaded in SAP GTS and is available for the product classification. The export/import attributes can be maintained in the product.

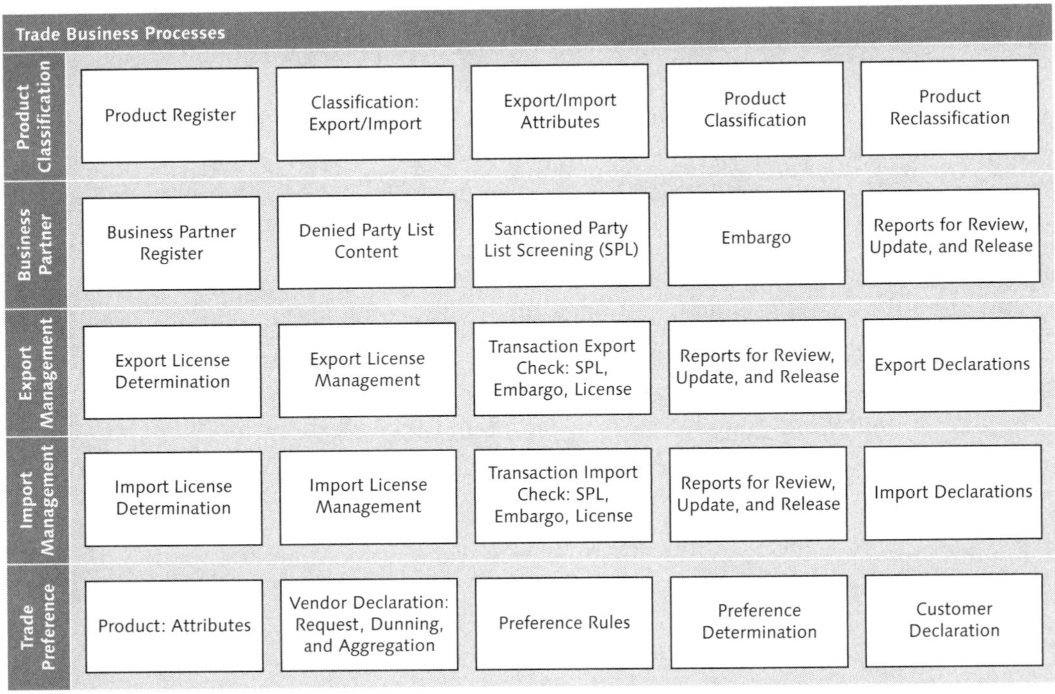

Figure 1.14 Business Process Alignment with Trade Services

Trade Compliance

SAP Compliance Management addresses the screening of business partners when they are created and when they are used within a transaction, sales order, delivery note, or PO. This functionality is called *sanctioned party list screening*, and it uses the denied party list content to screen the business partner addresses. The *import legal control* functionality addresses the import check requirements for products and services that are imported into a particular country based on the importing country regulations. *The export legal control* functionality addresses the export licensing requirements for products and services. The *embargo check* functionality is applied across both export and import legal controls.

Embargo checks are based on the country of departure for import transactions, and the country of destination for export transactions.

Embargo checks

The product number identifies the enterprise's materials or services; these parts are classified from export or import purposes. Products are classified according to their respective government guidelines and regulations; for example, in the United States, the export regulation (Export Administration Regulation) uses the Commerce Control List (CCL), which is comprised of export control classification numbers (ECCN). An ECCN is an alphanumeric code; in combination with the country chart, it provides the reason for control by destination country.

Legal control license determinations for products are based on the product classification for imports or exports. License determination is based on the legal regulation of the departure country for exports, and the destination country for imports, as well as the partner country, classification number, and license type.

Customs Declaration and Transit Procedures

SAP Customs Management in SAP GTS is a module that you can use to standardize electronic communication processes, including customs declarations. Communication in SAP Customs Management takes place by printing messages or creating Electronic Data Interchange (EDI) messages. You can connect SAP GTS to customs authorities all over the world to manage foreign trade activities. SAP GTS can communicate and set up electronic customs processes with European, US, and Australian customs authorities, and address the different filing formats, data transmission requirements, and other features. See Figure 1.15.

Custom Management communication options: print or electronic

In SAP Customs Management, you have two options: a printed form or an electronic communication. With a printed form, you have the option to print, mail, or fax. With electronic communication, the system converts the data into an Intermediate Document (IDoc) and sends the IDoc output file (text) to middleware. The middleware acts as a translator to convert the IDoc file into the format in which the receiving system expects it. Customs declarations can be created for export or import.

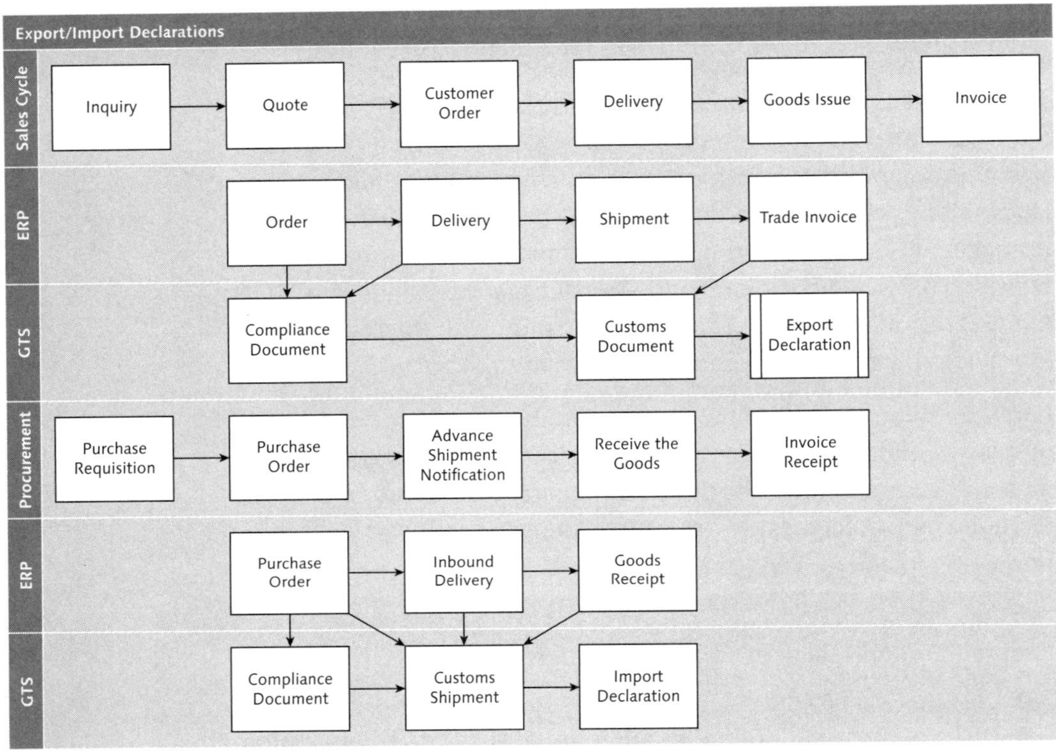

Figure 1.15 Customs Declarations and Reporting

Transit procedures

SAP GTS also has the functionality to support transit procedures. Transit is a facility available to operators that allows the movement of goods across international borders under customs control while ensuring that any changes due on those goods in their country of destination are secured. There are different types of transit; for example, community transit is a system that provides for the movement, under customs control, of goods that are not in free circulation through the community and also for the movement of free circulation goods in certain circumstances. It's comprised of two separate procedures: the *external community transit procedure* (T1) and the *internal community transit procedure* (T2).

Closely related to SAP GRC and SAP GTS is the SAP Environment, Health, and Safety Management (SAP EHS Management) module.

Environment Health and Safety

Environment, health, and safety (EH&S) are guidelines or codes of federal regulations within different areas, such as Environmental, Occupational Health and Safety, Community Health and Safety, Construction and Decommissioning, and so on. SAP EHS Management within SAP ERP includes several components: Basic Data and Tools, Product Safety, Hazardous Substance, Dangerous Goods Management, Waste Management, Occupational Health and Industry Hygiene, and Safety.

Hazardous substance checks

With SAP GTS 7.2 and higher, you can run hazardous substance checks for the items in your Logistics transactions. When you create a compliance document, for example, a sales order, delivery note, and so on, SAP GTS creates an equivalent document in the system and performs a check for EH&S with hazardous materials. These checks for hazardous materials can help companies with one or more of the following:

- Imported quantity restrictions
- Import restrictions for products from a specific country of origin
- Export restrictions to specific countries
- Export quantities restrictions

Based on the hazardous substance in the Logistics document, when transferred to SAP GTS, the system performs compliance checks and updates the status in the SAP GTS customs document. Within the Logistics document processing, you can check for this status; if it's not okay or blocked, you can stop the next process step. For example, if you have a sales order line blocked due to hazardous material, you can set up the system to stop the delivery note creation. If there are restrictions on the quantity, the system can check for the quantity that is allowed.

This same check can be also applied in the inbound for importing goods into the country through POs and goods receipts Logistics transactions. The function module that is used with the SAP ERP system for performing EH&S checks on POs is shown in Figure 1.16.

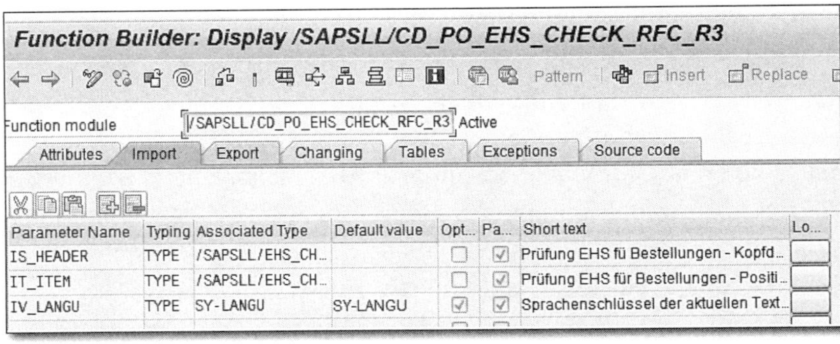

Figure 1.16 Function Module /SAPSLL/CD_PO_EHS_CHECK_RFC_R3 to Check EH&S with Purchase Orders

Preferential Processing

Preferential processing in SAP Risk Management helps exporters fulfill all of the legal requirements for customs tariff preferences, and to show that their goods are eligible for preferential treatment, thus enabling their customers to import these goods either duty-free or at a reduced rate of import duty. By providing evidence of eligibility for preferential treatment, exporters therefore gain a significant competitive advantage.

At a high level, preferential processing involves maintaining the following:

- Vendor declaration.
- Material or bill of material for usage indicator, if it's manufactured internally or sourced externally.
- The result of the threshold value for preferential treatment, stored in the product master.
- The threshold value of product with its Ex Works price. Depending on the result, the product is either eligible for preferential treatment or not.

If you have a bill of material (BOM), the preferential status is set for the main component in the product master. Results are determined and saved for each main component. On the sales document, the determined threshold value is compared with the Ex Works price and recognizes the preference situation for the current delivery (the Ex Works price must be greater than or equal to the threshold value). If the system determines a positive preference status, it allows you to print a preferential statement. This can be accessed in SAP GTS by choosing AREA MENU • RISK MANAGEMENT • PREFERENCE PROCESSING.

Vendor Declarations Management

Vendor Declarations Management provides functionality for requesting vendor declarations and sending reminders. Vendor declarations can be requested in email, via XML, or web-based via supplier self-service. These vendor declaration needs to be updated in the system, which allows you to aggregate them. The system allows you to issue or revoke vendor declarations, depending on the customer's purposes. For declaration to customs, the goods need to be classified according to a numbering schema. The numbering schema for the European Union is called *combined nomenclature* (CN). Imported and exported goods are identified by their classification number, starting with the subheading of the nomenclatures under which they fall. This determines which rate of customs duty applies, and how the goods are treated for statistical purposes.

Letter of Credit

SAP GTS risk management offers the *letter of credit* functionality. In a sales transaction, in compliance with the terms of payment that the exporter has requested, the importer opens a letter of credit at the bank of its choice. After approving the request for the letter of credit, the opening bank can contact the confirming bank's branch in the exporter's country to open the letter of credit on behalf of the importer and for the benefit of the exporter.

The letter of credit receipt gives the exporter the assurance of the importer's ability to pay, and the goods shipment is released. The exporter submits the shipping document and the letter of credit to the confirming bank, which checks the shipping documents for any discrepancies and pays the exporter the stipulated amount. The documents are forwarded to the opening bank in return for payment, and the opening bank then negotiates with the importer payment according to the stipulated terms in exchange for the shipping documents.

There are three different types of documentary letters of credit:

- Revocable
- Irrevocable confirmed
- Irrevocable unconfirmed

Figure 1.17 looks at the export and import process for Letters of Credit, referred to as LOC in the figure.

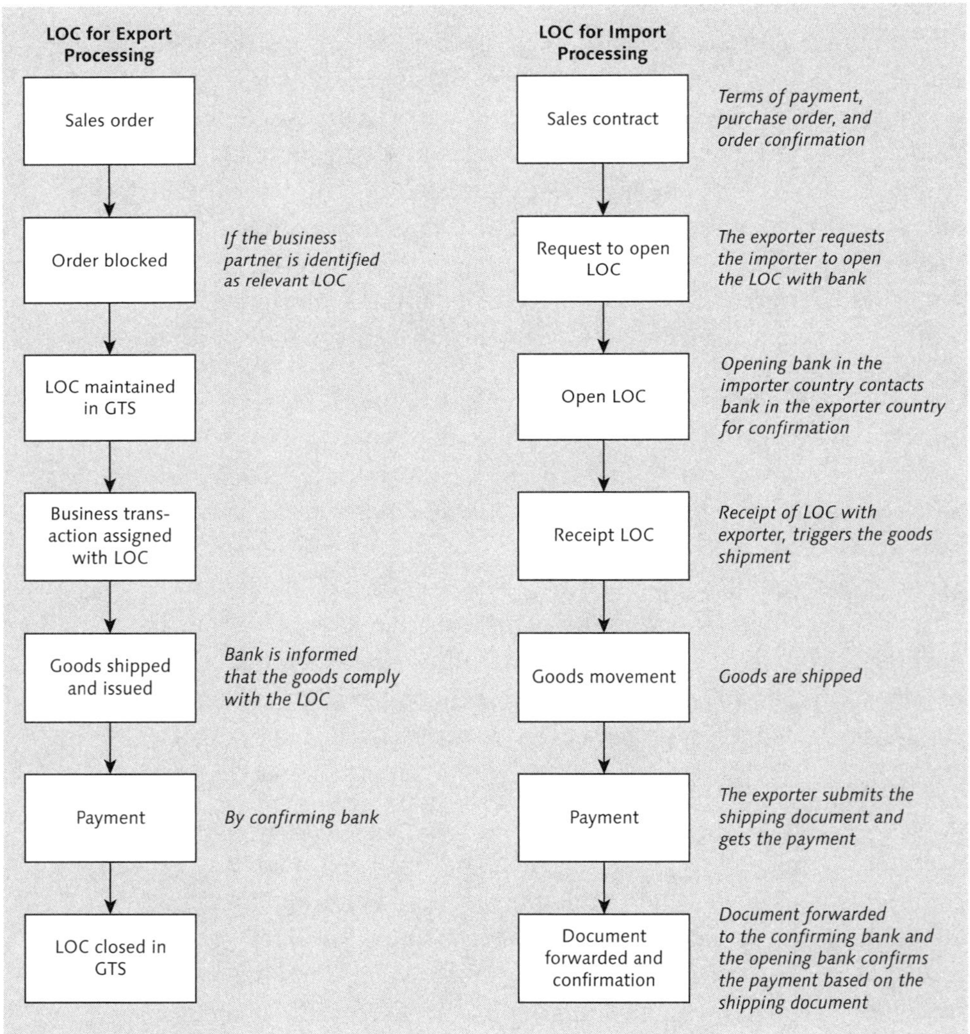

Figure 1.17 Letters of Credit Export and Import Process

Electronics Compliance Reporting

Intra European Community Trade Statistics (Intrastat) is a system for collecting statistics on the exchange of goods among member states of the European Union (EU). When the customs check on the EU internal borders disappeared, the opportunity to use the data from customs declarations for the compilation of the foreign exchange of goods statistics also disappeared. Consequently, the requirement for collecting data directly from the economic operator involved in the intra-community exchange of goods came into force. This system provides direct collection of information from economic operators and communities engaged in internal exchange of goods and registered in the Value-Added Tax (VAT) system. Statistics on the exchange of goods with non-EU countries are compiled by the *Extra European Community Trade Statistics* (Extrastat) system, based on customs declarations.

Arrivals and Dispatches for Intrastat declaration

Arrivals for Intrastat declaration include goods dispatched from another EU member state. *Dispatches* for Intrastat declaration include goods exported from one EU country to another. Operations that are subject to reporting need not necessarily have a commercial character. Return of goods and dispatch of replacement goods are reported in the direction in which the returned or replacement goods are actually dispatched. In practice, this means that an Intrastat declaration has to be prepared for the flow of incoming goods (arrivals) or the flow of outgoing goods (dispatches) for the following transactions:

- Selling from stock
- Procure to stock
- Inter-company selling
- Returns
- Inter-company stock transfer

The main components of ECR are Intrastat and Extrastat, commodity codes or classification, and master data. The Intrastat component allows you to edit documents, and display, import, or delete a worklist. Commodity codes or classifications let you maintain commodity codes and assign them to the products. Master data provides the functionality to edit the provider information, the default values, and business partners.

Trade processes are embedded within the SAP Supply Chain Management (SAP SCM) application, or an SAP ERP application is interfaced with a standalone trade application. SAP Foreign Trade is an example of the first scenario, and SAP GTS is an example of the second scenario. In both cases, trade processes go hand in hand with the supply chain process, and the supply chain process needs to comply with trade rules and regulations. The trade system and services are built to meet the trade requirement based on the system settings and business rules, which reflect the country-specific trade laws and the content to support the rules and regulations.

1.2 Shared Master Data

In Section 1.1, we explored all of the components of the SAP GRC suite, so now let's explore the common master data that supports the functionality across the platform. As we've mentioned, SAP GRC 10.0 provides master data as shared components between SAP Access Control, SAP Process Control, and SAP Risk Management modules. Providing shared master data such as organizational data is meant to reduce repetitive creation and maintenance of master data such as owners, controls, and organizations in multiple systems. At the same time, this shared master data helps in reporting the risks against individual organization unit levels or from the top level of the parent organization. This simplifies and enhances the user experience of managing and monitoring SAP GRC data centrally. Some examples for this shared data are organizational data, mitigation controls, drivers, impact and benefit categories for SAP Risk Management, HR relationships used for organization views, and so on. They all utilize a common SAP GRC repository to store and retrieve data.

Shared master data created from one component leverages the usage from other components. We'll discuss in later chapters how a mitigation control is created from SAP Process Control that can be utilized in risk mitigation, and how mitigation monitors and approvers are assigned in SAP Access Control.

Apart from shared master data, there are a few more technical components commonly used across SAP GRC 10. A few to mention here are connectors, connector groups, all workflow engine components (both basic and SAP GRC specific), policy management, surveys, and Continuous Control Monitoring (CCM).

Another SAP GRC tool to be aware of as an integration component is Content Lifecycle Management, which we discuss next.

1.3 SAP Content Life Cycle Management

Content Lifecycle Management (CLM) supports application content and managing that content, especially collaboration between partners and customers. CLM enables partners and customers to take a holistic view of package, version control, inspection, and import vendor content in SAP GRC applications. The master data types or vendor contents may include SAP Process Control controls, regulations, SAP Risk Management risks and KRIs, SAP Access Control rule sets, functions, and SAP GTS sanction party lists.

A complete list of CLM-managed master data types are given in Table 1.1, by SAP GRC application. While originally CLM had been expected to support Access Control content such as rulesets and functions, in the end this was not fully implemented.

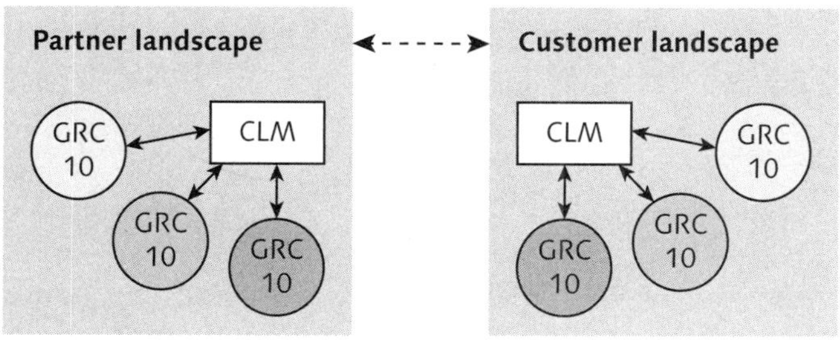

Figure 1.18 Content Lifecycle Management Content Sharing

The ABAP platform offers the Change and Transport Management system to address move content between systems within a single landscape. But as we will explain in greater detail in Chapter 10, those transport tools are quite cumbersome for customers to use, and in any case do not help move content (for example) between partner and customer landscapes. CLM helps both within-landscape and across-landscape content transport, as Figure 1.18 shows conceptually. CLM enables content providers establish a common channel for delivering application content and its subsequent changes in terms of content packages. For customers using those packages, CLM makes it possible to analyze the content coming from different vendors in a manageable way and to keep the content that fits closest to their business.

SAP Process Control	SAP Risk Management	SAP Access Control
Organization	Impact Category	
Central Risk Category	Driver Category	
Central Risk	Benefit Category	
Control Objective	Activity Type	
Account Group	Response Type	
Central Indirect Entity-Level Control Group	Risk Category	
Central Indirect Entity-Level Control	**Opportunity Category**	**SAP GTS**
Test Plan	Risk Template	Sanctioned Party List
Regulation	Opportunity Template	Delimiters
Regulation Group Regulation Requirements Central Process Central Subprocess Central Control	Activity Category	Aliases

Table 1.1 CLM Contents for Various SAP GRC Products

Now that we've reviewed the many components of SAP GRC and their shared master data, we need to touch on the general architecture and landscape of SAP GRC 10.0. Even a foundational knowledge of the technical components can lend an understanding of SAP GRC for business processes.

1.4 SAP GRC 10.0 Architecture and Landscape

SAP GRC 10.0 shares a common technology platform, which is a single SAP NetWeaver ABAP system. Most of the configurations are carried out here as this contains the Data Dictionary. We'll generally look at the backend system requirements, AS ABAP Components, Plug-in components and two-tier and three-tier landscapes, and frontend options.

1.4.1 Backend System Requirements

The SAP best practice recommendation is to install the standalone AS ABAP 7.02 SP06 or higher version. One important note here is that you don't install SAP GRC 10.0 in any SAP Business Suites, whereas all business suites connect to SAP GRC through plug-ins.

> **Note**
>
> SAP Access Control, SAP Process Control, and SAP Risk Management should not be installed with SAP Business Suite or with any SAP Business Suite components such as SAP ERP or any other satellite systems.

Following are the listed components of SAP GRC 10.0, which is installed on top of the previously mentioned base layer of AS ABAP. This removes a lot of hassle and cost from implementation, administration, and maintenance.

AS ABAP Components and Optional Components

Components to be installed on the standalone AS ABAP include the following:

- GRCFND_A is for SAP Access Control, SAP Process Control, and SAP Risk Management.

- SLL-LEG has its own add-on for SAP GTS.
- SLL-NFE is a separate add-on for SAP NFE.

Optional components include the following:

- In addition to the preceding components, CLM is an optional component that can be used for a variety of reasons as mentioned in Table 1.1.
- TREX can be added as an additional component to search and retrieve contents and documents from SAP GRC.
- SAP NetWeaver Portal 7.02 and Adobe Document Service (ADS) are also optional components.

Plug-In Components

You will note that throughout the chapters, we discuss the plug-in components of the GRC suite. It is these plug-ins to which we are referring. These are the components used in core SAP ERP or non-SAP ERP source systems to get the data for risk and compliance purposes. The source SAP systems should be 4.6C and above.

- GRCPINW holds SAP Access Control function modules for the SAP ERP system without SAP Human Resources (SAP HR/SAP HCM data).
- GRCPIERP contains SAP Process Control functions for automated controls and SAP Access Control functions pertaining to HR.
- SLL-PI holds all SAP GTS integration to the SAP ERP modules.
- Non-SAP ERP systems can be connected via adaptors provided by SAP partner companies or via custom built adaptors.

SAP GRC BI Content

This is an optional component, and SAP NetWeaver BW can be used for reporting via SAP GRC BI Content. BI Content 7.06 and SAP NetWeaver BW 7.02 must be used.

SAP NetWeaver PI

This is a required component for SAP NFE to exchange data with Brazil authorities. SAP NetWeaver PI 7.00 SP14 or higher version must be used.

SAP NetWeaver ID Management

This is a required component to connect with SAP Access Control 10 for risk analysis and provisioning purposes. SAP NetWeaver ID Management 7.2 must be used.

Adobe Documents Services

This is a required component for SAP GTS because it generates forms for SAP Customs Management. ADS can be an existing instance and be shared with other applications. For generating offline forms for SAP Process Control and SAP Risk Management surveys, it's recommended to share the ADS service. Most likely a portal instance running on AS Java may have ADS. SAP NetWeaver Java 7.02 Portal should be used.

TREX

A TREX instance is required for SAP GTS function sanctioned party list screening and some cases of search and classification of SAP Process Control and SAP Risk Management, but not for SAP Access Control. SAP NetWeaver 7.02 Search and Classification must be used.

To wrap up our discussion of the back-end system, and to help visualize the connections of the backend, please refer to Figure 1.19. This figure reflects the SAP GRC Landscape with the optional components.

Before we shift to the front end options available for the SAP GRC Suite, we would be remiss if we did not discuss the two-tier or three-tier landscapes available for SAP GRC. This is absolutely something you would want to consider for your implementation of the GRC suite.

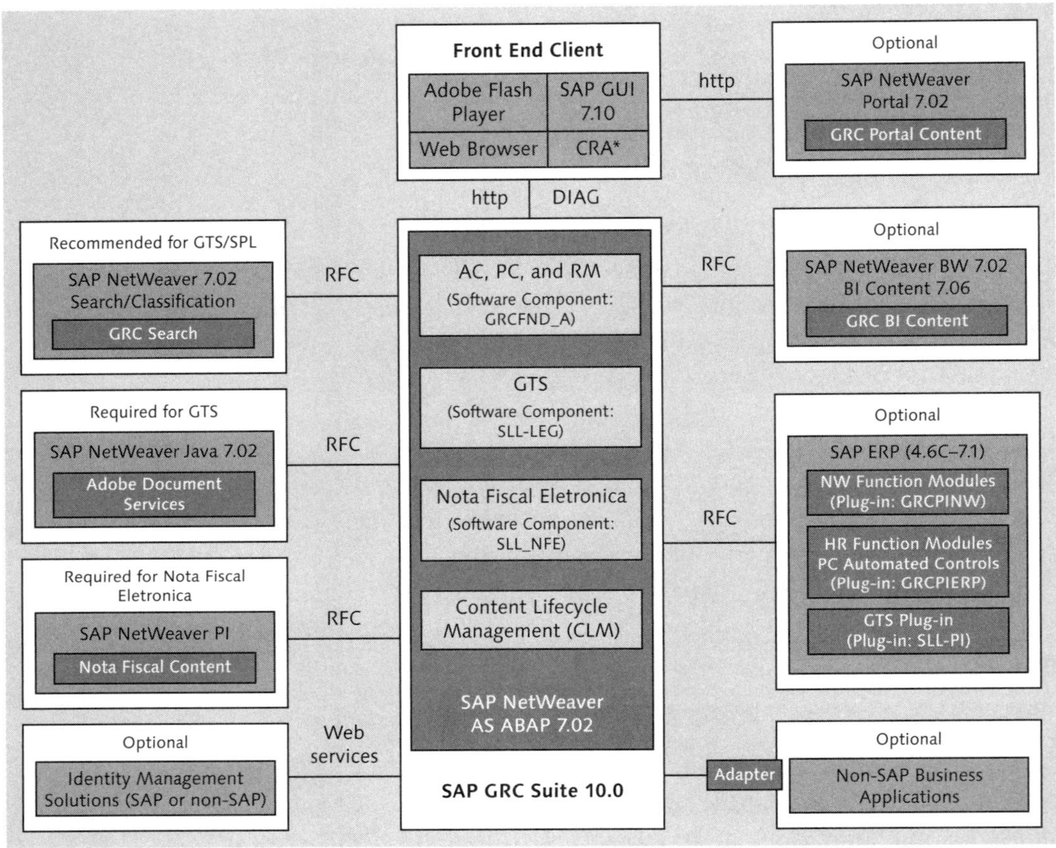

Figure 1.19 SAP GRC Landscape with Optional Components

1.4.2 Two-Tier versus Three-Tier Landscapes

A single SAP GRC system can be connected to various core systems globally across any enterprise to report, monitor, and comply in a reactive and proactive manner. This increase in complexity of the SAP GRC system demands a three-tier landscape to manage connected systems and enable them to meet various challenges during the implementation and maintenance phases. Remember, this is an ever-changing landscape and always coping with a company's IT systems, policies, and so on. Mostly larger enterprises use three-tier landscapes to tackle this complexity, whereas most small and medium enterprises prefer two-tier to reduce cost.

Now that we have review the back end system requirements, the two-tier or three-tier approach, let's look at the various front end options for the GRC suite.

1.4.3 Frontend Options

The SAP GRC system is a standalone system in which the presentation layer can be an Enterprise Portal (EP), SAP GUI, or NetWeaver Business Client (NWBC). The web browser can be used to access the embedded NWBC or SAP GRC via SAP NetWeaver Portal. The Adobe Flash Player 10 is used for displaying dashboards. The SAP Crystal Reports Adapter (CRA) is required for viewing SAP Crystal Reports in SAP GRC. See Figure 1.20.

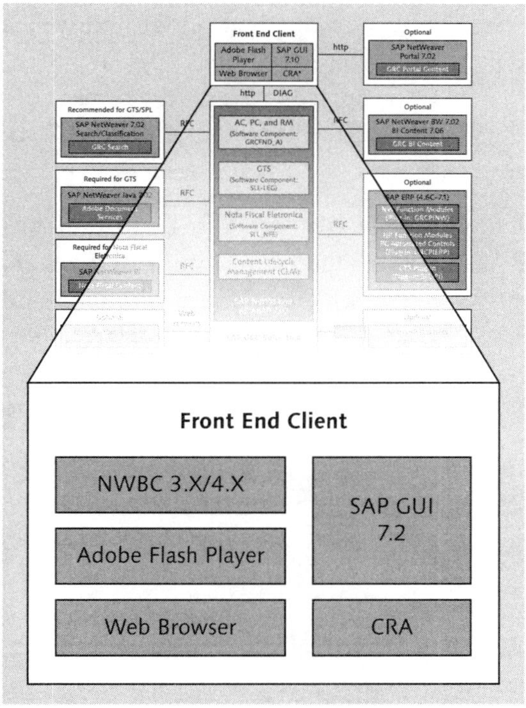

Figure 1.20 SAP GRC 10.0 Frontend Components

SAPGUI 7.20 or higher is required for administration or customizing tasks. Most of the implementation and configuration work is done at the backend during initial implementation. SAP GRC configuration and customizing are transported using the standard transport management system of the ABAP stack. Apart from the previously mentioned configuration, some additional setup, master data maintenance, and regular daily tasks can be carried out from NWBC or the portal frontend. NWBC can be installed at individual user desktops or centrally installed at the server and accessed from any web-based frontend.

1.5 Summary

This introductory chapter very briefly explained the nature of SAP GRC products and the value they bring to customers. We also touched upon the value of the integrated SAP GRC suite, over and above the value that the individual products bring. The rest of this book dives into much greater detail about the individual products. Chapters 2 through 8 address SAP Access Control, Chapters 9 through 14 cover SAP Process Control, Chapter 15 describes SAP Risk Management, and Chapter 17 addresses integration between the products.

In the next chapter, we will dive into the GRC suite, first with a discussion of SAP Access Control. We'll review the configuration and system settings of SAP Access Control, which will help you understand and make the SAP GRC system work for your enterprise effectively.

This chapter helps you start SAP GRC implementations via a hands-on introduction. We explain key real-world concepts critical to SAP GRC, and relate them to the terminology used by SAP GRC products.

2 Planning SAP GRC Implementations

This chapter is the first step toward an effective SAP Governance, Risk, and Compliance (SAP GRC) implementation. This chapter explores how to align your core business to build an effective SAP GRC implementation with a review of regulations and policies, the data structures that are in place to support your SAP GRC framework, the type of business processes and units in play, how to effectively manage IT compliance, and dealing with audits. Each module of SAP GRC has an individual overview chapter (Chapter 3 for SAP Access Control, Chapter 9 for SAP Process Control, and Chapter 15 for SAP Risk Management). This chapter does not aim to replicate those overview chapters but simply provide a foundation for business understanding and the implementation of SAP GRC.

From a SAP Access Control perspective, excessive access rights and segregation of duties (SoD) violations are key factors contributing to fraud. In this overview section, we examine some of the business challenges in typical system landscapes and how SAP Access Control helps to resolve the access and authorization issues.

Manually finding Segregation of Duties (SoD) violations in the system landscape of any company is cumbersome, slow, and inefficient. In the long term, giving users excessive authorizations (i.e., beyond their business needs) is more likely to harm the company than not. Further increases to system landscape complexity will likely increase SoD violations exponentially, making manual SoD verification virtually impossible.

Consider a simple situation in which your company is implementing an additional process within the existing system by adding a few custom transaction codes. After you start provisioning these transactions, SoD violations need to be verified for the users. Most companies in this situation check for SoD violations manually and only for core transactions. Some might only check currently provisioned roles and hence miss additional authorizations given to existing profiles.

If a later audit detects these violations, any subsequent process of finding and fixing all such problems will take more manpower at greater cost. Such inefficiencies lead to unidentified risks and missing mitigation controls, which can cost the company via penalties or losses due to fraud or avoidable errors. Compliance with regulations and good practices pay for themselves in many ways.

You'll see in Chapter 3 how SAP Access Control addresses all of the mentioned issues and manages the gaps and inefficiencies effectively with agility and flexibility in continuously changing IT and business environments. In forthcoming sections, you'll see some of the concepts that are used in SAP Access Control and how the tool is designed to handle your access and authorization analysis for SoD.

2.1 Regulations and Policies in SAP GRC

In this section, let's look at the various regulations and policies as they impact SAP GRC practices. We'll look generally at the different governing bodies of specific countries, regions, or multiple regions.

Sarbanes-Oxley Act

The Sarbanes-Oxley Act of 2002 (SOX) requires that US-listed companies have a system of internal controls and that directors monitor and report on operational risk. All companies must follow the US-specific Generally Accepted Accounting Principles (GAAP).

Similar standards have been adopted worldwide, and the spread of the International Financial Reporting Standard (IFRS) outside the United States means that a convergence is taking place in financial reporting and requirements. We've provided some of the SOX-equivalent regulations observed worldwide to govern internal controls in business.

To meet some of the SOX requirements, companies need to verify their system access and other processes in place, and they need to document the processes. According to SOX requirements, section 302 on IT general controls and Section 404 on internal controls need extensive documentation and testing of various practices held in companies.

CEO and CFO regulatory accountablity

Section 302 requires that when filing either an annual or quarterly report, both the CEO and the CFO must certify that they are responsible or accountable in the following ways:

- They need to have reviewed the annual or quarterly reports.
- They need to verify that the report doesn't contain any materially untrue statements, doesn't contain any material omission, and isn't misleading.
- They need to find that the financial statements and related information present the financial condition and financial results fairly and accurately.

In addition, the CEO and CFO must acknowledge that they are responsible for the following:

- Reviewing internal controls in the past 90 days, and reporting on these findings.
- Providing a list of all deficiencies in the internal controls and information on any fraud that involves employees who are involved with internal activities.
- Noting any significant changes in internal controls or related factors that could have a negative impact on the internal controls.

To meet the audit requirements mentioned here, IT and business teams need to put in lot of effort to establish and verify the controls. Beyond the SOX examples provided, globally there are other regulations to mandate internal controls. Let's see a few of those regulations next.

2.1.1 Japan's J-SOX

Global Regulations

The Japanese Financial Instruments and Exchange Law was promulgated as J-SOX. Also inspired by corporate scandals, J-SOX require that companies implement a management assessment of internal controls on financial reports. Like SOX, J-SOX is relevant to listed companies and their subsidiaries. It's expected that J-SOX will prompt mass audit automation, as it has in the United States.

2.1.2 Australia's CLERP-9

In Australia, Corporate Law Economic Reform Program (CLERP) aimed to strengthen Australia's financial reporting framework. The details of CLERP are less prescriptive than SOX. They contain reforms to the existing corporate governance provisions, including changes to financial reporting and executive remuneration. Provisions are in place to ensure auditor and analyst independence.

2.1.3 Canada's C-11

Brought into law in 2005, C-11 has established a procedure for the disclosure of wrongdoings in the public sector and ensures protection for the person who discloses these. Protecting the whistle-blower is also a vital point in SOX controls.

2.1.4 Basel II

Basel II has created an international standard for banking that regulators can use when making regulations on how much capital banks must have to offset potential risk. The more risk a bank has, the more capital it should have in place to ensure that it stays solvent. This requirement proactively provides a big safety net should things go horribly wrong.

Regulatory challenges—an organizational issue

For the companies to meet with various regulations is more laborious because there is no single information for compliance is available from single system or single business team. Siloed operations across different divisions and departments leads to more unproductive manual documentation, monitoring, and error-prone auditing processes. In the next section, let's check how SAP GRC tools provide you with a heads-up concerning risk alerts and monitoring controls with reporting to meet various compliance requirements.

2.2 Purpose of SAP GRC Tools

A SAP GRC system is designed to help organizations address various regulations and policies in an integrated approach to reduce cost, simplify GRC activities, easily adapt changes, and provide better visibility of risks and options to monitor them.

Achieving the core goal of preventing unauthorized access and SoD violations is possible using SAP Access Control tools that deal with the following:

- Perform a real-time fully automated security audit and SoD risk analysis and remediation for SAP and non-SAP software environments.
- Leverage the best-practice rule set for a quick start with easily adaptable custom changes to the rule set to monitor your SoD violations effectively and efficiently.
- Continuously monitor access risks and user assignments in a complex environment using single-system or cross-system violations.

Cost and time savings

At the same time, it helps to minimize cost and time by performing the following:

- Embed access risk analysis in user provisioning and role maintenance processes.
- Document and evaluate risk and controls in the tool and track all of their changes, along with rule set changes that are carried out.
- Streamline and automate reviews of user access using workflows.
- Integrate identity management solutions from SAP and non-SAP systems.

Real-time monitoring

Also it helps to achieve real-time monitoring by means of the following:

- Using centralized or decentralized options to manage emergency access and reporting from a central point.
- Empowering users with comprehensive capabilities for analysis, transaction access alerts, and reporting.
- Integrating with SAP Process Control for visibility into effectiveness of mitigating controls.

SAP Process Control provides comprehensive, end-to-end management of compliance and controls. Let's take a look at various options available in SAP Process Control to address section 404 of SOX compliance, and get a common understanding of what SAP Process Control does.

Documenting options

Documenting options include the following:

- As an initial step, you need to maintain your compliance and control structures, which include setting up organizations, business processes, risks, and controls.
- You need to establish the regulations and internal initiatives plus relevant company policies. Next you need to determine which structures will be shared across regulations such as SOX, J-SOX, FDA, NERC, or any other, as well as across SAP GRC.
- Then use rules to access SAP and non-SAP systems for automated testing and monitoring, and document the actions and results.

Scope options

Scope options include the following:

- You perform materiality analysis and assess risks to determine in-scope organizations and processes.
- You may use the resulting information to determine the level of evidence and test strategies that ensure you neither overtest (costly) nor undertest (unreliable) controls.
- You need to identify the scope of policies and methods of policy acceptance.

Monitoring options

Evaluating and monitoring options include the following:

- Evaluation starts with scheduled end-to-end, workflow-driven tests, assessments, and monitoring activities to execute your test strategies.
- Any issues raised (during automated or manual evaluations) are tracked through to completion of remediation activities and issue closure.
- Also, you need to distribute policies, and then receive and document policy acceptances.

Reporting options

Reporting options include the following:

- You can use embedded analytics and reports to provide continuous insight into the status of compliance and controls.
- You need to leverage hierarchical sign-off certifications to document acceptance of responsibility for internal controls and to freeze the status of data to ensure true historical reporting without the need for archiving.

To use these SAP GRC tools to get the maximum benefit for your company, you need to understand the master data that is used in SAP GRC systems and their relationship to real-world scenarios.

2.3 Business Processes and Controls

Businesses model their practices in business process models for various purposes: education and training, review and optimization of practices, audit planning, system implementation planning, user role assignments, workflow design and implementation, and so on. Naturally, the intended purpose determines the granularity of the business process model.

SAP GRC and the business process model

SAP GRC customers have a more focused goal—to identify controls motivated by the regulations and policies to be followed and to represent these controls in a business process hierarchy that shows their relationship to each other. Accordingly, SAP GRC products have a very simple data structure to represent the business process model. SAP GRC customers generally don't represent processes at as fine-grained a level as backend applications require. Unnecessary detail can confuse users and also adds overhead when updating the model after changes in the underlying business.

Business process hierarchies are SAP GRC master data shared among SAP Access Control, SAP Process Control, and SAP Risk Management. This sharing only occurs when any two (or all three) are installed together in the same system—the customer can choose to do so or run them separately in different systems.

As with business processes, so with organizational models—businesses maintain detailed models of organizational hierarchies in graphical modeling tools, Lightweight Directory Access Protocol (LDAP) software, and so forth. These models can combine geographical information, functional information, reporting lines, and personnel data to great level of detail. SAP GRC requires organizational models, but for a much more limited purpose: to tease out the variation in which regulations and policies apply and in the differences in control objectives by organizational structure. A related purpose is user role assignments by organization, for receiving workflows in SAP GRC business processes such as control assessments, defect remediation, and so forth.

2.4 Organizational Hierarchy and Local Controls

As a simple example, consider the purchasing process. Many companies configure purchasing approval limits by the organizational hierarchy. For example, if all employees can purchase supplies worth $50 without approval, first-line managers might be able to approve up to $1,000, the next level up to $10,000, and so forth. But these limits vary by organization; sales might have more liberal limits than, say, manufacturing. They will also vary by geography; purchasing limits for US employees will be set in US dollars, German employees in Euros. So the same control in the purchase requisition approval business process step will operate a bit differently, depending on the organization. In SAP Process Control terminology, this is a *local* control. SAP Risk Management has a similar concept of local risks.

In summary, SAP GRC products use organizational hierarchies to reflect variations in which regulations and policies apply and to capture so-called local variations in consequent compliance objectives, risk measures and impacts, and so on. This complicates the setup, but makes SAP GRC products much more useful to customers because this is the reality SAP customers face.

In Figure 2.1, you can see the details of the ORGANIZATIONS screen, the STANDARD HIERARCHY view, and the organization units and their reporting structure. You may choose a simplified reporting structure so that

SAP Access Control reports directly to your parent or root organization, or you can configure a more detailed structure that allows for both SAP Access Control and SAP Process Control go with their respective organizations to report risks.

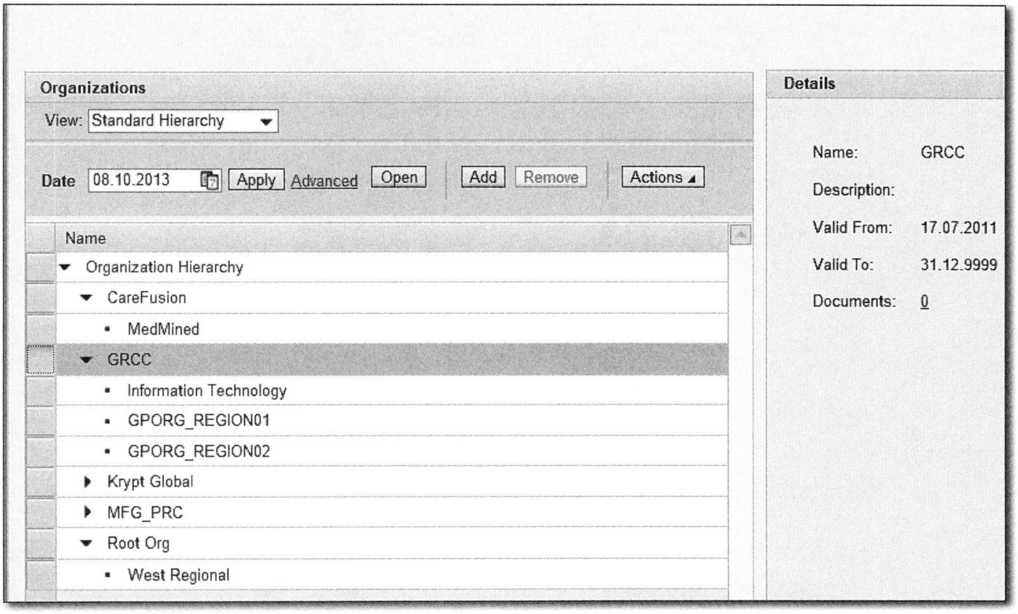

Figure 2.1 Definition of Root Organization

This decision should be discussed prior to implementation with your internal audit team to identify or utilize the current reporting structure used by the audit team. Figure 2.2 shows how the GRC organization has been configured.

As you can see in Figure 2.2, the root organization (GRCC) is created as the standard hierarchy, which will have a time frame with start date (VALID FROM) and end date (VALID TO) information. Multiple tabs are available at every organizational unit level, which hold all relationship data at their organizational level. These tabs holds detailed field level information on master data such as business processes, subprocesses, controls, owners, regulations, policies, and entity-level controls.

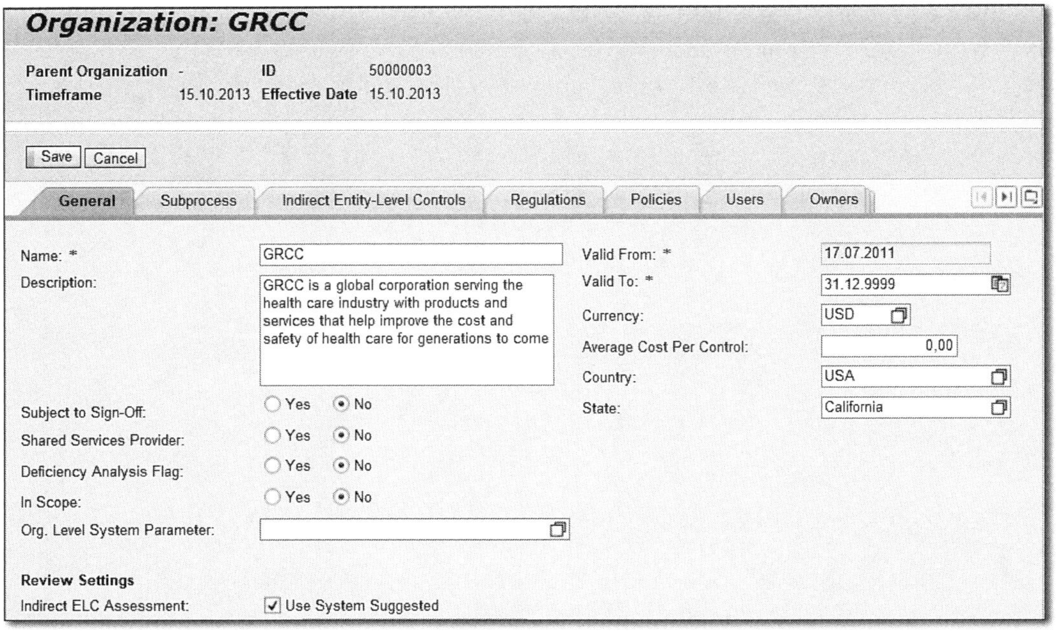

Figure 2.2 Root Organization Creation Initial Screen

We'll see some more details on the objects that are part of this root organization in Chapter 4. Overall master data flow is shown in Figure 2.3. You might be sharing some of this data, such as organization hierarchy, controls, risks and subprocesses with organization assignments in SAP Access Control.

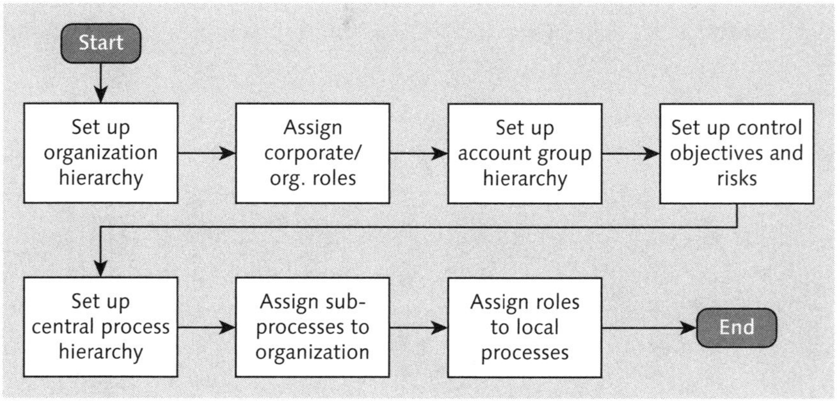

Figure 2.3 SAP Process Control Master Data Flow

We'll explore master data further in the subsequent chapters surrounding the SAP GRC modules, but let's review how you maintain other data such as subprocesses and controls. Also this is one of the places where you need to maintain SAP Access Control owners related to this organization too. You can also maintain multiple regulations and policies here. Most of the master data related to controls are created or maintained at the Controls and Control Owner Maintenance screen, shown in Figure 2.4.

Figure 2.4 Organizational Unit for Controls and Control Owner Maintenance Screen

The information configured in the organizational unit includes shared objects between SAP Access Control, SAP Process Control, and SAP Risk Management. In the next section, we'll introduce some basics of the user interface.

2.5 User Interface and Work Center

SAP GRC products can be presented to their end-users through either the SAP NetWeaver Portal or through the SAP NetWeaver Business Client (NWBC). NWBC is a rich frontend that is popular with many SAP GRC customers because it's much simpler to use and set up than the SAP NetWeaver Portal. The initial screen displays with work centers such as

My Home, Setup, and so on, based on your authorization. SAP GRC uses standard Transaction PFCG authorization to control access. You can also modify or hide different applications that are shown as links in this screen.

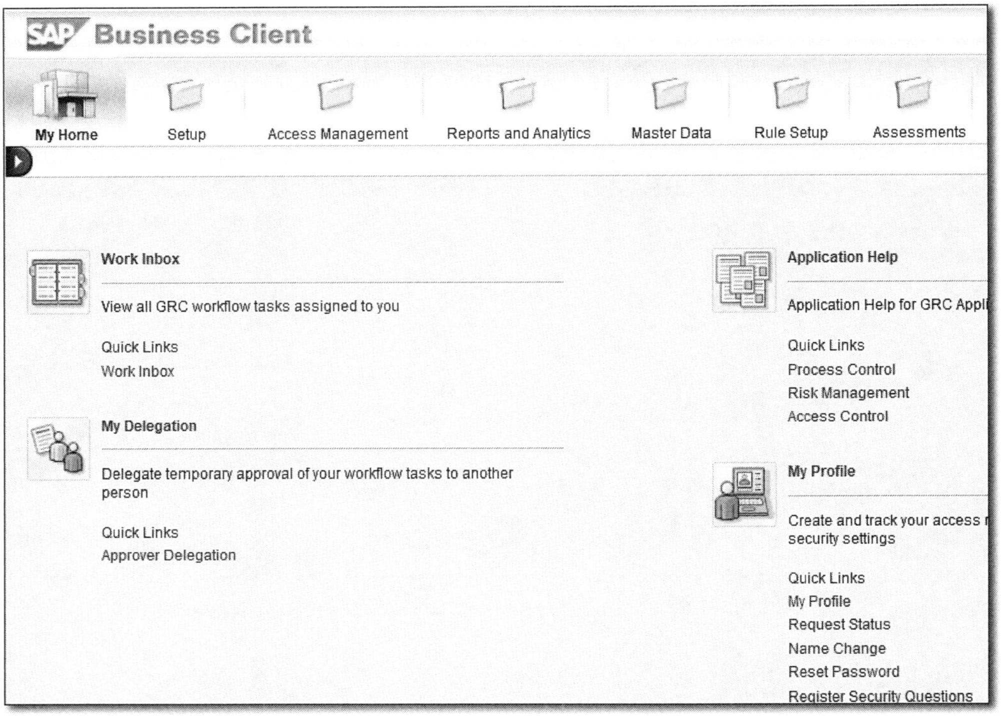

Figure 2.5 SAP NetWeaver Business Client Initial Screen

SAP NetWeaver Business Client planning considerations

We strongly advise some additional planning on how to use NWBC work sets with appropriate roles to reduce screen clutter. The added configuration effort is amply repaid by simpler training needs, reduced errors, and quicker adoption by end users. User interface (UI) screens focused around the functionality each user needs to do their jobs is a good thing. We suggest using Transaction PFCG and the customization of the launch pad options to customize the various roles in your environment. In the next section, we'll discuss different kinds of rules that are used in the SAP GRC system.

2.6 Rules

In SAP GRC, the core deficiency detection is done through setting up rules and finding and reporting these scenarios or risks that violate these rules. The rules set up in SAP Access Control are different from SAP Process Control and SAP Risk Management. In SAP Access Control, access rules are used to determine the underlying risks in any user profile. In other words, an access risk is identified with two conflicting *functions*, where each function contains underlying transactions and authorizations that are provisioned in the profiles of a single user. During the rule generation process, the system generates rule IDs that are uniquely named with two conflicting transaction combinations. This rule ID combines with the connecting system name to create a unique identifier that is used during access risk analysis.

Access Control rules

Other examples of SAP Access Control rules include critical access rules and exception access rules. Critical access rules identify roles and profiles that give access to particularly sensitive transactions and settings. Exceptional access rules are helpful in eliminating false positives based on organizational level restrictions. SAP Access Control rules and maintenance are discussed further in Chapter 5.

Process Control rules and Continuous Control Monitoring

SAP Process Control offers feature-rich and powerful Continuous Controls Monitoring (CCM) capabilities, covered in great detail in Chapters 11 through 14. CCM operates through business rules, which encode the logic of determining the correct operation of the control in question. When such a CCM rule executes, it can find violations of the control, which are called defects in SAP GRC. Upon finding defects, the rule creates a case management issue, which then routes to the control owner for remediation.

SAP Risk Management Rules

SAP Risk Management offers the capability to monitor key risk indicators (KRIs); the monitoring logic is encoded in business rules.

2.7 Reporting

SAP GRC 10.1 provides excellent reporting features and rich report content. This combines with a flexible reporting and analytics framework to offer SAP Access Control customers a greatly enhanced experience. The Reports and Analytics work center offers reports and dashboards covering the configuration, setup, and operation of SAP GRC products. Examples include issue status, control evaluations, risk analysis, mitigation, alerts, audit reports, user provisioning, emergency access reports for audit tracking, and so on.

Web Dynpro reporting framework

SAP GRC uses an ABAP Web Dynpro framework that is built with Floor Plan Manager (FPM), which is the newer UI framework that uses GUI building blocks to customize or modify the UI without changing the underlying code. It also enables personalization of end-user screens, including overview pages. In reporting, one advantage is that you can now personalize your reports and save them as variants.

In Figure 2.6, we've highlighted a few of the reporting features that will help you understand the newer capabilities of SAP GRC reporting.

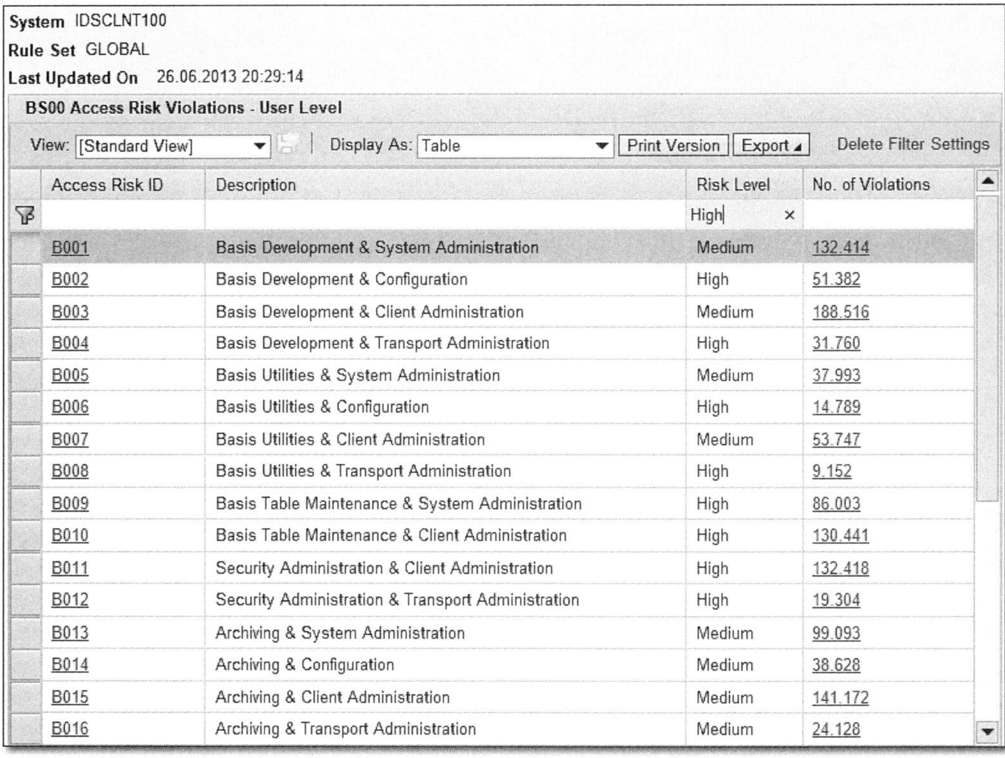

Access Risk ID	Description	Risk Level	No. of Violations
		High	
B001	Basis Development & System Administration	Medium	132.414
B002	Basis Development & Configuration	High	51.382
B003	Basis Development & Client Administration	Medium	188.516
B004	Basis Development & Transport Administration	High	31.760
B005	Basis Utilities & System Administration	Medium	37.993
B006	Basis Utilities & Configuration	High	14.789
B007	Basis Utilities & Client Administration	Medium	53.747
B008	Basis Utilities & Transport Administration	High	9.152
B009	Basis Table Maintenance & System Administration	High	86.003
B010	Basis Table Maintenance & Client Administration	High	130.441
B011	Security Administration & Client Administration	High	132.418
B012	Security Administration & Transport Administration	High	19.304
B013	Archiving & System Administration	Medium	99.093
B014	Archiving & Configuration	Medium	38.628
B015	Archiving & Client Administration	Medium	141.172
B016	Archiving & Transport Administration	Medium	24.128

Figure 2.6 Reporting Option to Filter a Column by Specific Values

Reporting capabilities within SAP GRC 10.0

SAP GRC 10.x has improved and enhanced your reporting results that are similar to SAP ABAP table services. You can do the following:

- Sort, arrange, or rearrange columns and filter them (refer to Figure 2.6).
- Use grouping and aggregation if any calculation values are available to find total count and so on (see Figure 2.7).
- Export to single or multiple spreadsheets for further analysis.
- Integrate with SAP Crystal Reports.

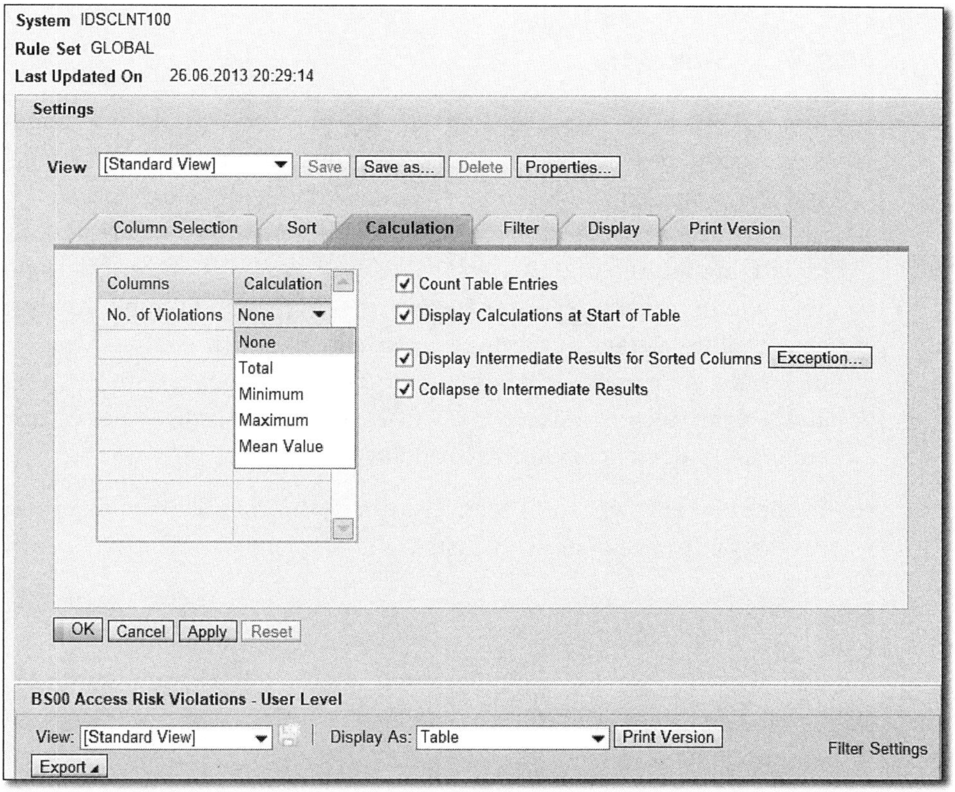

Figure 2.7 Reporting Settings with Calculation Option for Aggregation

All of the reporting links can be customized globally using Transaction LPD_CUST. This transaction allows you to group the reports differently from what SAP provides within the standard set, reorder the sequences of the reports, and hide unwanted reports from this screen.

In general, in the GRC suite, reports are related to a plug-in system, there is an audit report specific to the SAP GRC system itself. If you're in the REPORTS AND ANALYTICS work set, then select the link CHANGE LOG from AUDIT REPORTS. Here this report gives all change information related to SAP Access Control changes, including master data such as risk, function, rule set, role, criticality, firefighter ID, and so on. This report uses the CHANGED ON date field for the testing period to fetch the change log data between these specified dates.

2.8 Summary

In this chapter, we introduced terminology used in SAP GRC and hinted at the range of functionality SAP GRC offers customers in compliance and risk management. SAP Access Control, being the oldest product in the suite, offers the most mature functionality, which is widely used for identifying and managing access risks. SAP Process Control offers the ability to model any regulatory requirements, map their implications to controls, and establish monitoring to measure such compliance. SAP Risk Management models risks, along with their impacts and drivers, and it helps customers keep track of expected and actual costs of risks and plan mitigation responses to risk events.

In the next chapter, we'll look into the technical architecture of SAP Access Control and how to install and implement the solution efficiently.

This chapter is a hands-on guide to all of the mandatory and optional configurations and settings required immediately after installation of SAP Access Control. We'll review every step of the preliminary common configuration with details on how to prepare the system for different environments to suit your needs.

3 SAP Access Control Overview

In Chapter 2, we provided details on all of the master data used in different SAP Access Control tools. In this chapter, you'll see more of the technical details on preparing SAP Access Control to configure its tools. At this point, we assume that the SAP Basis team has installed all necessary components within the SAP GRC ABAP Stack and Java Stack (optional based on your company's requirement, if you need to use any Adobe forms). Also, we assume that the necessary components for any plug-in are installed in either SAP ERP systems or any other SAP or non-SAP systems that SAP Access Control needs to send and receive data. The required post-installation work will be carried out as part of the configuration in this chapter.

As we outlined in our GRC suite overview chapter, Access Control has four different tools and all of the concepts of those tools and explanations on implementation of all 4 tools will be explained in detail in this book. In this chapter, we'll explore the SAP NetWeaver Business Client framework, the access options, and the technical settings that need to be in place prior to implementation of SAP Access Control. These configurations ensure a successful SAP Access Control implementation. After these elements are addressed, we'll look at the specifics of configuring SAP Access Control in conjunction with SAP Process Control and SAP Risk Management. To get started, let's look at the technical requirements required to start your work.

3.1 General Assumptions during Implementation

By general assumptions, we mean the tools and system setup that should be in place prior to implementing and configuring SAP Access Control. There are four tools—Emergency Access Management, Access Risk Analysis, Business Role Manager, and User Access Management—that are part of SAP Access Control as discussed in Section 1.2. All of these tools share common master data and a common platform with other SAP GRC components—SAP Process Control and SAP Risk Management. In this chapter, we'll show you how to prepare technical components and set the stage for implementing all SAP Access Control tools on top of it.

Technical architecture that supports SAP Access Control

As discussed Chapter 1, SAP Access Control sits on top of the core ABAP component along with SAP GRC-specific software component GRFND_A, as shown in the SAP Access Control system architecture (see Figure 3.1). You need to check the basic requirement of the support pack level that is the minimum required SAP NetWeaver Application Server ABAP 7.02 system before proceeding to install core component GRCFND_A. GRCFND_A is the software component that is commonly used by SAP Access Control, SAP Process Control, and SAP Risk Management. You can install SAP NetWeaver Application Server Java 7.02 to have Adobe Document Services (ADS), which may be necessary based on your SAP Access Control requirement. Alternatively, ADS can be connected to any other SAP NetWeaver Portal component that is already present in your landscape. Discuss this with your Basis team, and then based on the requirement and usage level, either use SAP NetWeaver AS Java in a standalone SAP GRC system or connect it to any other existing SAP NetWeaver AS Java system. General configuration of SAP Access Control, SAP Process Control, and SAP Risk Management use core implementation Transaction SPRO. Some additional configuration work that involves master data maintenance should be done from the SAP NetWeaver Business Client; this includes frontend user interface (UI) visualization, defining owners, controls, risk maintenance, and so on.

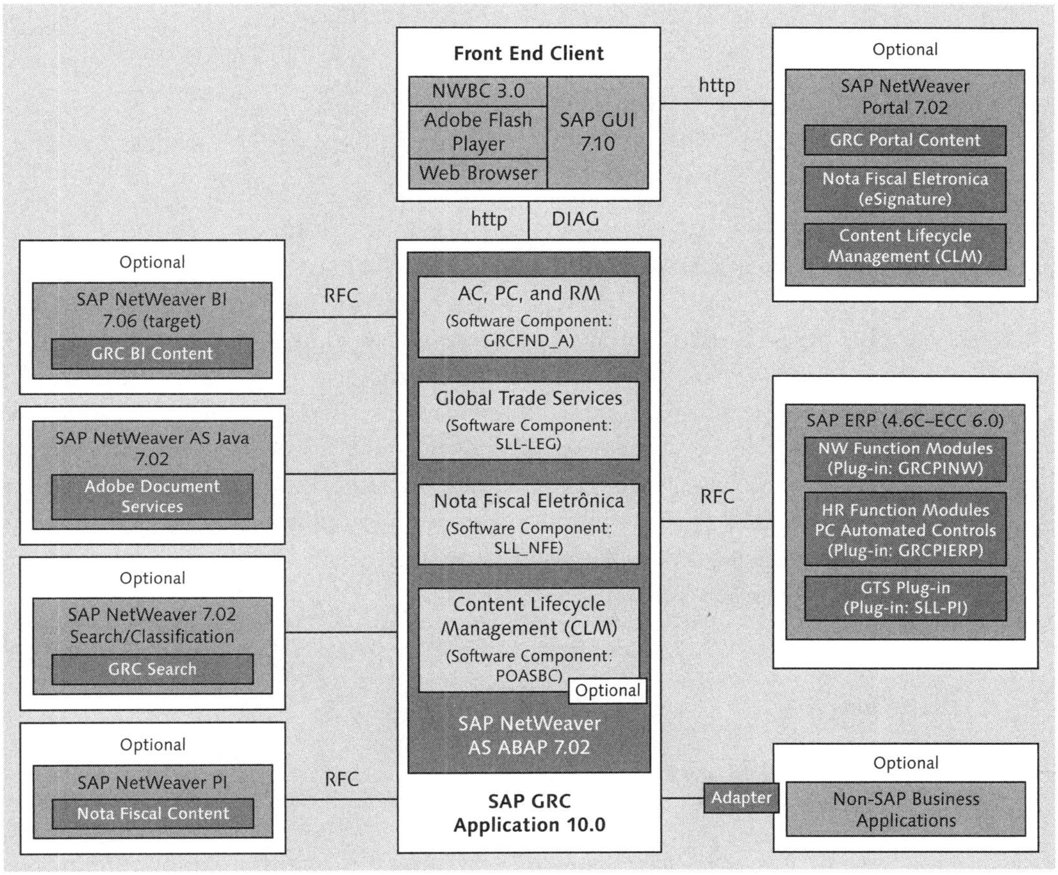

Figure 3.1 SAP Access Control System Architecture

In this section, we'll look at the SAP NetWeaver Business Client and the steps that need to be maintained, as well as explain a practical use case to further demonstrate how the SAP NetWeaver Business Client should be configured to support SAP Access Control. We'll discuss SAP NetWeaver Business Client and the basic SAP NetWeaver Business Client UI that is used for all of the SAP Access Control tools. You'll see how to activate the connection between core AS ABAP and SAP NetWeaver Business Client and how to invoke the services or Web Dynpro programs that are opened either in the SAP NetWeaver Business Client frontend or in a web browser. You can use SAP NetWeaver Business Client as a UI to maintain master data, execute risk analysis, create and approve user requests, schedule and execute background jobs, and execute reports that are used in SAP Access Control tools.

3.1.1 SAP NetWeaver Business Client as SAP Access Control User Interface

SAP NetWeaver Business Client is a rich frontend client program that serves as a single point of entry for user access to multiple applications and a harmonized secure entry point for the SAP UI. It harmonizes access to existing SAPGUI transactions in addition to providing SAP GRC worksets and work centers that are created using ABAP Web Dynpro. This UI is fully integrated with the browser and can be called by invoking Transaction SAP NetWeaver Business Client from SAPGUI directly. All SAP NetWeaver Business Client-related SAP Access Control applications and application links must be activated from the Internet Communication Framework—Transaction SICF. We'll see this later in the "Check SAP ICF Services" section.

Note

Make sure that your web browser/portal page display size is set to 100% zoom level. Due to technical complexities with Web Dynpro, a zoom level higher or lower than 100% can have an extreme impact on performance.

SAP NetWeaver Business Client comes in two flavors: SAP NetWeaver Business Client for HTML, which has zero installation on the client side, and the desktop client version, which is similar to SAPGUI but in a smaller footprint with plenty of functions.

SAP NetWeaver Business Client for HTML

SAP NetWeaver Business Client for HTML is a browser-based shell (available only for ABAP-based systems), in which all SAPGUI transactions are rendered using the SAPGUI for HTML rendering engine. You can invoke this from the ABAP system by executing Transaction SAP NetWeaver Business Client, which opens in your browser window. This runs from the default Internet browser, which is useful when you plan to run SAP NetWeaver Business Client without any add-on installations or you want to embed it with the portal frontend. SAP NetWeaver Business Client for HTML as a light version is only supported against ABAP systems, using established roles from Transaction PFCG.

SAP NetWeaver Business Client for Desktop

The SAP NetWeaver Business Client for Desktop is a .NET-based application, in which SAPGUI is used as the rendering engine if installed. SAP NetWeaver Business Client effectively replaces SAPGUI as main entry point to SAP applications; however, it does use SAPGUI to run existing applications, and this can be installed in individual desktops or at the server side at a central location. As mentioned, SAP NetWeaver Business Client UI is really a thin client because of its smaller footprint and memory to load and run; however, at the same time, it's a rich client because of its flexibility and the options available for the user. To start using the desktop client, you need to maintain some of the system parameters such as the system URL or host system and port, client number, and system description, which are the same as the SAPGUI parameters (see Figure 3.2) to start using the SAP NetWeaver Business Client frontend. This path and port are maintained as part of the Internet Communication Framework (ICF) setup. The desktop client has its own advantage when you plan to run it on the Windows platform with a full search function that enables you to search in SAP application servers as well as your desktop.

SAP NetWeaver Business Client for Desktop can also run against single ABAP systems with Transaction PFCG as a role repository, or against a SAP NetWeaver Portal using the Portal Content Directory (PCD) as the role repository. SAP NetWeaver Business Client related roles are maintained through Transaction PFCG in the SAPGUI like any other SAP ERP security roles. These roles and authorizations control what is visible and what the user can do within each application (Web Dynpro link) in the SAP NetWeaver Business Client frontend with comprehensive navigation functions. When you want to use SAP NetWeaver Business Client from the portal, it retrieves content from PCD via a set of web services.

Now that we've explored the different SAP NetWeaver Business Client options for SAP Access Control, let's look at how SAP SAP NetWeaver Business Client is used in a practical sense.

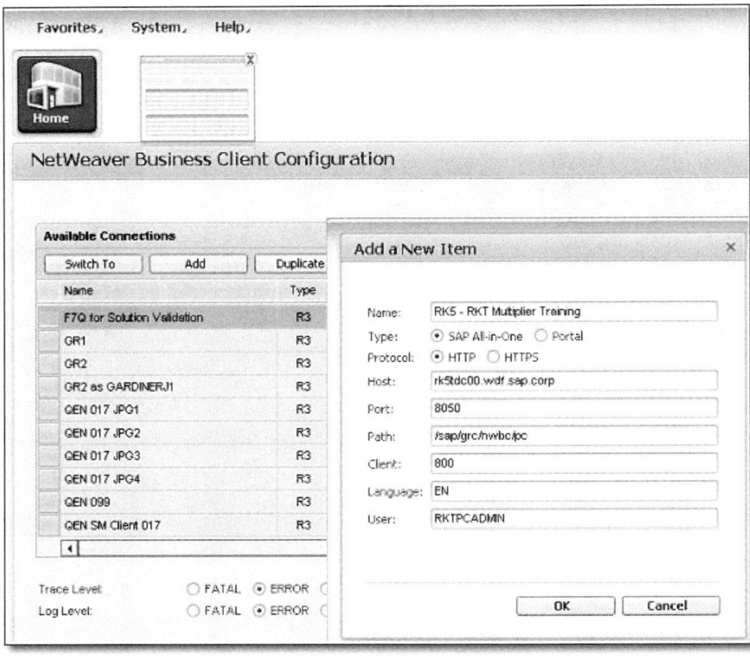

Figure 3.2 SAP NetWeaver Business Client Frontend Setup

3.1.2 SAP NetWeaver Business Client Use Case

The SAP NetWeaver Business Client frontend is used to maintain master data and tool usage from risk analysis, handle user access request creation, and provide access to the work inbox for approval or rejections, as well as provide access to various SAP Access Control reports and dashboards. Apart from Web Dynpro applications, SAP NetWeaver Business Client can be seamlessly integrated into conventional Dynpro applications such as generic SAP GUI-based transactions. These transaction authorizations and assignments can be maintained from Transaction PFCG roles. For some customers, this helps the user community to access SAP Access Control applications and other user maintenance and reporting options of the SAP GRC system from here.

Access options for SAP NetWeaver Business Client users

There are three access options for SAP NetWeaver Business Client available for the user. Most of these settings demand the involvement of SAP Basis consultants. Note that we're discussing the possible options and not the actual implementation. The actual implementation is beyond the scope of this book. There are three different access options from the frontend:

- **SAP NetWeaver Business Client on client side**
  This option requires the installation of the SAP NetWeaver Business Client GUI for logon as a desktop client. In this case, companies need to install them in individual desktops, and some basic user training might needed because the icons and navigation options are a little different from standard SAP GUI.
- **SAP NetWeaver Business Client on server side**
  By default, most clients prefer this because it eliminates additional installation work on individual desktops and has central maintenance. But there are some disadvantages to using this, such as no search, overflow menu, dropdown menus, or drag-and-drop function for work centers. Also this can be used in MAC OS and Linux. The initial SAP NetWeaver Business Client screen shows the My Home workset (see Figure 3.3). The first four worksets shown are used by SAP Access Control, and the last three worksets belong to SAP Process Control. The worksets shown in your initial screen are based on the assigned Transaction PFCG role to your user ID.
- **SAP NetWeaver Portal**
  If you have SAP NetWeaver Portal in place already this will be most suitable to run on SAP NetWeaver Java AS.

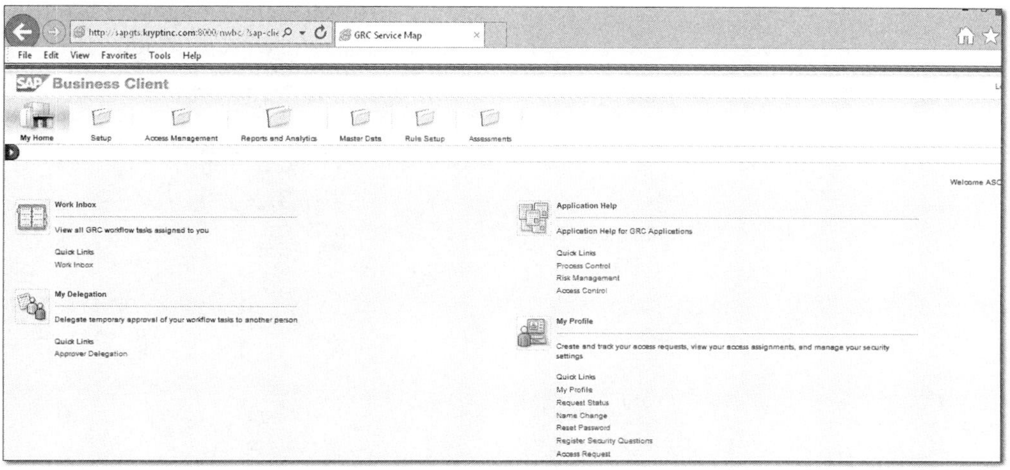

Figure 3.3 SAP NetWeaver Business Client Browser-Based Initial Page

Each access method has its own merits and demerits as discussed in the preceding list, so you should choose the one that best suits your environment. There are several consideration you should review when choosing an access method:

Access method considerations

- Operating systems users might use.
- Whether you prefer to install desktop applications or not.
- How extensively the full search option is required from the users' perspective.
- Whether you've already replaced SAPGUI with SAP NetWeaver Business Client for other SAP systems.

We've discussed some basic technical settings on activation of the Internet Communication Framework, which is mandatory to work with Web Dynpro applications that will be accessed or executed using one of the previously mentioned options. Now let's discuss the technical post-installation settings to start the SAP GRC implementation.

3.2 SAP Access Control—Post-Installation Technical Settings

Let's move forward with configuration details in the ABAP system after the initial installation of the SAP GRC system; this can be the installation of SAP Access Control add-on alone or installation along with SAP Risk Management and SAP Process Control. We'll walk through all of the necessary steps generic and sometimes basic steps that need to be carried out for either standalone or combined systems of SAP Access Control, SAP Process Control, and SAP Risk Management. Here, we assume most of the Basis activities will be carried out by your Basis team. We have listed them below as a checklist for SAP Access Control consultant and Basis consultant to perform on the installed system. For a big picture overview, the steps that we'll cover in the configuration are listed here:

Basis preliminary check workflow

- Performing the Basis preliminary check
  - Activating BC Sets
  - Activating the common workflow

- Troubleshooting task-specific customization
- Performing shared configuration of the SAP GRC system
- Activating the role profiles
- Creating the initial users

We'll review each of these tasks in the following sections. Let's first look at the Basis preliminary checks that should happen first and foremost before SAP Access Control can be used.

3.2.1 Basis Preliminary Check

In your SAP GRC system, you need to do an initial consistency check using Transaction SICK and confirm that post-installation activities using Transaction SE06 for transport organizer are completed by your Basis team. The Basis team should also complete the following:

Basis Team responsibilities

- Install the latest support packs.
- Check the license data to confirm there are no surprises later.
- Load the system profile to confirm that system-related parameter maintenance in Transaction RZ10 is carried out.
- Check the system time settings. All SAP GRC reporting, including SAP Access Control information, is based on this time setting so it's critical when your system landscape is spread across different time zones.
- Schedule regular background monitoring jobs such as those related to statistics and log collection.
- Check that the system logs are generated and available to view.
- Configure the SAP Service Marketplace setting to apply SAP notes.
- Apply any other SAP note recommendations.
- Schedule the load generator background job from Transaction SGEN.

This list is intended to be a verification checklist to ensure that your Basis team didn't miss anything during the post-installation process. Figure 3.4 details the support pack level from the Basis components. GRCFND_A is the SAP GRC system foundation component that comprises all core applications related to SAP Access Control, SAP Process Control, and SAP Risk Management.

Support Package Level for Installed Software Components

Component	Release	SP-Level	Support Package	Short description of the component
SAP_BASIS	702	0013	SAPKB70213	SAP Basis Component
SAP_ABA	702	0013	SAPKA70213	Cross-Application Component
PI_BASIS	702	0013	SAPK-70213INPIBASIS	Basis Plug-In
BI_CONT	707	0004	SAPK-70704INBICONT	Business Intelligence Content
SAP_BS_FND	702	0004	SAPK-70204INSAPBSFND	SAP Business Suite Foundation
SAP_BW	702	0013	SAPKW70213	SAP Business Warehouse
GRCFND_A	V1000	0011	SAPK-V1011INGRCFNDA	GRC Foundation ABAP
GRCPINW	V1000_700	0004	SAPK-10304INGRCPINW	SAP GRC NW Plug-in

Figure 3.4 Installed Components for the SAP GRC System

Additional Plug-Ins for SAP ERP Integration with SAP Access Control

Apart from the previously mentioned components, you need to install the following plug-ins on the backend SAP ERP system for integration of SAP Access Control with SAP ERP:

- GRCPINW plug-in for SAP Access Control for non-HR functions (VIRSANH RTA in SAP Access Control 5.X versions)
- GRCPIERP plug-in for SAP Access Control and SAP Process Control HR functions (VIRSAHR RTA in SAP Access Control 5.X versions)

After the preceding installation is over, don't forget to add both components in the SAP ERP system and any other plug-in system that needs to be connected to the SAP GRC system for monitoring. During the installation, check that the compatible versions and the technical details are provided in the SAP Service Marketplace as well as the installation guide. Note the additional disclaimer in the SAP GRC 10 Installation Guide stating that SAP Access Control, SAP Process Control, SAP Risk Management 10.0 should not be installed with SAP Business Suite or with any SAP Business Suite components such as SAP ERP, SAP Supply Chain Management (SAP SCM), SAP Customer Relationship Management (SAP CRM), and SAP Supplier Relationship Management (SAP SRM).

In the next section, we'll discuss the post-installation activities to prepare the foundation steps of the SAP GRC system. These post installation activities are generally completed by the Basis team and include:

- Creating Client Copy for SAP Access Control

- Activating Applications in the Access Control System
- Check SAP Internet Communication Framework Services

Let's review each of these post-installation steps in further detail.

Create Client Copy for SAP Access Control

After the SAP GRC components installation, you need to do a client copy for SAP Access Control, assuming that you're planning to implement SAP Risk Management and SAP Process Control as well. This activity is the same as preparing any other SAP system for actual use of the system that is a copy of master client 000. If you planned to have only SAP Access Control in your SAP GRC environment, then you can ignore this subsection; otherwise, you need to carry out this activity to get client-specific customizing data. Refer to SAP OSS Note 1505255 – Transfer Client-Specific Customizing for SAP Process Control, SAP Risk Management 10.0, which is specific to SAP Process Control, SAP Risk Management.

When you're ready to perform client copy from base client '000' to target client, you should perform it with instance profile parameter *login/no_automatic_user_sapstar = 0*. Also you will need to ensure that transport connection is setup within the landscape. This will help to move all of the configuration and changes you'll be carrying out in the development system to quality and production systems. This is similar to preparing any ABAP based system in your landscape.

Activating Applications in the SAP Access Control System

In this activity, you configure the SAP GRC system as to whether you want to activate the SAP Access Control alone or along with other components such as SAP Process Control or SAP Risk Management. Based on your requirements, either one or all of the components of SAP GRC can be activated in a single client or in respective clients if they are planned for different clients.

As you can see in Figure 3.5, you can activate this from Transaction SPRO, and then select SAP CUSTOMIZING IMPLEMENTATION GUIDE • GOVERNANCE, RISK AND COMPLIANCE • GENERAL SETTINGS • ACTIVATE

Applications in Client. In the Active Application in ClientArea, you can select the Active checkbox either only for GRC-AC or for all of the application components based on your requirements. If you plan to work on SAP Process Control or SAP Risk Management later in the same client, you can either set this as Active now or later when you start the other tool implementation.

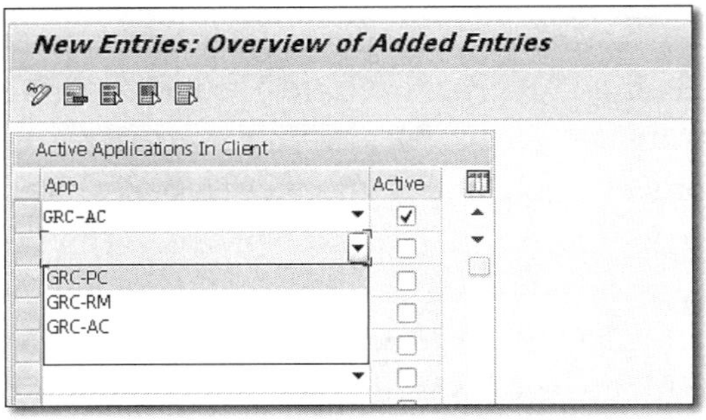

Figure 3.5 Application Component Activation

Based on the activated entries, the application functionality will be active in the current client. As you've seen earlier, some customers prefer to have SAP Process Control and SAP Risk Management maintained in different clients; basically, this setting in the SAP ERP system is client specific. After activation of the applications, you need to check that all Web Dynpro applications are active. Activation sequence of webdynpro applications is not an important factor. Next we will see how this can be performed.

Check SAP Internet Communication Framework Services

In this section, we'll see how to set up Internet Communication Framework (ICF) for all Web Dynpro services to view all ABAP Web Dynpro applications from SAP NetWeaver Business Client or SAP NetWeaver Portal. You can activate all of these application components by executing Transaction SICF. All of the services and application components can be viewed as shown in Figure 3.6. At the bottom of the window, the application hierarchy folder appears in a list with the services bundled together.

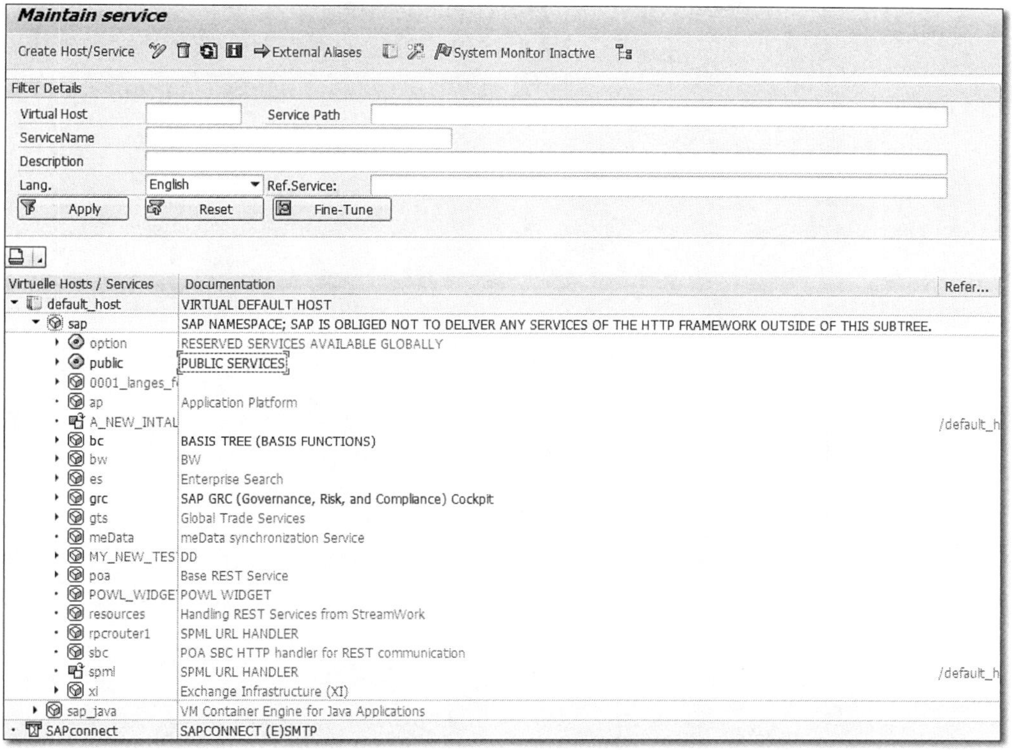

Figure 3.6 ICF Services Activation to Access the SAP Access Control Application from the SAP NetWeaver Business Client Frontend

Expand node DEFAULT_HOST • SAP • PUBLIC, right-click the node, and choose ACTIVATE SERVICE for all subnodes.

You can also activate all ICF services within the following:

- /SAP/PUBLIC: All subnodes.
- /SAP/BC: All subnodes.
- /SAP/GRC: All subnodes.

Advanced User and SICF activation

If you're an expert user and know specific nodes that need to be either activated or deactivated, then you can enter the service name and press the Enter button. At the bottom of the window, you'll see only the selected service. The cockpit subnode for SAP NetWeaver Business Client can be accessed by navigating down to SICF activation.

To deactivate any service, select the relevant service node(s), choose SERVICE/HOST, and then select DEACTIVATE. As shown in Figure 3.7, you can also choose DEACTIVATE SERVICE from the right-click context menu.

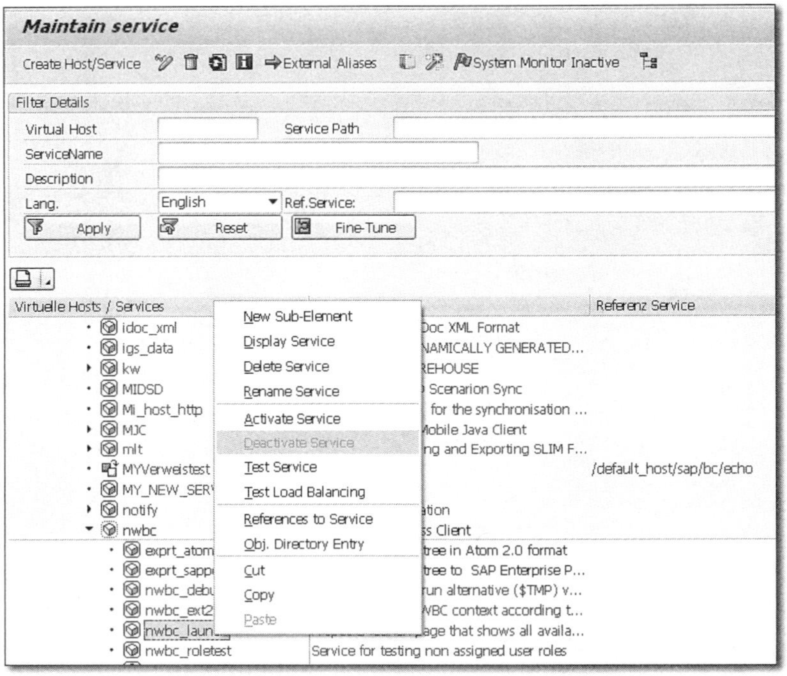

Figure 3.7 Deactivation of SAP NetWeaver Business Client Launch Screen

The relevant SAP NetWeaver Business Client nodes and the Internet Communication Framework

Table 3.1 lists some special SAP NetWeaver Business Client nodes in the ICF tree explained from a security viewpoint.

Node	Security Relevance
/SAP/BC/SAP NETWEAVER BUSINESS CLIENT	This must be active to use productively.
/SAP NETWEAVER BUSINESS CLIENT	This should be available to use productively.
/SAP/BC/SAP NETWEAVER BUSINESS CLIENT/SAP NETWEAVER BUSINESS CLIENT_LAUNCH	SAP recommends deactivating this node.

Table 3.1 SAP NetWeaver Business Client Services to Be Deactivated

Node	Security Relevance
/SAP/BC/SAP NetWeaver Business Client/SAP NetWeaver Business Client_test	SAP recommends deactivating this node.
/SAP/BC/SAP NetWeaver Business Client/SAP NetWeaver Business Client_testcanvas	SAP recommends deactivating this node.
/SAP/BC/SAP NetWeaver Business Client/SAP NetWeaver Business Client_debug	SAP recommends deactivating this node.
/SAP/BC/SAP NetWeaver Business Client/exprt_sapportal	SAP recommends deactivating this node, unless the functionality is explicitly used with an enterprise portal in your system landscape.

Table 3.1 SAP NetWeaver Business Client Services to Be Deactivated (Cont.)

At this point in the implementation of SAP Access Control, you have activated and deactivated most recommended ICF services to suit your business needs. So far, you've carried out SAP Basis activities and settings that are required to configure and implement SAP Access Control. In the next section, we'll discuss the purpose of Business Configuration Sets (BC Sets) and how to activate them.

3.2.2 Activating BC Sets

Most of the Basis activity was completed in an earlier section, so from this activity on, it's performed as part of SAP Access Control configurator or implementation consultant work. BC Sets are snapshots of customization settings or some master data that are captured by SAP and delivered as part of the software package. During the installation process, these BC Sets are available for customers to start their work swiftly without going through very detailed data creation or configuration work by manual process.

If you're familiar with the earlier SAP Access Control version 5.X, you might have dealt with various templates that are used to load master data or migrate configuration data from a development system to a quality control and a production system. Activation of a BC Set is similar to this activity. For example, you may want to create role sensitivity with three or four different values, and they can be created manually in the SAP Access Control configuration. Alternatively, instead of creating all of the generic master data from scratch in the SAP Access Control configuration, you can load these data into the SAP Access Control system by activating the corresponding BC Set in the system. You'll see the details of which BC Sets and relevant master data are loaded as a result of BC Set activation in later part of this section.

BC Set activation scenario

In a more complex scenario example for BC Sets, you might need to maintain multiple workflow processes and their relevant components in User Access Management (one of the SAP Access Control tools), and creating them individually as needed may take a long time and require a more skilled person. Instead, if you activate a BC Set related to workflow processes, all relevant tables and table views are populated, and you can customize the configuration to suit your needs. By doing this, you'll reduce a lot of resources and concentrate more on customizing that is specific to your enterprise rather than SAP Access Control tool components. At the same time, you have the flexibility to modify these values or descriptions. In other words, BC Set data are basically table entries that are populated in multiple tables and that can be extracted and repopulated in different systems directly from Transaction SCPR20. Some of the benefits are efficient group rollout, systems are easier to create and maintain, customizing can be performed at a business level, and change management is quicker and safer. The bottom line is that your upgrade will be simpler. Now that you understand the benefits of the BC Set, let's explore how to activate a BC Set.

BC Set naming conventions

In SAP GRC, BC Sets related to SAP Access Control have a naming convention that starts with GRAC; those related to SAP Process Control start with GRPC; and those related to SAP Risk Management start with GRRM. To activate the BC Set, go to Transaction SCPR20, and in the BC Set input field, enter "GRAC*". You can view when you select [F4] or Help values to list all available BC Sets in SAP GRC system. Alternatively this can be viewed by executing Transaction SPRO and selecting corresponding configuration node where BC Set Exists available in Additional Information (see Figure 3.8).

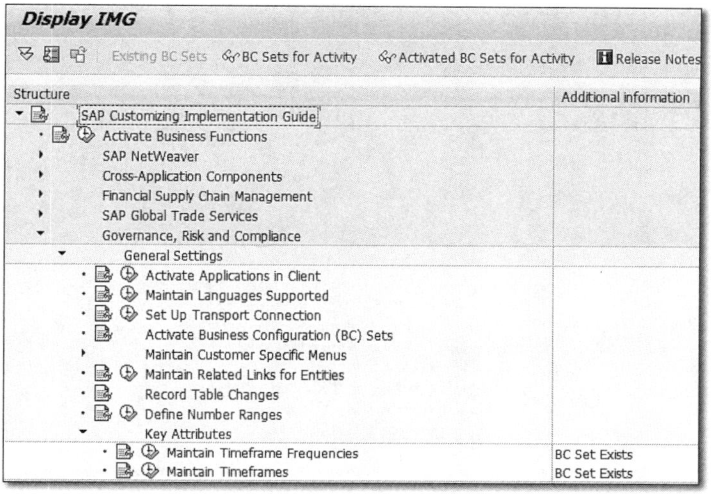

Figure 3.8 BC Set Activation from Transaction SPRO

BC Set activation

After you've selected the necessary BC Set, click on the BC SETS FOR ACTIVITY button. From this screen, click on the GOTO menu and select ACTIVATION TRANSACTION. This opens Transaction SCPR20, where you can activate all required BC Sets directly (as explained in the individual SAP Access Control tool configuration). Use expert mode for activation and make sure that you see the message ACTIVATION SUCCESSFULLY COMPLETED.

Error resolution

If you face any error on activation, refer to SAP OSS messages or contact SAP. Often, your issues can be resolved if you spend some time on the activation log and understand where the issue originates. You can access activation log details by using pressing Ctrl+F2, which shows you all of the activation logs. You can make a decision on this activation log data, which is hierarchically listed per date and time stamp. You can verify the earlier error or any warnings from here. If you want to overwrite the data or append data from a BC Set, you can turn expert mode on while doing the activation. In the screen shown in Figure 3.9, you can verify the latest activation details from the left side panel tree structure. You can drill down all of the way to various details such as database tables and records from this screen. This gives the details of any previous activation of the BC Set, including multiple activations with date and time stamp irrespective of whether they were successful.

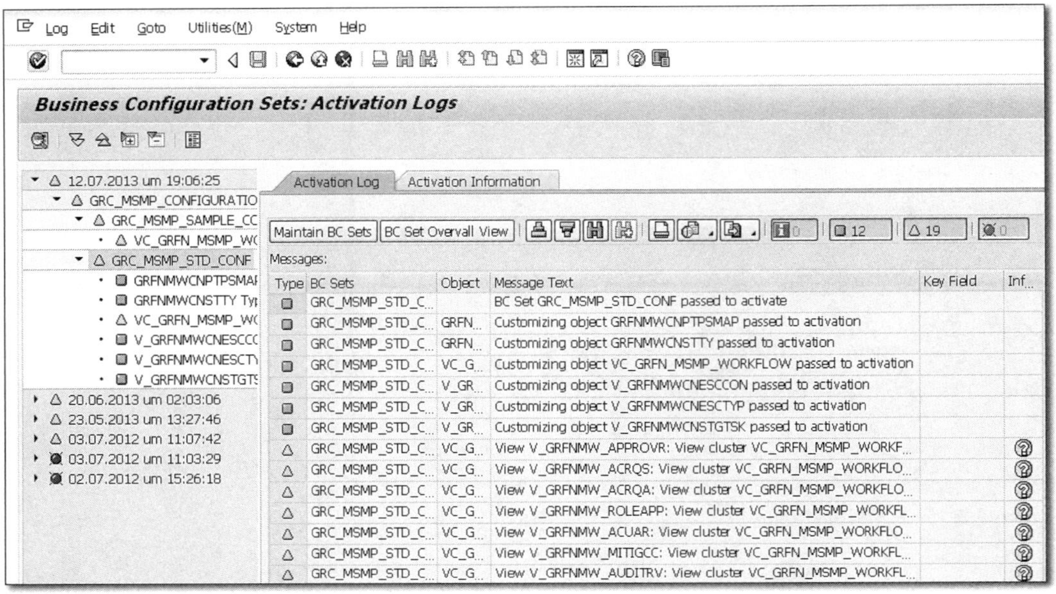

Figure 3.9 BC Set Activation Log

Reviewing all the available BC Sets in Access Control

In a GRC system the technical component naming conventions are often used like GRAC for SAP Access Control, similarly, GRPC naming convention is used for SAP Process Control, GRRM is meant for SAP Risk Management, and GRFN is meant all SAP GRC common functions such as workflow-related technical object values. If you want to view all of the SAP Access Control BC Sets then you can use Transaction GRAC*' to list out all the available BC Sets. You can activate all needed BC Sets from here as a baseline specific to your version of SAP GRC. In the product-specific chapters, we'll look at the individual tools, the data applicable, the BC Sets, and how to activate these elements. When you've activated the initial screen as shown in Figure 3.10 is shown with caution. Select the options 'OVERWRITE ALL DATA' and 'DEFAULT MODE(RECOMMENDED)' to activate very first time. In case, you are familiar with BC Set activation you can use 'EXPERT MODE' for activation and any data you want to append with already existing data then use 'DO NOT OVERWRITE DEFAULT VALUES'. Upon activation of the BC Set, you'll be asked to save this as a customizing request. Later all the activation details will be moved to quality and production system by such transport requests.

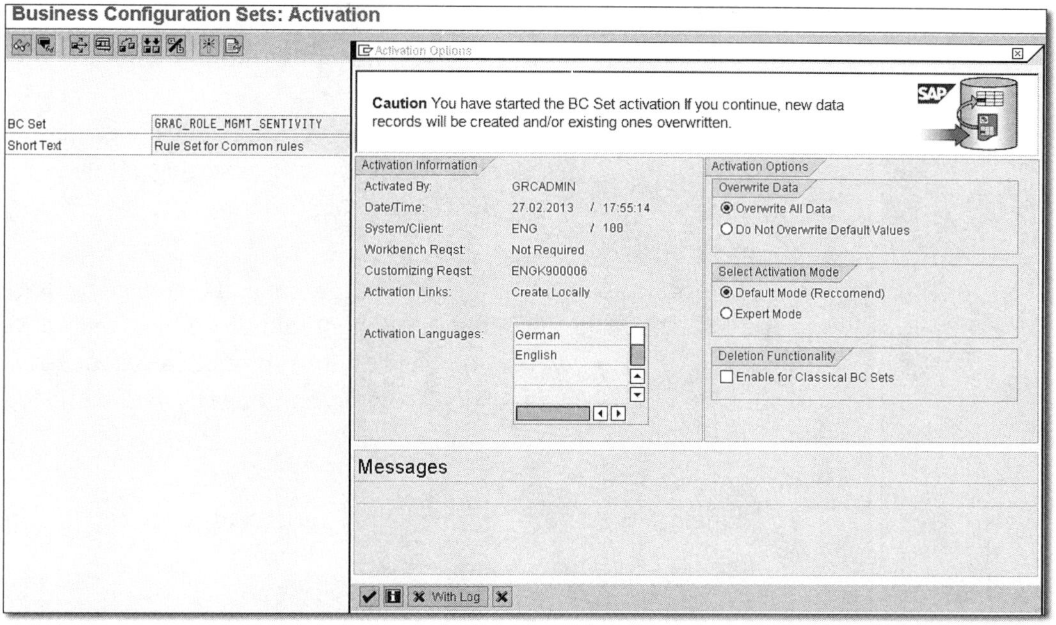

Figure 3.10 BC Set Activation

There are a few additional functions available in this screen and they are available as a menu button on top of the screen. The individual functions of this menu button are described in the following list and the corresponding icons for the functions are shown in Figure 3.11. You can use this screen to help you do a check of the BC Set and the activation log details. It's a best practice to run these checks before activation of any BC Set.

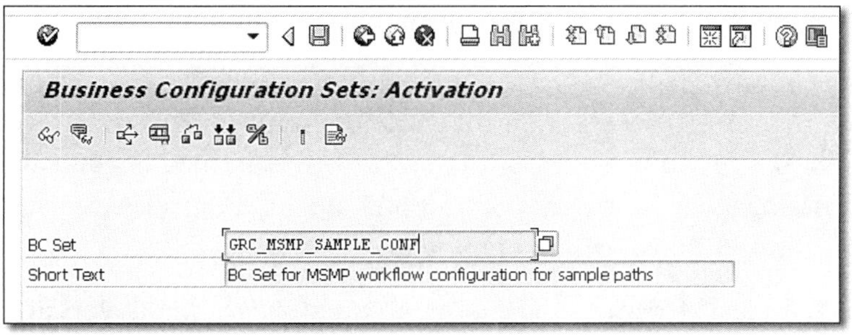

Figure 3.11 BC Set Activation Initial Screen and Various Check Icons

BC Set Activation Checklist

- Compare with Customizing Tables (with or without Variable Check)
  It's advisable to run this with variable check before activating any BC Set. You can compare customizing tables with the BC Set data to ensure that the BC Sets contain the actual system settings. If there are differences, you can copy the customizing table data into the BC Set.
- Compare BC Set with Another BC Set
  This helps to compare two BC Sets. For example, if you need to check between a Multistage Multipath (MSMP) sample and a standard BC Set to verify some values, you have options to select to see different attributes such as data records, activities and objects, variable fields, and so on.
- Consistency Check
  This function checks for any restrictions such as any problematic data records.
- Key Conflict Check
  Key conflicts occur if there are two data records in a hierarchical BC Set with the same key but different values; for instance, one is manually created and another one is delivered.

We've now covered the general BC Set activation, related activities, and various checking that needs to be carried out before activation and after activation to ensure that BC Set data is populated correctly in your system. In the next section, we'll cover how to activate basic workflow-related settings.

3.2.3 Activate Common Workflow

In this section, we'll discuss all of the tasks in detail that need to be carried out to make SAP Access Control workflow settings. This consists of two parts: the first one is part of the SAP ABAP workflow engine, and the other one is more specific to the SAP Access Control Multi-step Multi-path (MSMP) workflow component.

Activation of the common workflow engine

First we'll discuss activation and configuration of the common workflow engine. Though we assume that either you or your technical team member exposed to the common workflow engine settings related to

SAP ERP environment, we would like to give some detailed walk through on workflow engine activation. We've provided detailed steps on this activation to help those of you focused on working on SAP GRC workflow to design a better workflow configuration in your SAP Access Control environment. To start this from SAPGUI, execute Transaction SPRO, and select the menu path, SAP CUSTOMIZING IMPLEMENTATION GUIDE • GOVERNANCE, RISK AND COMPLIANCE • GENERAL SETTINGS • WORKFLOW • PERFORM AUTOMATIC WORKFLOW CUSTOMIZING. You can also directly execute Transaction SWU3. You can see this navigation in Figure 3.12.

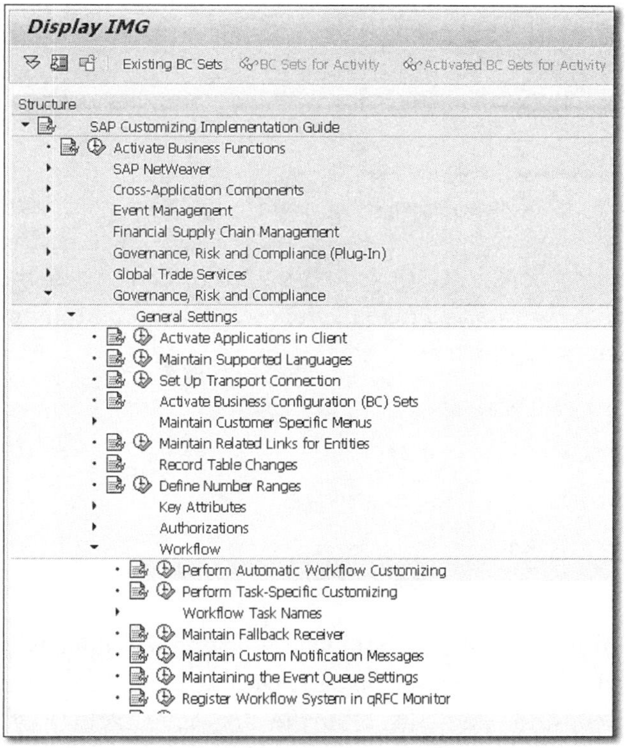

Figure 3.12 Base Workflow Engine Customization

From the PERFORM AUTOMATIC WORKFLOW CUSTOMIZATION option, you are taken to the AUTOMATIC WORKFLOW CUSTOMIZING initial screen, shown in Figure 3.13. Here you need to perform most of the steps that create and activate all workflow technical objects and make the whole workflow engine ready with all interconnections within the system and web service-related settings, triggering, scheduling events, and other background jobs during workflow runtime. Some of the activities are carried out automatically, and some of them may cause an error that requires you to handle with system-specific settings and configuration. These errors will cause a clear log entry on why there is an error and how to rectify it, with help readily available at every node level.

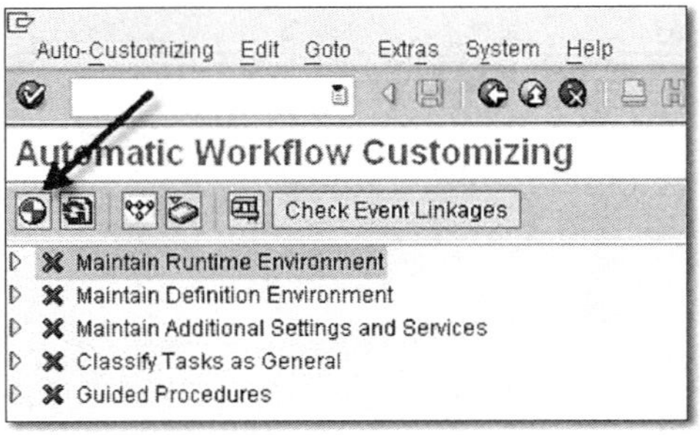

Figure 3.13 Automatic Workflow Customizing Initial Screen

Automatic workflow customization

From the AUTOMATIC WORKFLOW CUSTOMIZING initial screen, all the tasks under this activity is classified in to the following five sub-headings or sections as shown in Figure 3.13. They are:

1. MAINTAIN RUNTIME ENVIRONMENT.
2. MAINTAIN DEFINITION ENVIRONMENT.
3. MAINTAIN ADDITIONAL SETTINGS AND SERVICES.
4. CLASSIFY TASKS AS GENERAL.
5. GUIDED PROCEDURES.

You need to activate all of the steps from this transaction individually at all the five sub-heading level to complete basic workflow engine related settings. To do so, position the cursor on the first sub-heading, and choose function key F9. Now the execution will carry out automatic setting relevant to all the child nodes underneath the sub-heading MAINTAIN RUNTIME ENVIRONMENT

After the automatic configuration of the first sub-heading MAINTAIN RUNTIME ENVIRONMENT, carry out the following tasks as part of completion check:

1. Maintain your runtime environment.
2. Maintain definition environment.
3. Perform Additional settings and server maintenance.
4. Ensure that the Guided Procedures Process template has been applied.

Let's review each of these tasks in further details and review the customization needed for each of these tasks.

Tasks for the completion check

1. Choose Maintain Runtime Environment, and select Perform Automatic Workflow Customizing by selecting function key F9. This action executes all of the steps in automatic workflow customizing that are discussed below including generation of the user WF-BATCH.
   - Configure RFC destination.
   - Maintain system administrator for workflow.
   - Maintain active plan variant.
   - Classify decision task as general.
   - document generation/form integration.
   - Schedule background job for missed deadline.
   - Schedule background job for work items with errors.
   - Schedule background job for condition evaluation.
   - Schedule background job for event queue.
   - Schedule background job for clearing tasks.

Maintain definition environment

Now let's move to the second section of automatic workflow customization in Transaction SWU3.

2. Choose maintain definition environment. You have to execute the below mentioned three activities in this section manually. They are
   - Maintain prefix numbers
   - Check number ranges
   - Check entries from HR Tables

First, you must execute the link maintain prefix numbers, underneath the subheading maintain definition environment, the resulting screen is as shown in Figure 3.14. This enables the system to set up an internal number range that is required for workflow and organizational management relevant objects.

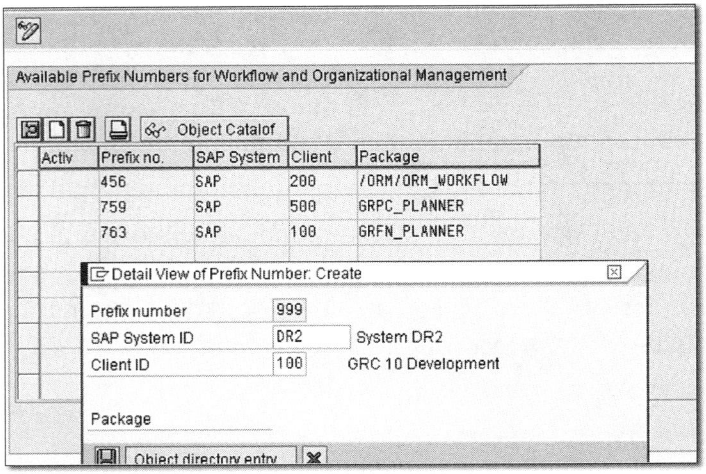

Figure 3.14 Maintain Prefix Number Range

Fixing HR control tables for the SAP workflow engine

After the number range maintenance task is completed, you need to run program RHSOBJCH from Transaction SE38 to fix HR control tables. Basically, the SAP workflow engine uses the HR organizational management system to manage routing workflows to identify different users dynamically based on their position, role, and responsibility. As a part of SAP GRC installation some of these organizational objects in HR tables are populated with preliminary data which might be a mixture of random test data that are not relevant to SAP GRC workflow. To start cleanup the pre-populated HR table objects, you need to execute program RHSOBJCH.

From the resulting screen you need to choose 'SELECT ALL' button to select all the resulting tables as shown in Figure 3.15. Click on the ADJUST button to carry out delete and recreate values in all HR tables, which are related to hierarchy and organizational management. As a result, all of the HR objects are adjusted as shown in Figure 3.16. These HR objects are related to organizational management and used in workflow engine to trigger or forward the work items from one decision node to the next.

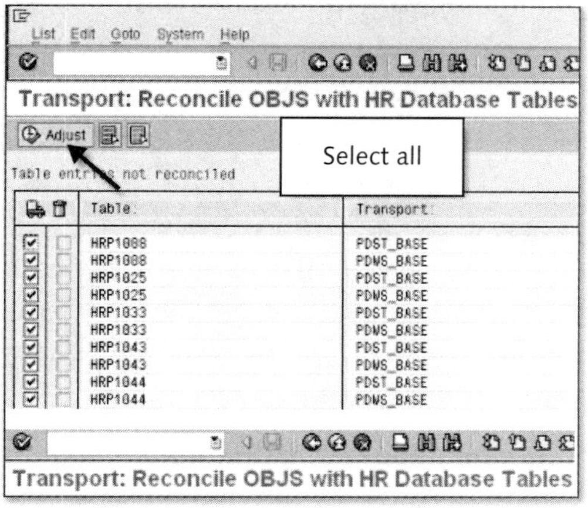

Figure 3.15 HR Database Clean for Workflow and Organizational Data

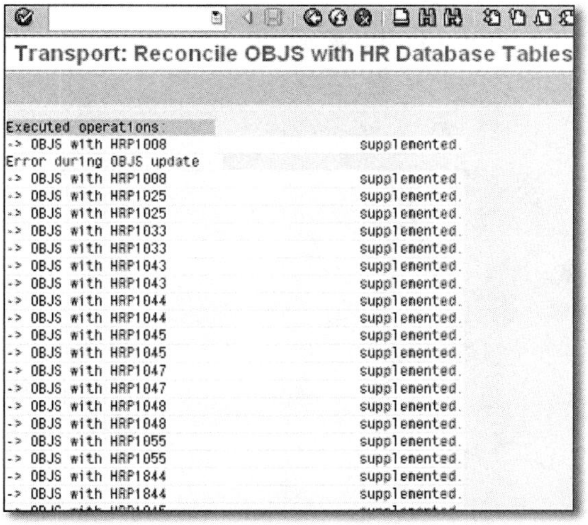

Figure 3.16 HR Database Clean in HR Data Tables

Additional Settings and Services maintenance

3. In the third sub-heading MAINTAIN ADDITIONAL SETTINGS AND SERVICES there are four activities that need to be performed:
   - MAINTAIN WEB SERVER
   - MAINTAIN STANDARD DOMAIN FOR INTERNET MAIL
   - ACTIVATE SEND TO OBJECTS AND HR OBJECTS
   - MAINTAIN DEMO AND VERIFICATION ENVIRONMENT

As shown in Figure 3.17, you have to maintain the web server, which enables web-flow services, such as a web-based workflow. This needs to be configured manually based on your system settings for web server details. The SAP Access Control system workflow is an enhanced version of the older workflow engine, and this uses the web service to send and receive web-based workflows, that is used in SAP GRC. After maintaining web server, most of the activities are performed automatically in the background and you no need to maintain any other settings manually. Similarly the fourth section or sub-heading CLASSIFY TASKS AS GENERAL will be set automatically with test workflows and other activities.

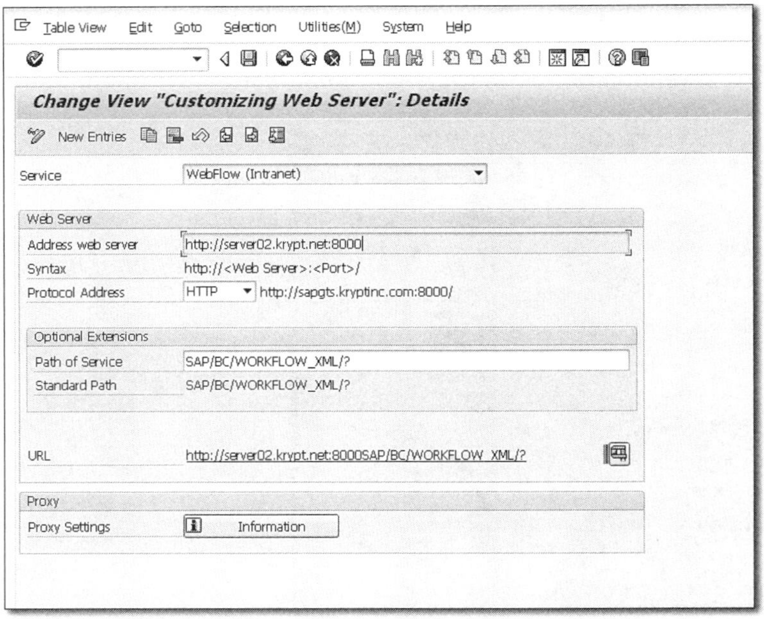

Figure 3.17 Web Server Setting

Guided procedures process templates

4. GUIDED PROCEDURES setting: Next, as a last section, you need to execute this setting so that guided procedures process templates such as MSMP can be executed on the business workflow engine. In this section, you need to activate the following three activities.
   - MAINTAIN GUIDED PROCEDURES GATEWAY
   - MAINTAIN GENERATION OF STANDARD TASKS
   - CLASSIFY GENERIC STANDARD TASKS AS GENERAL.

At the end of this activity, verify that all screen values have a green checkmark as shown in Figure 3.18. The HR control table has yet to be cleaned up in case if it's showing an error in its node.

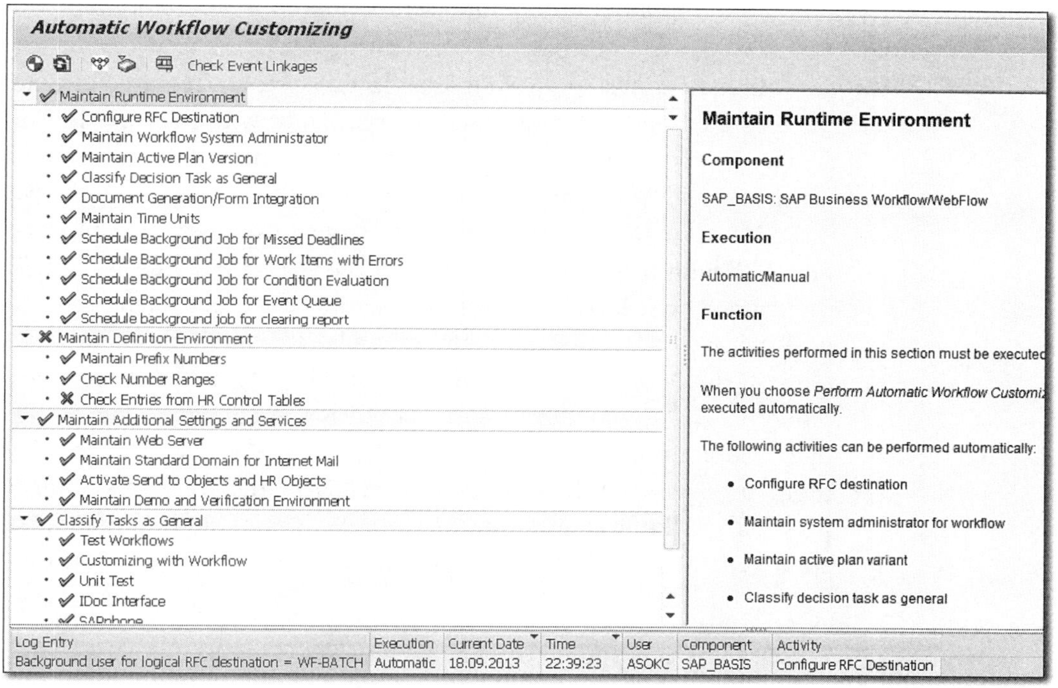

Figure 3.18 Automatic Workflow Customization Completion

Now you've finished automatic workflow customizing and press [F5] to begin the workflow verification in order to confirm that all are set correctly.

3.2.4 Workflow Verification

You've completed and verified your generic workflow customizing, as a last part of verification, you need to review if your workflow has been customized correctly. To ensure this is the case, choose GOTO • SAP BUSINESS WORKPLACE or press [Ctrl]+[F12]. Select the workflow under INBOX, and choose WORKFLOW TASK from the right side to execute the background step immediately. Now open the UNREAD DOCUMENTS folder, and you might see two messages in your inbox indicating the workflow has been customized correctly. In case of any issues, you can seek help from a technical person with workflow knowledge to troubleshoot the problem. With this verification, you confirm that the basic workflow setting is complete.

Task-specific customization

The next part of the workflow customizing activity is task-specific customization in which you need to establish the settings required to adapt the SAP tasks and SAP workflows in accordance with your needs. This activity sets up the tasks and workflows that you need during the implementation and to activate the triggering events for tasks and workflows in MSMP. You need to maintain possible agent variables for each workflow task with responsible processor of the task at every decision making stage or node level. A workflow can only be started in a dialog by its possible agents; in this case, for example, if you think of any user request, the possible agent is any user of the system who is creating a request. A task or workflow can be started as a reaction to events created by the application functionality. For this, specific events are declared as triggering events for the task or workflow. From the SAP Access Control perspective, this triggering event can be a submission of request or approval of request at any stage. Let's move on to complete this customization.

To start this activation from Transaction SPRO, select the menu path, SAP Customizing Implementation Guide • Governance, Risk and Compliance • General Settings • Workflow • Perform Task-Specific Customizing. Carry out the additional technical workflow object activation process that is specific to the SAP Access Control-related workflow objects.

This takes you to the screen shown in Figure 3.19 where you can see all available SAP applications tree structures that include SAP Access Control. If you don't see the GRC folder in this hierarchy, then you need to execute program RS_APPL_REFRESH either from Transaction SE38 or Transaction SA38. Execution of this program takes a while, and there is no output. If you go back to Perform Task-Specific Customizing again and open the GRC folder and GRC-AC subfolder, now you should be able to see both Assign Agents and Activate Event Linking links where you need to perform workflow customizing activation at the individual task or technical component level.

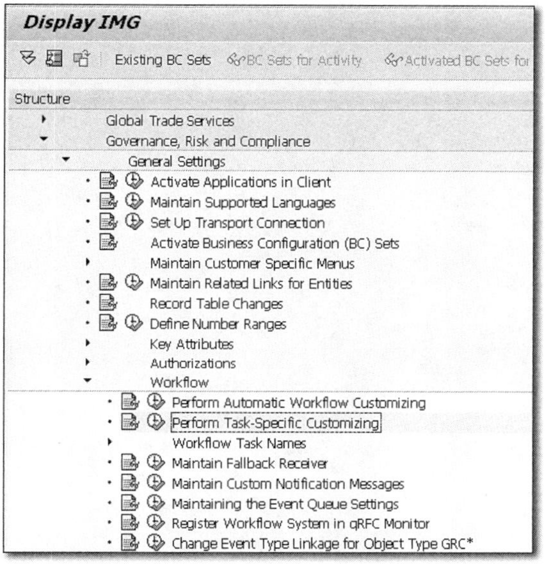

Figure 3.19 Task-Specific Workflow Customizing

When you expand the GRC folder (see Figure 3.20), if the GRC-AC subfolder has no links for ASSIGN AGENTS and ACTIVATE EVENT LINKING like the other GRC-SPC (SAP Process Control) or GRC-RM (SAP Risk Management) folders do—even after you executed program RS_APPL_REFRESH—then you need to carry out the troubleshooting steps discussed later in this section to get these entries as part of the task-specific customizing. When you have the links available, you can go ahead and execute the ASSIGN AGENTS activity.

Generally in this part of customization, you should set the listed standard tasks; that is, the IDs beginning with TS and not defaulted as BACKGROUND TASKS need to be set as GENERAL TASKS. To perform this, select a task that is blank, and then choose the ATTRIBUTES button. A subscreen appears that displays the details of the task's attributes. Select the first GENERAL TASK radio button, and click TRANSFER button (see Figure 3.21). Now you've completed agent assignment for the selected standard task.

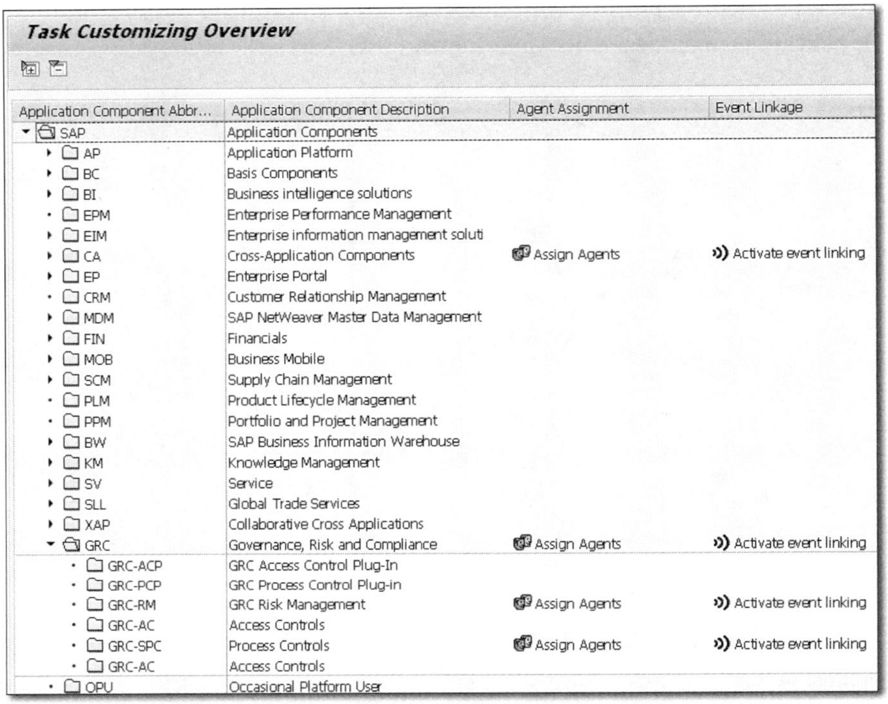

Figure 3.20 Task Customizing Hierarchy Overview

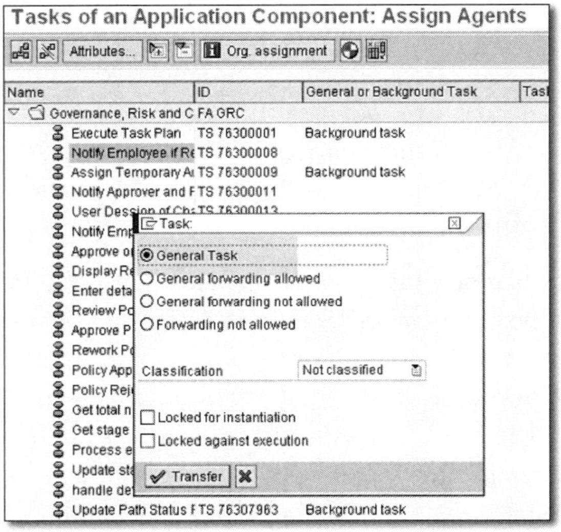

Figure 3.21 General Task Assignment

Carry out the previously mentioned general task assignment work for all standard tasks listed in Table 3.2. We'll troubleshoot any tasks that aren't carried out in Section 3.2.4.

Task Description	Task ID
Access Request Approval Dialog	TS76308026
User Access Review Workflow	TS76307964
Function Approval Workflow	TS76308029
Mitigation Control Maintenance	TS76308031
Risk Approval Workflow	TS76308038
SOD Risk Review Workflow	TS76308047
Role Approval Workflow	TS76307966
Fire Fighter Log Report Review Workflow	TS76308028
Control Assignment Approval Workflow	TS76308057

Table 3.2 General Task Assignment: List of Standard Task IDs

After you've completed the standard tasks agent assignment, you need to start activating event linking by selecting the top node of the hierarchy and choosing EXPAND ALL. Only some of the workflow templates have triggering workflow events. This is indicated by the EXPAND symbol in front of the name (see Figure 3.22).

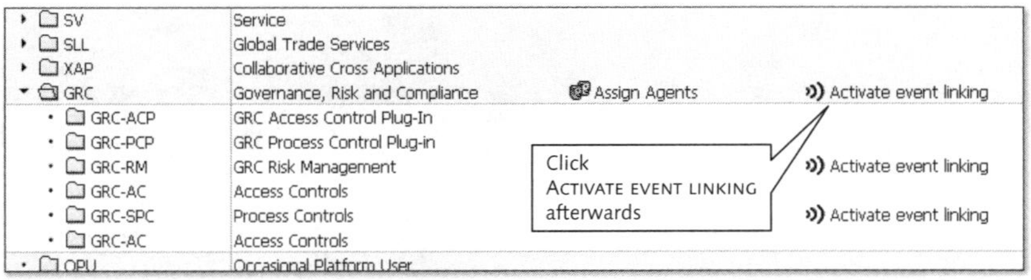

Figure 3.22 Activate Event Linking

Event Linking for Workflows

To activate event linking for workflows, select the required workflow task with a prefix of WS followed by numeric values. Select the small down arrow icon to expand this to show the event detail. From this line, choose the DETAIL VIEW button. This opens the PROPERTIES OF EVENT

LINKAGE subscreen. Set the LINKAGE STATUS value to NO ERRORS, select the EVENT LINKAGE ACTIVATED checkbox, and set ERROR FEEDBACK to DO NOT CHANGE LINKAGE, as shown in Figure 3.23.

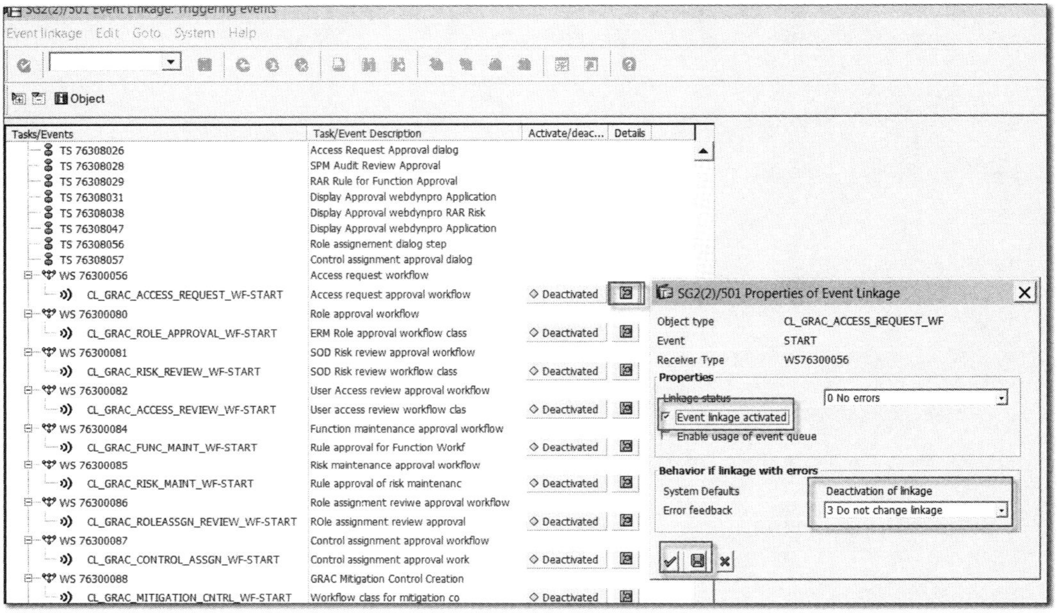

Figure 3.23 Event Linkage Activation

Save this and press [Enter]. At the end of this process, event linkage for this workflow task is activated. You need to carry out the same activation process for SAP Access Control workflow tasks detailed in Table 3.3.

Workflow Tasks Description	Task ID
Access Request Approval Workflow	WS76300056
Role Approval Workflow	WS76300080
Control Assignment Approval Workflow	WS76300087
Mitigation Control Maintenance	WS76300088
Function Approval Workflow	WS76300084

Table 3.3 Event Linkage Activation: List of Workflow Task IDs

Workflow Tasks Description	Task ID
Risk Approval Workflow	WS76300085
SOD Risk Review Workflow	WS76300081
User Access Review Workflow	WS76300082
Role Reaffirm Review Workflow	WS76300086
Fire Fighter Log Report Review Workflow	WS76300089

Table 3.3 Event Linkage Activation: List of Workflow Task IDs (Cont.)

At the end of the event linkage activation, you should be able to see that all of the workflow tasks appear as activated (see Figure 3.24).

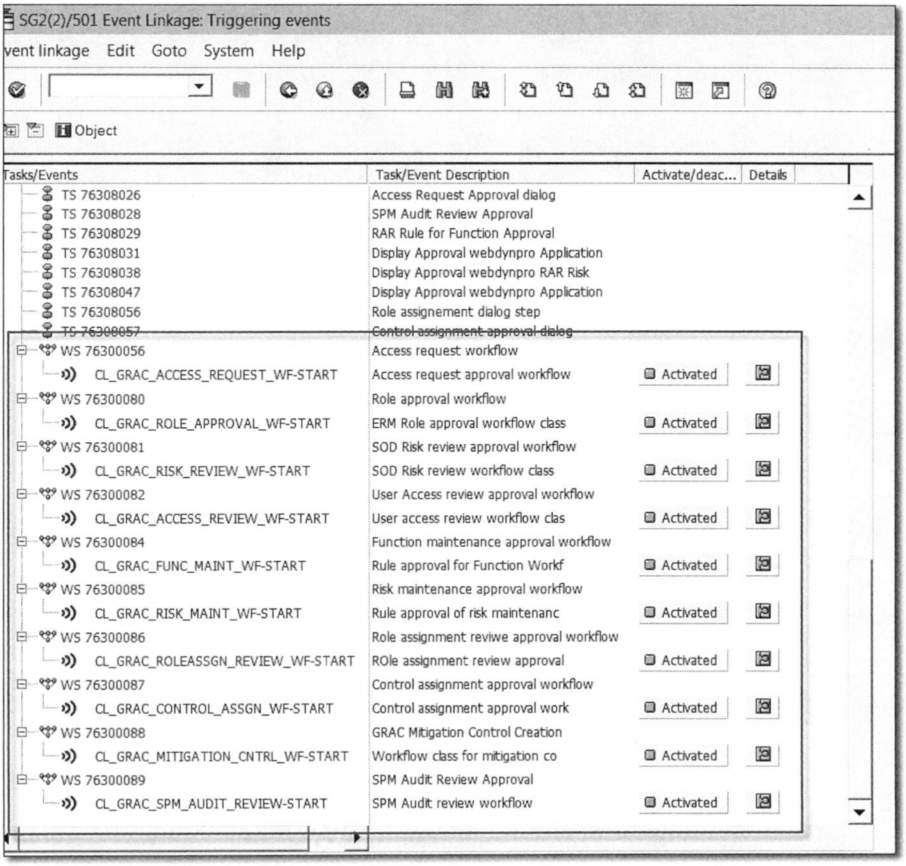

Figure 3.24 Event Linkage Activation Completed

Following the Basis preliminary checks and the activation of the BC Sets, you've successfully completed the task-specific workflow customization from the technical activation standpoint.

The next section provides some troubleshooting tips. This explains what to do if you searched for task-specific customization, and it didn't show up with the agent assignment and event linkage links. If you did not face any issues at that point in the configuration, you can skip this next section.

3.2.5 Troubleshooting for Task-Specific Customization

During workflow customization, a situation may arise where there are no links visible to activate assign agent and event linkage. This might happen if you have the SAP GRC plug-ins installed in the central SAP GRC instance as shown earlier in Figure 3.20a. To start this work, you need to execute Transaction PFTC for agent assignment by selecting the type and task as shown in Figure 3.25.

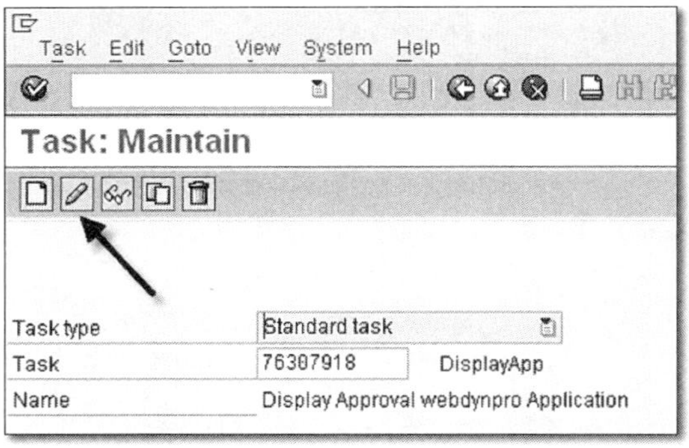

Figure 3.25 Standard Task Agent Assignment Initial Screen

In this initial screen (shown in Figure 3.25), enter the standard task listed earlier table in Table 3.2 as a numeric value without the prefix TS, and choose STANDARD TASK in the TASK TYPE text box. Ensure that you're in change mode by selecting the pencil/eye glass icon, and you are taken to the screen, shown in Figure 3.26. From this screen, you can maintain the agent assignments.

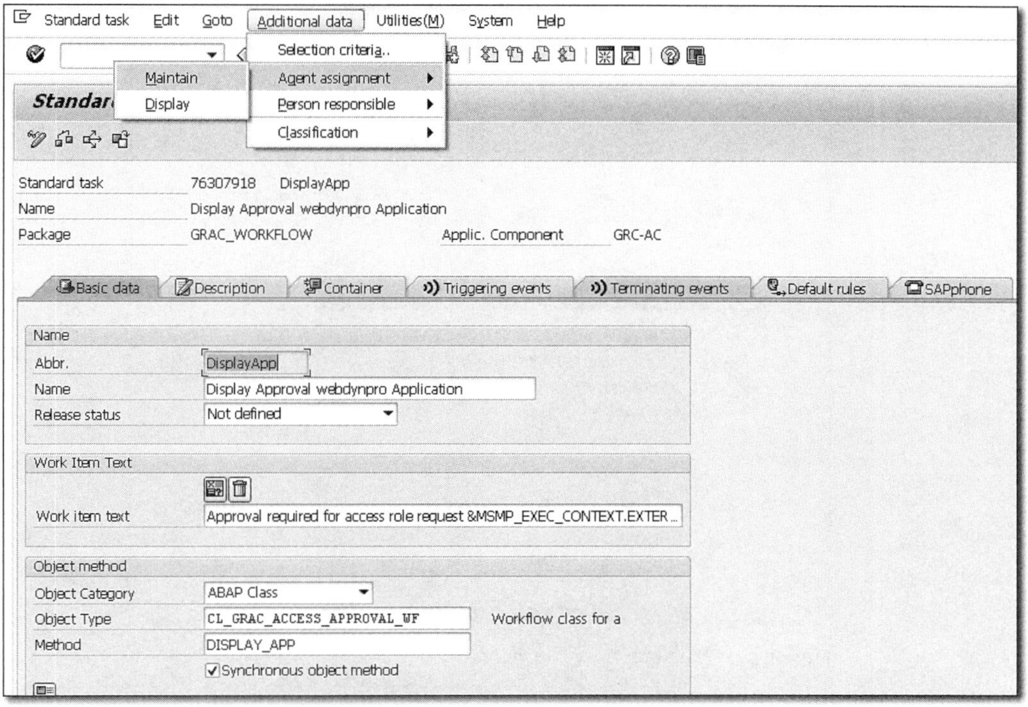

Figure 3.26 Agent Assignment Screen

On this screen, choose Additional Data • Agent assignment • Maintain from the menu bar. If the Transfer Container Elements pop-up appears, always choose No. Now you're taken to the next screen where you need to click on Attributes or press function key F8 to bring up the Task pop-up screen. In this pop-up, select General Task, and choose Not classified in the Classification field (see Figure 3.27). After you set these values, click on Transfer, then click on Back, and finally click on Save.

After saving, you need to perform all of the process steps to maintain all standard tasks that are listed in Table 3.2. After you're done with this troubleshooting step, you've completed the process of maintaining agent assingments that were invisible as shown earlier in Figure 3.20

Troubleshooting Event Type Linkage

The next activity in troubleshooting is activating the event type linkage from Transaction SWE2. You need to maintain the following linkages by double-clicking on each line item in change mode (see Figure 3.28).

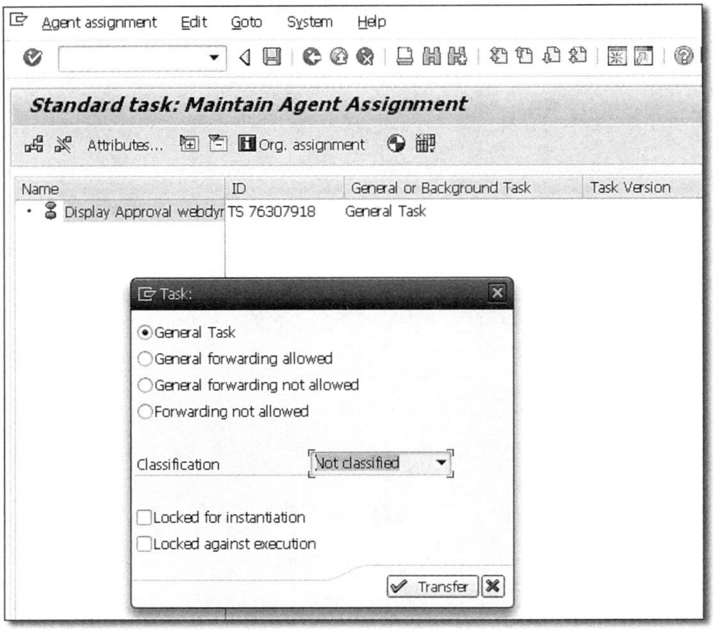

Figure 3.27 Maintain Agent Assignment

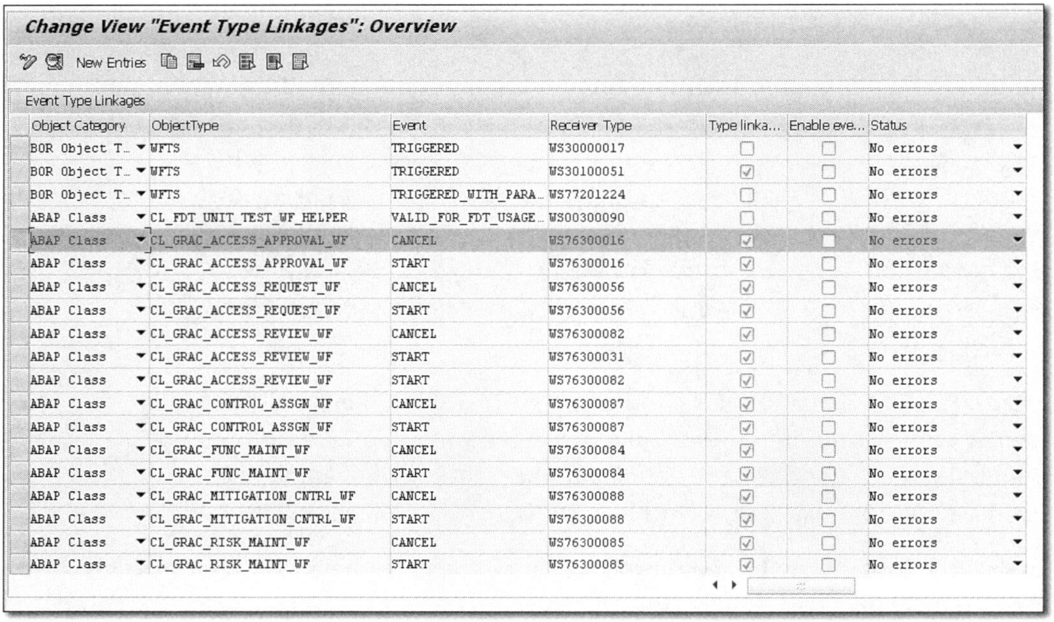

Object Category	ObjectType	Event	Receiver Type	Type linka...	Enable eve...	Status
BOR Object T...	WFTS	TRIGGERED	WS30000017	☐	☐	No errors
BOR Object T...	WFTS	TRIGGERED	WS30100051	☑	☐	No errors
BOR Object T...	WFTS	TRIGGERED_WITH_PARA...	WS77201224	☐	☐	No errors
ABAP Class	CL_FDT_UNIT_TEST_WF_HELPER	VALID_FOR_FDT_USAGE...	WS00300090	☐	☐	No errors
ABAP Class	CL_GRAC_ACCESS_APPROVAL_WF	CANCEL	WS76300016	☑	☐	No errors
ABAP Class	CL_GRAC_ACCESS_APPROVAL_WF	START	WS76300016	☑	☐	No errors
ABAP Class	CL_GRAC_ACCESS_REQUEST_WF	CANCEL	WS76300056	☑	☐	No errors
ABAP Class	CL_GRAC_ACCESS_REQUEST_WF	START	WS76300056	☑	☐	No errors
ABAP Class	CL_GRAC_ACCESS_REVIEW_WF	CANCEL	WS76300082	☑	☐	No errors
ABAP Class	CL_GRAC_ACCESS_REVIEW_WF	START	WS76300031	☑	☐	No errors
ABAP Class	CL_GRAC_ACCESS_REVIEW_WF	START	WS76300082	☑	☐	No errors
ABAP Class	CL_GRAC_CONTROL_ASSGN_WF	CANCEL	WS76300087	☑	☐	No errors
ABAP Class	CL_GRAC_CONTROL_ASSGN_WF	START	WS76300087	☑	☐	No errors
ABAP Class	CL_GRAC_FUNC_MAINT_WF	CANCEL	WS76300084	☑	☐	No errors
ABAP Class	CL_GRAC_FUNC_MAINT_WF	START	WS76300084	☑	☐	No errors
ABAP Class	CL_GRAC_MITIGATION_CNTRL_WF	CANCEL	WS76300088	☑	☐	No errors
ABAP Class	CL_GRAC_MITIGATION_CNTRL_WF	START	WS76300088	☑	☐	No errors
ABAP Class	CL_GRAC_RISK_MAINT_WF	CANCEL	WS76300085	☑	☐	No errors
ABAP Class	CL_GRAC_RISK_MAINT_WF	START	WS76300085	☑	☐	No errors

Figure 3.28 Event Linkage Activation from Transaction SWE2

Parameter Settings for Event-Type linkages

This takes you to the Change View "Event Type Linkages" Detail screen in Figure 3.29, where you need to select the Linkage Activated checkbox and select the Do not change linkage option for the Behavior upon Error Feedback field. The next step is to Save this entry and go back to the initial screen. You have to repeat the all of these steps again to activate all of the table entries that are listed in Table 3.3, or you can list and activate all ABAP classes that start with CL_GRAC, which are basically SAP Access Control workflow tasks (refer to Figure 3.28).

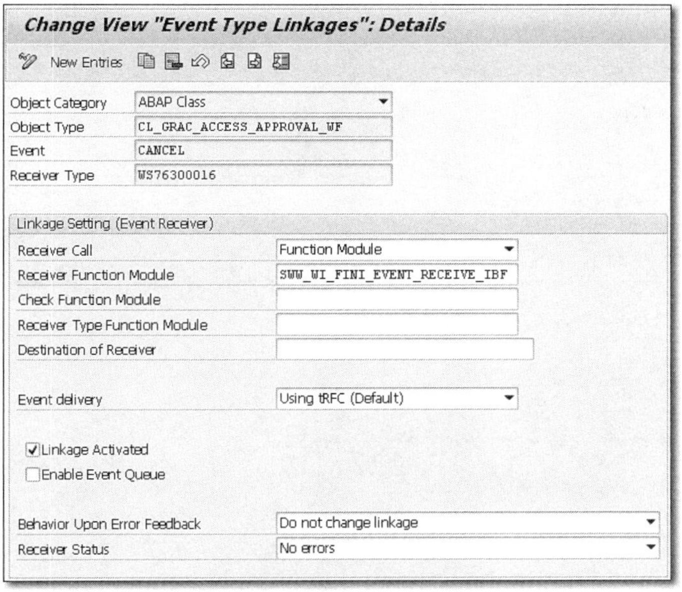

Figure 3.29 Event Linkage Activation Parameter Setting

You've now completed the agent assignment and linkage activation tasks through troubleshooting and activated those invisible workflow component event type linkages. The resulting screen will look like the screen shown in Figure 3.30.

Activating workflow tasks

After completing these two set of activities, you need to activate all of the workflow tasks from Transaction SWDD. From this screen, you can select search input by using an asterisk as the input for your search term to find the whole list of workflow templates. From the list, click on the Find button and enter "grac" to search the SAP Access Control workflow (see Figure 3.31).

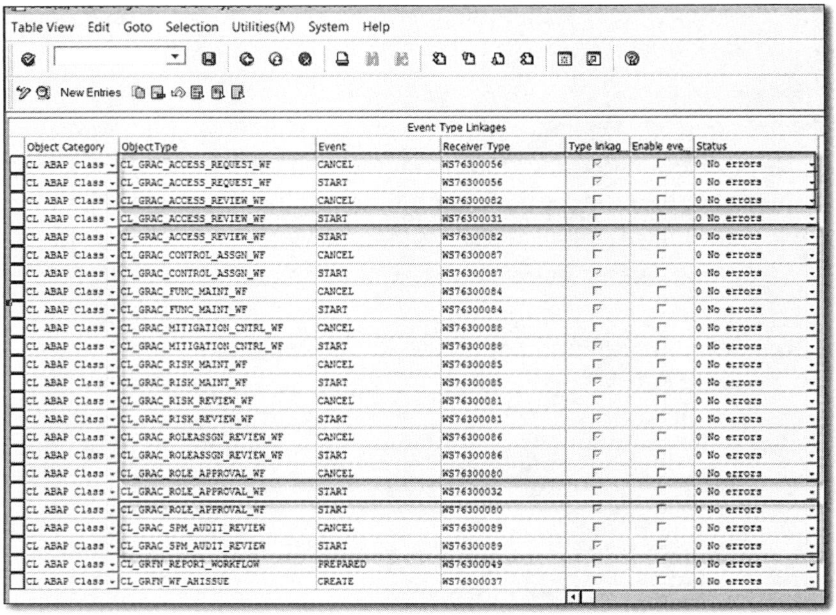

Figure 3.30 Event Linkage Activation Completed

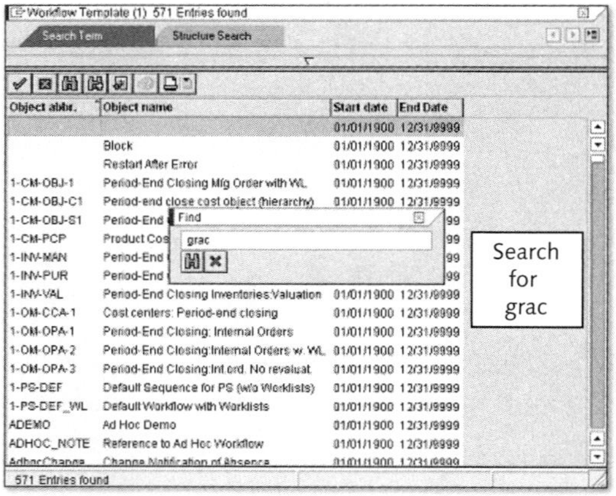

Figure 3.31 SAP Access Control Workflow Search for Activation from Transaction SWDD

From this comprehensive list, you are taken to the GRAC workflow list as shown in Figure 3.32. Choose one of these items and double-click on the line item to display the task in a subscreen along with all versions that belong to this task.

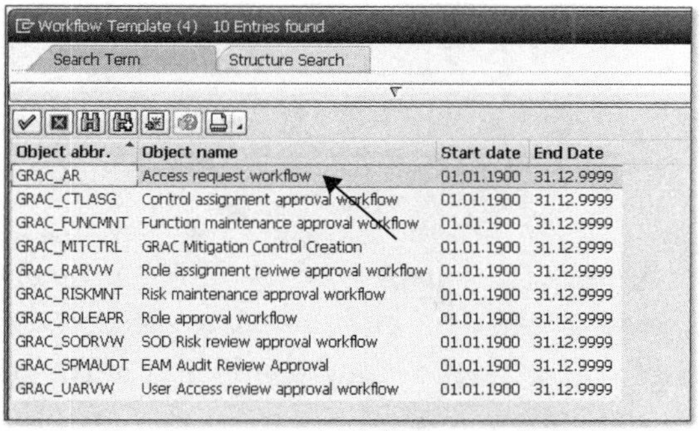

Object abbr.	Object name	Start date	End Date
GRAC_AR	Access request workflow	01.01.1900	31.12.9999
GRAC_CTLASG	Control assignment approval workflow	01.01.1900	31.12.9999
GRAC_FUNCMNT	Function maintenance approval workflow	01.01.1900	31.12.9999
GRAC_MITCTRL	GRAC Mitigation Control Creation	01.01.1900	31.12.9999
GRAC_RARVW	Role assignment reviwe approval workflow	01.01.1900	31.12.9999
GRAC_RISKMNT	Risk maintenance approval workflow	01.01.1900	31.12.9999
GRAC_ROLEAPR	Role approval workflow	01.01.1900	31.12.9999
GRAC_SODRVW	SOD Risk review approval workflow	01.01.1900	31.12.9999
GRAC_SPMAUDT	EAM Audit Review Approval	01.01.1900	31.12.9999
GRAC_UARVW	User Access review approval workflow	01.01.1900	31.12.9999

Figure 3.32 Search Result of SAP Access Control Workflow from Transaction SWDD

Select the highest version number of the workflow object from the VERSION field, and this is shown with all technical objects as workflow steps and a graphical represention in the side window. You need to activate this workflow version, and any error, warning, or success message as a result of activation will appear in the bottom-left corner of the window with a corresponding message (see Figure 3.33).

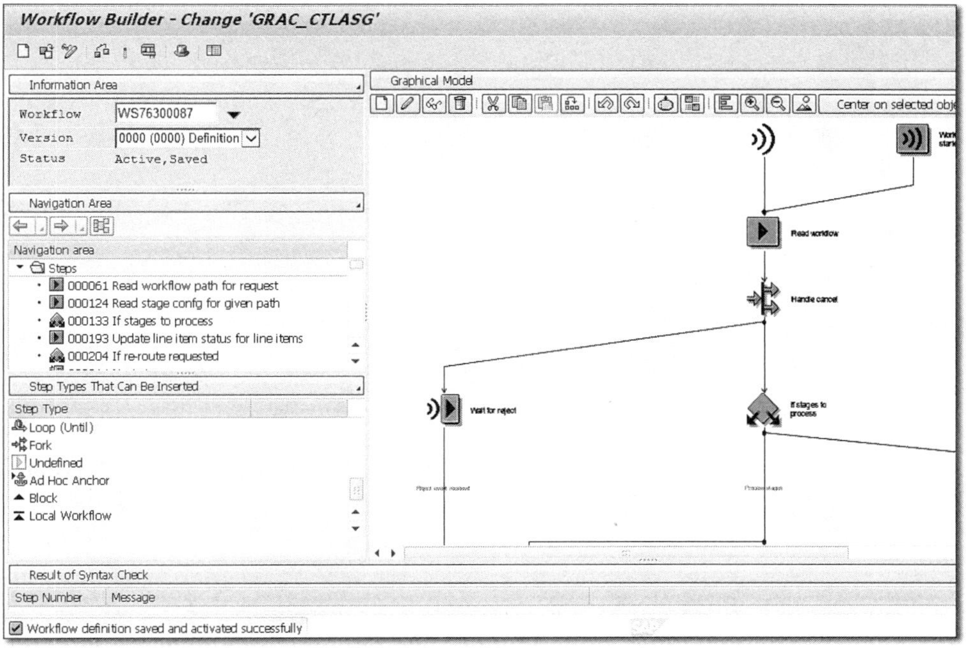

Figure 3.33 Selected SAP Access Control Workflow Object with Workflow Steps and Graphical Representation

Activating all SAP Access Control workflows

Similarly, activate all SAP Access Control workflows to complete the technical components that are active and connected. By doing this workflow activation process, now the system is ready to configure the MSMP workflow.

So far, you've worked on the workflow technical troubleshooting, which might arise in some customer installations based on the software components in their SAP Access Control system. In the next section, we discuss some of the commonly shared settings and configuration among SAP Access Control, SAP Process Control, and SAP Risk Management in detail.

3.2.6 Shared Configuration of SAP GRC Systems

In this customizing task list, you'll see some of the activities that need to be carried out initially in the system. These customizing activities are commonly shared among SAP Access Control, SAP Process Control, and SAP Risk Management. Some of the common components include RFC connection setup between SAP GRC and other SAP systems, organizational hierarchy, and so on. In other words, if your environment uses SAP Access Control, SAP Process Control, and SAP Risk Management in the same single client, then you may need to customize certain activities. The activities that we'll review as part of the shared configuration of SAP GRC are listed here:

Shared configuration activities for a multi-module GRC approach

- Clean up HR data.
- Configure root organization.
- Create connectors.
- Maintain connection settings.
- Use SAP Crystal Reports features.

We'll look at each of these activities in further detail in the following subsections.

Clean Up HR Data

You need to carry out this customizing activity to delete superfluous entries. After the system has been set up initially, the organization table

HRP1000 may contain entries that aren't relevant. By deleting these entries, the validity dates and texts for the delivered object numbers that are overlapped with newly created validity dates and texts will be removed.

Configure Root Organization

In this activity, you need to maintain the root organization for the SAP GRC system. This value is mandatory to maintain the core structure and root organization to which compliance and control reporting are made. In a standard system, there are multiple organization views available, or the standard hierarchy is maintained already. This hierarchy goes all of the way to relationship maintenance of organization structures, and organizational units that is used in the standard SAP workflow and HR structures that include the relationship between the organizations.

Multiple organization views

You can maintain multiple organization views for SAP Process Control, SAP Access Control, and SAP Risk Management to have different reporting hierarchy and remediation sign-off procedures. For general compliance reporting, if you're not sticking to any specific hierarchy—normally the HR relationship is used for organization views—the best practice recommendation is to use the standard hierarchy over any other hierarchy. After you select the organization view as '002' which is STANDARD HIERARCHY MAINTAIN IT IN the DETAILS area of the screen shown in Figure 3.34, you can create your ROOT ORGANIZATIONAL UNIT and CHILD ORGANIZATIONAL UNIT. These represent your control reporting structure in your company and are shared within the SAP Access Control, SAP Process Control, and SAP Risk Management components.

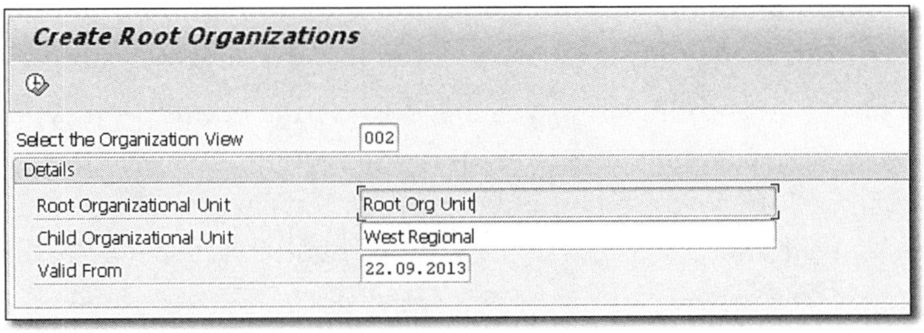

Figure 3.34 Root Organization Maintenance

Root organizations

Although these organizational value hierarchies are more important in SAP Process Control for the report and sign-off procedure that extends in relationship to control owners and organizations, it's encouraged to maintain those structures and use them for SAP Access Control as well. As mentioned earlier, however, it's mandatory to have at least a root organization; without this, you may not able to create, mitigate, or assign controls. Next we'll discuss how to enable create connectors to connect and receive data for SAP Access Control analysis.

Create Connectors

In this activity, we'll review how to create and maintain connector settings from a SAP GRC system to any SAP or non-SAP systems to get different data, execute risk analyses, or create and provide for roles. In SAP GRC, connectors and connector types are defined globally. These definitions can be used based on your required scenario anywhere in SAP Access Control, SAP Process Control, or SAP Risk Management with the same connector used for specific systems across your landscape.

To start creating and maintaining connectors and connector types, execute Transaction SPRO, and navigate through the following path: SAP Customizing Implementation Guide • Governance, Risk and Compliance • Common Component Setting • Integration Framework • Create Connectors. This takes you to the Transaction SM59 screen where you can create various connector types, such as the ABAP connection to SAP systems, HTTP connections, TCP/IP connections, and so on. This basically helps to define and establish connections between the SAP GRC system and other systems.

Defining a Connector Type

As a part of creating connectors, you need to define connection types and map the actual connectors with the connection types. Different types of connections that are available to use in SAP Access Control are SAP, LDAP, SPML, FILE, EP, and LOCAL, as shown in Figure 3.35.

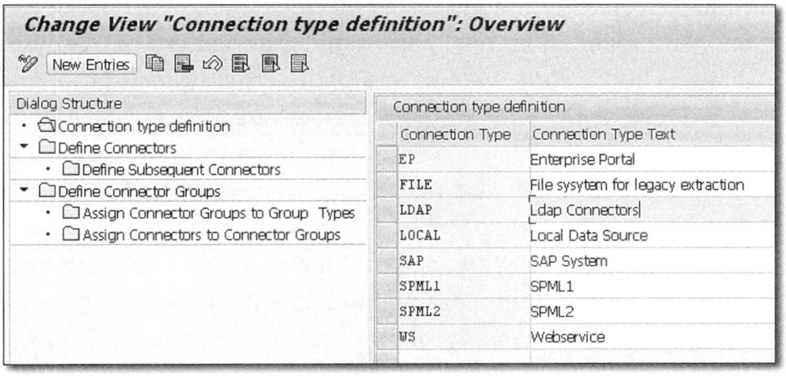

Figure 3.35 Connection Type Definition

The actual connectors with connector type and a few other parameters such as LOGICAL PORT, SOURCE CONNECTOR, and MAX NO. OF BG WP (maximum number of background work processes) to be defined are provided in Figure 3.36. If portal connectors are planned in your project, you need to maintain the subsequent connector definition. This subsequent connector is meant to maintain a logical port as an additional requirement to connect and get the data. For example, if you need data from SAP NetWeaver Portal, most of the actions, such as create user and delete user, are served by the standard Service Provisioning Markup Language (SPML) interface. But some actions like generate password aren't available with the standard SPML interface and therefore need a web service protocol. In this scenario, for SAP NetWeaver Portal, the standard SPML interface is the subsequent connector, and the web service protocol is the first connector.

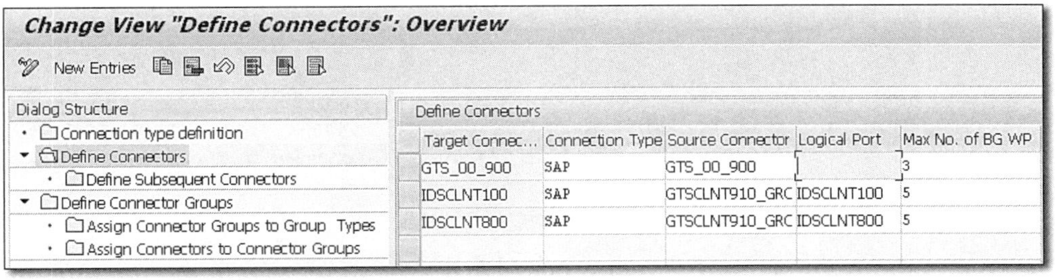

Figure 3.36 Define Connector

Logical Connector Groups

Next in the connector settings is the connector group, which is used to create and define logical groups. For example, in Access Risk Analysis, you want to logically group SAP ERP systems or cross-systems groupings such as SAP ERP and SAP SRM systems. In both cases, the system can use a single global rule set against one group. At the same time, you want to maintain user provisioning and role creation tasks targeted to serve a purpose, so you want to group SAP ERP systems specific to one instance and group development, quality, and production systems to move your role development and assignment within a specific logical group. This cross-system group and logical grouping will make maintenance work simpler and streamline the specific, task-oriented work. We've given an example connector concept in Figure 3.37.

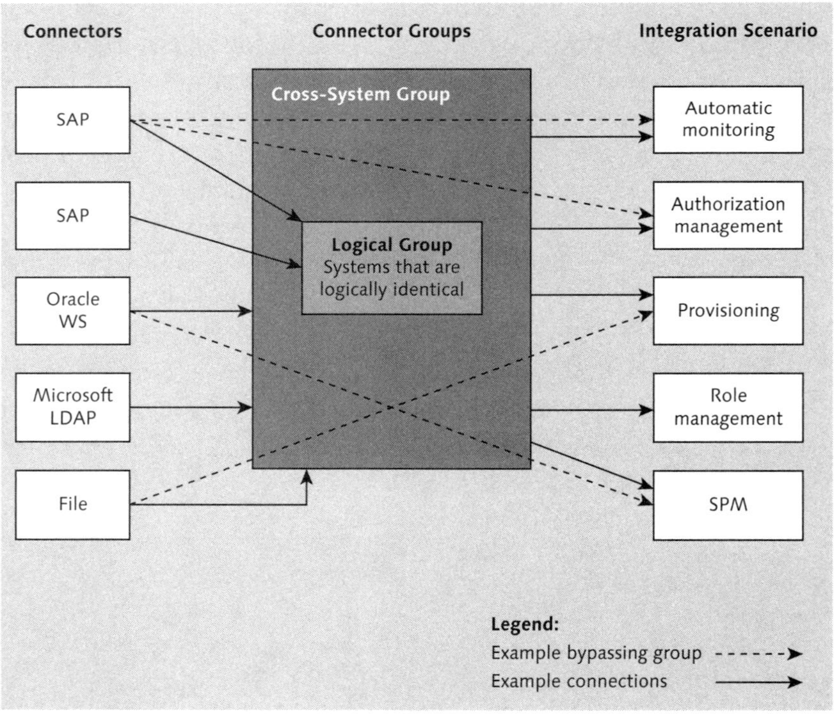

Figure 3.37 Example Connector Flow and Grouping

A logical group is the connector group type that consists of the systems that are logically the same, for example, all SAP ERP systems or Oracle systems. A cross-system group is a connector group type that consists of the systems with different environments, such as SAP CRM, SAP SRM, LDAP, and Oracle applications. In the same dialog structure where you defined connectors, you'll use the next links to assign connector groups to group types and assign connectors to connector groups.

You've now seen how to create, map, and group various connectors and connector types. Next, you'll establish connectors to various scenarios.

Maintain Connection Settings

In this configuration work, you'll assign integration scenarios and subscenarios to the connector. The integration scenario functionality is designed to work with different applications from SAP Access Control. It consists of SAP-delivered entries only and is also used by SAP Process Control for continuous control monitoring (described in Chapters 11, 12, and 13). You can use integration scenarios to define what kind of connector you want, how you want to maintain the connector, and how to technically deal with the connectors and connection types for each SAP Access Control tool or scenario, such as authorization, provisioning, and so on.

Integration scenarios and subscenarios

Let's move from integration scenarios to subscenarios. This consists of SAP-delivered entries, as shown in Figure 3.38. All of the subscenarios at this point have the same four names (except for Automatic Monitoring [AM]), but, technically, they are associated to classes defined in the system to fetch data associated with the scenario based on the connection type. This is used to classify how each and every component identifies the connector and how they want to process the connectors.

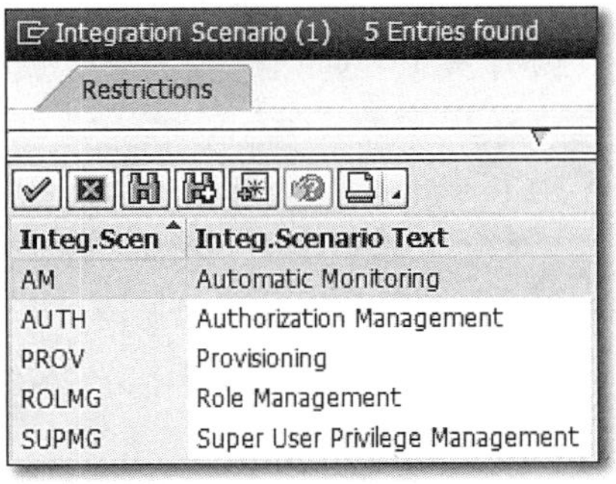

Figure 3.38 SAP-Provided Integration Scenarios

The ultimate goal of the subscenario is to connect with specific target connectors. Every subscenario is connected through a scenario connection type, which was created or predelivered (see Figure 3.39).

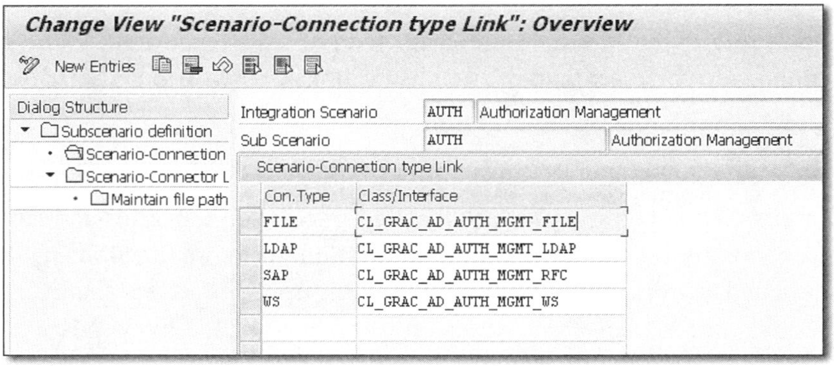

Figure 3.39 Scenario and Subscenario Link to Connection Type

The last subfolder is used to define the file path for logical connectors with connection types such as File. There is another set of connector settings available from menu path, SAP CUSTOMIZING IMPLEMENTATION GUIDE • GOVERNANCE, RISK AND COMPLIANCE • ACCESS CONTROL • MAINTAIN CONNECTOR SETTINGS. Rest of the configuration links from SPRO Transactions is explained later in Chapter 4 through Chapter 7 where individual tool configurations are explained.

Associating actions with scenario and default connectors

There is another configuration activity you need to complete is to associate the actions with scenario and default connectors. This is shown in Figure 3.39 with scenario and subscenario links to the connectors and connection types. This determines the type of affiliation between SAP Access Control and the plug-in system, such as any SAP system. For example, the AUTH scenario is meant for the Access Risk Analysis tool of SAP Access Control to connect with the target system. Basically, connectors are the links between SAP Access Control tools and target systems to fetch data into the SAP Access Control system.

So far, we've covered most of the core setting of the connectors, connector groups, and their links to different scenarios. Now let's discuss how to activate SAP Crystal Reports features.

3.2.7 SAP Crystal Reports Features

In this step, we'll cover how to activate the SAP Crystal Reports feature. Access Transaction SPRO, and follow menu path, SAP Customizing • SAP NetWeaver • Application Server • SAP List Viewer • Maintain Web Dynpro ABAP Specific Setting (see Figure 3.40).

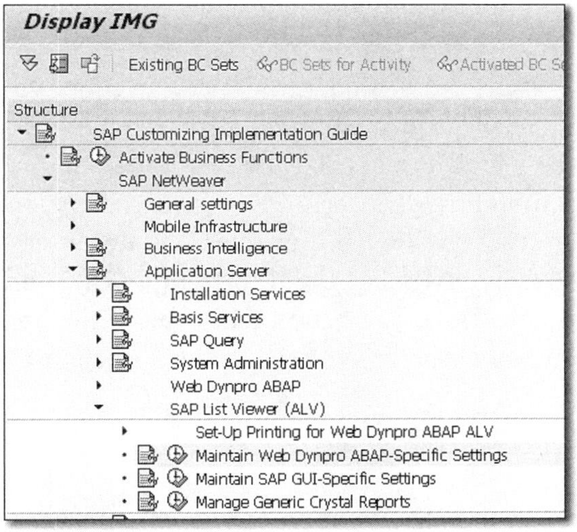

Figure 3.40 SAP List Viewer Options Configuration

You are taken to the Web Dynpro-specific setting for SAP List Viewer (ALV) screen with multiple checkboxes (see Figure 3.41). In this screen, select the Allow Crystal Reports checkbox.

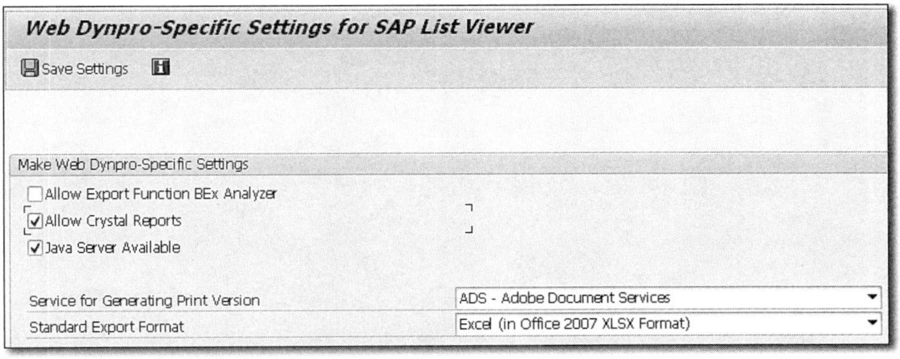

Figure 3.41 Enabling the SAP Crystal Reports Feature

As shown in Figure 3.41, by enabling this checkbox, you now have options to get various reports. SAP Access Control dashboard results can be viewed and stored in flexible and customizable SAP Crystal Report formats. Also customers can design their own reporting format and use full features of reporting in SAP Access Control data.

3.2.8 Activate Profile of Roles Delivered by SAP

Section 3.2.2 provided a brief introduction to BC Set activation, and individual activation of BC Sets is explained in the respective tools discussions. As a next step, let's look at mass activation of roles and profiles. There are definitely different security requirements based on your environment to define various provisioning user roles. It's always easy to start with standard SAP-delivered roles. Use Transaction SUPC, and choose UTILITIES • MASS GENERATION. This action takes you to the next screen as shown in Figure 3.42, where you have options to choose a range of roles.

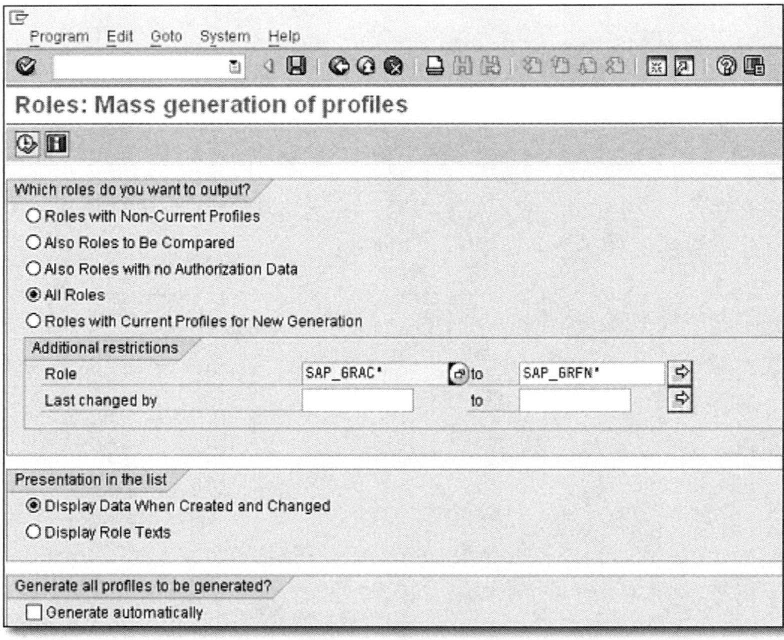

Figure 3.42 Mass Role Generation for SAP Access Control from Transaction SUPC

Mass role generation

If you want to activate only SAP Access Control related roles, enter only "SAP_GRAC*" in the ROLE text box with other options on the next subscreen PRESENTATION IN THE LIST select the option that you wish to see. If you choose the check-box GENERATE AUTOMATICALLY all the roles in your selection range will generate. Upon executing this screen, you are taken to the list of roles as shown in Figure 3.43 based on your selections. These are the roles available for you to generate profiles to start using them, so you need to either select all roles or choose selectively based on your requirements. Then execute with the F8 key or click the GENERATION icon (circled in Figure 3.43) to choose to generate selected roles either IN THE BACKGROUND or ONLINE.

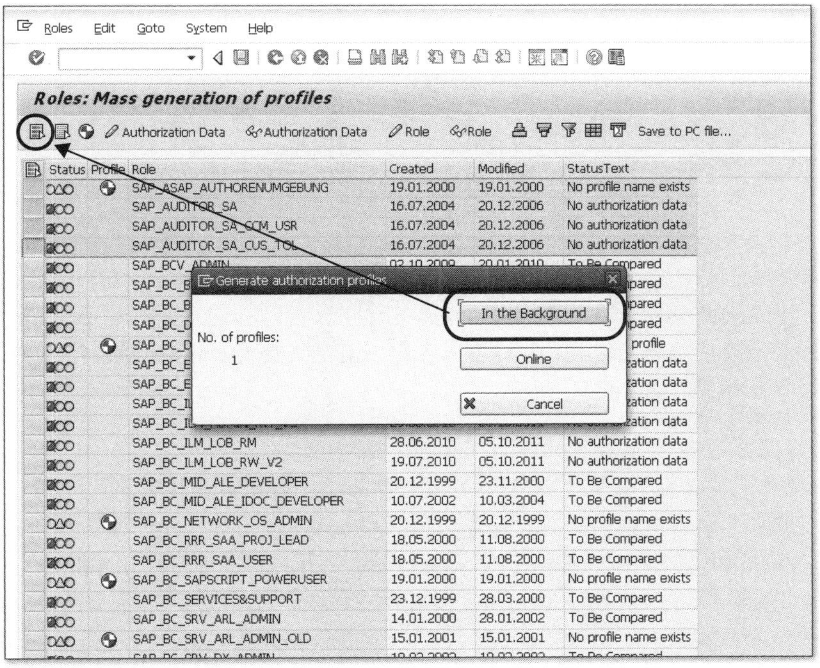

Figure 3.43 Mass Generation Selection and Execution Job

Role and profile activation

Roles and profiles are activated, and you get the detailed activation log on all of the roles with success or failure information as shown in Figure 3.44. You may use these roles directly or create roles under your custom namespace based on these generated roles as a starting point to define your own requirements in the SAP Access Control system.

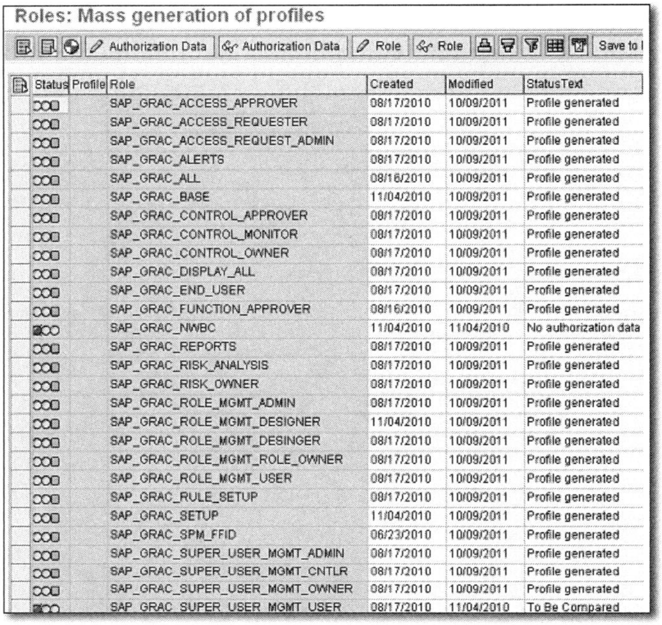
Roles: Mass generation of profiles

Authorization Data | Authorization Data | Role | Role | Save to l

Status	Profile	Role	Created	Modified	StatusText
		SAP_GRAC_ACCESS_APPROVER	08/17/2010	10/09/2011	Profile generated
		SAP_GRAC_ACCESS_REQUESTER	08/17/2010	10/09/2011	Profile generated
		SAP_GRAC_ACCESS_REQUEST_ADMIN	08/17/2010	10/09/2011	Profile generated
		SAP_GRAC_ALERTS	08/17/2010	10/09/2011	Profile generated
		SAP_GRAC_ALL	08/16/2010	10/09/2011	Profile generated
		SAP_GRAC_BASE	11/04/2010	10/09/2011	Profile generated
		SAP_GRAC_CONTROL_APPROVER	08/17/2010	10/09/2011	Profile generated
		SAP_GRAC_CONTROL_MONITOR	08/17/2010	10/09/2011	Profile generated
		SAP_GRAC_CONTROL_OWNER	08/17/2010	10/09/2011	Profile generated
		SAP_GRAC_DISPLAY_ALL	08/17/2010	10/09/2011	Profile generated
		SAP_GRAC_END_USER	08/17/2010	10/09/2011	Profile generated
		SAP_GRAC_FUNCTION_APPROVER	08/16/2010	10/09/2011	Profile generated
		SAP_GRAC_NWBC	11/04/2010	11/04/2010	No authorization data
		SAP_GRAC_REPORTS	08/17/2010	10/09/2011	Profile generated
		SAP_GRAC_RISK_ANALYSIS	08/17/2010	10/09/2011	Profile generated
		SAP_GRAC_RISK_OWNER	08/17/2010	10/09/2011	Profile generated
		SAP_GRAC_ROLE_MGMT_ADMIN	08/17/2010	10/09/2011	Profile generated
		SAP_GRAC_ROLE_MGMT_DESIGNER	11/04/2010	10/09/2011	Profile generated
		SAP_GRAC_ROLE_MGMT_DESINGER	08/17/2010	10/09/2011	Profile generated
		SAP_GRAC_ROLE_MGMT_ROLE_OWNER	08/17/2010	10/09/2011	Profile generated
		SAP_GRAC_ROLE_MGMT_USER	08/17/2010	10/09/2011	Profile generated
		SAP_GRAC_RULE_SETUP	08/17/2010	10/09/2011	Profile generated
		SAP_GRAC_SETUP	11/04/2010	10/09/2011	Profile generated
		SAP_GRAC_SPM_FFID	06/23/2010	10/09/2011	Profile generated
		SAP_GRAC_SUPER_USER_MGMT_ADMIN	08/17/2010	10/09/2011	Profile generated
		SAP_GRAC_SUPER_USER_MGMT_CNTLR	08/17/2010	10/09/2011	Profile generated
		SAP_GRAC_SUPER_USER_MGMT_OWNER	08/17/2010	10/09/2011	Profile generated
		SAP_GRAC_SUPER_USER_MGMT_USER	08/17/2010	11/04/2010	To Be Compared

Figure 3.44 Generated Roles from Import

The last activity that you need to complete for the shared configuration of the SAP GRC suite is to review the basic user ID and its privilege assignment required in the system to run various technical layers apart from regular users.

3.2.9 Creating the Initial User in the ABAP System

Apart from role creation and generic user creation with proper role assignments, some necessary user IDs with proper access privilege are required in SAP Access Control. Some of the activities, such as workflow trigger, background jobs, connectivity to plug-in systems to perform user provisioning or extract user, authorization data for risk analysis, access Web Dynpro application, email job, and so on, need these generic user IDs when they are invoked by users or approvers of SAP Access Control systems.

To start with, user ID WF-BATCH is required to perform all workflow-related activities to send and receive all work items. Normally, you can provide SAP_ALL and SAP _NEW profiles, but if your IT environment insists on restricting the authorizations of the background user WF-BATCH as part of SAP Business Workflow, then refer to SAP Note 73160.

The next user ID is the RFC User ID that needs to maintain in Transaction SM59 to establish connectivity between the SAP GRC system and the plug-in system, such as SAP ERP, SAP CRM, SAP SRM, SAP NetWeaver Portal, or authentication systems such as LDAP. This RFC User ID should contain all of the authorizations related to RFC privileges. You can use the RFC ID to the third user ID that is used in the ICF to log in and launch the SAP NetWeaver Business Client screen for general end-user logins or approvals by email link logon setup. You can also define this user ID based on different logon procedure options that can be set in Transaction SICF for Internet-based services to access the SAP NetWeaver Business Client screen in certain situations (see Figure 3.45). You'll see this in detail when we configure User Access Management in Chapter 7.

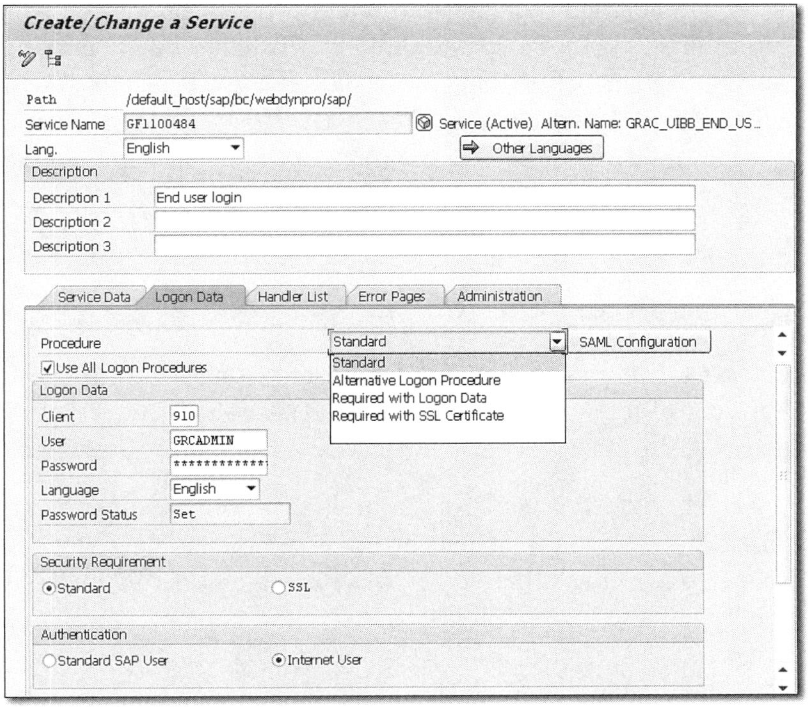

Figure 3.45 Transaction SICF Logon Procedure and User ID

Additional Basis system related tasks

There might be a few more Basis or system-related tasks, such as scheduling some regular background jobs, connecting to a non-SAP system if your implementation demands, a SAP Service Marketplace connection that might need one or more user IDs based on your system landscape plan and your company policies, and so on. Also you might need a developer user ID in the latter part of the implementation if you need to carry out any enhancements to SAP technical objects.

We've covered most user IDs that are required during the initial setup to carry out various tasks. Also you'll see at the individual tools level where user ID creation for actual end users and approver functions and their privileges and authorization details in Chapter 4 through Chapter 7.

In Section 3.2.5, we reviewed some core technical settings that are basically needed in SAP Access Control immediately after installation. Also we've performed some common connectivity settings between systems. Naturally, we should review the configuration that is specific to SAP Access Control that should be completed after the technical settings have been established with the help of your Basis team and after the shared configuration is complete. Up until this point, this chapter has focused on the general assumptions made and a good amount of post-installation work by the Basis team. Now we'll get into the specifics of Access Control Configuration with more details to come in the other chapters.

3.3 SAP Access Control Configuration

More than 100 entries are available for you to customize how your SAP Access Control tools should behave, the default values, and so on. To simplify, SAP logically grouped these parameters into parameter groups.

Parameters and parameter groups

Some of the parameters may work in conjunction with another, which means the combinations of two or three parameters may result in more than one or two different behaviors based on the combinations. We've listed these parameter groups in Table 3.4 and shown them in Figure 3.46.

Grp ID	Parameter Group Description	Grp ID	Parameter Group Description
01	Change Log	12	Access Request Role Selection
02	Mitigation	13	Access Request Default Roles
03	Risk Analysis	14	Access Request Role Mapping
04	Risk Analysis—Spool	15	SoD Review
05	Workflow	16	LDAP
06	Superuser Management	17	Assignment Expiry
07	UAR Review	18	Access Request Training Verification
08	Performance	19	Authorizations
09	Risk Analysis—Access Request	20	Access Request Business Role
10	Role Management	21	Management Dashboard Reports
11	Risk Analysis—Risk Terminator	22	Access Request Validations

Table 3.4 SAP Access Control Parameter Groups

As stated, there are more than 100 entries with self-explanatory descriptions given while selecting that parameter at the time of configuration. In Figure 3.46, we've provided a sample view of this screen with the parameter groups. The underlying individual parameter values for most of them are YES or NO and are available from a dropdown menu. There are some other parameters for which you may need to enter the correct values. Some important values are explained at the individual tool level in Chapter 4 through Chapter 7 so that it will help you understand them more clearly and configure the tools to meet your needs.

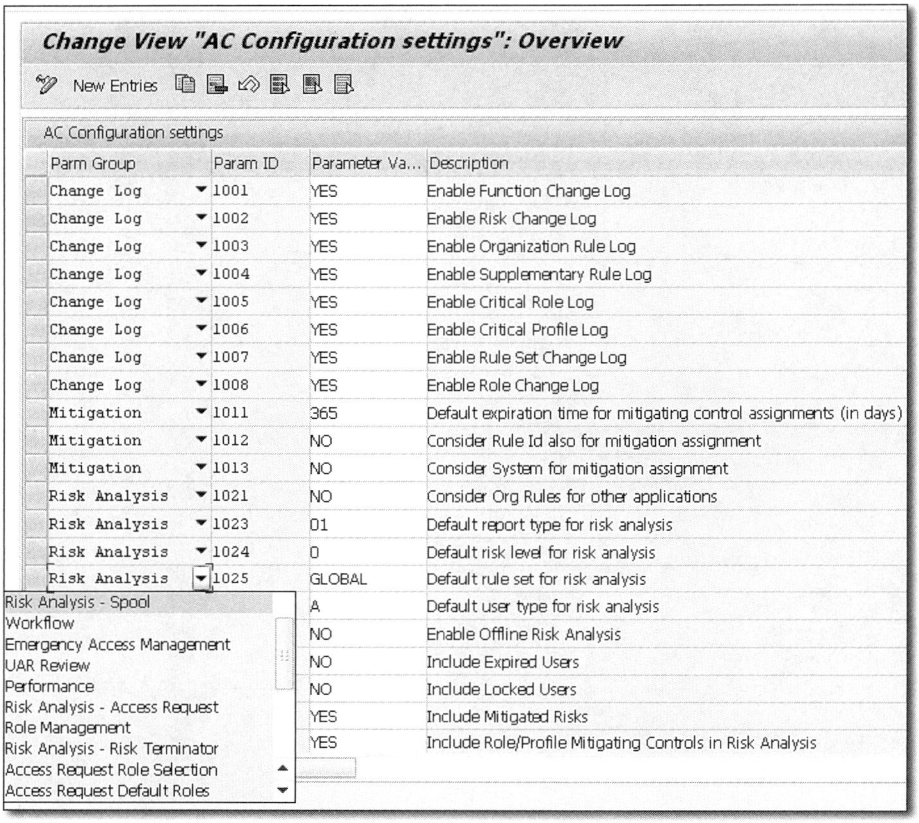

Figure 3.46 SAP Access Control Configuration Setting in Parameter Groups

Along with these details, we encourage you to check the SAP Services Marketplace, which is releasing documentation with individual explanations of these parameters from time to time based on newer releases of support packs, especially when they introduce any new parameters to improve the SAP Access Control functionality.

3.4 Summary

This chapter introduced you to the basic settings and technical preparatory steps that are required to start SAP Access Control configuration tools and the concepts behind those basic settings. In the following chapters, we'll go through the individual tool configuration in contrast to the current chapter, which covered more of the core-shared settings to start any SAP Access Control tools.

In the next chapter, we'll look into Emergency Access Management configuration and functionalities with various options that will help you implement Emergency Access Management effectively.

This chapter provides in-depth detail on Emergency Access Management configuration, firefighter ID usage and review, and reporting to help your organization maximize the full potential of this tool as part of your effort to maintain clean, risk-free IT environment from segregation of duties violations. Some extra features and future release options are also discussed.

4 Emergency Access Management Overview

This chapter looks at one of the most powerful tool sets of SAP Access Control, which is also simple to configure and use in customer environments. Emergency Access Management is used to perform some of the duties that users aren't normally privileged to do, but with appropriate approvals, users can carry out some business transactions for a specified period. Emergency Access Management mitigates the additional authorization risk by tracking changes made by users when they use Emergency Access Management to change or rectify some issues using business transactions in the SAP ERP system rather than at their own, less privileged logon. This tool is equally valuable in the normal environment to restrict authorizations such as the debugging authorization for developers in a production environment.

Short term authorizations and inherent risks

Also, period end closings such as month-end or year-end closings authorizations or transactions may be required for a short period of time to any business users and this authorization may not be as part of their regular user authorization in the SAP system. In other words providing those transactions are more liberal in an IT environment might lead to business risks and the opportunity to misuse such critical transactions. However, at the same time these actions may need to be used as part of business activities and if their usage may need to be tracked as emergency access action and audited to ensure that no intentional or unintentional risks are posed by using these transactions or activities. This kind of emergency action or occasional high risk transaction activities are carried out with business approval and self-check-out to enhance a smoother flow of business with minimized risks are achieved due to audit tracking in Emergency Access Management.

Role re-design and role remediation

This tool is also useful during role redesign and role remediation processes by enabling users to address some of the missing authorizations. This tool enables the user to continue with the business transactions while your security team addresses the regular authorization issues, which might take some time per your company policies and procedures. Basically, Emergency Access Management helps reduce your business downtime due to any authorizations-related issues while tracking all of the user activity at the same time.

Firefighter ID activity

The Emergency Access Management process workflow provides an auditable process for ensuring the log reports have been reviewed by supervisors (firefighter ID controller) following firefighter activity. The process assigns log reports to the supervisor's inbox where he can review and approve the firefighter activity. The supervisor also has the opportunity to request additional justification from the firefighter or forward questionable activity to others for review. This additional process step provides a complete process for evaluating exception base access.

In this chapter, we'll review how to use Emergency Access Management, including the different types of users and their responsibilities, the different types of firefighter application management, and how to configure, monitor, and report.

Firefighter role or Firefighter ID

Emergency Access Management can be used in two different ways—as a firefighter role or a firefighter ID. You may choose whether your application is ID based or role based and which is suitable to your environment. In this chapter, we'll explore how to configure the firefighter as ID based or role based by means of configuration parameters during implementation. In a role-based environment, the special role (firefighter role) is created in a remote system, and the assignment of one of the role to the users requested is approved and provisioned to perform emergency access in the target SAP ERP system from the SAP Access Control system. After the assignment is provided, the user can be logged on to the target SAP ERP system using his user ID and then use the firefighter role to perform emergency activities. This role is assigned with a specific time limit; after the time expires, the role privileges can't be used. We'll discuss how to use the firefighter role in Section 4.3.

In contrast to role-based firefighters, ID-based firefighters can log on from the SAP GRC system. The user needs to invoke Transaction GRAC_SPM to perform emergency activities by selecting the assigned firefighter ID against their user ID. This enables users to check in and check out the firefighter ID from the SAP GRC system as a single access point to multiple systems and clients as the centralized tool. The audit team can also verify various activity reports from a single SAP Access Control system. We'll first look at the different types of users, along with their roles and responsibilities in Emergency Access Management.

4.1 Using Emergency Access Management

The different types of users, their roles, and their responsibilities in using the Emergency Access Management tool are provided in Table 4.1. The table provides details on the firefighter ID, firefighter owner, reviewer, and firefighter ID user.

From Section 3.2.6, about role activation, we assume that you've populated and generated all GRAC roles, and they are available from Transaction SU01 for user assignments. All users who need to access the SAP NetWeaver Business Client (NWBC) frontend, irrespective of their roles and responsibilities, should be assigned the following roles: SAP_GRAC_NWBC, SAP_GRC_FN_BASE, and SAP_GRC_FN_BUSINESS_USER.

Type of User	Responsibility	Role
Firefighter ID (in SAP ERP)	Extra privileged user ID. All activities performed are tracked for audit.	SAP_GRAC_SPM_FFID *Any other functional role from the target system that has broader access to the system is meant to be used by the firefighter.*
Firefighter (in SAP GRC)	Person who performs some additional activities by checking out a firefighter ID.	SAP_GRAC_SUPER_USER_MGMT_USER
Firefighter ID owner (in SAP GRC)	Person who owns the ID and has authority to assign firefighter IDs to others.	SAP_GRAC_SUPER_USER_MGMT_OWNER
Firefighter ID Controller (in SAP GRC)	Person who reviews the reason code/description and audit trail to ensure that access was used appropriately. The user can be notified when firefighter IDs are checked in/out and notified of all activities performed via email trigger.	SAP_GRAC_SUPER_USER_MGMT_CNTLR

Table 4.1 Various Emergency Access Management User Types, Responsibilities, and Assigned Roles

Enhancements new to SAP Access Control as of version 10.0 and 10.1 include identifying firefighter IDs by criticality for workflow routing and the ability for a firefighter user to document additional activity about unplanned activity while firefighting. When viewing the transaction log report or reason code report, supervisors can bring up the log report directly, thus reducing unnecessary clicks while researching firefighter activity. This is best handled in the centralized Emergency Access Management tool, as shown in Figure 4.1.

Now that we've reviewed the different roles in Emergency Access Management, let's look at the types of logs that are captured from your SAP ERP system or any other target system during firefighter ID usage. This information will be shown as activities that are performed by the user using firefighter privileges, either in report form or sent as an email to the reviewer if workflow is activated in Emergency Access Management.

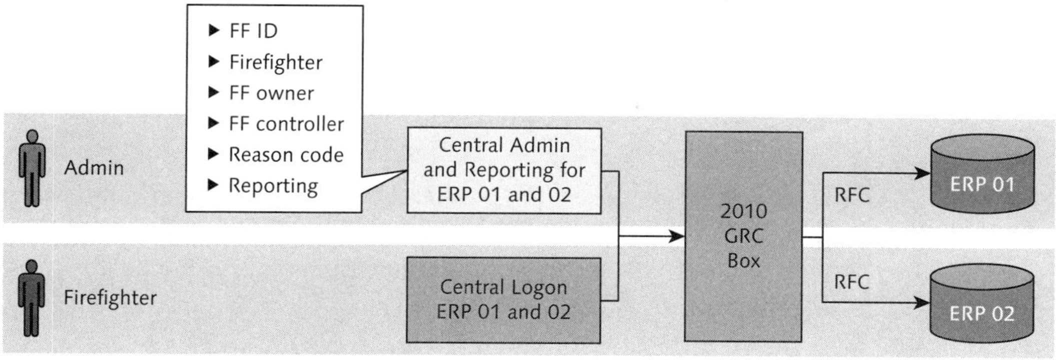

Figure 4.1 Centralized Emergency Access Management Tool

Log types in Emergency Access Management for auditing

Now let us see all the different types of logs that are captured by Emergency Access Management for auditing purpose. Most of the activities carried out by business team or technical team falls under one of the below mentioned log category.

- **STAD Transaction logs**
  All transactions that are tracked in statistics record from the system.
- **Change Logs**
  Transactional data from CDHDR and CDPOS tables that are captured for data changes.
- **Security Audit Log**
  Log details from Transaction SM20 that are relevant to security statistics.
- **System Log**
  Debug log details from Transaction SM21.
- **OS Command Log**
  Log details that are used at the operating system level and are invoked from Transactions SM49 and SM69.

Emergency Access Management uses a centralized log-on pad for several reasons:

- Display all predefined firefighter IDs assigned to the user.
- Firefighter can log on to the remote client system (older version needs to be logged on to the individual system).

- Reporting can be done from a centralized system.
- Messages can be sent to another firefighter who is using same firefighter ID.
- Unlock remote sessions being locked by a firefighter.

Now that we've looked at the different user roles in Emergency Access Management, as well as explored the types of logs that are pulled from your SAP ERP system, let's identify how to configure Emergency Access Management.

4.2 Emergency Access Management Configuration in SAP GRC

The configuration steps of Emergency Access Management are simple and straightforward. We've given all of the configuration steps, and, where necessary, we've provided additional details to help you better understand system settings. In this section, we'll review the following:

- Configuration parameters, both in the SAPGUI and the NWBC
- Email configuration
- The importance of properly setting up a background job

The implementation settings of shared components of SAP Access Control, preliminary checks, and requirements for implementation have already been explained in Chapter 3. These settings are applied to Emergency Access Management as a component of SAP GRC.

4.2.1 Configuration Parameters

Figure 4.2 shows configuration parameters that need to be set related to Emergency Access Management. These parameters are available under Superuser Privilege Management (SPM) in support packs prior to 8 and later as Emergency Access Management.

Parameter groups and parameter IDs

The parameter groups contain parameter IDs that start from 4000 to 4010. All of these parameter ID descriptions give the detail on what each parameter ID is meant for. A few of them are for retrieving and sending log details, and they have options for you to maintain with YES or NO. Parameter ID 4000 determines whether you want to use the ID-based or role-based firefighter application option. If you select the ID-based firefighter application, then you need to maintain parameter ID 4010 with the role name maintained in SAP ERP or any other target system to identify the firefighter ID. Also you need to add another parameter—1113—with the WF-BATCH value as ACCESS CONTROL E-MAIL SENDER, which is part of the WORKFLOW parameter group. This parameter setting is necessary to send email to the controller and owner about the emergency access activity with user and usage details.

Emergency Access Management configuration file path

To set these values, click on TRANSACTION SPRO. From here, navigate to GOVERNANCE, RISK AND COMPLIANCE • ACCESS CONTROL • MAINTAIN CONFIGURATION SETTINGS.

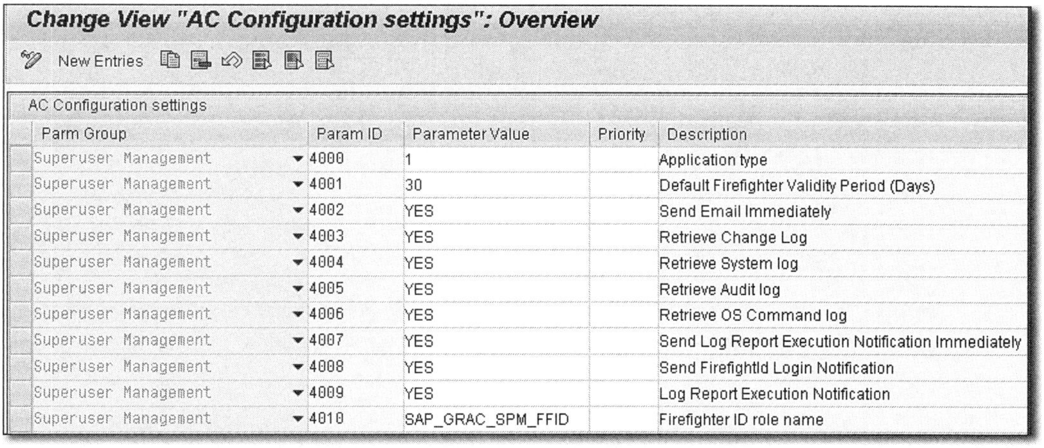

Parm Group	Param ID	Parameter Value	Priority	Description
Superuser Management	4000	1		Application type
Superuser Management	4001	30		Default Firefighter Validity Period (Days)
Superuser Management	4002	YES		Send Email Immediately
Superuser Management	4003	YES		Retrieve Change Log
Superuser Management	4004	YES		Retrieve System log
Superuser Management	4005	YES		Retrieve Audit log
Superuser Management	4006	YES		Retrieve OS Command log
Superuser Management	4007	YES		Send Log Report Execution Notification Immediately
Superuser Management	4008	YES		Send FirefightId Login Notification
Superuser Management	4009	YES		Log Report Execution Notification
Superuser Management	4010	SAP_GRAC_SPM_FFID		Firefighter ID role name

Figure 4.2 Emergency Access Management Configuration Settings with Detail

Now that we have explored some of the general configuration parameters, let's review the configuration steps for Emergency Access Management.

4.2.2 General Configuration Steps

Most Emergency Access Management configuration parameter usage details are self-descriptive as you've seen in the previous section. In this section, we'll look at the general configuration steps, both in the SAPGUI and in SAP NetWeaver Business Client.

Configuration in the SAP GUI

Step-by-Step Emergency Access Management configuration with SAP GUI

To configure Emergency Access Management with the SAPGUI, follow the following steps:

1. Define and assign all required user roles as listed in Table 4.1, in the SAP GRC system and in the target system (e.g., SAP ERP or any other SAP system).
2. In Transaction SPRO, define the following path: SAP CUSTOMIZING IMPLEMENTATION GUIDE • GRC • COMMON COMPONENTS SETTINGS • INTEGRATION FRAMEWORK • MAINTAIN CONNECTION SETTINGS.
3. Assign a connector to integration scenario of "SUPMG" in the INTEGRATION SCENARIO field shown in the SCENARIO-CONNECTOR LINK DIALOG STRUCTURE of the CHANGE VIEW "SCENARIO-CONNECTOR LINK": OVERVIEW screen (see Figure 4.3).

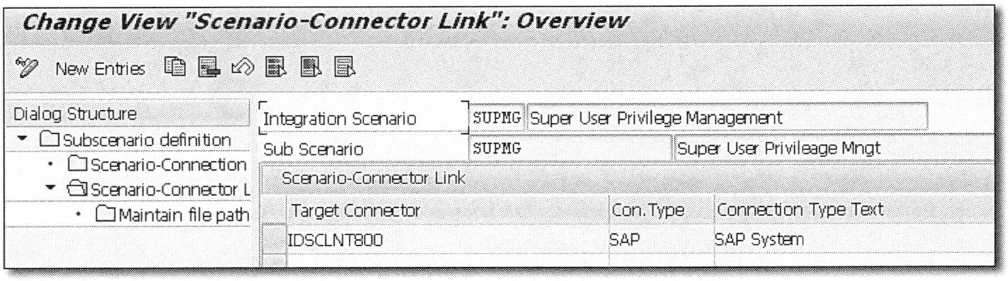

Figure 4.3 Emergency Access Management Tool: Integration Scenario Related to Connector

4. Set up email settings using Transaction SCOT, and schedule a job for email sending on a regular interval using parameter ID 1113 with a user ID value of WF-BATCH) (refer to Section 4.2.1). Section 4.2.3 shows how to perform these activities.
5. Schedule the REPOSITORY OBJECT SYNCH and EAM MASTER DATA SYNCH jobs to run on regular intervals to populate users, roles, and authorization objects from the target SAP ERP system to the SAP Access Control system. This is a mandatory activity to get any changes from the target system updated with changes in the SAP Access Control system; this is shared data among SAP Access Control tools. To perform this activity, execute Transaction SPRO, and follow menu path, GOVERNANCE, RISK AND COMPLIANCE • ACCESS CONTROL • SYNCHRONIZATION.

6. Schedule the FIREFIGHTER LOG SYNCH and FIREFIGHTER WORKFLOW SYNCH jobs to collect logs to get audit details from Transaction SPRO using menu path, GOVERNANCE, RISK AND COMPLIANCE • ACCESS CONTROL • SYNCHRONIZATION.

If you're not familiar with job scheduling, see Section 4.2.1 to see how to schedule a background job. Now that we've reviewed the configuration of Emergency Access Management through the SAPGUI, let's explore the technical backend and the configuration needed in the NWBC.

Configuration in the SAP NetWeaver Business Client

To configure SAP Emergency Access Management with SAP NetWeaver Business Client, you should follow these steps as outlined.

Step-by-step configuration of Emergency Access Management with SAP NetWeaver Business Client

The first step in configuring Emergency Access Management is to log in to the NWBC as the administrator. Administrator access allows you to set up SAP Access Control owners, set up superuser assignments, and maintain superusers.

From the initial page of the NWBC, you need to follow the menu path in the SETUP workset, and go to ACCESS OWNER • ACCESS CONTROL OWNERS to define owners and controllers of Emergency Access Management as having the generic owners privilege of SAP Access Control (see Figure 4.4).

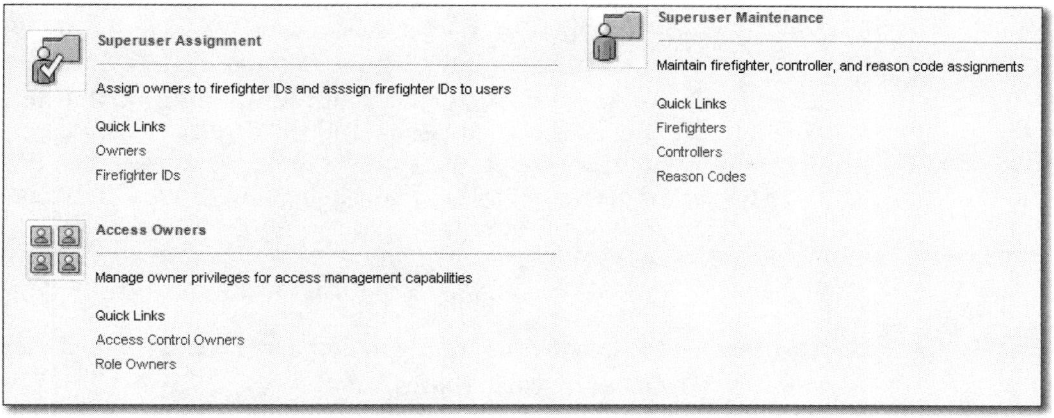

Figure 4.4 NWBC Configuration

Next, you assign firefighter ID owners to firefighter IDs using the OWNERS link under the SUPERUSER ASSIGNMENT heading as shown in Figure 4.4 those who will approve the firefighter ID or firefighter role activities in Emergency Access Management. You can assign firefighter ID controllers from the FIREFIGHTER IDs link shown in Figure 4.4. From firefighter IDs link, you can maintain the controller details, which is already defined as one of the SAP Access Control owners in the earlier step or this can be assigned from the link CONTROLLERS under SUPERUSER MAINTENANCE heading. And in the same detail screen you can set the options how the controller needs to be notified on firefighter activities by means of EMAIL, WORKFLOW, or LOG DISPLAY.

Next, in the same screen under SUPERUSER MAINTENANCE heading, reason codes and controllers are maintained by selecting the respective links. Also firefighter ID or role assignment to any SAP ERP user is performed manually from FIREFIGHTERS link shown in Figure 4.4 by entering userID and validity period to enable end user to access firefighter ID or firefighter role; alternatively, firefighter user access requests can be automated using User Access Management for access request and approval process and approval of this request will update the same set of tables that are manually maintained for firefighter ID or firefighter role privileges.

Multiple firefighter IDs can be assigned to the same controller; assuming that most companies may use an internal auditor, this works as a pooled resource to review firefighter access log data.

Note:

During the actual usage, the ID owner needs to assign the firefighter ID to the firefighter with from/to validity dates manually using NWBC. If a firefighter request workflow is configured as a part of User Access Management, the validity approval can be set while approving. Alternatively, a minimum time period can be set as one of the parameter values (4001) in SAP Access Control configuration with values in number of days.

Now that we've reviewed the configuration parameters, it's important to review how to set up email configuration.

4.2.3 Email Configuration

In SAP Access Control, you need to set up SAP email communication settings to send any notification emails. Here you're required to maintain your email host settings in the Simple Mail Transfer Protocol (SMTP) server details to receive automated email notification that is triggered as a result of background jobs related to emergency activities performed in Emergency Access Management. Let's see how these settings are made in SAPGUI.

SAPconnect Administration (Transaction SCOT)

You must configure the SMTP node in Transaction SCOT to enable SPM to send emails to firefighter users. Follow these steps:

1. Log on to the application backend.
2. Open Transaction SCOT.
3. Click CREATE.
4. Follow the prompts, and enter the information for your mail server.

User Configuration for Emails

You configure email messages the same way for both ID-based and role-based Emergency Access Management administration. To send notification and log messages as emails to a firefighter ID controller (internal auditor), you need to set parameter ID 1113 with user ID as workflow batch authorization (the same as WF-BATCH). Alternatively, a different ID with equivalent authorizations can trigger the workflow to send an email.

Also don't forget another setting mentioned earlier, which is setting the NOTIFICATION TYPE as EMAIL in the NWBC. You then choose SETUP • SUPERUSER MAINTENANCE • CONTROLLERS. If you set this value as WORKFLOW, then the controller can see this as work item in his workflow inbox from SAP NetWeaver Business Client. If you set this value as LOG DISPLAY, then controllers don't receive email notifications or workflow items, but rather they can view the log from firefighter log reports.

To receive log email messages, ensure that you schedule the background job as mentioned in the next section.

Scheduling a Background Job to Receive Log Messages

Periodic background jobs are scheduled to monitor the usage of emergency access activities using either firefighter IDs or firefighter roles. The background job records logon events and transaction usage. These jobs must be scheduled to generate and capture log data to view the firefighter log reports. As a best practice, it's recommended to have your background job run hourly, but this can be set to meet internal business and reporting requirements.

To maintain the background job, use Transaction SM36, or from Transaction SPRO (choose ACCESS CONTROL • SYNCHRONIZATION JOBS), you need to execute FIREFIGHTER LOG SYNCH or FIREFIGHTER WORKFLOW SYNCH per your parameter settings.

Background job and database table interaction

The background job updates the following listed database tables. These tables and their values feed the reports and send out emails with the firefighter log details.

- GRACAUDITLOG: Security Audit Log table
- GRACCHANGELOG: Data Change Log table
- GRACOSCMDLOG: Operating System Command Log table
- GRACSYSTEMLOG: System Security Log table
- GRACFFLOG: Details related to Firefighter ID Log On Information

Details related to Firefighter ID logon Information

If you've maintained the SEND LOG REPORT EXECUTION NOTIFICATION IMMEDIATELY parameter as YES, then it's updated during FIREFIGHTER LOG SYNCH; otherwise, it's updated during FIREFIGHTER WORKFLOW SYNCH. You maintain this in the CUSTOMIZING ACTIVITY MAINTAIN CONFIGURATION SETTINGS screen in PARAMETER ID 4007.

- GRACROLEFFLOG: This log is updated for role-based applications, when PARAMETER ID 4000 – APPLICATION TYPE equals role based.

Firefighter Workflow synchronization

The other background job in Emergency Access Management is the FIREFIGHTER WORKFLOW SYNCH as shown in Figure 4.5. This background job helps you generate requests for the firefighter ID log and sends the workflow to the controller. The FIREFIGHTER WORKFLOW SYNCH updates the GRACFFLOG and GRACROLEFFLOG tables, triggers the firefighter workflow, and creates firefighter work items.

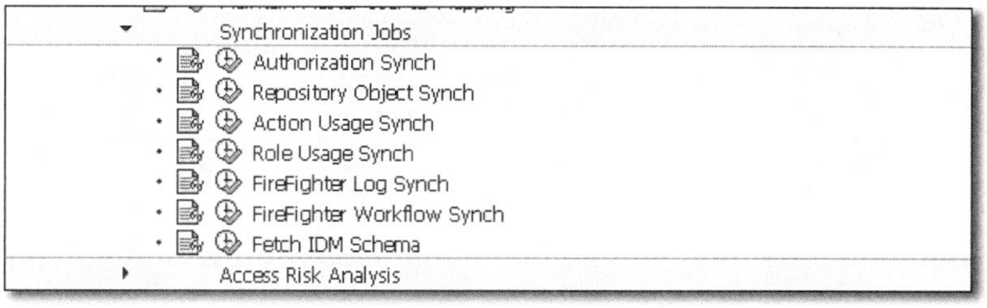

Figure 4.5 Emergency Access Management FireFighter Log Synch and FireFighter Workflow Synch

Alternatively these jobs can be directly scheduled from Transaction SM36.

4.3 Using a Firefighter ID

Before using the firefighter ID, make sure that you've implemented OSS Note 1545511 in the target system (e.g., SAP ERP) to enable the firefighter exit program to prevent anyone from using the firefighter ID to log in to the SAP ERP system directly. If someone does this, there is no log data captured for this type of login, which is riskier in most customer landscapes. Also make sure that the Access Control configuration parameter values of 1089 and 1090 in the plug-in system (SAP ERP) reflect the same parameter values maintained in the SAP GRC ABAP system's SAP Access Control configuration parameters of 4000 and 4010.

In the customer system, for any user who wants to use a firefighter ID, the respective ID owner needs to assign the ID to the firefighter who requested it with the dates from and to for this firefighter ID. The user who is allowed to use the firefighter ID logs on to the SAP ABAP system because the user is assigned a superuser management role. Transaction GRAC_SPM is available to use the firefighter ID as shown in Figure 4.6.

Firefighter user logon

Based on the firefighter assignment, the user can see all firefighter IDs assigned to this user (shown in the initial screen). Now the user can choose the LOGON button to open the target system using the firefighter ID, as shown in Figure 4.7.

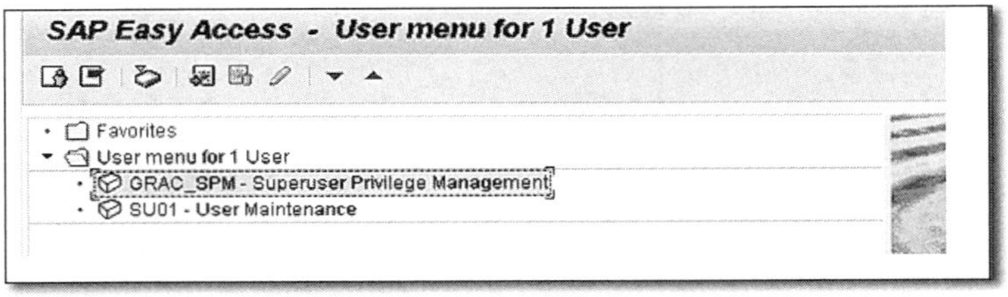

Figure 4.6 Firefighter Initial Screen

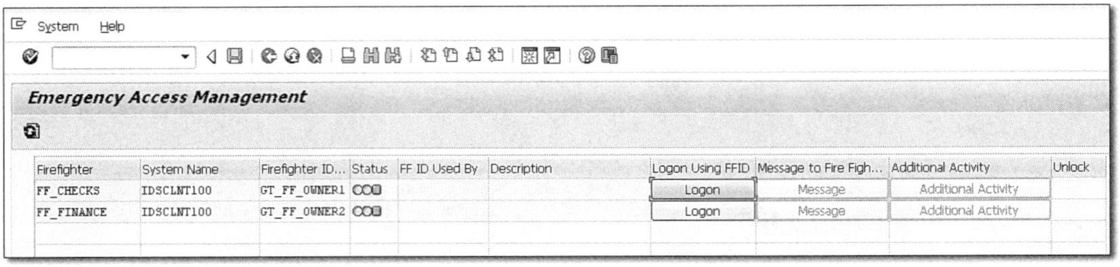

Figure 4.7 Emergency Access Management Dashboard to Check Out Firefighter IDs

Reason codes

Once logged on, the user needs to enter the Reason Code and an appropriate description of changes to start using the firefighter ID. The reason code is specific to Emergency Access Management, which is maintained in SAP NetWeaver Business Client, and the user need to choose the reason the user needs to use the firefighter ID as shown in Figure 4.8 as an example '0015 – emergency access management' chosen here. Similarly you may create many reason codes and reasons based on business requirements like month end closing activity, development fix – post go-live, etc. The user can enter anticipated actions and document any additional activity. All of these details will be shown in the Emergency Access Management report which we will discuss in Section 4.4. This data helps the controller or auditor understand who used the firefighter ID and why.

Once logged on to the SAP ERP system (the target system), the user will have all of the assigned access that has been authorized for that user's firefighter ID. All activities performed under this ID are captured and stored in respective database tables as a result of the background job after the firefighter logs out of the system.

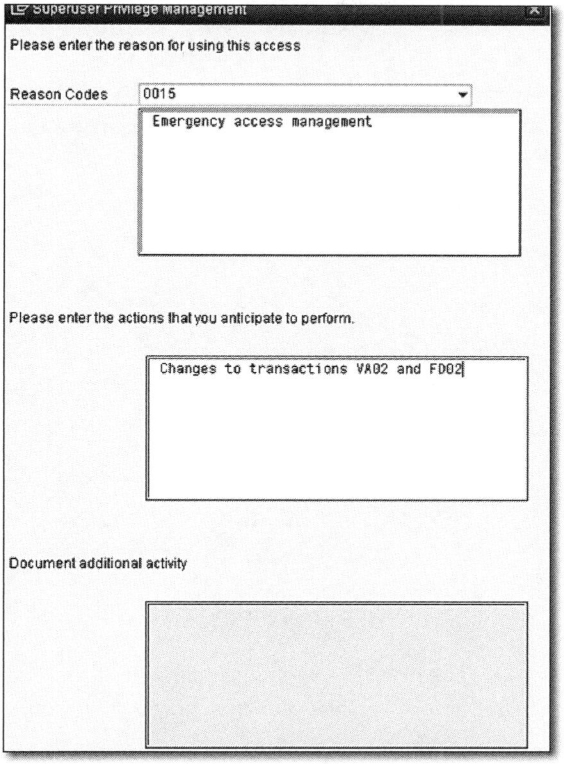

Figure 4.8 Emergency Access Management Mandatory Fields to Fill before Checking Out a Firefighter ID

Now that we've reviewed the types of user roles, the configuration of Emergency Access Management, and how to properly use a firefighter in a system, the next step is monitoring and reporting on any activity logged in Emergency Access Management.

4.4 Reporting

Multiple Emergency Access Management reports are available and accessible from the NetWeaver Business Client frontend component by the firefighter ID owner, controller, administrator, and auditors because these roles are authorized to access reports pertaining to Emergency Access Management.

Report access with SAP NetWeaver Business Client

To access these reports, users need to launch the NWBC either from SAPGUI by executing Transaction NWBC or by directly logging on to the NWBC frontend. From here, select the REPORTS AND ANALYTICS workset, and then choose CONSOLIDATED LOG REPORT under SUPERUSER MANAGEMENT REPORTS. Figure 4.9 demonstrates how to navigate to the reporting links for Emergency Access Management.

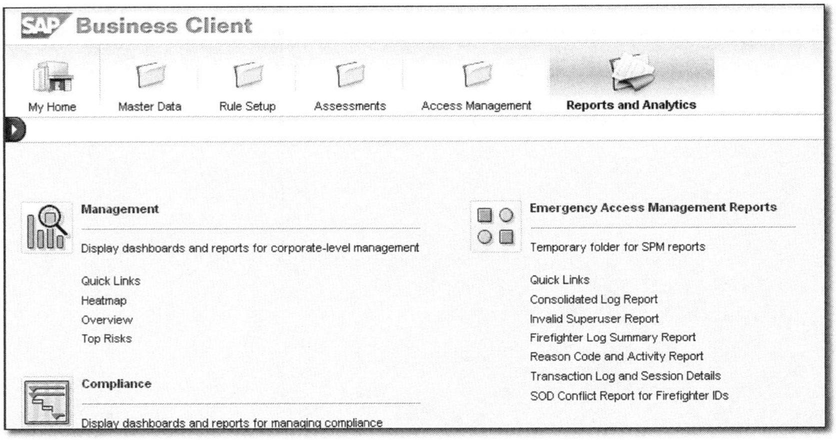

Figure 4.9 Emergency Access Management Reporting Links from the NWBC Reports and Analytics Tab

Emergency Access Management report types

Let's examine the following report types to understand the range of reporting capabilities in Emergency Access Management:

- CONSOLIDATED LOG REPORT
- INVALID SUPERUSER REPORT
- FIREFIGHTER LOG SUMMARY REPORT
- REASON CODE AND ACTIVITY REPORT
- TRANSACTION LOG AND SESSION DETAILS
- SOD CONFLICT REPORT FOR FIREFIGHTER IDS
- REASON CODE USAGE FREQUENCY REPORT

4.4.1 Consolidated Log Report

This report is one of the widely used Emergency Access Management report to get all systems emergency access activities using different input values to pull the data in reporting. This report provides the following:

- Output details of the firefighter ID
- Who used this ID on what system
- Transactions accessed, including old and new data if any business transaction changes were made
- Firefighter ID owner
- Reason code and from which terminal this firefighter ID is used
- Link to session details showing all activities performed on a specific login session along with date and timestamp

Next, let's see some of the options that can be used to extract the report.

Report by Date and System

Users can run a report based on the target system and date to get an overview of firefighter ID usage. You can enter a specific date as shown in Figure 4.10, or you can select a date range by choosing IN BETWEEN from the input field next to DATE, which opens two input fields to enter a from and to date range to extract Emergency Access Management data. Similarly, you can choose greater than a specific date or less than a specific date.

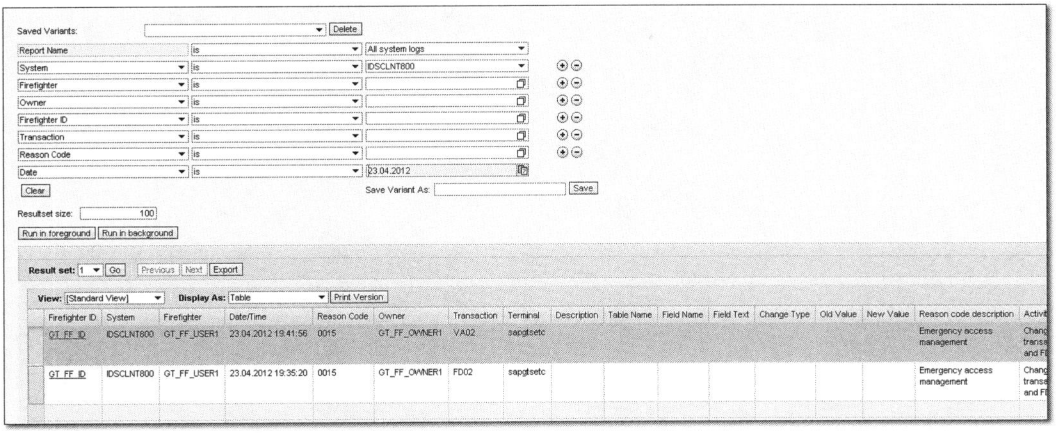

Figure 4.10 Consolidated Log Report: Report by System and Date

Report by Firefighter

The CONSOLIDATED LOG REPORT can be executed based on one user or multiple users who used fire-fighter IDs as shown in Figure 4.11. For those who need to access or monitor a group of users, this information can be saved as variants to run repeatedly in the future.

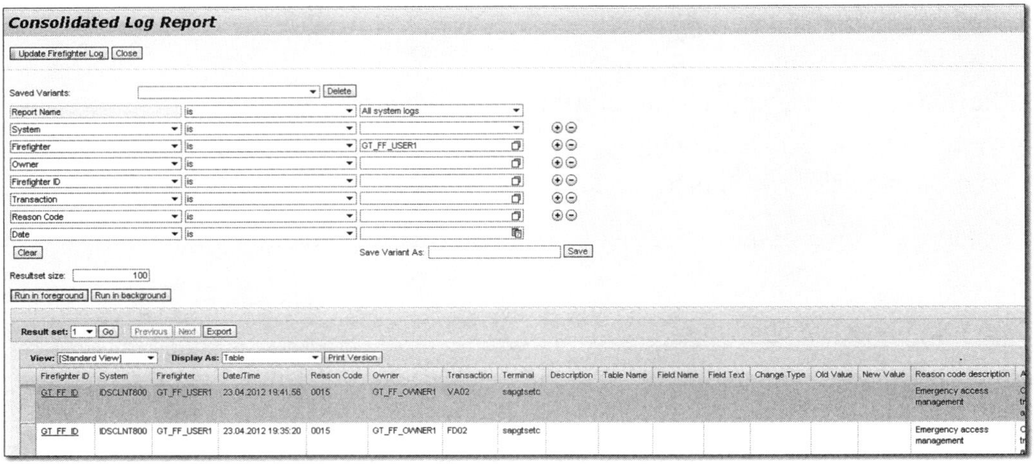

Figure 4.11 Consolidated Log Report: Report by Firefighter

Report by Owner

This report helps the firefighter ID owners quickly retrieve data specific to their firefighter ID usage by completing the OWNER field (see Figure 4.12).

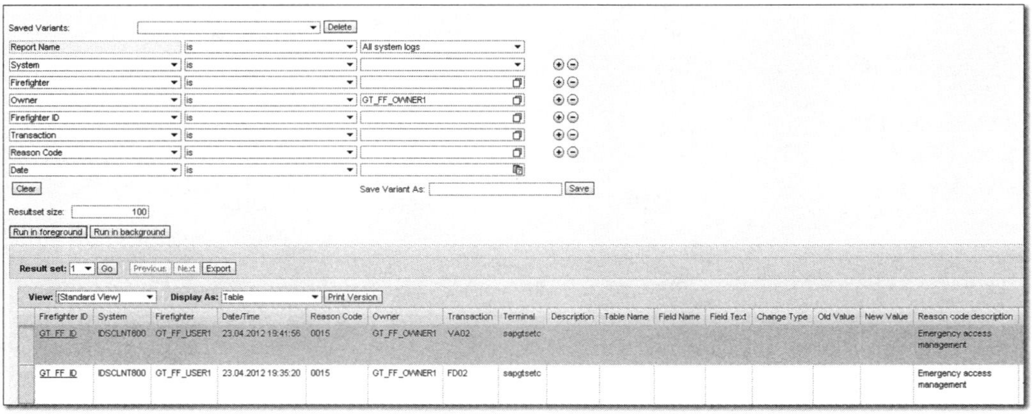

Figure 4.12 Consolidated Log Report: Report by Owner

4.4.2 Reason Code and Activity Report

This report is more helpful when an internal auditor needs to cross-check whether any specific reasons are used more frequently than others when firefighting. This report can detail when it's beneficial to a business to create more specific reason codes if a firefighter is using unique codes frequently (see Figure 4.13). This report can help you establish best business practices with Emergency Access Management.

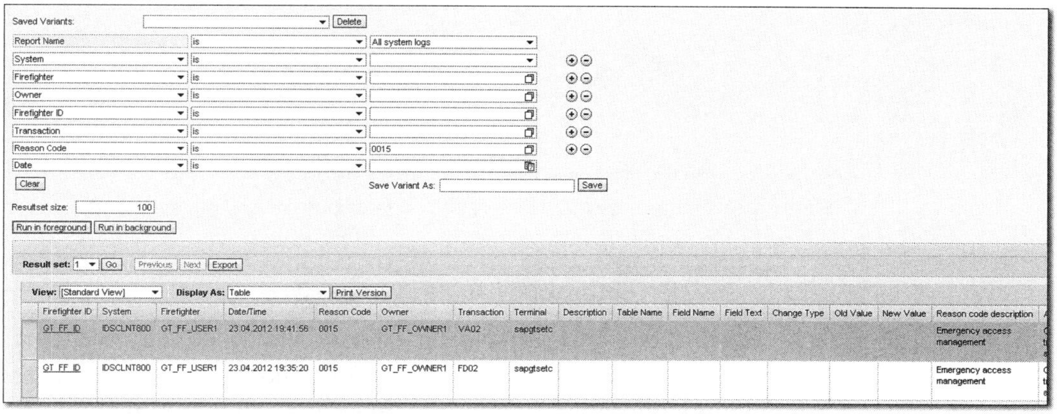

Figure 4.13 Emergency Access Management: Reason Code and Activity Report

4.4.3 Firefighter Log Summary Report

Similar to the CONSOLIDATE LOG REPORT, you can see the following columns in this report (see Figure 4.14): FIREFIGHTER ID, SYSTEM, FIREFIGHTER, DATE/TIME, REASON CODE, OWNER, REASON CODE DESCRIPTION, ACTIVITY DESCRIPTION, ADDITIONAL DESCRIPTION, and LOG REPORT. In this report, you can't choose the type of log individually, such as OS log, change log, or transaction log.

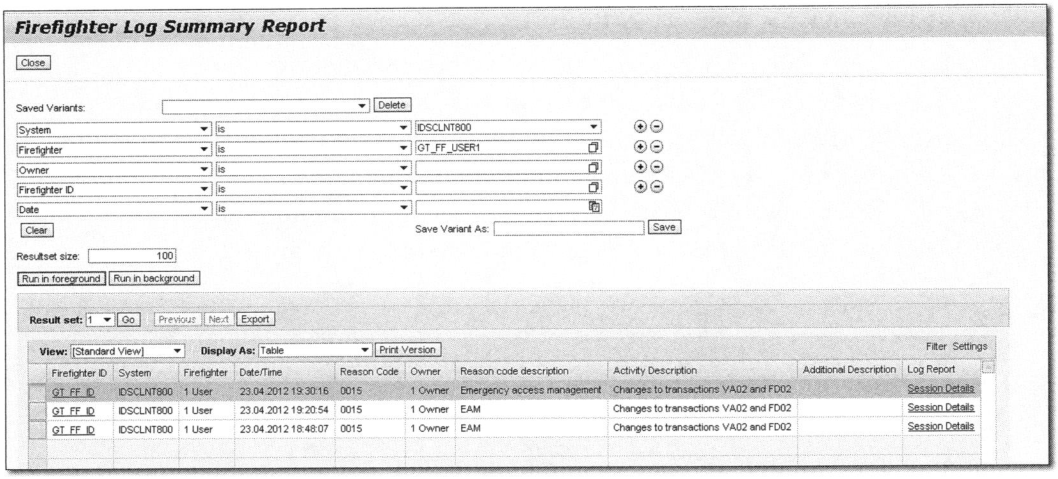

Figure 4.14 Emergency Access Management: Firefighter Log Summary Report

4.4.4 Invalid Emergency Access Report

This report allows you to find out any of the following Emergency Access user types like Firefighter IDs, Controllers or Owners that are expired, deleted or locked. This gives a quick detail to troubleshoot any issues in the usage or access approval of Emergency Access Management and also give details to auditing queries such as list of expired or deleted users/approvers for a specific date range.

4.4.5 Transaction Logs and Session Detail

This report provides transaction data for firefighter IDs and firefighters for specified system or range of systems. It gives the type of transactions and number of transactions per firefighter ID and for each user level. You may use filter the reports by transactions, reason code, and date.

4.4.6 SOD Conflict Report for Firefighter IDs

This report gives the detail and history of actions performed on SOD review tasks including mitigation for given system and firefighter IDs. You may use owner, firefighter and action as additional criteria as input values. The resulting risk analysis report can be obtained in different formats like summary, detail, management summary, and executive summary in technical view or business view. The risk analysis types can be set for action/permission level, critical action/permission, critical roles/profiles with an additional option to view executed transactions only. With this, we have completed all Emergency Access Management reports and before concluding the reports topic we have highlighted another reporting option in the next section.

4.4.7 Reason Code Usage Frequency

The Reason Code Usage Frequency report can be found from the Reason Code Assignment link from the Setup workset. You can execute this report specific to one or multiple systems to see how many times the emergency access had been used for a specific reason as shown in Figure 4.15. This information might help the security team decide whether the usage is so frequent that those kinds of activities or business transactions can be added to the regular role. This information can be reset across all systems or for each specific system.

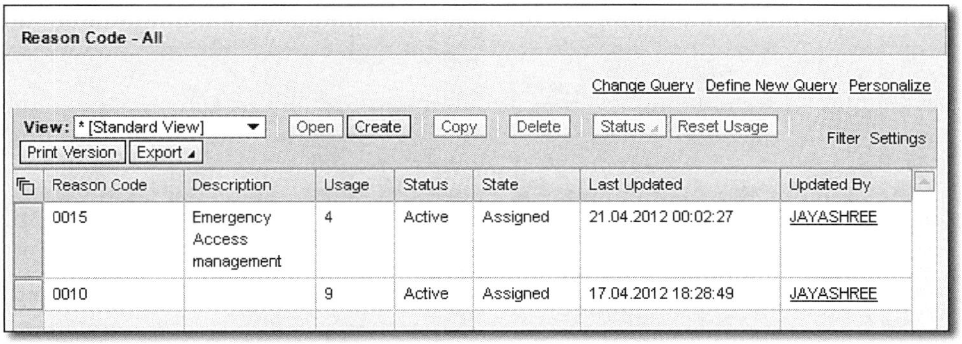

Reason Code	Description	Usage	Status	State	Last Updated	Updated By
0015	Emergency Access management	4	Active	Assigned	21.04.2012 00:02:27	JAYASHREE
0010		9	Active	Assigned	17.04.2012 18:28:49	JAYASHREE

Figure 4.15 Reason Code Usage Frequency Details

In this section, we've taken you through different options available to get results from different Emergency Access Management activities that are carried out in your landscape. This helps to address any audit issues and explanations that are needed for your internal or external audit.

4.5 Summary

In certain conditions, SAP_ALL authorization is required to handle business emergencies or critical conditions that may lead to SoD violations—the number one audit issue—and this extra privilege can jeopardize your business too. We've explained in this chapter how Emergency Access Management can be configured effectively to meet your organization's audit and compliance requirements.

In the next chapter, you'll see how to configure and use Access Risk Analysis.

The Access Risk Analysis tool is the backbone of SAP Access Control, which supports real-time compliance to detect, remove, and prevent access and authorization risks by means of reporting segregation of duties (SoD) violations before they occur. In this chapter, we'll walk through implementation, starting from loading default out-of-the-box rule sets to new reporting features, risk terminator, and alert monitoring options.

5 Access Risk Analysis Overview

The Access Risk Analysis tool is an automated security audit and segregation of duties (SoD) analysis application that is used to identify, analyze, and resolve all SoD and audit issues relating to regulatory compliance in your IT landscape, especially in an SAP ERP environment. You can perform risk analysis to identify risks associated with a user, role, profile, or human resources (HR) object. After SoD risk identification, this tool helps to create mitigating controls and monitors them. This can be performed by assigning these mitigating controls to control monitors. Approvers assign them to one of the specific controls that are used in the company.

Access Risk Analysis functionality

The Access Risk Analysis tool helps you to know and identify your IT environment risks and also helps to perform the following tasks:

1. Enforce SoD compliance from the start with enterprise-wide role design, documentation, and maintenance that prevents improper access to assets by automatically identifying and notifying the access- and authorization-related IT risks.
2. Support continuous real-time compliance to detect, remove, and prevent the access risks.
3. Use an internal control for a specified period to mitigate risk with reference to the user in the system when the risk identified can't be eliminated due to job nature or for some other reason.

4. Document and mitigate the business process risks by monitoring critical business function access.
5. Prevent security and access violations before they occur.
6. Use risk simulation to help identify risks in other SAP GRC tools such as Business Role Manager and User Access Management.

The Access Risk Analysis tool is designed to provide comprehensive capabilities to test and enforce SoD and monitor critical actions across enterprise applications proactively. Proper SoD and access control over key information assets are among the most effective safeguards against fraud and mistakes. However, these are some of the most difficult controls to deploy and sustain given the number of users, roles, and processes that require access, authorization, evaluation, testing, and remediation. In this chapter, we'll explore best practices for deploying and sustaining these controls using Access Risk Analysis.

Before we get into the basic configuration of Access Risk Analysis in Section 5.1, let's first discuss the SoD and how it can cause violation risks generally.

Segregation of Duties (SoD) violations

Based on Sarbanes-Oxley (SOX) requirements, the risk of the occurrence of irregularities in financial reporting is managed through enforcement of internal controls. SoD is a key internal control. Companies can mitigate risk by controlling access to corporate information, functions, and processes, and by segregating key duties to different personnel of the organization.

The following lists a few typical SoD violations that we've seen and how the Access Risk Analysis tool addresses these kinds of risks by using the out-of-the-box rule set provided by SAP:

- A person who maintains sales orders and credit memos has access to create a sales order, can generate fraudulent revenue, and then reverse the revenue in a subsequent period by issuing a credit memo.
- Conflicting transactions of maintaining a vendor master record and processing accounts payable leads to the risk that someone can create a fictitious vendor and generate fraudulent payments to the vendor.

The SAP GRC rule set is defined with risks which are defined by two or more conflicting functions. Each function is grouped with actions and underlying permissions. Actions are transactions of SAP ERP system and permissions are authorization objects maintained at individual transaction level. If any user is provisioned with conflicting actions and/or permissions, it poses SoD risk. You see this from our first example mentioned in our earlier paragraph, sales order creation and similar business transactions from SAP are grouped as one function as opposed to revenue posting, issue credit memo transactions are another function. Identifying any combination of these conflicting actions and permissions from user profiles would be more challenging if it's handled manually. To simplify this activity, the Access Risk Analysis rule set is created by grouping of transactions, functions and defining conflict between any of these kind of two or more functions are defined as a SoD risk to perform the Access Risk Analysis. This rule set is base to identify such SoD risks easily even in a complex environment which involves with more number of users, user profiles and systems.

SAP GRC Global rule set

As of now, there are about 154 risks identified and delivered in the SAP GRC system as part of the global rule set, across various business systems such as SAP ERP, SAP Supplier Relationship Management (SAP SRM), SAP Customer Relationship Management (SAP CRM), SAP Advanced Planner and Optimizer (SAP APO), and Enterprise Controlling Consolidation System (ECCS). These risks can be modified or switched on or off as part of rule set maintenance by setting the status of the functions, transactions, or authorization objects to 'ACTIVE' or 'INACTIVE' to suit customer business needs. We will cover the activation and de-activation in further detail in Section 5.1.3. Custom transactions can be added to the appropriate function and generating them to identify the standard risks for the custom transactions and standard transactions combinations. Additionally, you can create new risks based on business requirements. We'll discuss how to maintain these changes to the rule set in Section 5.1.4.

So far, we've discussed SoD violations, access risks, and how the Access Risk Analysis tool helps to protect and provides better IT governance.

Let's move forward on how to configure the Access Risk Analysis tool to support and carry out the previously mentioned tasks to work efficiently for your environment.

5.1 Access Risk Analysis Basic Configuration

In this section, we'll look at how to load the SAP-provided global rule set as a starting point to identify and eliminate risk in access and authorization. Also, we'll review the configuration parameters available for risk analysis. We presume that at this point, all of the preliminary common settings and connectivity between the SAP Access Control system and other plug-in SAP systems that need to be monitored are completed as described in Chapter 3.

This is a high-level look at the activities and actions that need to be completed by the implementation team before you start using the Access Risk Analysis tool. The following steps need to be completed before you can start to use Access Risk Analysis.

Step-by-step configuration process for Access Risk Analysis

1. Maintaining SAP Access Control risk analysis configuration parameters.
2. Adding a connector to the AUTH scenario and subscenario to link the Access Risk Analysis tool and target system.
3. Synchronizing users, roles, and profiles from the target or plug-in systems such as SAP ERP, SAP CRM, or SAP SRM systems.
4. Setting up/loading rule sets for risk analysis.
5. Assigning connectors to rule sets to name the correct rule IDs that will show the risk against the correct connectors and thus the target system.
6. Generating rules IDs to identify risks based on authorizations and transactions that are active specific to the target system.
7. Transporting rules from the development system (DEV) to the quality assurance (QA) systems and production (PRD) system.
8. Maintaining the rule set by adjusting with custom transactions or modify existing rules.

9. Setting up batch risk analysis.
10. Eliminating risks by using the role cleanup process.
11. Creating mitigation controls for risks that can't be removed.

In the following sections, we'll get into detailed explanation on these individual steps to help you understand Access Risk Analysis configuration, implementation, and use it effectively in your IT landscape.

5.1.1 Maintaining SAP Access Control Risk Analysis Configuration Parameters

As a first step in configuring risk analysis, the values listed in Table 5.1 need to be maintained in the RISK ANALYSIS parameter group based on your needs. To maintain configuration values in the IMG settings, use Transaction SPRO and access the following menu path: SAP CUSTOMIZING IMPLEMENTATION GUIDE • GOVERNANCE, RISK AND COMPLIANCE • ACCESS CONTROL • MAINTAIN CONFIGURATION SETTINGS. Table 5.1 provides you with the configuration parameter, the configured value, a description of the parameter and any other details needed to properly configure these values.

Configuration Parameter	Value	Description	Details
1021	No	Consider organization rules for other applications	Setting the value to YES automatically selects the CONSIDER ORG RULE checkbox on the RISK VIOLATIONS tab of the ACCESS REQUEST AND ROLE MAINTENANCE screens.
1023	2	Default report type for risk analysis	The risk analysis allows options such as analysis criteria, report options, and additional criteria. This parameter allows you to choose the type of report that is selected by default (02 = PERMISSION LEVEL). Note: This setting doesn't affect the RISK ANALYSIS TYPE fields on the BATCH RISK ANALYSIS screens; you must set these separately.

Table 5.1 Configuration Parameters Related to Risk Analysis

Configuration Parameter	Value	Description	Details
1024	3	Default risk level for risk analysis	Risk level that is selected by default (3 = CRITICAL).
1025	GLOBAL	Default rule set for risk analysis	This parameter allows you to choose the rule set that is selected by default.
1026	A	Default user type for risk analysis	This parameter allows you to choose the user type that is selected by default (A = DIALOG).
1027	NO	Enable offline risk analysis	Set the parameter value to YES to include offline data in risk analysis by default. On the RISK ANALYSIS screen, the OFFLINE DATA checkbox is selected automatically.
1028	NO	Include expired users	Set to YES to include expired users from plug-in systems for risk analysis.
1029	NO	Include locked users	Set to YES to include locked users from plug-in systems for risk analysis.
1030	YES	Include mitigated risks	Set the parameter value to YES to include mitigated risks in the risk analysis by default. The application displays the SoD violations, the mitigated risks, and the mitigating control assigned to it. On the RISK ANALYSIS screen, the INCLUDE MITIGATED RISKS checkbox is automatically selected.
1031	YES	Ignore critical roles and profiles	Set the value to YES to exclude critical roles and profiles for risk analysis.
1033	YES	Include role/profile mitigating controls in risk analysis	Set the value to YES to include the mitigating controls assigned to the user's roles and profiles for risk analysis.

Table 5.1 Configuration Parameters Related to Risk Analysis (Cont.)

Configuration Parameter	Value	Description	Details
1034	5	Maximum number of objects in a package for parallel processing	The application uses this parameter in conjunction with the NUMBER OF TASKS specified in the customizing activity DISTRIBUTE JOBS FOR PARALLEL PROCESSING to determine the distribution of objects that are processed per job. Note: The RZ10 parameter RDISP/WP_NO_BTC overrides this configuration. Therefore, if the RZ10 parameter is set to 2, then the application ignores the parameter in this setting and uses the value 2 instead.

Table 5.1 Configuration Parameters Related to Risk Analysis (Cont.)

5.1.2 Adding a Connector to the AUTH Scenario

After maintaining the preceding values, the other activity from Transaction SPRO is adding a connector to integration scenario AUTH, which uses the connector setting to perform risk analysis. Use the following menu path: SAP CUSTOMIZING IMPLEMENTATION GUIDE • GOVERNANCE, RISK AND COMPLIANCE • COMMON COMPONENT SETTINGS • INTEGRATION FRAMEWORK • MAINTAIN CONNECTION SETTINGS. The resulting screen shows the AUTH integration scenario (see Figure 5.1). You need to choose AUTH option and press Enter. From the next screen, select and assign the connector along with the AUTH subscenario. This is the same activity you've performed to configure Emergency Access Management in Chapter 4, Section 4.2.2, except that the scenario and subscenario are different for Access Risk Analysis.

After you continue, you'll see the subscenario with the default value AUTH. Select the SCENARIO CONNECTOR-LINK subfolder, where you create new entries and maintain all of the connectors that are used in your environment for risk analysis. Now that we've shown you how to configure the parameters for risk analysis, let's look at how to activate and upload these options.

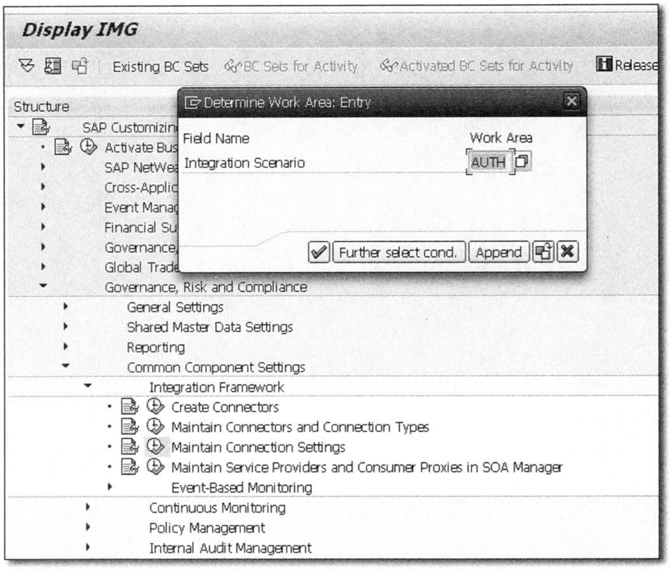

Figure 5.1 AUTH Integration Scenario

5.1.3 Risk Loading and Activation

The risk analysis process can be started by activating or uploading the out-of-the-box global rule set. This can be performed by two different approaches: executing Transaction SCPR20 or working with already created files. The first approach is to execute Transaction SCPR20, enter BC Set GRAC_RA_RULESET_COMMON, and then activate it. This populates the business process, subprocess, functions, and rule set. Figure 5.2 shows the Business Configuration Sets: Activation screen, from which you can select the GRAC_RA_RULESET_COMMON option from the BC Set dropdown list.

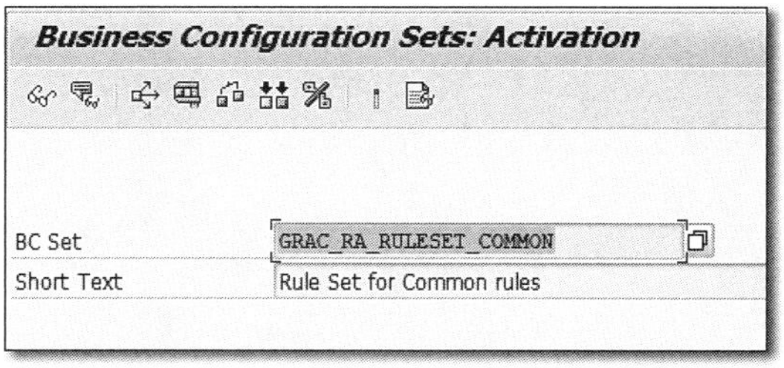

Figure 5.2 Rule Set: Common Activation

Uploading rule sets to your scenario configuration

After completing the scenario configuration, you need to load one of the rule sets that are available as a part of the standard BC Set. One of these rule sets should be activated based on your system environment. Upon successful activation, data will be created as table entries in respective database tables and views with respective logical group for conflicting actions, permissions, and risks. This first approach is applicable when you want to load the standard global rule set. To do this, you need to execute Transaction SCPR20, which shows you the screen in Figure 5.2. From the BC SET input field, enter "GRAC*RULESET" to get all available rule sets in the SAP GRC system (see Figure 5.3).

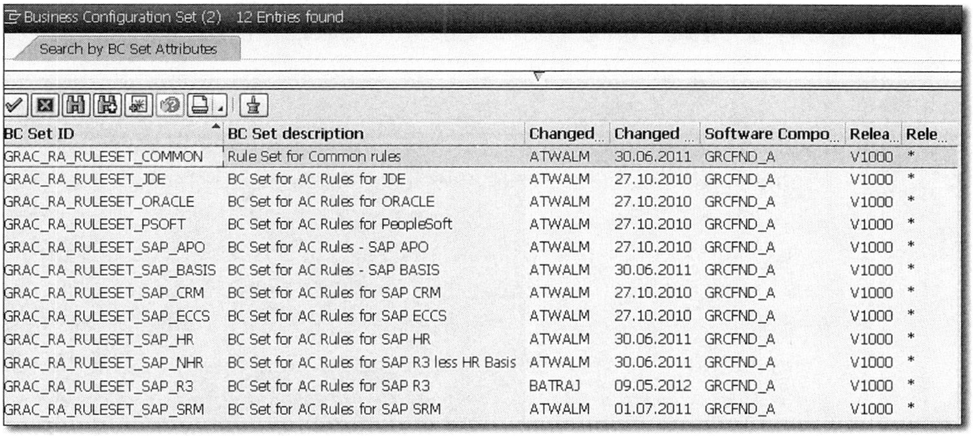
Business Configuration Set (2) 12 Entries found

Search by BC Set Attributes

BC Set ID	BC Set description	Changed...	Changed ...	Software Compo...	Relea...	Rele...
GRAC_RA_RULESET_COMMON	Rule Set for Common rules	ATWALM	30.06.2011	GRCFND_A	V1000	*
GRAC_RA_RULESET_JDE	BC Set for AC Rules for JDE	ATWALM	27.10.2010	GRCFND_A	V1000	*
GRAC_RA_RULESET_ORACLE	BC Set for AC Rules for ORACLE	ATWALM	27.10.2010	GRCFND_A	V1000	*
GRAC_RA_RULESET_PSOFT	BC Set for AC Rules for PeopleSoft	ATWALM	27.10.2010	GRCFND_A	V1000	*
GRAC_RA_RULESET_SAP_APO	BC Set for AC Rules - SAP APO	ATWALM	27.10.2010	GRCFND_A	V1000	*
GRAC_RA_RULESET_SAP_BASIS	BC Set for AC Rules - SAP BASIS	ATWALM	30.06.2011	GRCFND_A	V1000	*
GRAC_RA_RULESET_SAP_CRM	BC Set for AC Rules for SAP CRM	ATWALM	27.10.2010	GRCFND_A	V1000	*
GRAC_RA_RULESET_SAP_ECCS	BC Set for AC Rules for SAP ECCS	ATWALM	27.10.2010	GRCFND_A	V1000	*
GRAC_RA_RULESET_SAP_HR	BC Set for AC Rules for SAP HR	ATWALM	30.06.2011	GRCFND_A	V1000	*
GRAC_RA_RULESET_SAP_NHR	BC Set for AC Rules for SAP R3 less HR Basis	ATWALM	30.06.2011	GRCFND_A	V1000	*
GRAC_RA_RULESET_SAP_R3	BC Set for AC Rules for SAP R3	BATRAJ	09.05.2012	GRCFND_A	V1000	*
GRAC_RA_RULESET_SAP_SRM	BC Set for AC Rules for SAP SRM	ATWALM	01.07.2011	GRCFND_A	V1000	*

Figure 5.3 Different Rule Sets from BC Set

Table 5.2 details the generally available rule sets in the SAP GRC system, along with what the individual rule set means for what kind of systems.

Rule Set	Description
GRAC_RA_RULESET_SAP_R3	Rules for SAP ERP, including Basis and HR (SAP_R3_LG)
GRAC_RA_RULESET_SAP_HR	Rules for HR only (SAP_HR_LG)
GRAC_RA_RULESET_SAP_NHR	Rules for SAP ERP, excluding HR and Basis (SAP_NHR_LG)
GRAC_RA_RULESET_SAP_BASIS	Rules for Basis (SAP_BAS_LG)

Table 5.2 BC Sets Available for Activation from Transaction SCPR20

Rule Set	Description
GRAC_RA_RULESET_SAP_APO	Rules for SAP APO (SAP_APO_LG)
GRAC_RA_RULESET_SAP_CRM	Rules for SAP CRM (SAP_CRM_LG)
GRAC_RA_RULESET_SAP_ECCS	Rules for ECCS (SAP_ECC_LG)
GRAC_RA_RULESET_SAP_SRM	Rules for SAP SRM (SAP_SRM_LG)
GRAC_RA_RULESET_JDE	Rules for JD Edwards (JDE_LG)
GRAC_RA_RULESET_ORACLE	Rules for Oracle Apps (ORACLE_LG)
GRAC_RA_RULESET_PSOFT	Rules for PeopleSoft HRMS(PSOFT_LG)

Table 5.2 BC Sets Available for Activation from Transaction SCPR20 (Cont.)

Working with an existing rule set from SAP Access Control

Alternatively, if you've already built a rule set from an older SAP Access Control application, you can use the existing files instead of starting from scratch. In this process, you have to execute Transaction GRAC_UPLOAD_RULES and select the connector of the plug-in SAP ERP system or logical system that needs to be analyzed for SoD risks. Apart from the connector, there are nine input fields with field names that are available for you to enter as shown in Figure 5.4. Input the file path for all of the fields pointing to the correct file set from your desktop, and choose either the APPEND or OVERWRITE option. The APPEND option adds the rules, which you're loading, to the existing rules. If you choose OVERWRITE, this replaces all existing old rules.

Normally, the rules can be transported from development to quality and production systems. Instead of transporting these rules from one system to another system, you can use Transaction GRAC_DOWNLOAD_RULES to download respective files from the SAP GRC system. This screen is also similar to the screen shown in Figure 5.4 shown, except for the program used to download files into your desktop. These downloaded files can be altered to activate or deactivate certain combinations to yield a desired result on risk analysis. Later, you need to use Transaction GRAC_UPLOAD_RULES to load the roles specific to the new connector. This populates values in GRAC tables such as rule sets, business processes, risks, function actions, function permissions, and their relationships. All of these upload/download activities can be accessed from

Transaction SPRO by following the menu path, Customizing Implementation Guide • Governance, Risk and Compliance • Access Control • Access Risk Analysis • SoD Rules. You can choose Upload, Download, Delete, or Transport options from this node instead of executing the previously mentioned transactions.

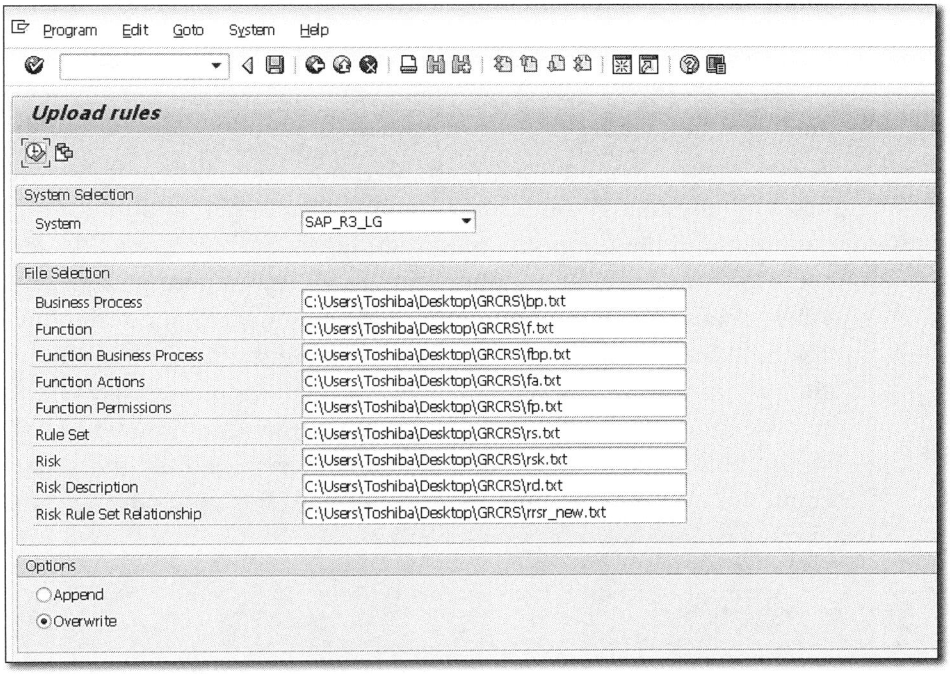

Figure 5.4 Uploading Risk Analysis Rules

Assigning Connectors to a connector group

After the rule set is loaded, make sure that you assign connectors to the connector group to link the system and the rule set that is loaded. This can be achieved from menu path, Customizing Implementation Guide • Governance, Risk and Compliance • Common Component Setting • Integration Framework • Maintain Connectors and Connection Types.

After defining the connection type as a SAP connection and from the Define Connectors folder, you can create entries for all your plug-in system connectors, as shown in Figure 5.5.

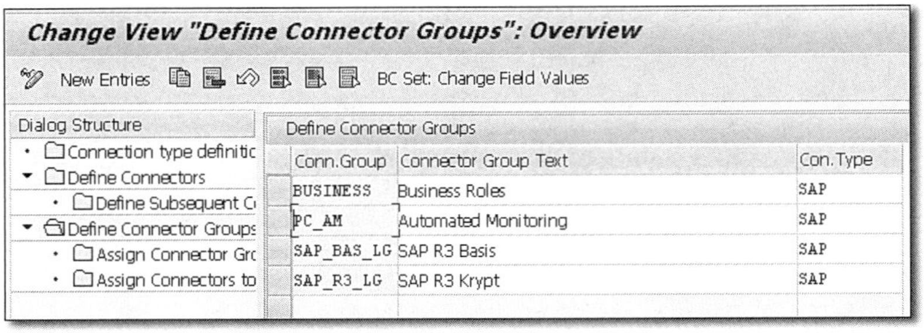

Figure 5.5 Defining a Connector Group

Defining a Connector group

Then select the Define Connector Groups folder, choose the correct logical group that you intend to use (see Figure 5.5), and then assign connectors to the connector group (see Figure 5.6). This links the rule set to the connector. Define Subsequent Connector need to be defined when a connector needs to trigger another connector. For example, in SAP NetWeaver Portal, most of the actions use standard Service Provisioning Markup Language (SPML), but a few actions (e.g., generating password) use the web service protocol. In this case, standard SPML should be defined as the connector, and web services is the subsequent connector. When the subsequent connector isn't applicable in your environment, you can leave this blank.

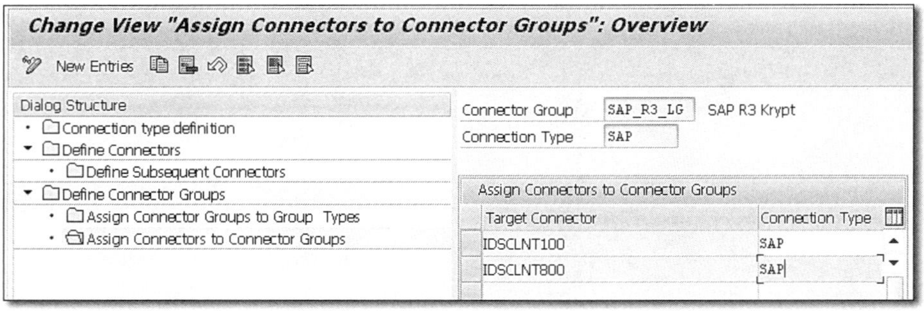

Figure 5.6 Assigning Connectors to the Connector Group

Generating a rule set

After completing the connector group and any subsequent connector assignments to the connector, you need to generate a rule set by executing Transaction GRAC_GENERATE_RULES or by using menu path, Customizing Implementation Guide • Governance, Risk and Compliance • Access Control • Access Risk Analysis • SoD Rules • Generate SoD

RULES from Transaction SPRO. This transaction is a generation of SoD rules that show up with input field options to enter RISK IDs. You can execute it by leaving input fields empty to process all risks the first time or for specific sets of risks by entering RISK IDs in input fields as shown in Figure 5.7. Normally, this transaction execution takes some time. After the execution is over, it creates rule IDs, which are system-generated values that represent a combination of two transactions that are based on your plug-in system as a physical connector or all connectors from a logical group, depending on which connector is used (refer to Figure 5.4) and your risk definition in the rule set. It's better to execute generation of rules in the background to process large datasets. The resulting generated rule IDs are system created and are available in tables GRACACTRULE and GRACSYSRULE. Alternatively, you can view this from the SAP NetWeaver Business Client in the SETUP WORK CENTER ACCESS RULE DETAIL under the GENERATED RULES work set, and then enter the system name, rule set, and risk ID. Run this report to view all generated permutations of actions and permissions for the risk.

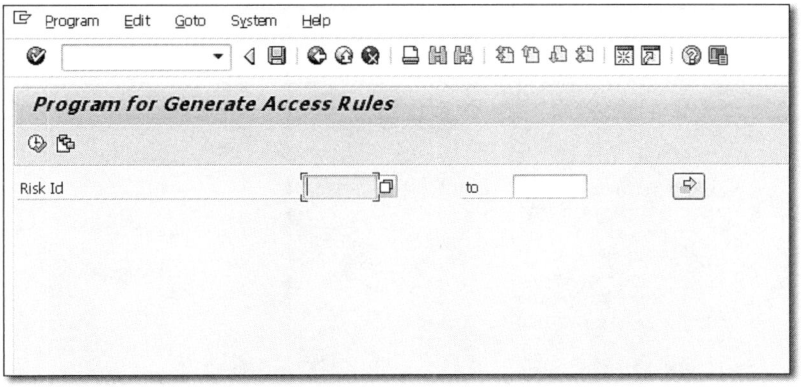

Figure 5.7 Rule IDs Generation

Rule ID creation

The preceding Access Risk Analysis, the rule ID generation is important. The Rule IDs are running numbers assigned by the SAP Access Control system internally for all combinations and permutations between all actions and permissions of two or more different functions that pose SoD risk. Every rule ID is attached to the connector for which the rule is generated. Based on this, the individual generated rule ID is unique in the system. During risk analysis, this value is compared against the authorization and transactions assigned to users, roles, or profiles, and all matched items are reported as risk analysis results.

Deleting a rule set

You've now seen how to maintain and generate SoD rules. If, for some reason, you need to delete the rules, you can execute GRAC_RULE_DELETE. After all of the rule sets are prepared well, generated, and tested in the development system, if you want to transport of all of the rules, this can be ported to the next system using transport management by executing Transaction GRAC_RULE_TRANSPORT. All of these transactions can be performed from the IMG menu path from Transaction SPRO also. The menu path for all of these activity links can be found under SAP Customizing Implementation Guide • Governance, Risk and Compliance • Access Control • Access Risk Analysis • SoD Rules (see Figure 5.8).

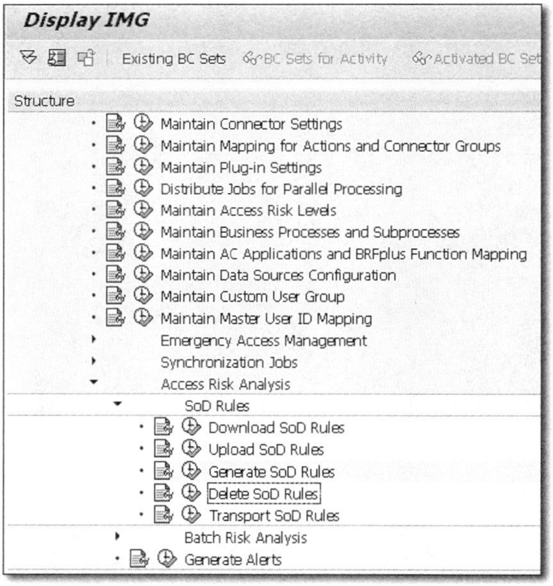

Figure 5.8 SoD Rules Generation Menu from Transaction SPRO to Perform, Download, Upload, Delete, and Transport SoD Rules Functionality

Now we've loaded all of these risks, and SoD rules are generated in the system with respect to the corresponding connectors. As a result of these activities, we've prepared the rule set for risk analysis. In the next section, we'll look into the synchronization of the plug-in system dictionary objects, such as users, profiles, and roles that need to be analyzed for risk.

5.1.4 Synchronization Jobs

The last step in the risk analysis process and working with Access Risk Analysis is to synchronize the users, roles, and profiles that bring plug-in system information to the SAP GRC system. To complete this, you need to execute Transaction GRAC_REP_OBJ_SYNC, or use Transaction SPRO and follow the path, SAP CUSTOMIZING IMPLEMENTATION GUIDE • GOVERNANCE, RISK AND COMPLIANCE • ACCESS CONTROL • SYNCHRONIZATION JOBS • REPOSITORY OBJECT SYNCH. In the REPOSITORY OBJECT SYNCH window (see Figure 5.9), select the PROFILE, ROLE, and USER checkboxes under SELECT SYNC JOB to synchronize from the connected plug-in system to use the SoD risk analysis of respective objects.

Maintain the CONNECTOR field with a single connector or multiple connectors, and select FULL SYNC MODE because you're going to synchronize the data from the plug-in system for the very first time and want to fetch all users, profiles, and roles into the SAP Access Control system. These data are stored in SAP Access Control system tables with respective connector names, and all SAP Access Control tools use these data for reporting, further analysis, or processing in their respective areas. For example, the Access Risk Analysis tool uses the data for risk analysis purposes, and the User Access Management tool uses these synchronized data for role-provisioning purposes.

Scheduling the Repository Object Synchronization frequency

After first time synchronization of all data is completed successfully, schedule this program to run in the background on a regular stipulated interval by choosing the INCREMENTAL SYNC MODE radio button, which is shown in the same screen. By setting this option, you synchronize only the data changed since the last synchronization activity. Any changes to users, roles, or profiles that happen in the plug-in system on a regular basis will be synchronized in the SAP GRC system based on the previously mentioned background job frequency. It's a best practice to schedule this incremental repository object synchronization more frequently, such as hourly or half hourly to synchronize the near real-time changes from the plug-in system to the SAP Access Control system.

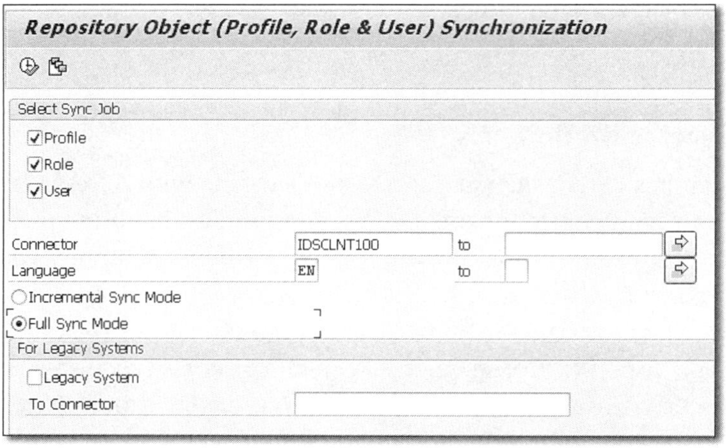

Figure 5.9 Repository Object Synchronization for the Plug-In System

5.1.5 Rule Set Maintenance

Now that we've discussed how to upload and generate the standard rule set, let's look at how to maintain the rule set after it's established. Those who plan to use *only* the standard out-of-the-box rule set may skip the process explained in this section; the intention of this section is to give a clear understanding to the Access Risk Analysis users for risk maintenance. This section deals more with how to make changes and maintain rule sets with custom transactions, functions, or risks.

Custom rule set creation or modifications to a global rule set

Basically, any rule set is a set of risks that is built by conflicting two or more functions. All functions are grouped with like business transactions, and the authorizations are called actions and permissions, respectively, in SAP Access Control. As a basic foundation before you create a custom rule set or change a global rule set, let's look into the step-by-step designing process for defining a risk:

Step-by-step process for defining a risk

1. Document the risk. The risk statement should clearly state the actions and the negative results.
2. Classify the risk. Rate the risk based on impact.
3. Identify the risk owners. Risk is related to a specific business, and business persons in the responsible area should be assigned to the risk.

4. Convert the risk into technical terms. Relate this identified business risk into IT terms such as transactions and authorizations.
5. Publish and deploy. Add this into the Access Risk Analysis tool in the correct segments and generate rules.

Correctly maintained risk and generated rule

Using the preceding best practice process steps as a risk-definition process, we'll show you how to maintain this information in Access Risk Analysis. IDs that are created as part of rule generation are the good foundation that will help you achieve your goal to identify risks and SoD violations related to authorizations and transactions maintained in your plug-in systems. One of the activities in maintaining a rule set is activating or deactivating certain transactions and/or authorizations from SAP NetWeaver Business Client. In certain cases of SAP ERP security, maintenance of these values and organizational rule maintenance might address some of the false positives shown in risk analysis results.

Avoiding false positives with Access Risk Analysis

False positives are misleading results shown in access risk analyses. These false positive could be avoided, if you perform risk analysis properly. To eliminate false positives in your risk analysis process you need to identify the cause. Let us walk through an example on what is false positive and how to identify and eliminate this. One of our earlier discussion point we have indicated SoD risk could be posed by the user profile who has authorizations to create vendor and create FI postings. Assume with same authorization in another situation where vendor creation is meant for company code '1000' and FI posting for company code '2000', in reality this is not an SoD risk for the user profile. In this case if you execute your analysis at action level then you may get a false positive, basically there is no SoD violation but the result will be showing that there is a SoD violation. In this kind of scenarios if you know about your landscape security environment has SoDs at authorization object and organization level authorization separations are in place then you need to perform your access risk analysis at permission level. By retesting various positive and negative tests of roles, profiles and fine tune your rule-set in order to confirm that you are not running into false positives in your access risk analyses.

Maintaining functions and activating or deactivating actions

For now, let's look in to the details of how to maintain functions and activate or deactivate actions (i.e., transactions) or permissions (i.e., authorization objects) to achieve correct risk analysis results. This process is performed from NetWeaver Business Client, so from the user interface (UI), select the SETUP workset and then choose ACCESS RULE MAINTENANCE • FUNCTIONS (see Figure 5.10).

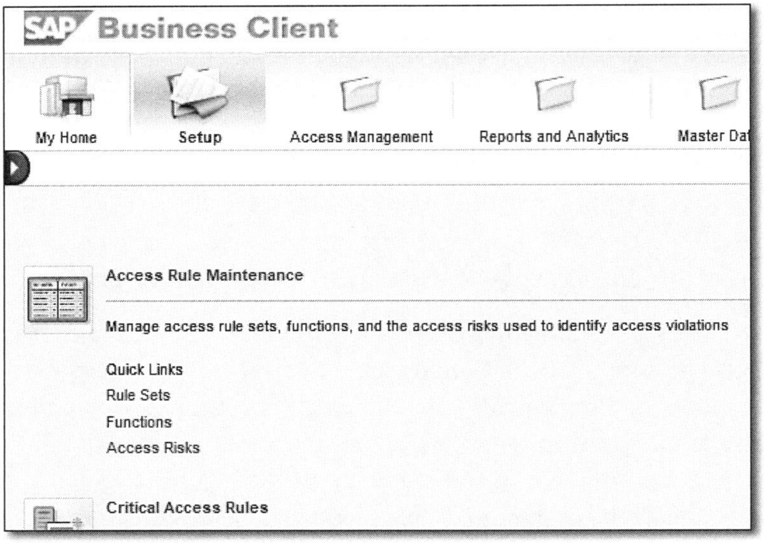

Figure 5.10 Rule Sets, Functions, Risks Maintenance: Setup Work Center

If this screen table contain no entries, click on the CHANGE QUERY link on the top-right corner, and enter specific values in the pop-up window—such as the risk ID or the process name—and execute. You can use a generic wild card search also. In the resulting window, you get a list of functions. Select any of the functions that you want to change, and click the OPEN button to go to the next screen where you should be able to maintain transaction codes and authorization objects. Figure 5.11 shows the list of functions in the background screen, and the foreground screen contains FUNCTION ID, BUSINESS PROCESS, and ANALYSIS SCOPE, along with actions and permissions in the two tabs. If CHANGLOG is enabled in SAP Access Control configuration, the CHANGE HISTORY tab in Figure 5.11 will show all of the changes that pertain to this function with the user ID and time stamp. If you want to add any additional transactions, maintain it in the ACTION tab by clicking ADD. This adds the transaction to the ACTION tab and relevant authorization objects to the PERMISSION tab. If needed, you can activate and deactivate the objects or permissions either to show the risk or hide the risk in your risk analysis result.

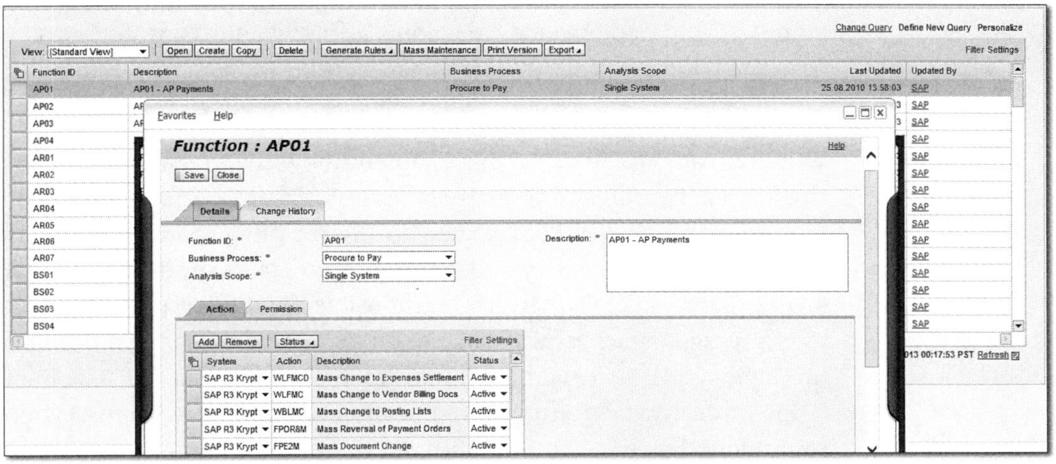

Figure 5.11 Function, Action, and Permission Maintenance in SAP NetWeaver Business Client

In Figure 5.11, the DETAILS tab captures changes to functions for auditing purposes. This is based on one of the configuration parameter id 1001 in the CHANGE LOG parameter group. After the changes are carried out at the function level or risk level, don't forget to execute GENERATE RULES. This rule generation triggers the changes to adjust or create new rule IDs, which are the backbone of Access Risk Analysis. Instead of changes to a single function, there is an option to do mass maintenance of functions.

Similarly, individual risk or groups of risks can be modified from the SETUP work center by choosing ACCESS RULE MAINTENANCE • RISKS. From here, you can create a new risk by defining two or three function combinations, or you can change a risk by selecting the risk and modifying the related function and underlying actions and permissions accordingly. Now that we have appropriate maintained our rule sets, let's review how we can maintain shared master data.

5.1.6 Maintain Shared Master Data

As the SAP Access Control administrator, you need to maintain SAP Access Control owners such as the risk owner, mitigation control monitor, and mitigation monitors from the Access Risk Analysis perspective. Maintaining this data is a mandatory process that should be carried out to create and monitor controls as part of Access Risk Analysis implementation; if this maintenance isn't done, it might impact any workflow-based activities such as risk maintenance, mitigation approval, monitoring automation, and user access review or SoD review.

Organization hierarchy across the GRC suite

We've already discussed in our Chapter 2 how the organization hierarchy is used as common master data in SAP Access Control, SAP Process Control, and SAP Risk Management. We'll see other shared master data such as mitigation control and assigning owners to controls in the following paragraph. Owners are responsible for the accuracy of risks, roles, mitigating controls, and so on with different responsibilities throughout SAP Access Control. SAP Process Control and SAP Risk Management deal with controls, so mitigation monitors and approvers are commonly shared.

Access Control Administrator role

As a SAP Access Control administrator, you'll maintain this master data in the NetWeaver Business Client UI. Prior to this maintenance, make sure that these owners are already created in Transaction SU01 with control or risk owner level roles that are equivalent to SAP_GRAC_RISK OWNER, SAP_GRAC_CONTROL_OWNER, SAP_GRAC_CONTROL_APPROVER, and SAP_GRAC_CONTROL_MONITOR, along with generic SAP Access Control user roles mentioned in Chapter 4.

After their user IDs are created with all roles, in the NetWeaver Business Client UI, click the Setup work center, and choose Access Owners • Access Control Owners. You'll see a central owner listed in a table format. From this screen, click the Create button to go to the Owner Assignment: New screen as shown in Figure 5.12. In this screen, the default selection in Group Type is Owner. In the Group Detail area, if you know the user ID enter it directly; otherwise, use the help function to get the desired user ID to fill in this field. Then select the checkbox in the Owner Type section that needs to be assigned to this owner, and enter comments as needed. Save and Close to exit from this maintenance screen.

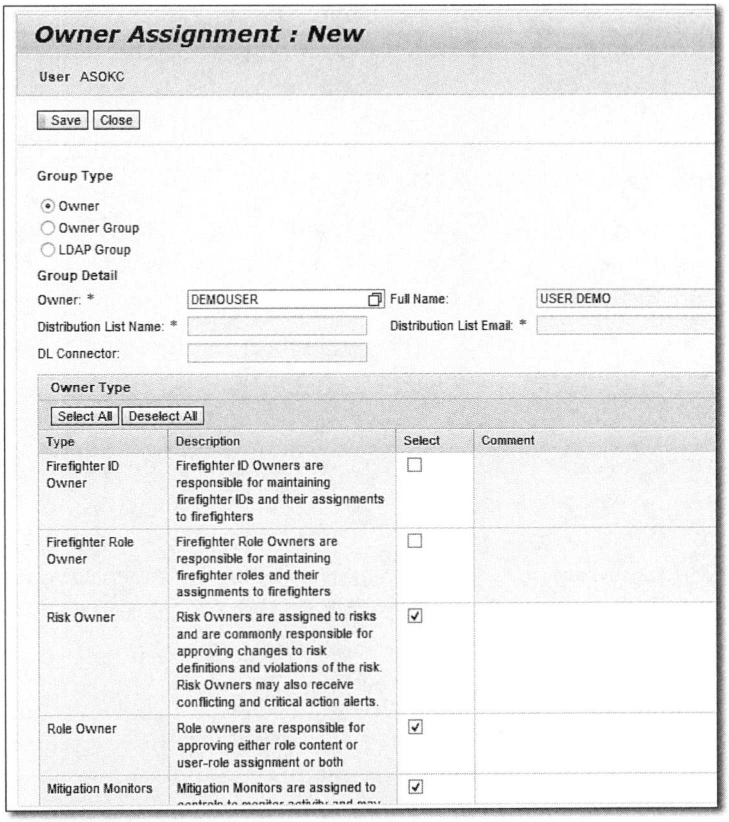

Figure 5.12 Centrally Assigning SAP Access Control Owners

SAP Access Control and the creation of multiple user IDs

Now this user ID is assigned with SAP Access Control owner responsibilities, and you can follow the same procedure to create it for multiple user IDs. One user ID can have multiple owner types and prepare the plan based on your SAP Access Control requirements. These owners can be assigned as mitigation controllers, monitors, or risk owners.

The role of risk owners

Mostly risk owners are business people who are responsible for maintaining functions, transactions, or approving the identified risks which possibly poses a threat in their functional area. Risk owners are the people those who should be notified about any risks in the roles or user profiles. Based on the risk owners' recommendations, either a user or role is mitigated for the risk or a risk-posing authorization or transaction can be recommended for removal from the user profile. Mitigation controllers and monitors can be from the business team or the audit team. These are the core responsibilities of SAP Access Control owners from the Access Risk Analysis perspective.

5.1.7 Perform Batch Risk Analysis

So far, we've carried out the necessary steps in Access Risk Analysis tool configuration to perform risk analysis. Now let's discuss how to run batch risk analysis. The risk analysis can be performed against single users or multiple users; similarly, this also applies to single or multiple roles or profiles from SAP NetWeaver Business Client.

If you want to perform this risk analysis across the entire system for users and roles, it's called a batch risk analysis. To analyze the entire system for risks the batch risk analysis can be scheduled from the SAPGUI using Transaction GRAC_BATCH_RA. You need to make sure that all authorization objects, roles, and user synchronization jobs mentioned in Section 5.1.4 are successfully completed before starting the risk analysis job. This ensures that you'll get the most accurate results for your risk analysis.

To run batch risk analysis, input fields are grouped into three different categories in this transaction. For simplicity, we split this into two portions as shown in Figure 5.13 and Figure 5.14. The first part is System Selection, in which you need to enter your batch risk analysis Job Name, System range (can be a single target system or multiple system depending upon your analysis), and RuleSet (based on the name of your rule set, which is usually Global).

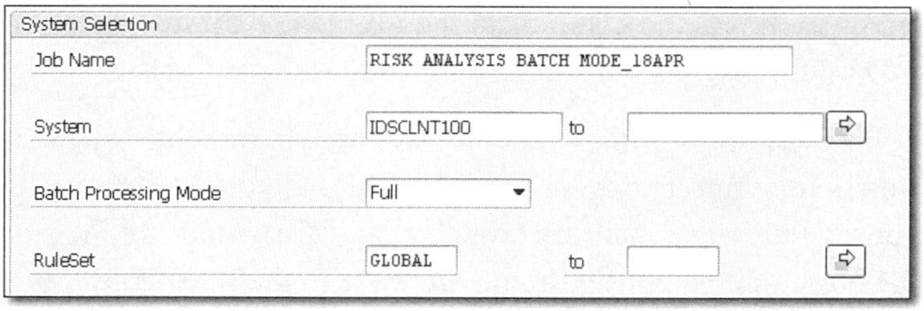

Figure 5.13 Risk Analysis: System Selection

Batch Processing

Also the BATCH PROCESSING MODE field should be set to FULL when you execute this batch risk analysis the first time to get a full scan of the system against all of the users, roles, and profiles for the risks defined in the rule set. For any subsequent scheduling, you can choose INCREMENTAL in the BATCH PROCESSING MODE field to reduce the load on the system for batch risk analysis; this will analyze only the changes to the user/role/profile objects that happened after the previous batch risk analysis. The best practice recommendation is to run batch risk analysis as a daily background job with incremental runs and then execute a full run once a month. This is a better use of the system resources and better management of risk analysis.

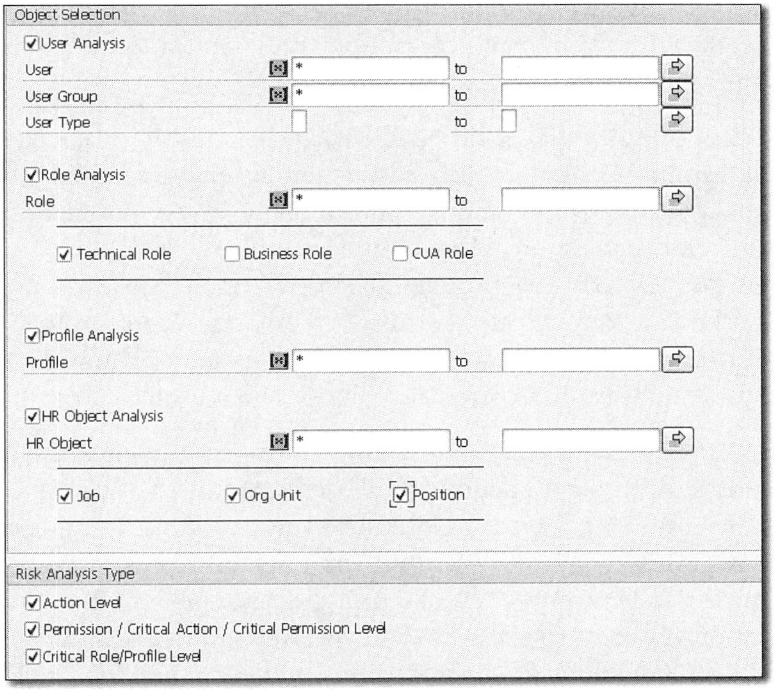

Figure 5.14 Risk Analysis: Object and Analysis Type

Figure 5.14 shows the OBJECT SELECTION and RISK ANALYSIS TYPE sections of the screen. OBJECT SELECTION contains four objects; all of the four objects or any combinations of USER ANALYSIS, ROLE ANALYSIS, PROFILE ANALYSIS, and HR OBJECT ANALYSIS can be selected for the object that gives sufficient risk data to meet your IT landscape demands. For example, if your company hasn't implemented SAP Human Capital Management (SAP HCM), and you won't get any data for HR objects, in this case, you may skip HR OBJECT ANALYSIS, or if partly implemented, you may enter those specific objects or range of objects that can be subjected to your risk analysis execution. Similarly, other objects such as users, roles, and profiles can be used with a wild card character to run for all data, or you can specify a range in the individual input fields.

Risk Analysis type selection

In the RISK ANALYSIS TYPE section shown in Figure 5.14, you can select any of the risk analysis reporting type options (e.g., ACTION LEVEL, PERMISSION/CRITICAL ACTION/CRITICAL PERMISSION LEVEL, and CRITICAL ROLE/PROFILE LEVEL), or you can analyze all of them at once. You need to select options based on your analysis result requirement to meet your company's risk and compliance needs.

Monitoring your Batch Risk analysis with the Access Risk Analysis reporting dashboard

Transaction GRACRABATCH_MONITOR will help to monitor the scheduled background job status. After completion of this background job, you should be able to view various reports from the Access Risk Analysis reporting dashboard. From SAP NetWeaver Business Client, go to the REPORTS AND ANALYTICS work center, choose ACCESS DASHBOARD, and execute the RISK VIOLATIONS report or USER ANALYSIS report to verify that all risks and risk analysis results are available for you. This dashboard uses Adobe Flash, so make sure your system is enabled for that.

Figure 5.15 shows the ACCESS RISK VIOLATIONS report with multiple options to select using dropdowns for the YEAR/MONTH, SYSTEM, ANALYSIS TYPE (USER, ROLE, or PROFILE), USER GROUP, and VIOLATION COUNT BY (by ACCESS RISK or by PERMISSION). The graphical representation of this data is shown as a pie chart, and data such as number of users and number of violations are also shown. Another set of graphs in the ACCESS RISK VIOLATIONS BY PROCESS half of the screen shows the violation counts based on business process. This report is interactive, so you can double-click any of this data to go to the next level screen to see the details at the risk ID level. You can find the user IDs that pose this risk by clicking on the number of violations.

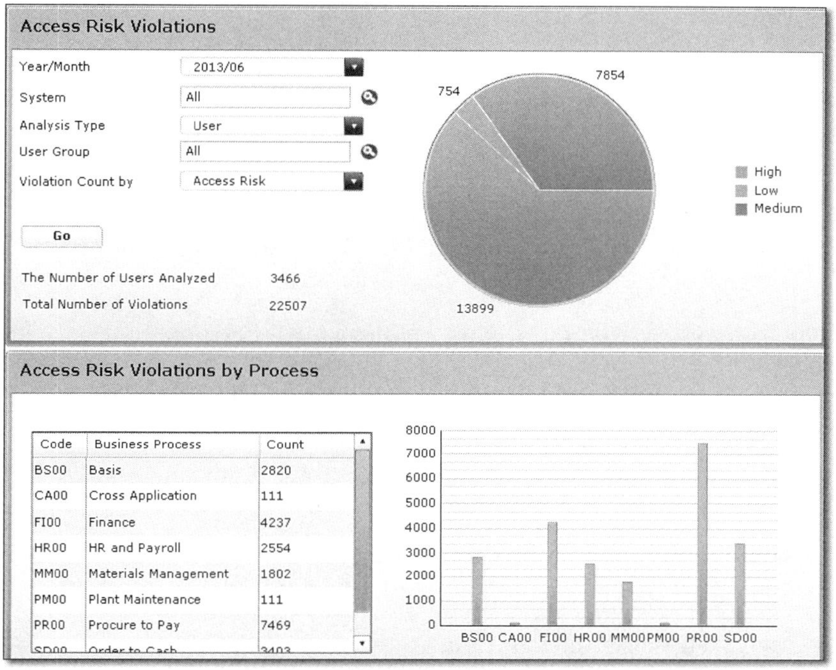

Figure 5.15 Access Risk Violations after Completing Batch Risk Analysis

We've now set a strong foundation by understanding Access Risk Analysis configuration and rule set preparation. With the proper approach to risk remediation, you'll have good controls in place for your internal audit and risk-free compliant IT environment. Next, let's take a look at risk analysis reporting.

5.2 Access Risk Analysis Reporting

Now that you've learned how to configure Access Risk Analysis and can run the risk analysis for the user level or role level assessment, let's look at the various reporting features provided in SAP Access Control 10.0, which uses the new risk analysis framework. The *risk analysis framework* includes various options such as the following:

Risk Analysis framework options

- Different conditions can be configured and combined.
- Multiple risk analysis reports can be run at the same time.

- Multiple selections can be imported from a file.
- Drilldowns are available across the reports.
- Columns in the report can be hidden and rearranged.
- Reports provide transaction execution data.
- SAP Crystal and PDF report the output.
- Reports have sort and filter options to view more specific sets of results.

Risk Analysis Framework benefits

The new risk analysis framework provides the following benefits:

- Provides a consistent interface with other SAP GRC modules on input and reporting features.
- Processes reports faster by including only the information required by the users.
- Saves time for users by allowing them to import report variables from files.

We've given a brief introduction to the risk analysis framework. Now let's explore it more by executing a user-level risk analysis using some of the new features. To invoke the screen shown in Figure 5.16, you need to be in NetWeaver Business Client and go to the Access Management work center. Click on the User Level link under Access Risk Analysis. In this initial screen, you can enter normal input fields such as System and Rule Set as Global. If you need to do analyses for specific users or user groups, enter the necessary entries, set user type as Dialog, and a dozen more input options become available.

After completing the input values, you need to select Report Options based on what type of risk analysis you want to perform and result set format like summary, details, executive summary or management summary in business view or technical view, available to view risk analysis result. Also you may set with other options like Access risk assessment, options for mitigation analysis, along with additional criteria such as Include Mitigated Risk, Show All Objects, Consider Org Rule, and Offline Data. All these data can be saved as variant in order to run the risk analysis repeatedly with same values. Based on these input and reporting options, you can either run this report in the foreground or as a background job.

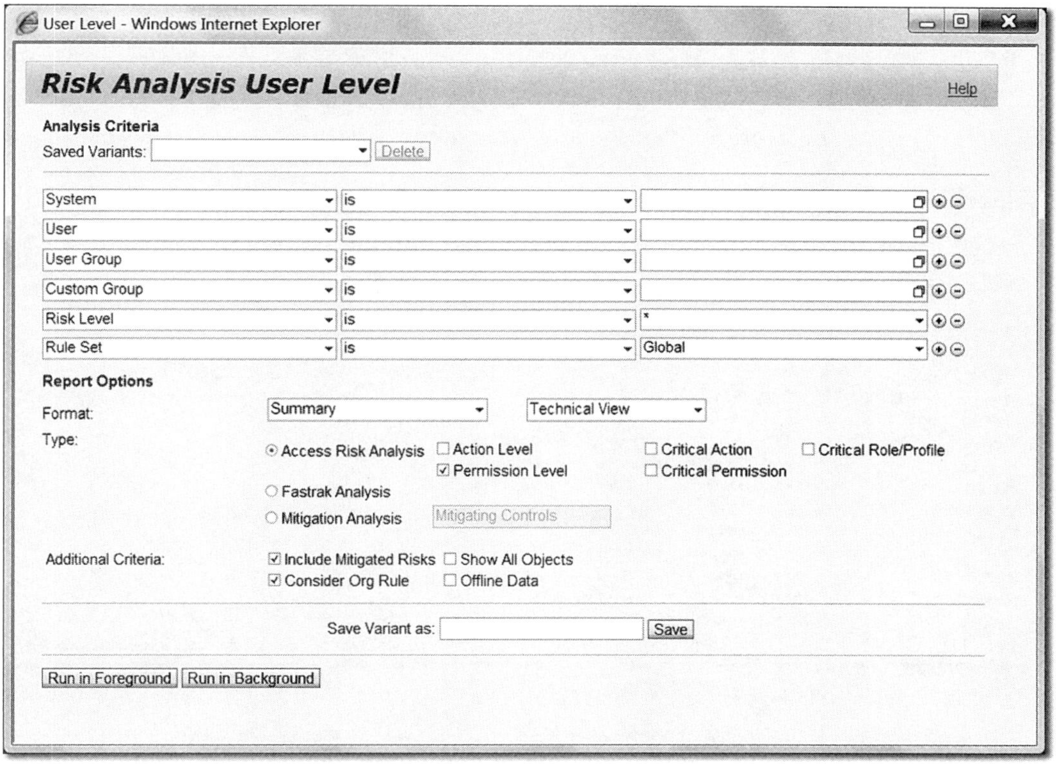

Figure 5.16 Risk Analysis User Level Input Screen

The result of the risk analysis view is shown in Figure 5.17. The result has options to sort and filter the columns to focus on specific results. The EXPORT RESULT SETS button on top of the result table enables you to download the result set. If the result set is very large, such as one of the reporting features, the files are split into downloadable multiple files that are all downloaded with a single click of a button and saved sequentially in the designated folder.

Risk Analysis results view

There is another option available in reporting that helps to view the results in different ways. To see the different report formats, choose one of the following from the FORMAT field above the table: SUMMARY,

DETAIL, MANAGEMENT SUMMARY, or EXECUTIVE SUMMARY. By default, the SUMMARY format is as shown in Figure 5.17. The DETAILS format provides all of the risk-related details, MANAGEMENT SUMMARY gives the users, risk IDs, controls, monitors, and SoD objects; and the EXECUTIVE SUMMARY shows the NO. OF CONFLICTS and NO. OF MITIGATION per RISKID. The basic purpose of risk analysis is to use Access Risk Analysis to leverage, identify, and clean access risks in your IT landscape.

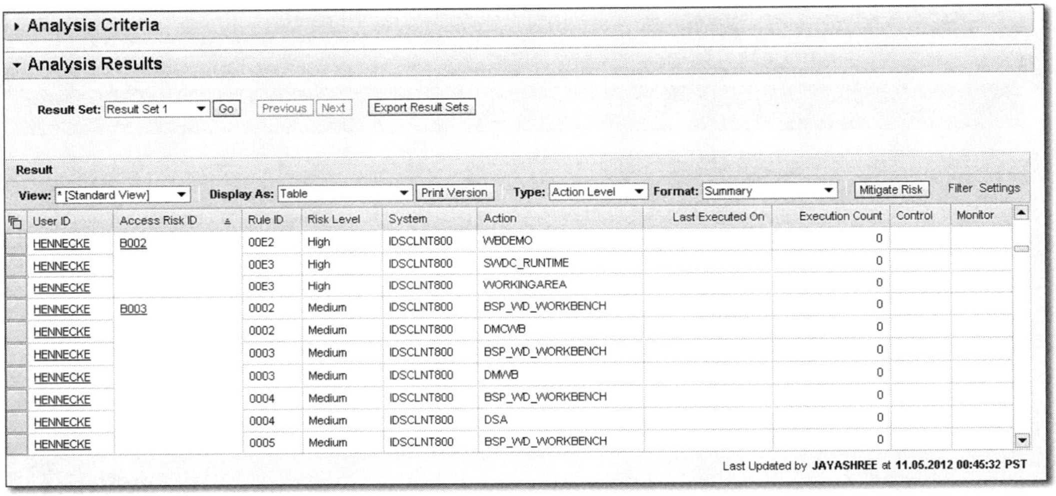

Figure 5.17 Risk Analysis Result View

Now, let's move on to the risk remediation process.

5.3 Risk Remediation Process

We've discussed how to perform SoD risk analysis, and as a result of this risk analysis, you get full detailed risk data view available against various metrics to focus on where you need to start the remediation of risks, which is the foremost reason for implementing SAP Access Control. Remediation processes eliminate risk from the IT landscape either by putting IT controls in place or by removing any extra privileges that are available to users beyond their general business functions in SAP ERP systems.

> **Note**
>
> Consider other alternatives such as SAP Business Workflow, user exits, modifications to configurations, and changes to business processes if those methods make a better option to eliminate risk on the business transaction level.

There are three ways to start the cleaning process. The first way is to remove access from the user. This might be cumbersome because of user access provided through roles, but if it's simple to remove the entire role from the user role assignment, then that is the foremost way to clean up IT access. The second option for the remediation process is to clean up the role by eliminating any high-risk objects from the role. Finally, the third option is to mitigate the risk using mitigation control assignment against the user and monitor on a regular basis. We'll see how to perform the latter two remediation processes using the Access Risk Analysis tool.

5.3.1 Role Cleanup Process with Access Risk Analysis

In the preceding section, we've seen a few options to do remediation work in SAP Access Control to remove access authorization risks. The whole remediation process can be started by analyzing single roles followed by composite roles in Access Risk Analysis. As a good starting point, a quick and easy way to eliminate these risks is to perform the following three steps as an initial role cleanup:

Step-by-step initial role cleanup process

1. Identify roles that are no longer used, and remove them from production system(s). Generally, you use Transaction SUIM reporting in the plug-in system to list the roles that aren't assigned to any users. If you're using master and derived roles in your environment, ensure that derived roles aren't assigned to users before deleting the master role.
2. Identify roles that don't require remediation, for example, roles that aren't assigned to end users (system users, communication users) such as firefighter roles.
3. Identify roles that can be defined as critical roles in SAP Access Control and can thus be monitored in SAP Access Control. In normal risk analysis, critical roles can be excluded on a regular risk analysis.

Upon completing these three initial steps on role cleaning, don't forget to document the approved reason for excluding these roles for audit purposes.

It's important to note that even after you've conducted the initial role cleanup and followed all of these steps, you may still have roles with risks that require discussion with role owners and business process owners to eliminate risks from them. With the role owner and business process owners, you may need to modify the roles by eliminating transactions and/or authorizations that are causing conflicts. Another option at this point, is to reconsider and adjust the rule set to give more precise results, avoiding false positives in your risk analysis by using organization rules or deactivating the actions and permissions that aren't used. If these corrective actions aren't workable, then you may go ahead with risk mitigation as explained in the next section.

5.3.2 Risk Mitigation as Remediation

If none of the remediation actions we've covered in earlier sections helped you clean up some of the SoD risks, mitigation is the last option to go with, and Access Risk Analysis has a few simplified activities to create controls and assign and monitor mitigation controls.

Mitigation controls

Mitigation controls are created for the risk, and the user/role/profile can be assigned to the mitigation control. SAP Access Control owners as mentioned in Section 5.1.6, such as the approver and monitor, are also assigned to the mitigation control. These mitigated risks need to be monitored on a regular basis. There are preventive mitigation controls that minimize the impact of a risk before it occurs and detective controls that alert the responsible person (risk owners) when a risk takes place to enable taking corrective measure are the two types handled in Access Risk Analysis.

System-specific mitigation and mass mitigation

Now, let's look at two ways to approach detective mitigation (system-specific and mass mitigation), which are improved in SAP Access Control 10.0.

System-Specific Mitigation

In this section, let's look at more new features like system specific mitigation that is less complex in nature and gives more flexibility to mitigate user/s for a specific system or group of systems. Also mitigating specific to a risk and rule-ID reduces risk compared to broader wide open controls that were provided in earlier versions of Access Control against risk level mitigation. While mitigating a risk, multiple controls can be created with system-specific and rule ID-specific mitigation or a combination of multiple systems and multiple rule IDs from single processing screen. During mitigation control assignment to a user, you can choose and assign multiple systems to the user as a simple way to assign many to one in a single process.

Benefits of system specific mitigation

This method provides more flexibility while creating mitigating risk with controls in a complex multiple system environments that needs mitigating control owners and less complexity while creating and assigning them with an easy UI.

Mass Mitigation

As a continuation of new features from SAP Access Control 10.0, mass mitigation provides an easy to mitigate multiple risks at once. This feature improves productivity with precise control that involves a single step to complete mitigation task.

Role or user level mitigation

When you perform risk analysis—either role or user level—the result are expanded to multiple line items. In this result screen, you can select all risks that need to be mitigated together and click the MITIGATE RISK button to complete multiple risk mitigation in the process. The simplified assignment of multiple risks at once reduces the number of steps required and the processing time, which reduces potential errors by users assigning mitigation controls. Mass mitigation is suitable for customers those who do not use system level or rule ID level mitigation. This need to be configured from SPRO transaction access SAP CUSTOMIZING IMPLEMENTATION GUIDE • GOVERNANCE, RISK AND COMPLIANCE • ACCESS CONTROL • MAINTAIN CONFIGURATION SETTINGS from here set the parameter IDs 1012 and 1013 as 'NO' to perform mass mitigation.

Now that you know how to remediate risk with all available options to eliminate risk and clean your IT environment. In the next section, you'll see how to alert respective control owners when critical risk or SoD risk is accessed by the users as a temporary mitigation controls and monitoring process.

5.4 Alert Monitoring

Alert monitoring is available in Access Risk Analysis to protect your IT environment from any other potential risks. Alert monitoring in SAP Access Control monitors critical or conflicting actions from rule sets; if any of these actions take place, it triggers an alert that sends an email to respective risk owners. These alerts are only sent if the user's permission level access violates the access rule, as defined in the rule set.

Alert Report frequency

The frequency (i.e., number of days) of the alert report depends on the criticality of the control that needs to be maintained. As a best practice, you'll want to monitor any critical actions or mitigated actions on a daily basis. If the number of risk alerts is high and more frequent, you can set the frequency on weekly in order to notify and monitor them less frequently for specific set of risks. So far we have seen how to remediate risks by means of mitigation and monitoring and in next section we will see how to use risk terminator from plug-in system to trigger alert when creating a role with SOD conflict (PFCG) or adding roles with conflict to Users (SU01, SU10 or PFCG). So far we've looked at options to alert users of any critical or risky business transactions to identify risk, but let's review how to stop this behavior in the system

5.5 Risk Terminator

In this section, we're going to see how to stop any unauthorized risky role creation or assignment in the plug-in system. The plug-in system is configured to connect with Access Risk Analysis and stop any further processing if you have risk during one of the following four scenarios:

- When transactions are added to a role and it's generated using Transaction PFCG.
- When users are assigned to a role using Transaction PFCG.
- When a role/profile is assigned to a user from Transaction SU01.
- When a role/profile is assigned to a user from Transaction SU10.

Scenarios where Access Risk Analysis will run the Risk Terminator

This is another way to stop risk at the entry point and prevent user risk. The Risk Terminator in SAP Access Control 10.0 is an optional setup that prevents any unauthorized role provisioning or role creation that contains risk in the plug-in system by validating new roles and user assignments. Risk Terminator settings consist of configuration in both the SAP GRC system and the plug-in system. First, let's look at the configuration in the SAP GRC system and then the plug-in system.

5.5.1 Configuration Setup in the SAP GRC System

The SAP GRC system is where the GRCFND_A package is installed. The Risk Terminator configuration parameters need to be configured in the IMG. Execute Transaction SPRO, and follow the menu path, SAP Customizing Implementation Guide • Governance, Risk and Compliance • Access Control • Maintain Configuration Settings. In the configuration settings, create new entries or make changes. If the entry has default values for the Risk Analysis – Risk Terminator parameter group, maintain the required parameter IDs from 1080 to 1088, with relevant values based on your system environment needs.

5.5.2 Configuration Setup in the Plug-In System

The SAP GRC plug-in system is where the GRCPINW/GRCPIERP package is installed. The Risk Terminator configuration parameters need to be configured here under the IMG. Execute Transaction SPRO, and follow the menu path, SAP Customizing Implementation Guide • Governance, Risk and Compliance (Plug-in) • Access Control • Maintain Configuration. Maintain the parameter values 1000, 1002, 1081, 1082, 1083, 1084, 1088, and other parameters to meet your environment needs.

Based on the preceding configuration in both the SAP Access Control system and the plug-in system, you can prevent risky role creation or risky role assignment to users. In next section, we'll discuss the Access Risk Analysis tool's additional features in the reporting area.

5.6 Access Risk Analysis 10.0: Additional Features

Building on the Access Risk Analysis tool set, configuration, and some of its functionality, let's look at some other additional features that may be helpful in reporting during the risk analysis process. We'll look at the initial access risk assessment and additional reporting options.

5.6.1 Initial Access Risk Assessment

To give a quick result of risks during risk analysis, this report is more efficient and useful. When you execute this report, the system analyzes, and after it finds a risk with a rule ID, it skips all other rule IDs related to the same risk and jumps to the next. Because of this action, the analysis process is quicker, but at the same time, it runs against all standard options such as action, permission, and critical action level, and it supports risk-level mitigation. In the risk analysis results, a secondary analysis can be run that shows all rule violations. You can do mitigation over the initial risk violations or at the secondary rule violation level.

5.6.2 Additional Reporting Features

Numerous reports are available in SAP Access Control, and considering Access Risk Analysis, most of the reports help the security team or audit team detect and develop risk-free IT access environments. The following lists may prove helpful to you:

- **Actions in roles but not in rules**
  This is an actionable report that enables you to track authorizations in roles that aren't tracked and reported by your rule set. This also provides due diligence for auditors that you've analyzed all role authorization.

- **Action usage by user, role, and profile**
  This report lists all transaction activity and target authorizations to transactions that aren't being used frequently.
- **Critical roles and profiles**
  This report identifies roles with the most sensitive and critical access, along with who is assigned to them. Separate reports for SoD violations are available to show conflicts executed by firefighter IDs.

Access Risk Analysis reporting framework

In addition to the preceding reports, we want to highlight some of the options that are available in the Access Risk Analysis reporting framework.

For instance, multiple user names or roles can be added during user analysis or role analysis. In the screen shown in Figure 5.18, you can select User options with Multiple Selections. On clicking the Add Selections button, a pop-up screen appears that enables you to enter multiple values using uploaded files. You can also enter generic reporting options also available through SUIM reports (ABAP-based report input options).

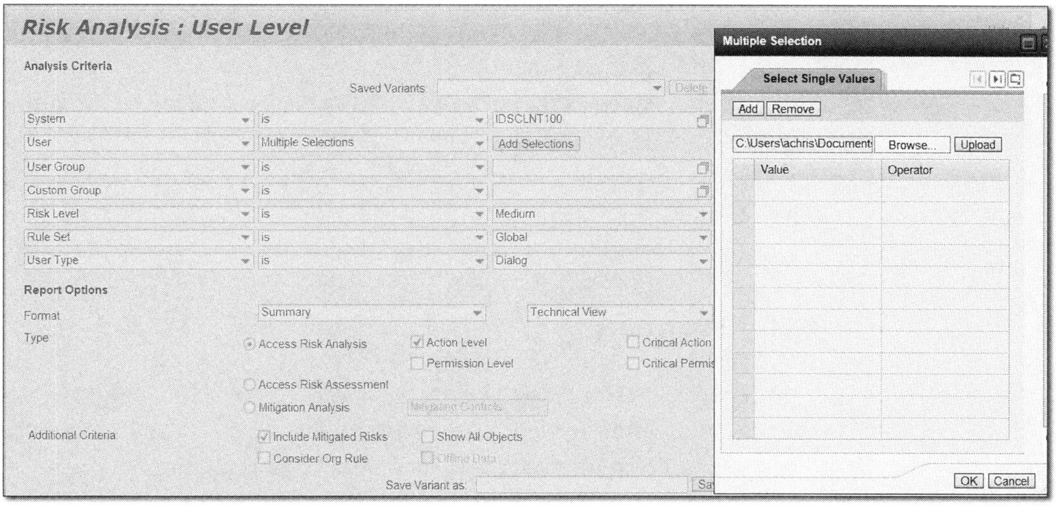

Figure 5.18 Adding Multiple Selections with the File Upload Function for Risk Analysis Input

If you need these uploaded variables regularly, then you have options to save them as variants as well.

Report generation with SAP Crystal Reports

You can generate reports as SAP Crystal Reports showing Access Risk Analysis results (see Figure 5.19). No additional software is required on the server, but the client's desktop or laptop requires installing SAP Crystal Report Adapter to view the risk analysis report or any other reports from SAP Access Control.

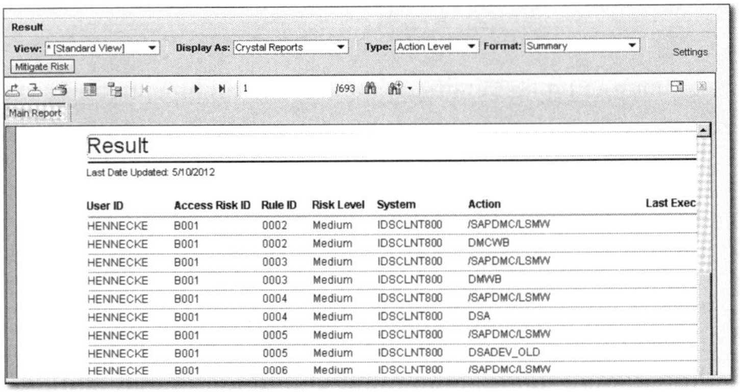

Figure 5.19 SAP Crystal Report Generated from Access Risk Analysis

In addition to SAP Crystal Reports, you can create a PDF version of the reports. You can do this from any report output by clicking on the PRINT VERSION button. This functionality requires an Adobe Document Services (ADS) instance in the SAP GRC landscape. This means maintaining ADS in any SAP NetWeaver Java Stack system such as SAP BI or SAP NetWeaver Portal that is within the landscape to connect with SAP Access Control.

5.7 Summary

In this chapter, we discussed all of the necessary steps to configure, prepare, and maintain rule sets, as well as how to run effective risk analysis to identify your risk. We also covered various remediation processes that address these risks with correct approach. We outlined some options that are available beyond risk analysis as well, such as risk terminator, reporting options, and mitigation. In the next chapter, we'll explain the configuration and usage of the Business Role Manager tool.

This chapter covers implementing the Business Role Manager tool in a risk-free role design environment to reach your organization's long-term goal of compliance and risk-free SAP Access Control in an IT environment.

6 Business Role Manager Overview

In this chapter, we explore how Business Role Manager helps to address SAP Access Control issues through centralized role design, testing, and maintenance. We provide detailed information on setting up different types of role creation, testing, and maintenance in an automated fashion starting from requirements, through conceptual design, to production ready roles, which are maintained free from access risks, to enforce compliance and to prevent access risks per regulations and company policies. During the role creation process, risk verification can be performed with the help of the Access Risk Analysis tool. The rule set defined in Access Risk Analysis works interactively, so the necessary corrective measures can be adopted by the role designer, and a new role can be vetted by the role owner based on the risk analysis result. Technical experts and business process owners can document role definitions, perform automated risk assessments, track changes, and conduct maintenance with ease, which increases consistency in collaborative environments.

Definition of the Business Role Manager

The Business Role Manager modeling tool is based on pattern analysis and policy validation, which is used to simplify the process for collecting, assessing, and analyzing established and existing roles. New roles also can be defined and analyzed for their risk using what-if scenarios with simulations of risk analysis in your landscape before testing your new roles. This activity helps you keep your IT environment as part of the clean phase of your SAP GRC initiative. It also acts as trusted system for reporting and an analytics tool to optimize roles by monitoring usage and effectiveness, reporting role risks and role usage, and tracking role changes for audit compliance.

Based on our experience, this tool wasn't popular because of some bad experience among customers due to some inabilities of its predecessor. In the newer 10.x versions, most issues are addressed and improved. Those who implemented the Business Role Manager as part of SAP Access Control 10.x implementations are able to manage SAP Access Control from SAP GRC tools very well.

Implementation considerations for Business Role Manager and Access Request Manager

It's always a best practice to implement Business Role Manager before implementing Access Request Manager. The basic reason for this is that both tools use roles and attributes from plug-in systems for the SAP Access Control system, and that information is stored in shared tables in the SAP GRC system. If you start the implementation with Business Role Manager, this tool will have enough information related to the plug-in roles during user provisioning. If you plan to skip Business Role Manager implementation and carry on only with the Access Request Manager, your overhead on maintaining role attributes will be very high due to the manually oriented process. If any single step is unknowingly missed in this manual process, it might lead to additional overhead from the troubleshooting view. SAP Access Control is a central repository for all SAP systems connected in the landscape to track the role status during design and maintenance, especially when multiple landscapes are introduced in an enterprise.

In addition to this, many more enhancement and add-on options are provided in the new version of Business Role Manager in areas such as managing Central User Administrator (CUA) roles, improved integration with Transaction PFCG, role certification, object level security, link test document via URLs, and a BADI to improve custom code integration with key integration points.

Apart from these reasons, here are a few more to justify the implementation of this tool:

Reasons to implement Business Role Manager

- Automated role certification, which ensures business managers participate and buy in to role assignments that are needed along with risk management during role creation.

- A trusted system of record for reporting and analytics so organizations are able to optimize roles by monitoring usage and effectiveness as well as track role changes for audit and compliance.
- Beyond technical roles such as single roles, composite, and derived roles, the introduction of business roles provides the following advantages to the customer environment:
  - Requesting role creation and assignment in business terms simplifies the process.
  - Business roles represent job functions.
  - Business roles hold one or more technical and/or business roles, providing easy maintenance to the security team to maintain few variants to satisfy a wide variety of users in a single business process.

So far, we've seen the general functions and benefits of the Business Role Manager. Now let's delve into the Business Role Manager configuration steps and the creation of a single role process.

6.1 Business Role Manager Configuration

Let's now walk through the scenario of implementing and creating a new single role, which helps companies manage enterprise roles with defined methodology and enforce compliance to prevent access risks per regulations and company policies. After you set this up, it's easier to create the rest of the role types using Business Role Manager, which is tightly connected to Transaction PFCG in the plug-in system. You have the flexibility to maintain the roles and track the role changes from SAP Access Control tools directly. Later, we'll discuss what needs to be done to this role to use it in a productive environment of SAP Access Control and plug-in systems.

Following are the basic requirements to start your configuration of Business Role Manager. By now, you might be more familiar with some of these activities. Also we've provided cross reference to earlier chapters for more on how to perform these steps.

- Basic configuration step.
- Assigning connectors to the connector groups (Section 3.2.5).
- Adding connectors to required scenarios (Section 3.2.5).
- Associating actions and assigning default connectors (Section 3.2.5).
- Activating Business Configuration Sets (BC Sets) related to Business Role Manager (Section 6.1.1).
- Entering configuration parameter values that suit your needs (Section 6.1.2).
- Assigning roles and maintaining SAP Access Control owners multistep process (see Section 6.1.5 through Section 6.1.7).

During the initial settings of Emergency Access Management, you may have already completed the basic configuration steps for most of the activities, such as connector-relevant configuration. As a continuation to the connector configuration, let's move on to the activation of BC Sets on our way to configure the Business Role Manager.

6.1.1 Activation of BC Sets

In Chapter 3, Section 3.2.2, we discussed BC Set activation and how to verify whether BC Sets are already active via Transaction SPRO. From BC Set maintenance, you can view the log details about already active BC Sets and see the content details. Five BC Sets are provided to simplify configuration and value population in the SAP GRC system to quickly start Business Role Manager configuration:

- **GRAC_ROLE_MGMT_LANDSCAPE**
  Activation of this BC Set loads data with respect to the business roles landscape. This information is stored in view V_GRFNCONNGRP and table GRACCONGRPSTAT. If you've defined this as part of the connector settings for your SAP Access Control landscape, you may not need to activate this.
- **GRAC_ROLE_MGMT_METHODOLOGY**
  Activation of this BC Set loads data related to role methodology process and steps. If you're comfortable in technical Data Dictionary

maintenance, then you may quickly access this information from Transaction SM34 and enter the view cluster GRACVC_MTH.

- **GRAC_ROLE_MGMT_PRE_REQ_TYPE**
  Activation of this BC Set creates data that are needed as role prerequisite types, such as certification or training requirements. These are populated in view GRACV_PRERQTYP.
- **GRAC_ROLE_MGMT_ROLE_STATUS**
  Activation of this BC Set populates values in view GRACV_ROLESTATUS, which helps to describe whether the table is in development or production-status that is available for provisioning.
- **GRAC_ROLE_MGMT_SENTIVITY**
  Activation of this BC Set loads data in view GRACV_RLSENS and connected tables to define role sensitivity.

Although it's possible to maintain all of these values manually from configuration, BC Set activation gives some standard best practice data to push forward your configuration work without much stress to define them in your SAP Access Control environment. After you've followed the same processes that are explained in Chapter 3 to activate the preceding BC Sets, you can move on to configure the values in the default configuration parameters related to the Business Role Manager tool.

6.1.2 Verifying Default Configuration Parameters

The next step in configuring Business Role Manager is to maintain configuration parameters. To maintain these configuration values in IMG SETTINGS, use Transaction SPRO to access the following menu path, SAP CUSTOMIZING IMPLEMENTATION GUIDE • GOVERNANCE, RISK AND COMPLIANCE • ACCESS CONTROL • MAINTAIN CONFIGURATION SETTINGS. From this configuration maintenance screen the following values in the ROLE MANAGEMENT parameter group,and WORKFLOW parameter group related to role management that need to be configured. Most of this configuration is related to role attributes and we have explained these parameter details in the following section.

Some of the values given in Table 6.1 mention parameters that can be adjusted later even after testing to reflect or adjust the role creation and maintenance process to suit your environment. Here we maintained Business Role Manager behavior-related configuration parameters. In the following sections, we'll list some of the key requirements to make Business Role Manager function properly from design to test to the transport phase in an automated environment.

Configuration Parameter	Value	Description	Details
3000	<empty>	Business process	Default business process
3001	<empty>	Subprocess	Default subprocess
3002	<empty>	Criticality level	Default criticality level
3003	<empty>	Default project release	Maintains project release
3004	Dev	Default role status	Role status: development, test, or production
3005	NO	Reset role methodology	YES value resets the role methodology step to the initial, irrespective of the type of change carried out
3006	YES	Add functions to authorization	Enables adding new functions to authorization
3007	NO	Editing organization level value of derived roles	Enables editing organizational-level values for derived roles
3008	YES	Ticket for authorization data change	Requires a ticket number after authorization data changes
3009	YES	Role deletion	Enables deleting of roles from the plug-in system
3010	YES	Attaching files	Enables attaching files to the role definition
3011	YES	Risk analysis before role generation	Conducts risk analysis before role generation

Table 6.1 Business Role Manager: Configuration Parameters

Configuration Parameter	Value	Description	Details
3012	NO	Role generation on multiple system	Enables role generation on multiple systems (useful for certain customers of global landscapes)
3013	NO		Uses logged-on user credentials for role generation
3014	NO		Allows role generation with permission level violations
3015	NO		Allows role generation with critical permission violations
3016	NO		Allows role generation with action level violations
3017	NO		Allows role generation with critical action violations
3018	NO		Allows role generation with critical role/profile violations
3019	NO		Overwrites individual role risk analysis results for mass risk analysis
3020	10		Provides role certification reminder notification in number of days
3021	<Empty>		Provides directory for mass role import server files
3022	21	Workflow	Provides request type for Role approval
3023	5	Workflow	Provides priority for role approval
3024	YES	Workflow	Enforces methodology process for derived roles during generation

Table 6.1 Business Role Manager: Configuration Parameters (Cont.)

Configuration Parameter	Value	Description	Details
3025	NO		Allows selection of organization value maps without leading organization
3026	YES		Saves role provisioning details while copying role

Table 6.1 Business Role Manager: Configuration Parameters (Cont.)

6.1.3 Maintain Role Type Settings

Now that we have configured the parameter settings of the Business Role Manager configuration, you need to maintain the Role Type setting. This provides the options to set various role types that can be designed in Business Role Manager. To set the role types that are needed in your environment, go to Transaction SPRO, and access the menu path, SAP Customizing Implementation Guide • Governance, Risk and Compliance • Access Control • Role Management • Maintain Role Type Settings • Deactivate Role Types. From this screen, complete the following configuration settings:

Role type Configuration Settings

- Deactivate role types by selecting which aren't required for your environment (mandatory).
- Maintain labels for role types. This is an optional step if you want to create descriptions for role types.
- Define the maximum length for the role types per application type (optional).

Continue the configuration steps that are shown in Figure 6.1 in the same sequence under Role Management, except the last four steps including Define Methodology Processes And Steps are excluded in this initial configuration to simplify the process. This excluded part uses Business Rule Framework Plus (BRF+) and help to address some complex scenarios in your landscape.

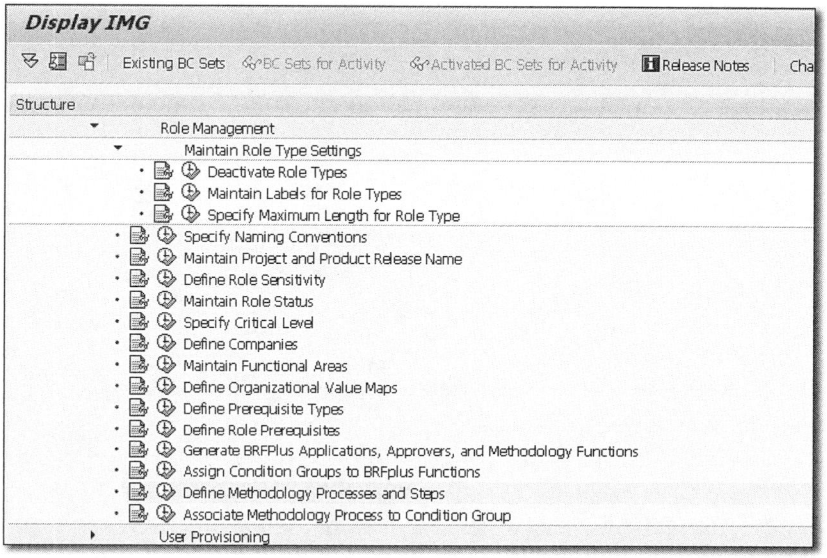

Figure 6.1 Maintain Role Type Settings

Now that you've set the default configuration settings and maintained your role types, let's look at the next phase of the Business Role Manager configuration, naming conventions.

6.1.4 Specify Naming Conventions

The role-naming convention should be followed by role types, and each role type can be set with its own rule for naming format and position. While creating new roles, this role mask reinforces the naming with some general guidelines:

General guidelines for naming conventions

- Maintain naming rules.
- Enter the naming convention description, role type, and relevant connector group.
- Maintain the naming convention format and position along with the sequence of the naming convention, number of characters, and type of information.

A sample role naming convention is given in Figure 6.2.

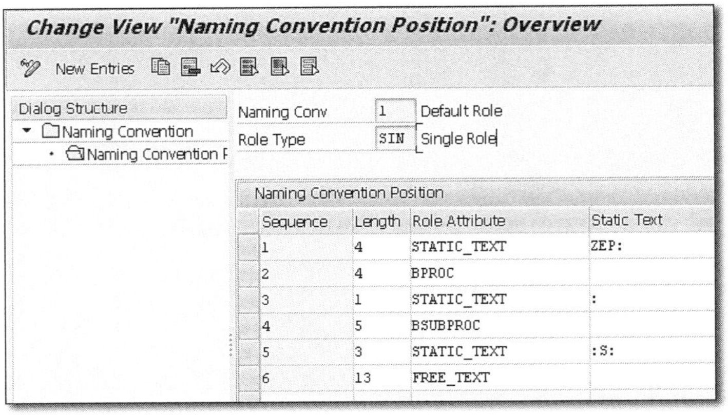

Figure 6.2 Role Naming Convention

In next set of configuration steps, we'll look at various role attributes that are part of Business Role Manager to determine approvers and related activities with respect to segregation of duties (SoD) violations and risk analysis.

Customizing Role Attributes

There are two sets of role attributes used in SAP Access Control content. One set requires customizing with options and predetermined values (discussed here), and another set is value maintenance specific to the role that you'll maintain along with role creation or role maintenance work such as maintaining role descriptions, role owners, parent roles if the role is derived, and so on. For the customization of a role attribute, we'll explain why this customizing is required and the purpose of each attribute. Some of these attributes are used in the role definition process and some attributes are used role approval process or helps to limit their appearance on user requests in User Access Management, for example, Business Process is either populated as part of a BC Set activation or is maintained during the configuration process. Some of these characteristics are mandatory and are used to determine certain characteristics in the workflow automation process to find correct approvers such as role owners or access request approving managers. In other case, this provides some detail about the role such as role status—whether this role is under development or in production status that is available for provisioning. We discuss some of these attributes in detail wherever we highlight those attributes.

Example of customizing a role attribute

Let's consider an example here in which a SAP GRC system and underlying plug-in system needs a clear differentiator between a role in the design phase and one in the testing or completed phase that moved to the quality system or production system of the plug-in environment. One of the role attributes, such as ROLE STATUS, gives this detail to the role. And this attribute restricts or allows further processing changes to the role in Business Role Manager or allows any user to request this role from Access Request Manager. These role attributes are shared data used across SAP Access Control tools and even in reporting to give more individualized reports.

Configuration options for role attributes

Let's consider this role's attributes and their various configuration options that you need to maintain. All of these activities are sequentially maintained from menu path, SAP CUSTOMIZING IMPLEMENTATION GUIDE • GOVERNANCE, RISK, AND COMPLIANCE • ACCESS CONTROL • ROLE MANAGEMENT. The role attributes are:

- MAINTAIN PROJECT RELEASE
  Maintain the list of projects and product releases. This data will be available as a dropdown list in ROLE MANAGEMENT screens. This attribute is used to specify that a role is relevant for a specific project or product.
- ROLE STATUS
  Create and edit a list of role statuses such as testing, development, and production. Only those plug-in system roles defined status as 'PRODUCTION' are the only roles available for the user to create a request in User Access Management. Any other role status considered as either 'DEVELOPMENT' or 'TEST' and they won't be available in User Access Management.
- ROLE SENSITIVITY
  Maintain role sensitivity by creating or editing role sensitivity values to suit your requirement. Available entries are populated from the BC Set. This attribute can help you restrict authorization to an intranet portal in conjunction with Transaction PFCG.
- CRITICAL LEVEL
  Labels how critical the role is for your enterprise. For example, payroll authorization roles might have a HIGH critical level.

- Companies
  Create or edit companies as a part of the role attribute. This allows your organization to group by companies and applies to the role-specific attribute.
- Functional Areas
  Create or edit functional areas to restrict your list of roles specific to a functional area, which reduces the list of roles shown on the user request creation. A functional area is a group or department in a company that performs a specific function or activity.
- Organizational Value Mapping
  Maintain the organization level mapping to maintain the parent organizational level and maintain parent or child organizational mapping to document organizational hierarchy and structure.
- Prerequisite Types
  Create or edit prerequisites from respective configuration links. This role prerequisite is defined to validate to the requestor whether the user has completed mandatory requirements before granting access. For example, basic training that needs to be completed to access the system can be validated here.
- Define Role Prerequisites
  Create or edit using the prerequisite type defined in an earlier step and enter the criteria, for example, if an HR administrator role must be completed as a prerequisite to HR training.

The first two attributes (Maintain Project Release and Role Status) are mandatory, and the rest of them are optional irrespective of role types or role methodology. By completing all of these steps, you've completed a portion of configuration of role attributes related to Business Role Manager that is sufficient to handle a single role type. Let's move on further to define role methodology and MSMP workflow configuration to complete the rest of the Business Role Manager configuration steps. There are a few more configuration steps that are relevant to advanced topics discussed in Chapter 8, as well.

6.1.5 Standard Role Methodology

Now that we've discussed role attribute configuration, the next step is to cover some details on what role methodology means, why you need to configure it, and how you can configure it to suit your enterprise needs to automate risk-free role creation.

Role creation process

In Business Role Manager, the role creation process consists of predefined methodology steps such as the definition phase, risk analysis phase, and so on. These steps or phases guide you through the role-creation process by using guided procedures. You've seen the standard methodology delivered with BC Sets shown in Figure 6.3, and this can be modified and overridden per your requirements. Role methodology enforces process flow and maintenance in a more controlled and uniform way to perform the sequence of activities involved in role creation or maintenance processes. At the same time, role methodology combined with CONDITION GROUP and BRF+ configuration leverage rules based on role attributes to dynamically select a methodology from the available list of methodologies. To define role methodology and steps, invoke Transaction SPRO, and go to menu path, SAP CUSTOMIZING IMPLEMENTATION GUIDE • GOVERNANCE, RISK AND COMPLIANCE • ACCESS CONTROL • ROLE MANAGEMENT • DEFINE METHODOLOGY PROCESSES AND STEPS.

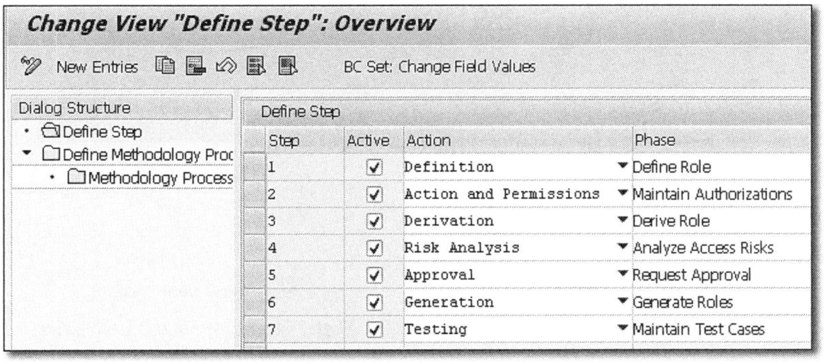

Figure 6.3 Role Methodology: Step Definition and Action Activation

If the DEFINE STEP folder isn't defaulted, double-click on this folder to see the define step options to which actions or phases are tied (see Figure 6.3). Make sure that all steps you want to perform as part of your standard methodology are active, or if you planned to skip any of these steps, deselect the Active checkbox.

Next define the methodology name and provide a description, status, and which methodology will be defaulted for role creation as shown in Figure 6.4.

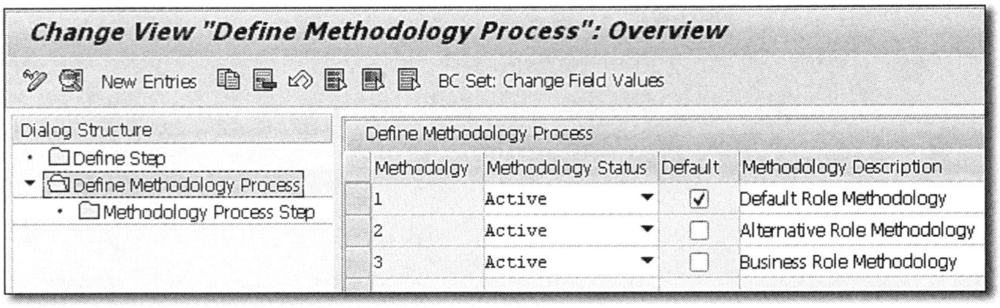

Figure 6.4 Role Methodology Definition Process and Steps

Step sequence for role creation

Next, you need to define the step sequence or phases of the processes under this methodology that the role creation process will undergo. The details are shown in Figure 6.5.

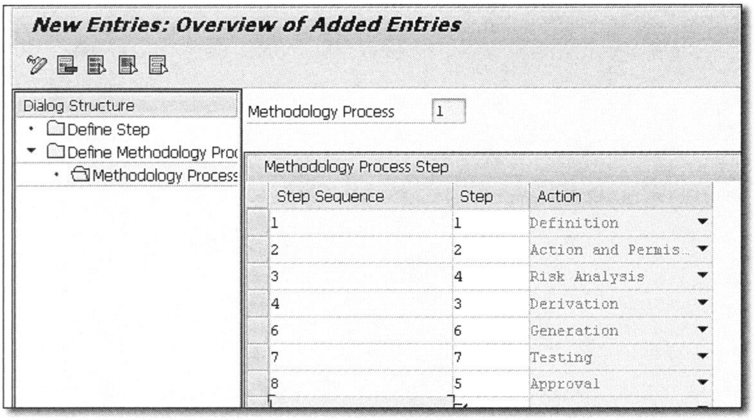

Figure 6.5 Step Sequence and Action Mapping for Methodology Process Definition

Applying different methodologies to meet your needs

Apart from the standard methodology provided as part of the BC Set, you can create different methodologies, and the process sequence or rules can be defined to suit your needs by switching the step sequences. If you think of your single role process methodology and the steps that need to be different from the business role or composite role process methodology, you have the options to define multiple and different customized methodology processes to meet your needs.

For example, you may need a sensitive role definition such as payroll-related role creation or change that requires an additional approval before role owner approval. Figure 6.5 shows the configuration STEP sequence 1 to 8 for methodology process 1. We'll look at more details on using the Business Rule Framework Plus (BRF+) rule configuration in Chapter 8 in advanced topics such as how to change rule methodology and using condition groups to help deal with more complex scenarios.

In this section, we've looked at how to configure and define the role methodology process that helps streamline the role definition process in your environment. Next, we'll guide you through how to configure a Multi-stage Multi-path (MSMP) workflow to define the workflow approval process.

6.1.6 MSMP Workflow Configuration

In this section, let's walk through the role approval workflow configuration details that are applicable to the approval phase of role methodology. Some of the detailed discussion about MSMP workflow is described in Chapter 8, so here we'll discuss very specific activity that you need to maintain and skip the rest of the configuration flexibilities for complex scenarios for now. SAP-provided MSMP workflow processes are delivered as part of BC Set activation as we discussed in earlier chapters.

To start this configuration action, start Transaction SPRO, and go to menu path, SAP CUSTOMIZING IMPLEMENTATION GUIDE • GOVERNANCE, RISK AND COMPLIANCE • ACCESS CONTROL • WORKFLOW FOR ACCESS CONTROL • MAINTAIN MSMP WORKFLOWS.

Executing this link takes you to a new browser window that shows the MSMP WORKFLOW CONFIGURATION initial screen as shown in the Figure 6.6.

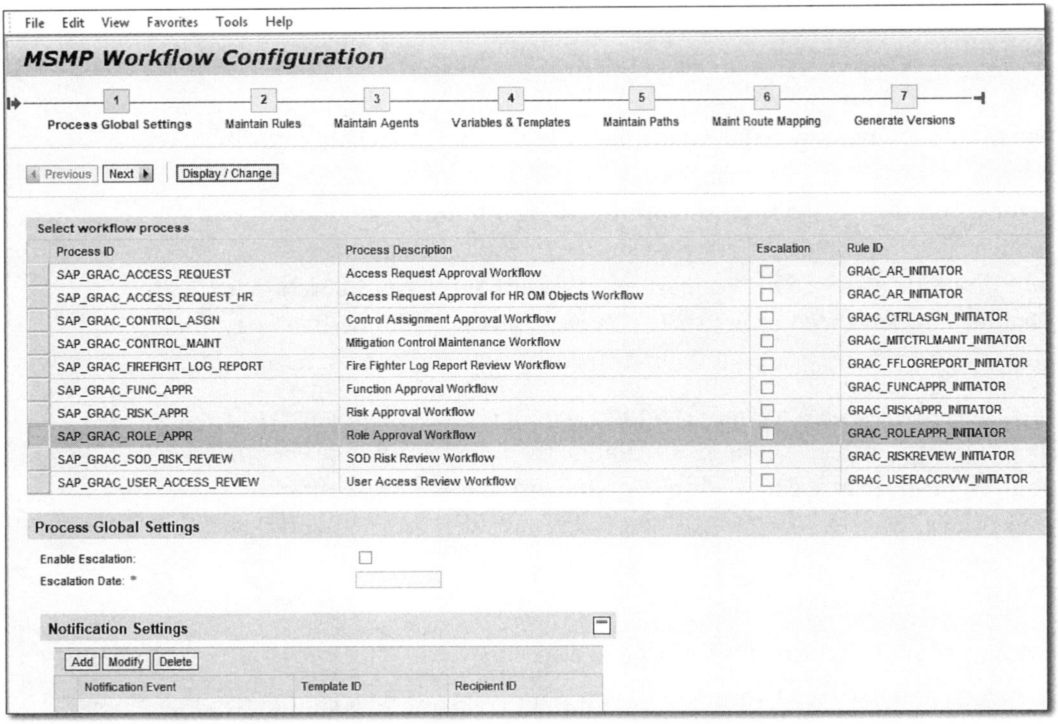

Figure 6.6 MSMP Workflow Configuration Initial Screen

Role approval configuration and the accompanying workflow configuration steps

For role approval configuration, you need to choose SAP_GRAC_ROLE_APPR under Process, and click on the Display/Change button to change the workflow configuration steps. This allows you to modify the process. As explained earlier, we'll go through only the necessary steps for this approval process, which means go to step 5 Maintain Paths, where you can configure details for the approval stage.

Maintain workflow paths

In process step 5 of the MSMP workflow, where you maintain workflow paths, make sure that default Path ID GRAC_DEFAULT_PATH is already populated as a result of BC Set activation. If there are no entries in the Maintain Stages section of the screen Figure 6.7, you need to add a stage and maintain the Agent ID as GRAC_ROLE_APPROVER by clicking the Add button for the stage GRAC_DEFAULT_STAGE.

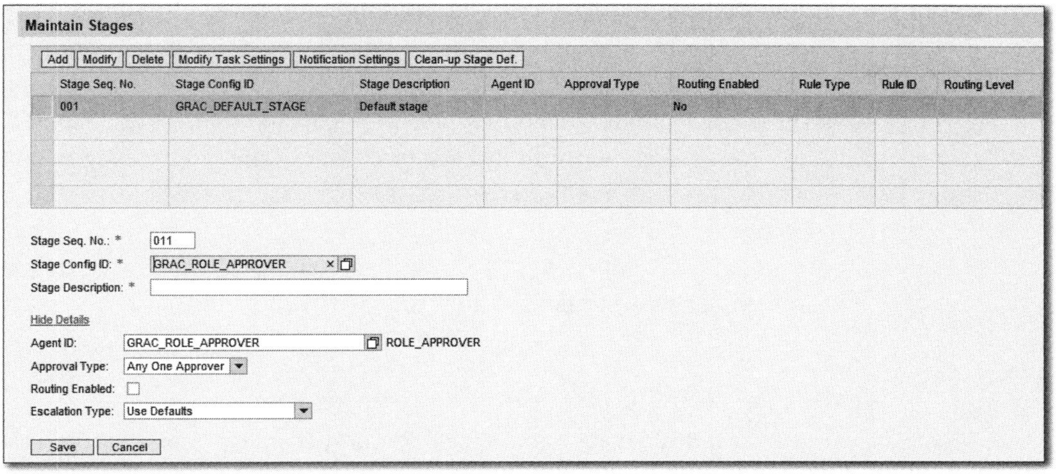

Figure 6.7 Maintain Stages for Role Approval Process

Maintain the tasks by Agent_ID

After you maintain the stage and agent, the next activity is to maintain the tasks that need to be performed by the AGENT_ID. For this, you need to click on the MODIFY TASK SETTINGS button and make the necessary task settings to be carried out as role approver (see Figure 6.8). Save your changes.

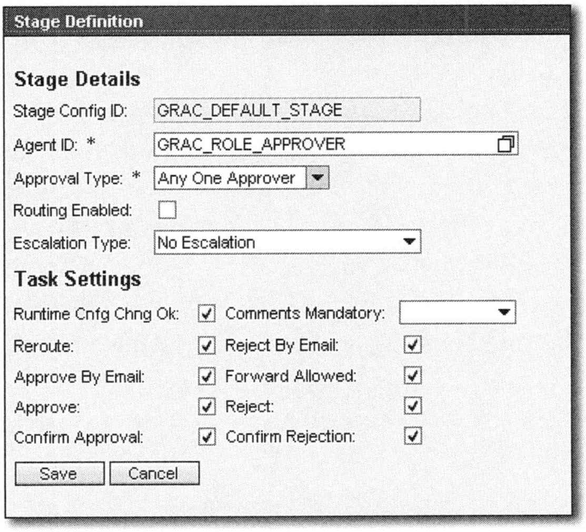

Figure 6.8 Role Approver Stage Task Configuration

Maintaining notification settings in the MSMP workflow

In the last step in this stage, you need to maintain notification settings that will be sent as email notifications to the respective work-item receivers. A detailed discussion on creating and maintaining notification settings and configuration is provided in the advanced topics of Chapter 8. After you're done with the necessary changes, save your changes, and you'll be taken to the last step—GENERATE VERSIONS—where you need to generate and activate the workflow process.At this point you have defined and generated Access Control role approval process workflow and ready to move to next section role owners creation.

6.1.7 Creating Role Owners

Business Role Manager and Access Request Manager tools require role ownership with the option of determining whether a person is allowed to approve content and/or assignment. To act as a role owner to perform approvals, this user needs to be assigned in SAP Access Control with the role SAP_GRAC_ROLE_MGMT_ROLE_OWNER. This approver also needs other base roles—SAP_GRC_FN_BASE and SAP_GRC_FN_BUSINESS_USER—as default roles for SAP Access Control access.

SAP NetWeaver Business Client role creation

From the SAP NetWeaver Business Client (NWBC) frontend, use the role owner user ID that is created in Transaction SU01 of SAP Access Control. To create role owners in SAP NetWeaver Business Client, these user IDs need to be set up as part of the central owners with role owner as the owner type. From the SAP NetWeaver Business Client frontend, select SETUP • ACCESS OWNERS • ACCESS CONTROL OWNERS, and maintain the owners as shown in Figure 6.9. After this is done, its role owners are created in the system. There is one more place, this will be maintained while creating a new role or while uploading the roles at first time in SAP Access Control, as owner attribute where the individual role owner needs to be maintained to complete the role owner maintenance task. After this role attribute information is provided, the SAP Access Control system and connected MSMP workflow can identify respective role owners and send approval workflows accordingly.

You've now maintained all of the necessary configuration steps to meet the basic requirements to create a new role using Business Role Manager. Next, let's create a new role from the Business Role Manager and see how a single role can be created from the beginning.

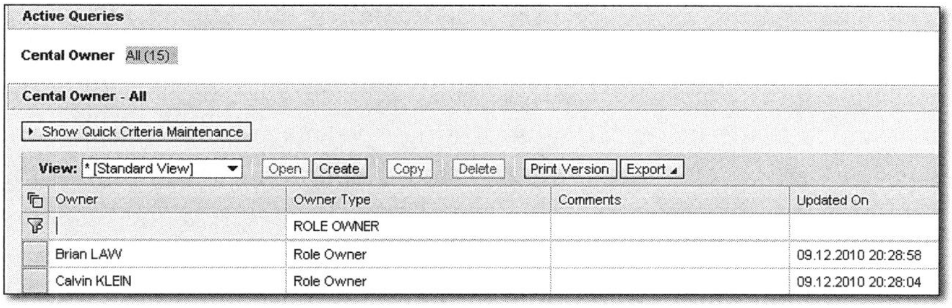

Figure 6.9 Role Owner Assignment in NetWeaver Business Client

So far, we've detailed the basic configuration steps that are all related to Business Role Manager to create risk-free roles for the plug-in system. In this section, we'll describe how to create a single role and then generate it in the plug-in system.

6.2 Business Role Manager Use: Creating a New Single Role

Creating a single role can be started from SAP NetWeaver Business Client. From NWBC, go to the ACCESS MANAGEMENT work set, and choose ROLE MANAGEMENT • ROLE MAINTENANCE.

The screen shown in Figure 6.10 is the starting point to creating a role in Business Role Manager. Click on the CREATE button, and it opens up a new screen with role types. Select SINGLE ROLE to start, which takes you to the next screen.

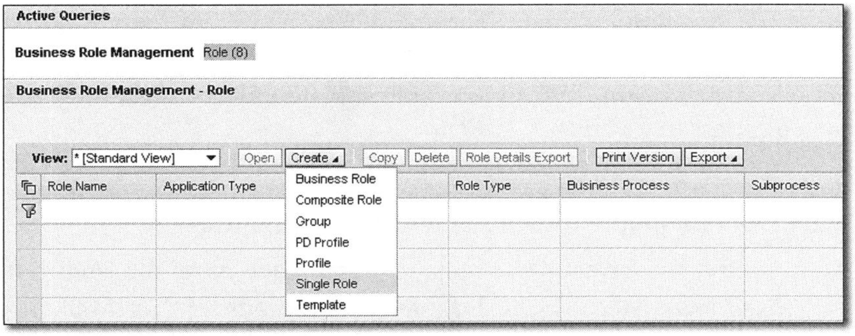

Figure 6.10 Role Creation: Initial Screen from NetWeaver Business Client

Role definition: guided configuration

You might have noticed that this initial screen is a guided procedure with all of the steps defined in our configuration with default role methodology. In the Define Role step, choose the Details tab, and fill in the mandatory fields by selecting appropriate values from the dropdown lists (see Figure 6.11). These values from dropdown lists are part of the initial configuration on attributes and their values. Role name is shown with the pattern defined in the role-naming convention configuration mentioned in Section 6.1.4.

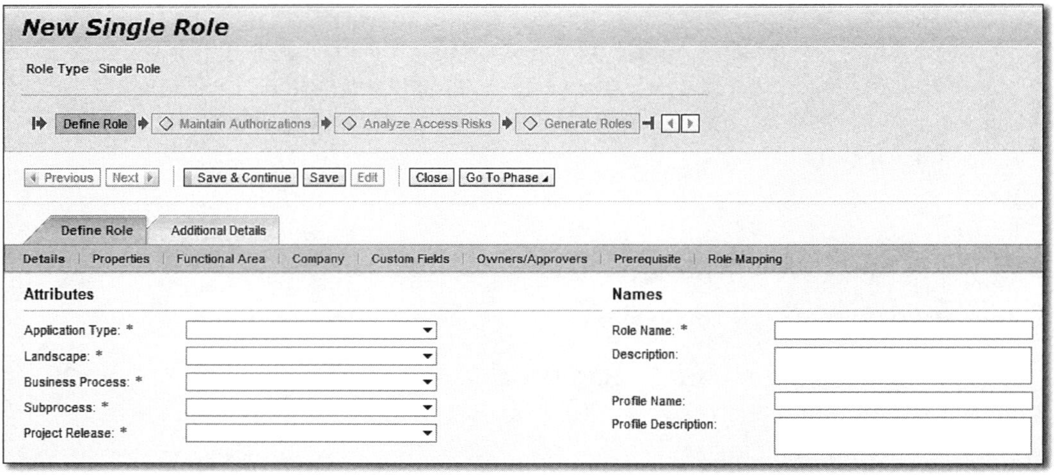

Figure 6.11 Role Definition Attributes Maintenance Screen

In addition to these fields, which are all part of the Details subscreen, there are a few more tabs to define in this step, including Company, Functional Area, Prerequisite, and so on, if they are all relevant to this new role. In the Owners/Approvers tab, you need to maintain Content Approvers as those who are the data object owners and Assignment Approvers as those who provide approval of role assignments to the end users in the plug-in system.

6.2.1 Assigning Authorizations to the New Role

After you set the Define Role step, you can move on to the Maintain Authorizations step by clicking Save & Continue. Select Maintain Authorization Data (see Figure 6.12) to open a pop-up screen that asks you to enter your user ID and password to log on to the plug-in system. This action opens Transaction PFCG in change mode.

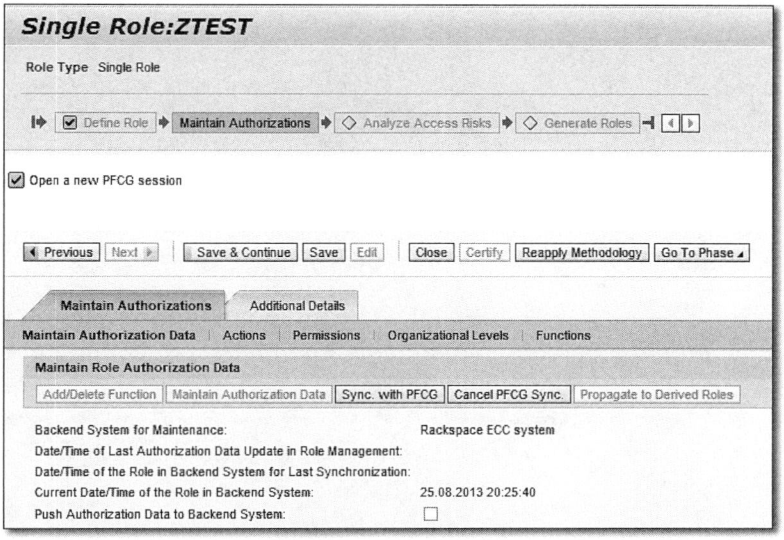

Figure 6.12 Authorization Maintenance Screen in NetWeaver Business Client

All of the following actions of maintaining transactions and authorization values in Transaction PFCG are carried out in the plug-in system, not in the SAP GRC system. After you've maintained all of the role-relevant authorizations and any organizational data, then save and generate the role that is shown in Figure 6.13. After this is done, you can log off the plug-in system.

Configuring actions and permissions for single role in the Business Role Manager

After logging off from the plug-in system, navigate back to the Business Role Manager tool from NetWeaver Business Client where you were creating roles as shown in Figure 6.12 and choose SYNC. WITH PFCG to get all of the actions and permissions from the plug-in system. This can be verified by checking the tabs in this step, such as ACTIONS, PERMISSIONS, or ORGANIZATIONAL LEVELS. In these tabs you will be able to view all the transactions, authorizations and organization units which were maintained in the plug-in system 'PFCG' Transaction. This is useful for you to verify consistency check between the SAP GRC system and the plug-in system.

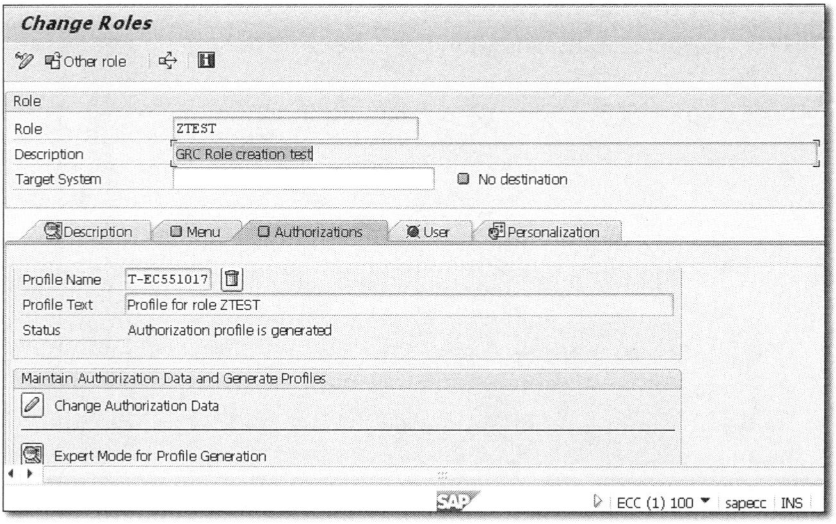

Figure 6.13 Transaction PFCG in SAP ERP (Plug-In) System Called from the Business Role Manager Tool

Now that you've completed the authorization assignment, click SAVE & CONTINUE, and stay on the current screen for the next step, analyzing access risks of the role.

6.2.2 Analyzing Access Risks and Remediation

This step allows the user to perform risk analysis at the role design stage to prevent risks in the plug-in system roles. From this screen, choose checkboxes for risk analysis types, such as ACTION LEVEL and required RULE SET, and SYSTEM, to analyze with options in foreground (see Figure 6.14).

Resolving risk violations

As a result of this risk analysis, if there are risks listed in the RESULT area, you can resolve the risk violation accordingly. The key purpose of using Business Role Manager to create a clean, risk-free role is achieved in this step. After you create a risk-free role, move to the next step by choosing SAVE & CONTINUE to stay on the current screen. Assuming that the next step involves role approval, at the end of this process step, an automatic workflow will be triggered, and the role owner will receive a role request approval work item in his inbox.

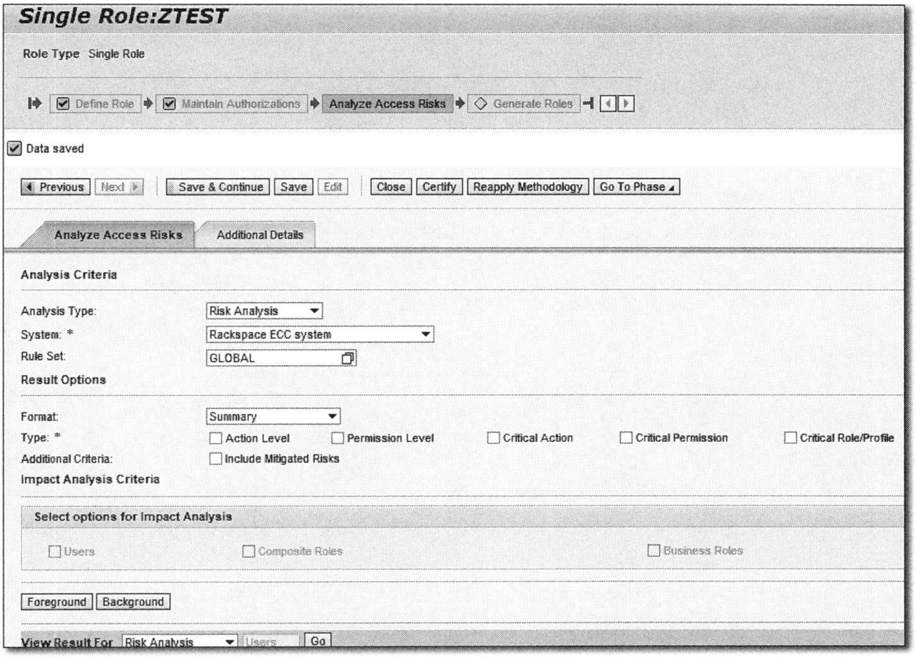

Figure 6.14 Performing Risk Analysis as Part of the Role Creation Process

6.2.3 Request Approval

As the role designer, after you've completed the role maintenance and risk analysis, your next step is to confirm that all necessary approvals are obtained before allowing the role to move on to the next step in the process. As mentioned earlier, the role owner should receive a work item or email regarding role approval. If the role owner approval is done, and per our workflow there is an additional approver defined, the system will send another work item to this additional approver. If all of the approvers of the workflow completed the approval, then this role is available to proceed to role generation, which is the next step.

6.2.4 Role Generation

The preceding approval process may be a discrete operation, but based on the notification setting in the MSMP workflow, the role designer gets the notification mail when the role approval is completed. Now the role designer can log in to the SAP GRC system and check for the role, that is in the 'ROLE GENERATE' step. In this step you click on GENERATE, button this takes you through a series of guided procedure screens to execute in foreground or schedule the background generation of the role in the correct plug-in system. After the role generation is completed, you'll get a success message, and you should be able to view the role in the bottom of the window with details (see Figure 6.15).

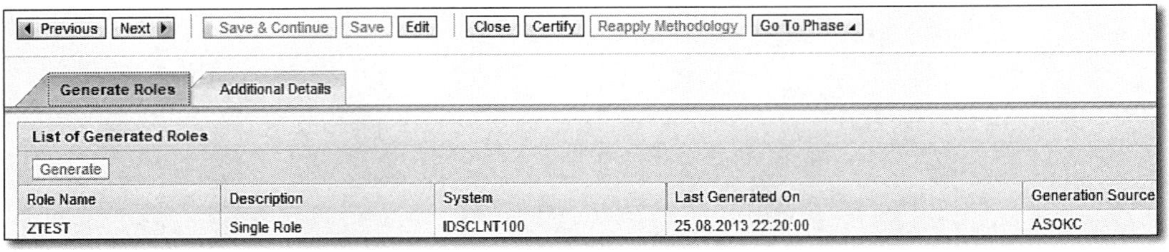

Figure 6.15 Role Generation from NetWeaver Business Client with System and Date

Now this new role is generated in the plug-in system, and you're left with one last step—testing the newly created role.

6.2.5 Testing the Role

Testing cases can be created according to real business situations. Upon successful completion of role testing, the document can be attached as a proof of role test for audit purposes.

In this section, we've seen how to create a new, clean, risk-free role with a role type of single role creation with specified methodology. Similarly, you can create various role types with the adoption of specific methodology in a seamless role creation using Business Role Manager, and these can be transported from the plug-in system in your landscape. Now that we've gone through the configuration and role creation process, let's move on to various reporting and maintenance tools available in Business Role Manager.

6.3 Role Maintenance and Reporting

Along with the role creation process, there are a few other requirements in the system that need to be carried out by performing regular maintenance of the roles, making changes to the process, or carrying out other attributes at a mass level. Also there is a definite need for an initial mass load of roles and reporting on various role metrics for auditing or general maintenance purposes.

These activities can be carried out by various reporting components that are provided as part of Business Role Manager. Figure 6.16 shows part of the ACCESS MANAGEMENT work set, in which there are three group of links provided to carry out the task: ROLE MANAGEMENT, ROLE MASS MAINTENANCE, and ROLE MINING related to Business Role Manager activities.

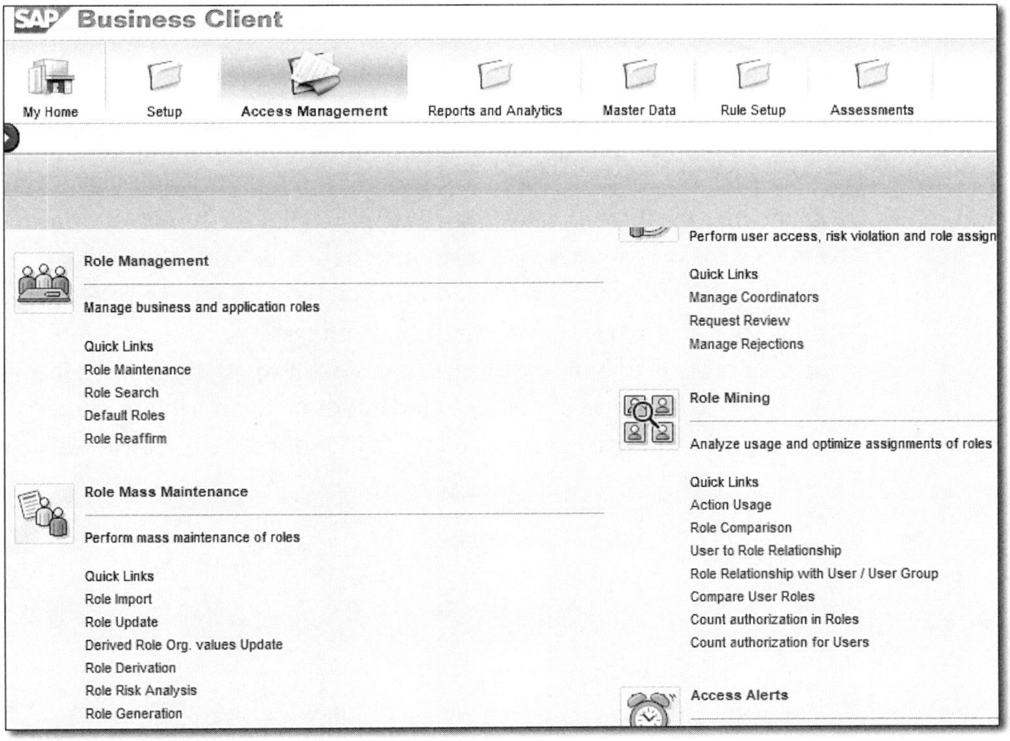

Figure 6.16 Role Maintenance and Reporting Options from NetWeaver Business Client Screen

Role Management task links

Role Management is more of a helping hand to SAP Access Control administrators or role designers to maintain the roles and their attributes on an as needed basis.

Role Mass Maintenance, as the name indicates, is used for mass maintainence of the roles such as role import into the SAP GRC system during initial implementation, any enterprise-wide reorganization caused by organizational value updates, or any other major attribute changes.

Role Mining task links are more related to various reporting options from the role perspective, which gives usage details or authorization details underneath the roles or compares the roles within the landscape to verify any difference between the roles or various versions of the roles. All of this reporting and maintenance tool help is really a very big leap in the tools functionality compared to previous versions of Business Rule Manager.

6.4 Summary

We've gone through various configurations and the creation of risk-free role development processes with some examples. This will help you to start using Business Role Manager with parallel execution of effective role design along with Access Risk Analysis. At the same time it provides seamless integration between various involved teams like role design, approval, security along with audit trail and testing documentation. The flexible process to build new roles or maintain roles with good controls boosts the confidence of the users and builds up the reliability of the system. We'll see more advanced additional options for the Business Role Manager in Chapter 8.

User Access Management concept, design, and core implementation steps are covered in this chapter, along with in depth details on User Access Management reporting. Various possible scenarios are explained to help your organization maximize the benefits of implementing this tool to provide a risk-free IT environment in the hire-to-retire cycle with the most monitoring functionality.

7 User Access Management Overview

User Access Management is the toolset to manage all systems access, user provisioning, and role assignments in your entire IT system landscape via an automated workflow approval process. This tool also provides an efficient way to handle risk simulations and improve collaboration between various business teams and IT teams involved in the provisioning process with speedier decision-making options.

User Access Management automates the access provisioning approval process and provisioning appropriate roles and permissions via workflow to the respective requested plug-in systems. When a user (requestor) requests resources (roles or access privileges) for which the user doesn't have permissions using User Access Management, it automatically forwards the access request to designated managers and approvers via workflow. At the end of the approval process, roles and permissions are automatically applied to the respective systems with requested privileges when the access requests are approved. During this process, User Access Management checks for segregation of duty (SoD) and critical access analysis for the user by combining the user's existing privileges with those requested using the integrated Access Risk Analysis tool. If there are any violations, these violations can also be dictated via workflow rules to handle them via additional workflow steps on how to handle these type of complex scenarios.

Figure 7.1 provides a snapshot of a typical workflow for the access request process that gives various approval and risk remediation processes that are customizable in User Access Management.

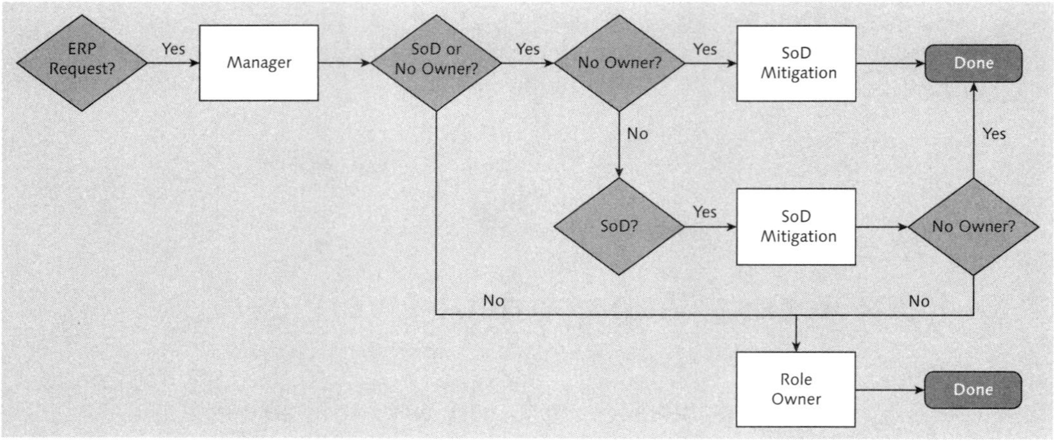

Figure 7.1 Sample Provisioning Workflow

In this chapter, we'll look at the different users in User Access Management, the configuration of User Access Management, how to configure your Multi-stage Multi-path (MSMP) workflow process details with a sample process on provisioning, and password self-service (PSS). Lastly, we'll touch on User Access Management reporting.

First, let's explore the User Access Management tool's capabilities and benefits for a business.

User Access Management capabilities

The User Access Management tool's capabilities help to improve your IT environment and increase the efficiency of managing a user's life cycle in your complex IT landscape in a way that ensures compliance and the smooth flow of user provisioning and deprovisioning in a timely manner. Current customer landscapes are often complex environments that comprise multiple SAP systems and non-SAP systems with various access combinations depending on the employer location and job position. Typically, user provisioning in this situation covers the entire hire-to-retire requirements in a manual process that is not only tedious but also error prone and makes it difficult to detect any SoD violations. You can automate the entire user life cycle management from hire to retire in your landscape using

User Access Management benefits

User Access Management offers the following benefits:

- Access request creation based on templates.
- Simplified access request creation using model by user or copy of earlier request.
- Automated workflow for efficiently approving various types of requests.
- Automated escalation process in case there are any missing deadlines in approval workflow process.
- Automatic triggering of provisioning and deprovisioning requests based on HR events such as a change in job or position.
- Risk analysis during the user-provisioning process and alerts to the approver about the risk of provisioning the requested roles.
- Comprehensive audit trails and reports for micro-level audit details that help to improve internal and external audit activities.
- Automate periodic user access reviews and SoD reviews for a clean environment.
- Integration with leading Identity Management vendors to leverage the seamless provisioning and deprovisioning process along with business roles to speed up the onboarding and retiring processes from a systems perspective.

Benefits of implementing User Access Management and Access Risk Analysis

The business benefits of User Access Management are numerous. Implementing this tool along with the Access Risk Analysis tool brings even bigger and better benefits to your company. User Access Management provides the following benefits to the implemented environment and business team that is already leveraging SAP GRC:

- Embedded Access Risk Analysis in the provisioning process to prevent introducing access risk
- Reduced IT workload with automated request and approval process
- Reduced cost of compliance, risk, and audit activities

We've now reviewed the basic concepts, purpose, and benefits of User Access Management. Before we shift into the specifics of configuring User Access Management, let's look at the types of users, their functions, and roles.

7.1 Different User Roles in User Access Management

Understanding the various users, roles, and responsibilities with respect to User Access Management will help the implementation team, business team, and IT team design a more efficient solution and train the different user teams appropriately. The available user roles for User Access Management are:

- General Users
- Requestors
- Approvers
- Administrators
- Auditors

We'll wrap up this section with a review of user maintenance but let's first review each of these roles in further detail.

7.1.1 General Users

When you consider user provisioning in an IT landscape, generally all user data resides in one of the systems such as Active Directory, Identity Management (IDM) system, SAP Access Control, or any other plug-in SAP systems or non-SAP systems. All user details may or may not exist in any of the user data involved in provisioning. For some customer's, the situation demands some or all of these new users to *not* have any other authorization, but still they need to create their user requests to have proper IT access to perform their duties. This can be performed by the user if the user can access a generic URL (as discussed later in Section 7.3.5. In other words, users aren't required to be maintained in the SAP Access Control system to create new user access requests. In some customer implementations, SAP GRC access request creation is designed in a way that all users are required to log on to the SAP Access Control system to create a new request or change a request. If you choose the latter design, all users should be maintained in the SAP GRC system and should be assigned with the following privileges, that is, SAP standard roles SAP_GRC_FN_BASE and SAP_GRC_FN_BUSINESS_USER, or equivalent authorizations, to authorize or identify them as general users of the SAP Access Control system.

7.1.2 Requestors

Sometimes, this role is confused with general users. The simple variation is that a requestor is the person who creates a request on behalf of others, whereas a general user is the terminology used to represent the person whose user ID is in the access request.

Requestor role in User Access Management

In general, most requestors and users are the same, but, in some cases, they can be two different persons when it comes to new user request creation. Sometimes, this user type can be related to an HR team or help desk that mostly initiates new users in the IT landscape. Managers also sometimes come under this category. For example, some companies allow the helpdesk team to create requests for new employees or contractors. In this case, help-desk team members should have access to the SAP Access Control system as a normal user to create new requests for others. Requestors should have privileges to access the SAP GRC system, and the roles are the same as mentioned previously for general users.

7.1.3 Approvers

In SAP Access Control there are different types of users in the system, such as firefighter IDs, firefighter users, owners, controllers, and so on. In this tool, there are approvers such as role content approvers, role assignment approvers, risk approvers, reporting managers and so on.

Approval role in User Access Management

Normally, the manager position is maintained in Lightweight Directory Access Protocol (LDAP) such as Active Directory or any other user detail data source defined in SAP Access Control configuration to get this information along with user details for approvals in User Access Management. A few of the various approvers discussed earlier (firefighter users, owners, and controllers) along with the SAP standard authorization roles to perform their activity as respective approvers. A few of the owners are listed here, and, depending on your design, you can combine a few responsibilities of the approvers in a single role to provide wider responsibilities, or they can be maintained individually as in standard roles. Various approvers in the SAP Access Control system are role content owners, role assignment owners, risk owners, function approvers, control owners, mitigation owners, and various access approvers that will be maintained in various stages in the MSMP workflow (discussed in Section 7.4).

7.1.4 Administrators

SAP GRC system administrators are privileged to configure, maintain master data or change master data, and troubleshoot some issues in the system. This type of user has all of the privileges of the SAP Access Control system. The relevant standard role authorizations can be narrowed down to handle very specific administrative tasks alone. While providing wide access to the system, make sure that all changes carried out by anyone who has privilege to change master data in SAP Access Control are captured in the change log of the system to monitor and audit them later.

7.1.5 Auditors

Auditors are those who verify whether IT or system access are provided correctly, and they are in place to meet the governance and compliance enforced in the company to avoid any access risks. Either internal auditors who are part of the company or external auditors of the company use most of the reports from SAP Access Control tools. These reports are used by auditors to verify that access controls are handled within stipulated company policy and in compliance. Their presence isn't an influential role in the user-provisioning process, but they should be mentioned along with other users of the system. These users will get only the reporting authorization to execute various reports in the SAP Access Control system.

7.2 Maintenance of Users

User maintenance requirements

For most user types, maintenance requires you to create user IDs in the SAP Access Control system with relevant SAP role assignments from the user maintenance screen in Transaction SU01. All users in the system should have valid email addresses irrespective of their roles; this enables the system to send notification emails and password information after provisioning. The maintenance of approvers requires an additional step that is a part of the configuration process where role owners, risk owners, mitigation owners, and backup approvers need to be maintained in the SAP NetWeaver Business Client (NWBC) correspondingly.

Implementation considerations for User Access Management and user roles

In the overview section, we've reviewed more general tool concepts and various types of users and their responsibilities. Prior to configuring User Access Management, you should prepare and design your implementation work by gathering all of the requirement details on the various systems that need to be provisioned, including how the user information will be populated, how any request will be created by a requestor or user, the process flow on approval, the mitigation control and assignment provisioning processes, and so on. This type of preplanning of your configuration will lead to a successful implementation. In Section 7.2, we'll look into the configuration of User Access Management, and then in the latter part of this chapter, we'll take you through an end-to-end request creation, approval, and provisioning process.

7.3 User Access Management Configuration

In this section, we'll consider a simple provisioning scenario to configure and use User Access Management as a first step. Some of the below mentioned common activities you might configure as part of the Access Risk Analysis tool in the beginning. These may also be performed as a quick verification point, as highlighted here again to confirm that these setting are already done in the system.

Configuration assumptions prior to implementing User Access Management

Based on the assumptions that you're now familiar with common settings such as connectors, connector groups, and scenarios, we don't explain much about these configurations. At some point, you need to configure all of these connector-related settings for LDAP systems and any other newly introduced plug-in systems whenever there is a new system introduced in the SAP GRC landscape for provisioning. In this case, currently we go forward with the assumption that the SAP GRC system and plug-in SAP ERP system connectivity is already established during the Access Risk Analysis tool configuration

Step-by Step process for configuring User Access Management

The following configurations steps should be established based on available options for User Access Management:

- Basic Requirements
- Activation of BC Sets
- Configuration parameters
- Maintain Connector settings
- Maintain Data source configuration
- Maintaining number ranges
- Defining number ranges
- Maintain end user personalization
- Maintain provisioning settings
- Maintain user defaults
- Activate End user log in

This list of User Access Management configuration steps will be more helpful in your planning and when you are preparing your requirements systems and various other options that you're going to use as a part of configuration. Let's step in to this process further with a simple possible scenario.

7.3.1 Basic Requirements

The first three steps of the configuration process listed here are common to all SAP Access Control tools. Because we've already gone through the connector settings between the SAP GRC system and plug-in systems such as SAP ERP, we'll jump directly to the fourth step—activating BC Sets—and onward for our discussion. The basic requirements include the following configurations:

Basic requirements for a User Access Management configuration

- Assigning connectors to the connector groups and adding connectors to the required scenario
- Associating actions and assigning default connectors
- Activating BC Sets related to User Access Management
- Setting up LDAP connectivity
- Verifying configuration parameters
- Assigning roles and maintaining SAP Access Control owners
- Setting up the MSMP workflow and notification templates

In the next successive topics, we'll look into the details of how to configure those individual steps and what options you have to work with.

7.3.2 Activation of Business Configuration (BC) Sets

You need to activate the BC Sets in Table 7.1 to populate basic data in the SAP Access Control system to start User Access Management configuration in Transaction SCPR20.

BC Set	Description
GRAC_ACCESS_REQUEST_APPL_MAPPING	Application function mapping
GRAC_ACCESS_REQUEST_EUP	End user personalization
GRAC_ACCESS_REQUEST_PRIORITY	Access request priority
GRAC_ACCESS_REQUEST_REQ_TYPE	Access request type

Table 7.1 Basic Data BC Sets

Along with the BC Sets, you can activate required MSMP Workflow relevant BC Sets also. Activate one of the three BC Sets listed in Table 7.2.

BC Set	Description
GRC_MSMP_CONFIGURATION	For standard and sample configuration
GRC_MSMP_SAMPLE_CONF	For sample paths
GRC_MSMP_STD_CONF	For standard configuration

Table 7.2 MSMP-Relevant BC Sets

7.3.3 Configuration Parameters

You only need to configure User Access Management related configuration parameter groups such as workflow, LDAP, role selection, and role mapping. Figure 7.2 is populated with the most generic values filled in, but all of these values depend on what type of setting you're planning for provisioning and how it will be dealt with in your environment.

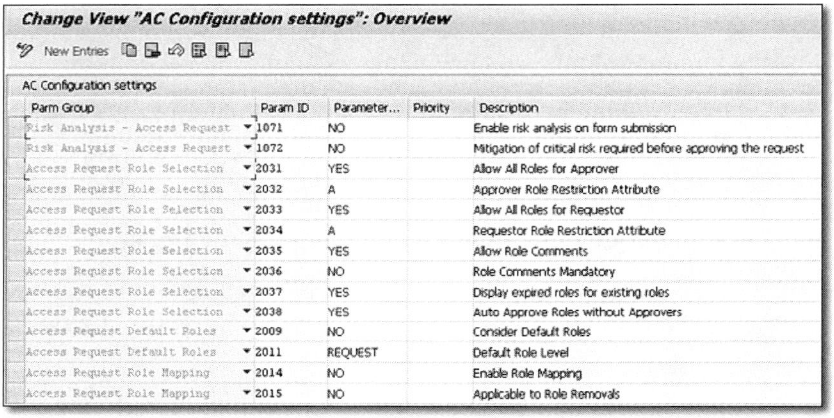

Change View "AC Configuration settings": Overview

New Entries

AC Configuration settings

Parm Group	Param ID	Parameter...	Priority	Description
Risk Analysis - Access Request	1071	NO		Enable risk analysis on form submission
Risk Analysis - Access Request	1072	NO		Mitigation of critical risk required before approving the request
Access Request Role Selection	2031	YES		Allow All Roles for Approver
Access Request Role Selection	2032	A		Approver Role Restriction Attribute
Access Request Role Selection	2033	YES		Allow All Roles for Requestor
Access Request Role Selection	2034	A		Requestor Role Restriction Attribute
Access Request Role Selection	2035	YES		Allow Role Comments
Access Request Role Selection	2036	NO		Role Comments Mandatory
Access Request Role Selection	2037	YES		Display expired roles for existing roles
Access Request Role Selection	2038	YES		Auto Approve Roles without Approvers
Access Request Default Roles	2009	NO		Consider Default Roles
Access Request Default Roles	2011	REQUEST		Default Role Level
Access Request Role Mapping	2014	NO		Enable Role Mapping
Access Request Role Mapping	2015	NO		Applicable to Role Removals

Figure 7.2 User Access Management-Related Configuration Parameter Values

Parameter groups

Each parameter groups has parameters available for you to define for your options. For example, when you choose RISK ANALYSIS – ACCESS REQUEST as a parameter group, you can choose parameters one by one from the PARAM ID column dropdown. If you select 1071 – ENABLE RISK ANALYSIS ON FORM SUBMISSION as the parameter to define, you have the option to choose YES. When you're creating a user request during the provisioning process, the risk analysis will be performed upon submitting the access request. When the next approver opens the access request, he will be able to see the risk analysis result related to the user and the user's profile along with newly requested roles. If you choose NO, then the risk analysis won't be completed.

Let's move on to the next important configuration setting to see how User Access Management connects to various systems via remote function call (RFC) connectors for the purpose of extracting data, provisioning, using a user data source, and so on.

7.3.4 Maintain Connector Settings

The user provisioning process in most customer environments starts with any one of three systems—SAP HR system, LDAP, or Identity Management systems—as a user data source. Let's first look at a very common environment such as how LDAP can be connected to the SAP Access Control system to provide user data during the user request process. This is an optional step because, as we've mentioned, the user data source can be LDAP, IDM, SAP HR, the SAP GRC system itself, or a combination of those systems. Depending on the type of connectivity, you need to set this up in the SAP Access Control system for connector settings.

> **Note**
>
> Remember that the integration scenario for provisioning is already set up. This is a mandatory configuration in the SAP Access Control system; all of the four integration scenarios need to be defined irrespective of their usage, as we mentioned in Chapter 3. As a part of the integration scenario, you might have completed a scenario and subscenario configuration with respective connectors. Similarly, all connectors, connector groups, and connection types should have been maintained. If the system, such as LDAP or IDM, isn't defined earlier in the landscape, then you should perform the connector settings now. Also, remember that the connection type can be different for LDAP and for IDM.

LDAP Connector Mapping

Creating LDAP connection and mapping properly is an important step in most of the user landscape. Most of the companies uses LDAP as primary source of initial user data maintenance system. In User Access Management configuration you need to follow these steps to create and map fields with LDAP:

Step-by-step for creating and mapping fields with LDAP

1. Create an RFC connection to the LDAP system from Transaction SM59 with connection type T.
2. After the RFC connection is established, use Transaction LDAP to configure your LDAP server.

3. Use Transaction LDAPMAP to set up the field mapping between the LDAP system and the SAPGRC system. This can be achieved from change mode in Transaction LDAPMAP and by pressing F6 (Proposal) to get the default mapping.
4. Use any existing old mapping XML file that can be loaded to map these fields accordingly. Figure 7.3 shows the LDAP field mapping to provisioning system fields for user details.

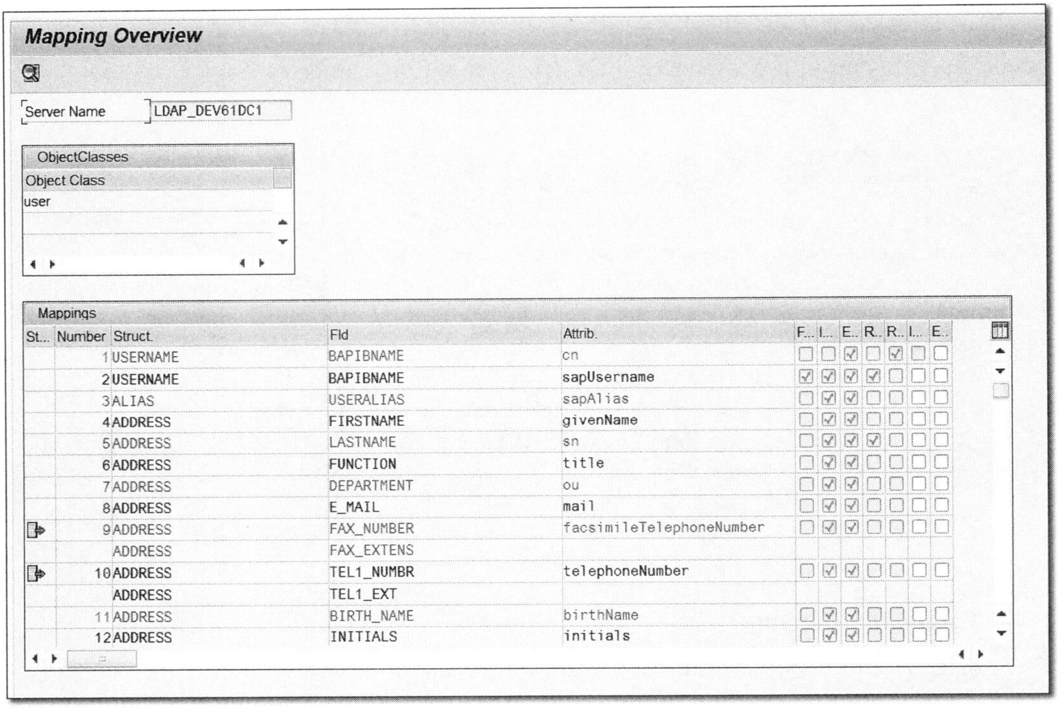

Figure 7.3 LDAP Field Mapping to Provisioning System Fields

Assign Attributes to Connector

As a part of the attribute assignment, the LDAP target connector needs to have GROUP PATH defined with respective attribute values. If the connector type is SAP, maintain some of the attributes such as PATH ID, as shown in Figure 7.4, which is meant to find a manager. This field is similar to the GROUP PATH attribute in LDAP to find and route mails to the AGENT manager. You need to select the suitable value from the dropdown menu—either A002 or B012—that helps determine the position to manager relationship in your environment. If you're not sure which one to use, check with the HR consultant in your company. If you plan to use password self-service (PSS) in your environment, then select the PSS indicator as well. We will discuss password self service in Section 7.6.

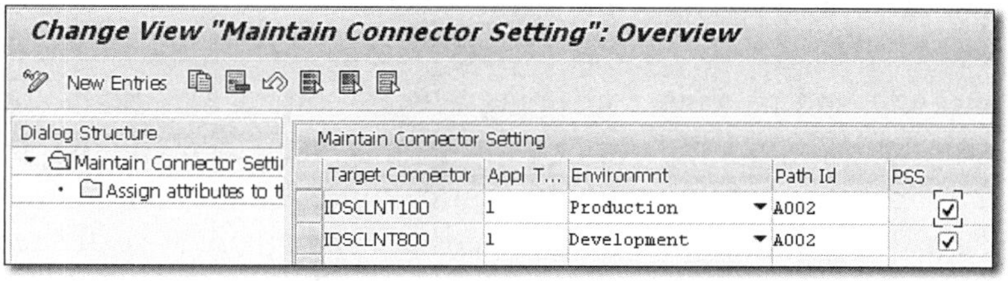

Figure 7.4 Maintain Connector Environment with Password Self-Service

Maintain Mapping for Actions and Connector Groups

In this customizing activity, connectors are grouped by application type, and these groups are assigned individually with five different actions that are related to SAP Access Control activities listed in the ACTION column shown in Figure 7.5. Select and save the default connector per group if you want to list that in the actual usage.

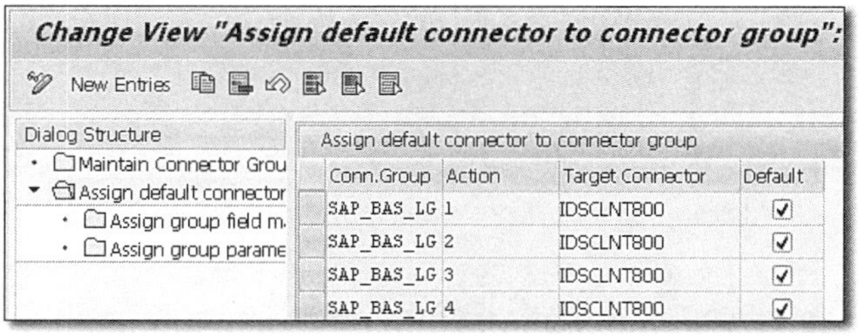

Figure 7.5 Default Connector Assignment to Connector Group

You need to assign all of the ACTIONS that you plan to use in the system for all connectors in the CONN.GROUP. As shown in Figure 7.5, all planned actions are defined along with the default connector. The following ACTIONS are available:

Actions available for mapping to connectors in Users Access Management

- 0001 Role Generation
- 0002 Role Risk Analysis
- 0003 Authorization Maintenance
- 0004 Provisioning
- 0005 HR Triggers

SAP application types don't require you to maintain field and parameter mapping, but LDAP does. Figures 7.6 and Figure 7.7 show the details of field mapping and parameter mapping between the LDAP system and the SAP Access Control system. This mapping is vital when you use the user data source or user detail data source. Information such as user name, email ID, manager, department, position, and more are extracted and shown in the initial screen of the user access request. Enter "LDAP" in the CONNECTOR GROUP field and "4" in the CONNECTOR ACTION field.

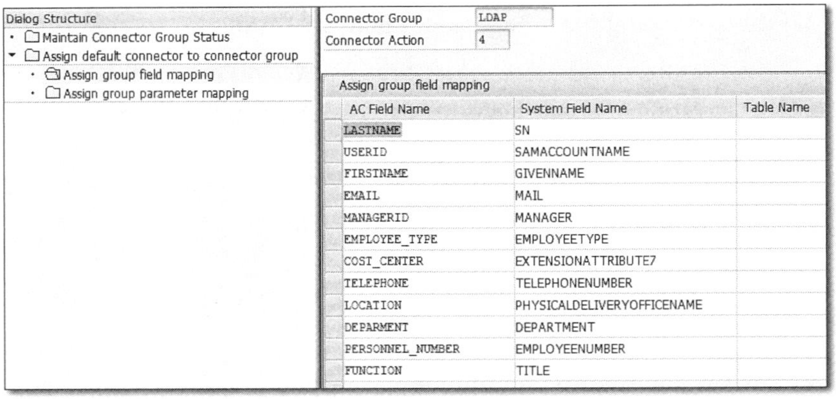

Figure 7.6 Provisioning Field Mapping for LDAP Connector

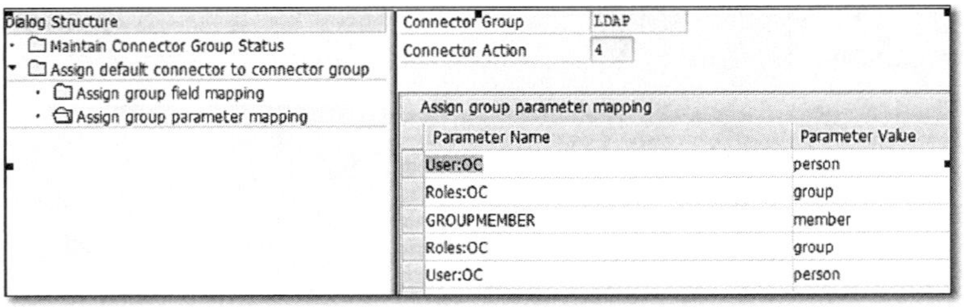

Figure 7.7 Provisioning Parameter Mapping for LDAP Connector

7.3.5 Maintain Data Sources Configuration

The data source configuration setting that is used in User Access Management can be more dynamic based on your environment and how you want to get user information in user request form. This is totally dependent on your environment and processes.

Improving access to user information

To get the user information in a more flexible way and to get better details, SAP provides options to get user data either from one source or from multiple sources. When you plan for multiple sources, the option is provided to put them in a sequence to perform a sequential search until the query hits a successful result to show in the request. You need to maintain four different information items related to the data source such as user search data source, user detail data source, user authentication data source, and end user verification. The first link related to user search data source is to find the user. Once you've configured search data source, this information can be validated by searching a new user from the access request screen. The most probable hit can be user ID from IDM, LDAP, SAP HR data, or Transaction SU01 data. As we explained earlier, the option to search sequentially from multiple data sources is the most flexible options for you to retrieve the unique user IDs by maintaining different connectors for each data source, and then assigning the appropriate sequences (see Figure 7.8).

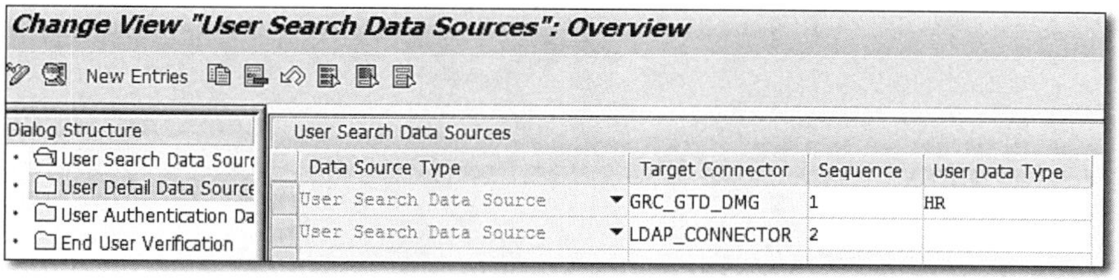

Figure 7.8 User Search Data Sources: Detail Data Source Setting

User detail configuration

Similarly, the next configuration for User Detail Data Source can be configured. This configuration is related to user details such as user email, department, position, and user manager details. This configuration also has similar options, as we mentioned in User Search Data Source, multiple connectors can be maintained with sequence numbers to search and get values from these connectors.

User authentication configuration

In the next configuration step, USER AUTHENTICATION DATA SOURCE is used for authenticating requestor identities for their access to create requests from the SAP Access Control system. User authentication can also be maintained with multiple connectors with sequence numbers to authenticate the end user (see Figure 7.9). If the user information is confirmed on one system, it's considered as authenticated for all systems; further confirmation on other systems isn't needed.

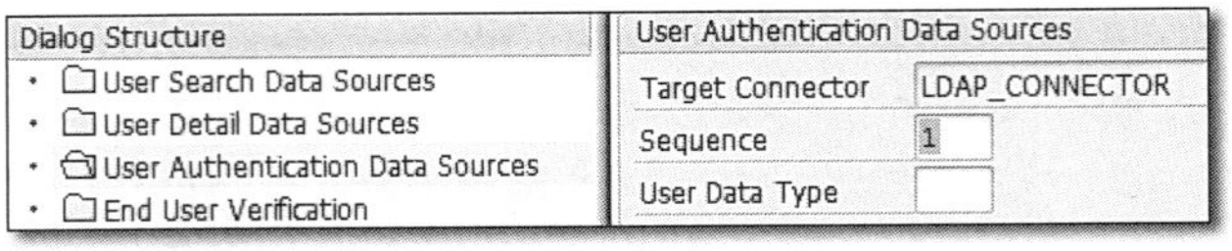

Figure 7.9 Maintenance Configuration of User Authentication Data Sources

For end users, SAP Access Control uses the connectors and authentication information to connect to the data sources and confirm the user IDs and passwords that the requestors use during end-user logon. This only applies to end users because they can also exist in remote systems, such as LDAP. The following is the URL for end users and requestors that exist on non-SAP GRC systems: *http<s>://<server>:<port>/sap/bc/webdynpro/sap/grac_uibb_end_user_login.*

You must maintain the entry and authorizations or the default user for this application logon at Transaction SICF. The details are outlined in Section 7.2.11 at the end of configuration process. For SAP HR authentication, you can use the personnel number as an alternative to the user ID, and you can use the Social Security number as an alternative for the password.

The last setting in user data source setting is END USER VERIFICATION, and this authentication is used if your environment uses Single Sign-On (SSO) as shown in Figure 7.10. This value should be set to 'NO'; if authentication is needed, then the PASSWORD/SSN field isn't displayed, and only the USER ID/PERSONNEL NUMBER is displayed on the login screen. The user can start using User Access Management by simply clicking on the Enter key.

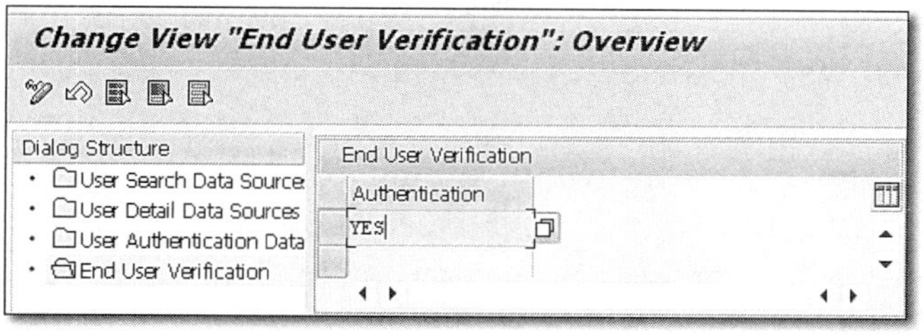

Figure 7.10 End-User Verification Related to Single Sign-On

7.3.6 Define Request Type

Activate the request types by clicking the ACTIVE checkbox, and then assign actions to the request types. SAP delivers several standard request types as part of BC Set activation, and you can maintain any new request types and connected actions as shown in Figure 7.11.

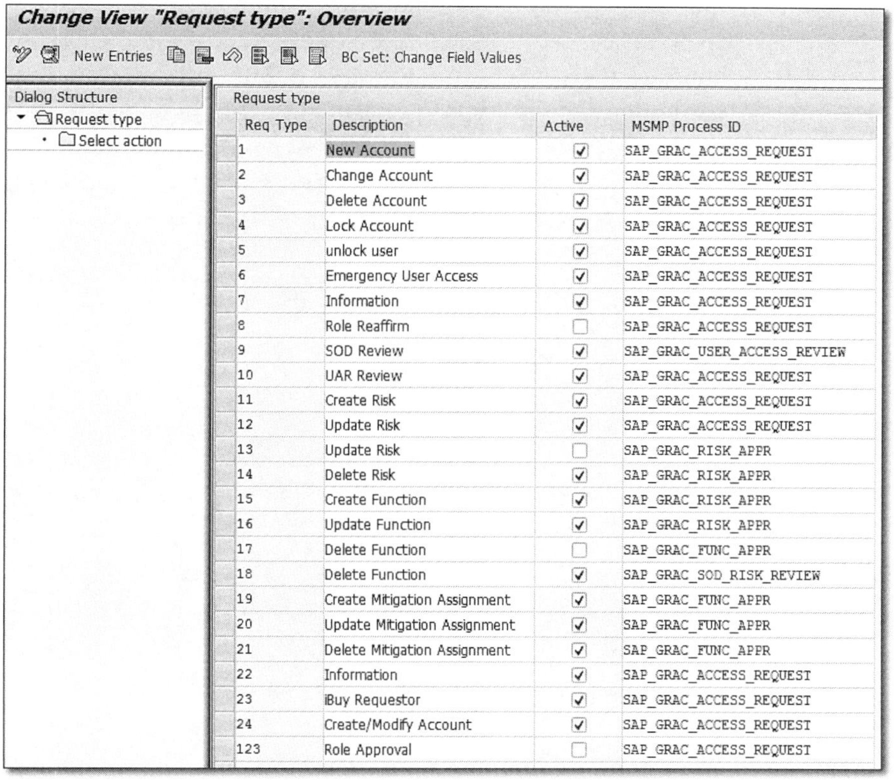

Req Type	Description	Active	MSMP Process ID
1	New Account	☑	SAP_GRAC_ACCESS_REQUEST
2	Change Account	☑	SAP_GRAC_ACCESS_REQUEST
3	Delete Account	☑	SAP_GRAC_ACCESS_REQUEST
4	Lock Account	☑	SAP_GRAC_ACCESS_REQUEST
5	unlock user	☑	SAP_GRAC_ACCESS_REQUEST
6	Emergency User Access	☑	SAP_GRAC_ACCESS_REQUEST
7	Information	☑	SAP_GRAC_ACCESS_REQUEST
8	Role Reaffirm	☐	SAP_GRAC_ACCESS_REQUEST
9	SOD Review	☑	SAP_GRAC_USER_ACCESS_REVIEW
10	UAR Review	☑	SAP_GRAC_ACCESS_REQUEST
11	Create Risk	☑	SAP_GRAC_ACCESS_REQUEST
12	Update Risk	☑	SAP_GRAC_ACCESS_REQUEST
13	Update Risk	☐	SAP_GRAC_RISK_APPR
14	Delete Risk	☑	SAP_GRAC_RISK_APPR
15	Create Function	☑	SAP_GRAC_RISK_APPR
16	Update Function	☑	SAP_GRAC_RISK_APPR
17	Delete Function	☐	SAP_GRAC_FUNC_APPR
18	Delete Function	☑	SAP_GRAC_SOD_RISK_REVIEW
19	Create Mitigation Assignment	☑	SAP_GRAC_FUNC_APPR
20	Update Mitigation Assignment	☑	SAP_GRAC_FUNC_APPR
21	Delete Mitigation Assignment	☑	SAP_GRAC_FUNC_APPR
22	Information	☑	SAP_GRAC_ACCESS_REQUEST
23	iBuy Requestor	☑	SAP_GRAC_ACCESS_REQUEST
24	Create/Modify Account	☑	SAP_GRAC_ACCESS_REQUEST
123	Role Approval	☐	SAP_GRAC_ACCESS_REQUEST

Figure 7.11 Request Types, Actions, and MSMP Process Relationships

MSMP Workflow Processes and request types

You also need to confirm that you've maintained the MSMP workflow process associated with the request type. Also you must maintain the relevant MSMP workflow process that is appropriate for your newly created request type. In the next step, you can select actions such as delete user, lock user, and change user, as necessary for your request type. In this way, the user provisioning action and request type are tied directly to the corresponding MSMP workflow. Some of the request types are meant for risk or function maintenance, which is related to the Access Risk Analysis tool, and request type Superuser Access is meant for requesting access to firefighter IDs.

7.3.7 Maintain Number Range Intervals for Provisioning Requests

Maintaining number ranges is one of the required activities because without maintaining number ranges, you can't create any type of request. To do so, access Transaction SPRO, and follow the menu path, SAP Reference IMG • Governance, Risk and Compliance • Access Control • User Provisioning • Maintain Number Range Intervals for Provisioning Requests. You can also use Transaction SNRO to maintain the number range intervals for the object GRACREQNO, which is meant for user access requests (see Figure 7.12).

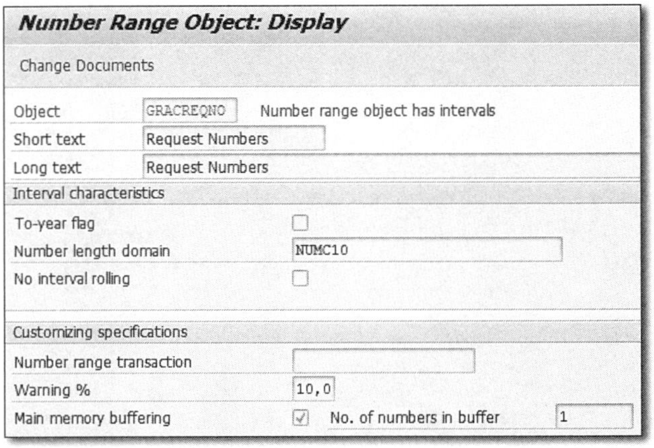

Figure 7.12 Number Range Maintenance

7.3.8 Define Number Range for Provisioning Requests

In this configuration section, you can maintain more than a set of internal number ranges, which means the numbers will be provided automatically in sequence by the application during the request creation. Although there is an option to maintain multiple number ranges, currently only one number range can be active at any point in time, which is used by the application to assign sequential internal numbers to all type of provisioning requests (see Figure 7.13).

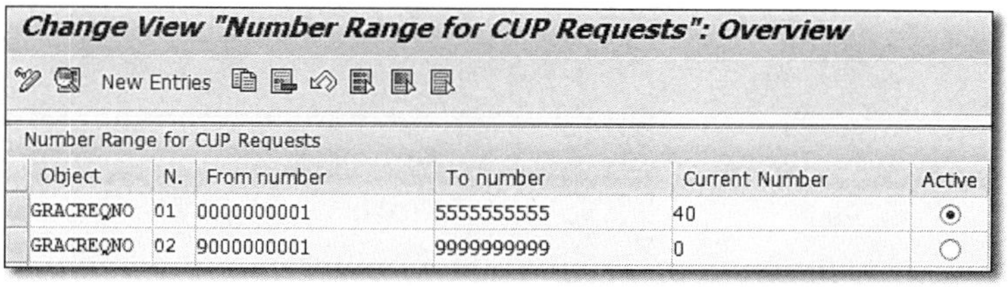
Change View "Number Range for CUP Requests": Overview

New Entries

Number Range for CUP Requests

Object	N.	From number	To number	Current Number	Active
GRACREQNO	01	0000000001	5555555555	40	◉
GRACREQNO	02	9000000001	9999999999	0	○

Figure 7.13 Number Range Maintenance

7.3.9 Maintain End User Personalization

To start this configuration, execute Transaction SPRO, and follow the menu path, CUSTOMIZING IMPLEMENTATION GUIDE • GOVERNANCE, RISK AND COMPLIANCE • ACCESS CONTROL • USER PROVISIONING • MAINTAIN ENDUSER PERSONALIZATION. The initial screen shows a default template as EUP ID "999" along with EUP CONFIGURATION NAME and DESCRIPTION. As a next step, select the child level folder MAINTAIN EUP FIELDS (see Figure 7.14).

BC Set Activation with End User Personalization data

This End User Personalization (EUP) data is populated by activation of one of the BC Sets. Instead of using this default EUP, you can create a new template with the necessary field settings. The MANDATORY, EDITABLE, AND VISIBLE columns can be set to YES or NO, the EDITABLE column can have additional information, such as YES, IF DATA IS MISSING. Default values such as LANGUAGE, USER TYPE, or DATE FORMAT can also be maintained here. All of these fields are part of the requestor initial screen that defines the behavior of the fields and the pushbuttons on the REQUEST ACCESS screen.

Templates for end user personalization

Multiple templates can be maintained, and only one can be set as defaulted in the system. Different options on choosing templates are possible when the requestor uses additional options while creating requests such as model user.

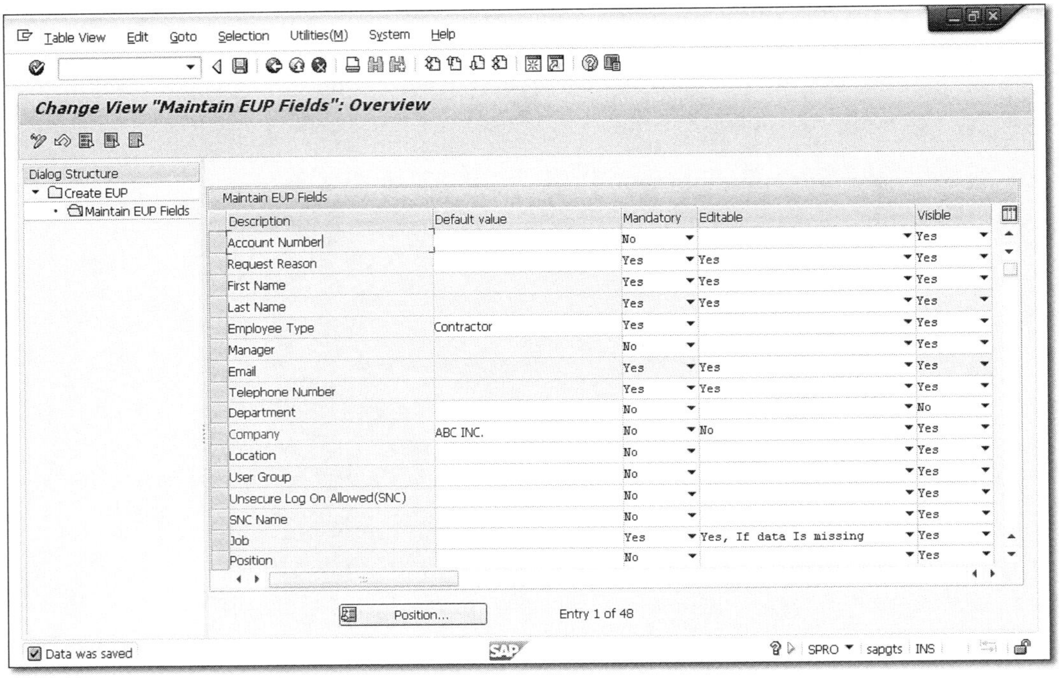

Figure 7.14 End User Personalization Template Configuration

Template based provisioning

Based on EUP, the initial screen's fields and tabs with their settings are shown in Figure 7.15. If your environment demands or you plan to provide more than one end user form for requests, this can be created and used in template-based provisioning. This template-based provisioning is very useful when you plan to separate different types of employees who might require different levels of data; for example, contractors may only need to fill in a few mandatory fields, whereas a full-time employee's details are already in the HR master or the LDAP system, which auto-populates the access request form. In this case, the custom-defined EUP form created for contractors can be set with a minimalist approach, which ultimately reduces the user input time. Eventually, this irons out new employee or contractor questions while they create new access requests and leads to a better and more efficient way to handle the provisioning process.

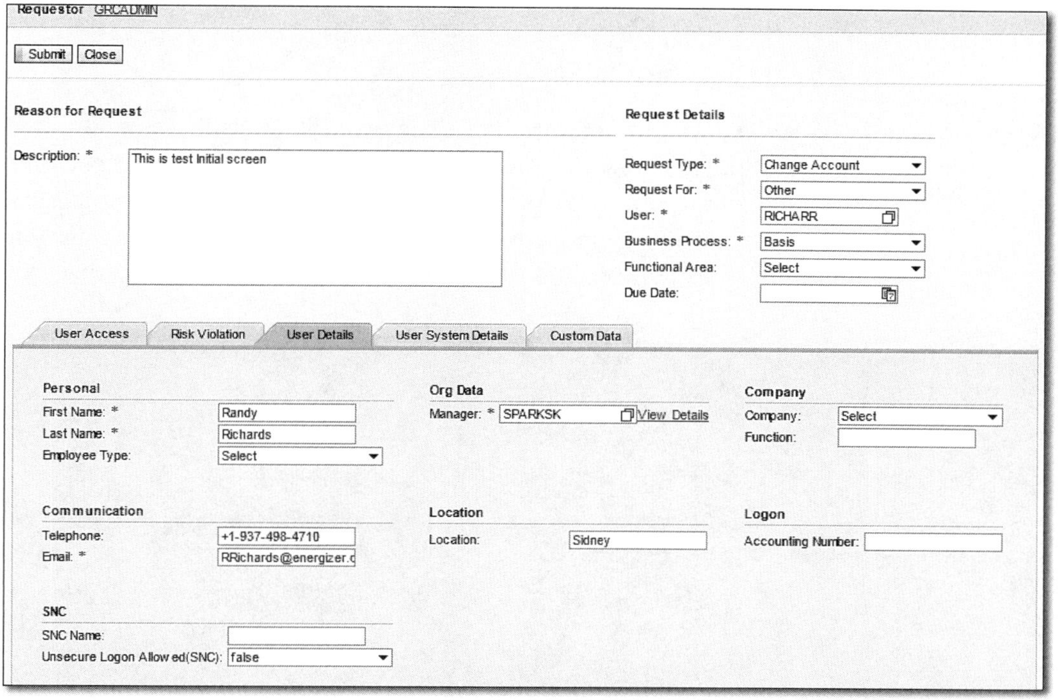

Figure 7.15 Initial Requestor Screen

7.3.10 Maintain Provisioning Settings

In this configuration step, you maintain global and system-specific provisioning settings. These settings impact the provisioning process flow at the end of user request approvals, and they should be provisioned in the plug-in system as direct or indirect provisioning, as individual role or request level, sending password via email, password expiration, and so on. Direct provisioning is a typical user creation process used in the SAP user master record by using Transaction SU01.

Indirect provisioning

Indirect provisioning is a request sent to the SAP HR system, and then the SAP HR system carries out the provisioning based on the job or position. You must use this method if you assign security roles based on the user's position in the HR organization. When you use indirect provisioning, you should configure by HR object types such as position based, organization type based, or job based, depending on your current security requirements. If this is the first time you plan to use indirect provisioning, then discuss this with HR and the security team on the possibilities that the HR object makes sense for your environment.

Use of both direct and indirect provisioning

In some cases, the customer environment demands to use both direct and indirect provisioning options, which is well handled in User Access Management. During this process, User Access Management application first uses indirect provisioning, and, if this fails, then the application uses direct provisioning. Provisioning settings are shown in Figure 7.16.

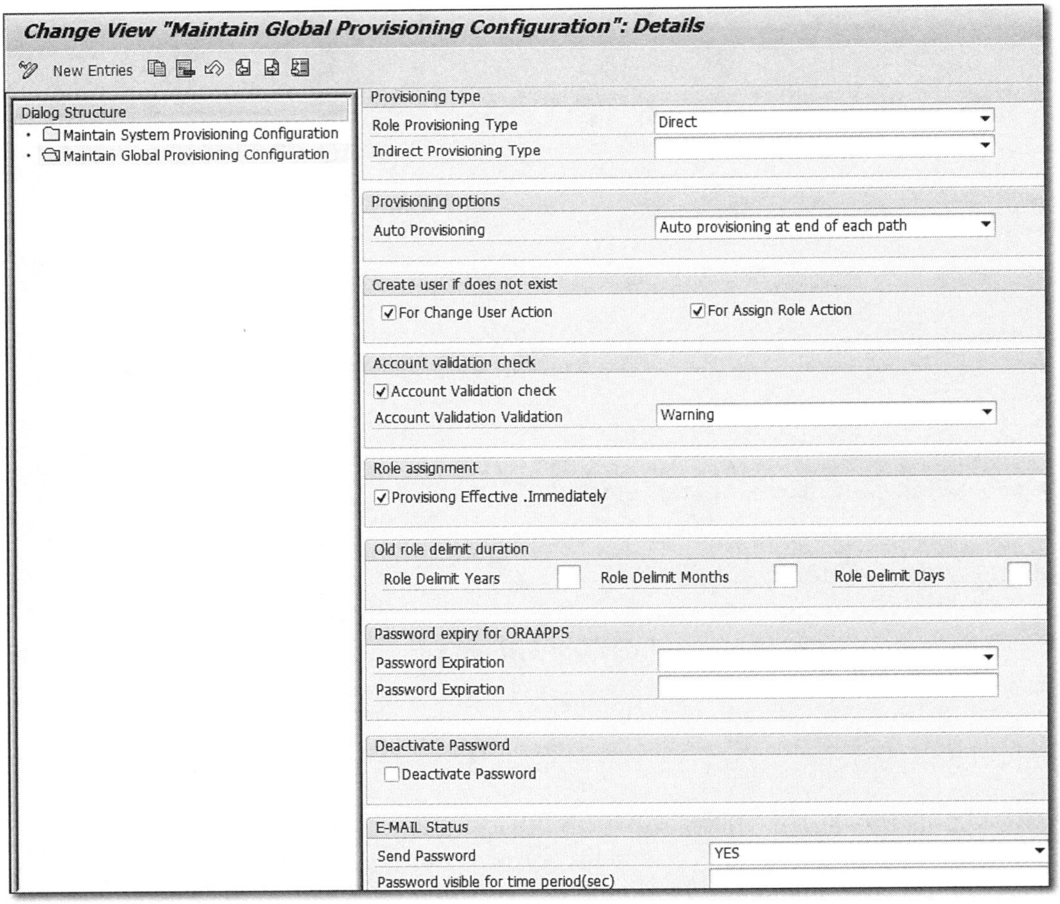

Figure 7.16 Global Provisioning Setting

System-specific provisioning

Some characteristics in provisioning enable you to maintain a system-specific setting separately from the global setting as shown in Figure 7.17. For example, a password can be deactivated to a specific system, an auto-provisioning option can be used, and so on. If you set to deactivate passwords here, but you've enabled PSS for the connector in the MAINTAIN CONNECTOR SETTING customizing activity, when the user tries to use PSS, the application displays a message indicating the connector isn't valid for password activation because of contradicting actions.

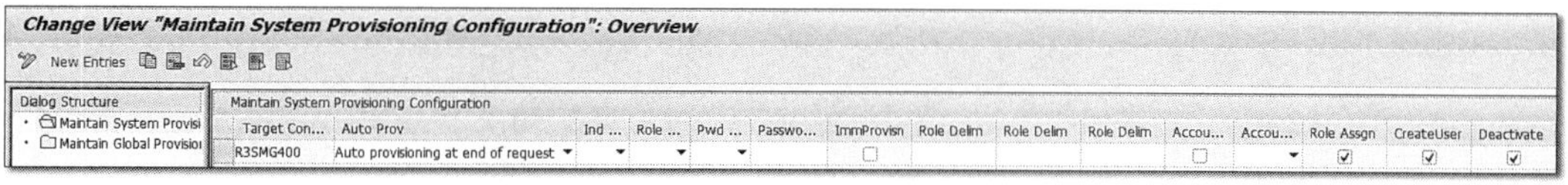

Figure 7.17 System-Specific Provisioning Setting

By default, user provisioning is done automatically by User Access Management. If you plan not to use auto-provisioning in your landscape, then you should select the NO PROVISIONING option from the AUTO PROVISIONING input field. Auto-provisioning is available for SAP systems and non-SAP systems only via plug-ins that are part of the SAP GRC component installed in the target systems. If your environment uses any systems based on Service Provisioning Markup Language (SPML), such as LDAP, it doesn't require plug-ins for auto-provisioning

7.3.11 Maintain User Defaults

In this setting, you need to assign user defaults that are needed for user creation in the SAP plug-in system, such as SAP ERP or any other SAP systems, for new users when they are created as part of provisioning. This includes logon language, date format, printer, and so on, along with user groups and parameter IDs that are required as user maintenance in Transaction SU01. User default maintenance is system-specific data that is maintained against an individual connector or target system.

7.3.12 Activate End User Logon

Activate the END USER LOGON screen for user provisioning, which is the last user provisioning configuration task. By executing this 'END USER

LOGON' link from Transaction SPRO, the maintain web service Transaction SICF and Web Dynpro link GRAC_UIBB_END_USER_LOGIN are displayed on the initial screen. The END USER LOGON screen allows users who don't have access to the SAP Access Control application to submit requests for access. GRAC_UIBB_END_USER_LOGIN is a Web Dynpro service that provides the option to log in via URL (discussed in Section 7.2.4). If you double-click this service, you are taken to the CREATE/CHANGE A SERVICE screen as shown in Figure 7.18. Select the LOGON DATA tab from this screen. To activate the automated log on procedure, you need to maintain the suitable logon procedure for logon in your landscape and its logon credentials if necessary.

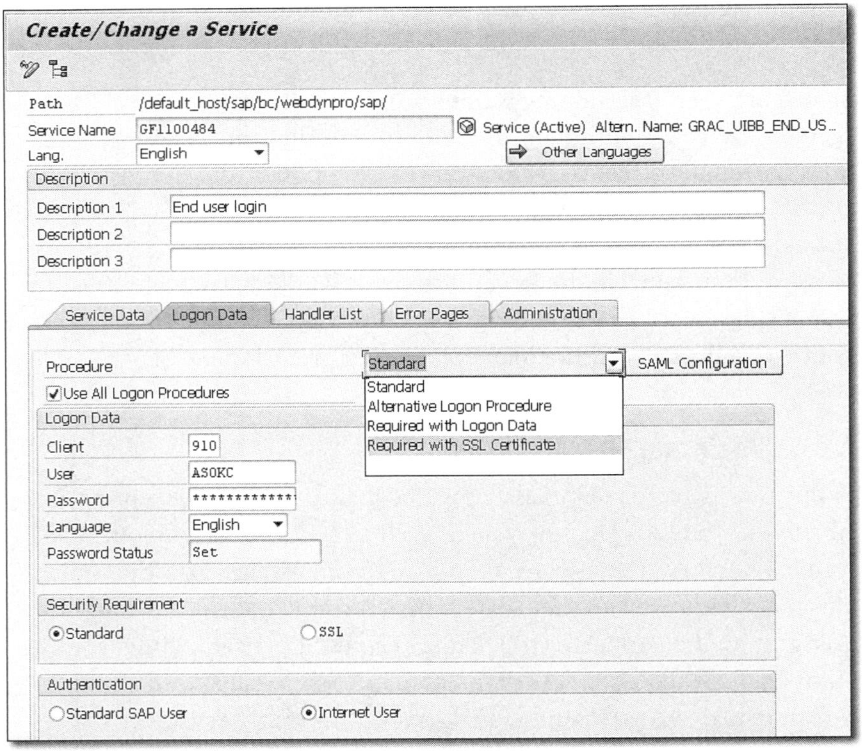

Figure 7.18 Multiple Logon Procedures to Enable End User Logons

Now that you've completed the basic configuration of User Access Management, the next step is to configure the MSMP workflow for the access request process. This is technically defined as a SAP_GRAC_AR process ID. We've provided detailed MSMP workflow maintenance and how to deal with your complex scenario for provisioning approval process and various MSMP processes in the next chapter. You may refer to Chapter 8 for step-by-step setup, combining the Business Rule Framework (BRF+), and other notification changes in detail.

7.4 Configure the MSMP Workflow

The Multi-stage Multi-path (MSMP) workflow is the key engine that moves the request from one stage to the next stage within the ABAP workflow engine. We'll start with a simple use case of the MSMP workflow for the user access request process configuration in this section.

Configuration process for MSMP workflow

To start configuring MSMP, go to Transaction SPRO, and follow the menu path, GOVERNANCE, RISK AND COMPLIANCE • ACCESS CONTROL • WORKFLOW FOR ACCESS CONTROL • MAINTAIN MSMP WORKFLOWS. Alternatively, you can execute Transaction GRFNMW_CONFIGURE_WD to open the MSMP application setup in a browser window. The initial screen shows all of the workflow processes with the global setting.

You might notice at the top of the screen that there are small boxes numbered 1 to 7. These correspond to the MSMP workflow configuration steps as listed here:

1. PROCESS GLOBAL SETTINGS
2. MAINTAIN RULES
3. MAINTAIN AGENTS
4. VARIABLES & TEMPLATES
5. MAINTAIN PATHS
6. MAINTAIN ROUTE MAPPING
7. GENERATE VERSIONS

At every step, you may need to configure or select some of the information relevant to your intended workflow process. It's not mandatory to complete all of the steps because the BC Set activation from steps 1 to 4 might have already prefilled some default options. You may consider modifying this if there is any change required to deal with your workflow regarding custom agents or custom variables.

Step 1: Process Global Settings

As a first step from the initial screen, select SAP_GRAC_ACCESS_REQUEST, and click on DISPLAY/CHANGE. It's a little tricky in this screen that you can identify the display or change mode by viewing the status of the ENABLE ESCALATION checkbox in this screen, under PROCESS GLOBAL SETTINGS. Click the ADD or MODIFY button in the NOTIFICATION SETTINGS area as highlighted in Figure 7.19. This global setting is required for the first two workflow processes only, and the rest may not require this NOTIFICATION SETTINGS because they send notification to pass information to the user or requestor about access request upon submission of the request, at the start of the workflow, and completion of request at the end of the workflow.

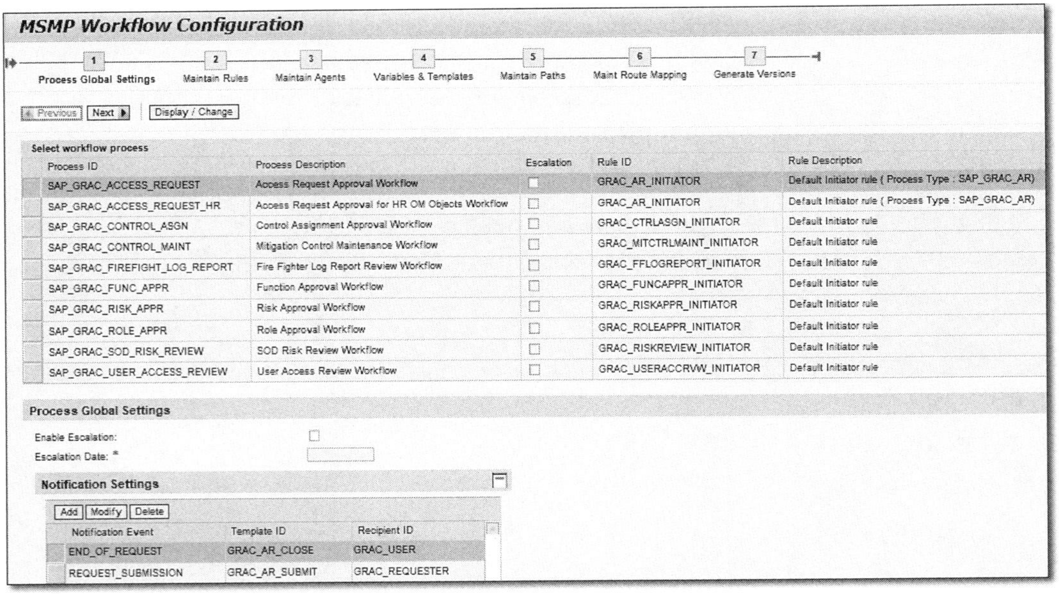

Figure 7.19 MSMP Initial Screen

Step 2: Maintain rules

After you've maintained the respective notification settings of REQUEST_SUBMISSION and END_OF_REQUEST with the appropriate template and recipients, click on the NEXT button to move to the next step—MAINTAIN RULES. This is a guided procedure, and you may jump between different steps after you're familiar with this MSMP workflow configuration. In this step, the available rules for the selected process are shown in Figure 7.20. These are the default rules for different rule types such as agent rules, initiator rules, notification rules, and so on. You need to maintain the global rules for the initiator and for notification. You can have one initiator per process.

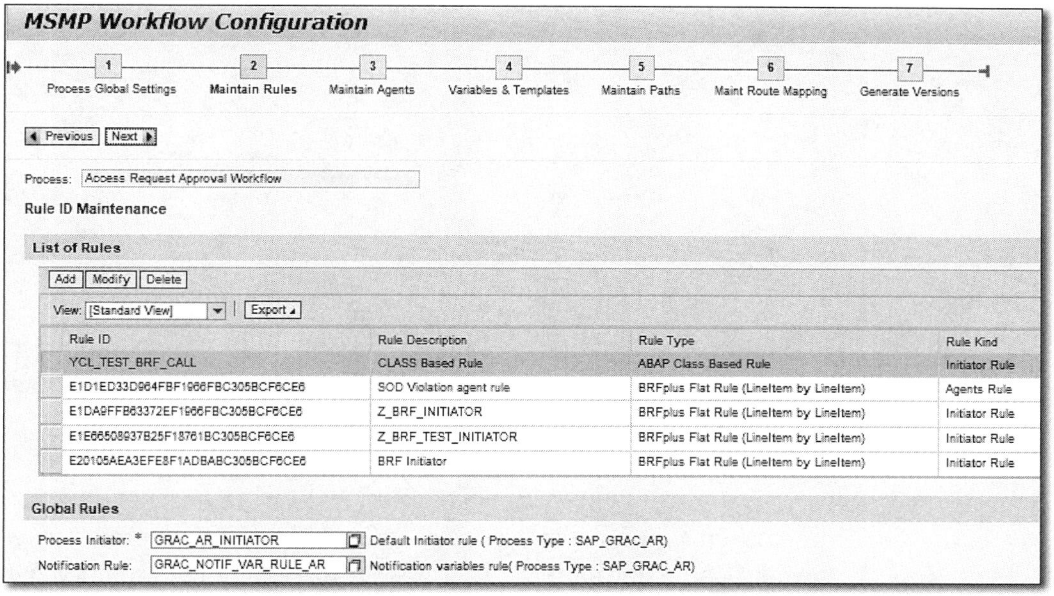

Figure 7.20 Maintain Rules

Steps 3, 4, and 5: Maintain Agents, Variables & Templates, and Maintain Paths

The next step—MAINTAIN AGENTS—is a more generic setting, and those who are approvers are actually defined in every stage and maintained in step 5—MAINTAIN PATHS. The next step is VARIABLES & TEMPLATES, which is used in notifications to various uses of User Access Management. The two steps—MAINTAIN AGENTS (step 3) and VARIABLES & TEMPLATES (step 4)—can be used with default SAP-provided values. In MAINTAIN PATHS (step 5), for the MSMP workflow configuration, you maintain the workflow path and define various stages as shown in Figure 7.21.

Assigning approvers or agents to the MSMP Workflow

Approvers or agents are assigned to these stages with the functions or tasks that need to be performed at every stage. You also define here what type of notification is sent to whom.

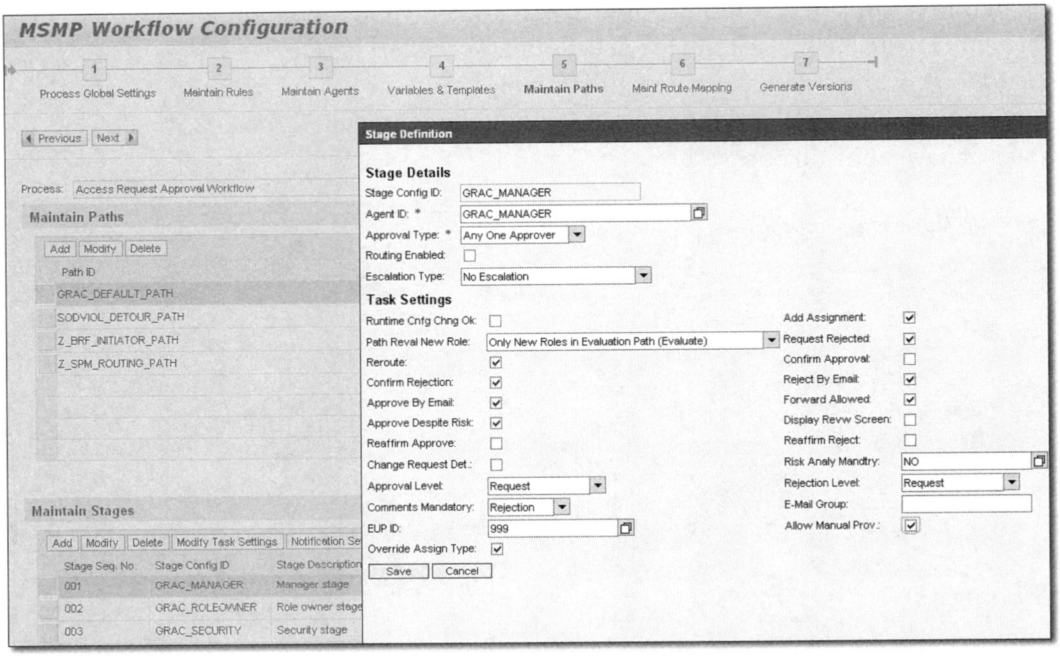

Figure 7.21 Maintain Path and Stage with Agents and Task Settings

After you maintain how the stage-specific configuration, approval, email sending, and so on are set, make sure that you've also maintained values for every stage with notification settings that include the following events:

- New work item
- Approved

Step 6 and Step 7: Maintain Route Mapping and Generate Version

Now that you've completed five steps in the MSMP workflow, the sixth step is Maintain Route Mapping, where you need to maintain RuleID, Path ID, and Rule Result Value mapped correctly. Now you've completed the MSMP workflow process configuration, so the next step is step 7, Generate Version. In this step, first execute Save and Simulate. This configuration won't be generated if there are errors in the MSMP workflow, and you need to rectify any of those before proceeding further. Activate the successfully generated MSMP configuration, and, at this point, you can assign it to a new transport request or existing transport request to transport these configurations to the production system.

Now you've fully completed all User Access Management tool configurations that are needed to create user requests, approvals in the system, and provisions to SAP ERP or any other SAP plug-in systems. The following list identifies given information that can be used as a quick checklist to verify that you've completed all tasks that are required to start creating request:

Verification checklist for access request creation and the MSMP workflow

- Connectors are defined.
- Connectors are assigned to scenarios.
- Data sources are configured.
- User search and details data source is configured and working.
- EUP is configured correctly for the request fields.
- Number range is defined.
- End user login service is enabled (for end users/non-SAP GRC users).
- Required sync jobs are run.
- Workflow is configured properly.
- Roles are imported into SAP Enterprise Risk Management (ERM).

Approver users are imported in the SAP GRC box—only users who have accounts in the SAP GRC box can approve workflow requests. In the past section, we worked on how to configure User Access Management and MSMP workflow to activate access request creation. With that, the User Access Management configuration is completed. In the next section, we'll go through the user provisioning process, including how to create user requests and how approvers review and approve the request using the User Access Management tool.

7.5 Process Details: Change/Create Access Request

As we discussed in Section 7.1, there are different kinds of users that will be using User Access Management with various authorization levels to perform a variety of functions. Now that we've properly configured the system, let's look at the change/create access request process details.

Request creation by user

First, we'll walk through the footsteps of request creation by user. A user can access the requesting page or landing page by directly clicking the link provided as part of the end user login implementation as mentioned in an earlier section. Alternatively, a user can log on to the SAP GRC system via regular SAPGUI and execute Transaction NWBC, or directly access SAP NetWeaver Business Client (NWBC) to access the landing page in the SAP Access Control system. From this initial page, you can click on the Access Request link to open the request creation page. This request page opens with fields and tabs that are defined on your EUP configuration and assuming you used the default 999 EUP template. Depending on your configuration and LDAP field mapping, some or most of the fields will be populated after you enter the User ID in the initial screen as shown earlier in Figure 7.15.

Optional modes for end users to create requests

Other than this access request link, three other optional modes are available for end users to create requests (activate all or some of them depending on your company needs):

- **Template-based requests**
  - Administrators need to define a template.
  - Different EUP settings can be used and thus multiple templates can be defined.
  - End users and requestors can use the template to create requests.
- **Copy requests**
  - Use the existing request number as reference.
  - Creating the user request is faster and most of the values are filled based on the selected request number.
- **Model users**
  - Most environments adopt this because if any new user comes as a replacement or a new user with the same job uses this function to create a new request, this is the most feasible and efficient way to create the new access request.
  - This link is used to request similar access by referencing any other user's access.

We've seen different kinds of request creation in this section, so next let's check through some necessary steps to view the roles in the requesting process. Chapter 6 discussed role maintenance and role loading in detail.

7.5.1 Role Availability for Provisioning

In this section, we'll look at the core steps needed to make sure the roles are available in the access request creation process. To ensure that you can see the role availability, follow these steps:

1. Making role availability visible. Make sure the role exists in the plug-in system with the respective connector name.
2. Complete the role synchronization job to bring all roles and their authorizations from the plug-in system to the SAP Access Control system.
3. Set ROLE STATUS to PRODUCTION in the SAP Access Control system's NetWeaver Business client frontend. Choose ACCESS MANAGEMENT • ROLE MANAGEMENT • ROLE MAINTENANCE, enter the role name, click on the ADDITIONAL DETAILS subscreen, and set the STATUS as PRODUCTION here.
4. In that same subscreen, set the PROVISIONING ALLOWED option to YES.
5. Check the role validity and also whether the role owner is defined.

Access request role extraction

By performing these steps, you have the option to extract the role during access request creation. Apart from this, there are two options in configuration to restrict the roles shown in the request screen based on the first screen selection. The attributes involved are FUNCTION and BUSINESS PROCESS. This option to limit roles by function or business process needs to be set in SAP Access Control configuration. The restriction of roles listing in the drop-down menu will be based on the function and/or business process that is entered in the initial screen of the user access request form.

SAP Access Control 10.1 functionality

The new SAP Access Control version 10.1 comes with a separate set of configuration to control the role list by manipulating and configuring various role attributes. It's very useful when you plan to provide the user with a less complex request creation environment. In the next steps, we'll go through the full cycle of the access request process from creation to provisioning, including the remediation process.

7.5.2 Access Request Process Steps

For a quick reference, the access request process and approval are explained in the following few steps:

1. **Complete the access request form**
   Either the end user or the requestor logs on to User Access Management and uses one of the previously mentioned four methods to complete the request creation. After the access request is completed and submitted, the user or requestor will be notified with a request number.
2. **Approval or rejection by first-line approver**
   After the request is submitted, this request sends information to the first-stage approver via a work item to the approver's inbox in the SAP Access Control system or to an email inbox, depending on the system setting. The approver can review this request and then approve or reject the request here. Apart from this, the approver can change or request a different role for the user based on the stage task settings.
3. **Role approver's review**
   After the request is approved by the first-line approver, the role approver receives the work item with the option to approve or reject the request. If there are multiple roles in a single request and these roles have different approvers, then the workflow sends different work items specific to the roles.
4. **SoD violation and mitigation**
   If this workflow is configured for any SoD violation exception with routing the workflow for the mitigation approver, and the user request contains any SoD violations, then this routing path is triggered to either mitigate the risk or reject the request. If there are no violations in the request, this routing path is skipped.
5. **Provisioning**
   After all of the configured stage approvals are completed, then based on the provisionnig configuration, either individual roles or complete requests are provisioned immediately after the last approval. At every stage, an approval or rejection notification will be sent based on stage setting.

All of this information is captured for the audit log, and upon provisioning, the end user is notified with password details if it's configured in the system.

You've now gone through the full cycle of a new user request or change request creation by any existing employee. We used this simple scenario to help you understand the process and do the configuration. In the next section, you'll see some additional functionality provided in User Access Management.

7.6 Password Self-Service

In this section, we'll look at the additional or extended Password Self-Service (PSS) as part of User Access Management. In most company landscapes, the major task handled by the help desk is resetting passwords. Enabling PSS to reset passwords not only reduces the workload of the help-desk team but also improves productivity of the user by changing passwords that start working on the system immediately.

7.6.1 Maintain Password Self-Service

In this configuration step, you need to set up PSS. When a user creates a request for a password reset, the application verifies the user based on the information the user maintained for his PSS settings. After the application verifies the user, it resets the password and sends an email to the user's configured email address. After the user resets his password, the application emails the new password to the user. For this purpose, you need to execute Transaction SPRO, and follow the menu path, Governance, Risk and Compliance • Access Control • User Provisioning • Maintain Password Self Service. See Figure 7.22.

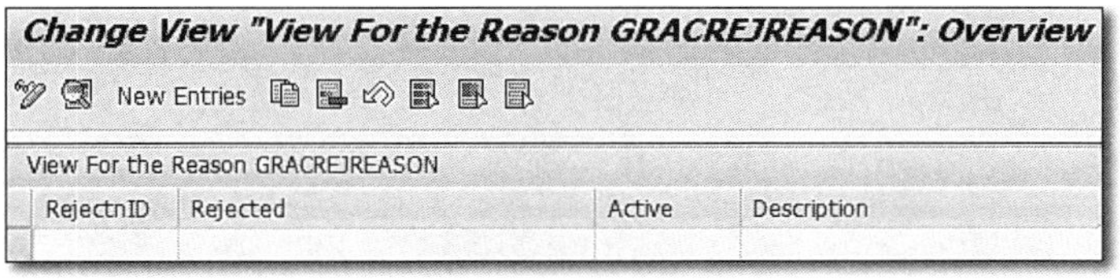

Figure 7.22 Password Self-Service Reason Maintenance

Connector configuration

One of the basic requirements for this self-service, configuration of connector, should be set to PSS or HR SYSTEM. According to this configuration, you'll later need to maintain PSS. From the PSS GLOBAL CONFIGURATION VALUES section, select either CHALLENGE RESPONSE with security questions or HR SYSTEM to verify personnel data against the system, as shown in Figure 7.23.

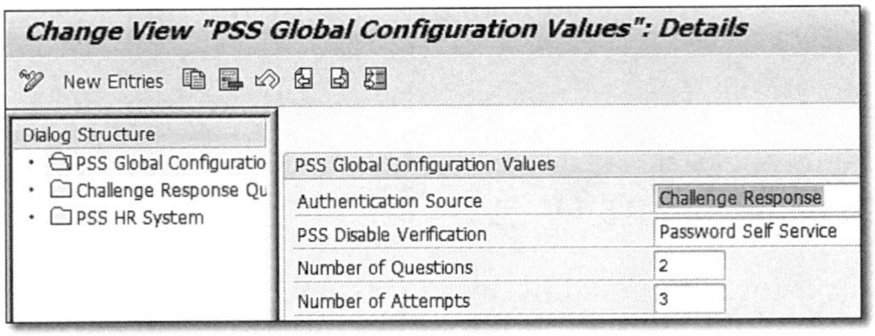

Figure 7.23 Password Self-Service Global Setting

Authentication sources for Password Self Service

If HR SYSTEM is maintained as the authentication source, then you need to maintain the PSS HR SYSTEM settings. Otherwise, you need to configure the security questions, and the users need to register their answers. A user who creates a request to reset his password must answer the questions as the user originally registered them, as shown in Figure 7.24. The application only resets the passwords if the user successfully answers all of the questions.

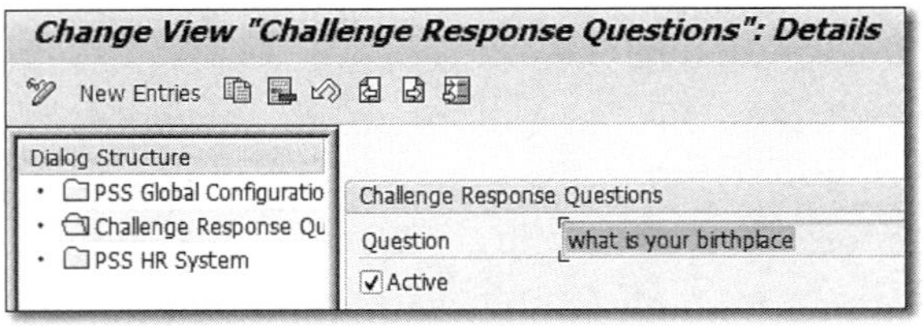

Figure 7.24 Maintain Challenge Response

After PSS is configured, users can access NetWeaver Business Client NWBC to use the link to create user-defined questions using the REGISTER SECURITY QUESTIONS link and another link to reset the password.

In this section, we've seen how to configure PSS and use this in the SAP Access Control environment. In the next section, we'll look at the options provided in the reporting features.

7.7 User Access Management Reporting

In earlier sections, we looked at User Access Management configuration, access request creation, and PSS. This section provides some details about the reporting features of User Access Management.

Search Report features

The foremost reporting tool from User Access Management is used to search different requests with a lot of flexible conditions. This search report input, as shown in Figure 7.25, has three segments, and the first column has about 33 fields for selection, located under the SAVED VARIANCE section. The second segment, RESULTS, has values to include various conditions related to input parameters and the last segment meant for the field values. This report helps to analyze various process IDs that are involved in request creation, such as access requests, User access reviews, SoD reviews, and so on.

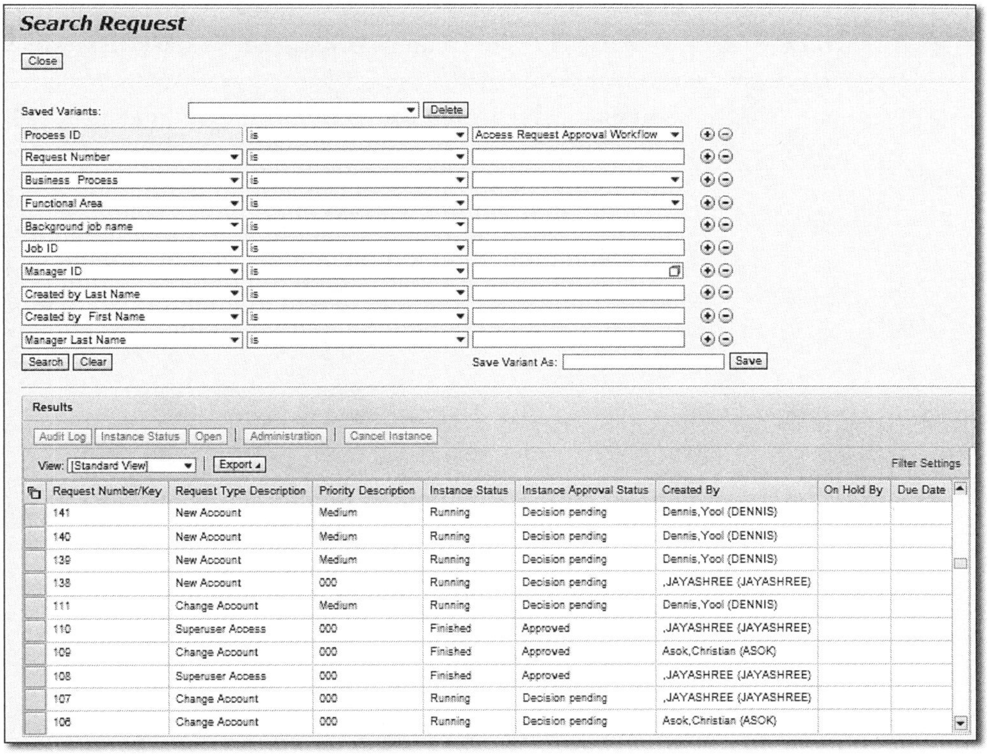

Figure 7.25 Search Request Screen

Value of reporting for administration of Users Access Management

This report shows the different statuses of the request; after it's executed, the result is shown in the bottom window based on your search criteria. This helps administrators filter any pending workflow to view and troubleshoot or reroute the request to a different stage. For this purpose, the ADMINISTRATION and CANCEL INSTANCE buttons help to route the workflow to a different position, cancel an instance of a request, or handle other administrative tasks from here.

Audit Logs

You might have noticed that there is another button—AUDIT LOG—that helps create the audit trail of the request, including all of the stage approval and rejection with a time stamp at every stage. These details give audit trail information to the audit team to verify various request types and their activity details.

The result window can be customized to show very specific columns to give a better picture of a certain scenario. One of the examples is to search a list of emergency access requests with the approval workflow result report. One of the result columns is REQUEST NUMBER/KEY, which reflects that although most of the requests are created with a request number, some requests are created with a key as shown in Figure 7.26.

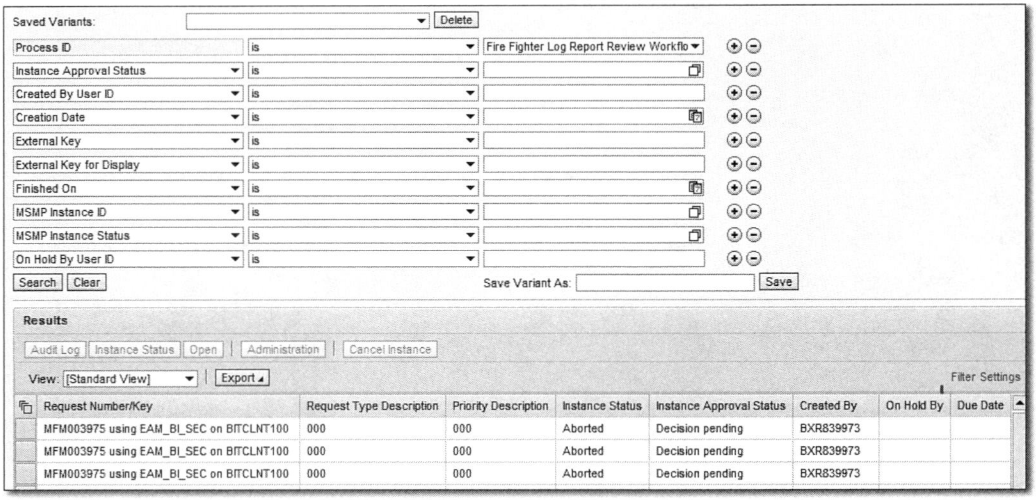

Figure 7.26 Firefighter Log Review Request Workflow Reporting Column

In this case, finding specific information may be a little complex. But this issue can be handled by selecting additional columns with the creation date and saving this as your default view. To do this click on the SETTINGS button at the far right corner above the table.

Report criteria selection

Choose the fields that are needed as output of the report, and click the ADD button to add the additional columns at the end by default. To manage the sequence of columns that are required, it can be adjusted by selecting the column name and clicking the change sequence button will move upward or downward to position that column as required.

After you make the above mentioned selection and/or changes click on the OK button. Now you will be shown with the same report with the modified columns as per our changes. Selecting these columns is limited to those available within the HIDDEN COLUMNS list. If you need more new fields, that might require modification to the reports. All these report layout changes can be saved and re-used repeatedly. For this you need to click on the SAVE AS button and use your own naming to store and retrieve this specific layout. You can switch between any of such layouts whenever you want to see the specific layout as report output.

The resulting selected column gives the date information; another column also comes with the date and time information (CREATION TIME STAMP). Choose whichever is more helpful. At the end, based on your selection setting, the output columns are shown in Figure 7.27.

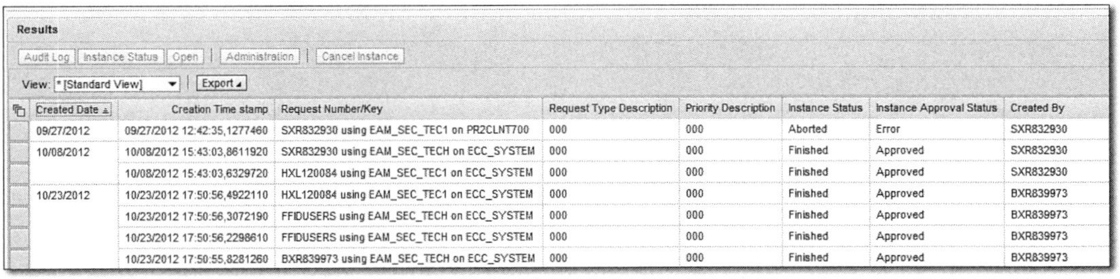
Results

Audit Log | Instance Status | Open | Administration | Cancel Instance

View: * [Standard View] | Export

Created Date	Creation Time stamp	Request Number/Key	Request Type Description	Priority Description	Instance Status	Instance Approval Status	Created By
09/27/2012	09/27/2012 12:42:35,1277460	SXR832930 using EAM_SEC_TEC1 on PR2CLNT700	000	000	Aborted	Error	SXR832930
10/08/2012	10/08/2012 15:43:03,8611920	SXR832930 using EAM_SEC_TECH on ECC_SYSTEM	000	000	Finished	Approved	SXR832930
	10/08/2012 15:43:03,6329720	HXL120084 using EAM_SEC_TEC1 on ECC_SYSTEM	000	000	Finished	Approved	SXR832930
10/23/2012	10/23/2012 17:50:56,4922110	HXL120084 using EAM_SEC_TEC1 on ECC_SYSTEM	000	000	Finished	Approved	BXR839973
	10/23/2012 17:50:56,3072190	FFIDUSERS using EAM_SEC_TECH on ECC_SYSTEM	000	000	Finished	Approved	BXR839973
	10/23/2012 17:50:56,2298610	FFIDUSERS using EAM_SEC_TECH on ECC_SYSTEM	000	000	Finished	Approved	BXR839973
	10/23/2012 17:50:55,8281260	BXR839973 using EAM_SEC_TECH on ECC_SYSTEM	000	000	Finished	Approved	BXR839973

Figure 7.27 Modified Column in the Result Window

In this reporting section, we've discussed a few options for using User Access Management reporting and customizing result columns. This helps to maximize your reporting capabilities and get the required result for a different kind of analysis for auditing and administrative purpose.

7.8 Summary

This chapter introduced you to the basic configuration, creation, and approval of user requests and reporting on User Access Management from various perspectives. This chapter should have given you a deeper understanding of the SAP Access Control Manager tool and its usage in conjunction with the GRC environment of your IT landscape. We'll discuss more advanced and complex User Access Management topics in the next chapter.

In earlier chapters, we've discussed the details on various SAP Access Control tools, including their basic implementation and usage. In this chapter, we'll delve in depth to handle some complex scenarios and advanced features provided in SAP Access Control to take your SAP Access Control environment implementation to the next level.

8 SAP Access Control Advanced Topics

This chapter discusses the advanced topics in SAP Access Control implementations to address the Emergency Access Management, Access Risk Analysis, Business Role Manager, and User Access Management tools, which we've discussed in previous chapters. SAP improved the SAP Access Control technical foundation on top of well proven ABAP technology and ABAP Web Dynpro and tightly integrated it with other SAP GRC products such as SAP Process Control and SAP Risk Management. SAP Access Control has many more enhanced functions and uses the improved ABAP-based workflow engine to suit various request flows to various users and configurations using guided procedures.

Also the MSMP workflow engine is integrated into the existing Business Rule Framework Plus (BRF+) to create rules on decision making to find approvers of these requests. These two areas are totally new to the SAP Access Control users and consultants who are implementing the User Access Management tool. This chapter introduces and explains these specific areas from the implementation and design perspective to help auditing team, security team, and SAP Access Control teams understand and design effective deployments of SAP Access Control in your environment.

Along with MSMP and BRF+, there are a few more technical areas that will help you understand and design better and effective solutions to meet your demanding IT landscapes and increase the return on investment (ROI). We'll first look at the MSMP workflow, BRF+, and then workflow notifications, including email notifications, and periodic reviews. Lastly, we'll review how to use HR triggers in your User Access Management tool. Most of these advance topics are aimed at dealing with cumbersome processes in User Access Management.

8.1 Multistage Multipath (MSMP) Workflow

Let's start working with how to define and configure the MSMP workflow with respect to different process IDs that are specific to one of the processes given, such as access requests, function or risk maintenance, user access review, segregation of duties (SoD) review, and firefighter log review. MSMP is the new workflow engine used within SAP Access Controls 10.0 and is capable of directing requests down multiple approval routes simultaneously. It's used for the management of automated approval workflows in User Access Management but can also be triggered for the other SAP Access Control modules, including Access Risk Analysis master data updates or role building approval workflows. The big change is that it works off of a multitude of different rules to govern what should happen to the requests. All of these rules need to be defined up front before they can be assigned in the configuration and used in the workflow processes.

Note

Before you begin here, make sure you've completed all required prerequisites related to workflow configuration as explained in Chapter 3.

As a first step, let's discuss the various steps involved in the MSMP Workflow Configuration. Based on the GRC_MSMP_CONFIGURATION BC Set activation, there are eight different processes and process IDs as noted earlier, such as access request, user review, and so on, and components of all these processes are populated with MSMP-related core values in these various steps to carry out configuration. To start configuration, you need to invoke Transaction GRFNMW_CONFIGURE_WD or from the IMG Transaction SPRO, and follow the menu path, Governance, Risk and Compliance • Access Control •

WORKFLOW FOR ACCESS CONTROL • MAINTAIN MSMP WORKFLOWS. This opens a browser window with a guided procedure, as shown in Figure 8.1. From this screen, you need to set up the following major steps to complete MSMP configuration for any one of the workflow processes mentioned here; the individual steps are discussed in later sections as noted in parentheses.

- Configure process and global settings (Section 8.1.1).
- Maintain rules for the MSMP workflow (Section 8.1.2).
- Maintain agents for the MSMP workflow (Section 8.1.3).
- Maintain notification variables and templates (Section 8.1.4).
- Maintain paths and stages for the MSMP workflow (Section 8.1.5).
- Map the workflow route (Section 8.1.6).
- Generate versions (Section 8.1.7).

Let's review how to configure the process global settings for MSMP, which is the first step in MSMP configuration.

8.1.1 Configure Process and Global Setting

Upon invoking the MSMP workflow, you might notice that the top part of the initial screen shown in Figure 8.1 shows seven steps with the first process SAP_GRAC_ACCESS_REQUEST highlighted. We'll take you through all of these steps with some explanations on their purpose and the options available for you to configure them to suit your needs.

Process IDs and Business configuration sets for MSMP configuration

Process IDs are predelivered as part of the MSMP BC Set GRC_MSMP_CONFIGURATION activation. They basically cover a specific scenario, and the process description for each process ID is self-explanatory for scenarios. You can start editing the entire MSMP process by clicking the DISPLAY/CHANGE button. In the PROCESS GLOBAL SETTINGS area of the screen, if the fields are editable, you know you're in change mode (this is the only indicator of whether you're in display or change mode). In our case, PROCESS GLOBAL SETTINGS area shows the settings applied globally to the process that selected from an earlier window.

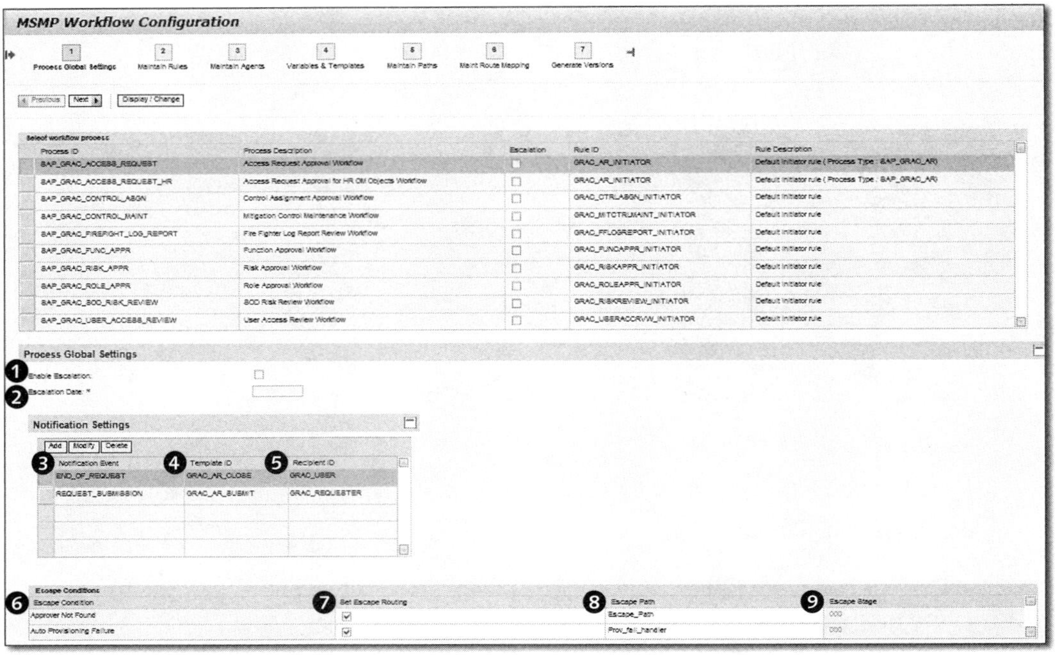

Figure 8.1 MSMP Workflow Configuration: Initial Screen

Let's review the individual fields that are found in Figure 8.1, some of which you can maintain. First select a workflow process and fields related to this process need to be populated. Under PROCESS GLOBAL SETTINGS there are two variables for you to set.

MSPM Workflow Initial Screen fields

❶ ENABLE ESCALATION
If this checkbox is checked, it enables global escalation on any workflow that was pending for approval and the deadline monitoring for the fixed date. After this date, all work items escalate for this process. We've given detail in MAINTAIN PATHS step, to configure escalation independently at each approval stage, and you have options to escalate to an alternative approver (a different agent) or to escalate directly to the next stage as a part of workflow deadline monitoring.

❷ ESCALATION DATE
This is the date on which all work items for this process are escalated. This field is required if escalation is enabled.

Under Notification Settings, the variables you should set are:

❸ Notification Event
There are two events like notification upon request submission and upon completion of request need to be configured in order to send the notification to the respective users at the trigger of these events.

❹ Template ID
The template is maintained for the message that has to be sent either at submission of request or at the end of request processing notifying the requestor or user of the outcome as message what is the request number that had been created with details or approval information after the end of the workflow process.

❺ Recipient ID
This is the recipient of the end of request notification message. (configured as an agent), which can be a user or requestor.

Under Escape Conditions, the variables you should set are:

❻ Escape Conditions
This table has two entries, one each for two escape conditions: Approver Not Found and Auto Provisioning Failure.

❼ Set Escape Routing
This checkbox need to be set to activate the respective escape paths. Activation is optional.

❽ Escape Path
Path the request follows if no agents are found for any stage or failure during auto-provisioning. This is set in step 5 and is required when Escape Routing is enabled.

❾ Escape Stage
This escape stage number dictates at which approval stage this escape routing should be triggered in case of if any escape condition arouse.

To maintain the escape path, it should be created in Step 5 to set the stage for the above mentioned escape path to which the request should follow. The next step in the configuration of MSMP is to maintain rules and rule results.

8.1.2 Maintain Rules and Rule Results

This section discusses how to maintain various rules and rule results that help to identify agents in the workflow and condition-based determination of different workflow paths.

Rule types applicable for MSMP configuration

Four different rule types are available to maintain in the system: BRF PLUS, FUNCTION MODULE BASED, ABAP CLASS BASED, and BRF PLUS FLAT RULE. In Figure 8.2, BRF PLUS FLAT RULE is maintained. These rules are used to find the correct path, agents, or routing to a different path based on logic designed in the rules. For example, if the user request to a role in system A, then the workflow should go to Path_1; if the system is different, then the workflow should route to Path_2. For our example, we've Path_1 and Path_2 are logical paths. Figure 8.3 shows the rule and rule result, but the path definition based on the results discussed in Section 8.1.5. Let's discuss some more details on each and every field (attribute) and their functionality next specific to rule maintenance and rule result maintenance.

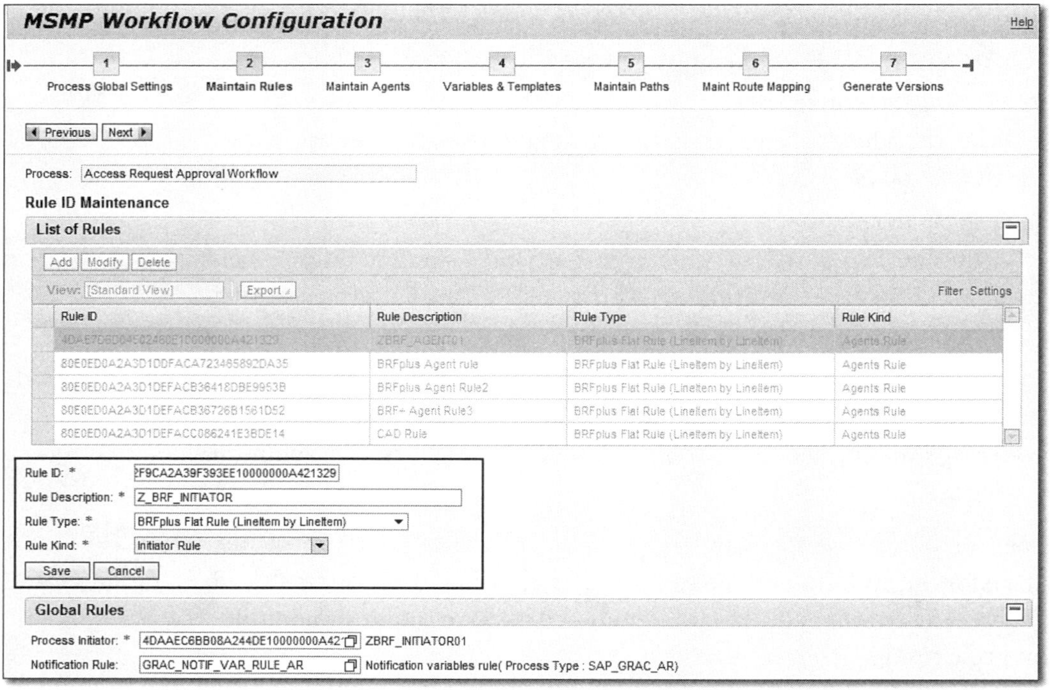

Figure 8.2 Maintain Rules: MSMP Workflow Configuration Screen

Under the RULE ID MAINTENANCE table, a list of rules is provided by default, which can be modified, or new rules can be added as needed. The fields in the table are described:

Default Rules within the MSMP workflow

- RULE ID
  Unique name for the rule to identify different rule types and rule kinds that are used in the MSMP workflow process. This is a mandatory field.
- RULE DESCRIPTION
  Meaningful description to the purpose of the rule.
- RULE TYPE
  There are four rule types based on the underlying technology that helps to make decisions. In SAP Access Control, there are several out-of-the-box ABAP class-based and function module-based rule types available. If you need any additional rule types based on any of these, they can be generated with the help of a technical resource in the custom namespace and then used in the MSMP workflow process. The BRF+ rule is a more simplified rule engine that helps the business user define the rules without much technical skill. In Section 8.3, we explain how to create the BRF+ rule and how to attach it in the MSMP workflow to simplify your complex decision-making process in User Access Management tool. In other words it's a technical component or underlying technology used to define the rule. The following rule type options are available:
  - BRF PLUS RULE
    Rule defined in the BRF+ application to get rule results depending on conditions inside the rule.
  - FUNCTION MODULE BASED RULE
    Function module coded to output rule results.
  - ABAP CLASS BASED RULE
    Class method coded to output rule results.
  - BRF PLUS FLAT RULE (LINE-ITEM BY LINE-TIME)
    BRF+ rule defined for only one line item. (This rule is called once for each line item in the request.)
- RULE KIND
  Four different rule kinds are used during the execution of the MSMP workflow process to determine results for initiator, agents, routing

and notification variables. The rule kinds in the workflow process are described here:

- INITIATOR RULE
  This rule is used to direct the workflow path based on the rule, result which is defined by the rule type. Only one initiator rule per process can be defined in the bottom window GLOBAL RULES area with the PROCESS INITIATOR field. In SAP Access Control 10.x, rather than specifying an initiator for each workflow path, you now only have one that contains all of the different possible variations that can be achieved by rule result values.
- ROUTING RULE
  You can use this rule to route a request from one path to another based on the rule result.
- AGENT RULE
  You can create multiple rule IDs for the agents rule kind based on your definition of multiple agents such as role owner, risk owner, or any other custom agent.
- NOTIFICATION VARIABLES RULE
  This is also defined once per process in global settings. This rule helps to send notifications to various agents.

As shown in Figure 8.3, you can maintain multiple agent rules, routing rules, initiator rules, and notification rules based on any rule type.

Rule result maintenance

In the bottom part of the screen shown in of Figure 8.3, you can maintain RULE RESULTS. Here you need to maintain rule result values for a selected rule. The rule result value can be a single result or multiple results, which is used in workflow paths or stages to determine either agents or paths depending on the rule kind. In this screen, both the result value and its description are mandatory fields, as described here:

- RULE RESULT VALUE
  Initiator or routing rules have rule results which are results derived from rule types. The result value is configured as the path to be taken by the workflow or used to determine.
- TRIGGER VALUE DESCR
  Rule results require meaningful description, which you maintain here.

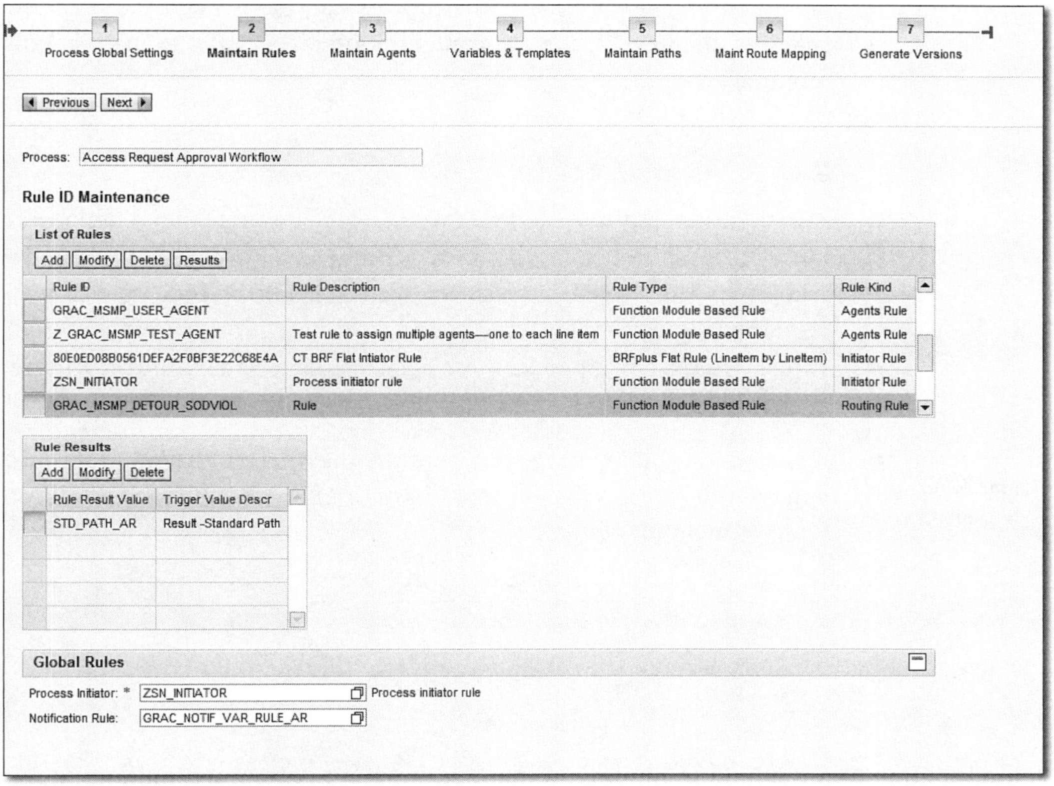

Figure 8.3 Maintain Rule Results: Rule ID Maintenance Screen

Also at the bottom part of the screen shown in Figure 8.3, you need to configure Global Rules. The fields that are important in the configuration of global rules are described in further detail here:

Global Rules fields

- Process Initiator
  Associate the rule comprising possible initiators to a process. There can be only one active initiator per process. This initiator needs to cover all paths defined for the process that are to participate in the process.
- Notification Rule
  Rule to determine notification variables used in notification templates.

Now that you've configured the process and maintained the rules and rule sets, the next step in the configuration of MSMP is to maintain different agents.

8.1.3 Maintain Agents

After maintaining rules and rule results, let's discuss how to define various access request approvers such as immediate managers, role owners who own the business, security team or notification agents (e.g., requestors and users involved in the workflow process) and how individual users are mapped to these agents to determine the correct stage approver.

Adding and modifying agent approval roles

If you want to add new agents or modify their determination procedure, you can select respective buttons either to Add or Modify in the Agents screen shown in Figure 8.4.

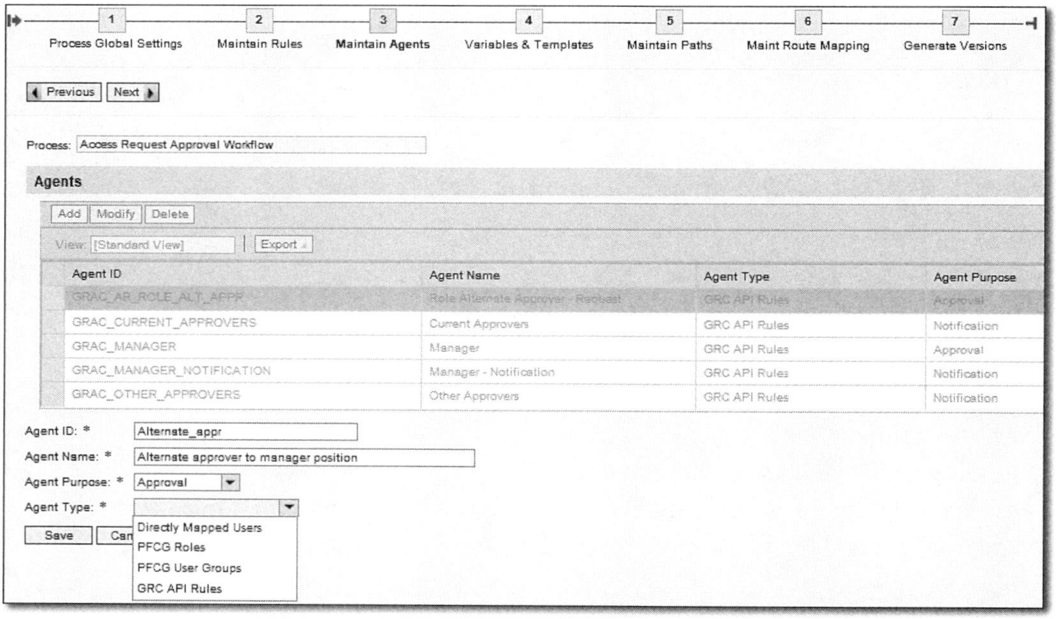

Figure 8.4 Maintaining Agents

Several fields shown in Figure 8.4 may need to be maintained; some are maintained as part of the BC Set activation. Let's review these fields in further detail to help you create new agents and maintain respective values to serve their purpose:

New Agent fields and their configuration

- Agent ID
  Define the logical approver ID, which is a required field.
- Agent Name
  Give a description of the logical approver ID.
- Agent Purpose
  Agents are defined in the MSMP workflow for either approval purposes or to notify about the activities.
  - Approval
    This can be selected from the dropdown list, which is as shown in Figure 8.4 and this agent will get work item from workflow for approval purpose.
  - NOTIFICATION
    Apart from approval agent, there could be another type of agents in the system for notification purpose to convey the information about the workflow.
- Agent Type
  Define dynamic approvers that can be assigned to any workflow stage. Agents are logical approvers determined or supported by the following mapping:
  - Directly Mapped Users
    Approvers selected from the Approver definition. Don't select By pass Approver Mapping for fixed approvers. This configuration is used for defining static user groups used within workflow processes for example, to define a security group consisting of one or more SAP users. This group can be assigned to any approval stage for a workflow process. The Approver list definition is required only if the Agent Type is Directly Mapped Users.
  - PFCG Roles
    PFCG roles assigned to a user as agent and workflow determines the agent based on the role assignment.

Various Agent types for notification and workflow

- PFCG USER GROUPS
  PFCG groups assigned to a user; for example, this can be specific process owners that are defined in a user group.
- GRC API RULES7
  This is used to fetch rule-based approvers such as manager, role owners, risk owners, and so on via associated function modules. This field is mandatory if AGENT TYPE is defined as Function Module BASED RULE in an earlier step. An example of this can be defined for the manager approval stage with GRAC_MSMP_MANAGER_AGENT as the RULE ID or any other custom agent RULE ID as shown in Figure 8.5.

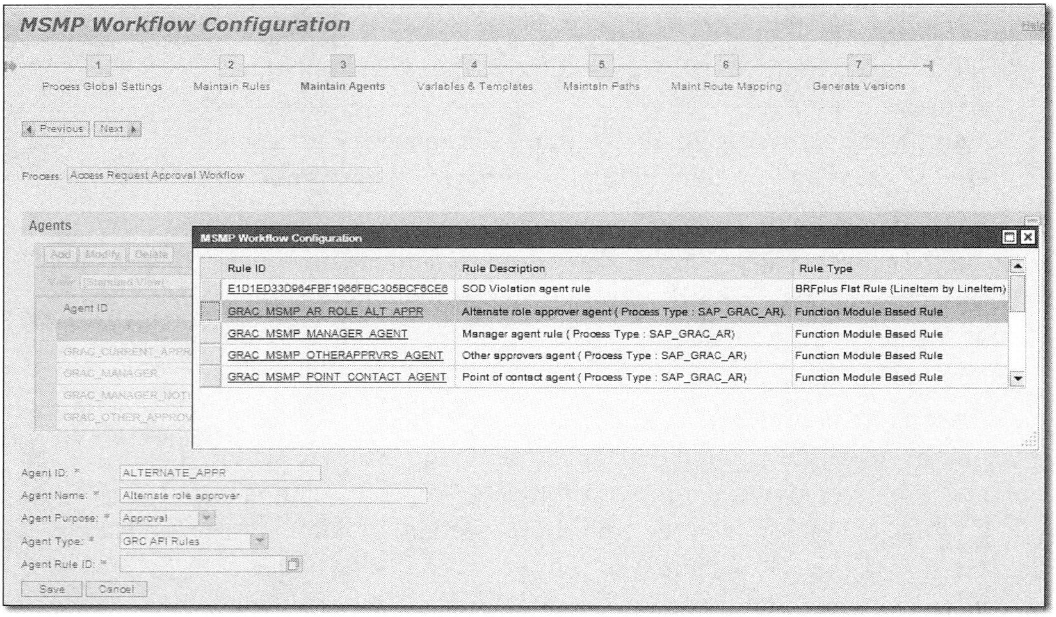

Figure 8.5 Agent Maintenance-SAP GRC API Rule Configuration

So far, you've defined various agents who need to be notified or act as approvers. In the next step, let's add templates and notification variables that are needed for approval, notification work items, or email.

8.1.4 Variables and Templates

Along with the previously mentioned agents, notification variables and templates must be configured to be used as part of a specific MSMP workflow. These templates are used to send email messages to the approvers/notification receivers that contain some fixed texts and variables, such as user ID, user name, request type, role or provisioning details, system name, to give the message to the receiver of this workflow content for decision making on approval or rejection. All of the customization can be done to these templates and variables from the ABAP stack using Transaction SE61, which we'll discuss in Section 8.5.1.

Customization with template fields

Here we'll discuss how to maintain the customization using standard templates and variables. Figure 8.6 shows the fields in the MSMP workflow step 4, as described here:

- Notification Templates
  Templates for each notification type are configured here along with the corresponding messages class/number for each template. In this area of the screen, you can either add a new template or delete one if you don't need it.
- Template ID
  Unique ID that identifies each template.
- Message Class
  ID where the message is stored.
- Message number
  Number assigned to the message.
- Notification Variables
  Variables used in the notification message that will be replaced by valid values in the runtime by the MSMP engine.
- Temp. Variable
  Unique name for each variable used in the template message.
- Variable Description
  Meaningful description for the variables used in the message.

In this step, you've learned about the necessary notification templates and variables. The next section reviews how you can maintain paths and assign stages to paths for your MSMP configuration in its support of SAP Access Control.

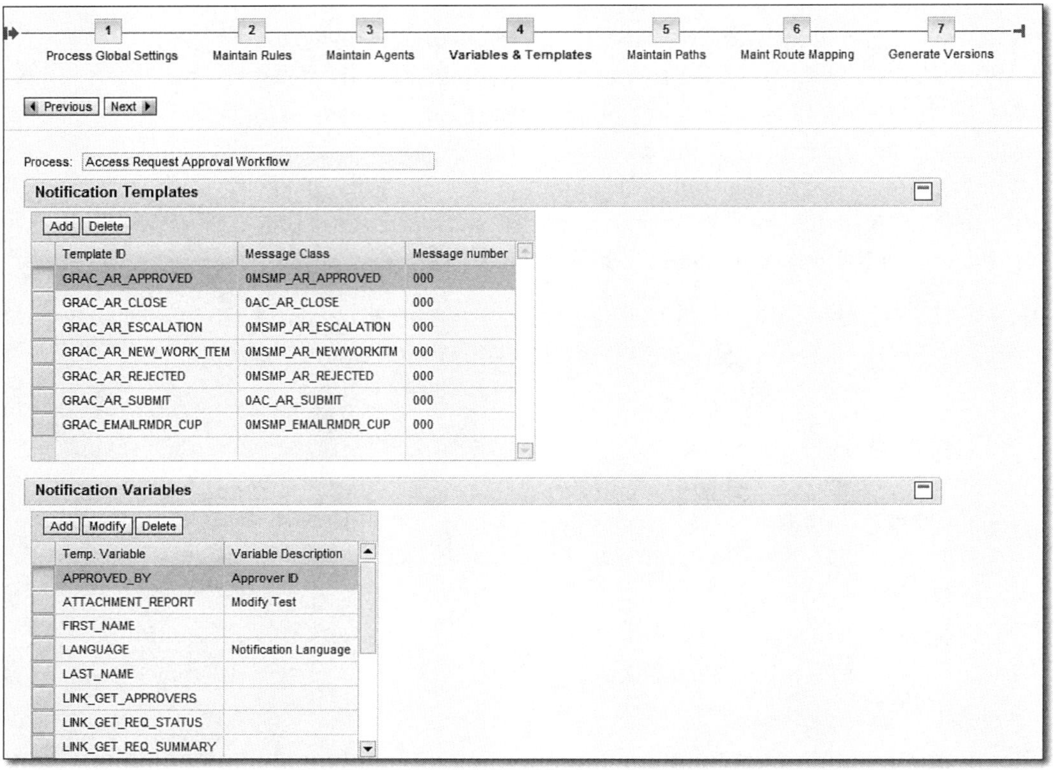

Figure 8.6 Configuration of MSMP Variables and Templates

8.1.5 Maintain Paths and Assign Stages to Path

After defining notification templates and variables, you start maintaining and configuring MSMP workflow paths. Every workflow path contains one or more intermediate nodes for the decision-making process called *stages* in the SAP Access Control workflow. You can create stageless workflows also. At every stage, you need to define various parameters that are important for decision making and workflow processes. Dynamic conditions such as segregation of duty (SoD) violations identified in making the request or type of request, changing the stage owner, or adding a role might require switching the entire workflow path to a different one. For this reason, you need to maintain multiple workflow paths within the process. At the approval stage level, if there is any SoD risk violation, you need to define whether any routing is required. These details will be maintained in the next step, MAINTAIN ROUTE MAPPING, with approval stage information and paths where it is routing from and to. If you take another example on type of request, then the process initiator decides which path to follow for the workflow process to complete the task. We've explained with some how to define BRF+ based initiators to determine this in Section 8.3 with an example. You may choose ADD, MODIFY, or DELETE button from MAINTAIN PATHS window to carry out the required actions (see Figure 8.7).

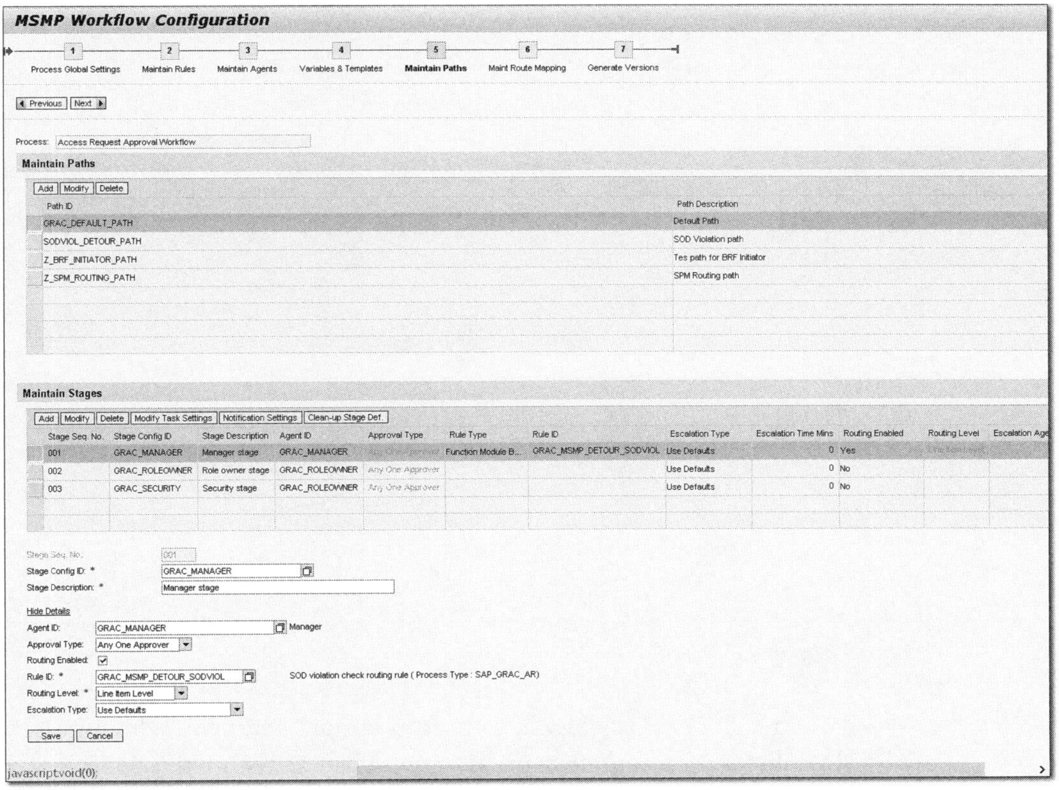

Figure 8.7 Maintain Paths for MSMP Workflows

In the MAINTAIN PATHS section of the screen, you'll define the PATH ID, which is the path name, and the PATH DESCRIPTION; both are mandatory fields. You can maintain multiple paths as needed. Also note the MAINTAIN STAGES area of the screen; let's review how to maintain stages next.

8.1.6 Maintain Stages

In the MAINTAIN STAGES area of the screen, you'll maintain approval stages and stage-relevant task and notification settings, which can be associated to the workflow path. You can configure the application-specific actions/tasks for a process in MODIFY TASK SETTINGS and maintain notifications by selecting the NOTIFICATIONS SETTINGS button (see Figure 8.8).

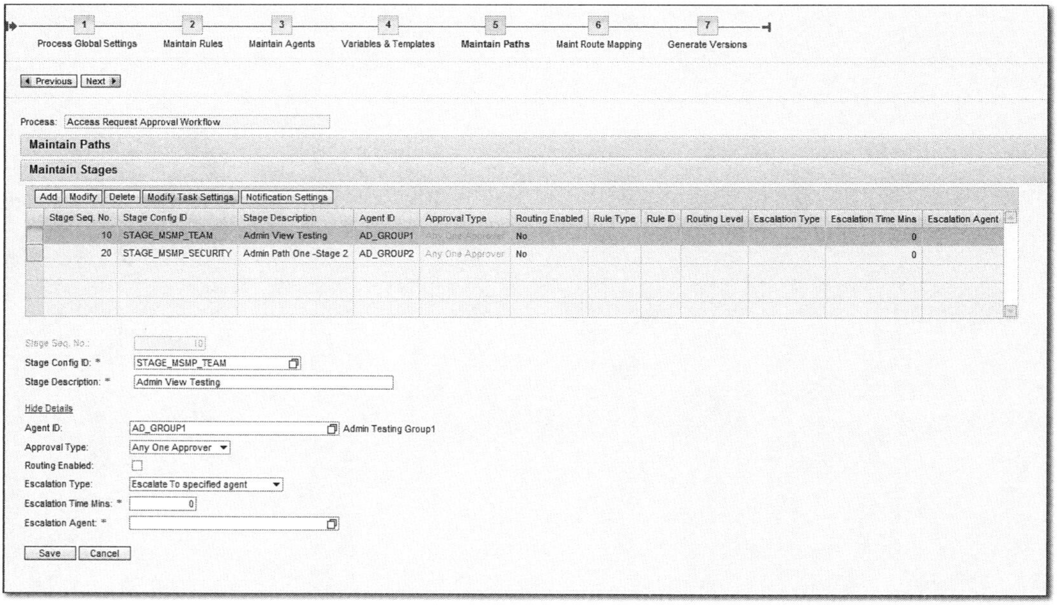

Figure 8.8 MSMP Stage Maintenance

Creating a new stage

To create a new stage, select the ADD button, and define the necessary attributes. You can maintain as many stages as required for the chosen path and maintain all stages one by one in the correct sequence with numbering for the approval process. You need to review and define the following attributes when you create a new stage:

New stage attributes

- STAGE CONFIG ID
  This is a unique ID that can be used to identify the stage, and it can be used in multiple paths, for example, for manager, role approver, and so on.
- STAGE DESCRIPTION
  Maintain meaningful text to describe the stage.
- AGENT ID
  The dropdown menu shows all of the agents that are maintained in the MAINTAIN AGENTS step. LOGICAL APPROVER ID can be chosen from this dropdown menu.
- APPROVAL TYPE
  Maintain the value that this stage level needs; either all approvers or any one of the approvers is sufficient to move the workflow to the next stage.
- ROUTING ENABLED
  Select this optional checkbox if routing needs to be enabled for this stage. If this checkbox is chosen, the following additional two fields will be shown on the screen.
  - RULE ID
    Maintain based on what routing rule is needed at this stage.
  - ROUTING LEVEL
    Indicate in routing whether to route the entire stage or only the failed line items as a result of routing. This is mandatory if routing is enabled.
- ESCALATION TYPE
  When you select USE DEFAULT, then the default settings defined for the process are used for escalation:
  - ESCALATE TO SPECIFIED AGENT
    If this value is selected, then an additional field is shown in the same screen to escalate to provide agent that is maintained in AGENT ID field.
  - SKIP TO NEXT STAGE
    This selection escalates the request to the next stage.
  - NO ESCALATION
    This is an optional setting to use if you don't want to escalate.

- ESCALATION TIME MINS
  Escalation should start after a specified time in minutes. This field is required if ESCALATION TYPE is set with ESCALATE TO SPECIFIED AGENT or SKIP TO NEXT STAGE.
- ESCALATION AGENT
  Agent ID is used to determine approvers for escalation. This field is required if ESCALATION TYPE is set to ESCALATE TO SPECIFIED AGENT is chosen.

Now that we've reviewed how to create a new stage affliated with maintaining paths, let's look at how you can maintain the stage task settings you've just created and the specific task settings that are applicable.

8.1.7 Maintain Stage Task Settings

As shown in Figure 8.9, the task settings for the stage is another important place where determine what is and what isn't possible at the stage level, such as whether at this stage as approver you're allowed to change the request, do you need to enter comments if you reject, and so on. After the stage is defined, click the MODIFY TASK SETTINGS button to open the STAGE DEFINITION screen. In this stage definition, you need to maintain the values for application-specific configuration for actions that can be performed in a given stage and activities that are needed to be performed by the stage approvers.

Task Settings for chosen stages

In the top portion of the screen, STAGE DETAILS is populated based on the chosen stages defined earlier under the MAINTAIN STAGES screen area. Let's review the attributes that need to be configured in the TASK SETTINGS section of Figure 8.9:

- PATH REVAL NEW ROLE
  Checks whether path revaluation is to be performed if a new role is added. The following possible values are available from the drop-down list:
  - ONLY NEW ROLES IN EVALUATION PATH (evaluate)
  - ALL ROLES IN EVALUATION PATH (reevaluate)
  - NO PATH REVALUATION FOR NEW ROLE (continue)

- Risk Analy Mandtry
  Ensures that risk analysis is performed for a stage.
- Rejection Level
  This value allows the stage level approver to reject either one of the defined level such as Role, Request, System, and Role.
- Approval Level
  This setting allows the stage approver to approve either one of the difined level such as role, request, system, and role.
- E-mail Group
  Email ID for a group of users that need to be notified at this stage level.
- Comments Mandatory
  Makes adding comments mandatory while approving or rejecting.
- EUP ID
  End User Personalization (EUP) template that should be shown at this stage level.

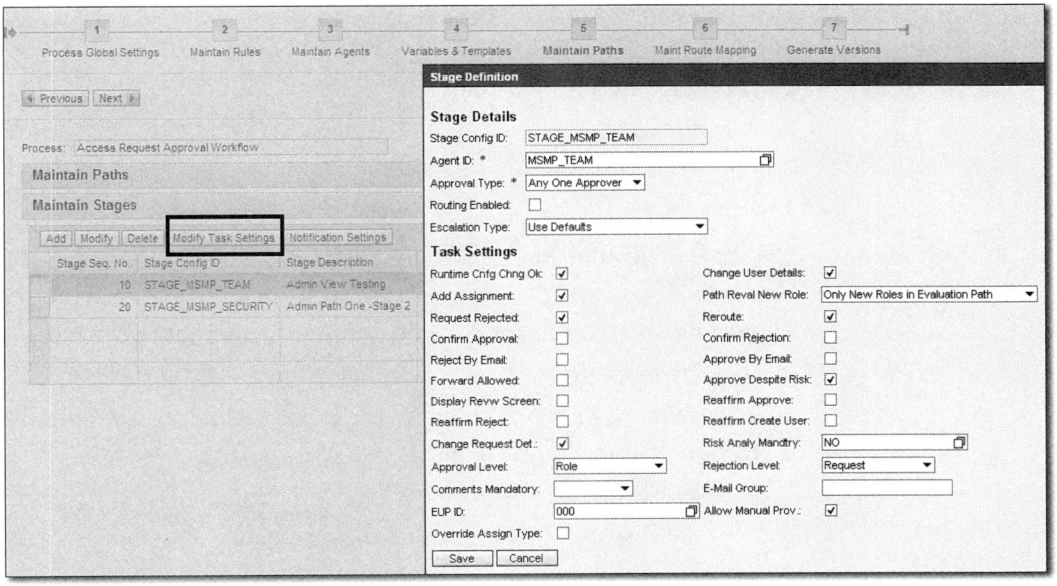

Figure 8.9 Maintain Task Settings Specific to the Stage

Besides these parameters, the other settings located in the TASK SETTINGS section are checkbox values that activates the respective attributes as explained here:

- RUNTIME CNFG CHNG OK
  If there are any configuration changes in the stage settings, should it be considered for any workitems that are already in process path effected with these new changes.
- ADD ASSIGNMENT
  Enables this stage approver to add new roles.
- REQUEST REJECTED
  Enables the stage approver to reject a request.
- REROUTE
  Enables the request to be rerouted manually by the stage approver.
- CONFIRM APPROVAL
  Once approved, this enforces approval confirmation by pop-up window.
- CONFIRM REJECTION
  Enforces rejection confirmation by pop-up window.
- REJECT BY EMAIL
  Enables the approver to reject the request via emails by clicking the link received in the approver's inbox.
- APPROVE BY EMAIL
  Enable the approver to approve via email.
- FORWARD ALLOWED
  Allows the approver to forward the request to another approver.
- APPROVE DESPITE RISK
  Enables request approval though risk exists in the request without mitigation or remediation action.
- DISPLAY REVW SCREEN
  Enables the display of the request review screen.
- REAFFIRM APPROVE
  Enables approvers to confirm their identities before approving requests by means of logon with a user ID and password.

- Reaffirm Reject
  Enables approvers to confirm their identities before rejecting.
- Change Request Det
  Enables changing of the request parameter.
- Allow Manual Prov
  Allows approvers to provision directly from the stage approval screen.
- Override Assign Type
  Enables the override of the default setting of direct, indirect, or combined provisioning. For this function, manual provisioning should be checked.

After you set these task settings for a stage, you can move to the notification settings that are required at this stage.

8.1.8 Notification Settings

From the Notification Settings screen, you need to configure the notification templates mapping to the notification event and recipients (see Figure 8.10).

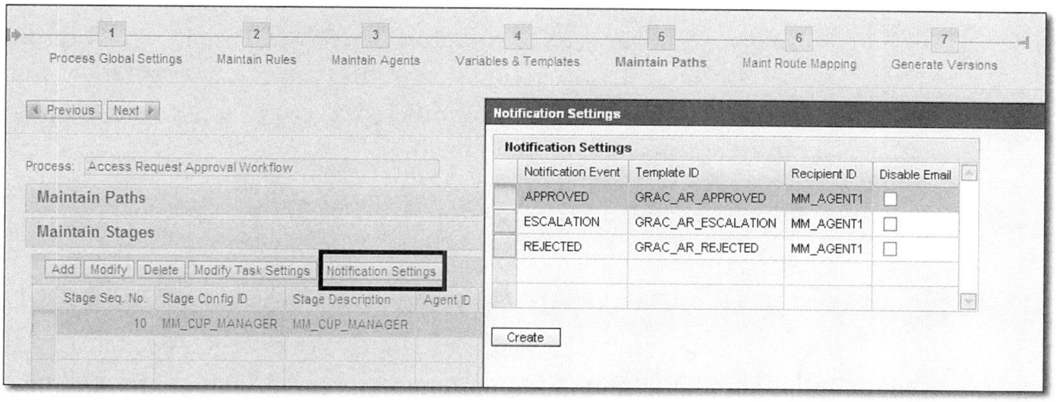

Figure 8.10 Configuring the Notification Templates in the Notification Settings

Field configuration for notification templates

The fields that should be configured for the notification templates in the MSMP workflow are listed here:

- **Notification event**
  Notification triggering events such as APPROVED, REJECTED, and so on.
- **Template ID**
  Notification template to be used for getting the message. If you select a new work item as the event, this template might be the approval or rejection notice.
- **Recipient ID**
  Any agent who may be an approver of this stage or receiver of this stage activity result, such as a requestor or user.
- **Disable email**
  If this checkbox is enabled only workitem from workflow will be sent to the agent but not email.

Now you've maintained the configuration for stage-related maintenance activities for one specific workflow path. If your workflow path contains more than one stage, then follow the same processes as explained in this section to complete other stages in the workflow path. Remember, every stage is a decision-making point for the request in the process. If you've defined multiple workflow paths for the same process, select all of the paths involved in this process one by one, and define the entire stage level configuration to complete this step configuration. For example, in the access request workflow process, you can create more than one workflow path to deal with different systems, an SoD escape path, or an emergency access request path.

Next, let's discuss how to maintain route mapping.

8.1.9 Maintain Route Mapping

In the Maint Route Mapping step shown in Figure 8.11, you map logical paths such as initiator or routing rule to an actual path. As you saw in Section 8.1.5, the actual path is defined and mapped to the path ID defined per the rule result value.

To maintain the MSMP route mapping as shown in Figure 8.11, there are several attributes that need to be defined:

Route mapping attributes

- **Rule ID**
  Rule ID of the path.
- **Rule Result Value**
  Result returned by the rule.
- **Path ID**
  Path ID to be started in case this trigger value is returned by the rule.

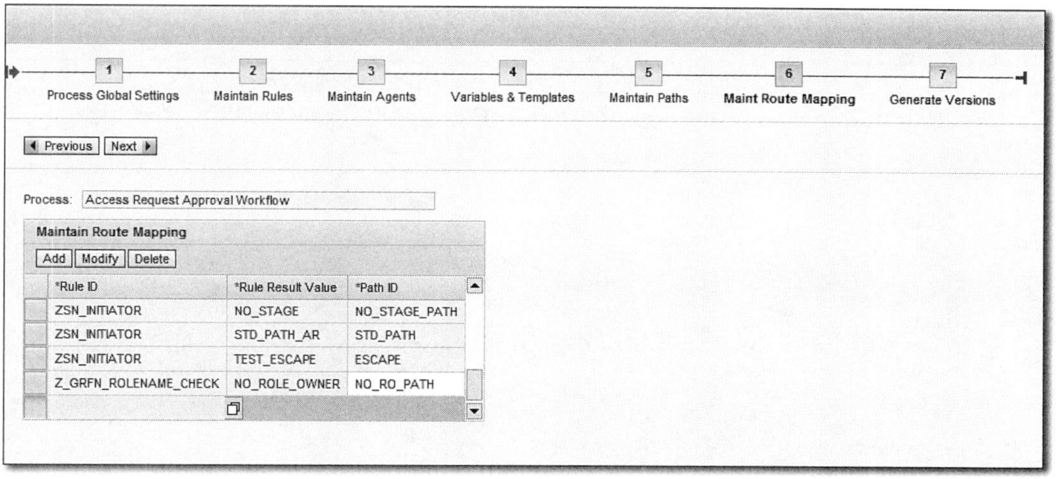

Figure 8.11 MSMP Route Mapping

Route mapping is quite straightforward. Now that you've configured the process, maintained the rules and rule sets, maintained the agents, reviewed the variables and applied a template, and maintained the paths and route mapping, you can finalize the last step in the MSMP Workflow Configuration: generating versions. Generating workflow versions enables you to change the workflow configuration while there are other active running paths.

8.1.10 Generate Versions

Other than agent, approver, and process global settings, all other workflow configuration settings are versioned by SAP Access Control to track the changes as well as transport them to other systems, which is similar to a technical object in the ABAP system. If you select the Save/Simulate button shown in Figure 8.12, this action will simulate generation to confirm that there are no errors in the MSMP workflow process so far. If there are errors that need to be addressed, the error message will give some lead to resolve the issue. Once completed with this action, ACTIVATE this process to make it ready to use in the specified workflow process. During the save and simulation phase, a popup screen will ask whether to save against new or old transport requests or without transport. Save this to transport all of the settings to another environment of the SAP Access Control system.

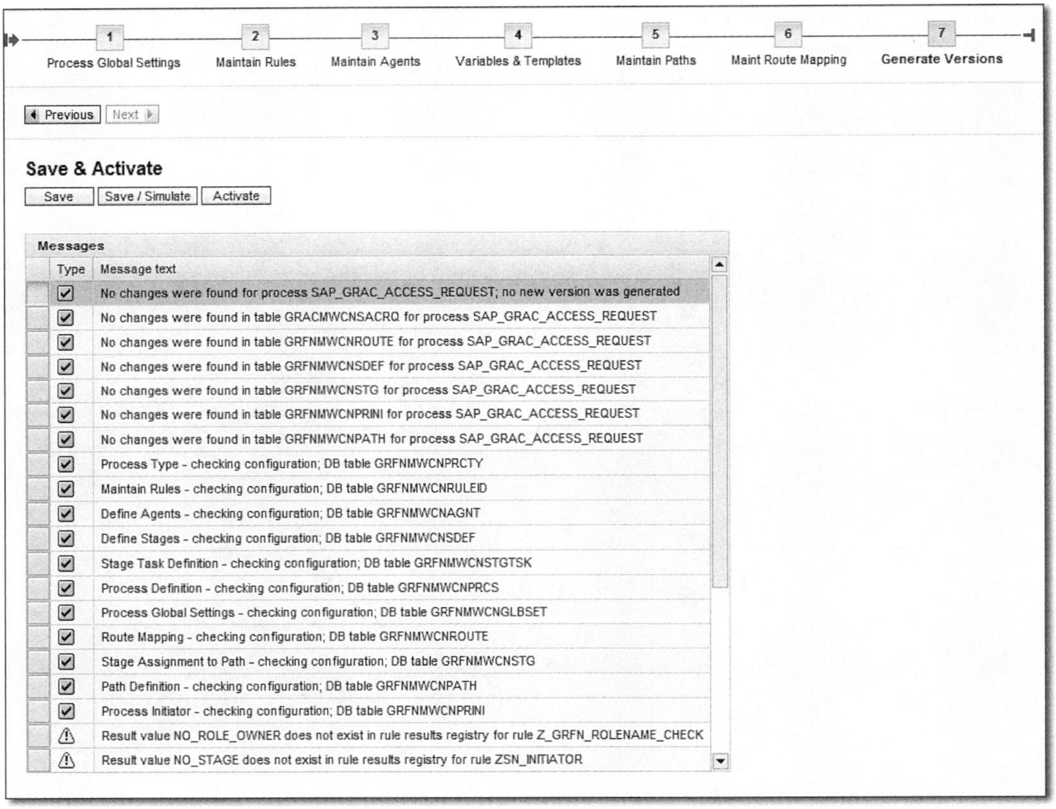

Figure 8.12 MSMP Version Generation

You've now seen how to configure the MSMP workflow using all of the seven steps maintained with various components, generated with a new version, and ready to work with the approval and notification processes.

Now let's review how to debug MSMP, which might be handy if you encounter some issues while processing a request.

8.2 Debugging MSMP

This section provides some technical help on how to debug the MSMP workflow as a part of troubleshooting. Generally, any user can view his own request status in the application, but there is also an improved instance status available for users who have an additional authorization to search access requests in User Access Management. Also, the user can see the full status and history of the request as well as the current approvers. However, if there are multiple approvers (such as a few role owners), it doesn't dynamically update to show which of the current approvers have already approved and who is waiting for whose approval. Because this whole workflow is running on the core ABAP-based workflow engine, MSMP is built on top of that to give some flexibility. Even though it's possible to troubleshoot part of the workflow issues in the traditional way, due to the MSMP addition, there is an extra setting required to troubleshoot and debug MSMP.

Debug logging activities and customization

The following procedure outlines the activities/customization you need to perform to enable debug logging for MSMP requests:

1. Enable the MSMP debug log.
2. Select the granularity of the MSMP debug log.
3. Add log categories.
4. Review the log.
5. Turn off the log.

Caution

We strongly recommend that you take extra caution to enable this log only in exceptional situations and disable the log after the problem is resolved.

To start the debugging, you need to enable the MSMP debug log. Execute Transaction GRFNMW_DEBUG to activate debugging as shown in Figure 8.13. You can enable the MSMP file debug log in this transaction for the situations in which the MSMP audit log or Transaction SLG1 isn't sufficient to analyze the problems. You can customize the debug logging for each of the MSMP processes. You customize the location of log file GRFN_MSMP_RUNTIME_LOG, which can be accessed using standard Transaction FILE. Change this only if required.

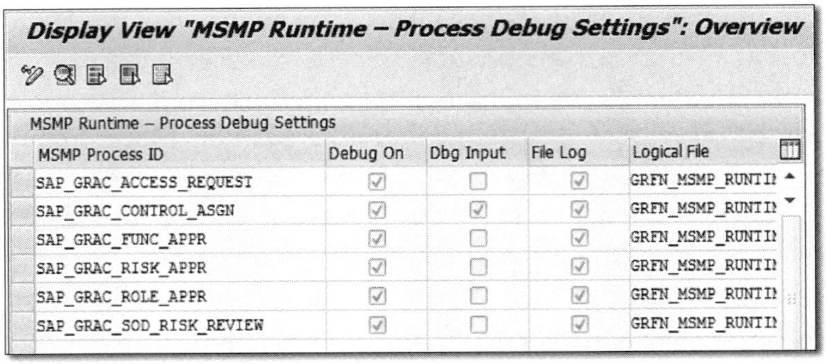

Figure 8.13 MSMP Debug Setting Activation

You can execute Transaction GRFNMW_DEBUG_MSG to choose the granularity of MSMP debug log messages from low to high. You need to add the log categories for the MSMP process to be able to log them to the file log configured in the previous step (see Figure 8.14).

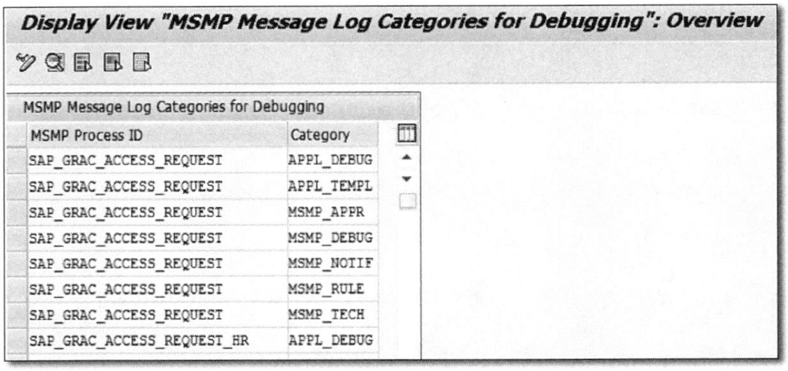

Figure 8.14 MSMP Debug Log Categories

You can view the content of the log files in standard Transaction AL11 in the directory that was configured earlier. Double-click on the file to view the log messages. Each one of the MSMP requests is generated in an individual file. After the successful submission of a request to MSMP, the logging process begins. Remember to turn off logging when you're finished troubleshooting.

Now that you know the important steps for troubleshooting the MSMP process using debugging, you've completed the MSMP process. Let's move on to using BRF in the MSMP process decision making without writing code.

8.3 Business Rule Framework Plus (BRF+)

Business Rule Framework Plus (BRF+) is a business rules system developed in the ABAP Stack. This provides a comprehensive application programming interface (API) and user interface (UI) for defining and processing business rules by business users to meet agile business conditions without much dependency on the IT development team. It's been used in various application areas in SAP systems and support features such as simulation, trace, transport, and XML export or import. Business rules describe the operations, definitions and constraints that apply to an organization in achieving its goals. Business rules include basically everything that runs a business, for instance, business habits, manuals, policies, lines of computer code, and minds of experienced employees. BRF+ supports the definition of business rules. BRF+ usage in SAP Access Control gives the flexibility to model rules in an intuitive way, and it reuses these rules in the MSMP workflow to initiate and decide various access request paths and/or find the correct approval agents in the workflow process. In advanced cases, it can actually be like writing code, but for SAP Access Control functionality, the uses are often more simple to derive agents or specific results that can be linked to workflow route decision points.

In this section, we'll look at a BRF+ use case for SAP Access Control to ground our discussion of BRF+ practically. After we've reviewed the use case, we'll look at the chaining route rule and at the BRF+ function in the Business Role Manager.

8.3.1 BRF+ Use Case in SAP Access Control

For an example, BRF+ can be used to make a decision based on the access request type. If it's emergency access related, then the workflow should be routed to the emergency approval workflow path; otherwise, this should route to a different path. This routing rule can be defined in BRF+ as an initiator rule. Similarly, any specific agent determination such as department head or custom approver can also be defined with the help of BRF+ rules. Let's discuss BRF+ rule creation in depth, including how to create new BRF+ rules and attaching them to the MSMP workflow as shown in Figure 8.15.

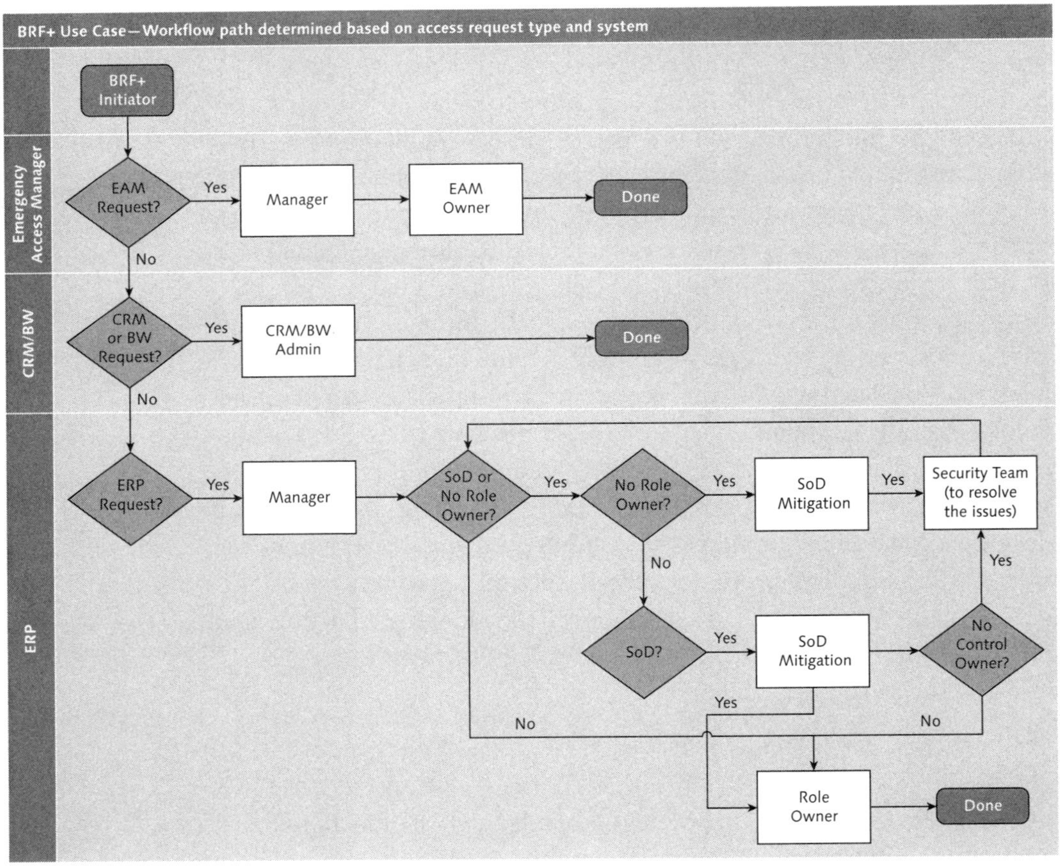

Figure 8.15 MSMP Workflow Sample Path Selection Based on the BRF+ Initiator Rule

Logging into SAPAccess Control and BRF+

Let's get started by logging on to SAPGUI in the SAP Access Control system. Select SAP Reference IMG from Transaction SPRO, follow the menu path, GOVERNANCE, RISK AND COMPLIANCE • ACCESS CONTROL • WORKFLOW FOR ACCESS CONTROL • DEFINE WORKFLOW-RELATED MSMP RULES, and execute. You'll be taken to the GENERATE MSMP RULE FOR PROCESS screen.

Selecting the process ID and Rule types

As shown in Figure 8.16, you need to maintain the relevant MSMP process ID that needs a BRF+ rule. In our case, we've selected SAP_GRAC_ACCESS_REQUEST as the process from the 10 different process IDs that are available in the standard GRAC process. Similarly, there are four different RULE TYPES available: BRFPLUS based, FUNCTION MODULE based, ABAP CLASS based, and BRFPLUS FLAT RULE. This rule type is used to define what kind of rule generation process is used. For illustration purposes, we use BRFPLUS FLAT RULE (LINEITEM BY LINEITEM).

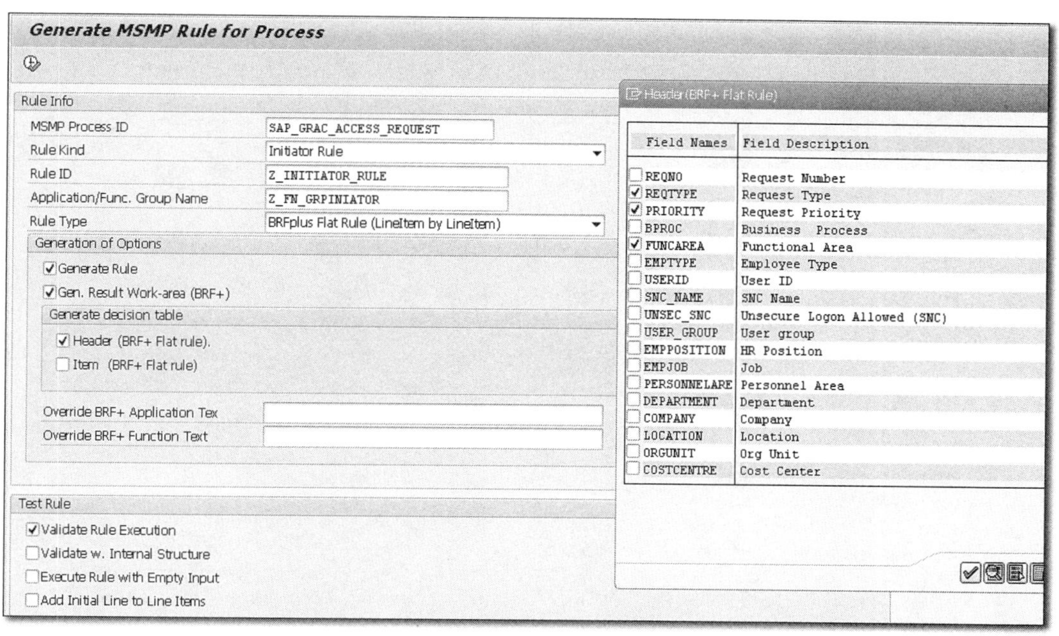

Figure 8.16 Maintain MSMP Process Related to the New BRF+ Rule

The next field shown in Figure 8.16 is RULE KIND, which is used to get results from one of the types such as agent, initiator, routing, or notification variables. This needs to be maintained accordingly in the MSMP workflow depending on the requirement. After maintaining these values, enter any appropriate name for the RULE ID and APPLICATION/FUNC. GROUP NAME, and follow the customer namespace that starts with Y or Z. At the same time, check the default GENERATE RULE and GEN RESULT WORK-AREA (BRF+) checkboxes, along with VALIDATE RULE EXECUTION. While preparing this shell for the actual BRF+ rule, you need a decision table to make decisions based on request header characteristics such as request type and request priority. Choose the HEADER (BRF+ FLAT RULE) checkbox. Now you've maintained all of the required entries, so click on EXECUTE to generate the rule.

As a result of successful generation, shown in Figure 8.17, you'll be able to view a log with details of the activity carried out along with an APPLICATION ID and FUNCTION that are created in the BRF+ with Z names you entered and the GUID that is returned. This long alphanumeric GUID is referred to repeatedly in the message, which is the rule ID/function generated here. If there are any red lights in the log generation, you might need to do some troubleshooting work before proceeding further.

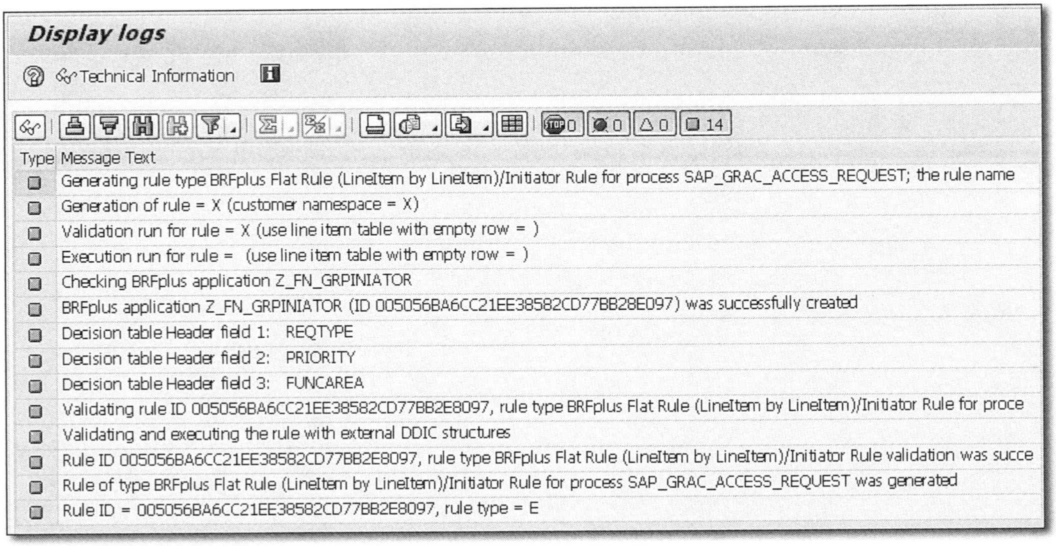

Figure 8.17 BRF+ Log with Application ID, Function, and Result Data

Creating a rule in BRF+

The next step in working with actual BRF+ is to create a rule to suit your needs. In this use case, the rule you need to create is a decision table based on a request type and system combination. To achieve this, you need to define a business rule using the BRF+ Workbench in combination with the decision tree. The steps for creating, saving, and activating rules are listed here:

1. Create the top expression.
2. Select the result data object.
3. Select the condition items.
4. Define the condition parameters and result set.
5. Save the condition parameters.
6. Activate the condition parameters.
7. Save the rule.
8. Activate the rule.

To give a little introduction on the BRF+ Workbench, let's start by executing Transaction BRF+, or follow the menu path, GOVERNANCE, RISK AND COMPLIANCE • ACCESS CONTROL • WORKFLOW FOR ACCESS CONTROL • DEFINE BUSINESS RULE FRAMEWORK from Transaction SPRO. This action opens a new Web Dynpro application in a browser window as the BRF+ Workbench, and you can see the rule GUID that you've created. If you don't see any, select it from MY APPLICATIONS on the bottom-left part of the window. Figure 8.18 shows various options, such as REPOSITORY, RECENTLY USED, FAVORITES, and CATALOG, which are available for you to work on.

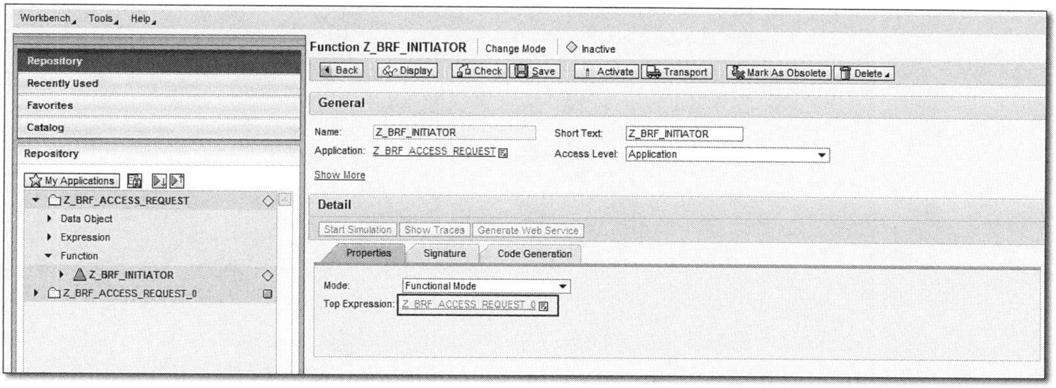

Figure 8.18 BRF+ Workbench Options

Alternatively, you can click on OPEN OBJECT as shown in Figure 8.19, and enter the GUID that you created earlier in this discussion. On the left side panel of the application, you can open the APPLICATION ID node via the arrow icon to display all objects created under the APPLICATION ID ZBRF_ACCESS_REQUEST, which you created from an earlier step. Double-click on the function name to display the details of the function from the right side. You can toggle between hyperlinks SHOW_LESS OR SHOW_MORE to see the details of the function to include the unique GUID. Similarly, you can toggle between DISPLAY AND EDIT to go between display and change mode.

From the PROPERTIES tab, click and create the DECISION table in the TOP EXPRESSION, and you'll see the DECISION TABLE created earlier as shown Figure 8.20. Insert new rows as required to enter and create your decision table. Each line will match a specific condition based on the request attributes depending on the columns you selected. Each line will be mapped to a path in the MSMP workflow configuration, so make sure you give it a unique result value in the RULE_RESULT column, which is used in MSMP WORKFLOW CONFIGURATION to get the result from here.

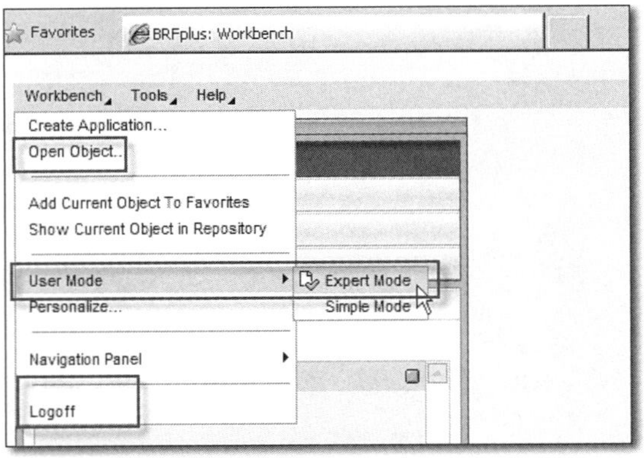

Figure 8.19 BRF+ Workbench: Maintain Top Expression

Decision tree rule activation

After you've maintained all of the rules in the decision tree, select SAVE, and activate all technical components that belong to your custom BRF+ application, functions, expressions, and so on. Make sure that all are active and showing up as green. Also make a note on the GUID that it needs to be entered in the MSMP workflow as a BRF+ function name.

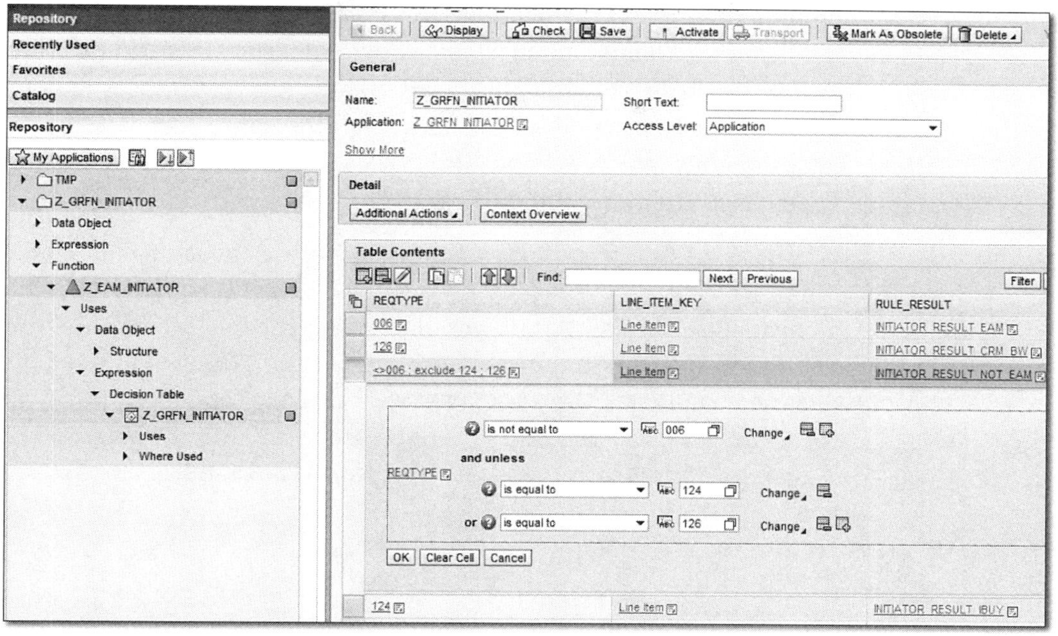

Figure 8.20 BRF+ Decision Tree Rule Creation

To ensure that everything is working fine, you may use simulation with values to check whether you're getting the expected results in the RULE_RESULT table. To start using simulation from an existing BRF+ menu, click the option as shown in Figure 8.21.

Rule simulation

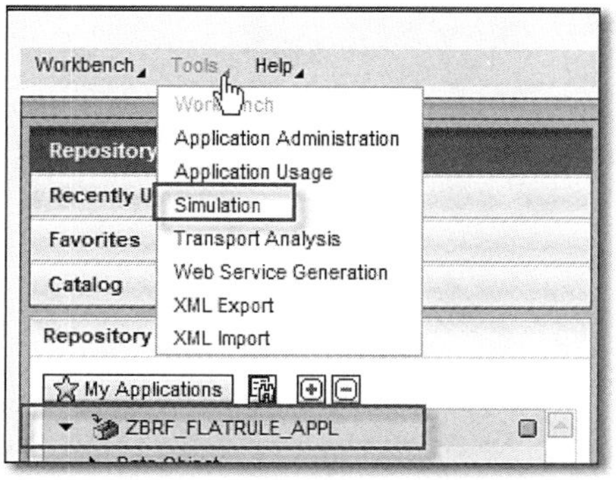

Figure 8.21 BRF+ Simulation to Test Rule Result

Enter all planned input values in the initial screen and execute it; based on the input, your result table will show the result. This will help you determine that your BRF+ rule determination has no errors. Also don't forget to activate the BRF+ function after everything is fine and confirm that the function, application, and decision table are all marked with a green light to show that they are active.

So far, we've looked at how to create a BRF+ rule based on a few conditions. Now, let's move further into this functionality and check how this is maintained in the MSMP workflow to trigger the correct workflow with a BRF+ rule as an initiator rule. Execute Transaction SPRO, and follow the menu path, GOVERNANCE, RISK AND COMPLIANCE • ACCESS CONTROL • WORKFLOW FOR ACCESS CONTROL • MAINTAIN MSMP WORKFLOWS. The MSMP initial screen with all processes is shown in Figure 8.22.

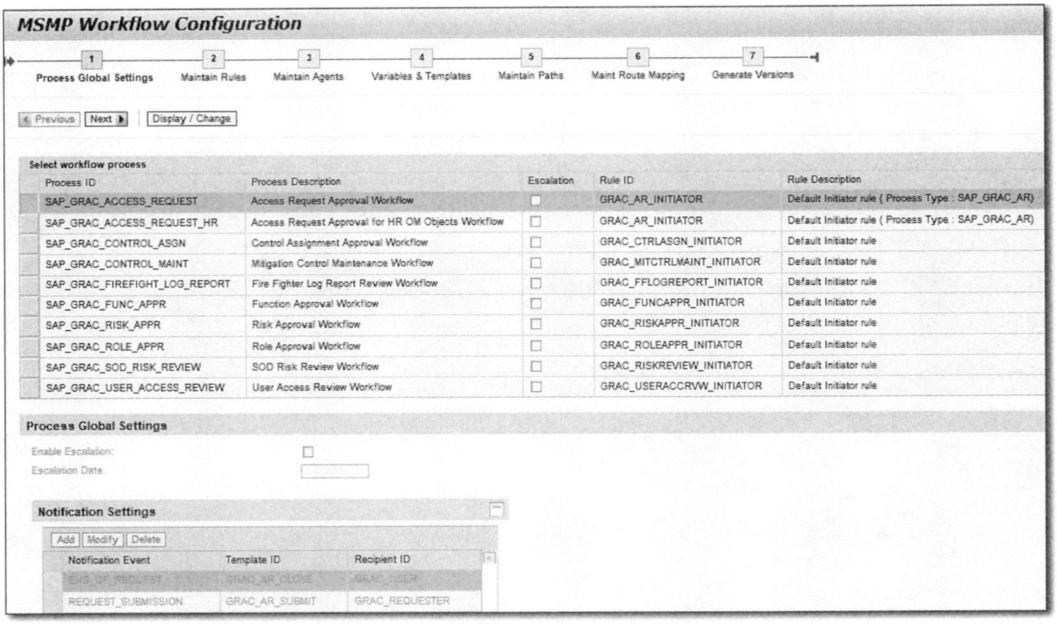

Figure 8.22 MSMP Initial Screen: Maintain BRF+ Initiator Rule

Click on the DISPLAY/CHANGE button to maintain the BRF+ initiator rule configuration. Select the correct PROCESS ID, and choose the MAINTAIN RULES step. Click the ADD button from the LIST OF RULES window, add the BRF+ RULE ID, and enter the RULE DESCRIPTION, RULE TYPE, and RULE

KIND, which is INITIATOR RULE, as shown in Figure 8.23. Save the settings. In the same window, click on the RESULTS button to add all of the result values that are created in the BRF+ result tab.

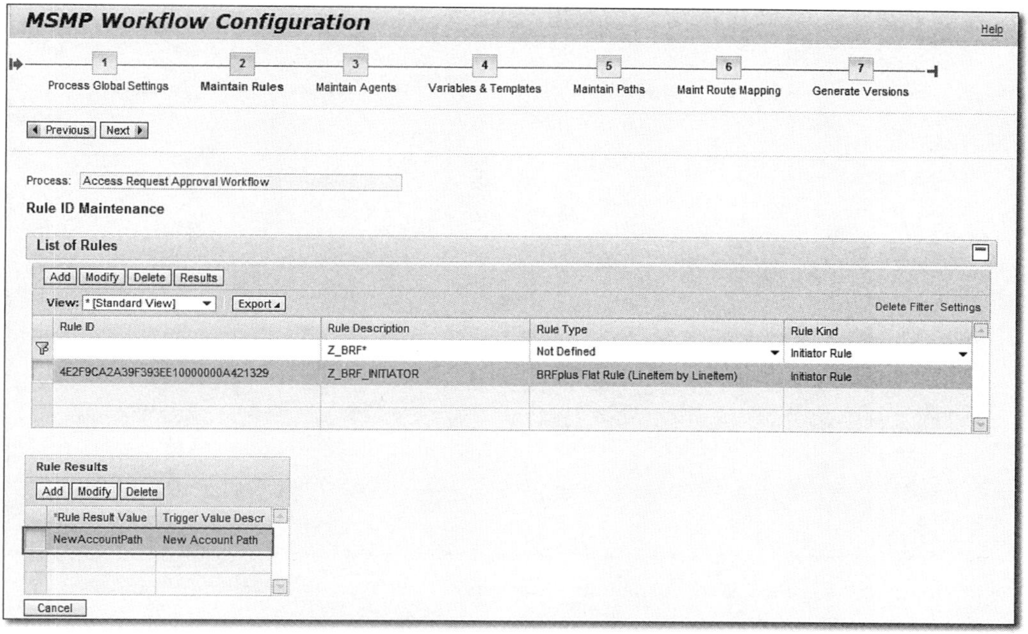

Figure 8.23 BRF+ Rule Maintenance for the Initiator Rule and Rule Results

After you've created the initiator rule, you need to maintain the GLOBAL RULES and the PROCESS INITIATOR along with this BRF+ RULE ID. These global rules values are for the INITIATOR RULE and NOTIFICATION RULE only because they meant global to the workflow process selected. And you can maintain only one rule per process ID. In contrast to this, other rules, such as agent rules, can be defined with multiple rules per agent type. As shown in the workflow diagram earlier in Figure 8.15, the example scenario assumes that you've maintained three results that route to three different workflows.

Initiator rule maintenance

As a next step to initiator rule maintenance, you need to maintain three different paths and their respective stages with configuration as a RULE_RESULT from the initiator in the MAINTAIN PATHS step of the MSMP workflow, detailed in Section 8.1.5. After all of the paths are maintained, go to the next step, MAINTAIN ROUTE MAPPING, as detailed in Section

8.1.9. You need to map the RULE_RESULT with the path in this step, and based on the result value passed by the BRF+ rule, the resulting path will be chosen to execute the workflow (see Figure 8.24).

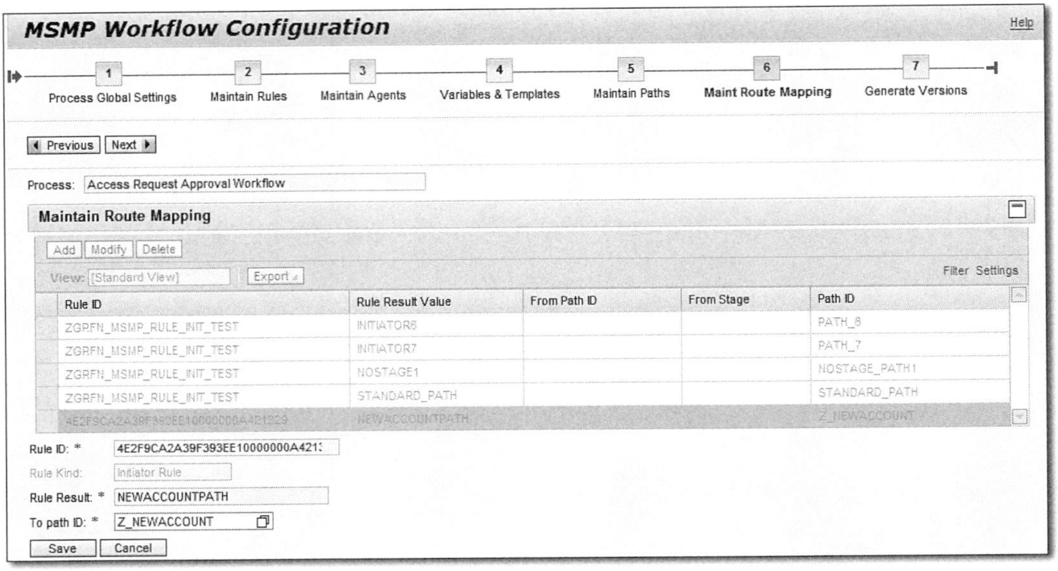

Figure 8.24 Maintain Route Mapping

Activation of the MSMP Workflow

After maintaining all of these values, now you're ready to generate the MSMP workflow and activate the workflow with your own BRF+ rule as the initiator to determine the approval workflow path based on the access request type and any other characteristics defined in the business rule.

In Section 8.3.1, we've walked through a use case on how to create and maintain a business rule in BRF+, maintain a decision table with a rule result, and embed this rule in the MSMP workflow to serve the purpose of routing to different workflows based on the initiator rule. Similarly, BRF+ rules can be used to create agent rules or notification rules. The routing rule is another rule kind that can be used to take a different route based on an SoD violation result. The same example diagram shows the additional option of verifying for any SoD violation after the manager stage approval. After the workflow determines that there is an SoD violation, then the workflow uses this different workflow routing upon completing the manager's approval. If there is no violation, then the workflow is processed in the regular path defined in the MSMP process.

Building on this use case for BRF+, we'll highlight at the very high level some extraordinary options that you can use with the BRF+ decision table to set up rules that don't need any kind of coding. In this section, we highlighted how some complex scenarios can be handled. In the next section, we'll look at the chaining routing rule using a function module. This can be helpful to some companies for dealing with complex decision-making processes in their Access Request Management tool implementation.

8.3.2 Chaining Routing Rules Using a Function Module and BRF+

The MSMP workflow allows only one routing rule to be attached after stage execution (approval) happens, and some scenarios might need to use multiple routing rules to resolve the business cases. There are two different function module-based routing rules for no role owner and SoD violation detour.

Forming new rule logic with combined rules and routing

To have several routing rules participating in routing, you can combine the rules together by defining a new rule logic that uses those predelivered rules as building blocks by means of MSMP rule chaining. The customer is responsible for the chaining logic by defining the order of execution and translation of rule results. (Only MSMP rules of the same kind can be chained together (because they have same signatures).

Segregration of duty violation routing rule and no role owner routing rule

In this example, you'll combine the SoD violation routing rule and the no role owner routing rule into a new rule that has the following logic:

1. Execute the SoD rule to check whether the SoD exists. If yes, then return result SOD_VIOLATION.
2. If no SoD violation exists, then execute the no role owner rule to check whether the role owner is defined. If yes, then return result NO_ROLE_OWNER.
3. If neither of these are true, then return SPACE (meaning continue to the next stage).

To complete the task, you need to perform the following to make the previously mentioned logic work. As a first step for this, you need to generate an empty shell of a new function module that will implement the logic just mentioned. After this function module is ready, then register this new function module-based rule for the access request process ID. After this, define the three new rule results in the rule registry. This is done either via standard MSMP configuration Transaction GRFNMW_CONFIGURE_WD as mentioned earlier to start your configuration work from the browser window, or via expert maintenance Transaction GRFNMW_CONFIGURE, which is from the SAPGUI. If you're an expert, you can use configuration from SAPGUI. Figure 8.25 shows how to define this new function module in the MSMP process and how to maintain the rules in the SAPGUI.

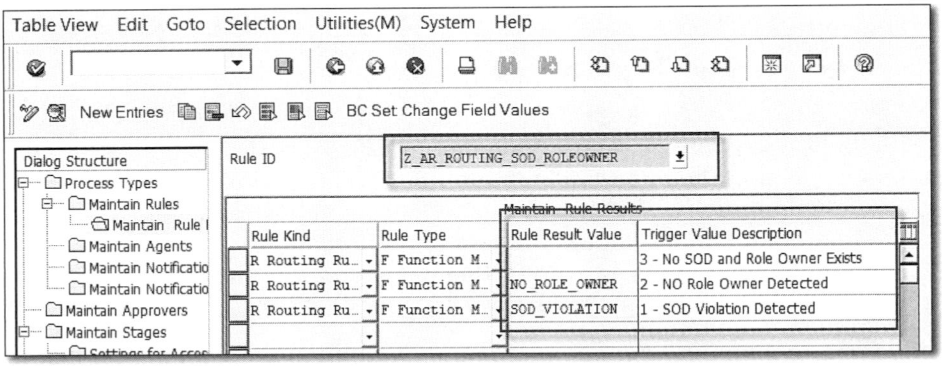

Figure 8.25 MSMP Maintenance for Routing Rule Chaining

We've shown you how to deal with some of the complex workflow routing using function modules at a very high level. Even at this high-level review, this functionality will be helpful for most advanced users to deal with some complex scenarios in your environment. In the next section, we'll look at the BRF+ function usage in the Business Role Manager tool.

8.3.3 BRF+ Function in Business Role Manager

You've seen earlier how to use BRF+ to streamline the access request workflow based on certain business rules. Just to refresh your memory on the Business Role Manager tool, the role methodology is defined with multiple steps involved in the creation of roles.

Role Methodology and mapping

You can define multiple methodologies in Transaction SPRO and use specific methodology depending on role types, department-specific policies, and other company policies. The BRF+ rule and rule result are required to determine the condition group to find the role methodology function and/or approvers. Mapping of this condition group to the role methodology process determines the appropriate role methodology to be carried out as designed. Let's walk through the process of creating the BRF+ and associating it with condition groups. For example, you can have the role methodology for technical roles, and the derived roles definition methodology can follow some processes, but, at the same time, the business role may skip some of the steps in the role definition methodology. Let's look at these steps at a high level in the following list and then get into further specifics about configuration:

1. Create the BRF+ application and rule shell.
2. Create BRF+ rules.
3. Map BRF+ rules to the condition group.
4. Define the methodology processes and steps for role maintenance.
5. Create condition group IDs and associate them with methodology.
6. Access the MSMP maintenance screen, select the SAP_GRAC_ROLE_APPR process, and maintain all of the necessary the MSMP workflow configurations.
7. Maintain the stage settings, and select the AGENT ID as the approver rule that is created in BRF+ or the standard GRAC_ROLE_APPROVER, and activate the workflow.

BRF+ application and rule shell creation

As specified, the first step for this process is to create the BRF+ application and rule shell by running the program GRAC_GENERATE_ERM_BRFRULE. You can also access this from Transaction SPRO, and by following the menu path, GOVERNANCE, RISK AND COMPLIANCE • ACCESS CONTROL • ROLE MANAGEMENT • GENERATE BRFPLUS APPLICATIONS, APPROVERS, AND METHODOLOGY FUNCTIONS. The initial screen appears as shown in Figure 8.26. After you've maintained the RULE INFO settings with the customer namespace, execute this to create the BRF+ applications and rules shell. If you face any errors, they need to be rectified before proceeding to the next step.

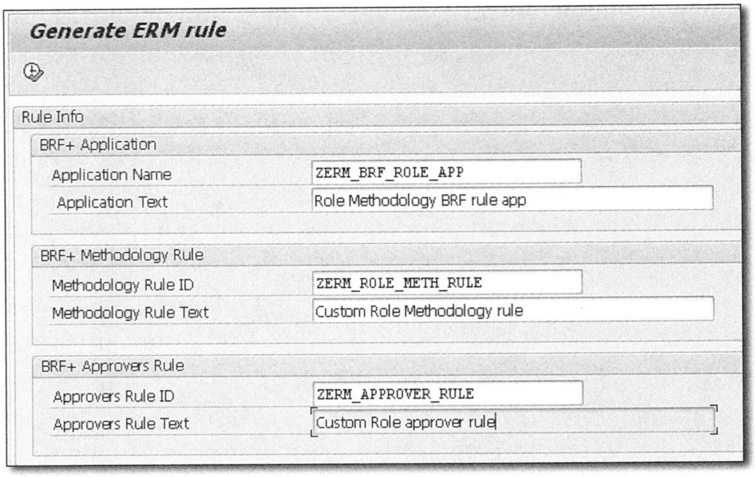

Figure 8.26 Business Role Manager BRF+ Rule Generation Initial Screen

Now you need create rules (see Section 8.3.1) by carrying out all of the eight steps involved in BRF+ rule creation and simulating these rules to confirm that the rules are working fine in Transaction BRF+.

Mapping to a condition group

After you've finished the rules creation, you need to map these BRF+ rules to condition groups from Transaction SPRO. Follow the menu path, GOVERNANCE, RISK AND COMPLIANCE • ACCESS CONTROL • ROLE MANAGEMENT • ASSIGN CONDITION GROUP TO BRF+ RULES. After executing this, the screen shown in Figure 8.27 appears, where you select CONDITION GROUP and maintain the BRF+ application and relevant rule ID or function name. Two different condition groups are available: APPROVER and METHODOLOGY. You can maintain these mapping based on your requirements.

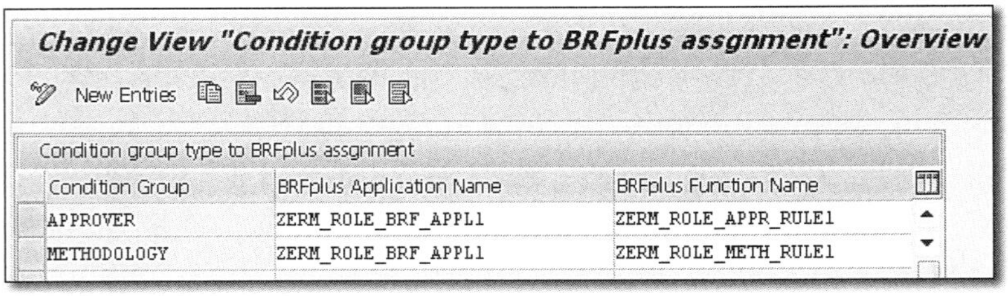

Figure 8.27 Condition Group Type to BRF+ Rule Assignment

Defining the methodology processes and steps for role maintenance

After the rule ID mapping to condition group is done, you need to define the methodology processes and steps for role maintenance. The application provides a set of actions that can be used for role maintenance, such as definition, generation, and so on. You can select which actions to use, the order, and the frequency. This is called your methodology. For example, you can define that six steps are required to maintain a role and that approval is required after each step. The detailed configuration activity of this step was covered in Chapter 6.

To continue further to the next step, follow the menu path, GOVERNANCE, RISK AND COMPLIANCE • ACCESS CONTROL • ROLE MANAGEMENT • ASSOCIATE METHODOLOGY PROCESS TO CONDITION GROUP. In the screen shown in Figure 8.28, you need to create CONDITION GROUP IDs and associate them with the methodology that is maintained in the earlier step. These condition groups link the BRF+ rules and the role METHODOLOGY to determine whether to carry out role METHODOLOGY 1 or role METHODOLOGY 2 based on the BRF+ methodology rule defined with the result based on the role type of either single role or business role.

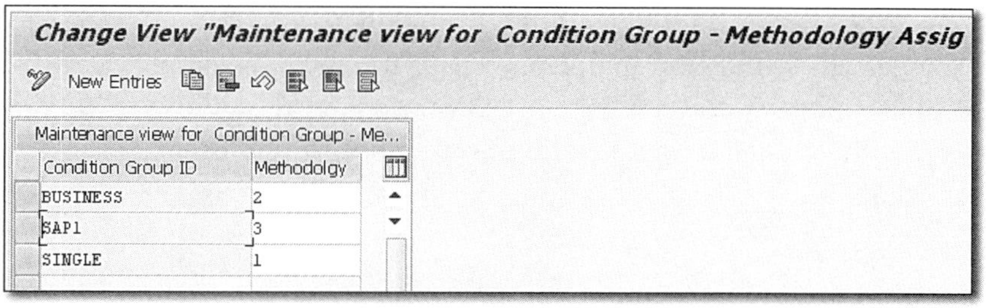

Figure 8.28 Condition Group to Methodology Assignment

Configuration maintenance and MSMP

Now you need to access the MSMP maintenance screen, select the SAP_GRAC_ROLE_APPR' process, and maintain all of the necessary MSMP workflow configurations as we've discussed in the first part of this section. You need to maintain the approver agent rule that had been created in BRF+, if any, in MSMP process step 2, MAINTAIN RULES. In step 5, maintain the stage settings, and select the AGENT ID as the approver rule that is created in BRF+ or the standard GRAC_ROLE_APPROVER, and then activate the workflow.

In this section you've seen how to create BRF+ rules and assign condition group types to the BRF+ applications and functions, along with the role methodology process and the steps to associate the condition group to role methodology. You've also configured the role approver based on BRF+, attaching BRF+ rules to the MSMP workflow process and rule chaining to achieve a complex resolution using BRF+.

In the next section, we'll build upon the MSMP configuration and get into the details of how to maintain workflow notification as part of the advanced SAP Access Control topics.

8.4 Workflow Notification Maintenance in MSMP

In the MSMP Workflow Configuration, you've seen how to maintain or configure various variables at different steps such as workflow paths, stages, approval agents, and rule IDs. In this section, let's get into the little details of how to create or maintain notification. This is another important topic to most of the customer environment because it's a vital communication between various players in User Access Management, and most companies prefer to define it according to their company policies, other needs, and regulations. To maintain various templates, SAP provides all notification templates out of the box. We've provided the detailed information on available notifications in the following subsections with detailed usage. Later, in Section 8.5, you'll learn how to customize them.

8.4.1 Available Notification Templates

Every workflow event in one of the workflow processes that will trigger an email notification (work item) corresponds to exactly one predefined message class. Each message class is attached to one document object containing a predelivered message body for the corresponding workflow event. The link between the message class and the predelivered document object can be viewed but can't be altered in table view GRFNVNOTIFYMSG. Customers, however, can create custom document objects, that is, an object name starts with Y or Z with message bodies that are better tailored to the customer's need and replace the predelivered document objects in the IMG customizing. Almost every process comes with only four different events that can be configured to send an email notification:

- New Work Item
  This notification is sent to the inbox of the responsible approver(s) at every stage level.
- Approval
  This notification is sent when the request or line item is approved.
- Rejection
  This notification is used to send rejection information when the request or line item is rejected.
- Escalation
  This is used to send an escalation message at each approval stage to an alternative approver (a different agent) or to escalate to the next stage agent.

Event configuration and e-mail notifications with MSMP

Table 8.1 lists each process and each of the four events of the respective message class.

Process ID\Event	New Work Item	Approved	Rejected	Escalated
SAP_GRAC_ACCESS_REQUEST & SAP_GRAC_ACCESS_REQUEST_HR	0MSMP_AR_NEWWORKITM	0MSMP_AR_APPROVED	0MSMP_AR_REJECTED	0MSMP_AR_ESCALATION
SAP_GRAC_CONTROL_ASGN	0MSMP_CNTLASGN_NEWWI	0MSMP_CNTLASGN_APPR	0MSMP_CNTLASGN_REJC	0MSMP_CNTLASGN_ESCL
SAP_GRAC_CONTROL_MAINT	0MSMP_MITCNTRL_NEWWI	0MSMP_MITCNTRL_APPR	0MSMP_MITCNTRL_REJC	0MSMP_MITCNTRL_ESCL
SAP_GRAC_FIREFIGHT_LOG_REPORT	0MSMP_LOGRPT_NEWWI	0MSMP_LOGRPT_APPR	0MSMP_LOGRPT_REJC	0MSMP_LOGRPT_ESCL
SAP_GRAC_FUNC_APPR	0MSMP_FUNCAPPR_NEWWI	0MSMP_FUNCAPPR_APPR	0MSMP_FUNCAPPR_REJC	0MSMP_FUNCAPPR_ESCL
SAP_GRAC_RISK_APPR	0MSMP_RISK_NEWWI	0MSMP_RISK_APPR	0MSMP_RISK_REJC	0MSMP_RISK_ESCL

Table 8.1 Process to Notification Type Relationship

Process ID\Event	New Work Item	Approved	Rejected	Escalated
SAP_GRAC_ROLE_APPR	0MSMP_ROLEAPPR_NEWWI	0MSMP_ROLEAPPR_APPR	0MSMP_ROLEAPPR_REJC	0MSMP_ROLEAPPR_ESCL
SAP_GRAC_SOD_RISK_REVIEW	N/A	0MSMP_RISKREVW_APPR	0MSMP_RISKREVW_REJC	0MSMP_RISKREVW_ESCL
SAP_GRAC_USER_ACCESS_REVIEW	0MSMP_USERACC_NEWWI	0MSMP_USERACC_APPR	0MSMP_USERACC_REJC	0MSMP_USERACC_ESCL

Table 8.1 Process to Notification Type Relationship (Cont.)

There are always some exceptions in definitions, and two processes have additional workflow events that send email notifications. The first process is the Access Request Approval Workflow (for both users and HR Organizational Management objects) with process IDs SAP_GRAC_ACCESS_REQUEST and SAP_GRAC_ACCESS_REQUEST_HR, respectively. This process comes with the following additional events and message classes:

- **Request submission: 0AC_AR_SUBMIT**
  This message is sent to the user or requestor upon request creation.
- **Request approval by mail: 0MSMP_AR_APP_REJ**
  This message with URL is sent to the approver's email inbox. This is an alternate to message class 0MSMP_AR_NEWWORKITM.
- **Request forwarded: 0MSMP_AR_FORWARD**
  This message is sent to agents (approvers) whom the request should be forwarded to.
- **Request closed: 0AC_AR_CLOSE**
  This message is sent to the user upon completion of the workflow process.
- **Email reminder: 0MSMP_EMAILRMDR_CUP**
  This message is sent to responsible agents as a reminder to approve any pending work item that needs to be approved. This is sent based on configuration.

The other exception is the SoD risk review workflow, which comes with an additional message class for an email reminder event:

- **Email reminder SoD: 0MSMP_EMAILRMDR_SOD**
  This message is sent to responsible agents to remind them of an outstanding SoD review.

You can look up the names of the predelivered document objects for each message class in table view GRFNVNOTIFYMSG as shown in Figure 8.29. By double-clicking on the message class, you can view the details.

Display View "Notification Messages (Defaults)": Overview

Notification Messages (Defaults)

Message Class	Msg.no.	Description
0AC_AR_CLOSE	0	CUP Provisioning Notification
0AC_AR_SUBMIT	0	CUP Notification
0AC_AR_USER_PROV	0	CUP Provisioning Notification
0AC_CONTROL_ALERTS	0	Mitigation Control Alert
0AC_CONTROL_ASSIGN	0	Control Assignment
0AC_CONTROL_ASSIGN_D	0	Control Assignment Delete
0AC_CUP_NAME_CHANGE	0	Name change notification
0AC_CUP_PSS_NOTIFY	0	PSS Notification
0AC_CUP_ROLE_NOTIFY	0	Notification on role expiry
0AC_RISK_TERMINATOR	0	Risk Terminator
0AC_ROLE_REF_INST	0	Message Class for Role reaffirm Instructions
0AC_SOD_ALERTS	0	SOD Alert
0AC_SPM_INSTRUCTION	0	SPM workflow instuction
0AC_SPM_LOG_NOTIFY	0	SPM Log notification
0AC_SPM_NOTIFICATION	0	SPM Login Notification
0ERM_ROLE_CERTIFY	0	Role certification reminder
0FN_OBSOLETE_SURVEY	3	Obsolete survey
0FN_OWP_DELIVER	0	Offline working process deliver mail content
0GRFN_BRFP_ACT	1	BRF plus action: Email notification 1
0GRFN_BRFP_ACT	2	BRF plus action: Email notification 2
0GRFN_ISSUE_NOTIFY	0	Send notification to object owner
0GRFN_POLICY_SEND	0	Policy send
0MSMP_AR_APPROVED	0	Approved - Access Request
0MSMP_AR_APP_REJ	0	New Work Item - Approve/Reject by email
0MSMP_AR_ESCALATION	0	Escalation - Access Request
0MSMP_AR_FORWARD	0	Forward - Access Request
0MSMP_AR_NEWWORKITM	0	New Work Item - Access Request
0MSMP_AR_REJECTED	0	Rejected - Access Request
0MSMP_CNTLASGN_APPR	0	Approved - Control Assignment Request
0MSMP_CNTLASGN_ESCL	0	Escalation - Control Assignment Request
0MSMP_CNTLASGN_NEWWI	0	New Work Item - Control Assignment Request
0MSMP_CNTLASGN_REJC	0	Rejected - Control Assignment Request
0MSMP_CN_APPROVED	0	Mitigation Control Maintenance Request Approved
0MSMP_CN_REJECTED	0	Mitigation Control Maintenance Request Rejected
0MSMP_EMAILRMDR	0	Reminder Notification

Figure 8.29 View GRFNVNOTIFYMSG: Message Class View

In Figure 8.30, you can see the detail and the relationship of MESSAGE CLASS 0AC_AR_CLOSE and DOCU. OBJECT GRAC_AR_CLOSE with description, subject, and title information.

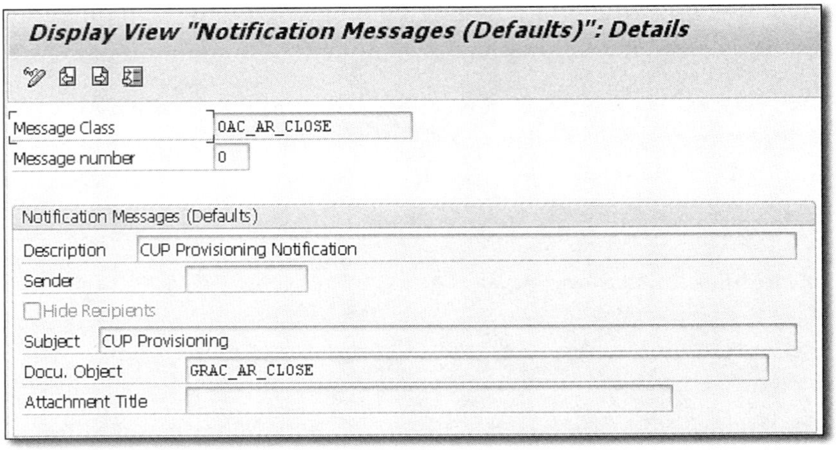

Figure 8.30 Document Object Maintained in the Message Class

If you need to see the contents of this document object, execute Transaction SE61, which is standard SAP Script text maintenance. In this transaction, you need to select the document class as GENERAL TEXT and enter the document object NAME. Click on DISPLAY to see the details (see Figure 8.31). If your system supports it, and these objects are maintained in multiple languages, then you'll be able to view the content based on the logon language.

Notification Messages: multiple language output

The SAP predelivered document object, shown in Figure 8.32, is the content that will be sent to the agents as a notification message via email. If you maintain this in multiple languages, the recipient receives the access control notification email based on their logon language. You can customize the message with your own message content using the variables available. You'll see in Section 8.5.1 how to customize the contents of notification messages.

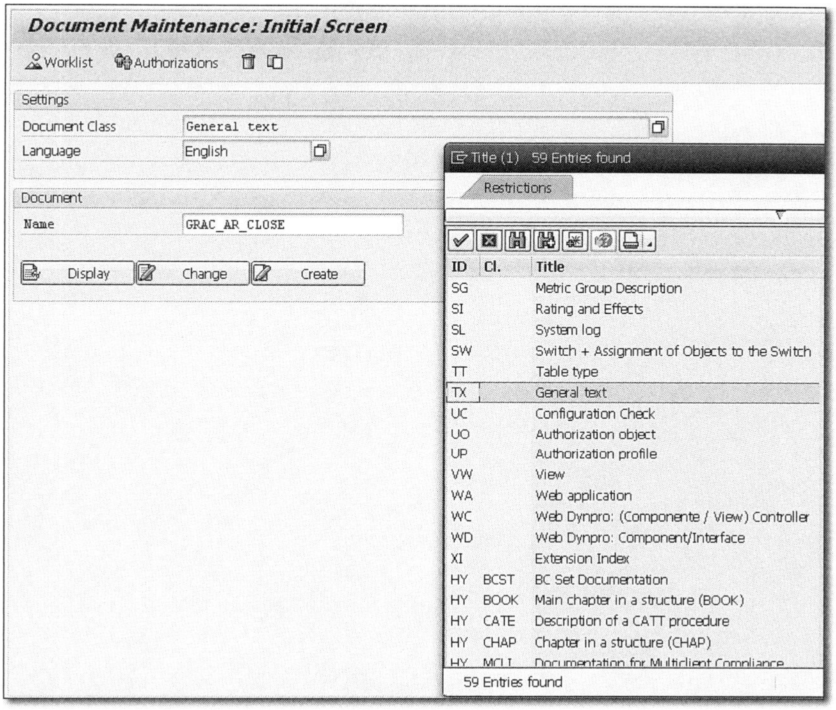

Figure 8.31 Text Maintenance

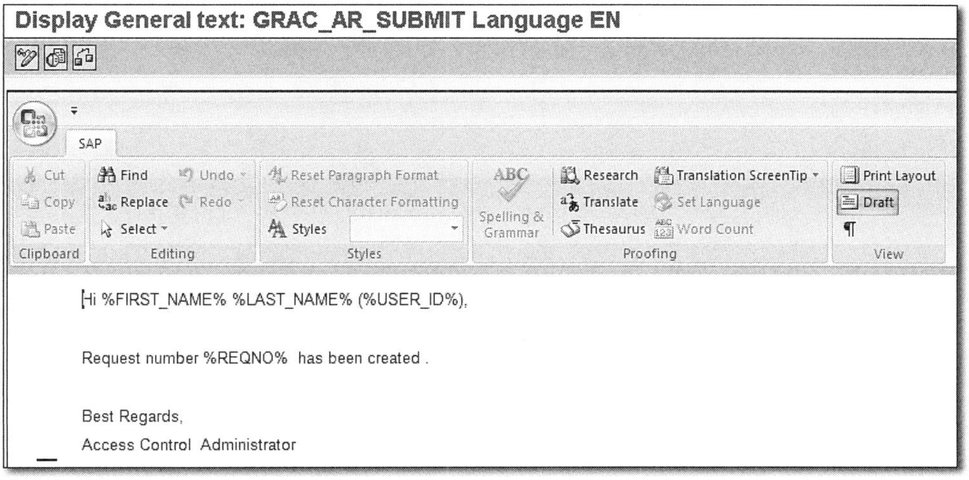

Figure 8.32 Message Content

You'll be using this document object against the message class used in the VARIABLES AND TEMPLATES step 4 in the MSMP workflow process that is provided against the TEMPLATE ID discussed in Section 8.1.4. Also the variables that are defined as %FIRST_NAME% %LAST_NAME% are the variables available from the bottom part of the window of this step 4, as shown in Figure 8.6. The template ID is attached in step 5, detailed in Section 8.1.5, while defining stages with various notification or approval messages.

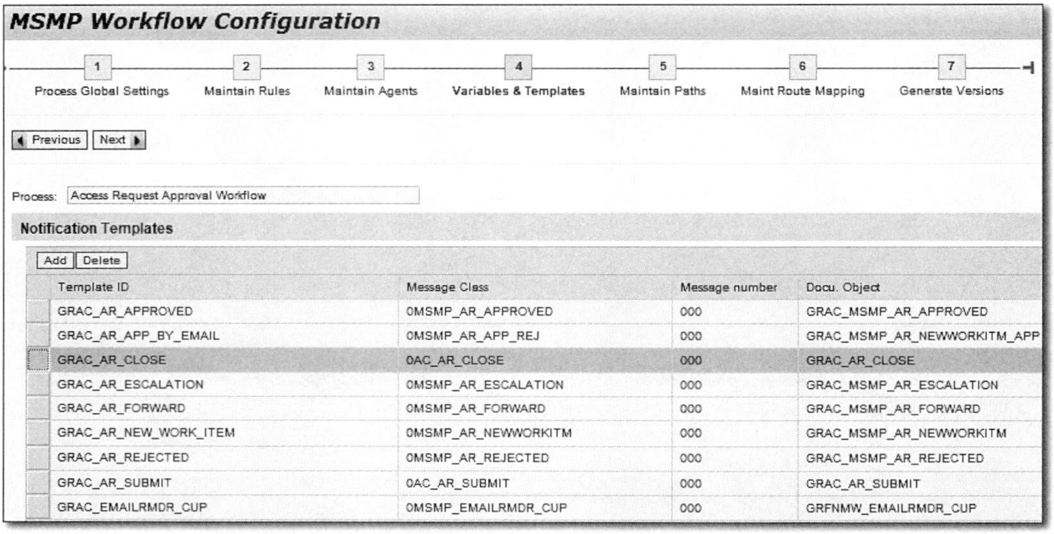

Figure 8.33 Template, Message Class, and Document Object Relationships in the MSMP Workflow

You've seen the notification templates and how they are connected to the message class and document object that are available in the standard SAP Access Control system. Also you've seen different processes, triggering events, and message classes that are connected to each other and how they are maintained to send email message to notification agents. In the next section, we'll discuss the available notification variables.

8.4.2 Notification Variables

In Section 8.1.4, we discussed notification templates, and this section, we'll discuss the available notification variables that will help you define your own message using these variables. As we've discussed earlier, this notification message doesn't only contain static text but also uses notification variables to refer to the user name, request number, and other pieces of information that depend on attributes and content of the request and triggering events. As part of workflow when the triggering event sends notification to the approver, this notification email should be formatted in business content and should contain all of the previously mentioned variables and convey the detailed message to the approvers. To prepare this template, you need to know what variables are available for the various MSMP processes.

Pre-delivered documents to support workflow processes and notification variables

Each workflow process comes with a number of notification variables that are available to all notification templates that belong to it. They are displayed on the bottom of the screen in step 4 VARIABLES & TEMPLATES in the MAINTAIN MSMP WORKFLOWS customizing activity. These variables are used in the predelivered document objects as shown in Table 8.2and can also be used in custom document objects. They appear in the message with the % character, for example, %REQNO%.

Notification Variable	SAP_GRAC_ACCESS_REQUEST & _HR	SAP_GRAC_C ONTROL_ASGN	SAP_GRAC_CONTROL_MAINT	SAP_GRAC_FIREFIGHT_LOG_REPORT	SAP_GRAC_FUNC_APPR	SAP_GRAC_RISK_APPR	SAP_GRAC_ROLE_APPR	SAP_GRAC_SOD_RISK_REVIEW	SAP_GRAC_USER_ACCESS_REVIEW
APPROVED_BY	Y	Y	Y	Y	Y	Y	Y	Y	Y
FIRST_NAME (requestor)	Y	Y	Y	Y	Y	Y	Y	Y	Y
LAST_NAME (requestor)	Y	Y	Y	Y	Y	Y	Y	Y	Y
LINK_APPROVE_REJECT	Y	N	N	N	N	N	N	N	N

Table 8.2 Notification Variables Availability against MSMP Processes

Notification Variable	SAP_GRAC_ACCESS_ REQUEST & _HR	SAP_GRAC_C ONTROL_ASGN	SAP_GRAC_ CONTROL_MAINT	SAP_GRAC_ FIREFIGHT_LOG_REPORT	SAP_GRAC_ FUNC_APPR	SAP_GRAC_ RISK_APPR	SAP_GRAC_ ROLE_APPR	SAP_GRAC_ SOD_RISK_REVIEW	SAP_GRAC_ USER_ACCESS_REVIEW
LINK_GET_APPROVERS	Y	N	N	N	N	N	N	Y	Y
LINK_GET_REQ_STATUS	Y	N	N	N	N	N	N	Y	Y
PATH	Y	Y	Y	Y	Y	Y	Y	Y	Y
REQNO	Y	Y	Y	Y	Y	Y	Y	Y	Y
REQUESTOR_NAME	Y	Y	Y	Y	Y	Y	Y	Y	Y
REQUEST_TYPE	Y	Y	Y	Y	Y	Y	Y	Y	Y
SENDER (user ID)	Y	Y	Y	Y	Y	Y	Y	Y	Y
STAGE	Y	Y	Y	Y	Y	Y	Y	Y	Y
USER_ID	Y	N	N	Y	N	N	N	Y	Y
LINK_GET_ROLE_STATUS	N	N	N	N	N	N	Y	N	N
ROLE_NAME	N	N	N	N	N	N	Y	N	N
ATTACHMENT_REPORT	N	N	N	N	N	N	Y	Y	Y
CO_ORDINATOR	N	N	N	N	N	N	Y	Y	Y
REVIEWER	N	N	N	N	N	N	Y	Y	Y
PROVISIONING	(Y)	N	N	N	N	N	N	N	N

Table 8.2 Notification Variables Availability against MSMP Processes (Cont.)

The variables mentioned in Table 8.2 are used in the MSMP workflow in step 4 VARIABLES & TEMPLATES as discussed in Section 8.1.4. It's possible to create additional notification variables and add them to the list via the ADD button. This, however, requires an enhanced version of the predelivered notification variables rule assigned to the workflow process in step 2 MAINTAIN RULES, as discussed in Section 8.1.2. Pre-delivered notification variable rule GRAC_NOTIF_VAR_RULE_AR is a function module that evaluates the actual values at runtime of each one of the notification variables. A technical person should be able to create enhanced versions of notification variables and sample screen shot is shown in Figure 8.34.

The list of available notification variables by workflow process is provided in Table 8.2, shown earlier. The variable PROVISIONING is a multivalue variable listing users and roles provisioned to one or multiple systems. The variable isn't listed in the MSMP WORKFLOW CONFIGURATION interface, but is used in the document object tied to message class 0AC_AR_CLOSE, shown in Figure 8.34.

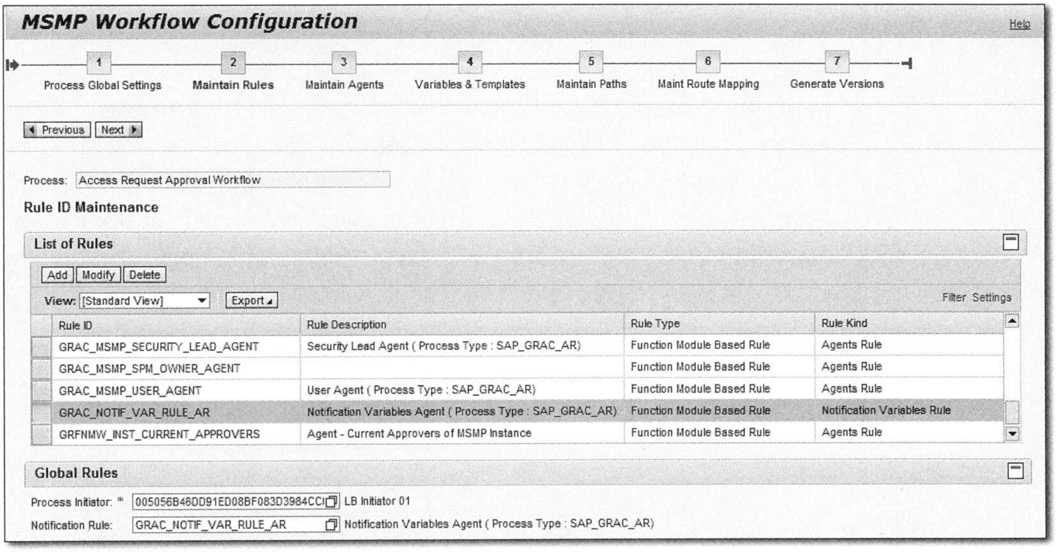

Figure 8.34 Notification Variable Rule Definition in MSMP Workflow Configuration

We've discussed the basic technical objects of notification messages in the past few sections that are used in various the MSMP workflow processes, including their usage and configuration details. In the next section, we'll take you through the steps of customizing email notifications.

8.5 Customizing Workflow Processes: Email Notifications

You can customize email notifications sent to approvers and requestors in the workflow process. As you've seen earlier, to replace the predelivered standard messages for a particular workflow event by customized email notifications, you need to create a custom document object in Transaction SE61 and associate this custom document object with the selected message class in view GRFNVNOTIFYMSG. The following subsections describe in detail how to create and associate custom document objects.

8.5.1 Creation of Custom Document Objects

To create a custom document object, either execute Transaction SE61 directly or from the IMG customizing activity by following the menu path, Governance, Risk and Compliance • Access Control • Workflow for Access Control • Maintain Text for Custom Notification Messages. This takes you to the screen shown in Figure 8.35. Select General Text as the Document Class, and enter your custom object Name that starts the customer namespace with either Y or Z. Click on the Create button to go to the next screen.

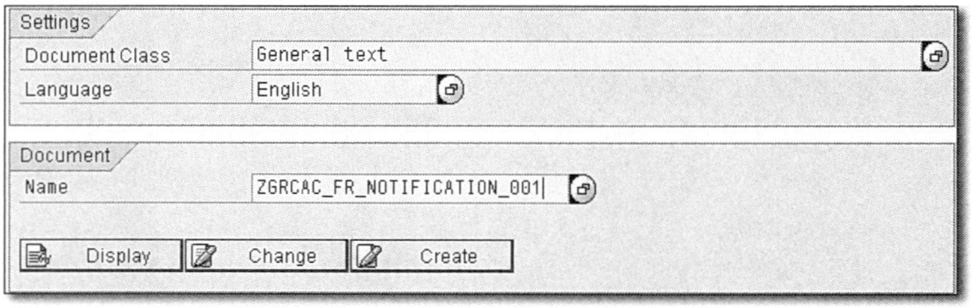

Figure 8.35 Document Object Maintenance

Text maintenance and message customization

Figure 8.36 shows part of text maintenance in SAPGUI. In this screen, you can customize the message body, including variables that are required to suit your needs. Although you can customize the variables, generally most of the predefined variables, as shown in Table 8.2, can be used directly without much technical knowledge.

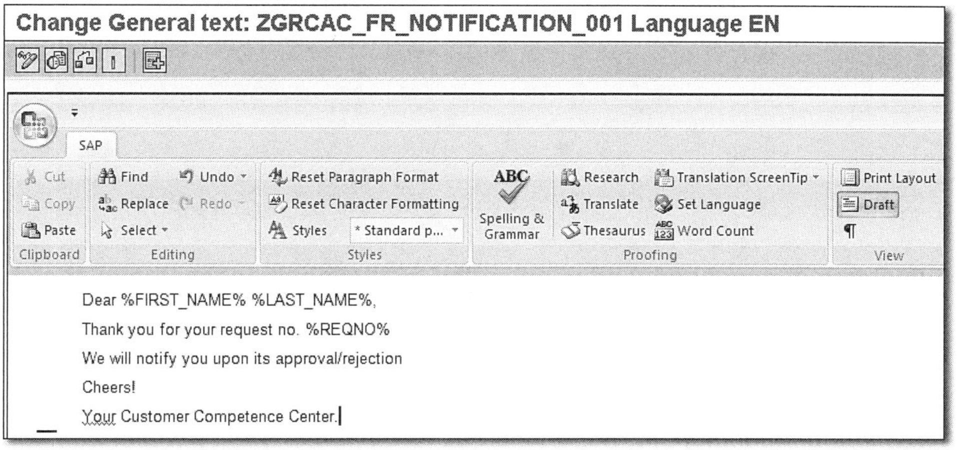

Figure 8.36 Message Content Maintenance

After you maintained the message, you can format, save, and activate it. Now the message is ready to associate with the message class for the workflow event. Let's go through these steps next.

8.5.2 Associate Custom Document Object with Message Class

After you create the customized notification content, you can associate a message class in SAP Access Control. For this association purpose, only one document object to a single message number 000 is available, and it's associated with predefined standard objects. You've already seen that these predelivered document objects can be viewed in table view GRFNVNOTIFYMSG. You need to overwrite this assignment in the IMG customizing by using menu path, Governance, Risk, and Compliance • Access Control • Workflow for Access Control • Maintain Custom Notification Messages. Click on New Entries from this screen, and then enter the following fields with their respective values:

Custom notification messages and configurable fields

- Message Class
  Enter the relevant message class of the predelivered document object that you need to maintain.
- Message Number
  Prefilled, and only 000 is permitted.

- **Description**
  Provide a description of what the message is used for and its generic usage purpose for the technical object. This information doesn't appear in the email notification.
- **Hide Recipients**
  If checked, the email displays an empty list of recipients.
- **Subject**
  Enter a subject that will appear in the subject line of the email notification.
- **Docu. Object**
  Enter the name of the custom document object you created in the previous step.

After maintaining all of these values, save the notification message. These changes are captured in a transport request based on your client settings to be transported to quality and production SAP Access Control systems. The next step is maintaining this document object mapped to the selected message class in step 4 of the MSMP Workflow Configuration, detailed in Section 8.1.4.

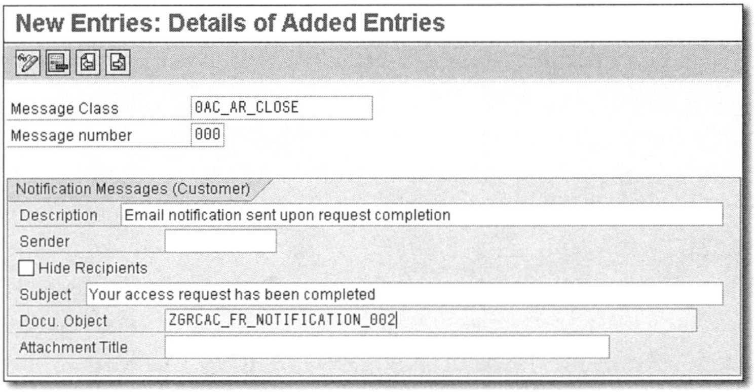

Figure 8.37 Custom Document Object Maintenance

Now you've saved this value and the custom object is assigned against the standard message class and message number, as shown in Figure 8.37. In the next step, you map and embed this customized document object which is modified notification templates in the workflow processes by attaching them to the respective stage level notification recipients.

8.6 Select Notification Templates and Recipients

You've seen how to create custom messages in an earlier section, and this section, you'll see how to maintain these custom messages to specific templates and assign these templates to different agents specific to triggering events. This needs to be performed from the MSMP WORKFLOW CONFIGURATION step 4 VARIABLES & TEMPLATES, detailed in Section 8.1.4. As shown in Figure 8.6, you choose the required template, enter the custom document object, and save. You might notice that the owner column shows CUSTOMER, whereas all other standard objects show SAP as the owner.

After this step is saved, you should follow the steps in the step 5 MAINTAIN PATHS, detailed in Section 8.1.5, where you maintain workflow stages. Select the stage for which you need to maintain notification. In general, you can select from four different pre-delivered agents of PURPOSE NOTIFICATION to determine the recipients:

Options for 4 pre-delivered agents to determine recipents

- Current approvers (of current stage)
- Other approvers
- Requestor
- User (affected by the request)

You can add additional agents with the PURPOSE NOTIFICATION in the same way as you do for agents with the PURPOSE APPROVAL by choosing from the same available AGENT TYPES: DIRECTLY MAPPED USERS, PFCG ROLES, PFCG USER GROUPS, and GRC API RULES. Again, the AGENT TYPE GRC API RULES supports the following RULES TYPES: BRF PLUS RULE, FUNCTION MODULE BASED RULE, ABAP CLASS BASED RULE, and BRF PLUS FLAT RULE. This gives you full flexibility to determine recipients for workflow notifications.

MSMP notification templates

In the MSMP WORKFLOW CONFIGURATION interface, notification templates are always selected by their TEMPLATE ID, which defers in its name from the respective message class by the prefix that is always "GRAC_" instead of "0MSMP_" or "0AC_" used for message classes. If you create a custom document object for the message class/TEMPLATE ID you select, the system always uses the custom text rather than the predelivered text. SAP_GRAC_ACCESS_REQUEST and SAP_GRAC_

ACCESS_REQUEST_HR are the only workflow processes that come with a message class for request submission (TEMPLATE ID GRAC_AR_SUBMIT) and completion (TEMPLATE ID GRAC_AR_CLOSE). You can select them together with their recipients in the PROCESS GLOBAL SETTINGS area of the screen as explained earlier in the first step of the MSMP WORKFLOW CONFIGURATION guided procedure.

Notification templates for events at stage selection

Notification templates for the events NEW WORK ITEM, APPROVED, REJECTED, FORWARD, and ESCALATION are selected by stage in step 5 MAINTAIN PATHS. Select the stage for which you want to select notification templates and recipients, and click the NOTIFICATION SETTINGS button from shown Figure 8.38. Then, click on CREATE, and select NOTIFICATION EVENT, TEMPLATE ID, and RECIPIENT IDs as needed for the selected stage.

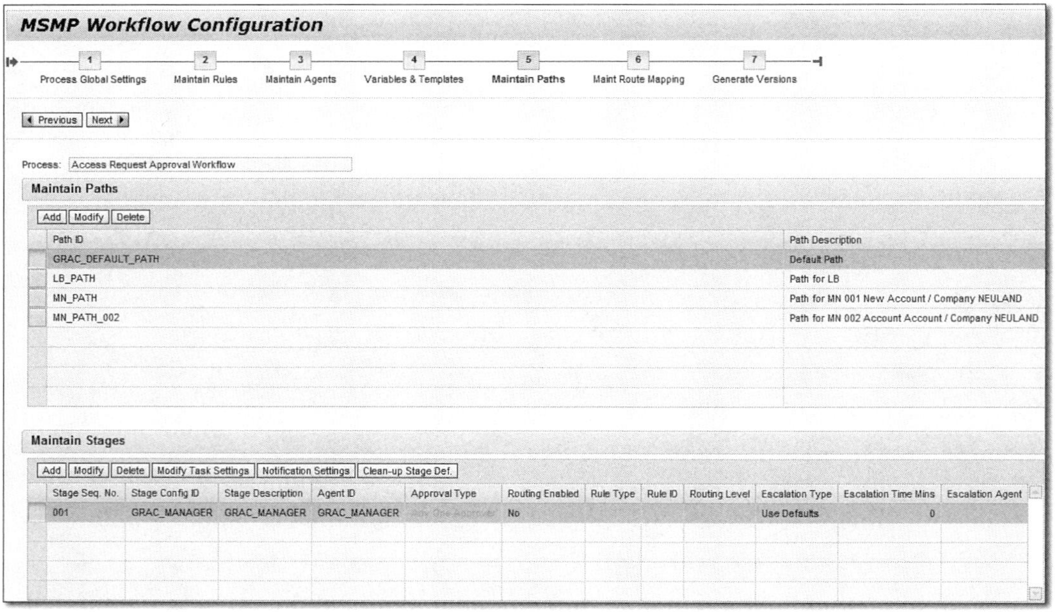

Figure 8.38 Notification Template Configuration at the Stage Level

As we mentioned, every stage can be maintained with all notification events, corresponding templates, and recipients as shown in Figure 8.39. All new work items need to be maintained for current approvers to receive the work item notification for the stage approvers or alternate approvers.

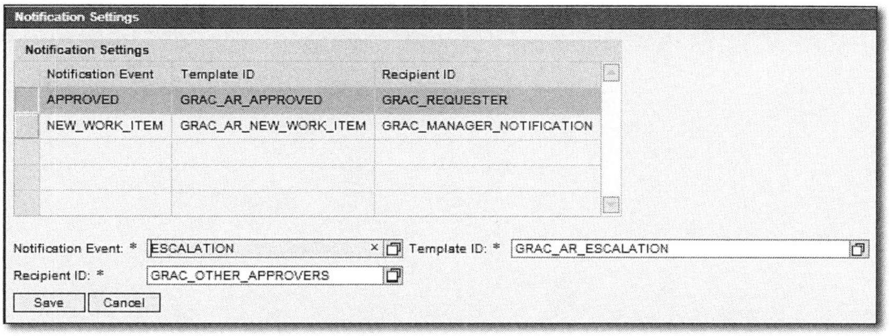

Figure 8.39 Notification Events, Template IDs and Recipient IDs

In the same way, you need to maintain notification in every stage available in the workflow path. After all of these settings are done, the agents will receive customized notification message content in their work inbox or email inbox. In the next section, we'll cover how to set email reminder notifications.

8.7 Setting Up Email Reminders

Email reminders are used to send reminders concerning the approval notifications that are pending to the stage approvers. These emails can be scheduled on regular interval, till the approver acted on the outstanding workitem, for each individual workflow process. This section describes how to use periodic email reminders and select a notification template. Three predelivered templates are available in SAP Access Control:

Pre-delivered templates for email reminders in SAP Access Control

- GRAC_EMAILRMDR_CUP (for access request approval workflows)
- GRAC_EMAILRMDR_SOD (for SoD risk review workflows)
- GRCC_EMAILRMDR

In the system, each email reminder comes with a period in number of days indicating how long any uncompleted workflow task will wait before it sends a reminder notification to the same notification agent.

Again, you can create custom document objects containing customized message contents against these template IDs or message classes.

Job definition and scheduling as related to e-mail reminders

To schedule these reminder notifications in the system, the job definition must already exist in the system, and this can be scheduled from Transaction SA38. You need to enter the program name as "GRFNMW_BATCH_EMAIL_REMINDER" in the ABAP PROGRAM field, and then click EXECUTE. Select MSMP process that you want to trigger an email reminder, and enter other values such as PERIOD (IN DAYS) and TEMPLATE ID (see Figure 8.40).

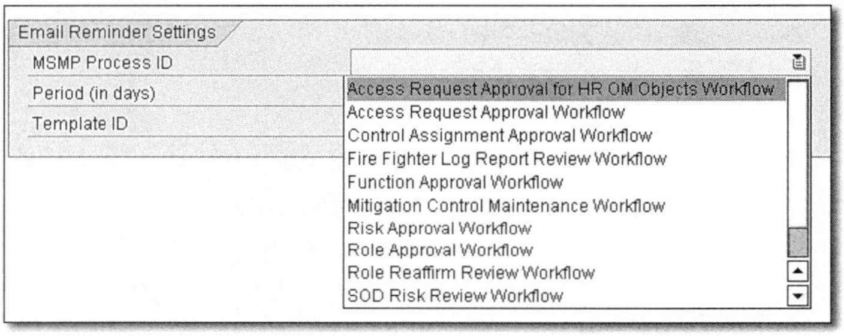

Figure 8.40 Email reminder

After the values are entered, save this as a variant and schedule this in the background to run in a regular interval as required in your environment. Normally, this can be hourly or daily jobs, which can be monitored from Transaction SM37.

Now you've completed most integrated components of the MSMP WORKFLOW CONFIGURATION. The next section deals with some of the additional options that can be achieved by combining some functions from Access Risk Analysis and User Access Management.

8.8 Periodic Reviews

This section gets into the details on reviewing access risk and monitoring user and role access in the company as part of compliance certification reviews. Let's discuss configuration, implementation, and usage of the SoD/user access review process. Implementation and usage of SoD/

user access reviews streamlines the internal control process with collaboration among business managers, internal control, and security teams. Also this increases improved efficiency and visibility of the internal control process to the company.

The SoD review process gives a decentralized review to managers or risk owners of SoD violations based on users' authorization profiles and their access privileges over a period. Also SoD review reaffirms any mitigating control assignment to the user community.

Segregation of duty risks and monitoring

SoD risks or critical risks of all the users, can be monitored on regular interval for a prolonged period. This ensures any unmitigated or mitigated risks can't be missed unnoticed rather all these details are triggered as workflow and reports for business users and audit team. The user access review features automating and documenting the periodic decentralized user access review by business managers or role owners. User access review requests can be generated on regular intervals and sent to respective managers to review role assignments of users in the organization.

Segregation of duty preliminary steps for a review: Synchronization steps

Before executing an SoD review job, there are a few preliminary measures that you need to take. First, ensure that the batch risk analysis job is executed and completed with the management report and that risk owners are assigned to risks. Second, make sure to run the following synchronization and action usage jobs in the listed sequence as preconditions for performing SoD reviews in SAP GRC Access Control 10.x:

1. GRAC_ROLEREP_PROFILE_SYNC
   This job synchronizes all profiles from the plug-in repository in SAP Access Control tables with updated values.
2. GRAC_ROLEREP_ROLE_SYNC
   This job synchronizes all roles from the plug-in repository in SAP Access Control tables with current values.
3. GRAC_ROLEREP_USER_SYNC
   This job synchronizes all users and roles used by these users.
4. GRAC_BATCH_RISK_ANALYSIS
   This job updates the risk analysis result based on an update of the repository data from previous jobs so that the risk values will be up to

date. SoD violations are taken from these table entries and thus it's essential to update them before you run the SoD review job.

5. GRAC_ACTION_USAGE_SYNC
   This job retrieves the transaction usage for users.
6. GRAC_ROLE_USAGE_SYNC
   This job retrieves and updates the role usage.

After running all six of these jobs, you'll have enough data to execute the SoD review job generation. Next, let's walk through the SoD configuration and review process.

8.8.1 Configuration for SoD Review

This section describes the configuration steps and other activities, such as background jobs, that need to be carried out to trigger the SoD review. After login to SAPGUI in the SAP Access Control system, execute Transaction SPRO, select the SAP Reference IMG option, and follow the menu path, Governance, Risk and Compliance • Access Control • Maintain Configuration Settings. Maintain the values for SoD review in the shown in Figure 8.41.

SOD Review	2016	9	Request Type for SoD
SOD Review	2017	1	Default priority for SoD
SOD Review	2018	MANAGER	Who are the reviewers?
SOD Review	2019	YES	Admin. review required before sending tasks to reviewers
SOD Review	2023	YES	Is actual removal of role allowed

Figure 8.41 SoD Review Configuration Parameter Settings

Segregation of duty review configuration parameter fields

The fields that you'll need to review for the SoD review configuration parameter settings are as follows:

- Request Type: Parameter ID 2014
  This parameter is the request type that will be associated with SoD review workflow requests. Request types can be reference points for initializing a workflow and determining the actions to be performed.
- Request Priority
  Set a priority for a request to determine how quickly a request is to be approved. The request priority is also one of the workflow request attributes.

- Reviewers
  This term refers to the approver at the reviewer stage. For the SoD review, the reviewer can be the user's direct manager or the risk owner as maintained in the Access Risk Analysis tool master data.
- Admin Review
  This configuration option provides an opportunity for the administration to review the request data for completeness and consistency prior to sending the request to reviewers. If any manager or risk owner information is incorrect or missing, the administrator can modify the data prior to generating workflow tasks and notifications. The administrator can also cancel the requests. An administrator can perform SoD review-specific administrator tasks, such as cancelling SoD review requests and regenerating requests for rejected users. The configuration options are available to set with Yes or No.
- User Detail Data Source
  If there are users with no manager identified in the User Detail Data Source and the Reviewer is defined as the user's manager, then administrator review is required. This allows the administrator to maintain the missing data, such as reviewer, or if there is a need to change different reviewers prior to sending workflow tasks to reviewers.
- Removal of Roles
  In SAP Access Control, reviewers can actually remove a role if any risk is associated with it and if the option is set to Yes. But the recommended best practice for this option is to set it to No so that the security team can handle the recommendation or outcome of the SoD review workflow approvals.

Service level agreement maintenance

Apart from these settings, navigate to Governance, Risk and Compliance • Access Control • User Provisioning • Maintain Service Level Agreements to maintain the service level agreement (SLA) to create a due date for the workflow. This SLA maintenance is specific to the MSMP workflow process, and SLA type variables can be chosen from the dropdown list as shown in Figure 8.42.

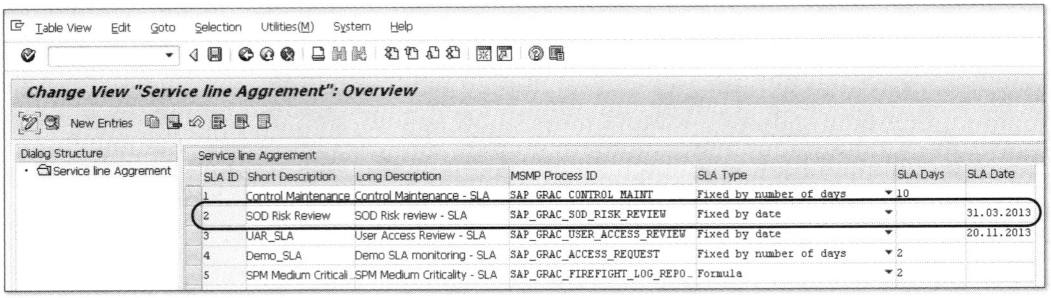

Figure 8.42 Due Date Configuration via SLA Monitoring

Service level agreement type determinations

Based on this SLA type determination, fixed date, number of days, or formula can be set, and the corresponding values need to be maintained and saved either in SLA DAYS or in SLA DATE. Now this value will serve to set the due date for the corresponding process.

You've now completed the configuration for the SoD review. In the next section, let's discuss how to maintain reviewers and coordinators for this SoD review workflow.

8.8.2 Maintain Reviewers and Coordinators

In this step, you need to maintain two different types of owners or agents for SoD reviews. The first set of owners are the reviewers and the actual approvers of the SoD review workflows. The second set of owners are coordinators. The coordinators are the SAP Access Controls owners, and they will be notified with the SoD review workflow.

Using the SAP NetWeaver Business Client frontend to update coordinators and reviewer roles

To access this page, log on to the NetWeaver Business Client frontend in the SAP Access Control 10.0 system, and follow the menu path, ACCESS MANAGEMENT • COMPLIANCE CERTIFICATION REVIEWS • MANAGE COORDINATORS. In the MANAGE COORDINATORS screen, you can create, import, or delete coordinators and reviewers. If you want to change a coordinator-to-reviewer mapping, choose the OPEN button. This opens the CHANGE MAPPING screen, where you can modify the settings, as required. Choose SAVE to complete the change coordinators and reviewers.

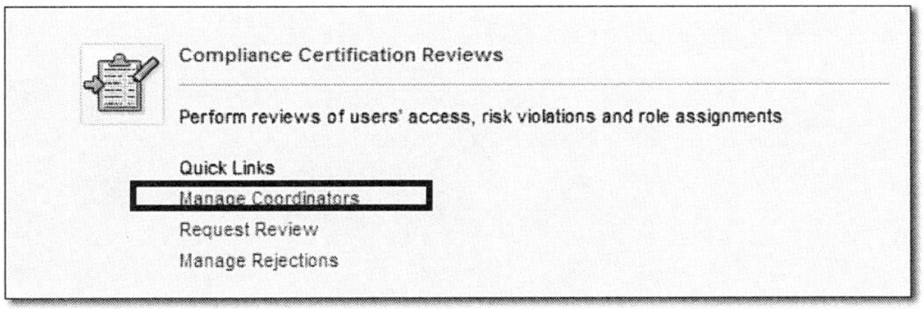

Figure 8.43 Maintain SoD Reviewers and Coordinators

When you click on the Manage coordinators link as shown in Figure 8.43, it takes you to the next screen, where the system shows the earlier assigned reviewers and coordinators. Click on the Create button, and the Create Mapping screen appears when you want to create new coordinator and reviewer combination (see Figure 8.44).

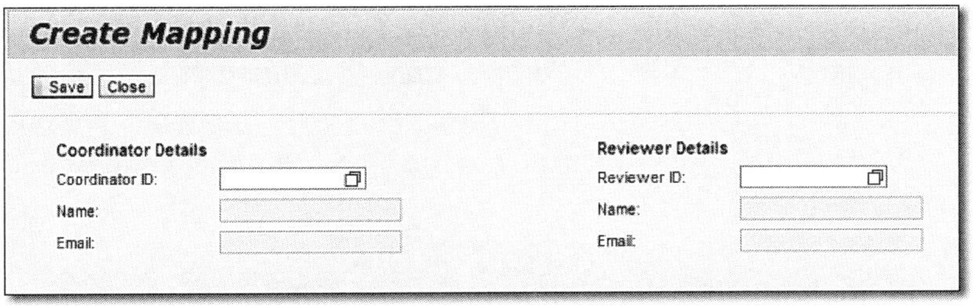

Figure 8.44 Create Reviewer and Coordinator

Maintain the values for the fields Co-ordinator ID and Reviewer ID shown in Figure 8.44 use help values to list users, which lists only those users who are already defined as SAP Access Control (Risk) owners from the Setup work center. This activity can be performed manually in Figure 8.44, or you can use Download Template, maintain the records in the template file, and click the Import button to import all of the values as a mass maintenance functionality (see Figure 8.45).

Now we assume that all SoD risk owners are defined in the system and are mapped with coordinators and reviewers. Also don't forget to configure the MSMP workflow process SoD risk review workflow. In this process, maintain all necessary workflow settings by following the same procedure explained in the Section 8.1. In the next step, you need to run the background job that generates the SoD review data and prepares the data for review.

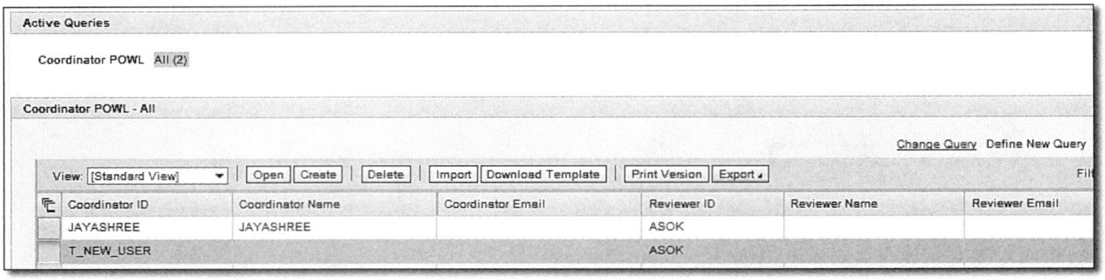

Figure 8.45 Mass Maintenance via Download and Import Buttons

8.8.3 Generate Data for SoD Review

After you set the coordinators and reviewers, you can generate the SoD review contents. For this scheduling, select BACKGROUND JOBS from the SCHEDULING workset in the ACCESS MANAGEMENT work center, Figure 8.46 showing the scheduling screen details. To test generate SoD review data, this can be scheduled once, but after all configuration and SoD reviews are tested, this can be set in the production system in a periodic fashion such as monthly or quarterly to meet your internal audit or SOX requirement.

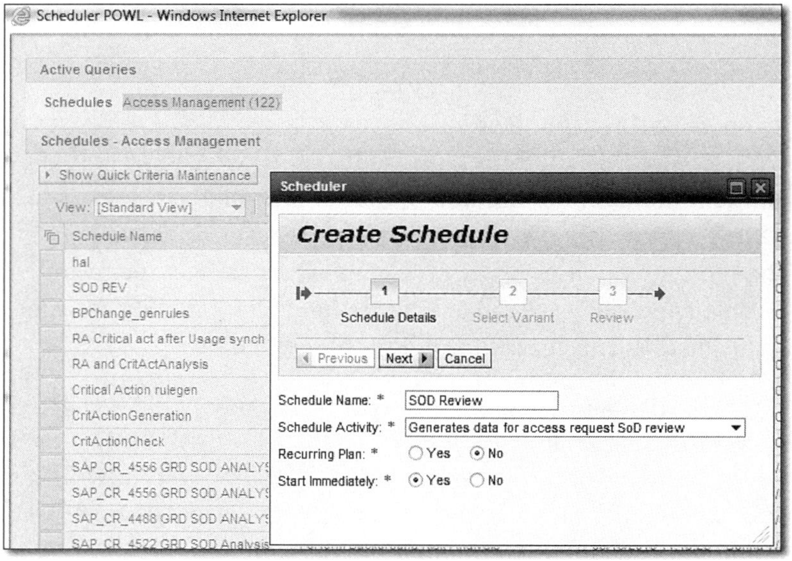

Figure 8.46 SoD Background Job Scheduling

Segregation of duty background job scheduling

As a second step in scheduling, you need to select variables as needed from the larger selection screen and save this variant (see Figure 8.47). You may create variants specific to systems, risk levels, or risk types, and the outcome result can be grouped by users or risks.

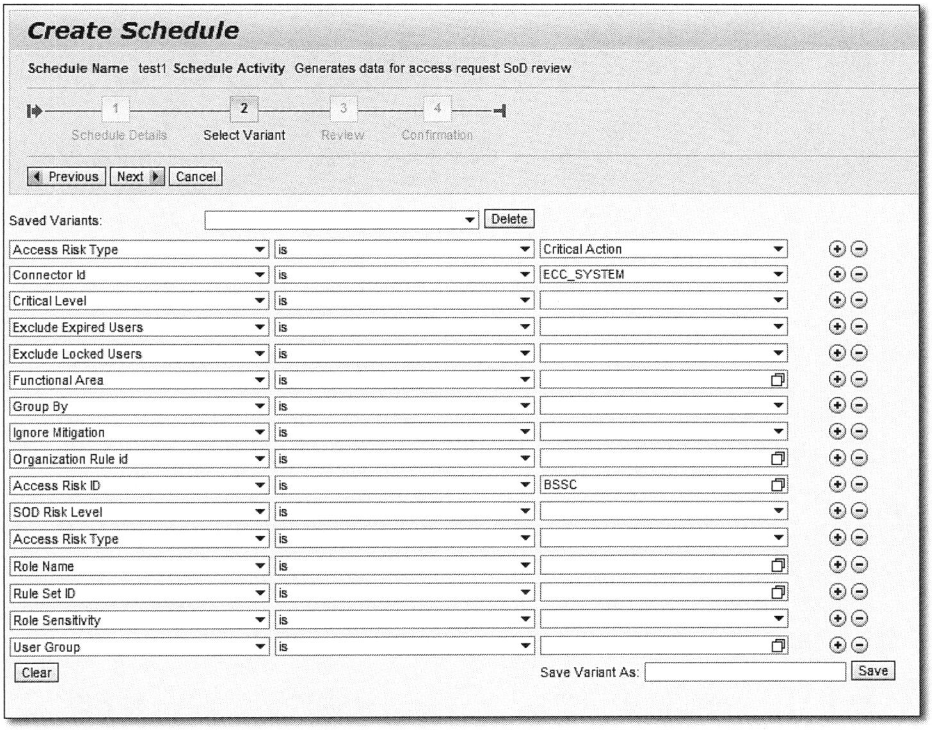

Figure 8.47 Background SoD Risk Review Selection Screen

Execution of the background job for Segregation of duty risk review

After maintaining the selection criteria, further review your selection and confirm to execute this job in the background. As a result of this background job and configuration, if you set the value to Yes for the administration review required before sending requests in the SoD review configuration, the result is created as a request and waits for an administrator's review. After the job is completed, check the status and if it's completed, you should be able to view the number of requests that are generated (see Figure 8.48).

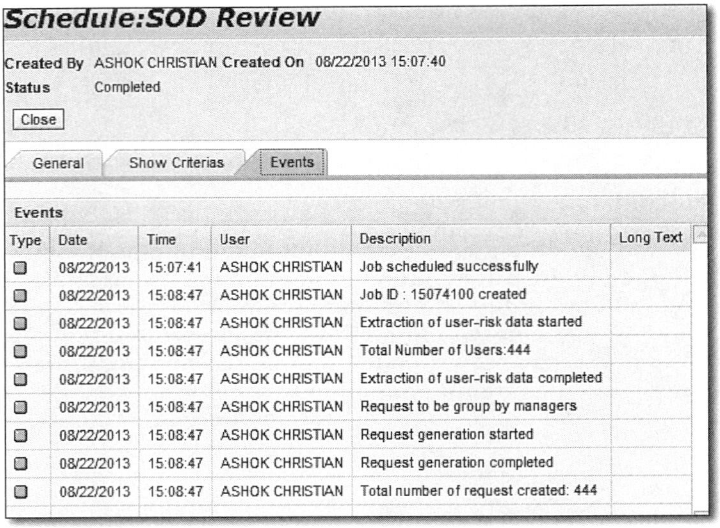

Figure 8.48 Background Job ID and Status

Administrator review of Background Jobs

After the job is completed, the administrator can review the coordinators, reviewers, and generated data from the REQUEST REVIEW link from the COMPLIANCE CERTIFICATION REVIEWS workset. A request review query can be listed out to get specific results when there are few input parameters available. If an administrator is interested only to review the requests that don't have any reviewers, this can be selected by choosing the NO REVIEWER checkbox.

Missing reviewer or changed reviewer maintenance

If you want to maintain any missing reviewers or change reviewers for requests by a SAP GRC administrator, those tasks can be performed here that is shown in the Figure 8.49. If an administrator feels that there are a few inappropriate requests, he can cancel or change reviewers. Because the SoD review process is an automated process to create requests based on input criteria, sometimes it might push a very large amount of data as the result of wrong selection criteria. To avoid this, the administrator review helps to verify all of these requests as having the correct reviewers. If they have some issues, then the administrator either cancels them individually or changes reviewers before scheduling these requests to execute the workflow for actual review.

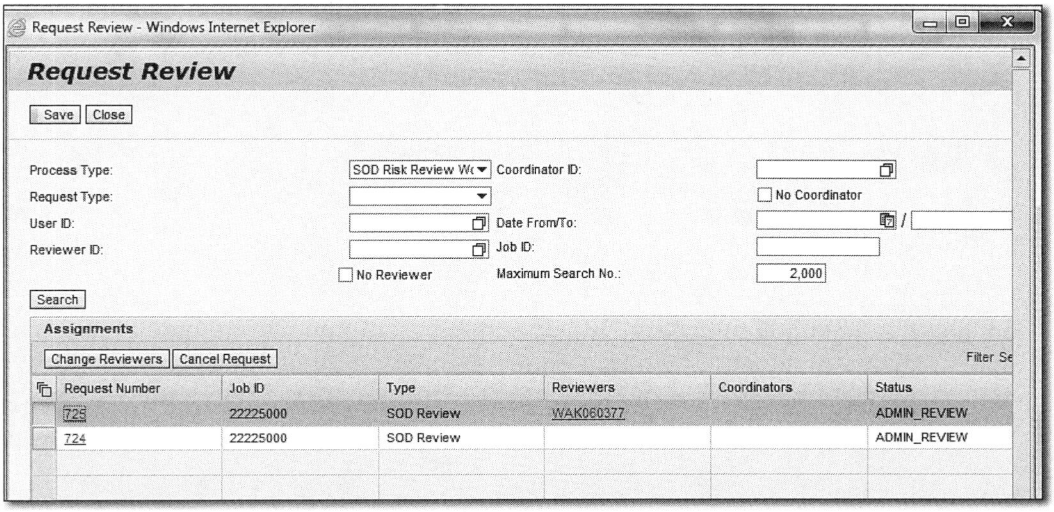

Figure 8.49 Administrator's Review Screen

We've changed both reviewers and coordinators and saved for both requests, which were generated from the SoD data generation background job. Now schedule the next background job as shown in Figure 8.50, Update Workflow for SoD Risk to trigger the workflow.

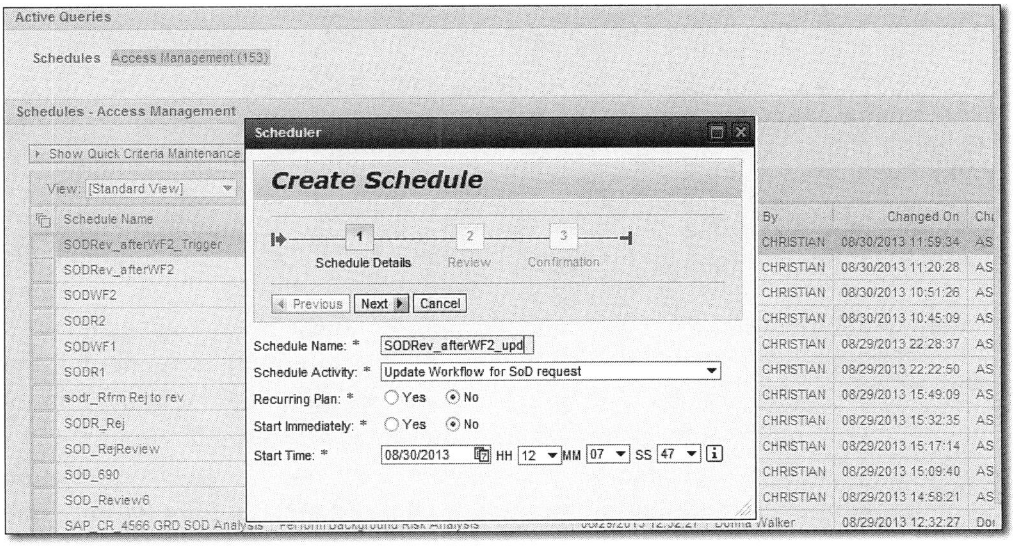

Figure 8.50 SoD Request Review Update Workflow

Figure 8.51 shows you the SoD Review screen, which gives the details on risks associated with user IDs. This can be switched to view groups by risks instead of groups by user.

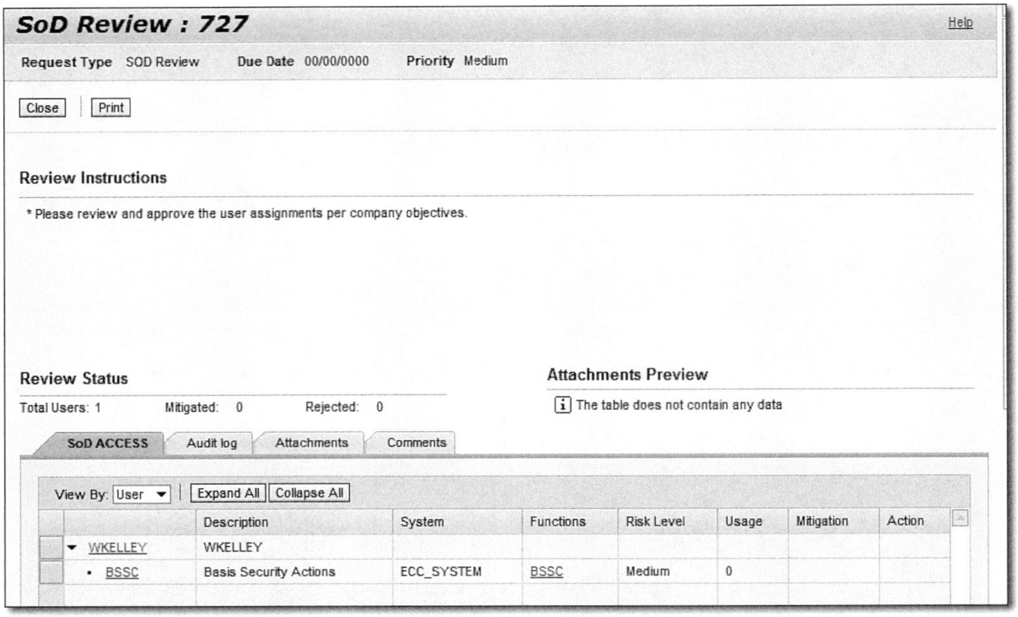

Figure 8.51 SoD Review by SAP Access Control Administrator

Work Inbox notifications upon Segregation of Duty risk review

Successful completion of the background job should trigger all SoD risk review requests to be sent to the work inboxes of all reviewers. As a reviewer, you may log on to the SAP NetWeaver Business Client frontend and click on the Work Inbox link in the Work Inbox work set in the initial screen. Reviewers can select individual requests and act on these requests.

Approval and mitigation by the segregation of duty request reviewer

As an approver, once you open the work-item or request, you'll see the above shown Figure 8.52, select the one to review and either mitigate this critical risk for the user or propose removal. The actual removal should be carried out manually by the security team. If you set the configuration parameter that allows the SoD request reviewer to delete the role from the user assignment, then a best practice recommendation is to set this value as a propose removal option for the SoD request reviewer.

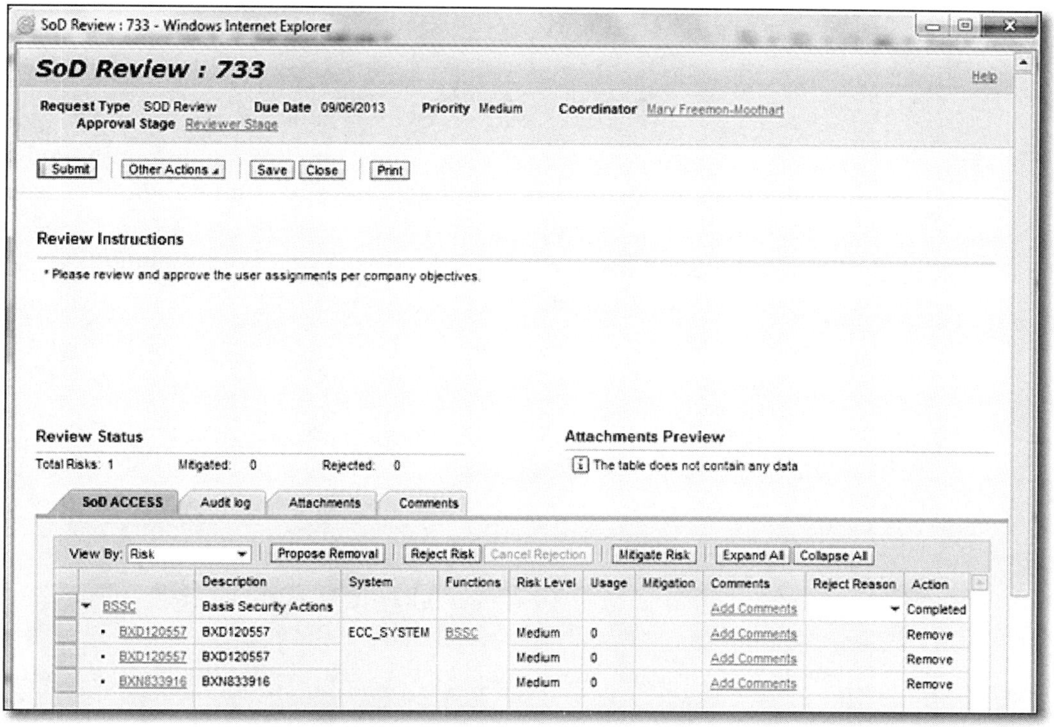

Figure 8.52 SoD Request for Approval or Mitigation

You've now completed the SoD review. User access review is configured, reviewed, and executed in a similar way. The only difference is that user access reviews are normally sent to the manager to get consent concerning whether the user still needs all of the access under his privileges. At some companies, they use HR functions and indirect provisioning via the job or position. Although user access reviews aren't much use to them, it might be helpful to deal temporary workers those who usually not under HR position-based provisioning. In the next sections, we'll discuss how to use HR triggers to automate your entire hire-to-retire cycle provisioning or authorization management fully, which is possible when you're using the HR module in the SAP ERP system.

8.9 HR Triggers

This section covers how HR triggers help to automate new user request creation or change user request creation when a user's job changes. Users don't need to create a request; instead, when an event in the HR module occurs, such as hiring activity, rules are applied, and the corresponding action to create a workflow request executes in the User Access Management tool. As a subsequent activity, this request passes through one of your predefined workflow processes for approval, and per the User Access Management configuration, the provisioning is completed.

Integration of HR and SAP Access Control

Let's go through the basic flow of this process. All users should be in the SAP ERP HR system, if any event from the HR system will trigger a function module GRAC_GET_HR_TRIGGER_DATA in SAP Access Control to create the request.

The role of BRF+ and the Users Management tool in request creation

In the next step, the HR trigger BRF+ rule evaluates the changes and gives out the result. Based on this result, the equivalent actions maintained in the User Access Management tool creates the request. At this point, this action is similar to the discussion in Section 8.3 on how the BRF+ rule result decides what type of request needs to be created.

To start this configuration, you need to execute Transaction SPRO, select the SAP Reference IMG option, and follow the menu path, Governance, Risk and Compliance • Access Control • User Provisioning Maintain Settings for HR Triggers. You'll be taken to the screen HR trigger Maintain Action Overview screen as shown in Figure 8.53. In this screen, click on the Maintain Action folder, and then click on New Entries to open the details screen. Enter the Action ID, Description, Request Type, and Priority ID under Action Details. You're maintaining the action ID that is equivalent to the request type, which we've discussed in Chapter 7, Section 7.2.6. This action ID will be the entry sent from the HR trigger rule. Other areas of this screen, such as Address, Parameter ID, Default, and User Group, need to be entered with Yes or No information. Based on these settings, what should be updated during the HR trigger is passed from the HR data.

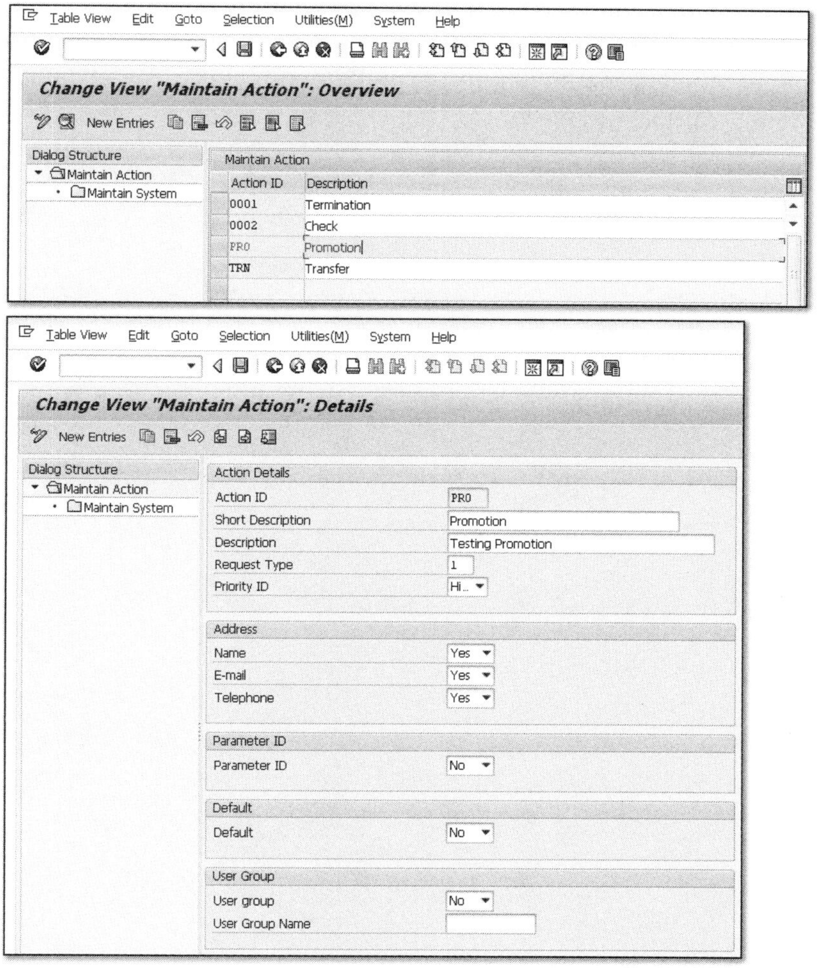

Figure 8.53 HR Trigger Maintain Action Overview and Details

Connecting an HR Event with BRF+

Now that you've set what request types should be triggered at which event information, the next step is connecting the HR event with BRF+. For this, execute Transaction SPRO, and from the SAP Reference IMG option, follow the menu path, GOVERNANCE, RISK AND COMPLIANCE • ACCESS CONTROL • MAINTAIN AC APPLICATIONS AND BRFPLUS FUNCTION MAPPING. From this screen, you copy the predelivered BRFplus rule, mentioned against APPL ID HR TRIGGERS. Go to the BRF+ transaction, choose WORKBENCH, click on OPEN OBJECT, AND then paste the BRF+

application ID. In BRF+, the next step is to create your own rules, conditions, and decision tables with results. After you're finished, make sure that you simulate the BRF+ function and that you're getting the desired action ID for the provided input.

8.10 Summary

In this chapter, we've discussed SAP Access Control advanced topics such as MSMP maintaining and debugging, BRF+ function creation and MSMP connections, workflow notification, email notification, notification templates, reminders, periodic reviews, and HR trigger. This completes the discussion of SAP Access Control. The next chapter provides an overview of SAP Process Control, including its implementation and how to maximize ROI.

Chapter 1 introduced SAP Process Control, and this chapter extends that brief overview to a more detailed introduction. It also sets the stage for the following chapters on continuous controls monitoring features of SAP Process Control.

9 SAP Process Control Overview

With financial concerns, anti-corruption focus, food and drug safety, worker safety, trade sanctions, and environmental concerns, businesses worldwide face ever-tighter regulations that are being strictly enforced. Proper attention to, and management of regulatory risk and compliance is no longer solely a question of avoiding fines or jail terms for executives—compelling as even those motivations are. Rather, effectively managing compliance can give a company a true competitive edge, especially in mature industries. Operating efficiently while managing risks and avoiding unpredictable hits from adverse regulatory action can be the hallmark of a well-managed and competitive business.

Process Control efficiencies

SAP Process Control can be a real asset in helping companies achieve such efficiencies. A classic problem companies face is that regulations apply top-down, but compliance has to be achieved bottom-up. That is, the Security Exchange Commission (SEC) requires the company as a whole to follow financial regulations, but each purchasing agent and salesperson must understand what obligations this imposes on their daily job and act accordingly. At the end of the year, the affected compliance officers need to be able to pull together such information globally to be audit-ready and to report on the company's compliance.

Capturing the regulations and company policies in one place is a start. SAP Process Control enables customers to do this at varying levels of granularity, depending on the size of the organization, the scope of its operations (in this context, to how many regulatory jurisdictions it must report), and the maturity of its governance, risk, and compliance (GRC) practices.

Improving employee awareness

SAP Process Control helps inform affected employees of regulatory requirements and obligations, documents employees' acceptance, and even tests their understanding and awareness. SAP Process Control also enables many best practices. A sound compliance program prioritizes efforts by impact. SAP Process Control offers risk-based scoping, which establishes formal evaluations of various risks as the basis of compliance-monitoring activities. Compliance managers can cascade their assessments, testing and monitoring activities down to individual business process steps, thus mitigating risks in order of likelihood and impact.

9.1 The Evolution of SAP Process Control

SAP Process Control replaced SAP's Management of Internal Controls (MIC) product. The first release of SAP Process Control was numbered 2.5, in part reflecting this continuity. SAP Process Control 2.5 was largely a Sarbanes-Oxley (SOX) compliance product, and many early customers continued to use SAP Process Control through successive releases mainly for SOX compliance.

SAP Process Control's appearance and behavior reflects its upbringing among auditors, even though SAP Process Control 10.1 is far more than a SOX compliance tool. It has included explicit support for multiple regulations, extensive modeling of corporate policies, and increasing emphasis on Continuous Controls Monitoring (CCM)—all quite far evolved from SAP Process Control's original value in planning for SOX compliance.

9.2 SAP Process Control Features

SAP Process Control is very much a compliance-centric product. All monitoring, for instance, is assumed to be motivated by compliance to regulations, corporate policies, or both. SAP Process Control risks and mitigating controls all require a tie back to a regulation. Naturally, this doesn't mean that SAP Process Control can't be used by customers with motives other than regulatory compliance, but it does mean that even such customers have to use placeholder regulations because they don't have actual ones to track. This reflects itself in two features, date validity and views, briefly described next.

9.2.1 Date Validity

Almost all SAP Process Control master data has effective dates (from and to). The upside of effective dates is that it makes explicit a fact of life in most situations: regulations, business process models, organizational structures, controls, monitoring rules, test plans, assessments, surveys, and so on all change over time. But even as they change, executed surveys, monitoring results, issues, and remedial actions all make sense only in the context of master data as it existed at the time. So it's necessary to keep track of master data settings as they existed in the past; otherwise, past transactions can lose referential data integrity. For instance, an organizational unit called California Branch Office may later get merged into West Coast Regional Office. While the former existed, some controls and monitoring rules might have executed and found problems that were then fixed. All these results lose their context and meaning if the old California Branch Office organizational unit is deleted or just renamed.

Validity dates and master data

SAP Process Control (and SAP Risk Management) addresses this by requiring most master data to have validity dates. The usage pattern then is that even the relationships such master data objects have to each other is subject to effective dating. This is why all reporting and data maintenance displays must begin with an explicit statement of the "as of" date, as illustrated in Figure 9.1. That figure shows the ORGANIZATIONS modeled in SAP Process Control and which master data is shared with SAP Access Control and SAP Risk Management, if the customer has chosen to use SAP solutions for GRC as an integrated suite. In Chapter 10, we address this and other master data in more detail, and show this picture here only to illustrate the concept of timeframes and validity dates.

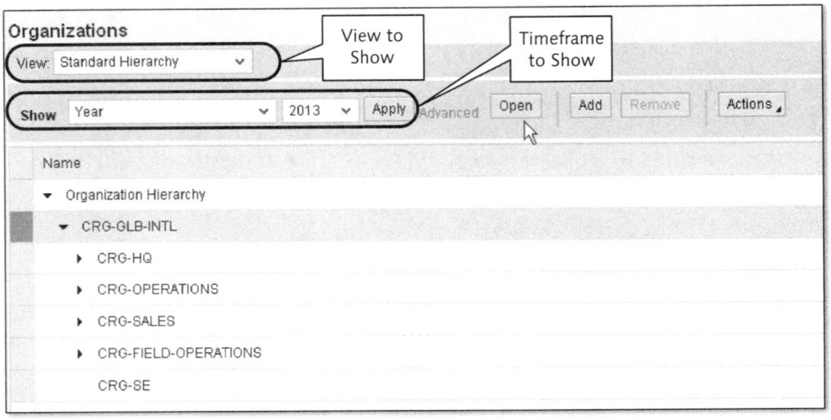

Figure 9.1 Time Frames and Views Govern the Appearance of Organization Master Data

9.2.2 Views

Multiple perspectives can bear on a SAP GRC implementation in general. Further, some basic master data such as organizational structures are shared between SAP GRC products. To accommodate these variations, SAP GRC allows multiple views of the organizational structure to exist in parallel. Clearly, customers using this flexibility need to exercise due care when using these structures in other parts of SAP Process Control because otherwise it can cause confusion. Now that we've explored some of the many features of SAP Process Control, let's shift our focus to the technical architecture of the module.

9.3 Architecture

The term *architecture* reflects many viewpoints, including components, processes, deployments, and so on. For our purposes here, Figure 9.2 shows a simplified component and deployment architecture of SAP Process Control 10.1.

This will help you understand the different SAP GRC components, and where and how they can be deployed.

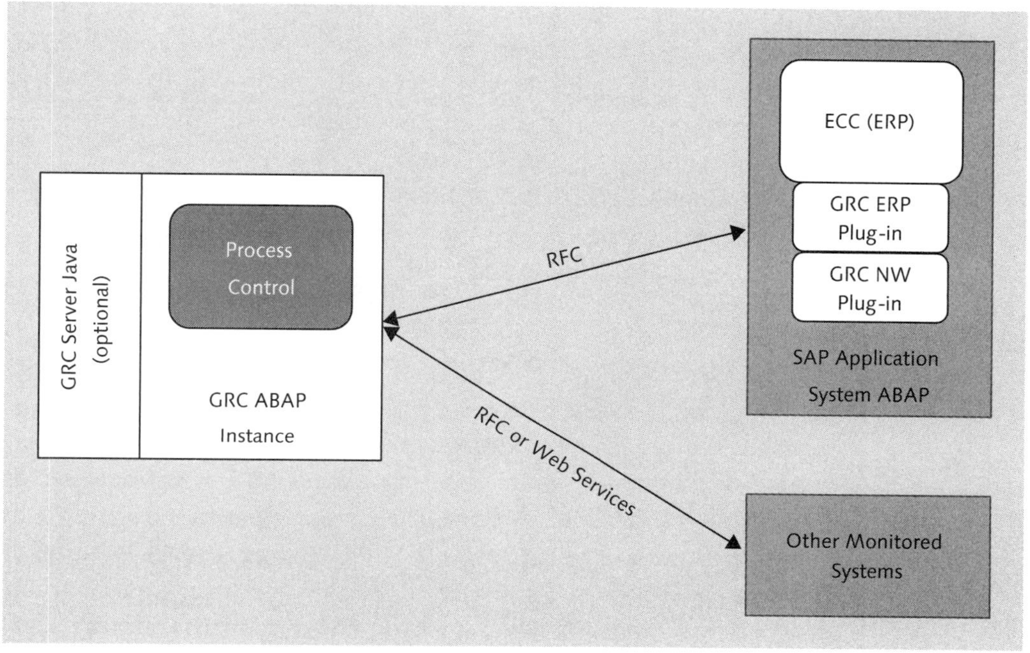

Figure 9.2 Component and Deployment Diagram

Deployment architecture and SAP NetWeaver

In theory, SAP GRC can coexist on the same server as a monitored system such as SAP ERP. In fact, technically it may even be possible to have them operate in the same server instance, assuming SAP NetWeaver dependencies are compatible. A server (e.g., a computer with a network address) can have multiple instances of SAP NetWeaver running on it. In practice, SAP discourages same instance server deployment for many reasons: performance and sizing, SAP NetWeaver release dependencies, release frequency, implementation schedule differences, and so on. Perhaps the most important, though, is that most customers consider their production SAP ERP instance to be mission-critical and best isolated from other applications. SAP GRC users typically form a more tightly defined group than for monitored systems, and given SAP's user-based pricing, this also aligns with the customer's interests.

SAP NetWeaver Configuration for GRC

The preceding architecture should also help customers understand, at a glance, the need to configure multiple SAP NetWeaver system stacks, networks, remote logins, privileges, security, and so on. To the experienced administrator, it should also immediately bring home the issues involved in setting up SAP GRC to fit into a standard corporate portal setup, or Single Sign-On (SSO) authentication system. To better understand the architecture of SAP Process Control and its implementation, let's review the installation and setup.

9.3.1 Installation and Setup

SAP GRC, SAP Access Control, SAP Process Control, and SAP Risk Management ship in several software components and together cover many scenarios. All these components, service packs, and so on are found on SAP Service Marketplace, as usual. The main component installs into the server and instance, which hosts the SAP GRC products; others install in backend application systems to be monitored or managed via SAP GRC products. Still other components correspond to optional features such as offline forms (via the Adobe Document Server), TREX search support, and so on.

Service Marketplace support

Installation, upgrades, and configuration is very well addressed in official SAP documentation, as shown in Figure 9.3. This book aims to complement official documentation with additional suggestions and guidance. Because the initial installation and configuration of SAP software follows standard Basis practices, there is little value to be added in recapitulating the process here, so please refer to SAP standard documentation.

Naturally, after you've installed the latest iteration of SAP Process Control, you'll want to configure SAP Process Control and set basic settings to support your workflow.

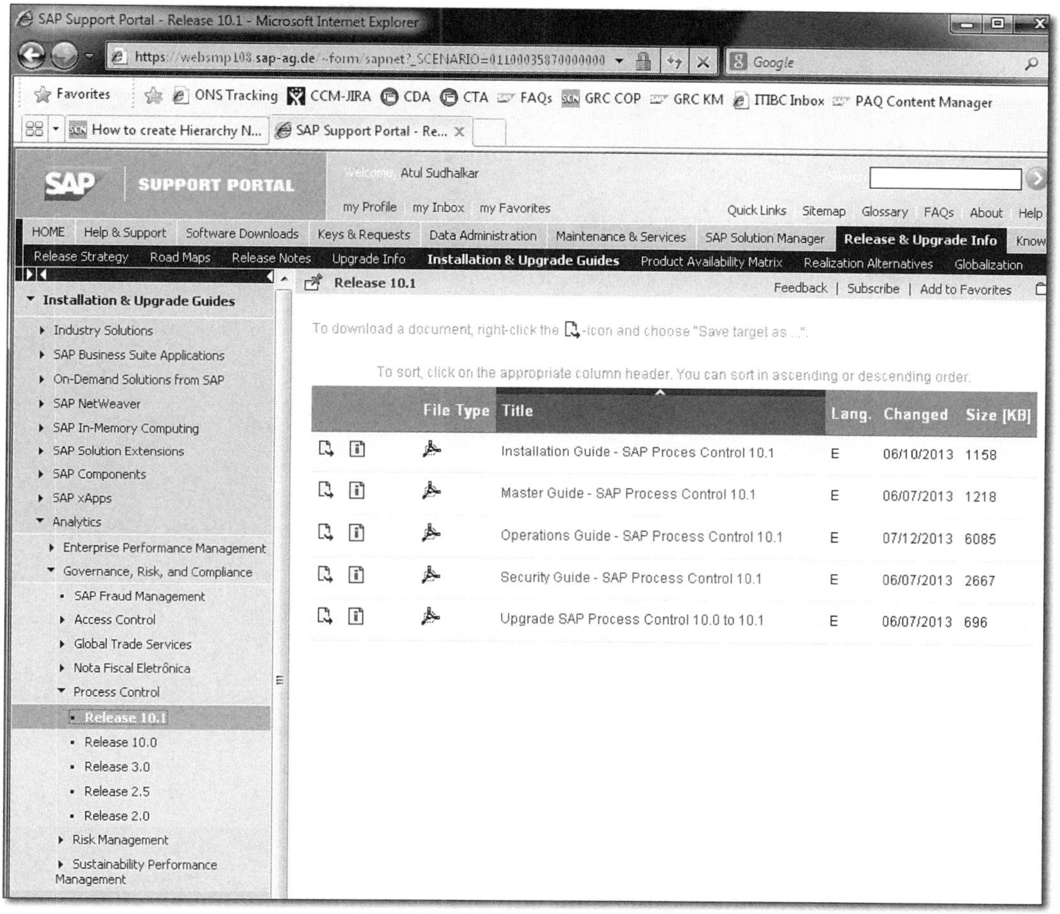

Figure 9.3 SAP Process Control 10.1 Documents on Service Marketplace

9.4 Configuration and Basic Settings

As always, the IMG provides documentation and links to complete configuration and setup for all SAP GRC applications, including SAP Process Control.

IMG configuration

IMG configuration is, of course, documented in the IMG itself. SAP Solution Manager content provides additional guidance. Even more, understanding the SAP authorization model (Transaction PFCG), workflow configurations, and application management in general will give

SAP GRC customers a very good general understanding of what is needed to get SAP Process Control up and running.

Business Configuration Sets

Note

SAP delivers some Business Configuration Sets (BC Sets) that populate configurations to an initial state to get customers started. Customers are, of course, free to use them or not, or to modify the SAP-provided starter configurations to suit their own needs.

Figure 9.4 shows the SAP GRC configuration settings in the SAP standard IMG.

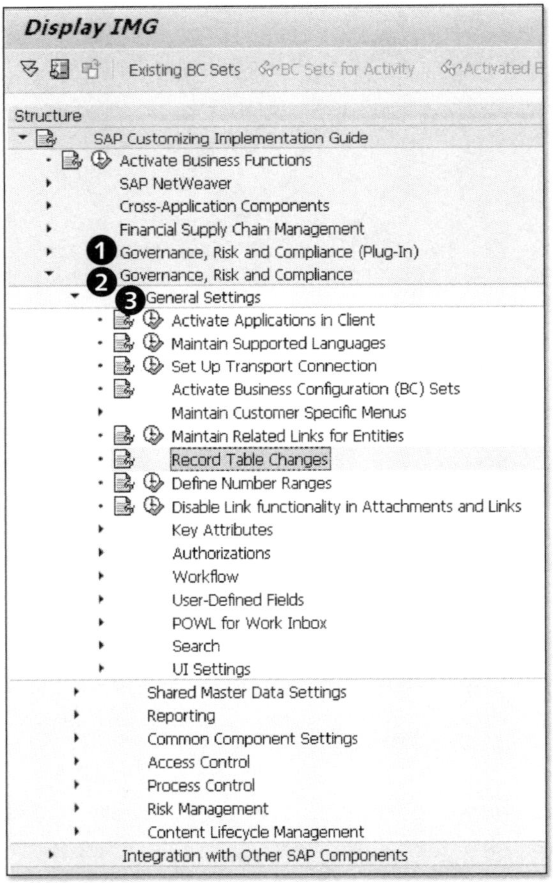

Figure 9.4 SAP GRC Configurations Page in SAPGUI

The numbered labels in Figure 9.4 anchor our descriptions here. First of all, the unlabeled items aren't specific to the SAP GRC applications and so won't be addressed here.

The settings (labeled ❶) actually apply to the SAP GRC plug-in used to monitor an application such as SAP ERP (refer to Figure 9.2). These settings typically don't exist in the SAP GRC system itself (the fact that our demo system has the plug-in deployed is an artifact of a specific scenario we were testing, and not relevant to this discussion or to the vast majority of our readers).

The remaining settings are relevant to SAP Process Control installations, and most of them are documented in the IMG. In the rest of this section, we only add comments to complement SAP documentation, where necessary. Let's start with the GENERAL SETTINGS option in the IMG.

9.4.1 General Settings

As mentioned, we won't explore all there is to review in the GENERAL SETTINGS section in the IMG ❸ but simply comment on the different settings that will impact your implementation of SAP Process Control. We'll review the following settings:

- MAINTAIN SUPPORTED LANGUAGES
- SET UP TRANSPORT CONNECTION
- MAINTAIN CUSTOMER SPECIFIC MENUS
- RECORD TABLE CHANGES
- DISABLE LINK FUNCTIONALITY IN ATTACHMENTS AND LINKS
- KEY ATTRIBUTES
- AUTHORIZATIONS
- WORKFLOW
- USER-DEFINED FIELDS
- POWL FOR WORK INBOX
- SEARCH
- UI SETTINGS

This list isn't intended to be exhaustive. Refer to the IMG and the SAP Help documentation to support your understanding of other fields. Let's review each of these fields in further detail.

Maintain Supported Languages

SAP GRC software ships by default with the major European languages enabled. In addition, SAP provides many other language packs, and obviously which ones are supported varies with SAP's strategy and time.

Set Up Transport Connection

SAP NetWeaver supports transporting configuration data between systems, and this configuration affects what can be transported and to which target systems. While transporting master data isn't an intended purpose of the SAP NetWeaver transport facilities, most SAP Process Control master data is technically an HR Infotype derivative (for its validity date features), which can be transported.

Transporting HR Infotypes across systems or clients is tricky, for several reasons. For one, there can be multiple versions for a given object, identified by different validity periods. Not only can the attributes vary by validity periods but so can relationships to other objects. Finally, HR Infotype objects are identified by their technical object ID, not their name. Because these IDs are generated in the system in which they are created, transporting them runs the risk of ID clashes. Transporting these objects is thus not an easy task and requires some preparation and planning.

To avoid errors, customers are advised to disable transports until they have fully understood HR Infotype ID management across their landscape.

Maintain Customer Specific Menus

The settings in the MAINTAIN CUSTOMER SPECIFIC MENUS are extensively populated via SAP-delivered baseline configurations, and most customers don't deviate significantly from these. Figure 9.5 illustrates two of the menu options that are subheadings under the MAINTAIN CUSTOMER SPECIFIC MENUS setting.

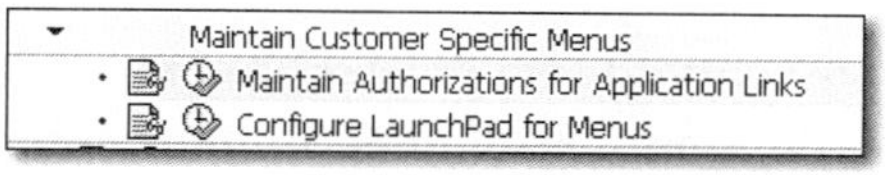

Figure 9.5 Customer-Specific Menus

Delivered configurations and role access

Making major changes to these settings requires a very thorough understanding of the SAP Basis authorization concept. The delivered configurations have a lot of flexibility; most customers then only need to carefully grant appropriate roles (also from the delivered set) to specific users.

Record Table Changes

Basis applications and change logging

Record Table Changes enables Basis change logging for customizing and some other key, low-volume tables. Changes to such tables can greatly affect the proper performance of your SAP application, and SAP recommends enabling such logging only in production, and only for such critical and low-volume tables.

In fact, this is a unique but often underutilized feature of Basis applications. Experience has repeatedly shown that tracking changes to configurations and master data isn't a performance or space (memory) drain. At very little cost, such logging lets customers trace changes to critical settings.

Disable Link Functionality in Attachments and Links

Many SAP Process Control and SAP Risk Management objects allow customers' end users to define external links when creating or editing such objects. Most customers find this useful, but some worry about malicious links being added deliberately or unknowingly. This configuration allows customers to disable link creation.

Key Attributes

As described, time frames govern much of the appearance and behavior of SAP Process Control master data. The KEY ATTRIBUTES setting establishes the range of options available to end users creating master data entities, and using them in other SAP Process Control functionalities. As you can see in Figure 9.6, the user can choose to MAINTAIN TIMEFRAME FREQUENCIES, MAINTAIN TIMEFRAMES (in general), and MAINTAIN TIMEFRAME YEARS.

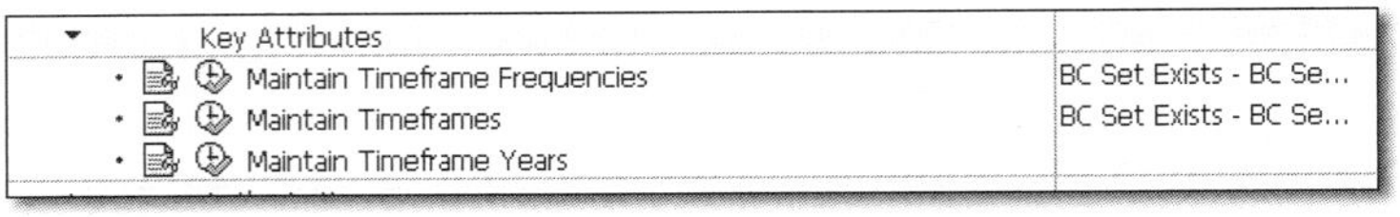

Figure 9.6 Key Attributes: Time Frames and Frequencies

Time frame frequencies and user options

Time frame frequencies as configured here determine, for instance, the options available to users establishing the frequency of monitoring or testing of automated rules. Time frames are named chunks of time, such as specific months or weeks of the year. These must not overlap, and together must span an entire year. Time frames also allow for offsets, which are useful when fiscal years are different from calendar years, for instance. Time frame years define how many years prior to the current year are on offer in various TIMEFRAME dropdown menus in the application.

Authorizations

The SAP-delivered defaults for these configuration settings work for most customers, at least initially. As customers gain experience and insight, they can use these settings for more fine-grained control over which users and roles can access or modify which entities, or execute which functions in SAP Process Control.

Business Workflow

SAP Process Control uses SAP Business Workflow (also known as ABAP workflow) for moving and tracking tasks for assessing, testing, and monitoring controls, among other things. Figure 9.7 shows various IMG settings available to customize workflows.

Business Workflow customization

Warning

Changing these settings within the SAP Business Workflow IMG can require an SAP_ALL authorization profile, emphasizing that this isn't a task to be undertaken lightly! Because SAP Process Control uses underlying Case Management functionality to route and manage issues, it's not easy or safe to extensively customize workflows beyond the parameters offered in the standard customization. While some customers have tried customizing at the SAP Business Workflow level, this doesn't take into account Case Management modules that lie between SAP Business Workflow and SAP Process Control, and this can lead to very difficult administrative challenges.

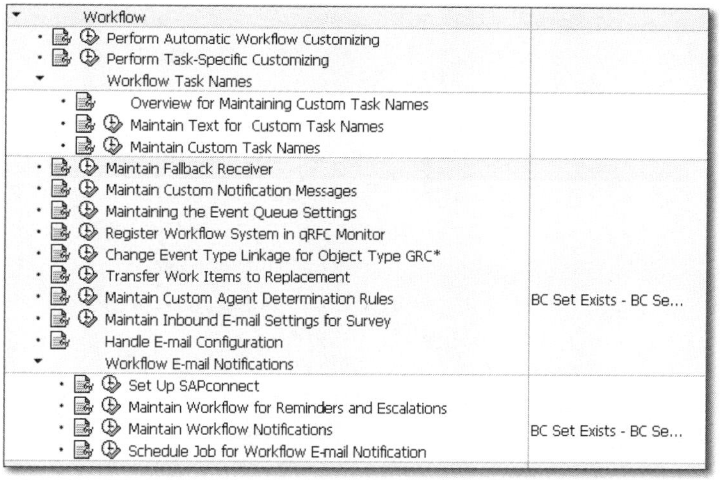

Figure 9.7 Configuration Settings for Customizing Workflow

Note, however, that walking through these steps during installation and configuration is an essential step, without which none of the key features of assessment and testing will work correctly.

User-Defined Fields

User-defined fields have a certain popularity because they allow annotations of SAP Process Control objects with attributes unique to each customer's existing practices. They do, however, come at the cost of some effort in setting up during customizing, as illustrated in Figure 9.8.

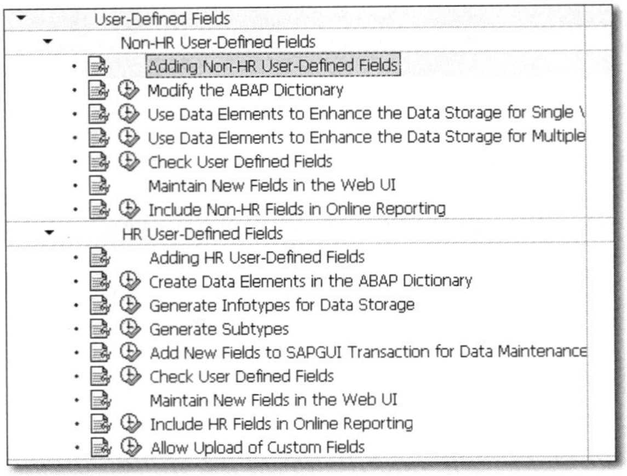

Figure 9.8 User-Defined Fields in IMG, Featuring Both HR User-Defined and Non-HR User-Defined Fields

Validity date ranges and master data objects

Note again the bifurcation between HR (with date validity ranges) and non-HR (without date validity ranges). This is because most SAP Process Control and SAP Risk Management master data objects (though not all) require validity date ranges, while SAP Access Control objects don't support the concept. Because the handling of date-enabled data types is so different, the IMG works very differently for each type.

POWL for Work Inbox

Figure 9.9 shows the configuration options for the Personal Object Worklist (POWL).

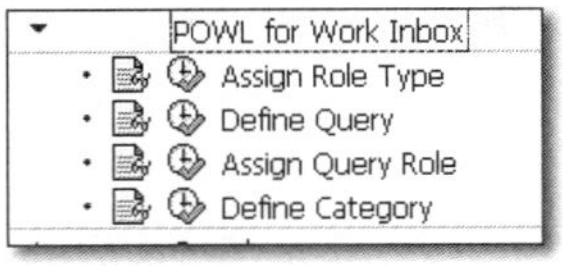

Figure 9.9 Personal Object Worklist (POWL)

Almost every entity screen in SAP Process Control (e.g., regulations, controls, rules, etc.) is based on a POWL, which is a Web Dynpro application. These customizing activities contain the default SAP-delivered methods of populating these pages with data (e.g., a list of CCM rules) when the pages are opened.

Personalization of the Personal Object Worklist

Figure 9.10 shows the POWL PERSONALIZATION screen. Because extensive personalization is possible on most of these pages (e.g., the query, order of display of columns, sort order for rows, etc.), it's advisable to not change these settings.

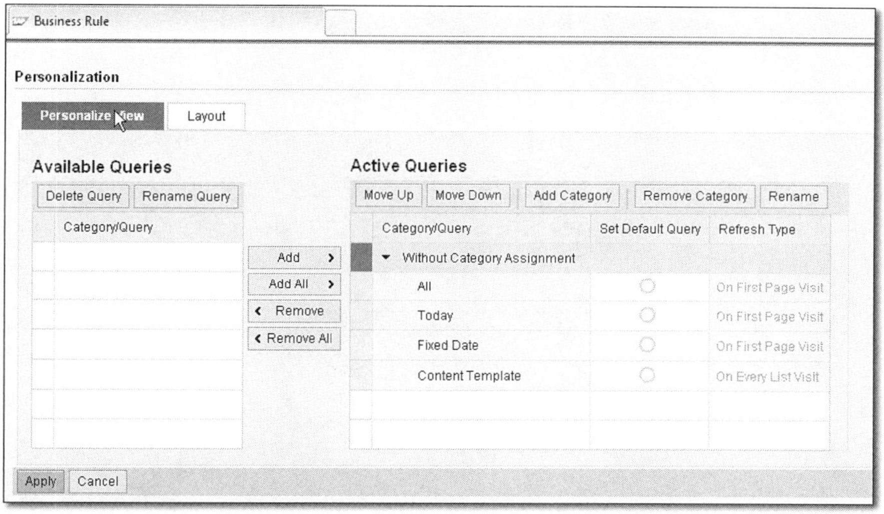

Figure 9.10 POWL Personalization

TREX Search

In SAP Process Control, search is supported via TREX. New to the 10.1 release, such search extends to all attributes of objects, leading to a "Google-like" search. Figure 9.11 shows the SEARCH customization settings.

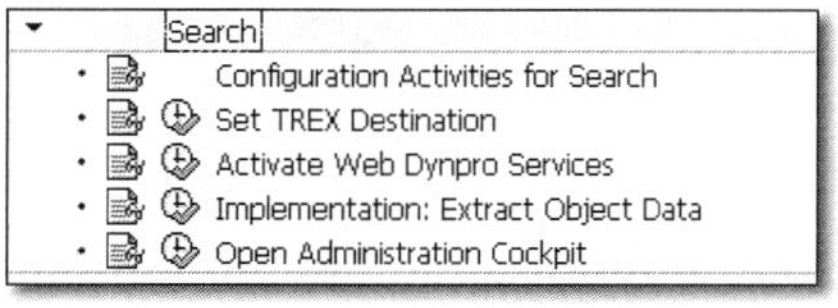

Figure 9.11 Search Customization

TREX Search Customization

This SEARCH customization requires the mediation of a separate TREX server. Of course, whether or not this is a physically separate server is a matter of trading off costs against performance, which can't be addressed here.

UI Settings

The only customizing activity under this category is to set up the *side panels*, which are new to SAP GRC 10.1. If configured, these show up next to the usual SAP Process Control POWL displays, taking their context cues from such main pages to show related information.

Side panels

Figure 9.12 shows an example side panel that displays alongside business processes, showing the percentage of such processes with issues and the evaluation status for the set.

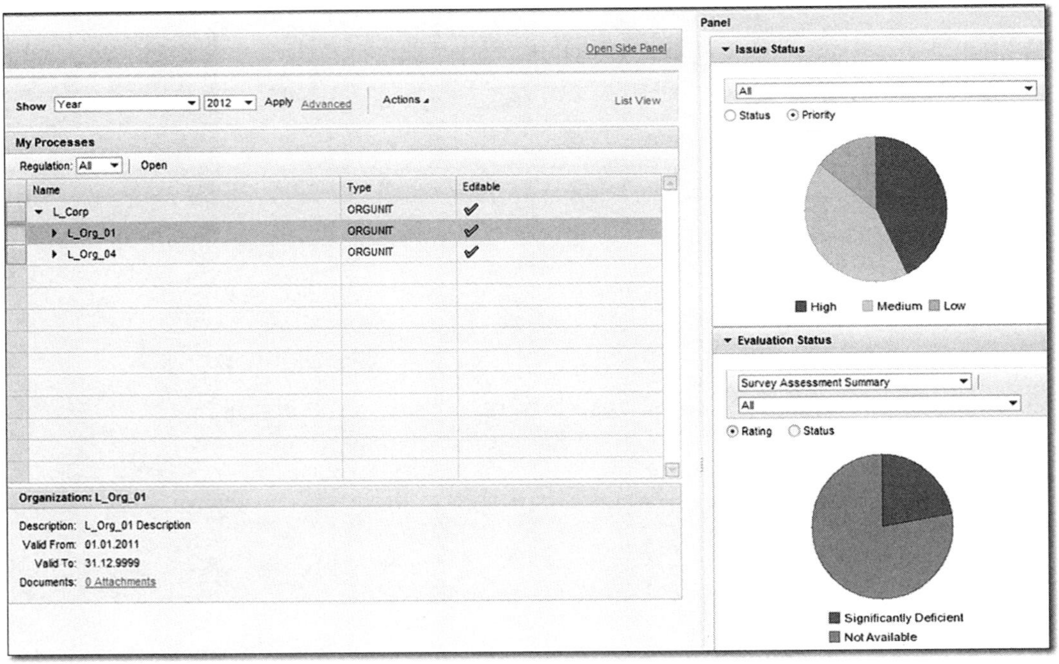

Figure 9.12 Example of Side Panels in SAP Process Control

9.4.2 Shared Master Data Settings

Figure 9.13 shows the shared master data settings customization activities.

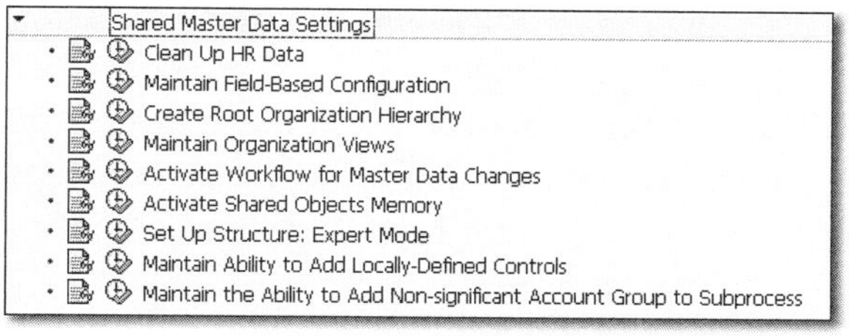

Figure 9.13 Shared Master Data Settings

Master Data Upload Generator

Although the root organization views can be set up or maintained here, the SAP Process Control Master Data Upload Generator (MDUG) can also be used to upload these from the template spreadsheet, so it's not necessary to always use this customizing activity for maintenance. See the next chapter for details.

Organization views

Alternate organization views are useful in some specific cases, such as having an organization not subject to sign-off, or where the SAP Risk Management product is installed together with SAP Process Control, and requires a different organization view.

Master data changes can be better controlled by activating workflow for changes. This isn't really optional, except that many customers consider this too sensitive to be routinely allowed even with workflow activated. Such customers reserve changes for well-planned and extensively reviewed change projects that happen infrequently.

Master data settings

Most settings shown in Figure 9.14 are relevant for SAP Risk Management rather than SAP Process Control, but with each release, customers who are using the two products integrated will find increasing overlap.

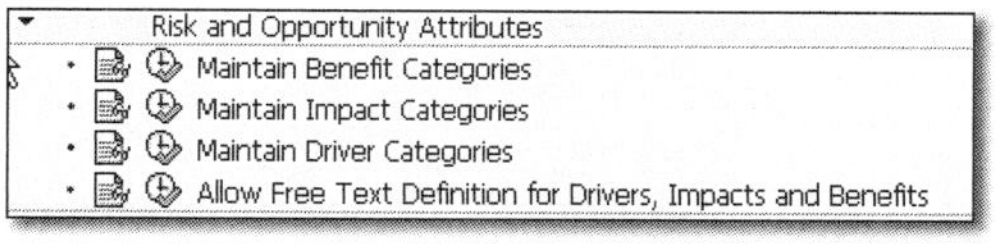

Figure 9.14 Risk and Opportunity Attributes

9.4.3 SAP Process Control Reporting

SAP Process Control master data can change appearance with different validity periods, which complicates reporting considerably. Reports can run directly against database tables for other data types, but it's much more complicated to read HR Infotype objects. In the REPORTING IMG, you can maintain user responsibility, maintain dashboard file paths, configure your reports, and maintain report column settings Figure 9.15 shows some of the configuration settings for reporting within SAP Process Control.

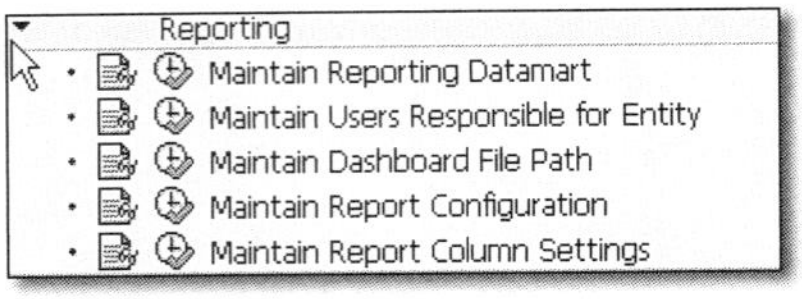

Figure 9.15 Configuration Settings for Managing Reports in SAP Process Control

Reporting datamart and SAP Process Control

SAP Process Control provides a reporting datamart, which holds SAP Process Control objects as of a particular time frame, against which reports can be defined and run.

9.4.4 Common Component Settings for SAP Process Control

The COMMON COMPONENT SETTINGS, shown in Figure 9.16, affect software modules that are shared across the SAP GRC applications.

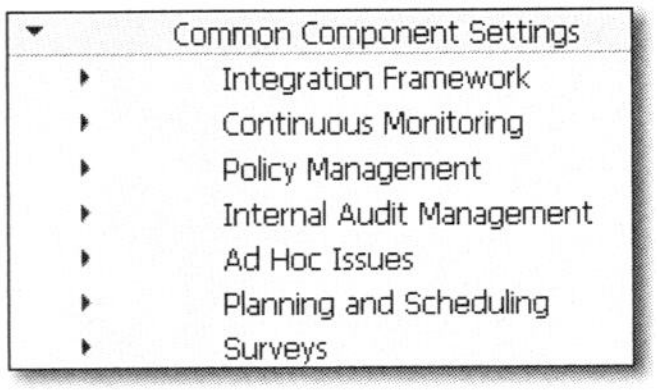

Figure 9.16 Common Component Settings

Common component settings

The integration framework mediates all SAP GRC communications with remote backend systems. For SAP Process Control, this is relevant only for CCM. Because it's quite critical for the operation of that functionality, it's treated extensively in Chapter 11.

Import and export functionality

The section on CCM itself deals with minutiae of the behavior of the CCM modules, except for the activities that enable export and import of CCM business rules and data sources, shown in the last two rows of Figure 9.17: EXPORT DATA SOURCES AND BUSINESS RULES and IMPORT DATA SOURCES AND BUSINESS RULES.

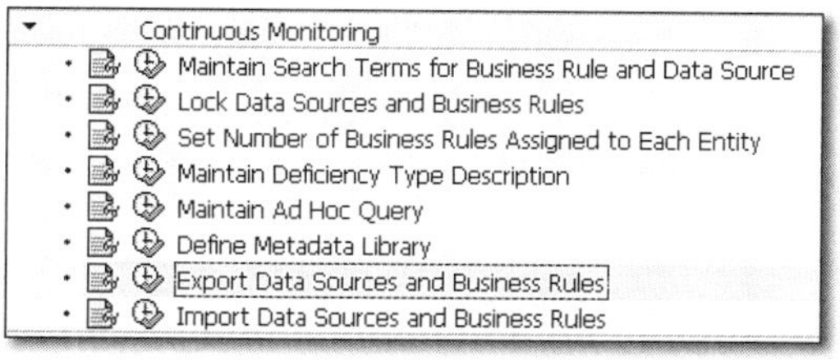

Figure 9.17 CCM Content Export and Import

SAP Process Control 10.1 functionality

This is a significant improvement new to SAP Process Control release 10.1. Customers who use CCM, and particularly customers who have developed their own monitoring rules, consider such rules to be some of the most high-value content in their SAP Process Control systems. Moving such content reliably between test and production systems has been highly sought, and SAP Process Control 10.1 delivers this functionality.

Business rules (and the data sources upon which they depend) can be exported to the user's local disk as XML files. Such exported rules can then be uploaded to another SAP Process Control instance. The files in question can be moved around by any convenient means, including email, FTP, portable media, and so on

Global Unique ID and HR Infotypes

SAP Process Control 10.1 avoids the problems of HR Infotype ID management (number ranges) by using a globally unique ID (GUID) for these objects. This makes it safe to move CCM content back and forth without fear of unintended duplication.

Where the business rule in question uses BRF+, SAP Process Control helpfully extracts and includes the BRF+ rule itself. CCM content export and import is fully described in Chapter 13.

Policy management setttings

Policies aren't new to SAP Process Control 10.1, but their creation, revision, propagation, and tracking of acceptance represents very powerful and useful functionality. Figure 9.18 details the settings found under the POLICY MANAGEMENT node. Note the LDAP server settings, which are new to release 10.1. SAP Process Control can send policy disclosures and collect survey responses via offline forms using SAP Process Control's integration with Adobe Document Server. In many cases, the recipients aren't SAP Process Control users, and SAP licensing models make customers reluctant to expand the list of SAP Process Control users where avoidable. By using LDAP directories, SAP Process Control can send policy disclosures and collect survey results from participants who aren't SAP Process Control users.

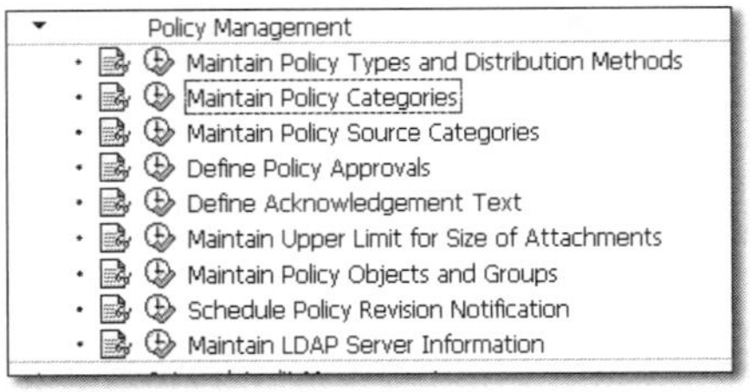

Figure 9.18 Policy Management Settings

Now that we've reviewed the technical architecture and configured the system settings, let's now review the SAP Process Control implementation process by taking a high-level look.

9.5 Implementation Overview of SAP Process Control

Customers new to SAP Process Control are well advised to first set up a sandbox system, and use the SAP-delivered BC Sets as the baseline or first iteration configuration.

SAP Process Control implementation and the business blueprint template

SAP provides a business blueprint template to guide customer implementation efforts. The goal of this chapter isn't to duplicate the information in that template but to complement the template with an overview and specific advice based upon our experience as consultants and implementation experts. We've found that clearly establishing your business goals is key to the success of your implementation. First, you need to review and set the goals of your implementation. We recommend a phased approach to implementation that is followed by data collection and management, and then user and role settings. Let's look at each of these areas in further detail.

9.5.1 Setting Business Goals

SAP Process Control is a tool to help organizations document their regulatory or policy compliance needs, plan compliance initiatives, assess and test the degree of their compliance, and document any deficiencies and steps taken to remediate them. A SAP Process Control implementation can only succeed to the extent that the customer's goals match these SAP Process Control capabilities.

Alignment of business goals and SAP Process Control functionality

As we said in Section 9.1, SAP Process Control started as a financial regulatory compliance tool. Since then, its capabilities have evolved, especially in CCM. It can now be used for operational compliance as well, although the notion of controls, issues, remediation, and so on still carry a strong regulatory compliance flavor.

SAP Process Control can certainly be used for purposes other than regulatory compliance, but customers have to be prepared to adapt their plans to suit SAP Process Control's architecture and approach.

Apart from Continuous Control Monitoring (CCM), SAP Policy Management is another feature with which SAP Process Control has started evolving beyond regulatory compliance.

9.5.2 Phased Approaches

As will become clearer in Chapter 10, SAP Process Control requires a considerable amount of master data to be set up. Customers find it helpful to deploy SAP Process Control in phases, initially limiting themselves to one regulation, for example, applied only to a small part of the company and, perhaps, to only one business process. The point is to gain experience with SAP Process Control implementation, roll out to users, and train in a limited setting before impacting others.

While this has proven a successful strategy for many (if not most) SAP Process Control implementers and users, IT departments have slightly different sensitivities. SAP Process Control installations have some optional components, as shown in Figure 9.19.

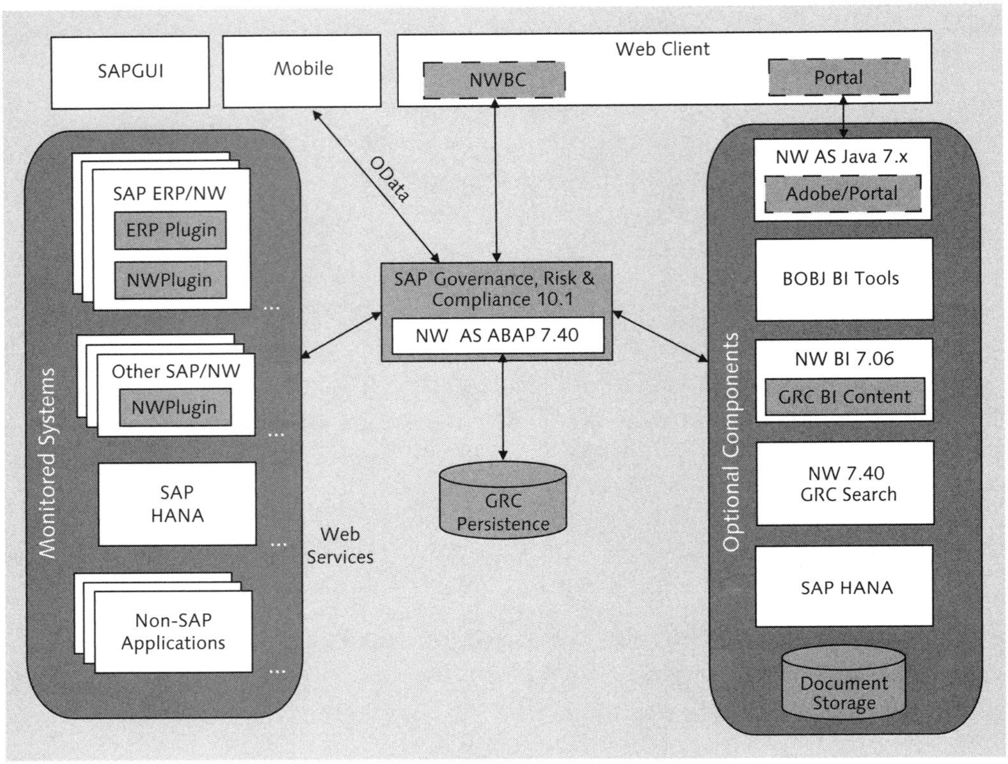

Figure 9.19 Process Control Deployment Architecture

SAP Process Control deployment architecture

While the deployment architecture diagram of Figure 9.19 appears complex, comparison to Figure 9.2 shows that it presents the same information but in greater detail. For this section, our goal is to point out that, depending on which functionality is to be used, different optional system landscape components have to be installed and set up. For instance, if CCM isn't needed, then the SAP ERP and SAP NetWeaver plug-ins need not be installed.

Master data and role assignment considerations during phased implementation

A phased implementation succeeds well if the only changes between phases affect the master data, users, and role assignments of SAP Process Control. If customers want to defer implementation of optional components such as the Adobe Document Server, TREX search, and so on to a later phase, they need to take care to reflect the IT impact in terms of additional servers, Basis configuration, and so on, at later stages of the project.

9.5.3 Master Data Collection

In Chapter 10, we describe SAP Process Control master data in more detail, in terms of how it's to be entered into SAP Process Control. But the collection of the appropriate information is very much part of the planning and preparation stage of SAP Process Control implementation.

Compliance versus operational considerations during implementation

Organizational structures, business process models, business process controls, regulations, policies, and so on all exist outside of SAP Process Control. It's tempting to think that SAP Process Control users only need to type these into appropriate SAP Process Control data structures, but experience suggests otherwise. The compliance perspective of these objects is quite different from, say, the operational perspective. To use a recent customer example, two distribution centers in the same city are two nodes in the organization operationally because they have two managers to whom workers report. But for regional compliance and reporting, it may serve no purpose to treat them separately.

Similarly, business processes have very nuanced and layered meanings, but the main purpose they serve in SAP Process Control is to anchor controls and regulations. You can see that this leaves off many levels of meaning.

Process flow hierarchies

The SAP Process Control implementation team should view these hierarchies from the SAP Process Control process flow perspective and decide on a minimal representation that still captures the level of detail they need.

9.5.4 Process Control Users and Roles

The IMG customization activities as detailed in Section 9.4, especially for authorizations and workflow, are the definitive repositories of active roles in SAP Process Control. Most implementations start with fewer users who assume too many roles; with experience and increasing sophistication, customers learn the right level of granularity in role assignments.

Managing role conflicts

The key driver here is always the original goal. If SAP Process Control is being used primarily as a compliance monitoring tool, then stricter attention must be paid to keeping role conflicts at bay.

Offline forms and Adobe Document Server

Note that offline forms (via Adobe Document Server) make it possible for many people to interact with SAP Process Control without becoming SAP Process Control users (i.e., without having a login account in SAP Process Control). So only those people who are business process or control owners, have sign-off authority at various organization levels, or play a role in maintaining regulations, risks, policies, and so on must have accounts. Occasional participants, such as those to whom policies are disclosed or who respond to risk or control assessments need not have SAP Process Control accounts. Now that your system is implemented, let's review how Process Control can be used effectively.

9.6 Overview of SAP Process Control Usage

You're likely interested in implementing SAP GRC, and our guidance in this book focuses mostly on that. However, it's important to note that particularly in SAP GRC, the implementation of the product always evolves over time. If SAP delivered no more updates to the product, and if your business changed no further, you would still find yourself updating your SAP Process Control implementation on a regular basis. You can think of this as the wheel shown in Figure 9.20.

Figure 9.20 SAP Process Control Usage Cycle

SAP Process Control usage cycle

Thinking of SAP Process Control use in terms of such an evolving cycle will help you understand how SAP approached the design and development of the product. Each of the following sections describes activities that fall within such a cycle, describing SAP Process Control usage at a slightly finer grain. We'll start with documentation activities then shift our focus to scope, evaluation, monitoring, and reporting activities. Figure 9.20 details the SAP Process Control usage cycle.

9.6.1 Documenting

Documenting regulations, regulatory requirements, risks, control objectives, and so on is the start of the SAP Process Control process flow cycle, as shown in Figure 9.20.

Documentation types and the user role

Documentation includes capturing regulations and regulatory requirements, risks, responses, controls, control objectives, and so on. In addition to the descriptions and attributes of such SAP Process Control master data objects, customers can also add links and attached documents to further enrich the context of their compliance or control initiatives. This is the job of the user setting up such master data, although other SAP Process Control users can read such documents and follow the links. For instance, US utilities regulations modeled in SAP Process Control can have a link to formal regulations maintained by the Federal Energy Regulatory Commission. When conducting control design assessments or remediating detected control violations, SAP Process Control users might find it both helpful and necessary to review the details in such links.

9.6.2 Scope

Scoping process

Scoping is the SAP Process Control process that determines which organizations in the organizational hierarchy are relevant (material) for financial compliance. Account balances, risk assessments, and so on contribute this determination.

Planner functionality

The *Planner* is the functionality used to schedule activities such as assessments, sign-offs, and surveys. The steps in a plan can be manual, which typically works by routing workflow to a user. Alternatively the step can be automated, which works by invoking a monitoring rule on a backend system (see Chapters 11 through 14 for more detail).

9.6.3 Evaluation

Manual assessments and tests obviously require a workflow recipient to be configured for the task. This is part of the user and role customization in IMG. Risk assessments include evaluating both the likelihood and the impact of a risk. Control design assessments, on the other hand, only evaluate a single metric of whether the control in question is well-designed and will prove adequate to meet its stated objectives.

9.6.4 Monitoring and Remediation

After key risks and controls have been identified during assessments, it's the job of compliance officers to monitor these, to head off trouble if possible, or to at least limit the adverse impact if problems are encountered. In SAP Process Control, this is achieved via monitoring of controls. SAP Risk Management has a corresponding concept of monitoring risks.

Automated versus continuous monitoring

In the simplest terms, monitoring means keeping an eye on the implementation of various controls in backend applications to make sure they are correctly setup, are faithfully followed, and are updated in a timely manner when needed. Such monitoring can be manual, meaning that SAP Process Control users are expected to periodically review configurations and transactions in backend applications to evaluate compliance. In contrast, automated monitoring means a business rule has been created and scheduled to run periodically, which extracts data from backend applications and evaluates compliance. Semi-automated monitoring means a rule extracts data and presents it to a SAP Process Control user for review, while tracking activities via workflow.

Monitoring is a rich and varied topic. Because automated or continuous monitoring is also a key differentiator for SAP Process Control, this topic is addressed at great length in Chapter 11 through Chapter 14.

When a problem or an issue is found, it should be addressed. Either it should be fixed, or if that proves impossible, its ill effects should be limited. Remediation is the formal recognition that such steps taken to fix a detected problem also need to be justified, followed faithfully, and the actions taken audit-trailed.

Remediation Plan

In SAP Process Control, remediation can be a formal plan, which a control owner (see Chapter 10 for more details on what constitutes a control) assigns from a previously approved list of such plans). The job of executing the remediation plan can then be delegated to an issue owner. This is the standard method of addressing problems and is called the standard remediation process.

9.6.5 Reporting

Extensive reporting is available for various processes within SAP Process Control. Status and results of evaluations, issues, and remediation can be examined. Hierarchical reports allow owners of higher level organizations to view rollups of evaluations of organizations under them.

SAP Process Control's (and SAP Risk Management's) use of validity-period layering of objects has always made reporting a challenge. Most query and reporting engines expect objects to map to relational database tables in ways that (a) capture object relationships in table relationships, and (b) have a set of fields that together serve as key fields. SAP Process Control validity-period objects violate these two expectations, which makes it impossible to use standard reporting and analytical tools directly against SAP Process Control master data tables.

Master data tables and the datamart

Even SAP-delivered reports for SAP Process Control typically first extract data from master data tables to a set of intermediate tables (colloquially called the datamart), and then run reports against those. The datamart is populated "as of" a specific date or time frame.

Custom reporting

Customers have always had the option of writing custom reports against the datamart directly. But SAP has always insisted that the datamart isn't a public API, so customers should not expect SAP to keep the datamart design stable from release to release. SAP has also never provided customers or partners with any documentation of the datamart schema. This has discouraged most customers from investing in custom reporting.

SAP NetWeaver Business Warehouse (SAP NetWeaver BW) has instead been SAP's preferred solution for customer-defined reports. Because all the SAP BusinessObjects BI tools run against SAP NetWeaver BW, this strategy certainly had good thinking behind it, except that many SAP GRC customers never implemented SAP NetWeaver BW.

SAP Process Control 10.1 reporting functionality

With SAP Process Control 10.1, two other options have become available for customers who want to customize reports. Operational Data Providers (ODP) is a feature of SAP NetWeaver, available since release 7.31. This allows SAP BusinessObjects BI tools to connect directly to ABAP application systems. From the SAP Process Control side, such SAP BusinessObjects BI tools still see a datamart, but with release 10.1, SAP has made this datamart a public API, so that customers may develop reports against it, secure in the knowledge that following standard SAP rules, SAP GRC will keep the datamart schema stable.

SAP Process Control and HANA

Finally, SAP Process Control 10.1 also includes support for SAP HANA. For one thing, SLT replication can populate a sidecar installation of SAP HANA. For another, all of SAP GRC 10.1 runs directly on SAP HANA. Note that either of these options still relies on the equivalent of the reporting datamart mentioned earlier. That is, the validity-period dependency of SAP Process Control master data must still be unraveled first, during datamart population. But because the datamart is now a public feature, customers can take advantage of SAP HANA analytics capabilities.

9.6.6 Certification

Organization owners certify the state of compliance for their organizations. This process is also called sign-off, and it proceeds hierarchically up the organizational structure until, at the root node, the owner's sign-off certifies the results for the entire company. Because the process is hierarchical, higher levels in the organizational structure can certify only after all their subnodes have completed sign-off. Higher levels in an organization can see the certifications for their lower levels and will only get the appropriate workflow routing after all their subnodes have finished the sign-off process.

9.6.7 Policy Management

SAP Process Control 10.0 introduced a very powerful set of Policy Management capabilities. This complements the regulatory-compliance flavor of SAP Process Control usage because policies aren't necessarily motivated by regulations.

Policy Management functionality

SAP Process Control provides a comprehensive set of tools for policies. Customers can collaborate on drafting policies, review them, and approve them before making them active. Revising policies creates new versions, so that historical information is never lost. They can arrange for policies to be distributed to users (and those recipients don't have to be SAP Process Control users—LDAP integration, new to SAP Process Control 10.1, enables policies to be distributed via email to non-SAP Process Control users).

Planner functionality

The Planner as discussed in Section 9.6.2 can be used to send surveys to affected users; they can be asked to acknowledge or accept the policy, and can even be required to take a quiz to ensure that they've read and understood it. Completion of such surveys can be tracked as a metric and be made visible to appropriate management levels.

Document Management Systems integration

Policy management can also leverage integration to document management systems (DMS) as an optional feature. This allows policies (as represented in SAP Process Control) to be linked to policy documents maintained on DMS servers.

9.7 Summary

SAP Process Control 10.1 has a rich set of features to help companies document and track compliance to regulations and policies. The capabilities of SAP Process Control are so rich that customers have found SAP Process Control useful in monitoring for reasons other than compliance, such as operational monitoring.

Implementing SAP Process Control is made easier by starting with the SAP-supplied BC Sets and accepting the default behavior first. Collaborating with colleagues in all affected departments to collect all the master data needed to implement SAP Process Control reduces effort in the long run because it better enables users to pick the right level of granularity at which to represent organizational and process hierarchies, the right set of accounts, risks and controls, and properly prioritize which processes and controls require assessments and monitoring.

Reporting and analytics in SAP Process Control 10.1 is very rich and made much richer by support for ODP, which delivers SAP BusinessObjects BI analytic capabilities in the application itself (i.e., it enables BI without SAP NetWeaver BW). SAP Process Control 10.1 also supports SAP HANA (either via replication to, or by running directly on SAP HANA), which enables the rich and growing set of SAP HANA analytic capabilities.

Having read this relatively brief introduction to SAP Process Control functionality, you now better understand the purpose, nuances, and life cycle of various SAP Process Control master data types, which we describe next in Chapter 10.

This chapter describes in more detail SAP Process Control master data and provides some tips on how to set it up for an optimally configured SAP Process Control scenario.

10 SAP Process Control Master Data

Before SAP Process Control functionality can be used, customers need to set up SAP Process Control master data. In this chapter, we describe the key master data elements, and highlight some of the unique features of SAP Process Control master data that impact how SAP Process Control functionality behaves. Once again, the goal is to add value beyond SAP-provided application documentation and to avoid mere repetition.

Importance of an organizational structure

SAP Process Control requires a model of your organizational structure. The organizational hierarchy is fundamental to almost all SAP Process Control functionality (described in Chapter 9): assessments, monitoring, and, of course, the reporting and analytics based on those. Section 10.1 describes how to create and maintain the organizational hierarchy.

SAP Process Control and regulatory modeling

Because so much of regulatory modeling and monitoring is date dependent, SAP Process Control (and SAP Risk Management) explicitly tag most master data with validity date ranges. We describe these first in Section 10.1.2 in the context of organizations, but note (as we emphasize in that section) that validity date ranges apply broadly across most master data types.

In this chapter, we will cover a wide range of content as related to Process Control master data. Let's review what each of the sections will cover.

Business process models

Section 10.2 describes business process models as used in SAP Process Control. While many SAP ERP and other applications have rich and detailed business process models, SAP Process Control takes a minimalist approach. The only information SAP Process Control holds on business processes is the hierarchy, which always ends in a control at the leaf node.

Regulations

Section 10.3 describes regulations. SAP Process Control assumes that regulatory compliance motivates all SAP Process Control usage. Most assessments and all monitoring happen with respect to a control, as applied in the context of a particular organizational node, and as relevant to one or more regulations. So along with business processes and organizational hierarchy, regulations are a fundamental master data type in SAP Process Control.

Policies

Section 10.4 describes policies. New since release 10.0, policies aren't critical to the operation of the assessments and monitoring functionality of SAP Process Control. They do represent a very useful and sometimes critical part of compliance, however, because effectively capturing, disseminating, and measuring acceptance of policies is certainly fundamental to a compliance program.

Accounts and Account Groups

Section 10.5 describes accounts and account groups. All financial applications depend on having multiple accounts for running the business, preparing standard financial filings, financial reporting, and so on. For operational and other reasons, businesses typically have many more accounts than account types or groups; for instance, there may be multiple cash accounts, receivables and payables, assets, and so on. For compliance monitoring, it's convenient to lump similar accounts together into account groups and apply materiality thresholds to such groups.

Master data content management

Section 10.6 discusses the interesting and difficult topic of master data content management and transport. Implementing SAP Process Control requires collecting a large amount of information to populate the SAP Process Control master data types described here. This often requires people with different expertise to collaborate on the right information at the correct level of granularity. The usual SAP Process Control user interfaces (UIs) can be very tedious because they support creation of master data element by element. SAP Process Control itself also provides few tools for collaborating on the implementation phase. To address all of these challenges, SAP provides two tools, external to SAP Process Control, for helping customers create, upload, download, and update master data en masse. This contrasts with some other products such as SAP Access Control, which provides facilities to upload data from spreadsheets as part of the product functionality itself.

Figure 10.1 shows the MASTER DATA tab of SAP Process Control. Note that for the purposes of this book, we've used a login with wide access and high levels of authorization. The level of detail visible on any given screen (such as Figure 10.1) reflects this exceptional situation. Much more commonly, users will see fewer links and a cleaner UI, consistent with their role in SAP GRC processes.

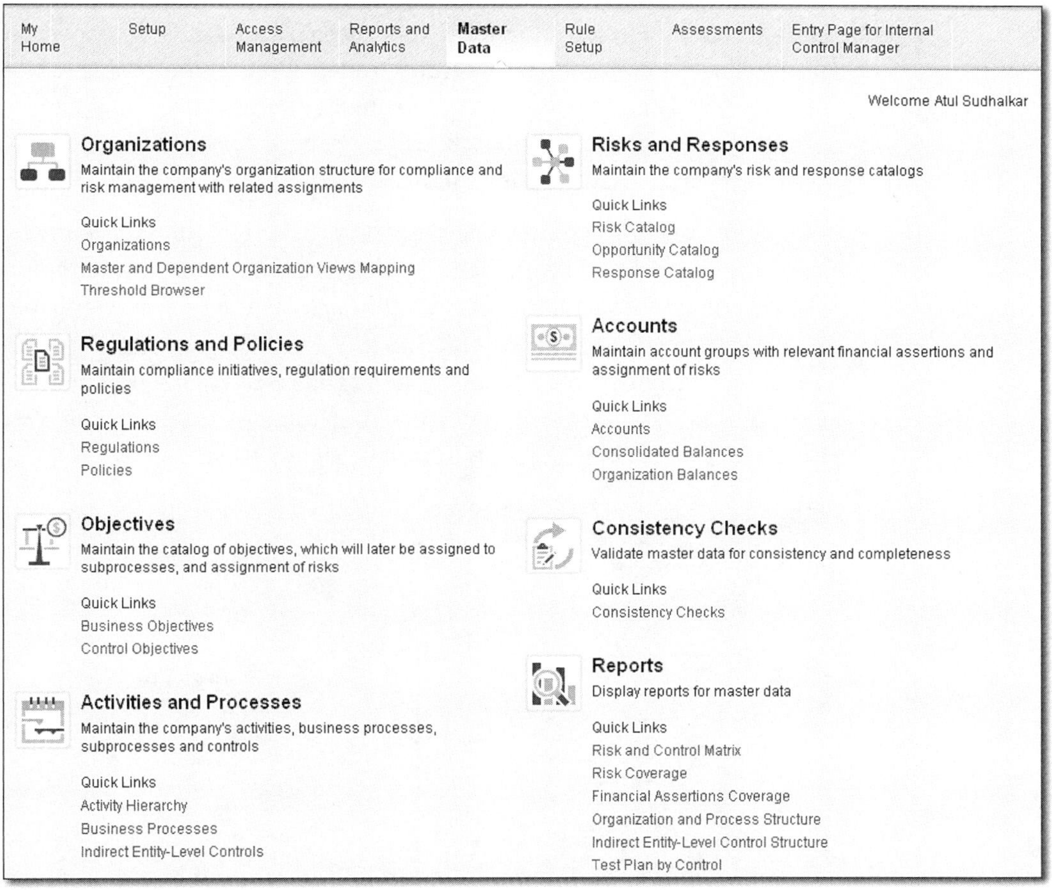

Figure 10.1 Master Data Settings Page in SAP Process Control

In the following sections, Sections 10.1 through Sections 10.6, we will describe the key master data elements. These include Organizations, Business Process Models (Found in the OBJECTIVES Tab), Regulation and Policies, Account Groups (listed in the ACCOUNTS Tab), and Master Data Content Management (Found in the CONSISTENCY CHECKS Tab). The links to which are shown in Figure 10.1.

10.1 Organizations

All companies have organizational structures, and all business process configurations and policies vary within such structures. This is especially true where organizational structures reflect geographic or regulatory boundaries. The ORGANIZATIONS tab under the MASTER DATA page is pretty straightforward. This tab allows companies to maintain their organizational structures for compliance.

Modeling the organizational and business process structures is central to assessing and risks and compliance. SAP Process Control allows multiple organizational views to be created—although (as the figures in this section show) our demo system only has one. The root of every organizational hierarchy has to be created via the IMG (see Figure 10.2 and Figure 10.3), although nodes under the root can be created in the Web Dynpro UI by clicking the ADD button in Figure 10.4.

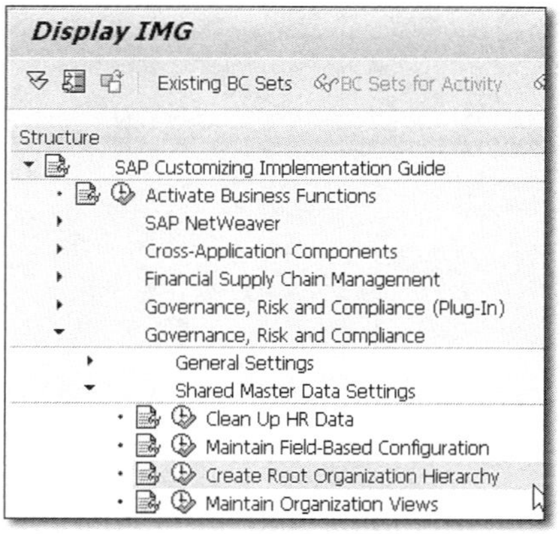

Figure 10.2 IMG Node to Create the Root Organization Hierarchy

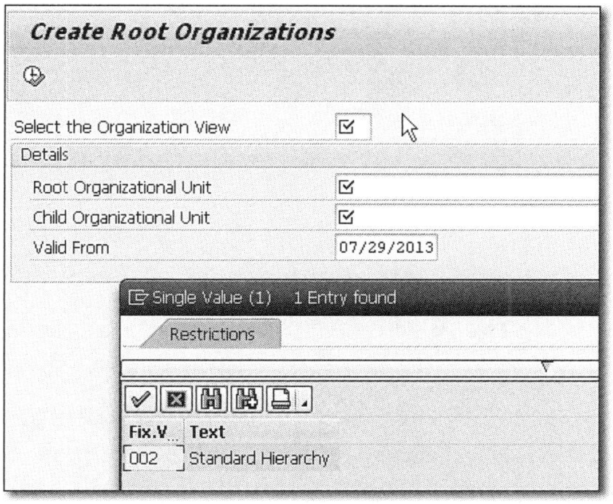

Figure 10.3 Creating the Organizational Root in SAP Process Control

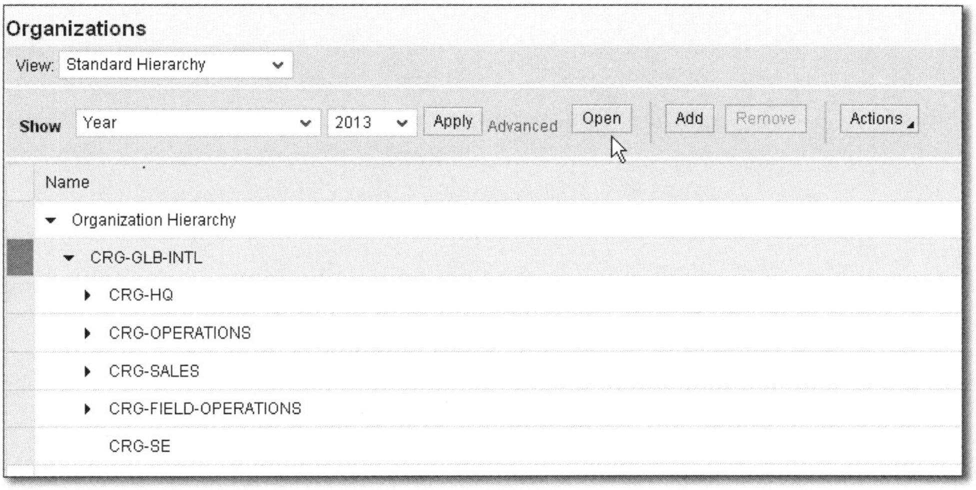

Figure 10.4 Detailed Look at the Organization Root and Organizations in SAP Process Control

In the context of organization hierarchies, we next explain two features: multiple hierarchies, which are unique to organizations, and validity dates, which are widely used in SAP Process Control for master data types.

10.1.1 Multiple Hierarchies

Organization Structure hierarchy example

Organizational structure can vary in the level of granularity, depending on its purpose. For example, a well-known bottler in North America has two warehouses in a major city, each with a manager overseeing several employees. The warehouse managers report to a regional manager, who also manages office employees for a sales office. Because the customer wants to use SAP Process Control for regulatory compliance monitoring, representing the organizational structure down to the level of individual warehouses is overkill. Nor do the company's remediation plans vary between the warehouses. The customer therefore chose to keep its organizational model at a coarser level, which better reflected the company's needs.

Parallel hierarchies

Similarly, different regulatory frameworks might make it worthwhile to have parallel hierarchies. SAP Process Control's multicompliance framework allows customers to reuse business processes and controls for multiple regulations, but organizational structures might well be very different for financial regulations than for, say, worker safety regulations. Finally, because organization hierarchies can be shared between SAP Access Control, SAP Process Control, and SAP Risk Management, this is another reason to have multiple hierarchies.

These are some of the reasons why SAP Process Control allows multiple hierarchy views, as evidenced by the Views dropdown box shown earlier in Figure 10.4.

Organization nodes

Figure 10.5 shows details of a particular organization node, reached by selecting one such node in a particular time frame and view, as in Detailed look at the Organization Root and Organizations in Figure 10.4. The core attributes of an organization node are shown in the figure; relationships to other master data entities are in the various tabs. Most core attributes shown in the figure are for documentation only; that is, they either don't affect the behavior of SAP Process Control functionality, or they affect it only slightly. The exceptions are validity dates, which are described next; and the Org Level System Parameters, which are described in Chapter 14.

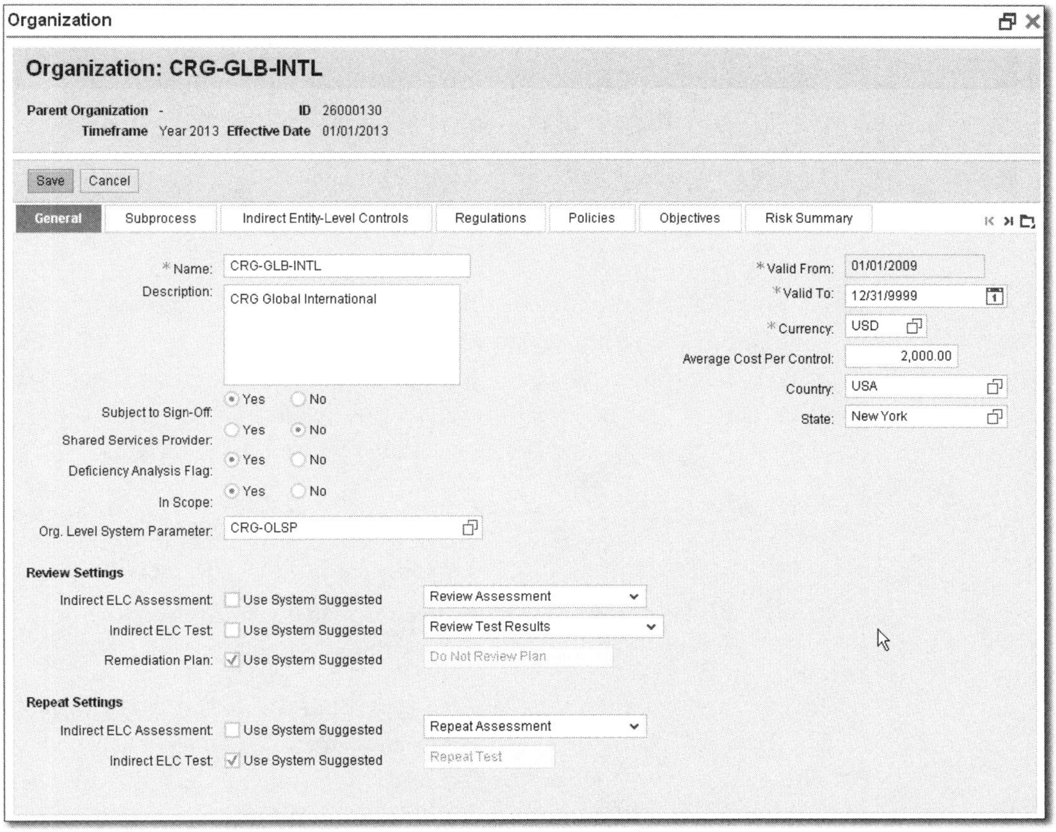

Figure 10.5 Organization Details

10.1.2 Validity Dates and Time Frames in the Organization Structure

Validity dates are a recurrent theme in most SAP Process Control master data structures. The point is that as these entities change, it's nevertheless necessary to maintain a record of their previous values. This is necessary for documentation purposes because SAP Process Control is intended to be used as a regulatory compliance tool.

Furthermore, because many of the attributes of these master data entities are actually their relationships (both hierarchical and associative), the relationship graph between these can also change over time. Because SAP Process Control transactions (e.g., assessments, remediation, etc.)

depend on such master data and interrelationships to make sense, it's essential to be able to link back to "old" structures and relationships. Otherwise, it would be impossible to allow these entities to vary over time because that could lead to inconsistencies in transactional data.

This is why so much of SAP Process Control master data is effective-date enabled. That is, there is always a VALID FROM and VALID TO date, as Figure 10.5 shows for ORGANIZATIONS (top right of the figure).

An effective-dated entity can have multiple values for the same name and ID. But the effective dates have to have disjoint ranges. That is, for a given time frame, there shouldn't be two or more valid versions of the same entity. This logic is enforced in the code, so that users are prevented from saving changes that violate this validation logic.

The usual practice in such cases is to create entities with a meaningful START or VALID FROM date, but an END or VALID TO date in the year 9999. Later, if a different version of the entity is to be stored, the end validity of the previous version is truncated to be the same (or a day before) the start validity of the new value.

This section on date validity applies to most of the master data entities of SAP Process Control and SAP Risk Management, so take particular note. Now that we've reviewed the ORGANIZATION tab and the structural hierarchy of organization units within SAP Process Control, we turn next to the business process, which is another data type fundamental to almost all aspects of SAP Process Control functionality.

10.2 Business Process Models

Business process models are commonplace in business IT. With roles, authorizations, approvals, systems, and other details, Business Process Modeling) software vendors can capture very fine-grained levels of detail about many aspects of a business.

SAP Process Control business process models are far more limited, focusing on the only aspects of business process models that SAP Process

Control can effectively use—the hierarchy. This will become clearer as we examine the screens used to create these models.

To illustrate, we reach the process hierarchies in our demo system via the ACTIVITIES AND PROCESSES group of the MASTER DATA tab shown earlier in Figure 10.1. The PROCESS STRUCTURE page is shown in Figure 10.6.

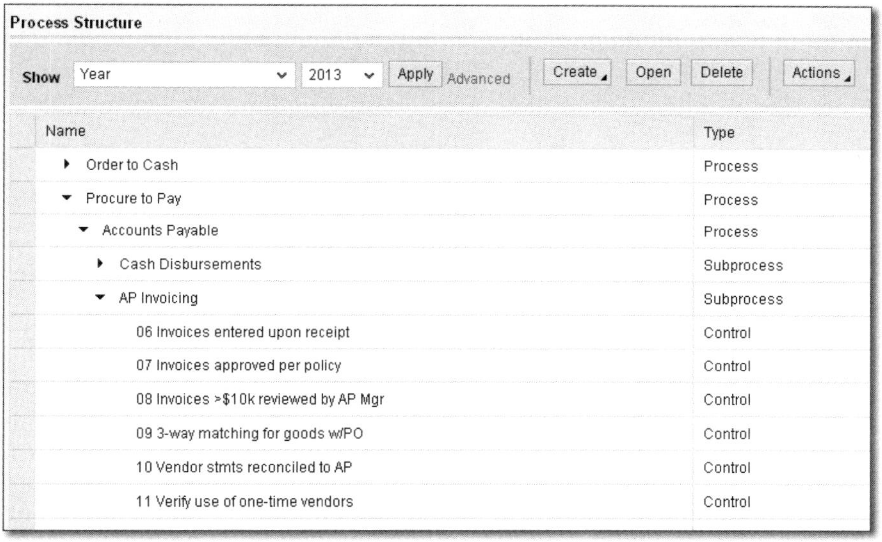

Figure 10.6 Business Process List

Figure 10.6 shows a simple hierarchy: a process node can have any level of nested child process nodes, or one child level of subprocess. A subprocess can only have a control as a child. Selecting any one node in this hierarchy and clicking the OPEN button brings up the details of that node, as shown in Figure 10.7.

Process nodes

Figure 10.7 shows details of a process node. Other than a description, and hooks for attachments and links documenting aspects external to SAP Process Control functionality, there is little room for any other information. It exists mainly as a means of allowing SAP Process Control business process structures—at least in depth of hierarchy—to align with more detailed business process models the customer might have stored elsewhere, for instance, in specialized process modeling tools.

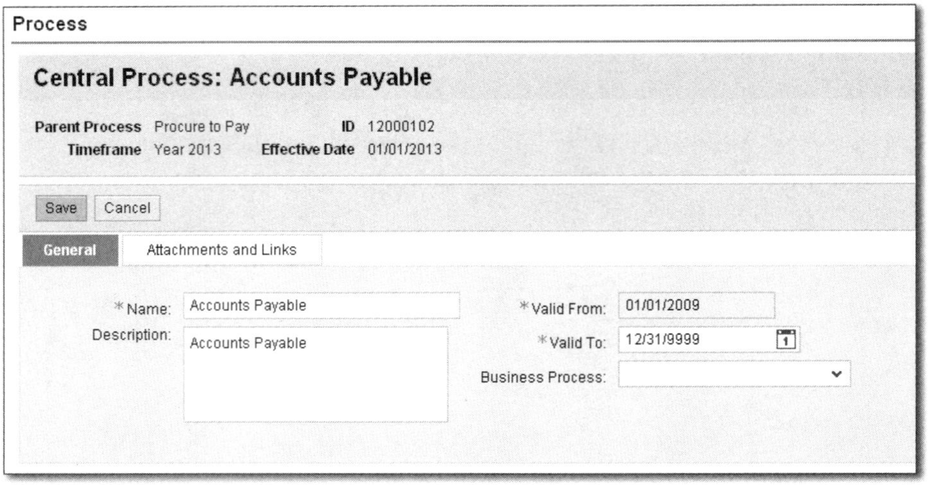

Figure 10.7 Business Process Detail

Subprocess nodes

Figure 10.8 shows details of a subprocess node. Again, such a node's details are reached by selecting the node in the PROCESS STRUCTURE shown earlier in Figure 10.6, and clicking the OPEN button. Clearly, subprocess nodes are also pretty lightly instrumented with SAP Process Control functionality, although more so than process nodes. Master data types mentioned on the tabs in Figure 10.8—CONTROLS, REGULATIONS, and so on—link to subprocesses in the execution of SAP Process Control functionality.

Controls

Figure 10.9 shows details of a control in SAP Process Control. Note again that this is the leaf node of a process hierarchy as shown in Figure 10.6. It can almost be said that the entire business process hierarchy exists mainly to provide context for the control—the control is the main SAP Process Control master data type through which so much of SAP Process Control functionality is presented. It should be immediately obvious that controls are central to a lot of SAP Process Control functionality. Fields such as SIGNIFICANCE, LEVEL OF EVIDENCE TO BE TESTED, and so on serve to document the control itself, but some fields, such as TEST AUTOMATION, also affect how assessments, testing, and continuous control monitoring (CCM) work.

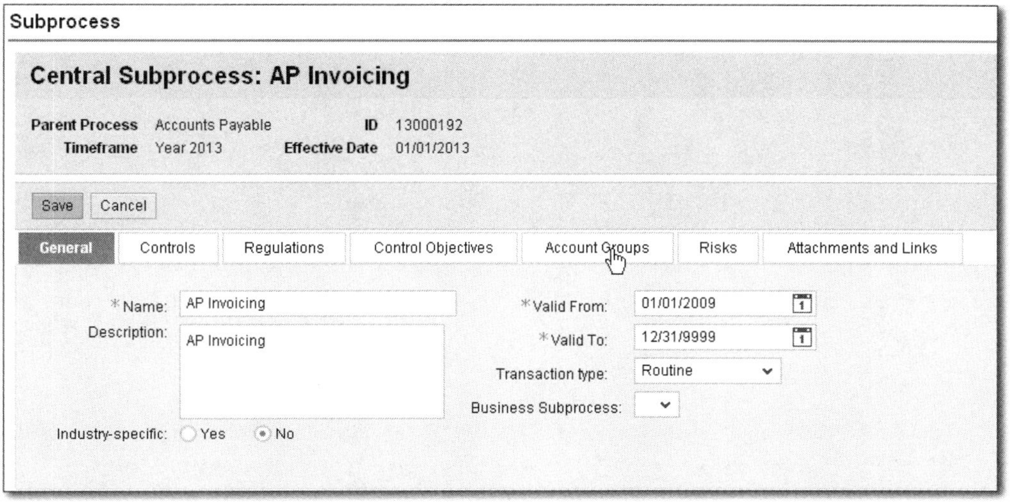

Figure 10.8 Subprocess Details

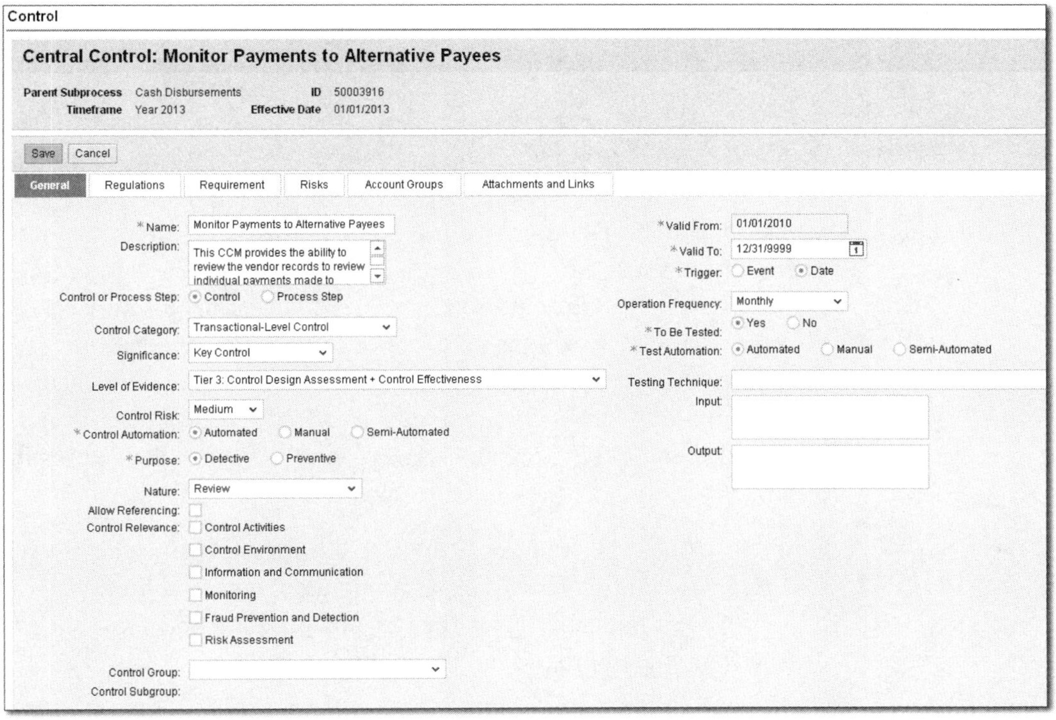

Figure 10.9 Control Details

Now that we've explored the subnodes and process nodes with the business process, let's look at the REGULATIONS AND POLICIES tab shown earlier in Figure 10.1.

10.3 Regulations

Like organizations, regulations are a fundamental master data type. Regulations don't depend on other data types, but many others depend on regulations to be complete or to participate in SAP Process Control functionality.

Regulatory hierarchies

Much like other master data types, SAP Process Control models regulations via a hierarchy. Customers construct regulatory hierarchies in many ways, depending on the regulations, customer practices, geographic spread, and even the job profile of SAP Process Control users. In general, our recommendations are two-fold: represent regulations at the level of granularity you need to generate reports based upon regulations, and place them in hierarchies how you may want to roll data up.

Regulation hierarchies organized by regulatory authority

Common uses of regulatory hierarchies include grouping under labels such as Financial, Worker Safety, and so on. This can also be colored by regulatory authority: Sarbanes-Oxley (SOX) and FCPA in the United States, BilMoG in Germany, Anti-bribery Act in the United Kingdom, and so on. In short, how to structure the regulatory hierarchy is more a matter of what suits the customer usage: if different people are going to be responsible for managing compliance to different regulations, work in different countries, and so on, then chances are they will manage different parts of SAP Process Control and will want to see reports restricted to their own area. Proper segregation begins with the regulatory hierarchy.

Regulation groups and nodes

Figure 10.10 shows a simple REGULATION HIERARCHY in the demo system. Regulation groups are the root node type, whose child nodes can either be other regulation groups or regulations. A regulation node can only have regulation requirements as child nodes.

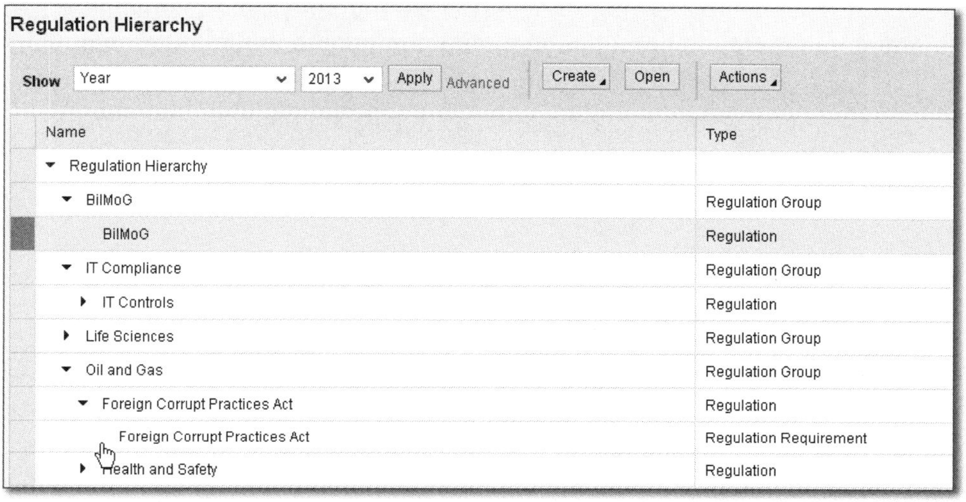

Figure 10.10 Regulation Hierarchy

A regulation group is an extremely simple object, whose only purpose in SAP Process Control is to group together related regulations. Figure 10.11 shows a regulation linked by issues because issues (reported or detected problems requiring remediation and documentation) are required to link to a regulation.

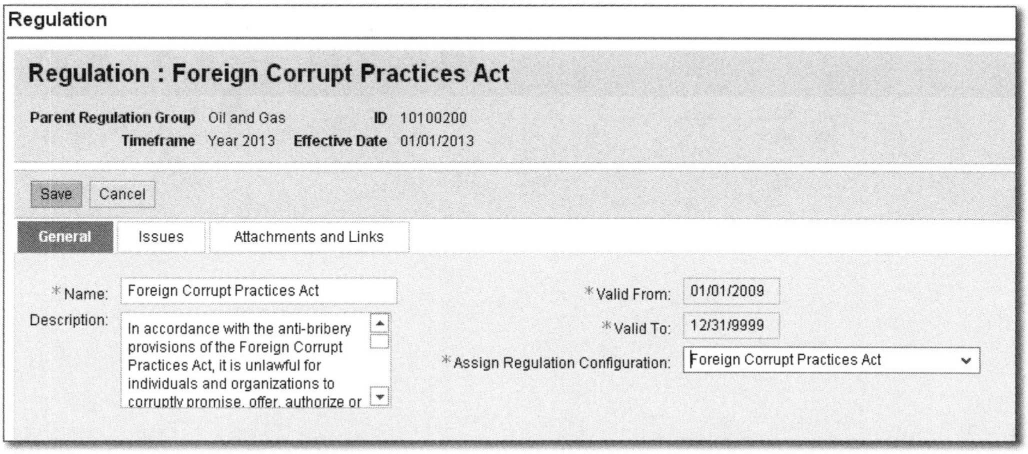

Figure 10.11 Regulation Detail

Finally, the leaf nodes in this hierarchy are regulation requirements, which is another very simple data type that only serves to capture a specific requirement on the business, arising from the regulation in question. Now that we've explored the regulation functionality on the REGULATIONS AND POLICIES section detailed earlier in Figure 10.1, let's shift our focus to policies.

10.4 Policies

Policies were added to the SAP Process Control functionality in release 10, and further enhanced in 10.1. Following the pattern so far, you likely won't be surprised to learn that the policy hierarchy starts with policy groups at the top, which can have child nodes that are also policy groups, nested to any level. A policy group can also have a policy as its child, which marks the end of the tree down that branch. Figure 10.12 shows this for our demo system. Note that the second column, TYPE, shows only two types of nodes, POLICY and POLICY GROUP. Once again, the higher level group is useful for lumping together individual policies by attributes such as common motivations, geographic or functional area of applicability, and so on. This can be useful during reporting, if (for instance) results of policy acknowledgement surveys are to be grouped by geographic region or by functional areas within the company, such as sales or development.

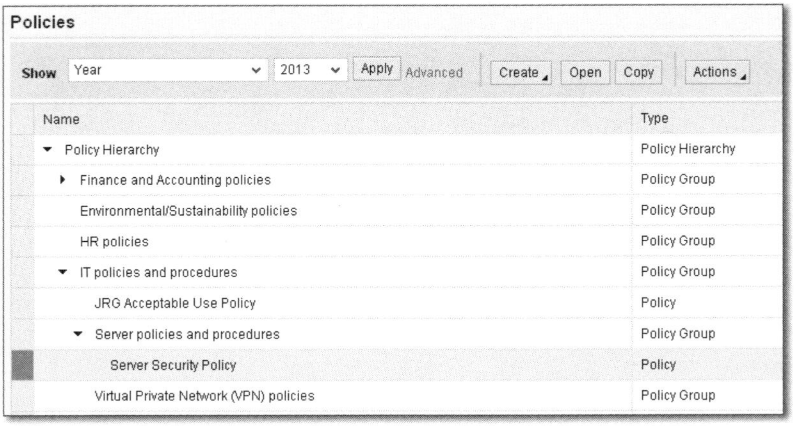

Figure 10.12 Policy Hierarchy

Policy node details within a policy hierarchy

Figure 10.13 shows details of one policy node, JRG ACCEPTABLE USE POLICY. The figure shows rich details in the use of policies: life cycle data such as who created the policy and when, when it was revised and by whom, to whom it applies, how it was communicated, whether any controls to which it applies has failed, and so on. This shows substantial participation in SAP Process Control functionality. As always, the tabs reflect relationships to other types of data objects such as risks, controls, roles, issues, and so on. The attribute called DISTRIBUTION METHOD suggests another functional (as against purely documentary) link: policies can be communicated to employees, and their acknowledgement and understanding measured by a few different methods.

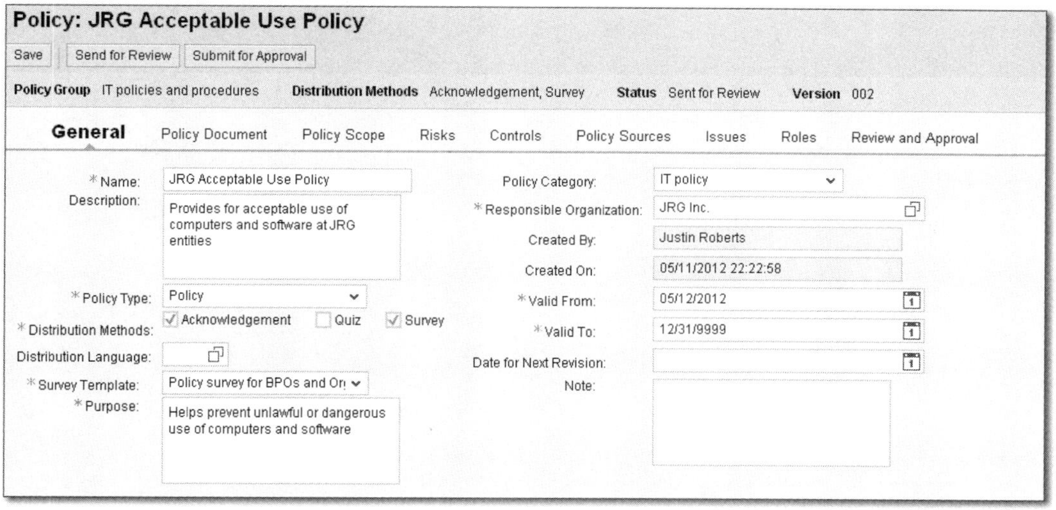

Figure 10.13 Policy Detail

10.5 Accounts and Account Groups

Once again reflecting its lineage as in financial risk management and regulatory compliance, SAP Process Control allows customers to categorize their chart of accounts into key account groups, which have distinct risks and compliance profiles. All cash accounts, for instance, can be in a Cash Account group; all debts owed to the company can be in a Receivables group. The point is that from a finance perspective, there might be a functional or meaningful difference between two different cash accounts but not necessarily so from a compliance and monitoring perspective. SAP Process Control therefore allows customers to lump finer-grained General Ledger accounts into coarser-grained SAP Process Control account groups, as shown in Figure 10.14. The page shown there is reached via the ACCOUNTS group in the MASTER DATA tab shown earlier Figure 10.1.

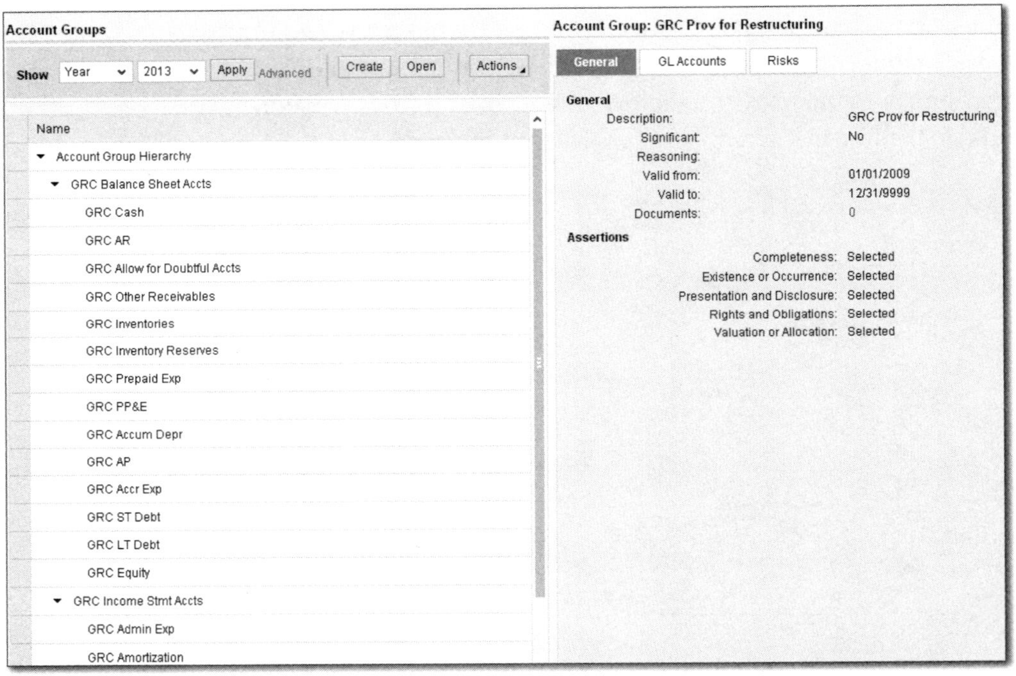

Figure 10.14 Account Groups

Figure 10.15 shows a more detailed view of one such account group, and the main level of detail to note is the ASSERTIONS attribute—the checkboxes in the lower left of the screen. These assertions reflect the nature of compliance concerns the customer has with that account group.

In Figure 10.1, also under the ACCOUNTS group, are links to the maintain materiality thresholds for account groups, and uploading actual account balances periodically. From this, SAP Process Control can judge which accounts require heightened scrutiny, and from the assertions enabled for each, judge to which risks the customer faces heightened exposure.

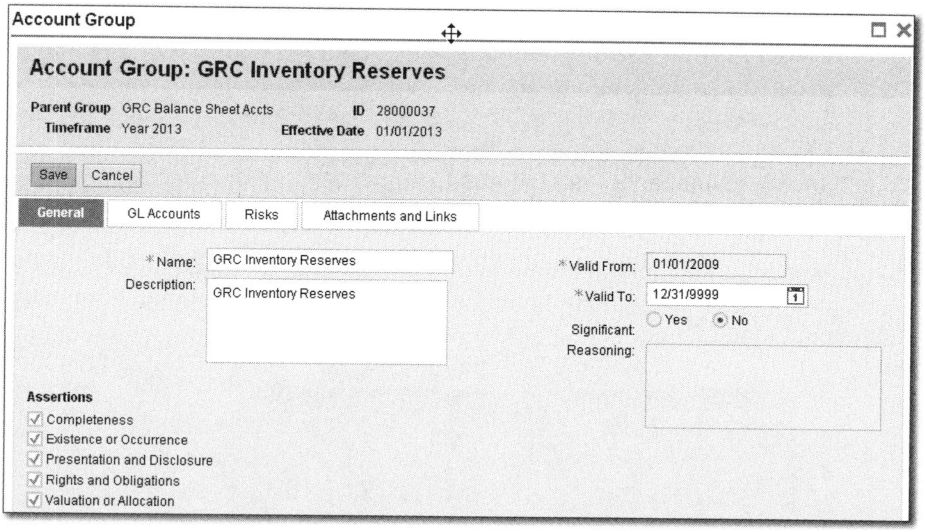

Figure 10.15 Account Group Detail

10.6 Master Data Content Management and Transport

Getting the right master data into applications is a sensitive matter—getting it wrong affects many downstream transactions and is painful to subsequently correct. Customers take great pains to pull together the right information first and extensively review and test it before populating the production system with master data.

Many SAP applications provide shortcut tools to facilitate the loading of master data into applications. Going back to the Management of Internal Controls (MIC, the precursor of SAP Process Control) days, SAP Process Control has supported a tool called the Master Data Upload Generator (MDUG). In the next section, we'll look at MDUG more closely.

MDUG is a very useful and relatively quick tool, but it suffers from one major limitation: it really only helps customers manage content in one system. To address the need of moving master data between systems (e.g., from test to production, or from a partner's test system into a customer's test system), SAP Process Control 10.0 introduced SAP Content Lifecycle Management (CLM) (described a bit later in Section 10.6.2).

Finally, because two tools for similar purposes are obviously a confusing choice for any customer, Section 10.6.3 compares MDUG and CLM, and discusses when to use which.

10.6.1 Master Data Upload Generator

MDUG creates a Microsoft Excel template for SAP Process Control master data, as shown in Figure 10.16. The main point to understand is that the Excel file contains several tabs, as the code view in Figure 10.17 shows.

	Organization	Parent	Orgunit View
3	CRG-HQ	CRG-GLB-INTL	002
4	CRG-C-FINANCE	CRG-HQ	002
5	CRG-Controllers-Office	CRG-C-FINANCE	002
6	CRG-General-Accounting	CRG-C-FINANCE	002
7	CRG-Financial-Reporting	CRG-C-FINANCE	002
8	CRG-C-INSURANCE	CRG-HQ	002
9	CRG-C-TREASURY	CRG-HQ	002
10	CRG-C-LEGAL	CRG-HQ	002
11	CRG-C-FACILITY-MGMT	CRG-HQ	002
12	CRG-C-INFO-TECHNOLOGY	CRG-HQ	002
13	CRG-C-INFO-CHAN-CNTL	CRG-C-INFO-TECHNOLOGY	002
14	CRG-C-INFO-SECURITY	CRG-C-INFO-TECHNOLOGY	002
15	CRG-C-INFO-SYSMGMT	CRG-C-INFO-TECHNOLOGY	002
16	CRG-SALES	CRG-GLB-INTL	002
17	CRG-EURO-REGION	CRG-SALES	002
18	CRG-DE-FR-REGION	CRG-EURO-REGION	002
19	CRG-NORTHSEA-REGION	CRG-EURO-REGION	002
20	CRG-AMERICA-REGION	CRG-SALES	002
21	CRG-N-AMERICA-REGION	CRG-AMERICA-REGION	002
22	CRG-CANADIAN-REGION	CRG-N-AMERICA-REGION	002
23	CRG-US-REGION	CRG-N-AMERICA-REGION	002
24	CRG-US-CALIFORNIA	CRG-US-REGION	002
25	CRG-US-SANDIEGO	CRG-US-CALIFORNIA	002
26	CRG-US-FLORIDA	CRG-US-REGION	002
27	CRG-US-ORLANDO	CRG-US-FLORIDA	002
28	CRG-US-MIAMI	CRG-US-FLORIDA	002
29	CRG-US-NEWJERSY	CRG-US-REGION	002
30	CRG-US-MEADOWLANDS	CRG-US-NEWJERSY	002
31	CRG-US-TEXAS	CRG-US-REGION	002
32	CRG-US-DALLAS	CRG-US-TEXAS	002
33	CRG-US-HOUSTON	CRG-US-TEXAS	002
34	CRG-S-AMERICA-REGION	CRG-AMERICA-REGION	002
35	CRG-CHILE	CRG-S-AMERICA-REGION	002
36	CRG-ARGENTINA	CRG-S-AMERICA-REGION	002
37	CRG-CENTRAL	CRG-S-AMERICA-REGION	002
38	CRG-APJ-REGION	CRG-SALES	002
39	CRG-YEMEN-REGION	CRG-APJ-REGION	002
40	CRG-AP-ALL-REGION	CRG-APJ-REGION	002
41	CRG-DEVELOPING-REGION	CRG-SALES	002
42	CRG-RUSSIA-REGION	CRG-DEVELOPING-REGION	002
43	CRG-INDIA-REGION	CRG-DEVELOPING-REGION	002

Figure 10.16 MDUG Excel File

Master Data Upload Generator and Microsoft Excel

In fact, there are 29 different master data types in an MDUG Excel file, each in its own tab. This enables customers to capture all of their master data in a single place, which is useful for collaborative implementation projects. It also makes reviews and signoffs more convenient because all of the material is collected together in one file.

Customers sometimes ask for a list of entities supported by MDUG. Figure 10.17 has that list, but more importantly shows a simple way to generate that list.

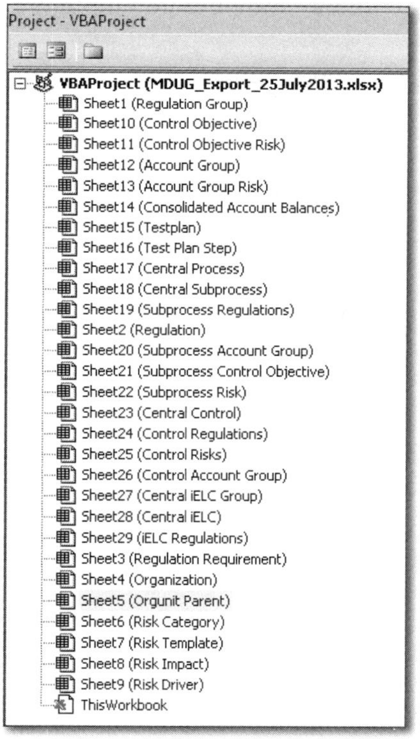

Figure 10.17 List of Tabs in a MDUG Excel File

Master Data Upload Generator and data types

This does have one disadvantage—data types that necessarily have nested relationships and that support one-to-many relationships between objects aren't so easy to represent in a flat spreadsheet format. As users gain experience with MDUG, they will realize that some compromises had to be made. For example, multiple child nodes in a parent-child relationship are accommodated by replicating parent data across every child row. As another example, multiple values distinguished by different effective dates can't be managed in a single MDUG Excel file.

MDUG is launched via the ABAP Editor, Transaction SE38. The program name is GRFN_MDUG, as shown in Figure 10.18. Note that this is the only SAP Process Control functionality shown so far that can't be launched by clicking on a link displayed in a UI page. Presumably, MDUG is considered advanced enough functionality that its users won't be unduly concerned by having to fire up the ABAP Workbench to launch it.

> **Note**
>
> Click the Clock icon (or press [F8]) to execute the named program.

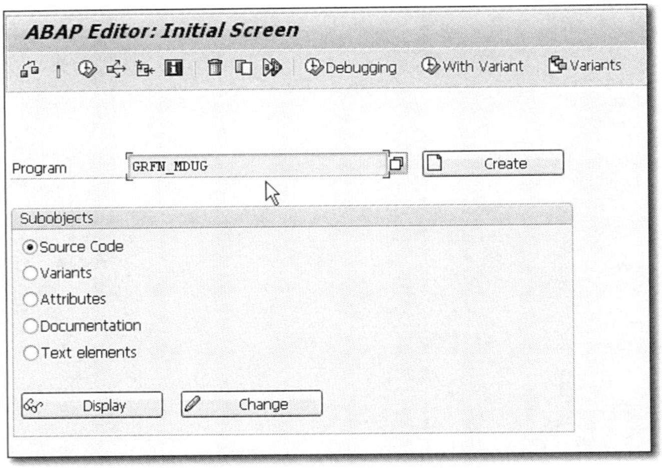

Figure 10.18 MDUG Launch

GRC 10.1 Functionality and Master Data Upload Generator

In previous releases, MDUG allowed users to upload data; with 10.1, MDUG allows both download as well as upload. This is a crucial step forward because so many customers like to do phased implementations of SAP Process Control. In other words, they implement on a smaller scale first, take it all of the way into production, and then apply the lessons learned for the next incremental advance in the implementation. Figure 10.19 shows this download option in MDUG.

With the new version of MDUG as part of GRC 10.1, customers can download the previous phase's master data, and then modify it, add to it, or even delete it to create the right master data set for the next phase of SAP Process Control implementation.

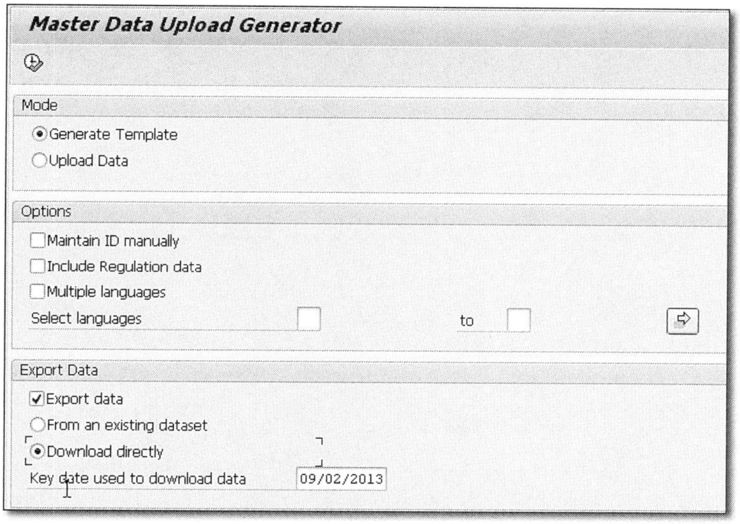

Figure 10.19 Downloading Data via MDUG

One very important constraint to note about MDUG is that it may only be used to download and upload data from a single system. That is, you can't download data from system A, edit it, and upload it to system B. The upload of edited data may only be to the system from which the data was originally downloaded. Now that you have an understanding of MDUG, let's focus on Content Lifecycle Management and the value it brings to the SAP Process Control module.

10.6.2 Content Lifecycle Management

The Content Lifecycle Management (CLM) set of features was first released with 10.0 of SAP GRC. Like MDUG, it also helped manage master data but was intended to work across all four SAP GRC applications: SAP Access Control, SAP Process Control, SAP Risk Management, and SAP Global Trade Services (SAP GTS). In the event, SAP Access Control did not release CLM integration, and GTS customers were already used to established methods of importing sanctioned-party and other master data supplied by partners, and CLM adoption has been restricted to SAP Process Control customers for the most part.

Contract Lifecycle Management functionality

Figure 10.20 shows the main screen of the CLM application. The EXTRACT, DEPLOY, and MASS EDIT buttons encompass the main functionality CLM offers. EXTRACT pulls master data out of a SAP GRC system, storing it in the CLM repository. DEPLOY sends content already in the CLM repository to a SAP GRC system.

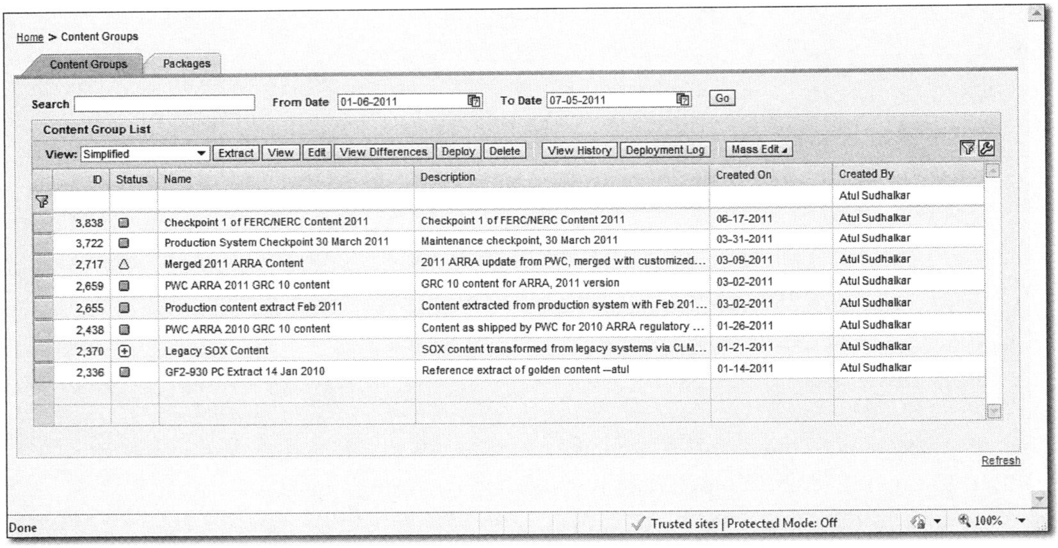

Figure 10.20 Content Lifecycle Management

Because CLM itself operates outside of any particular SAP GRC system, it can be used to populate more than one SAP GRC system with master data.

MASS EDIT in CLM (see Figure 10.21) enables downloaded and uploaded content in CLM's repository to be moved to the local disk of the computer being used to access the CLM UI. Such downloaded content is in an XML file, conforming to a CLM-specified format for each SAP GRC application. Such files can then be edited, loaded back into CLM, and subsequently deployed into SAP GRC applications.

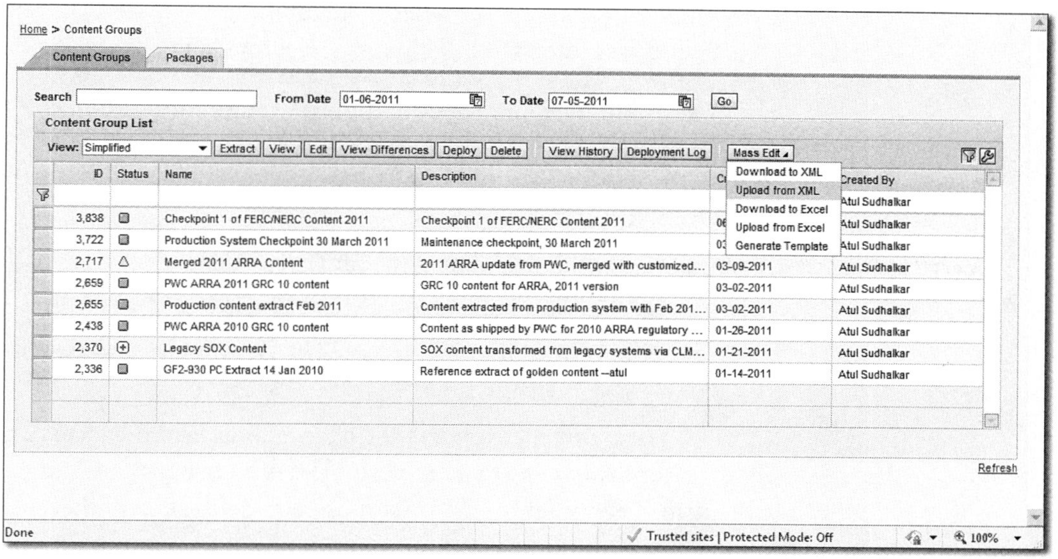

Figure 10.21 CLM Mass Edit

MASS EDIT is a key feature of CLM and was expected to help customers in several ways. Like SAP Process Control MDUG, CLM supports a flattened format suitable for use with Excel, although this feature is only available for SAP Process Control data, not for other applications. New customers can start with an empty template file, XML or Excel, and populate it with master data for upload. Customers some way into their implementation can use CLM to first download data already in the application (whether previously uploaded via CLM or not), and continue their implementation from that point forward, changing the old data, adding new data, and so on.

So how do you choose between using CLM and MDUG for your compliance and risk needs? Let's compare these two tools in the next section.

10.6.3 CLM versus MDUG

The following differences will be immediately obvious to you, even with the brief descriptions just given:

- CLM was intended to work with all SAP GRC applications, although, in practice, CLM for SAP Access Control was never officially released.

- CLM works with explicit knowledge of multiple SAP GRC system instances and was intended to help move master data between different SAP GRC systems.
- CLM keeps past versions of master data content in a versioned repository, allowing users to compare two versions of similar content and merge differences.

Master Data Upload Generator advantages

MDUG does offer two big advantages over CLM:

- The validations MDUG performs are more in tune with SAP Process Control configurations, in part because MDUG only services one SAP Process Control system at a time.
- MDUG 10.1 also offers customers the chance to upload the local controls: an essential benefit to large customers who have organizational restructurings every few months with cascading effects on other SAP Process Control master data.

Although CLM originally was expected to support all SAP GRC applications, the SAP Access Control implementation of CLM was never completed and officially released. Because SAP GTS had prior relationships with third-party content vendors, its long-established import-export APIs for such content kept down wider adoption of CLM.

CLM was originally conceived as a master data versioning and management system with applicability across multiple applications. Due to this, its integration with SAP GRC applications was always at arm's length. Because the code itself had other dependencies, the SAP Process Control development team chose to invest in MDUG going forward, rather than CLM. As of this writing, while CLM remains a supported application, ongoing development efforts are all focused on MDUG, and only limited support is available for CLM.

10.7 Summary

Most of the master data in SAP Process Control consists of information readily available to SAP GRC customers. Every customer uses process models, controls are ubiquitous in SAP ERP implementations, and no modern business can operate without a very good understanding of regulations with which they must comply. SAP Process Control models this information fairly minimally, requiring only such information as is directly used either for documentation, testing, monitoring, or reporting.

Entering master data into SAP Process Control can be very time-consuming, and mistakes can be costly to correct. SAP Process Control 10.1 therefore supports two different tools, MDUG and CLM, to improve productivity in managing and uploading master data.

Having described the main master data types used in SAP Process Control, in the next chapter, we begin examining a very rich and powerful set of features in SAP Process Control, Continuous Controls Monitoring (CCM). This topic will occupy the discussion for the next four chapters.

Continuous Controls Monitoring is a very important part of SAP Process Control functionality. In this chapter, we give an overview of CCM and full details of the configuration and setup of the feature.

11 Continuous Controls Monitoring

In previous chapters, we introduced the topic of Continuous Controls Monitoring (CCM), its goals, and how it fits into SAP Process Control functionality and data structures. Monitoring is about looking at business processes, transactions, and master data, and asserting your expectation of how it should be. In this chapter, we'll look at the architecture of CCM, the different data source types, how to create a data source and business rules, and then how to assign these rules to controls.

Continuous Control Monitoring process overview

The overall process of using CCM follows a simple pattern, which we describe in detail in this chapter. The steps are easily summarized as follows:

1. Create a data source object in SAP Process Control, which usually points to a query (or equivalent) in a remote system to be monitored. Creating a data source takes some knowledge of the monitored system: business process, transaction, tables, fields, and so on.
2. Create a business rule tied to the data source. A business rule may only use one data source, while a data source can serve any number of business rules.
3. Assign the business rule to a local control (see Chapter 10) in the context of a regulation. A business rule can be assigned to any number of local controls.
4. Schedule the rule to execute in the context of the regulation and local control to which it has been assigned.

In the next section, we look at the key architectural features of CCM: SAP Process Control assumes there's a remote system to which it must connect, and from which it will extract data. Then in Section 11.2, we explain some critical configuration steps specific to CCM, after which the remaining sections explain how to set up actual monitoring rules.

11.1 Continuous Monitoring Architecture

Architecture diagrams serve many different purposes, from technical to marketing. To understand how CCM works in SAP Process Control, you must understand how SAP Process Control relates to other systems when live. The literature sometimes refers to this as runtime architecture, or deployment architecture. Figure 11.1 shows such a diagram for SAP Governance, Risk, and Compliance (SAP GRC) in general.

Figure 11.1 implies that SAP Process Control is separate from the backend systems it monitors, which applies even when SAP Process Control is being used to monitor an application co-located in the same application stack. So monitoring always requires the configuration of a remote connection: SAP's remote function call (RFC) protocols in most cases, but also web services connections in other cases. There's a third type, called local system, which is used only when SAP Access Control risk analysis is triggered from SAP Process Control as a monitoring rule.

Over the years, customers have occasionally asked about using SAP Process Control to monitor itself or other SAP GRC applications. While this should certainly be possible, there's very little information about scenarios where such SAP GRC self-monitoring would add value. Note, however, that even in such scenarios, conceptually SAP Process Control would still treat the monitored system as remote, requiring one of the two supported connection scenarios (RFC or web services).

Functionally, the architecture of SAP Process Control is as shown in Figure 11.2.

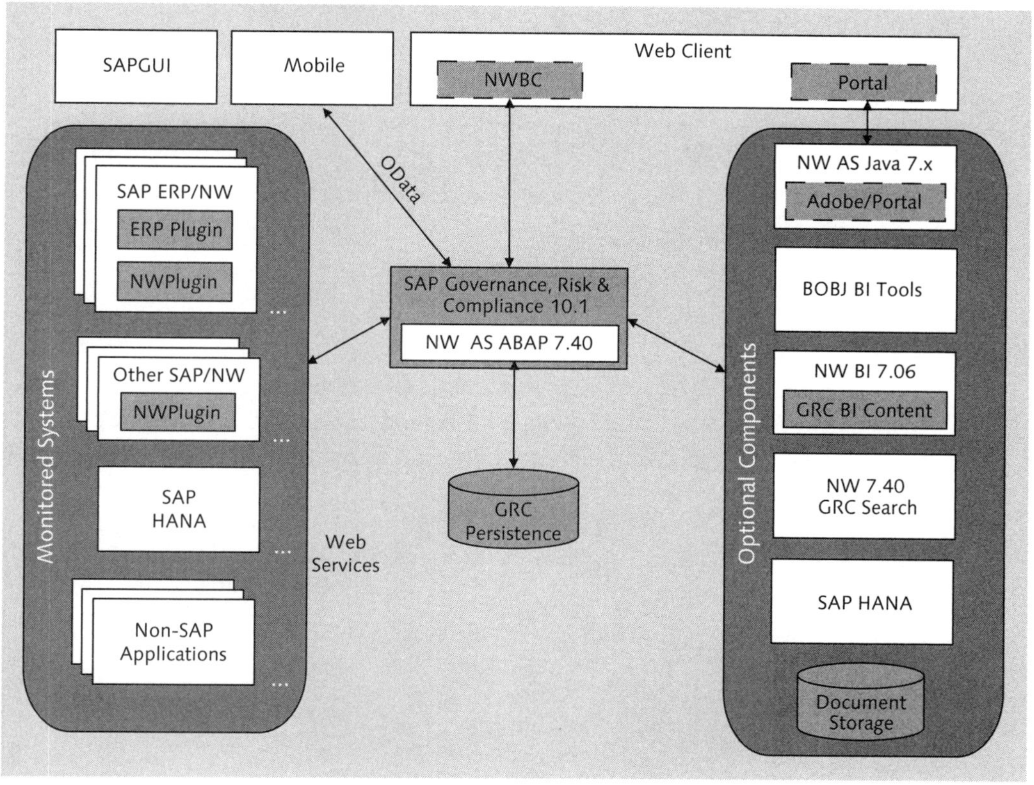

Figure 11.1 SAP GRC 10.1 in the System Landscape

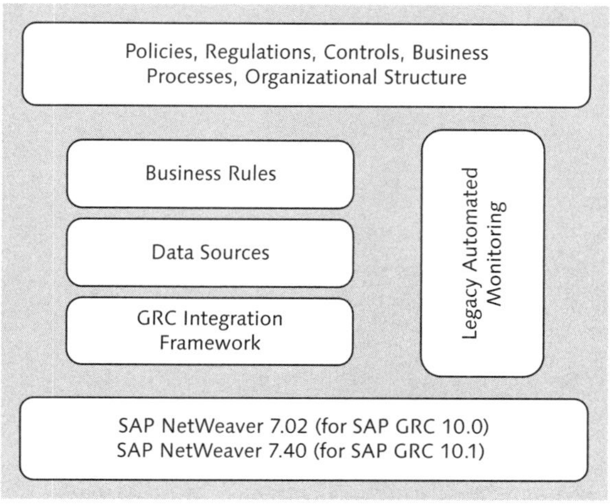

Figure 11.2 SAP Process Control Component Model

Continuous Control Monitoring process flow within SAP Process Control

Using CCM functionality follows a certain process flow in SAP Process Control, as outlined in Figure 11.3 and listed here:

1. Create the data source.
2. Create the business rule.
3. Assign the business rule to a local control.
4. Schedule the rule to run.
5. Analyze and remediate detected problems.
6. Report.

If a monitoring rule executes and finds problems, it creates issues, which get routed to control owners for remediation. All this is then captured in SAP Process Control audit trails and is available via reports and dashboards.

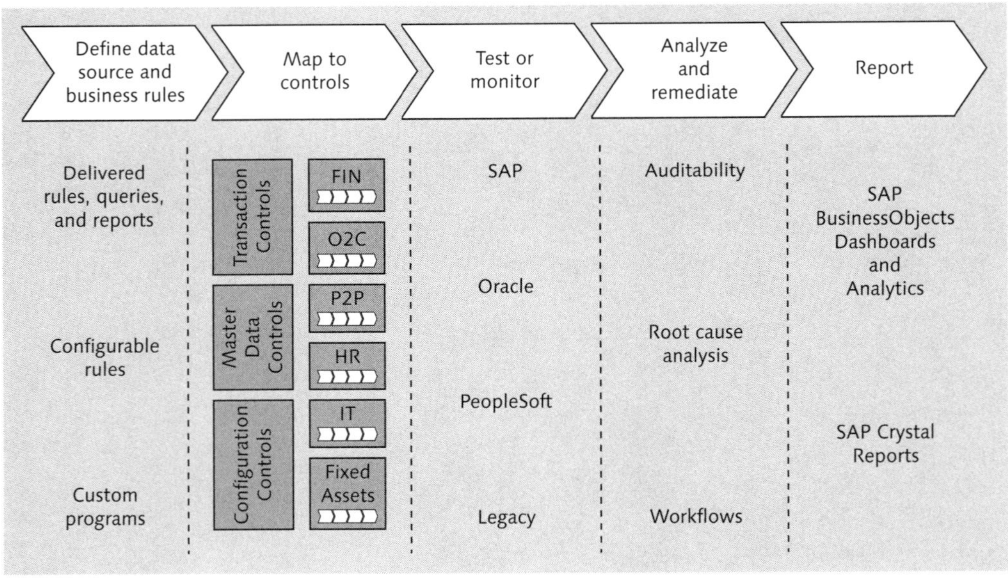

Figure 11.3 Continuous Controls Monitoring Process Flow

Figure 11.4 shows the Rule Setup tab of SAP Process Control. As we explain CCM functionality throughout this chapter, we'll refer to various user interface (UI) pages for different elements, all of which can be accessed from links on this page. We'll refer to it as we describe each element of CCM.

Data Sources

Data sources are SAP Process Control objects that hold information about a specific data source in a remote system to be monitored. The CONTINUOUS MONITORING group in Figure 11.4 (labeled ❶) has a link to the DATA SOURCES page. In SAP GRC, this is abstracted into the connector, which SAP traditionalists will know by the name of SM59 destination. Hence, it includes information about the system address, login credentials, communication method, and so on. We'll explore data sources in more detail in Sections 11.3 and 11.5.

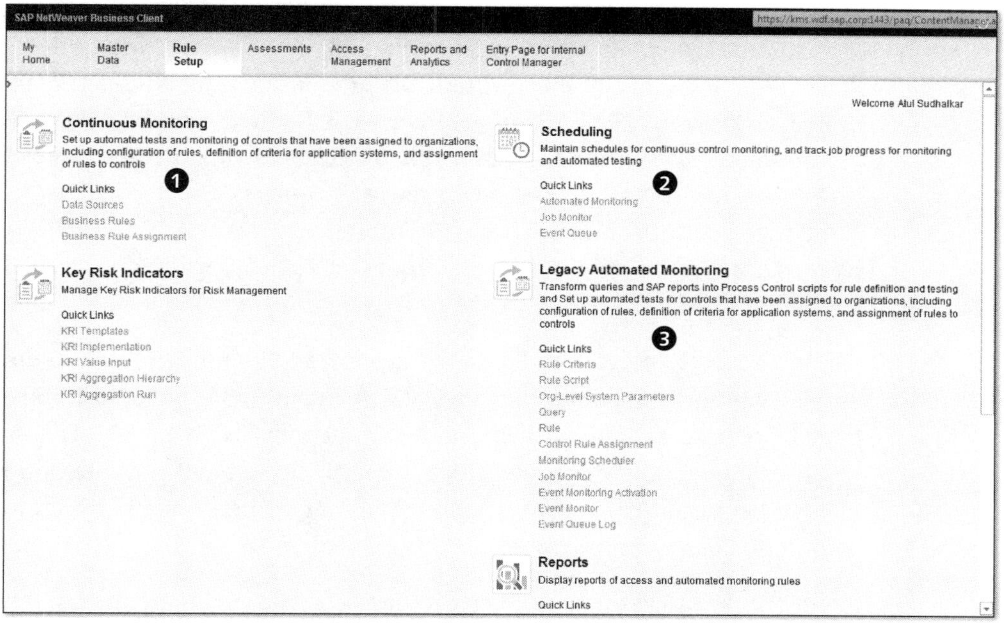

Figure 11.4 Rule Setup Tab for SAP Process Control

Business rules

Business rules encapsulate the actual monitoring logic, including the key functional notion of what constitutes a problem to be remedied—a deficiency, in SAP Process Control parlance. Business rules are accessed by a link in the CONTINUOUS MONITORING group of the RULE SETUP tab of SAP Process Control ❶ of Figure 11.4. We'll further explain business rules in Sections 11.4, 11.6, and 11.7.

Job Monitoring

Actual testing and monitoring is executed via the SCHEDULER ❷ shown in Figure 11.4. The set of links there is intended to be used by a user in a technical or administrative role, and is concerned with scheduling, monitoring and maintaining batch jobs. CCM jobs have two components, one part which runs on the SAP Process Control system, and a related job which executes on the remote monitored system. When things go well, the JOB MONITOR link in this group provides a page which suffices for tracking scheduled rules. If there are problems, it is sometimes necessary to look in the logs of both the SAP Process Control system, and also in the remote or monitored system's logs.

Legacy Automated Monitoring is a compatibility module used to run monitoring rules carried over from releases 2.5 and 3.0. SAP GRC also delivered several ABAP queries designed to run in the SAP GRC plug-ins for SAP ERP. Links to this functionality are found on the RULE SETUP tab of SAP Process Control ❸ in Figure 11.4. These were popular for early adopters of SAP Process Control, and this compatibility module is meant to provide a smooth transition for those customers. In fact, ABAP-coded queries are difficult to change, and in releases 10.0 and 10.1, SAP GRC enhanced other monitoring techniques to reduce customers' need to rely on ABAP.

SAP GRC Integration Framework visiblity

The SAP GRC Integration Framework, shown in Figure 11.2, is a technical component that underlies all SAP GRC applications' communications with remote systems. It's invisible to functional users of SAP Process Control but we have shown it in the component model and mention it here because it is relevant when maintaining configurations, which we describe in the next section.

Before we discuss data sources and business rules in greater detail, let's look at how to properly configure CCM.

11.2 Configuring Continuous Control Monitoring

Apart from the general configuration steps covered earlier, CCM requires the setup of various connectors, and their association with the different data source types. As always, configuration begins in the SAP standard IMG, accessed via Transaction SPRO. Although in general SAP IMG has its own documentation, the CCM configurations are rather unique, and it helps to walk through the process here. Figure 11.5 shows the starting screen.

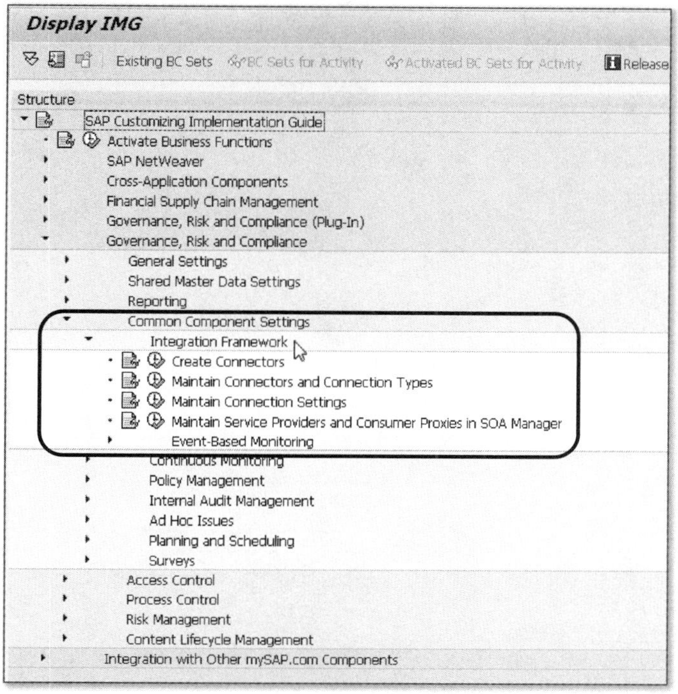

Figure 11.5 IMG Page Showing Continuous Monitoring

> **Note**
>
> In Figure 11.5, you'll note the confusing fact that we have highlighted an area of IMG that is different from the one labeled CONTINUOUS MONITORING. The INTEGRATION FRAMEWORK is a grouping of settings fundamental to both continuous monitoring, and other GRC Risk Management and GRC Access Control features which require communication with remote systems. The CONTINUOUS MONITORING section of IMG, on the other hand, contains non-critical settings which are unique to SAP Process Control Continuous Monitoring.

The first node in the highlighted area of Figure 11.5, CREATE CONNECTORS, is just a link to the standard Transaction SM59. Because that's standard SAP NetWeaver functionality, we won't describe it further here. The next link in the IMG, MAINTAIN CONNECTORS AND CONNECTION TYPES, takes you to the screen shown in Figure 11.6, which starts you down the path to defining connections to remote systems. The INTEGRATION FRAMEWORK is a grouping of settings fundamental to both continuous monitoring, and other Risk Management and Access Control features which require communication with remote systems. The CONTINUOUS MONITORING section of IMG, on the other hand, contains non-critical settings which are unique to SAP Process Control Continuous Monitoring. The connection types ❶ are defined with the delivered software and should not be changed.

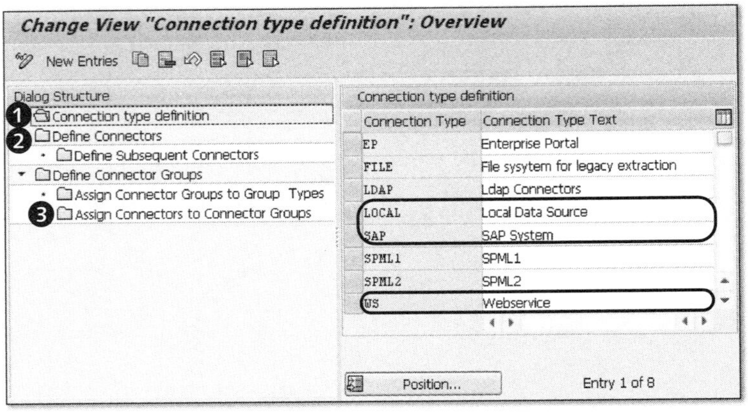

Figure 11.6 Connector Types

There is no configuration to set or change here; we show the figure only for your information. Note that the highlighted connection types shown are the only ones SAP Process Control CCM uses (SAP Process Control 10.1 includes one more, for monitoring SAP HANA systems).

The next step is DEFINE CONNECTORS, which is in the same IMG node in Figure 11.6. As you can see, the second link ❷ in the DIALOG STRUCTURE column in the figure directs you to a screen to define connectors. Figure 11.7 shows the resulting screen.

Defining connectors

Figure 11.7 shows all of the SAP GRC-relevant Transaction SM59 destinations in the system. We've highlighted one of these, the SMEA5_100 TARGET CONNECTOR, which points to the backend SAP ERP system that we plan to monitor. Because it's an SAP ERP system, note that the second column, CONNECTION TYPE, holds the value SAP—it just means that RFC is the expected communication protocol. Again, note that the other connection types visible in these figures—FILE, EP, and so on—aren't relevant to SAP Process Control CCM and won't be explained further here.

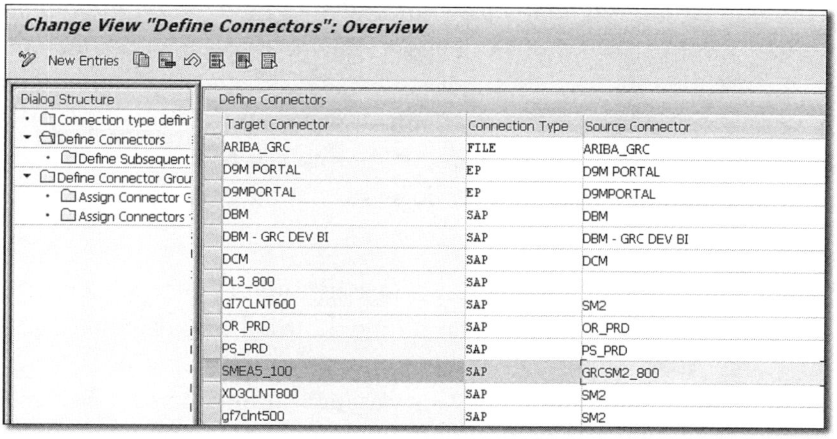

Figure 11.7 Define Connectors

Note, in particular the third column, SOURCE CONNECTOR. This is a tricky concept that requires careful configuration. The source connector attribute of a connector is the name of another connector—and this is the tricky point.

In Figure 11.7, the source connector is SM2, but that isn't a connector in this (SAP Process Control) system. Rather, it's an RFC destination in the SAP ERP system pointed to by the TARGET CONNECTOR SMEA5_100. This source connector in the remote (monitored) SAP ERP system points back to the SAP Process Control system that we're configuring here.

The source connector is, in fact, a callback channel. Certain monitoring rules cause SAP Process Control to connect to the SAP GRC plug-in on the monitored system. In asynchronous situations, the plug-in needs to call back to SAP Process Control, and the initial call from SAP Process Control into the plug-in sets this up by naming the callback connector to use.

Source Connectors

To recap, the source system in this case is the SAP Process Control system we're configuring. There are several remote systems the source system can reach, of which one system is to be monitored via SAP Process Control CCM for our purposes. We refer to that SAP ERP system as the target system, or monitored system. The connector that points to the target system is called the target connector; in our example here, its name is SMEA5_100. One of the attributes of the connector is called SOURCE CONNECTOR, whose value is the name of an RFC destination, which exists in the remote target system. That RFC destination points back to our source SAP Process Control system. It will be used by the SAP GRC plug-in in the monitored system to call back to SAP Process Control, if and when it needs to do so during the execution of a CCM rule.

Assigning a connector to a Continuous Control Monitoring function

The next step in configuring CCM is to assign the selected connector to the CCM function. CCM code was internally called automated monitoring or the Automated Monitoring Framework, and the technical name of the connector group is AM. This variation in the name of the functionality and internal code modules has caused some mild confusion. The way to think of this is that the automated monitoring capabilities of SAP Process Control support CCM by customers.

Now, click the last link in the DIALOG STRUCTURE shown earlier in Figure 11.6 ❸: ASSIGN CONNECTORS TO CONNECTOR GROUPS. A popup asks you to select the connector group to which you want to assign connectors; type in the name "AM", as mentioned earlier. As you can see in Figure 11.8, the CONNECTOR GROUP "AM" has been assigned with the correct connection type and assignment.

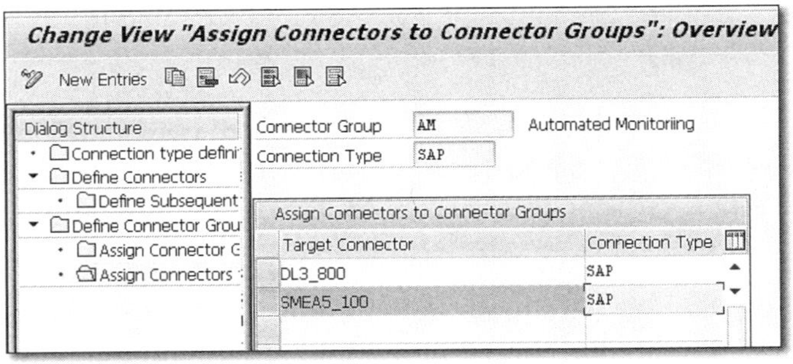

Figure 11.8 Assigning a Connector to a Connector Group

In this case, the connector of interest, SMEA5_100, highlighted in Figure 11.8, is already assigned to the AM group. If it were not, you click the NEW ENTRIES link at the top of the screen and add it.

Next, step out to the original IMG display shown earlier in Figure 11.5, and click on the MAINTAIN CONNECTION SETTINGS node. A popup appears asking you to select the integration scenario. Select AM. A screen similar to Figure 11.9 appears.

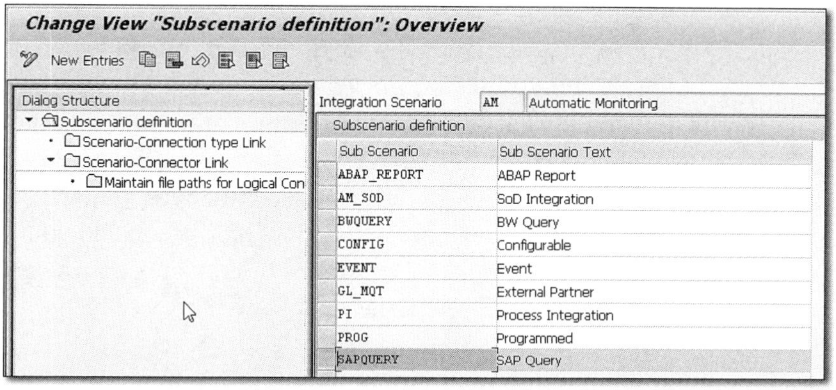

Figure 11.9 Scenario-Connector Link

The right side of the figure lists nine SUB SCENARIOS, reflecting the different types of data sources SAP Process Control 10.0 supports; SAP Process Control 10.1 supports an additional type for SAP HANA (not shown in the figure). The implications of these different types are explained later, but for now, just note that for each data source type, the relevant connectors need to be explicitly enabled. This configuration step accomplishes that.

Select the SUB SCENARIO (data source type), and then click in the left half of the screen on the SCENARIO-CONNECTOR LINK. This brings up a screen like Figure 11.10.

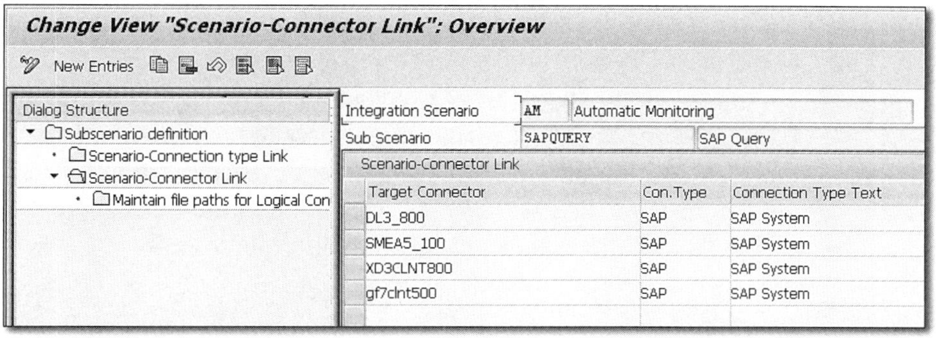

Figure 11.10 Scenario-Connector Details

If the connector you want isn't already in the list of connectors in the TARGET CONNECTOR column, then you must click the NEW ENTRIES link and add the connector you want.

In general, this level of granularity is something of an overkill for data source types. For instance, if the monitored system is SAP ERP, then it's highly likely that you'll want to associate its target connector to each of the following data source types: CONFIGURABLE, SAP QUERY, ABAP REPORT, and PROGRAMMED. Still, this is how the configuration IMG is set up, so this is what needs to be done. Also, data security considerations (addressed more fully in Section 14.2) require a finer granularity in connectors and their access privileges in the remote systems to which they connect.

For the original SAP Process Control 10.0 release, the SAP NetWeaver Business Warehouse (BW) query DS type could only connect to SAP NetWeaver BW system connectors. With the new Operational Data Provider (ODP) facility in SAP applications on SAP NetWeaver 7.3 (or later), the SAP NetWeaver BW Query DS type can also connect to SAP application systems directly—since service pack 9, SAP Process Control 10 (and, of course, SAP Process Control 10.1) support using ODP to treat application systems (such as SAP ERP) as SAP NetWeaver BW query targets. The PI data source type works only with SAP NetWeaver Process Integration (SAP NetWeaver PI), and the web services connector is used as the catch-all category for any other system that can match the SAP-provided Web Services Description Language (WSDL) (see SAP Note 1549031).

SAP HANA and the database connector

As we mentioned, SAP Process Control 10.1 offers an additional data source type, HDB, which is designed for monitoring SAP HANA databases, as shown in Figure 11.11. There are many nuances to the use of SAP HANA as the underlying database for backend applications such as SAP ERP (or its use as an analytics database). But we're concerned primarily with how to use SAP HANA as a source of monitoring data. SAP Process Control 10.1 enables this to fit neatly into the overall CCM framework, as we describe in Chapter 12.

The odd man out in the list of data source types is the EVENT (refer to Figure 11.9). Events are different from all other types of data sources, in that an event originates in external systems. Every other data source type is invoked by SAP Process Control either on a schedule or when a user triggers it; events are raised by external systems as they judge appropriate. So there isn't really a connector for it—rather, there is an inbound web service, described in detail in the user guides on SAP Service Marketplace.

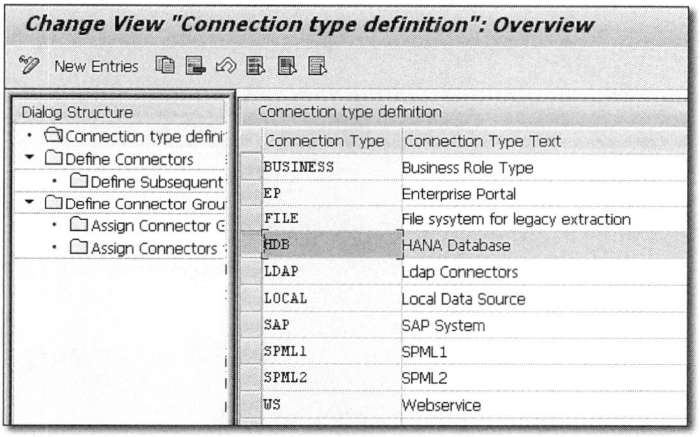

Figure 11.11 SAP HANA Database Connector

Note

CCM User Guides are found in the SAP Process Control 10.0 release section of the SAP Service Marketplace at *https://service.sap.com/~form/sapnet?_SCENARIO=01100035870000000202&_SHORTKEY=01100035870000735637*.

We've looked at how to properly configure and define a connection type and ensure that the correct connector is affiliated. Now let's take a look at how to create data sources.

11.3 Creating Data Sources

As we mentioned earlier, data sources encapsulate methods of extracting data from backend systems. For the most part, they have semantics similar to queries in that they follow a defined logic, take filter parameters, and return results of a schema fixed at the time of data source definition. Based on this known schema, you can define business rules (described in the next section).

As also mentioned previously, SAP Process Control 10.0 offered nine types of data sources; SAP Process Control 10.1 adds a new type, for monitoring SAP HANA-based data. In this chapter and section, we'll describe how to define one specific type of data source: SAP Query. That's a good introduction to the basic flow of creating and using CCM rules. The use of other types of rules and data sources is described in Chapter 12.

Step-by-step process to create a data source

Creating data sources follows this simple process, which we first outline and then describe in detail:

1. Click the CREATE button on the DATA SOURCE LISTING page.
2. Enter the usual information such as a name, description, validity dates, and so on.
3. Select the type of data source from one of the 10 data source types mentioned earlier.
4. Point to the monitored system on which the actual data will be found via a suitable connector (see Section 11.2).
5. Select the specific source of the data on the monitored system. This will depend on the type of data source you selected in step 2 here and will be described in detail later in this chapter and the next.
6. Save and activate the data source.

Data sources are created and maintained on the DATA SOURCES page, found in the RULE SETUP tab of SAP Process Control, in the CONTINUOUS MONITORING area (refer to Figure 11.4). Note that creating data sources is the first step in the four-step process for CCM, outlined in the introduction to this chapter. Figure 11.12 shows the DATA SOURCE page.

Click on the CREATE button as shown in Figure 11.12. This brings up the first screen of the DATA SOURCE creation process, as shown in Figure 11.13.

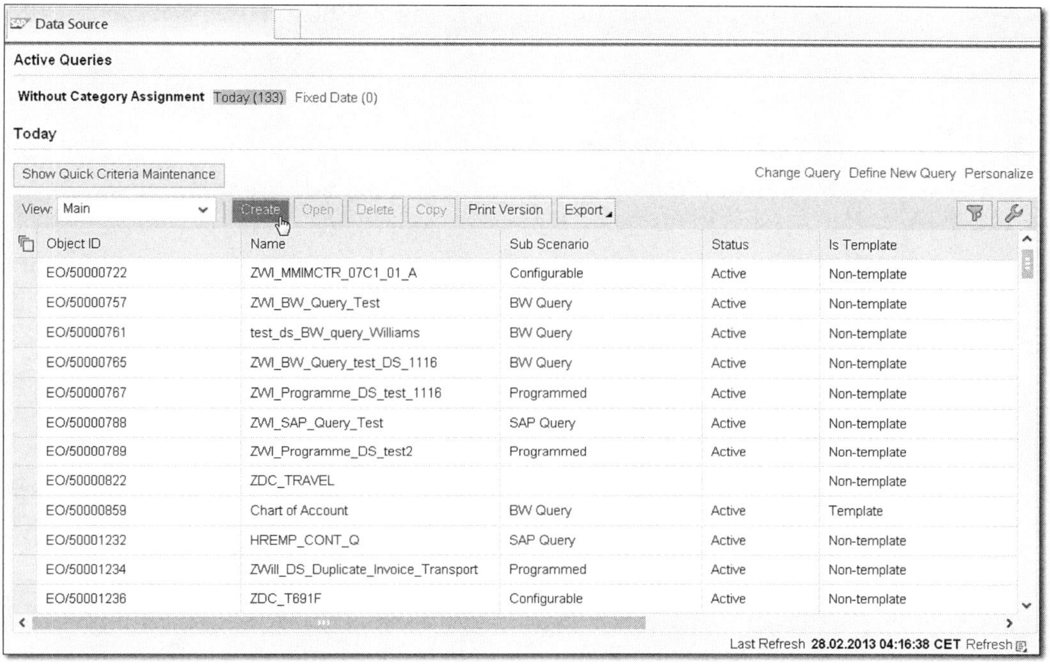

Figure 11.12 Data Sources List

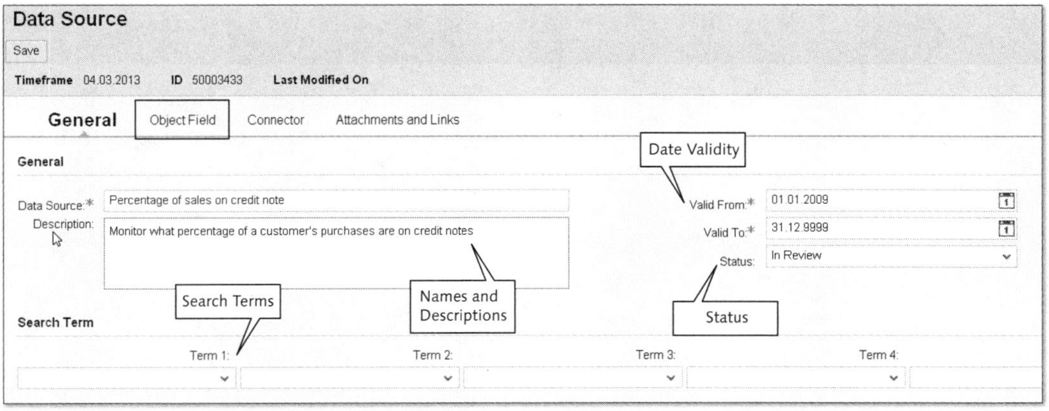

Figure 11.13 Data Source Creation: Step 1

11.3.1 Adding Data Source Information

As the first step in creating a new data source, the information in this screen is fairly simple, but it serves as a good starting place for some general advice. The titles of the following subsections correspond to the labels in Figure 11.13.

Data Source and Description

SAP Process Control objects have a name, a description, and an ID. The ID is system-generated and is unique. Even though the separation of name and description suggests that the name might be unique while the description is for, obviously, descriptive purposes, this isn't quite correct. The name itself is also treated as a descriptor field, and SAP Process Control doesn't require the name to be unique. Customers need to take care to keep names distinct; otherwise, they will have difficulty telling apart different data sources (or, for that matter, other objects) that have similar names.

Valid From and Valid To

The date validity ranges are for customers to use as their business needs dictate. But the default value of the Valid From field is the current date. People tend to accept defaults unless they have clear and specific reasons to change them, and our experience is that this causes problems. Because the validity of monitoring in actual rules is governed by the date validity of all of the associated objects (i.e., data sources, rules, controls, business processes, organizational structures, etc.), inadvertent acceptance of the default validity start has caused many a customer confusion. A typical symptom is the inability to find a monitoring rule in various contexts, with no clear explanation of why an existing business rule isn't visible all of a sudden! A rule of thumb we follow is to push the validity start well back into the past, say the first of January a few years back. Again, you should make the validity start to be whatever makes business sense; however, if your business logic doesn't suggest anything specific, it's best to make this date the first of January of a few years ago, giving yourself some wiggle room.

Status

CCM objects such as data sources and business rules have a Status field; the system allows status values of New, In Review, and Active. Only active data sources are available for building business rules (see the next section). But on the other hand, active data sources can't be changed!

Status changes can only go in step increments: New to In Review, In Review to Active, and vice versa. For instance, a newly created data source will be in status New by default. The user has to save it, close it, and reopen it to change the status to In Review, and repeat the process to make it Active. Experienced users tend to change the status from New to In Review immediately on creation of a data source or business rule to avoid the annoyance of an extra cycle of editing.

Note also that while Active data sources and business rules can be set back to In Review (and then changed), this demotion from Active status is somewhat restricted for objects that are referenced by other objects. For instance, a data source must be active for users to be able to define a business rule that references it. After a business rule is created which references that active data source, the status of the data source can be changed back to In Review but very few attributes can be changed even so.

Search Term

Up to five search terms or tags can be set on the data source (and also on business rules and some other objects). The values of these are set in the IMG (see the IMG node marked Continuous Monitoring shown in the previous section), and users may only choose between the tags previously defined there.

11.3.2 Defining the Technical Details

With these preliminaries out of the way, we proceed with the business of actually creating a data source. The next step is to define the technical details of the data source, which is on the Object Field tab of the data source. Click the Object Field tab link in Figure 11.13, resulting in the screen shown in Figure 11.14.

Object Field Tab

The first action on the Object Field tab is to select the data source type (labeled Sub Scenario, purportedly in keeping with SAP NetWeaver terminology). Select the SAP Query type here; we'll discuss the rest later.

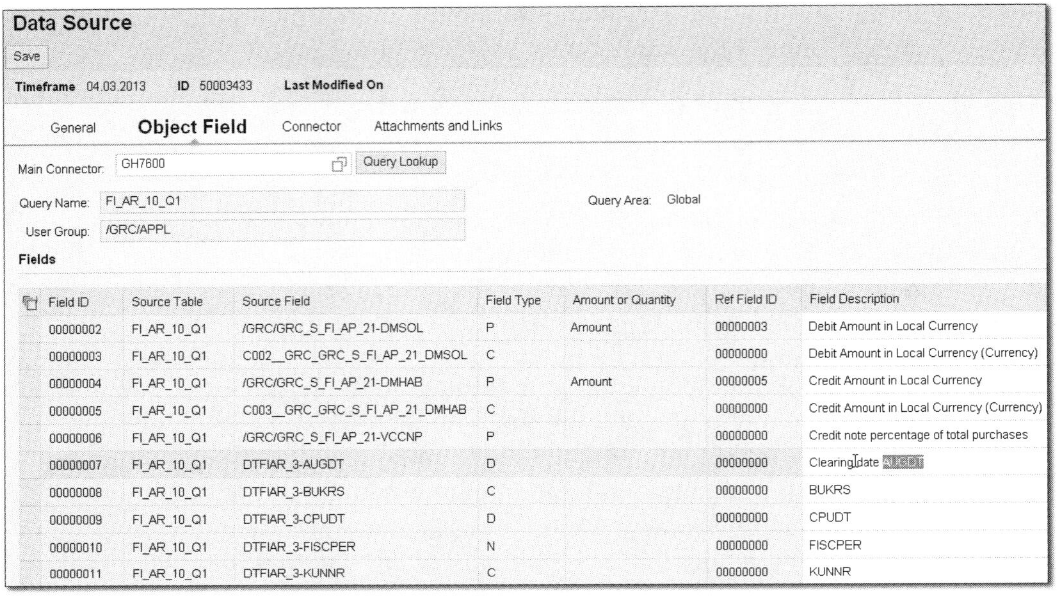

Figure 11.14 Data Source Step 2: Technical Settings

Because SAP queries only exist in SAP ABAP applications, SAP Process Control automatically sets the CONNECTION TYPE to SAP SYSTEM as shown in Figure 11.15.

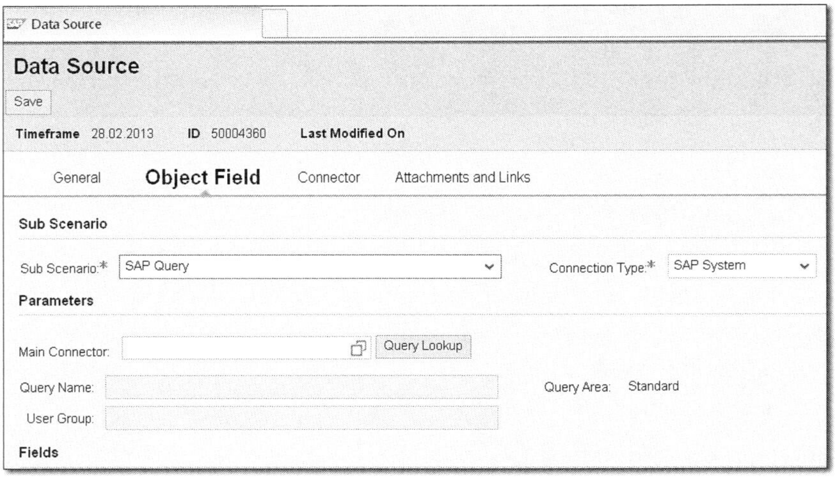

Figure 11.15 Data Source Configuration Step 2: SAP Query Type

Note that while the CONNECTION TYPE field looks like a user-selectable dropdown, it really isn't. The next step is for you to select a connector, which requires a little diversion to explain the design-time versus runtime aspects of CCM in SAP Process Control.

Connection Type Field

CCM is, perhaps, the most technical and challenging feature of SAP Process Control. Providing early validation and prompts is critical to avoid user confusion later, so where possible, at design time, SAP Process Control tries to validate the correctness of data sources against backend systems. Once created, at runtime, data sources can be applied against other backend systems as well, provided validation works. This is why you have to point to a specific backend SAP system here while you are defining the data source.

11.3.3 Pointing to a Connector

Your next step in this exercise is to point SAP Process Control to a connector (which is SAP Process Control's way of referring to a monitored backend system). The connector you select must have been set up to work against the SAP QUERY data source type (because that is our example here). Figure 11.16 shows that SAP Process Control relies on the connector configurations explained in Section 11.2, and offers only those connectors that apply to SAP Query data sources.

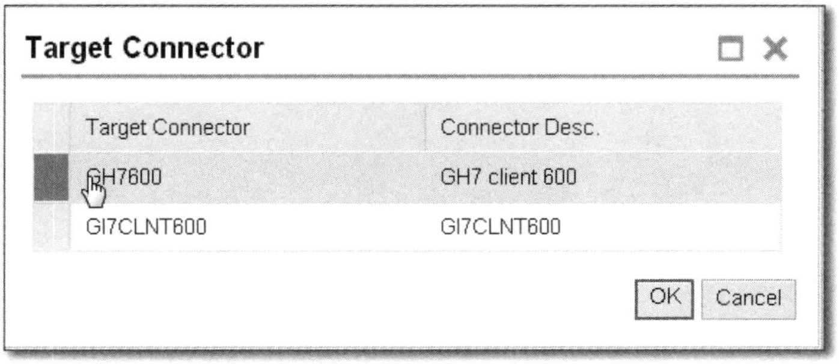

Figure 11.16 Data Source Step 2: Target Connectors

Then next step is to look up available SAP queries by clicking the QUERY LOOKUP button shown earlier in Figure 11.14.

Searching for queries

In Figure 11.17, note that you can search for queries by name, user group, and query area; wild card searches are also possible. After you select a query, SAP Process Control automatically looks up the associated InfoSets and populates the FIELDS area of the screen, as shown in Figure 11.18.

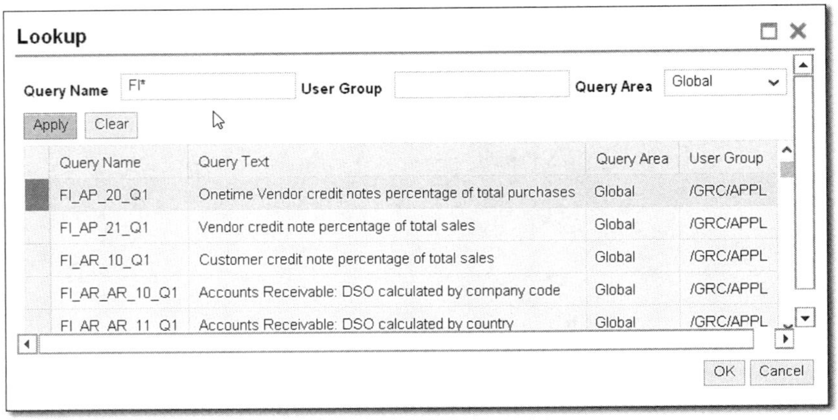

Figure 11.17 Data Source Step 1: Query Lookup

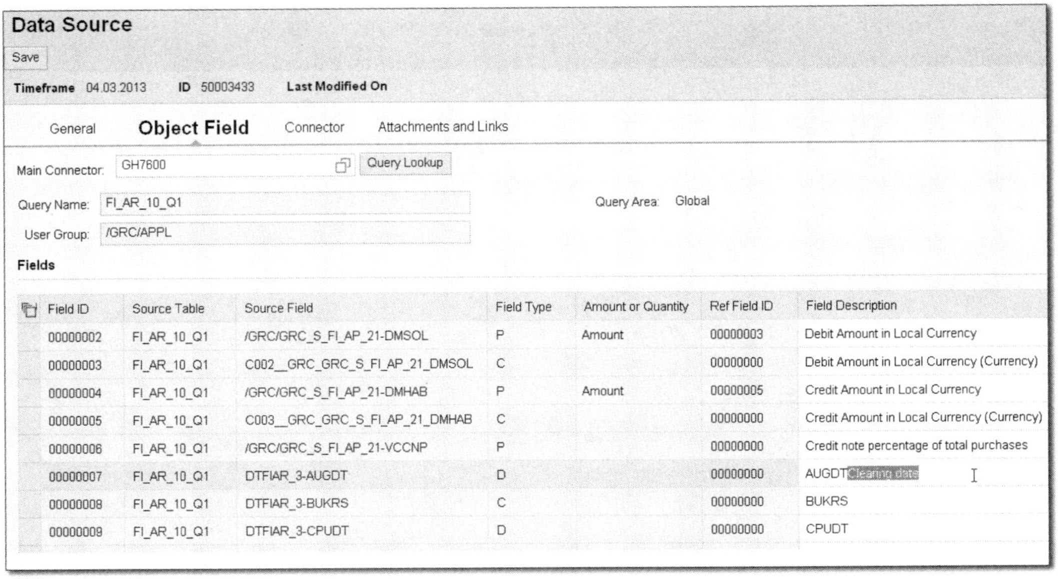

Figure 11.18 Data Source Step 2: Query Parameters

Note that the DESCRIPTION column is populated with the description extracted from the query InfoSet in the monitored system but can be overwritten here if appropriate. Sometimes it's necessary—as shown in Figure 11.18, the highlighted text is what we typed in, while the default description was just the technical field name.

Additional connectors

The next step is to add additional connectors to the data source. Every additional connector added to a data source should point to a (presumably distinct) system that has the same backend source of data—in our present example, a SAP query. The page for this is accessed via the CONNECTOR link, and the page that appears is shown in Figure 11.19.

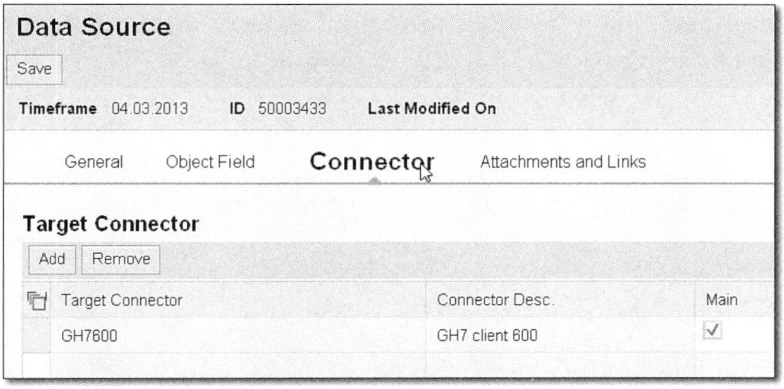

Figure 11.19 Data Source Step 3: Additional Connectors

11.3.4 Adding Documentation

The final step is to add documentation to the data source, if appropriate. Documentation in this case can be an attachment or a link to a document on the network. This is accessed via the ATTACHMENTS AND LINKS link.

The next step, of course, is to save the newly created data source. After this, you'll have to reopen it to change the STATUS to ACTIVE (which will require two steps, if you originally saved the data source in NEW status rather than IN REVIEW).

Only active data sources are available for the next step—creating business rules—which we describe next.

11.4 Creating Business Rules

Business rules are designed to fit particular data sources. They invoke the data source, passing it parameter values to filter the data. The business rules then take the data returned by the data source, do some processing depending on the type of data source in use and how the business rules are configured, and, in most cases, lead to the creation of a remediation issue if the business rule logic determines that there is a deficiency.

Business rule caveats

Note that there are several caveats—the nature and behavior of a business rule can vary a lot, depending on the data source type, type of analysis the business rule is designed to perform, and so on. This chapter only presents the business rule variations relevant to the SAP Query data source type. Other variations will be mentioned as relevant to other situations.

Creating a business rule is longer, more complicated, and much more dependent on the type of data source and business rule being defined. You'll find it helpful to remember that, even so, the process of creating business rules follows the same general steps:

Step-by-Step business rule creation

1. Click the CREATE button on the BUSINESS RULES LISTING page.
2. Select the DATA SOURCE (previously created and active) on which this business rule will be based.
3. Enter the usual general information: name, description, validity dates, and so on.
4. Select the CATEGORY and ANALYSIS TYPE for the rule.
5. Select which data fields (from those made available by the data source) are relevant to this business rule. Remember that one data source can serve many business rules, but each business rule can choose to operate on a subset of the fields the data source provides.
6. Define any filters to be passed down to the data source. For instance, the business rule may only want to look at data for certain company codes, in a specific date range, and so on.

7. Define the deficiency fields. These are fields, on the values of which you'll define deficiency criteria, which determine whether the data row in question is deficient and requiring remediation or review.
8. Define any additional logic. This relates to advanced BRF+ features, which we discuss in detail in Chapter 13.
9. Examine some technical settings, which most customers can ignore for most rules.
10. Test the rule logic in ad hoc query mode.
11. Save and activate the business rule.

Business rule maintenance

Business rule creation and maintenance is done on the BUSINESS RULE page, found in the CONTINUOUS MONITORING section of the RULE SETUP tab of SAP Process Control (refer to Figure 11.4). Having reached the BUSINESS RULE page, you start the process by clicking CREATE. This brings up the first page in the BUSINESS RULE creation wizard, as shown in Figure 11.20.

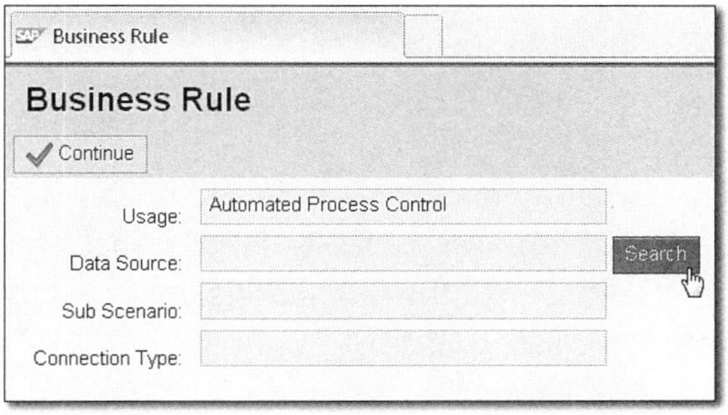

Figure 11.20 Business Rule Creation Initial Screen

The business rule creation process depends very strongly on the data source type, so the first step is always to select the data source for this business rule. Click the SEARCH button next, which brings up the SEARCH page shown in Figure 11.21.

This SEARCH screen allows users to filter the available data sources by many attribute criteria, as Figure 11.21 shows. It also allows wild card searches on the name, which is very handy.

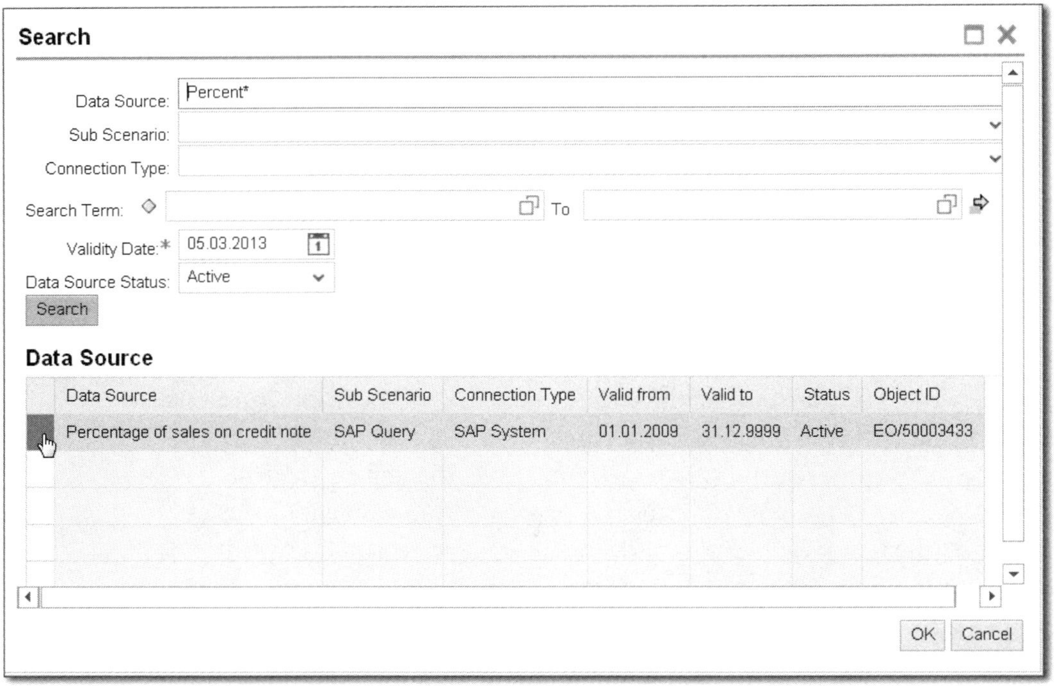

Figure 11.21 Business Rule Creation: Data Source Search

Data sources and business rules

A business rule can only be based on one data source (although a data source can drive any number of business rules). Note, too, that even though the SEARCH dialog offers to search for data sources in any status, rules may only be based on active data sources.

Having found the data source, you select it, and click OK. This takes you back to the previous screen, where you click CONTINUE, as shown in Figure 11.22.

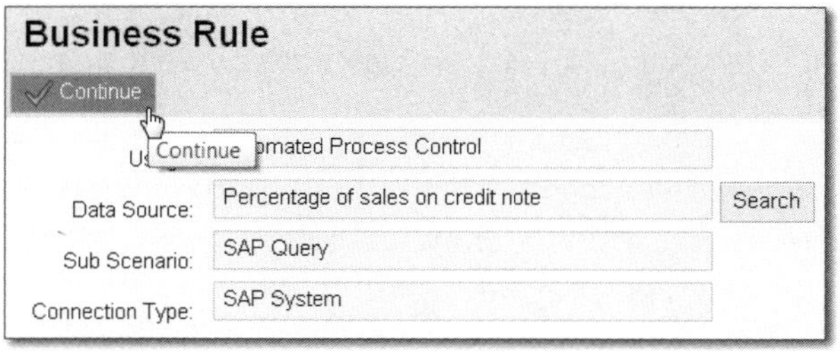

Figure 11.22 Business Rule Creation Continued

The information sought in the first screen in the business rule creation process is identical for all business rule types, although the process bar at the top will show different steps for business rules based on different data types. We'll focus only on the relevant steps for the SAP Query DS type for now, and complete the business rule creation process for this example.

The following subsections walk through most of the steps of the rule creation process, in the sequence in which the user will see them.

11.4.1 Basic Information

Figure 11.23 shows the BASIC INFORMATION screen for the business rule setup.

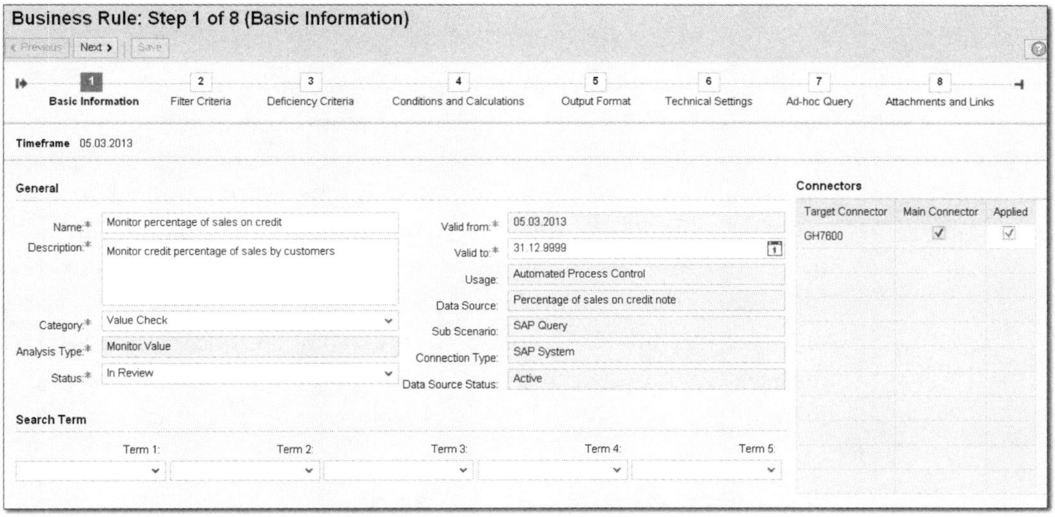

Figure 11.23 Business Rule Creation: Basic Information

The NAME, DESCRIPTION, STATUS, and VALID FROM/VALID TO fields mean the same here as they did for the data source creation process. Because these fields are fairly self-explanatory, we won't go into further detail as to complete these fields. Beyond the fields similar to data sources, the CATEGORY and ANALYSIS TYPE fields shown in Figure 11.23 are unique to business rules and require some explanation.

Business rule categories: exception and value check

For SAP Query business rules, there are two categories: Exception and Value Check. For business rules of category Exception, SAP Process Control treats every row of data as being a problem, requiring human remediation. Value Check category business rules carry further evaluation logic (described later in this section), by which the user will configure SAP Process Control to judge whether rows returned by the business rule represent problem scenarios (called *deficiencies* in SAP Process Control).

The Analysis Type depends on the Category. For the Exception category, two types of analysis are available, Set Deficiency Indicator and Review Required, as shown in Figure 11.24.

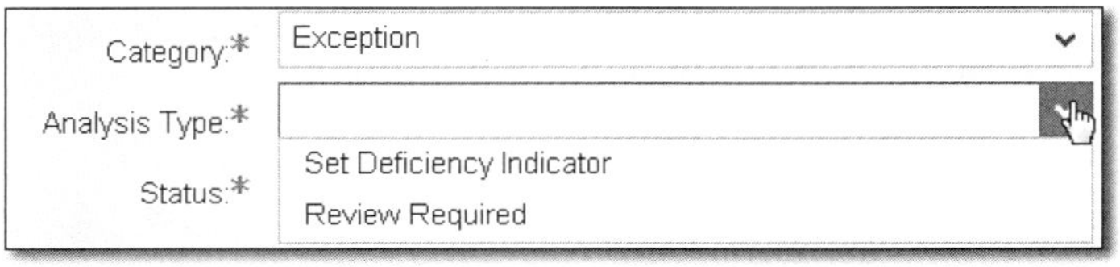

Figure 11.24 Business Rule Exception Category Analysis Types

Setting the deficiency indicator

The status Set Deficiency Indicator means every returned row is a problem scenario, or deficiency. In this case, all returned rows can be set to a Deficiency Indicator, which can be one of Low, Medium, or High (the display changes to offer an additional dropdown box for selecting one of these values). In contrast, the Review Required Analysis Type means SAP Process Control will make no judgment on the meaning of the returned data but will route it to a human for evaluation.

11.4.2 Filter Criteria

Various parameters in the underlying SAP query that can be assigned filter conditions appear on this screen, as shown in Figure 11.25.

Typical filter fields for CCM rules include dates, company code, plant code, and so on. This will be somewhat clearer after Section 11.6, but the simple reason is, when scheduling monitoring rules, SAP Process Control customers typically fix these values from the test time frame, the organizational unit, and so on.

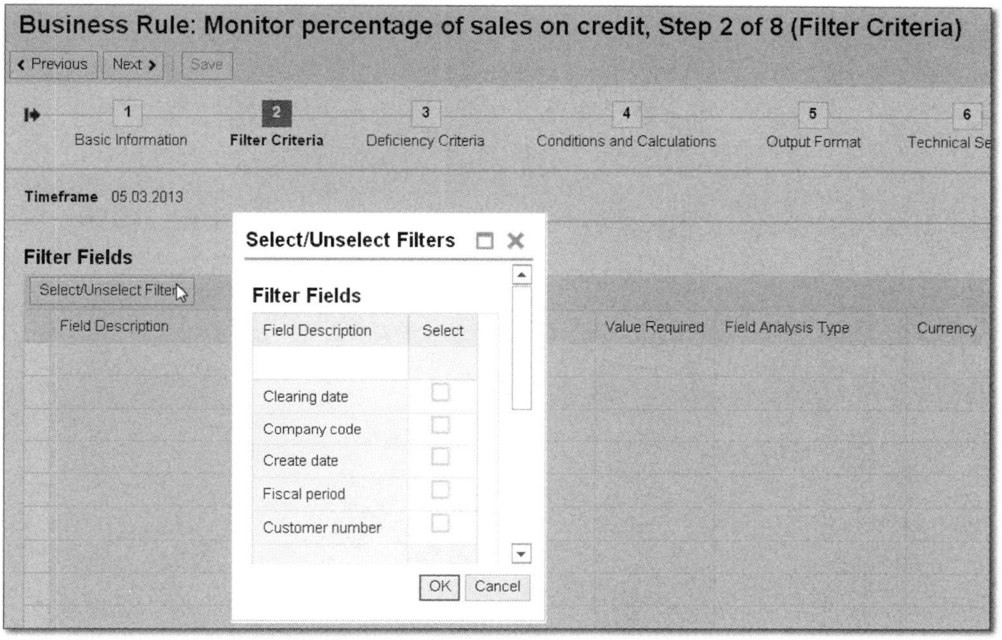

Figure 11.25 Business Rule: Filter Conditions

11.4.3 Deficiency Criteria

The deficiency criteria is the heart of a monitoring rule. You define criteria that the rule engine applies to data returned by the data source. Any data rows that match these deficiency criteria are considered deficiencies, also called defects or problems to be remedied.

The simplest deficiency criteria are set up on a single field. You click on the SELECT/UNSELECT DEFICIENCY button as shown in Figure 11.26. Note that to better highlight relevant details, Figure 11.26 shows both the original screen and the modal popup together; the right side of the figure is the popup.

Deficiency criteria and analysis types

For each deficiency criterion thus selected, you have a choice of two ANALYSIS TYPES: BLANK CHECK and VALUE CHECK. BLANK CHECK tells SAP Process Control that a blank value of the selected field is a deficiency; VALUE CHECK tells SAP Process Control that you intend to define specific conditions on the value of the deficiency field, which will be considered deficiencies. This is shown in Figure 11.27.

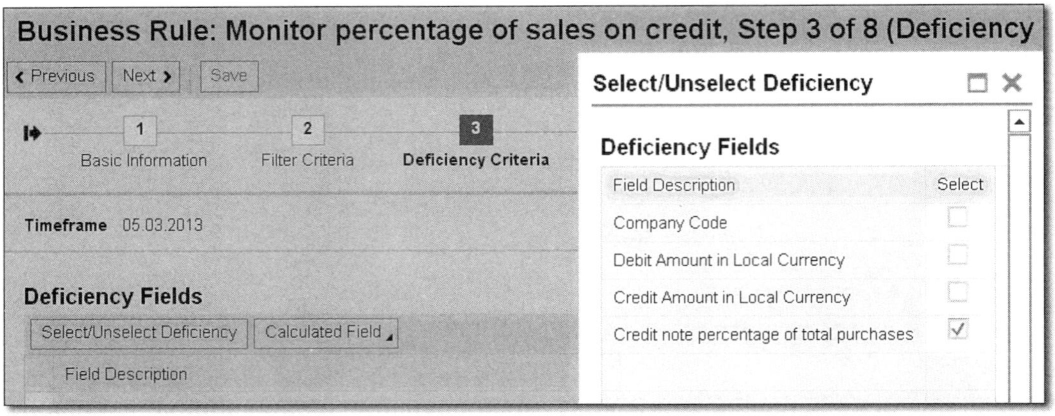

Figure 11.26 Business Rule: Deficiency Criteria Selection

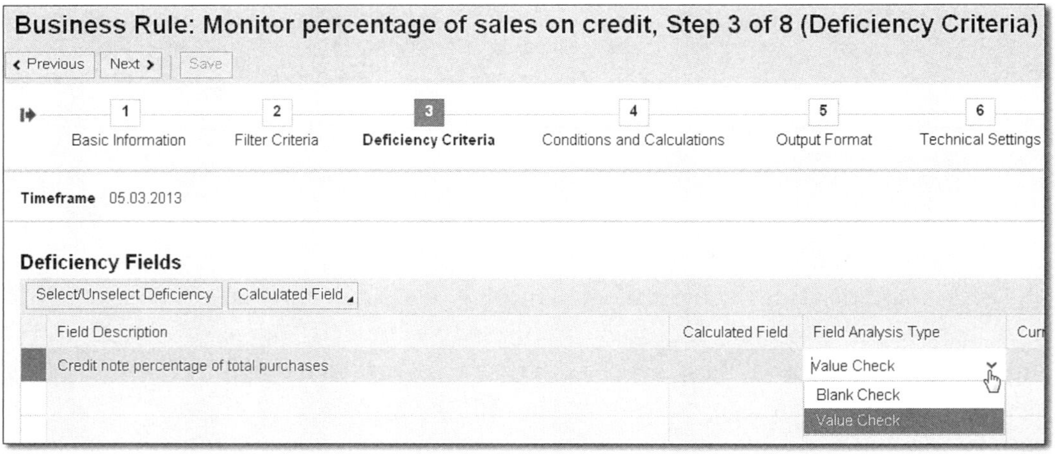

Figure 11.27 Business Rule: Deficiency Analysis Types

Note the Calculated Field button on the Deficiency Criteria screen—that button helps set up additional computations using the SAP NetWeaver standard BRF+ rule engine. We describe that in more detail in the next chapter.

After a Value Check Deficiency field is defined, the lower half of the screen requires configuration of the actual deficiency conditions, as shown in Figure 11.28.

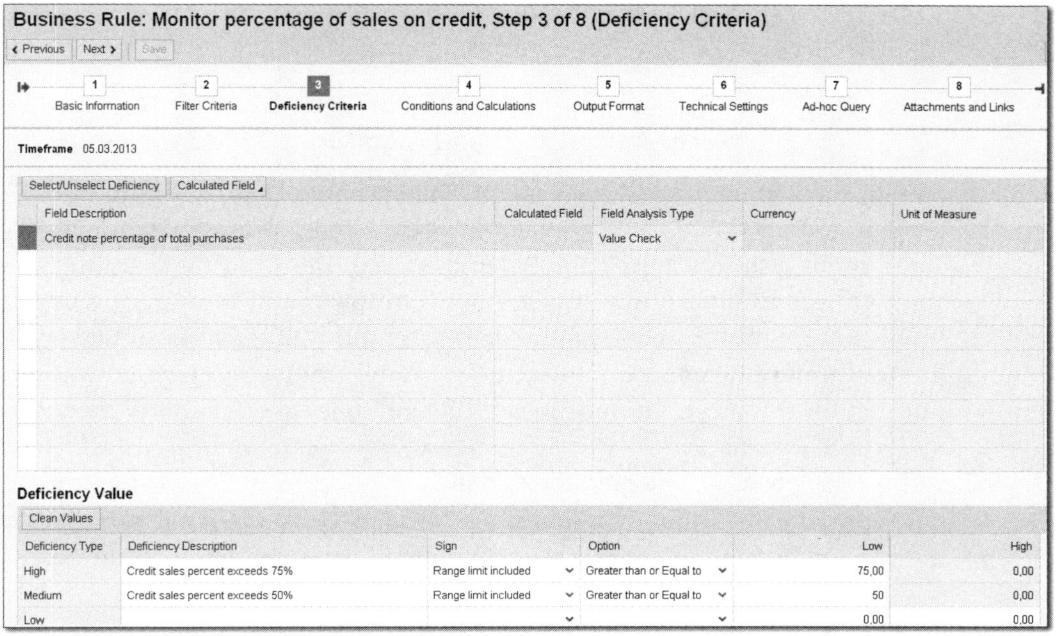

Figure 11.28 Business Rule: Deficiency Thresholds

Deficiency types

Note that three levels of deficiency type are on offer: HIGH, MEDIUM, and LOW. You can see them in the bottom of the figure, in the first column. Customized descriptions can optionally be set for each. You don't have to configure all three, but you do have to configure at least one.

11.4.4 Conditions and Calculations

The CONDITIONS AND CALCULATIONS tab relates to SAP Process Control integration with the SAP NetWeaver BRF+ rule engine. The SAP Process Control rule designer can define calculated fields (i.e., fields whose values aren't retrieved from a data source but instead computed during the execution of the rule). SAP Process Control calls on BRF+ to handle the computation, and this tab is used to set up the calls to BRF+ and to handle the values returned by BRF+. This will be addressed in great detail in the next chapter.

Output Format

When defects are found, an issue or case is created, the problematic data rows are presented to the user. The OUTPUT FORMAT tab lets the rule designer make some small adjustments to how the data is presented. Because the flexibility is fairly minimal, we won't focus on this.

11.4.5 Technical Settings and Monitoring Rule Behavior

Technical settings control how monitoring rules behave at runtime. In SAP Process Control 10.1, this section has been cut down to just one setting—how many data rows are examined. This is the usual performance impact limiter with its advantages (mainly that it's easy to specify and apply in the code) and disadvantages (relationship between number of rows examined and the actual performance impact varies by rule and data source). Previous releases offered finer-grained control over synchronous versus asynchronous execution and whether data filtering happens on the monitored system or on the SAP Process Control system. But feedback from customers and partners was that these other settings were too technical and confusing, so in release 10.1, they aren't offered.

The default number of rows to be examined is usually 100, which is too low for practical use. In general, setting such limitations is poor practice because its application is technical, and the semantics are therefore arbitrary. Setting the rows examined to zero disables this feature, forcing SAP Process Control to examine all of the data that meets the filter criteria.

Of course, performance issues can't be ignored because SAP Process Control customers typically like to monitor production backend systems directly. Chapter 14 describes a more strategic approach to CCM, in which we discuss the options more fully.

11.4.6 Ad Hoc Query

The ad hoc query facility is very useful for rule designers. It allows you to execute the rule—and hence the underlying data source or query—immediately, so you can verify that the data it brings back meets your expectations. It can be run in one of two modes, Data Collection or Apply Rule, as shown in Figure 11.29.

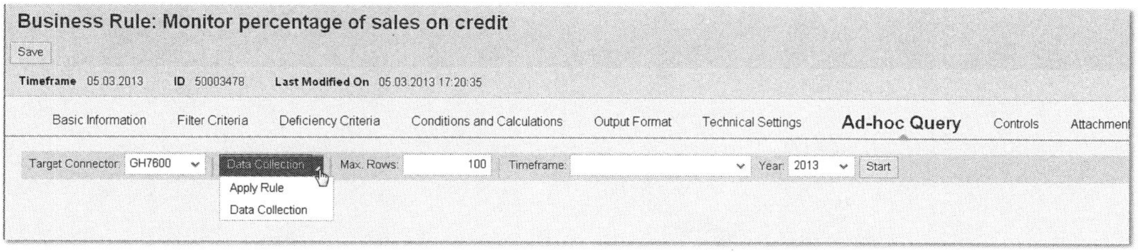

Figure 11.29 Business Rule: Ad Hoc Query

In DATA COLLECTION mode, the query applies filters as configured but just returns all of the data that the data source finds. APPLY RULE, in contrast, actually applies the rule logic—any additional (BRF+) calculations, deficiency evaluations, and so on. APPLY RULE shows only rows that are finally judged to be deficient. It shows what would route in an issue, if the rule were to be scheduled and executed.

The TIMEFRAME dropdown shown in Figure 11.29 requires additional explanation. Its behavior isn't always easy to understand. For one thing, it's often asked for even when the underlying data source or the business rule applies no time filter to the data it examines. So sometimes you'll be asked for a value for this field, and it will have no discernible effect on the results.

11.5 Data Source Types and Related Rules

Section 11.4 described the SAP QUERY data source type and its associated business rules. There are nine other data source types, and their associated business rules have several categories and analysis types.

Figure 11.30 shows a screenshot of the available data source types. Table 11.1 summarizes the different data types and their meanings. Details about how these data source type should be used will follow in Chapter 12 and Chapter 13.

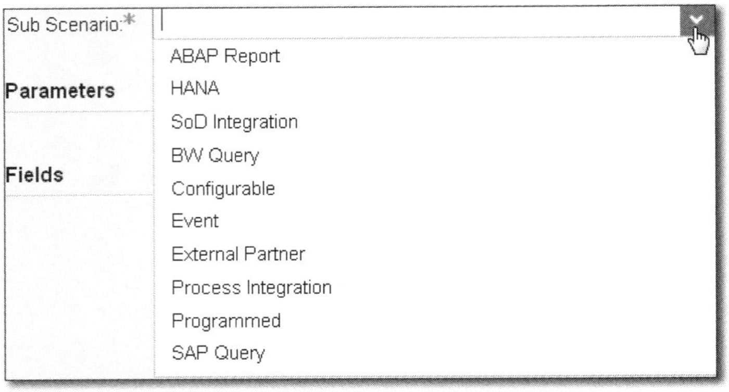

Figure 11.30 Data Source Types

Dropdown Text	Short Description
ABAP REPORT	ABAP reports—SAP delivered or custom—have long served to help users monitor business processes and compliance. This data source type invokes ABAP reports on the monitored system and presents the results for user review in SAP Process Control.
HANA	SAP Process Control can look up SAP HANA Virtual Data Model (VDM) views and pull data from such views for monitoring.
SoD INTEGRATION	Invokes SAP Access Control risk analysis as a SAP Process Control monitoring rule.
BW QUERY	Allows customers of SAP NetWeaver BW to use their analytic models as the basis for monitoring. Particularly useful when monitoring rules require substantial (in performance and complexity) analysis, data harmonization across multiple systems, or the analysis of large amounts of data.
CONFIGURABLE	This data source lets users define queries in the SAP Process Control system to be run against tables in the monitored system. The queries are much simpler than what SAP Query (SQ01/02) can do, but so is the user experience. This also avoids modifications to the monitored system, which is a key roadblock to quick definition/adjustment of monitoring rules.

Table 11.1 Data Types and Description

Dropdown Text	Short Description
EVENT	Every other data source type in SAP Process Control is triggered from SAP Process Control, either manually or via the scheduler. Events, in contrast, are raised by systems outside of SAP Process Control when they judge it appropriate. SAP Process Control receives and processes them as they are received.
EXTERNAL PARTNER	This is an outbound web services API. The design-time methods look up a list of queries at the destination and the details (parameters, results) of each query. The runtime methods invoke the query and make the data available to the rule engine in SAP Process Control.
PROCESS INTEGRATION	SAP NetWeaver PI is the SAP standard Integration Framework. Customers and partners can use SAP NetWeaver PI to call out to other applications or to ODBC/JDBC supporting databases, and construct any query they want. SAP Process Control can connect to SAP NetWeaver PI, treating such integration modules as data sources for monitoring purposes.
PROGRAMMED	Reaching back to the earliest releases of SAP Process Control, ABAP programmed queries can be deployed on backend systems. SAP Process Control can invoke these like other rules, and their results are returned to SAP Process Control for monitoring.
SAP QUERY	SAP Query (Transactions SQ01/02) is a standard SAP NetWeaver query tool and engine. Widely used (e.g., in the Audit Information System), SAP Query is a powerful query engine. SAP Process Control can invoke SAP queries defined in backend (monitored) systems and present the results to business rules for monitoring.

Table 11.1 Data Types and Description (Cont.)

Of course, there are various nuances to the use of most of these data types, which are addressed in Chapter 12.

Having created a business rule and tested it ad hoc, several more steps are needed to use this rule for CCM. First, the rule must be assigned to a local control, which provides the rule with the proper compliance context in which to execute. This is described in the next section.

11.6 Assigning Rules to Controls

In Chapter 10, we discussed how to create master data such as process and organizational hierarchies. As you saw, a SAP Process Control central control is at the leaf node of the process hierarchy. When localized to a particular organizational node, the central control becomes a local control. CCM rules can only be assigned to local controls via the BUSINESS RULE ASSIGNMENT link in the CONTINUOUS MONITORING area.

Figure 11.31 shows the page for assigning rules to (local) controls. Find your local control by filtering on process, organizational unit, previously assigned business rules, and so on, as shown in the top of the figure.

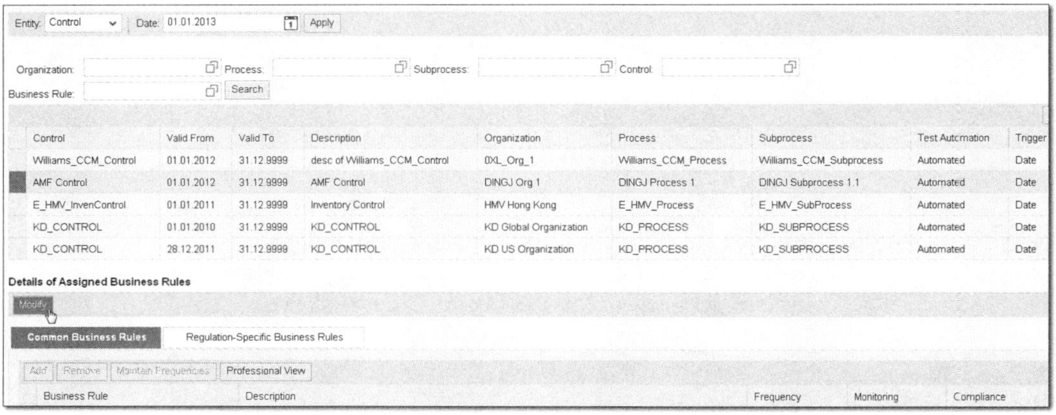

Figure 11.31 Business Rule Assignment: Find Local Control

Next you must click the MODIFY button, highlighted in Figure 11.31, and then click the ADD button (just below the MODIFY button). Note that the assignment occurs in the context of one or more regulations. Here we're about to assign it as a cross-regulation, or common business rule, but it's also possible to make the assignment only in the context of specific regulation(s).

After a CCM rule is assigned to a local control, it's finally ready for actually monitoring backend systems. To actually start monitoring, it's necessary to schedule the rule for actual monitoring, at which time you'll specify which system to actually monitor, how often, and so on.

11.7 Scheduling Monitoring Rules

Scheduling happens from the SCHEDULING area of the RULE SETUP page, via the AUTOMATED MONITORING link. The CONTINUOUS MONITOR SCHEDULER is shown in Figure 11.32.

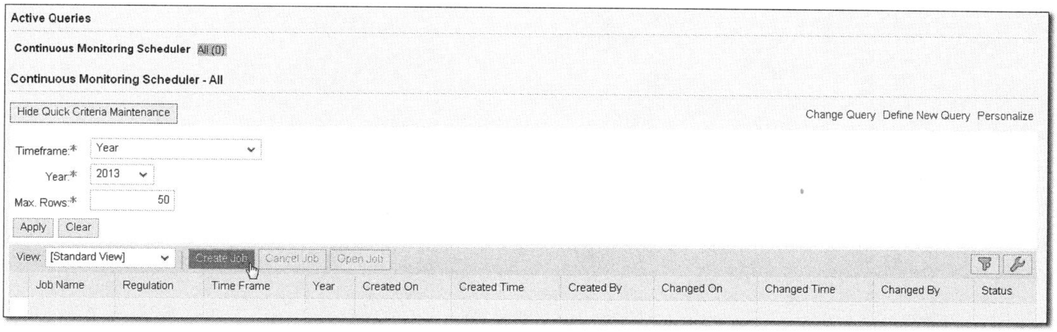

Figure 11.32 Continuous Monitor Scheduler

Note the QUICK CRITERIA MAINTENANCE area, shown expanded in Figure 11.32. When the page first comes up, this area is collapsed, and users are advised to always verify that the TIMEFRAME and YEAR settings match their own intentions, or else they will find the scheduler's display and behavior confusing.

In our continuing example, the next step is to create a new job by clicking on the CREATE JOB button. Figure 11.33 shows the first page of the create job process.

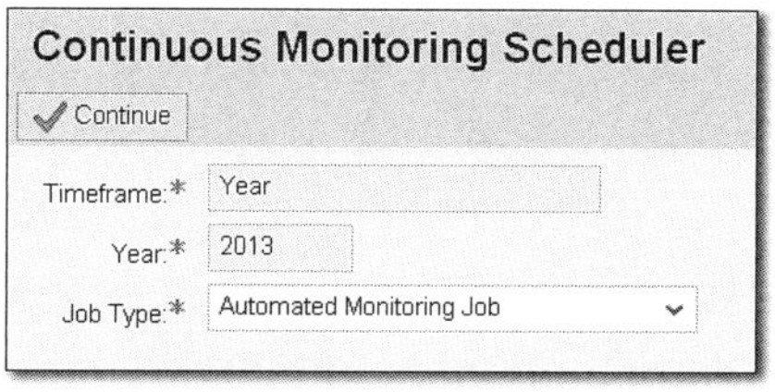

Figure 11.33 Assigning a Job Type: Create Job Process

New job creation process

Note that the TIMEFRAME and YEAR are grayed out in Figure 11.33. These are copied from the QUICK CRITERIA MAINTENANCE section of Figure 11.32 and can't be changed here. Clicking CONTINUE brings you to the CONTINUOUS MONITOR SCHEDULER page shown in Figure 11.34.

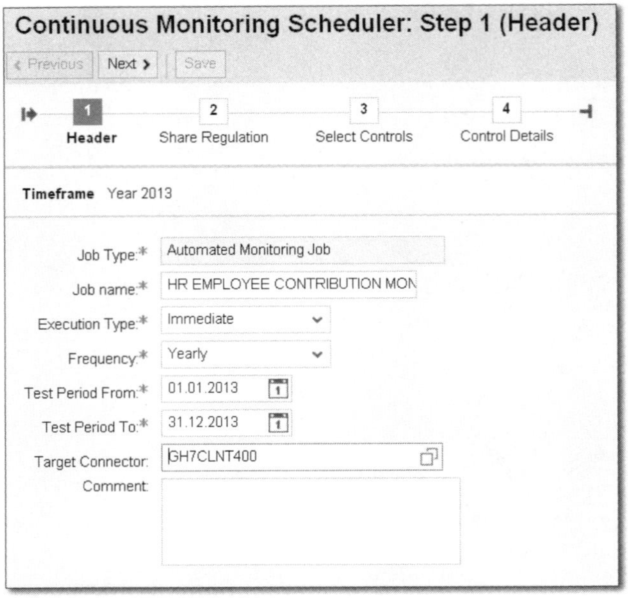

Figure 11.34 New Job: Step 1

New job features

There are several noteworthy features here. First, note that the test period appears to be entirely up to the user here, but in fact must lie within the TIMEFRAME and YEAR shown earlier in Figure 11.32. The user is free to use any supported frequency, but the FREQUENCY choice made here will restrict the user in the next step, when the user selects the business rule (as assigned to a local control) to schedule.

The choice of a TARGET CONNECTOR here will similarly restrict users to rules that have the chosen connector associated with them. Note that only one connector can be selected—one job can only connect to one monitored system.

The EXECUTION TYPE of IMMEDIATE is likely used more often for demonstration and testing purposes than in actual practice. In actual practice, you're more likely to choose to run monitoring jobs at the end of a period such as week, month, quarter, and so on. And the time of execution is likely to reflect your opinion of when the monitored system is least likely to be under load.

Selecting a regulation

The next step requires you to select a regulation, as shown in Figure 11.35. Even if you're scheduling a cross-regulation business rule, you have to select a specific regulation for which monitoring is to nominally occur. You can then choose to share the results with other regulations.

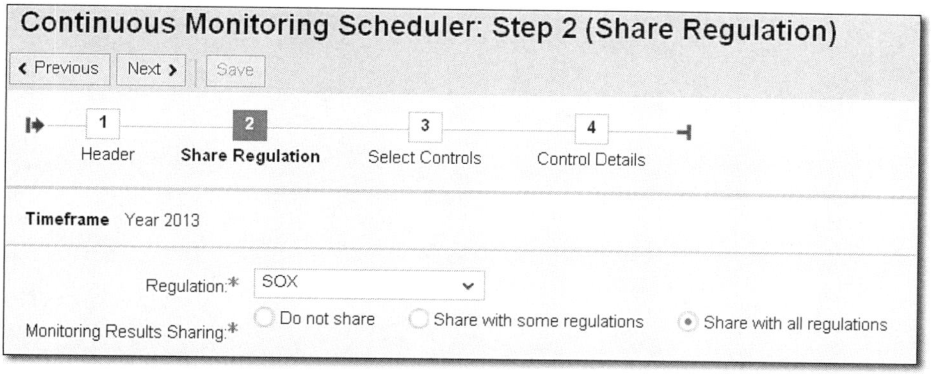

Figure 11.35 New Job Step 2: Regulation

Selecting the actual control-rule assignment for monitoring

Finally, the last step in the scheduling process allows you to select the actual control-rule assignment to schedule for monitoring, as shown in Figure 11.36. In addition to the search fields shown in Figure 11.36, all of the choices made so far—timeframe, year, regulation, and so on—constrain the search. So if the results are contrary to your expectation, you're advised to go back and check whether all of the explicit and implicit search constraints match the rule and control you expected to see. Examples of implicit search constraints include effective date ranges of rules and controls, scheduler timeframe, whether the rules in question are in active status, and so on.

The overview of CCM presented so far in this chapter presents a very mechanistic or how-to approach to monitoring. Useful as that undoubtedly is to customers, our experience has shown that success in CCM is best achieved by those customers who begin with a clear business goal for their monitoring efforts, and systematically work their way through the CCM features to find the best means of implementing CCM. In the next section, we offer some high-level advice to help customers find the best path through this complicated but rewarding topic.

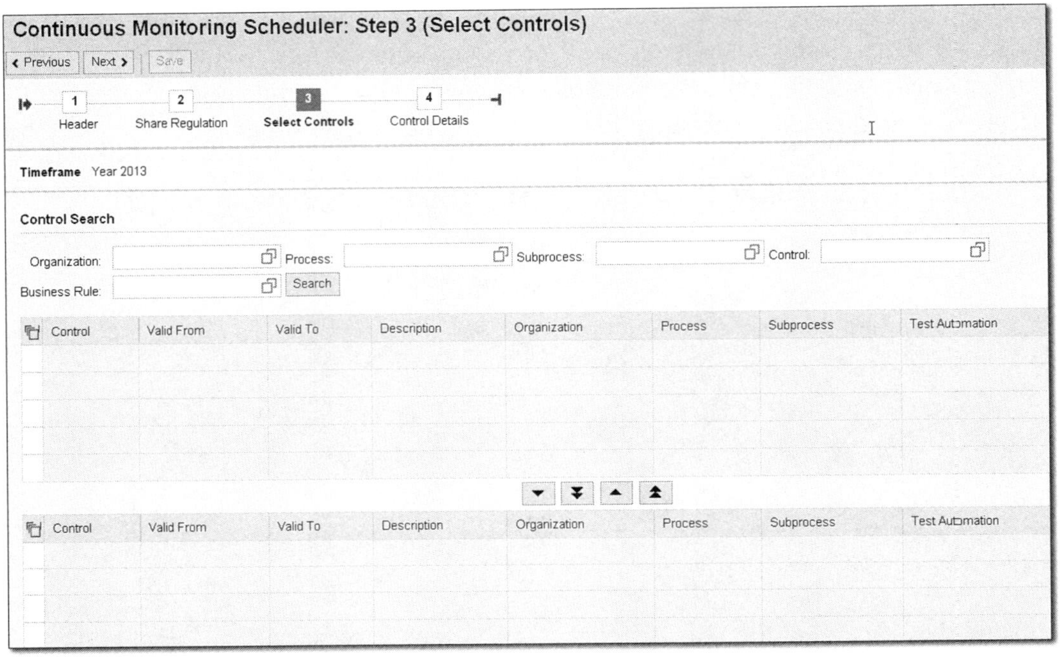

Figure 11.36 New Job Step 3: Select Controls

11.8 Structured Approach to Continuous Controls Monitoring

Customers new to CCM are often at a loss to know where to begin. Regulatory and policy compliance, fraud detection and internal controls, process optimization and operational control, loss prevention, and so many other worthy business goals might benefit from CCM. All lines of business can profitably be subject to monitoring, too—HR, finance, supply chain, purchasing, logistics, and so on can all have problems, and certainly all have to respond to regulatory requirements, meet internal control objectives, and may be victims of some type of fraud or the other.

Monitoring a backend system with SAP Process Control 10.1

SAP Process Control 10.1 offers ten different methods of monitoring backend systems and processes. These overlap in some ways and offer radically different monitoring methods in other ways. The system requirements, performance characteristics, reliability, timeliness, skills required, and so on can be very different, and customers sometimes find themselves going down blind alleys. They start using a monitoring technique, only to discover later that they strayed far outside the sweet spot for that technique and trespassed well into the proper domain of another. Such missteps can be costly—they waste time and resources, lead to lost opportunities, and affect reputations.

Our goal here is to present a philosophy and approach to CCM that has motivated SAP Process Control for the past few releases. Obviously, this isn't the only possible approach and goal, nor should it be. But if nothing else, it provides you with one approach, with which you are free to agree or disagree; either way, we hope reading this gets thoughts flowing, and ideas germinating in your mind. We hope that having read this and related chapters, you can define your own preferred approaches. Regardless of how closely your approach matches the presentation here, we hope to contribute to your thinking, and hence to a fruitful implementation of CCM in SAP Process Control.

11.8.1 The Nature of ERP Controls

Enterprise Resource Planning processes in general follow certain patterns of configuration and use, which we illustrate with a highly simplified example of the purchasing process, as shown in Figure 11.37.

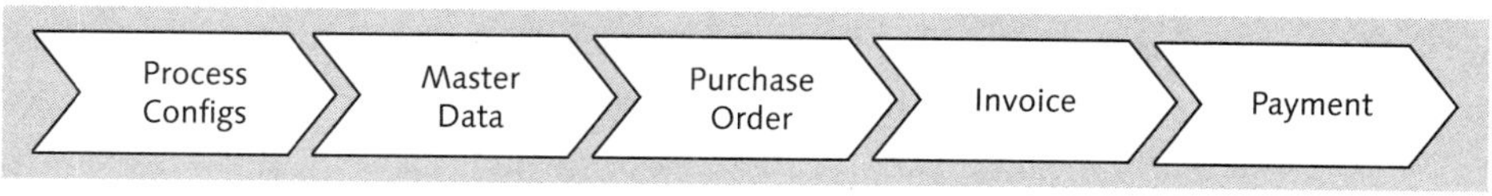

Figure 11.37 Abstract Model of the Purchasing Process

Configurations define what options and choices are available for creating requisitions, what approval and purchasing authorizations are granted to which users, what budgetary constraints are to be imposed on cost centers, whether tolerances are to be applied to differences between POs and invoices, and so on. Master data settings on vendors, for example, might allow a particular vendor's invoices to be accepted with minimal validations or approvals when there is a long-established relationship coupled with frequent purchases.

The strength of long-established and reputed vendors such as SAP lies in the extensive configurability of their processes and master data. SAP boasts, with great justification, that following its recommended best practices leads its customers to highly reliable business process implementations. Company policies can be accurately captured, so that transactions that violate the customer's intent are prevented, without costly and error-prone human controls and intervention.

Such preventive and inherent controls are the best option available to businesses. Set the systems up right, and bad news is prevented—the value of that can't be overstated.

But what if the configuration is wrong? Or worse, what if a configuration is weakened to allow a bad transaction through, either as a deliberate fraud or as a mistake? The entire value proposition of an expensive and complex ERP solution rests on correctly configuring the processes.

As explained earlier, the best controls are those built into a process. Such controls—configuration settings, really—allow valid transactions through and prevent bad ones from being created. Good applications cover a wide range of real-life business needs in this respect, and great ones do so in most cases, over a range of industries and lines of business.

11.8.2 The Goal of Monitoring

Where process experts have fine-tuned ERP applications to precisely reflect their business needs in the configurations and master data settings of their applications, the business comes to rely on the system to remain compliant to its regulatory needs and policy mandates. This no doubt leads to efficient and lean operations, but a reliable tool, if corrupted, can cause great harm.

The first goal of monitoring, then, is to explicitly monitor those configurations which, if invalid, would cause great harm. Misconfigured sales settings can expose the business to excess risk of customer defaults; weakened oversight of vendor payments can lead to fraud.

In some cases, it's not the settings themselves that need to be monitored but excessive use of certain exceptional settings. Many businesses allow one-time vendor accounts to be used to process payments for rare expenses as an efficiency measure. But paying the same vendor multiple times, or in large amounts, violates the spirit of this facility. Quick payments to vendors or tardy billing of customers costs very little each time, but a pattern of such transactions can add up to significant costs over time.

Scaling your monitoring

Large businesses or those that frequently undertake mergers and acquisitions face another challenge: a fragmented system landscape. Many SAP customers have multiple instances of the same SAP application active in production. Sometimes there are even version mismatches between these applications. No single configuration or master data repository can reliably capture the intent of the business. In such cases, the business tends to develop elaborate manual processes, analytic solutions via data warehousing, or a mix of such approaches to ensure compliance.

11.8.3 Effective Monitoring

What can a SAP GRC customer monitor? The possibilities are endless: all aspects of a business are supported by IT systems, and all of these can and should be monitored. Monitoring can be expensive: setting up SAP Process Control and maintaining the monitoring schedule itself can take a lot of implementation time and expense. Furthermore, monitoring rules impose a time and memory cost on the systems being monitored: monitoring queries usually are quick to run individually, but the more customers monitor, the more time and memory burdens are placed on their systems.

Risk-based approach to monitoring

Effective monitoring, then, must begin with a risk-based, quantitative approach. What situations expose the business to the greatest risk of noncompliance? Which risks have the largest impact in terms of financial losses, fines, reputation loss, and so on? A structured approach to these questions can quickly focus the organization on the most sensitive data to be monitored.

Secondly, a clear understanding of the business goals helps identify the best method of monitoring. Is the problem caused by bad transactions or improper configurations? Are roles and authorizations cleanly compartmentalized? After bad situations are identified, what corrective actions are possible? How will these be assigned and tracked? How can the organization learn and avoid repeating past mistakes?

Customer examples of monitoring

A couple of customer examples might make this a bit clearer. One large bottler in a competitive industry sought to track sales performance by measuring the ratio of the number of customers recently purchasing to total number of customers. This is certainly a valid metric, and a low number points, perhaps, to ineffective or insufficient marketing. But note that detecting this is more properly a SAP Risk Management Key Risk Indicator (KRI) monitoring opportunity—when the risk is identified as too high, the response is initiated by upper management, and the steps taken can't be tracked in SAP GRC applications.

On the other hand, duplicate payments to vendors, misconfigured credit checks, lax payment terms enforcement, and so on can all be traced to individual settings or transactions. These can then be corrected at the very least going forward. Remedial actions can be prescribed, assigned to specific responsible individuals, and tracked. These are more properly the domain of SAP Process Control CCM.

11.8.4 The Importance of Proper Configurations and Master Data Settings

As outlined in the previous section, proper configurations and master data settings yield great dividends by permitting good transactions and preventing bad ones. Conversely, misconfigurations and bad master data settings expose the business to errors and fraud, causing losses, adverse regulatory action, fraud, and so on.

SAP customers are particularly interested in these examples because one of the biggest virtues of SAP ERP (and related) applications is their extreme degree of configurability. Elaborate configurations make SAP applications difficult to set up, but once properly configured, SAP applications are extremely reliable.

SAP GRC has invested heavily in developing monitoring techniques specifically tailored to such settings. SAP applications offer a very unique feature for configurations and master data: change tracking at a very detailed level. Indeed, the granularity of change tracking of configurations is itself configurable.

SAP Process Control can reconstruct past configuration and master data settings from such change logs, and does so transparently to the users of SAP Process Control. The rule designer in SAP Process Control merely captures the business intent in the rule: what makes a configuration setting valid (or rather, how to identify invalid settings). SAP Process Control then applies this logic not only to configurations in effect when the rule is run but to reconstructed past settings as well, over the entire test time period. This is explained in detail in Chapter 12.

Where appropriate, such change log monitoring rules represent the best return on investment for SAP Process Control customers. The monitoring rules impose very little burden on the backend system (configuration and master data tables aren't large), and due to reliability of the change tracking mechanisms, the rules need not run very frequently.

11.8.5 Transactions

Sometimes, it's not possible to set configurations and master data to fully implement controls. Perhaps the system landscape is fragmented, with multiple systems implementing a single business process—a common enough situation in practice, especially for businesses which often undertake mergers and acquisitions. In some other cases, the logic of the control is simply outside the capabilities of the configurations.

Master data monitoring

Whatever the reason, if configuration or master data monitoring isn't sufficient to the needs, transaction monitoring is the only option. The techniques are similar, except that change tracking of transactions is typically never enabled for transactions, primarily due to high volume of data. Another reason is that applications often encode special mechanisms to track changes to transactions, so changes are tracked in a separate table.

Transaction monitoring

Transaction monitoring is then mainly a matter of querying several tables, and usually involves joins to master data tables. This is the main disadvantage to transaction monitoring: computational expense. SAP GRC advises customers to use the most efficient technique possible for transaction monitoring, due to the risk of high volume or computationally expensive table joins. For instance, the Configurable rules described in Chapter 13 are very easy for SAP Process Control users to set up and test. But because they involve additional layers of interpretation, they are rarely the most efficient query mechanism. SAP Queries in the backend are definitely more efficient.

In some cases, such as those involving pool or cluster tables, SAP's OpenSQL (which underlies both SAP Process Control configurable rules and SAP NetWeaver queries) isn't an option, and ABAP-coded queries are the only choice. In some cases with multiple joins, using a little ABAP to cleverly sequence or nest SQL can yield large time savings.

In our experience, it's best to start with configurable rules, where feasible, to test the concepts on a small test system. Then proper performance/load testing might suggest a shift to SAP queries, ABAP reports (see the next section), and SAP NetWeaver BW queries (where all of the computational burden is shifted to offline systems). With the 10.1 release, it's also possible to leverage the high speed and large volume capabilities of the SAP HANA in-memory database.

11.8.6 Reports and Analytics

Over the years, SAP has developed many reports for SAP ERP (and similar) customers. Many SAP customers have also invested time and money to develop their own reports. Where used, these reports presumably reflect customers' practices for (manual) monitoring of transactions. If such a report is useful and performs well enough for a customer's regular use, it obviously has value as a data source for SAP Process Control CCM.

Analytics is another area where content being developed, by SAP, partners, or customers, can be leveraged for monitoring. This is especially true where the monitoring logic involves statistical analysis of data to determine deficiency thresholds for monitoring.

11.9 Summary

This chapter has been a quick tour through the essential steps of defining and scheduling CCM rules. We swept through the steps, and mentioned several areas that need to be visited in more detail. Moreover, there are many variations on the simple theme we showed in the examples of this chapter. We go into more of these details and variations in the next chapter.

We judged it necessary to present this topic in this two-phased manner, because while the details can be confusing in the level of variation, the underlying theme is still common: define data sources, then business rules, assign these to local controls, and finally schedule them for execution.In Chapter 12, we examine the details of the different data source types and the business rule options for each.

Chapter 11 introduced the topic of continuous controls monitoring. This chapter dives deeper, describing more data source types—and associated business rule types—in detail. The chapter ends with a handy summary of different data source and business rule types, and the variations between them.

12 Continuous Controls Monitoring: Data Source Types

In this chapter, we continue our tour through the topic of Continuous Controls Monitoring (CCM). We explain many more types of data sources and business rules, discussing the nuances of each in some detail. We pay particular attention to configurable data sources and the associated rules because these are very unique to SAP Process Control. We leave for the next chapter two advanced topics: ODP-based and SAP HANA-based monitoring.

All of the material presented here serves as a good introduction to the rich and sometimes technical topic of SAP Process Control 10.1 CCM. Rule designers who want to implement any of the specific techniques described here will occasionally need more detailed and step-by-step guidance. This is best obtained from SAP's published documentation, available from the SAP Service Marketplace. As the product evolves, updates to these documents will also be published there.

Before reading further, please recall that both data source and business rule creation follow a standard pattern, with minor variations depending on data source type, rule analysis type, rule category, and so on. We listed the basic steps in context of SAP Query data source types (Section 11.3) and associated business rules (Section 11.4).

Configurable data sources and business rules were intended to allow SAP Process Control users to define queries against monitored backend systems, without modifying those systems directly (as described in the next section, Section 12.1). The change log check rules refers to a special category of configurable rules, in which SAP Process Control reconstructs past configuration and master data settings (see Section 12.2).

Following these descriptions, we describe several more data source types.

12.1 Configurable Data Sources and Rules

In Chapter 11, we showed how a query defined in the standard SAP Query tool (T SQ01/02) can be consumed in SAP Process Control CCM as a data source. The challenge for many customers is that their IT department views the creation of a new SAP query as a system modification. In most places, production backend system modifications are very rare; IT procedures and policies can very easily frustrate an ambitious CCM agenda.

SAP Process Control and remote backend system tables

In response, SAP GRC came up with the idea of allowing SAP Process Control users to define queries against remote backend system tables, while working in the SAP Process Control user interface (UI). That is, SAP Process Control looks up tables and their relationships on the monitored system, and then presents the SAP Process Control user with choices. The user then chooses the tables, either accepts or overrides the known relationships between them, and chooses the fields of interest. At runtime, SAP Process Control constructs a query from this information, and sends it to the SAP GRC plug-in on the monitored system, which then executes it using the SAP Query toolset.

Configurable queries and their limitations

Does this violate your IT rules? Not so, not even in spirit. The queries SAP Process Control allows its users to construct are severely limited:

- These *configurable* queries, so-called because they are configured during the definition of the SAP Process Control data source, are read only. They never update, delete, or insert into backend tables, and hence are safe queries from that perspective.

- Configurable queries only permit inner joins on up to five separate tables to safeguard against performance problems at the monitored system.
- Configurable queries only allow equi-joins on fields of matching types—this avoids other types of performance problems and also many errors.

Note that the word "configurable" refers to the fact that users can configure the logic of the query, rather than have to program it in ABAP or SQL. The term is a little unfortunately chosen because it's also true that customers often use configurable rules to monitor configuration settings, especially using the change log check category of configurable rules. Whether used to monitor configurations or not, "configurable" only refers to the fact that SAP Process Control users define the underlying query in the SAP Process Control UI. Configurations in the monitored system can be monitored via any other data source types as well, although the change log features make configurable rules particularly suitable for monitoring configurations.

12.1.1 Configurable Data Sources

As explained, configurable data sources allow a query to be defined in the SAP Process Control system, but the query is intended to run against tables in the monitored system. In effect, the SAP Process Control system inspects the monitored system and brings back table definitions and relationships between tables as captured in the monitored system's data dictionary. SAP Process Control then uses this information to help guide the data source designer.

Data source creation process

In what follows, we're walking through the data source creation process for configurable data sources. This is analogous to the process shown in Chapter 11 for SAP Query data sources, so we focus here on steps that are different. As you read this section, please keep in mind that the overall flow here is comparable to the SAP Query case from Chapter 11.

For instance, the designer can search for the appropriate table by name or description using wildcards, as shown in Figure 12.1. This step is a variation on the query lookup described in Section 11.3, specifically referring to Figure 11.14 through Figure 11.17. Although Figure 12.1 doesn't show this, the lookup could also have occurred via the Table Description field, which also accepts wildcards.

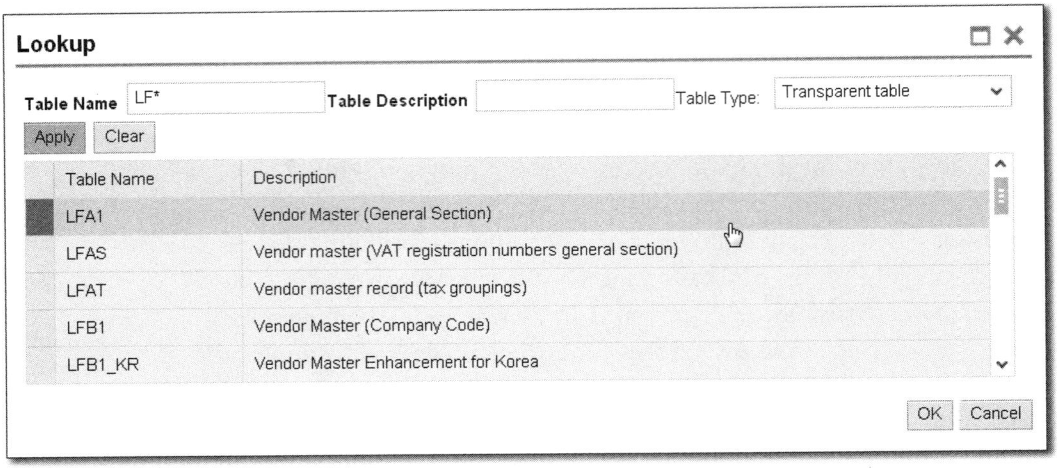

Figure 12.1 Looking Up Tables to Build a Configurable Data Source

The prompting and validation help that SAP Process Control provides extends to also knowing related tables when defining joins. Once the user has selected a "main" table for the data source, looking up related tables is guided by the known relationships (from the monitored system's data dictionary). For instance, and continuing the example of Figure 12.1, LFA1 is the primary table, and LFB1 is a dependent table for vendor master data (see Figure 12.2).

SAP Process Control continues to help the user by interpreting the Join Conditions gleaned from relationships captured in the data dictionary of the remote ABAP system. Again continuing the vendor master example, you see that SAP Process Control finds some ambiguity in the data dictionary of SAP ERP, as shown in Figure 12.3. The highlighted text box message warns the user of the ambiguity; although the warning doesn't explicitly describe the ambiguity, the highlighted box at the lower right of the screen shows that LFA1:LIFNR can be equated to one of three related fields in LFB1. The user needs to select one of these to avoid overconstraining the join.

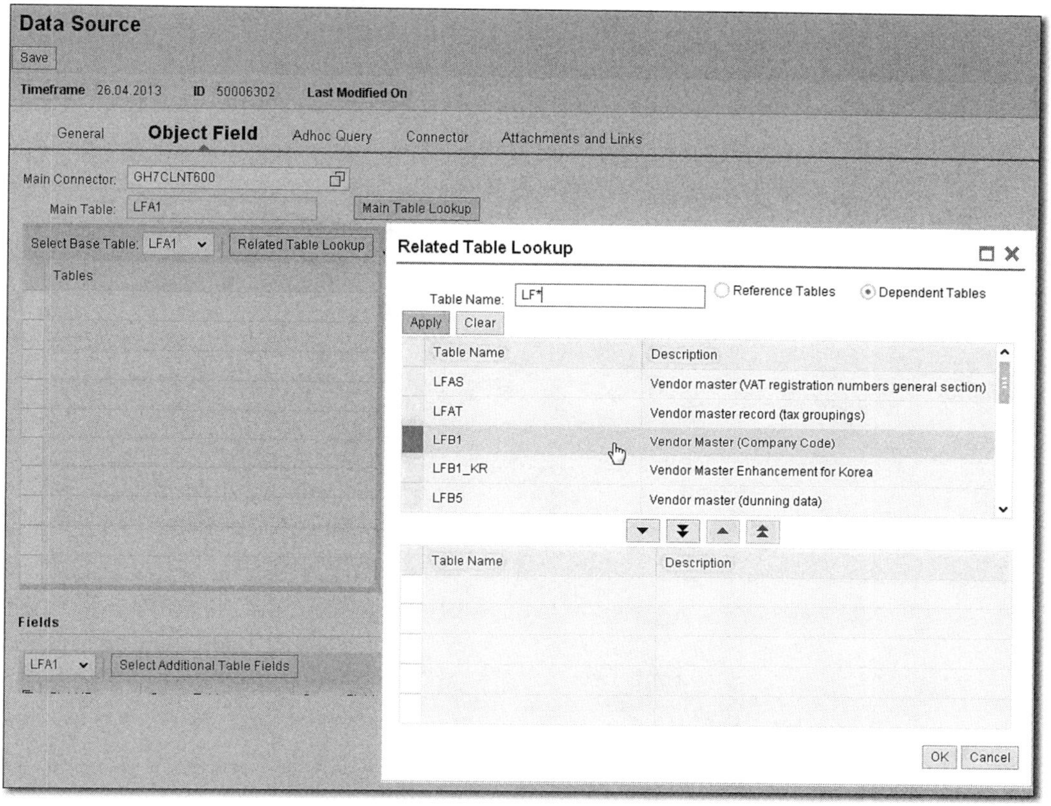

Figure 12.2 Looking Up Related Tables

SAP Process Control recognizes that multiple join conditions are available, but not all of which can be applied simultaneously. The ambiguity is reflected in the first three join conditions shown in the figure, which all relate tables LFA1 and LFB1, but via equality conditions from LFA1:LIFNR to three different fields on LFB1. SAP Process Control invites the user to remove redundant JOIN CONDITIONS, as shown in the message area at the top of the screen in Figure 12.3.

The next step is to select fields from each of the tables being joined together, to include in the data source. Fields referenced in the JOIN CONDITIONS (LIFNR and MANDT) are automatically included; others have to be explicitly selected. Figure 12.4 shows all of the fields which were selected for inclusion in the data source being created. Note that the last column, FIELD DESCRIPTION, is editable.

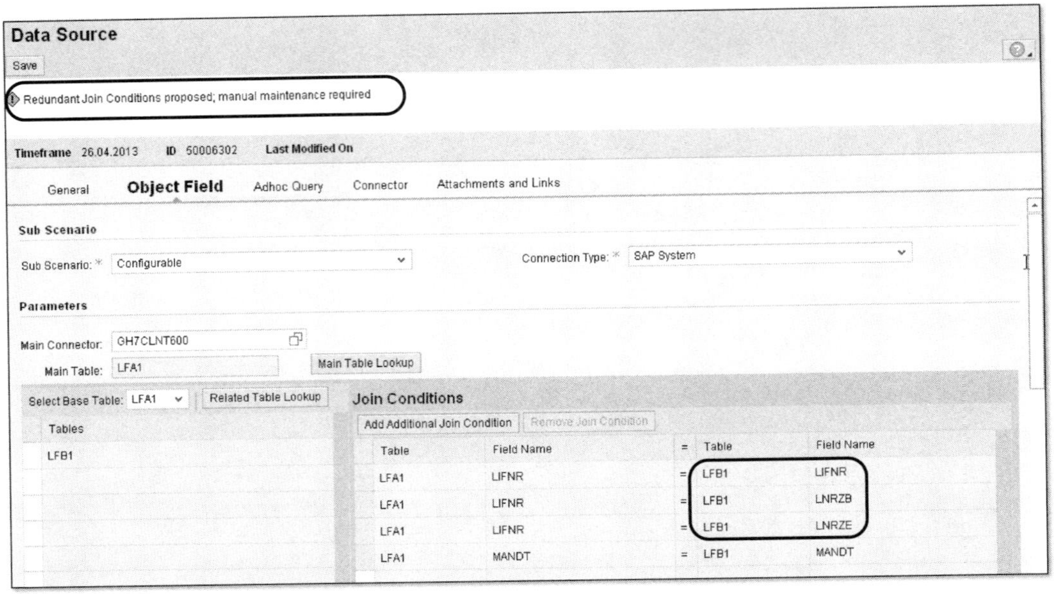

Figure 12.3 Join Conditions for a Configurable Data Source

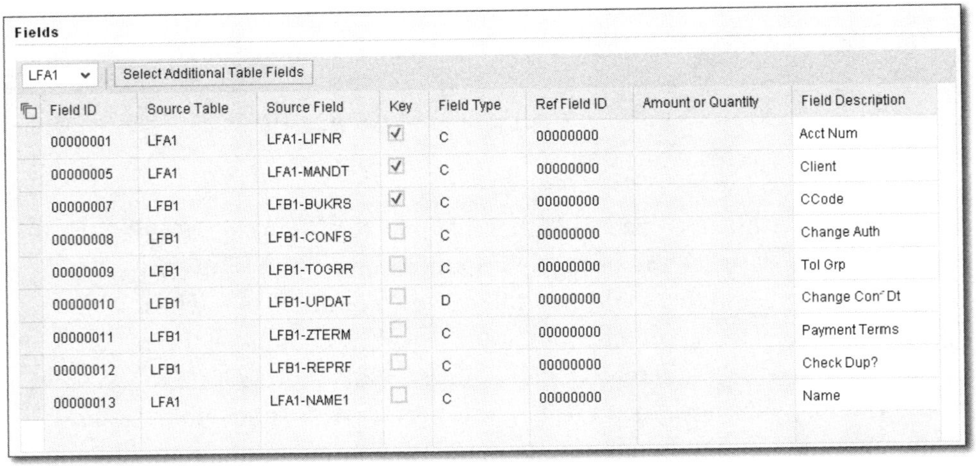
Fields

LFA1 | Select Additional Table Fields

Field ID	Source Table	Source Field	Key	Field Type	Ref Field ID	Amount or Quantity	Field Description
00000001	LFA1	LFA1-LIFNR	✓	C	00000000		Acct Num
00000005	LFA1	LFA1-MANDT	✓	C	00000000		Client
00000007	LFB1	LFB1-BUKRS	✓	C	00000000		CCode
00000008	LFB1	LFB1-CONFS		C	00000000		Change Auth
00000009	LFB1	LFB1-TOGRR		C	00000000		Tol Grp
00000010	LFB1	LFB1-UPDAT		D	00000000		Change Con' Dt
00000011	LFB1	LFB1-ZTERM		C	00000000		Payment Terms
00000012	LFB1	LFB1-REPRF		C	00000000		Check Dup?
00000013	LFA1	LFA1-NAME1		C	00000000		Name

Figure 12.4 Adding Fields to a Data Source

Warning

Please make sure you've selected all of the tables to be joined before you select additional fields—changing the join erases previously selected fields, even for tables whose participation in the join hasn't changed!

Now that we've reviewed configurable data sources, let's take a look at the associated business rules. Any rule based upon a configurable data source is called a configurable business rule.

12.1.2 Configurable Business Rules

Configurable business rules come in two categories: value check and change log check. The rule category really controls the behavior of the underlying data source in this case. Change log rules cause the data source to parse change logs and reconstruct past settings (more on this in Section 12.2). Value check rules only ask the data source to read what's in the referenced database tables at the time of rule execution.

Value check categories

In this section, we describe the value check category as the base type of configurable business rules; the later section on change log rules expands on this for the more powerful change analysis capabilities.

Figure 12.5 shows the Basic Information for the rule being written: Name, Description, Valid from/Valid to, Status, and so on. Note that the value check category of configurable rules only allows one Analysis Type: Monitor Value (more on that later in Section 12.1.3).The rest of the rule definition closely parallels the process shown in Chapter 11, so we won't belabor the matter here.

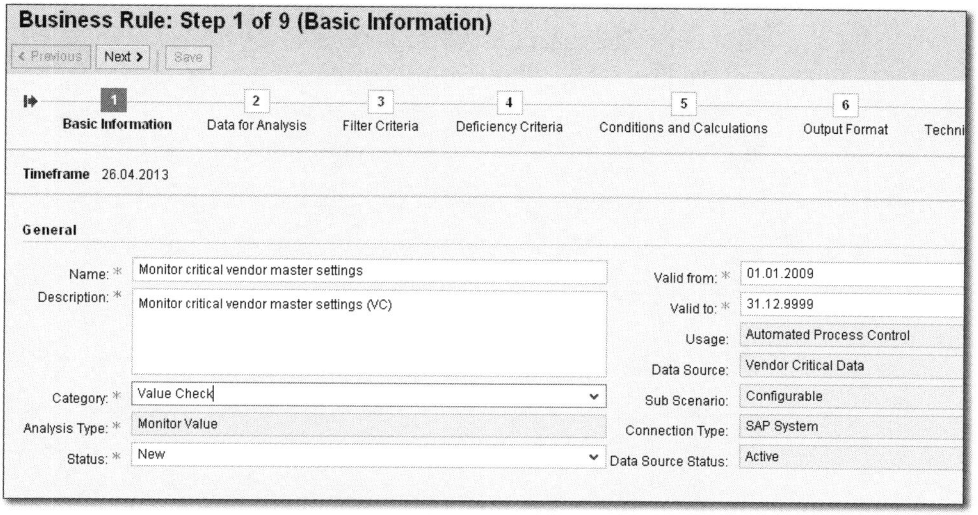

Figure 12.5 Value Check Configurable Rule: Basic Information Screen

The remaining steps for creating configurable rules of CATEGORY: VALUE CHECK/ANALYSIS TYPE: MONITOR VALUE are identical to the SAP Query rule shown in Chapter 11, Section 11.4, so we omit the details here. We next look at some important limitations in the use of configurable data sources and rules.

12.1.3 Limitations of Configurable Data Sources and Rules

In this section, we will review some of the limitation of configurable data sources and rules. In particular, we will look at following limitations in further detail:

- Pool and Cluster tables can't be joined.
- Configurable Data Sources Limit Joins to Five Tables.
- Value Check Category Doesn't Offer Review Required Analysis Type

These limitations are general system limitations that the general user should be aware of prior to configuring rules. Let's first look at the limitation of pool and cluster tables.

Pool and Cluster Tables Can't Be Joined

Configurable data sources are limited to the three table types shown in Figure 12.6: transparent, pooled, and clustered. These details are generally far too technical for most SAP Process Control users, but the limitation around cluster/pool tables is something a rule/data source designer is almost sure to encounter, especially for monitoring SAP ERP systems.

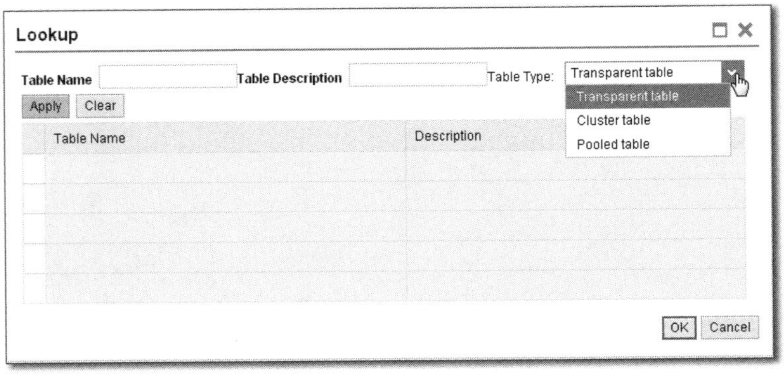

Figure 12.6 Table Types for Configurable Data Sources

Pooled and cluster table schema

Pooled and cluster tables have an apparent schema that differs from the actual, underlying schema. Typically, several fields in a row of data are concatenated together in their string representation and stored as a string. This compacts the representation and reduces disk storage at the expense of query power. Because the database layer has no knowledge of the intended representation of the data but only knows about the shrunken form, SAP's standard query tools (including SAP Query) can't handle pool or cluster tables. Such tables can only be handled in ABAP code.

Defining data sources against pool and cluster tables

SAP Process Control 10.1 allows users to define data sources against such pool and cluster tables but not to join these with each other or any other table types. In contrast, transparent tables have no such limitations. Their actual schema as stored matches their apparent schema as presented in various screens.

Defining data sources is perhaps the most technical challenge facing SAP Process Control users, and the distinction between transparent and other table types is obscure. We explained this in some detail just so readers understand the nature of the challenge, and know the right questions to ask if they run into this limitation.

Configurable Data Sources Limit Joins to Five Tables

Configurable data sources allow the user to define queries with table joins. SAP NetWeaver query tools (e.g., SQ01/02) allow users to define joins with any number of tables, but the assumption is that the user is an expert who knows the performance implications of any query he defines. Or, at least, the user recognizes that performance impacts must be gauged before deploying such queries in production systems.

Since the PC configurable data source is designed to help perhaps less-skilled users to nevertheless define simple queries, PC architects wanted to limit any unintended performance hits to monitored systems. They imposed a hard limit of five tables which can be joined in configurable data sources.

Value Check Category Doesn't Offer Review Required Analysis Type

As shown in Figure 12.7 later in this chapter, the Change Log Check Category of configurable rules offers several analysis types, including Review Required for Changes. This forces SAP Process Control to route any data to a user for review without making any judgment about whether there is a defect to be remedied. In some situations, the determination of whether or not there's a defect is very context-dependent and difficult to encode in the rule's logic.

The Value Check category of configurable rules doesn't offer this analysis type, which is a limitation that has forced some customers to work around by voiding SAP Process Control-created issues. This works well enough but can cause spurious defect reports that then have to be explained.

12.2 Change Log Check Rules

SAP applications have extensive change-tracking mechanisms for database tables, which guarantee that all changes are captured, even if they last for a very short duration. That is, even if one change is quickly followed by another, both changes are reliably logged. These mechanisms, usually configured by Basis administrators, cover changes made directly in the system and also changes transported into the system. This guarantee is very important for SAP GRC customers, whose primary goal is to ensure that business processes comply with policies.

The next few paragraphs go into some level of detail about change logs, but readers not interested in the technical details may safely skip them. The only point to remember is that changes to configuration settings and master data are tracked by SAP Basis, and using change log check category business rules to monitor changes is an easy and reliable way to monitor changes.

The function of Change log check business rules

The change log check category business rules parse the data in the change logs of configuration and master data tables, and reconstruct any past settings over the time frame of the control. So a change log business rule allows you to check the validity of a configuration or master data setting at any time, with confidence that all changes made to that setting will be found and tested for correctness—a correct setting being one that accurately reflects customer intent. Wrong configurations are caught, no matter how transiently they were in effect.

In addition, transported changes are also tracked. Configuration changes can be transported in and are covered by the Basis change tracking mechanism. Master data can only be changed directly in the system. Configuration and master data tables have different change tracking mechanisms, and SAP Process Control 10.1 parses the correct information for appropriate table types. Master data uses the change document mechanism of SAP Basis, while configuration tables rely on DBTABLOG-based change tracking.

Many SAP competitors offer a less reliable method of tracking changes, called polling. We examine the differences between these methods next.

12.2.1 Change Tracking: Logs versus Polling

In SAP Basis, every time a table is changed, the change is logged as long as logging is enabled, and the table being changed is marked for logging. This eases the challenge of change monitoring: instead of more and more frequent monitoring to make sure even transient changes aren't lost ("lost" in the sense of not showing up on review), customers can feel secure that they will catch every single change.

Polling

Some other products use *polling*, in which the table in question is queried frequently, and the state is compared to prior states to detect changes. But it's only half a solution—you can check any reported changes for correctness, but you can't be sure that more changes didn't happen between two polling snapshots. With polling, you always run the risk that a fraudulent change was made and then obscured by another change. Basis change logging misses no change, no matter how transient.

Scheduling polling

Some customers' IT policies disable change logging by default, usually over performance concerns, which we address directly in Section 12.4. In the meantime, if Basis monitoring isn't enabled, customers must schedule the polling program as a background job in the monitored system (this capability is delivered with the SAP GRC software, as a plug-in deployed in monitored systems—see Figure 11.1 and Figure 11.2 in Chapter 11), choosing a polling frequency that best balances the need to catch changes against the impact on performance. If Basis change logging is enabled after polling has been scheduled, the SAP GRC plug-in recognizes the redundancy and stops polling. The history reconstruction module of SAP Process Control 10 then looks at polled snapshots as well as the change log, so as not to miss any known changes regardless of the tracking mechanism.

The process of defining change log check category of business rules closely follows the same pattern shown with SAP Query business rules in Chapter 11. We look at the details next, again focusing on what's unique.

12.2.2 Defining Change Log Rules

Change log rules can be based on either "configurable" data sources or "programmed" ones. Such change log rules can be used to monitor either configurations (via the DBTABLOG functionality mentioned earlier) or via master data (by a different document master system of tracking changes). The design of this feature shields the rule designer from the complexities of log analysis; they simply find the right tables and fields to monitor, and the SAP GRC code tracks down the additional information needed to reconstruct past settings from change logs.

Defining a monitoring business rule

After the data source is ready and active, you can define a monitoring business rule on it. During the process of defining the rule, the user must indicate that the rule in question is a change log type rule. Thus, change log rules can only be defined:

- For configuration and master data tables.
- Based on either configurable or programmed type data sources.

Analysis types for business rules

In Figure 12.7, you can see all of the available analysis types (CHANGES, NUMBER OF CHANGES, REVIEW REQUIRED FOR CHANGES, MONITOR, and PATTERN) for the CHANGE LOG CHECK CATEGORY of configurable business rules.

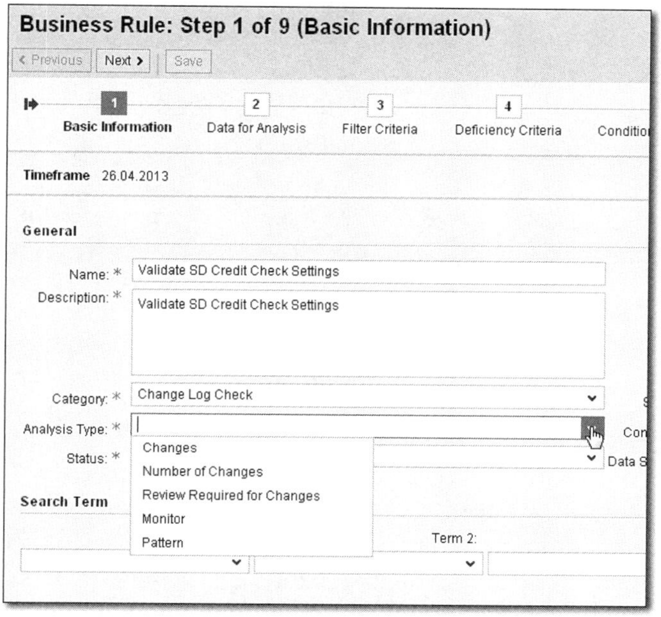

Figure 12.7 Defining Change Log Configurable Rules: Step 1

For change log rules based on configurable data source types (but not for programmed data source types), SAP Process Control provides an analysis type of pattern, which allows users to define a multifield deficiency criterion using a decision table. In fact, this "pattern" analysis is a decision table, powered by the SAP NetWeaver BRF+ rule engine (see Chapter 13).

Table 12.1 explains each of these analysis types.

Analysis Type	Description
CHANGES	Allows designer to select several fields to watch; any change to these fields is reported as a deficiency.
NUMBER OF CHANGES	Deficiency condition limits the number of times a field can be changed within the test time frame.
REVIEW REQUIRED FOR CHANGES	Any change to selected fields is routed for review but without marking it as an issue. It differs from the CHANGES analysis type only to this extent.

Table 12.1 Analysis Types for Change Log Check Category Business Rules

Analysis Type	Description
MONITOR	Allows the designer to define specific logic to determine if the new value of a changed field is acceptable.
PATTERN	Uses BRF+ decision table functionality, presented in the SAP Process Control user interface as a table of logical expressions. This is more fully explained in the text.

Table 12.1 Analysis Types for Change Log Check Category Business Rules (Cont.)

The first four analysis types operate natively, while PATTERN uses BRF+ decision table functionality. We defer discussion of BRF+ details to Chapter 13.

Technical details of how change log check category business rules operate are mostly hidden from users. One aspect of which they need at least some understanding of is the existence of the table handlers, which mediate change tracking of tables. We describe these next.

Table Handlers

When using change analysis, one configuration requires additional explanation. When interpreting the change log, the SAP GRC backend plug-in needs a handler to interpret the change log entries. This roughly corresponds with the methods for changing that setting, as registered with the Basis change tracking functionality. Sometimes more than one table handler is registered for the table in question, and it can be difficult to determine which handler to use, as shown in Figure 12.8.

Table handler selection

Sometimes, you may have to choose between two or three handlers to determine which one is appropriate. In most cases, handlers of type SCU3 will prove appropriate. Experienced SAP users will recall that SCU3 is a transaction code that displays change information in SAPGUI—the related handler, if it exists, is usually the most useful. More generally, the correct handler for your situation will be the one that makes your deficiency fields available for use in the change analysis rule.

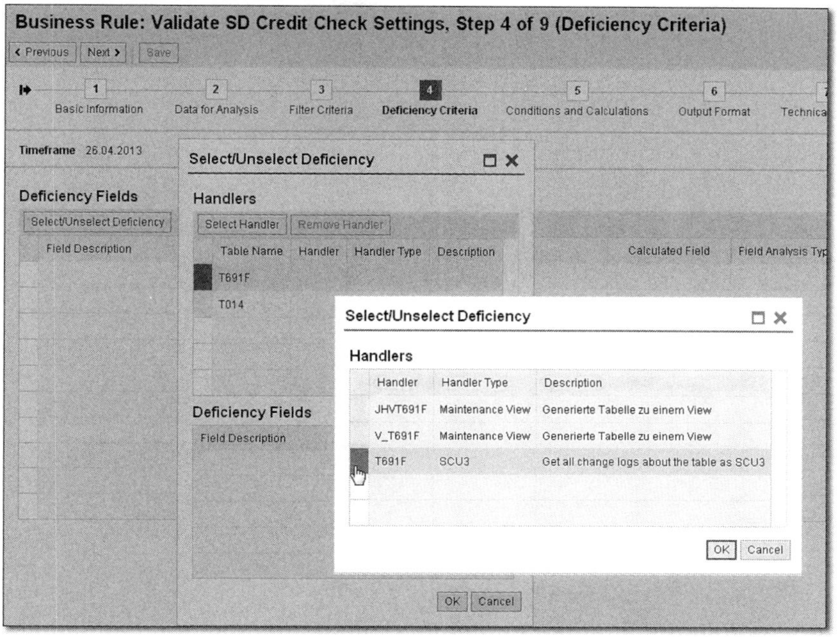

Figure 12.8 Handlers for Changes to SD Credit Check Settings

After you choose the handler, you can then select the fields for which you want to define a deficiency condition, as shown in Figure 12.9. As you can see, we've selected the CREDIT CHECK: SET CREDIT STATUS (BLOCK) field.

Field selection for monitoring changes

After a field is selected (or a calculated field is defined—see Section 13.3 and Figure 13.4), you must choose one of the options in the FIELD ANALYSIS TYPE dropdown: VALUE CHECK or BLANK CHECK (see Figure 12.10). VALUE CHECK lets you define an explicit condition on the value of the field in question. BLANK CHECK is a check for whether the field is blank or has a null value. Once again, note that this applies to the new value—the value after each reported change.

We've devoted considerable space to describing configurable business rules because they are unique to SAP Process Control. Experience has shown that they are also highly popular with customers. But SAP Process Control CCM can also use many other types of data sources, which we describe next.

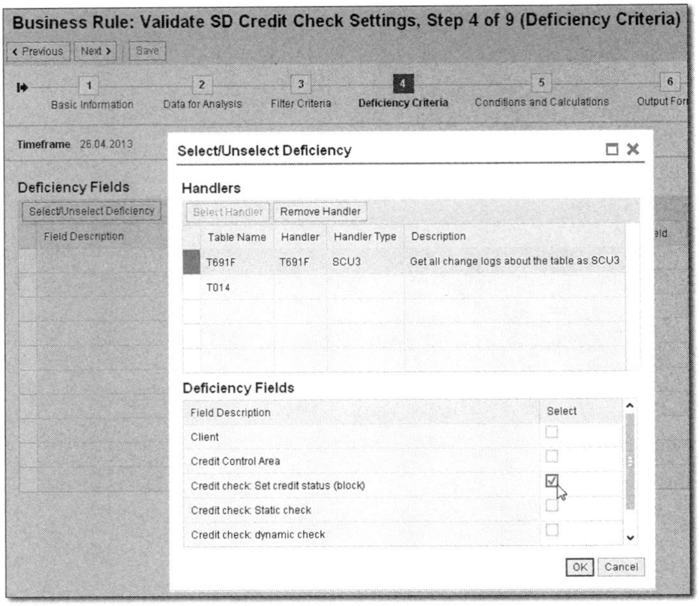

Figure 12.9 Selecting Fields for Monitoring Changes

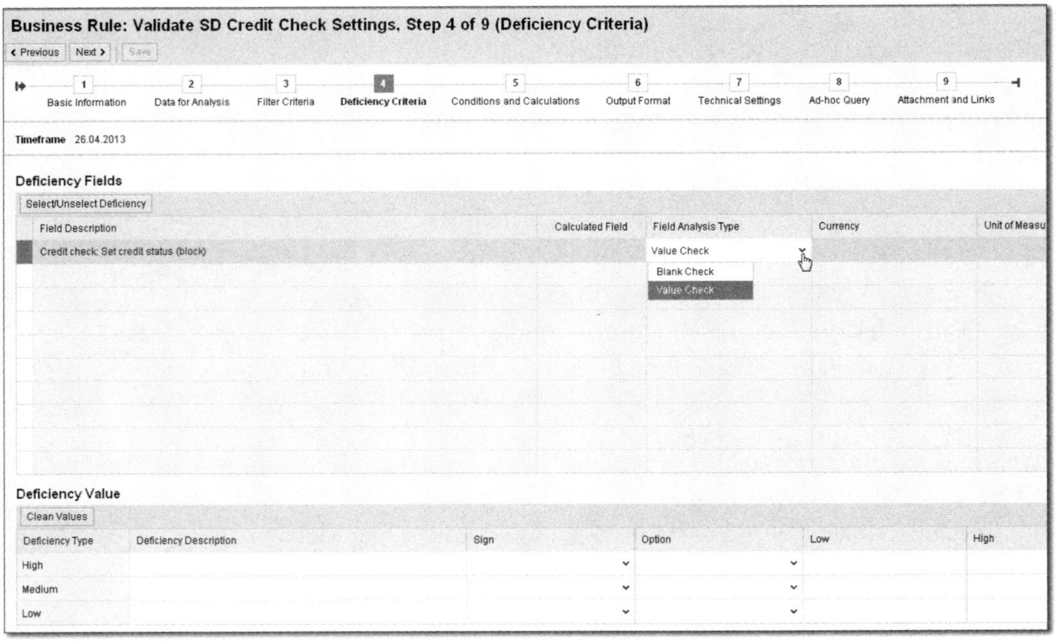

Figure 12.10 Value Check versus Blank Check

12.3 Other Data Source Types and Rules

Configurable data sources are defined by the SAP Process Control user and then used by associated business rules. But many other types of data sources leverage existing queries and reports, and it was always a key goal of SAP Process Control designers to allow customers to reuse any investments they had previously made in such content. We will look at several data sources in this section:

- ABAP Reports
- Segregation of Duty integration
- SAP NetWeaver BW query
- Event-driven data sources
- SAP NetWeaver Process Integration (SAP PI)
- ABAP Program data sources
- External partner sources

The first such data source type uses ABAP reports, which we describe next.

12.3.1 ABAP Reports

ABAP reports are widely used to monitor transactions, configurations, master data, and so on, in SAP applications. SAP Process Control 10.1 can use such reports for CCM. SAP Process Control can run such reports on a user-defined schedule, bind values (e.g., company codes, dates) to report parameters, and present the results to SAP Process Control users for review. Use of report variants is supported but not always needed. Results are viewable as an image, PDF document, or spreadsheet.

ABAP reports have a range of behaviors, some of which aren't suitable for SAP Process Control 10.1 CCM. SAP Process Control 10.1 must invoke ABAP reports remotely, so first of all, the report must be able to run as a background job on the monitored system, and its results must be able to be stored as a spool job. Secondly, it must not use additional popup screens for user input, after its declared parameters are bound to values. It's difficult to know which reports qualify under these circumstances, so the SAP Process Control team has written a program to help qualify ABAP reports for use in CCM.

Most SAP Process Control customers are also customers of SAP Access Control, and with release 10.0 (and continuing into 10.1), SAP Process Control CCM can integrate very tightly with SAP Access Control. We describe the related data source type next.

12.3.2 Segregation of Duty Integration

The SAP Access Control 10.1 solution includes extensive rules covering segregation of duty (SoD) conflicts, critical actions, permissions, and so on. These rules conform to the rules interface of the SAP Process Control CCM framework. Such rules can be run in the context of SAP Process Control local controls, as described in Chapter 11. One key constraint is that the two SAP GRC products—SAP Process Control and SAP Access Control—should both be installed in the same system.

SAP Access Control and Process Control integration

SAP Access Control provides one rule to use with SAP Process Control 10.1 for monitoring, which takes a fixed set of parameters and returns a single set of results. This can only be used as-is within SAP Process Control 10.1.

The SAP NetWeaver Business Warehouse (SAP NetWeaver BW) has powerful analytical capabilities and can aggregate data from multiple backend systems. We discuss the monitoring opportunities with SAP NetWeaver BW next.

12.3.3 SAP NetWeaver BW Query

SAP NetWeaver BW has a query tool that you can use to define queries against SAP NetWeaver BW InfoObjects and InfoCubes. If you want to monitor your business processes by looking at data extracted to SAP NetWeaver BW, you can create SAP NetWeaver BW queries. Definition of SAP NetWeaver BW query data sources is very similar to SAP Query data sources as described in Chapter 11.

Setup of SAP NetWeaver BW queries

However, there is one critical difference in the way the SAP NetWeaver BW queries must be set up. Unlike transactional systems, the whole purpose of data warehouses is to enable users to analyze data intensively.

SAP NetWeaver BW queries can be designed to allow follow-on analytics even after the query returns results. Automated monitoring can't use those features because the recipient of the results in this case is the SAP GRC product, not directly the user. So the SAP NetWeaver BW query used for SAP Process Control 10.1 CCM must be of a more restricted type. For use with SAP Process Control 10.1 CCM, SAP NetWeaver BW queries should be constructed with the following constraints:

SAP NetWeaver BW Query constraints

1. SAP NetWeaver BW characteristics of interest must be arranged in the row area in Query Designer. The characteristics are a list of output fields, which will appear as DATA FOR ANALYSIS in a SAP GRC data source.
2. SAP NetWeaver BW key figures must be arranged in the columns area in Query Designer.
3. Free characteristics in Query Designer may not be used.
4. Characteristic restrictions should not be used for query filters.
5. Only SINGLE VALUE and SELECTION OPTION variable presentations of query filters should be used.
6. All query filters and selection fields must be optional—SAP GRC monitoring rules don't require filters to be specified, so the underlying SAP NetWeaver BW query must also make this optional.
7. In Query Designer's row area, the result row setting must be ALWAYS SUPPRESS.

12.3.4 Event-Driven Data Sources

Event-driven data sources and rules are different from all the others in one respect—they aren't initiated by SAP Process Control on a schedule (or by the SAP Process Control user). Instead, some external program or agent must decide when an event has occurred and needs to be communicated to SAP Process Control for monitoring and evaluation.

Event registry and event payload

Process Control provides a web services interface that a partner product can call to raise such events to SAP Process Control. SAP Process Control must first be configured to expect such an event in the Event Registry (part of IMG customizing), and the configuration includes a description of the event payload, or the contained attributes and their data types.

When actual events are received, SAP Process Control first validates the payload (XML) against the registered event metadata, and only those events with payloads that pass muster are processed further. The event interface is a synchronous method, and only success or failure is communicated back.

Details about how to configure these data sources, how to obtain the Web Services Description Language (WSDL) for the web service, and so on can be found in the associated user guide on SAP Service Marketplace.

12.3.5 SAP NetWeaver Process Integration

SAP GRC can monitor non-SAP applications, and the SAP NetWeaver Process Integration-based data source is one of several suitable for this purpose.

Database protocols for SAP NetWeaver Process Integration

SAP NetWeaver Process Integration (SAP NetWeaver PI, formerly known as SAP NetWeaver XI) is SAP's preferred platform for integrations. SAP NetWeaver PI supports common database access protocols such as JDBC and ODBC, and customers who have non-SAP applications in their system landscape can use SAP NetWeaver PI to either query directly against the underlying databases of these applications via JDBC/ODBC, or even integrate at the code level, if appropriate.

The Monitoring API

SAP Process Control 10.1 provides a four-method monitoring API to integrate with SAP NetWeaver PI, grouped into two design-time functions and two runtime functions. Design-time functions are useful to rule designers, and runtime functions are used to execute the rules so defined. This section describes the API at a conceptual level, although the technical names of implementing functions and proxies may well be different. The descriptions in this section are also relevant to other data source types described here.

The four methods can conceptually be called GetQueryList, GetSignature, TestQuery, and ExecuteQuery. The actual names are shorter, and not so descriptive. The first three are the design-time methods—that is,

SAP Process Control calls these as needed while the rule designer is creating or editing the rule. The last method is only called at runtime, when a scheduled rule executes.

- **GetQueryList**
  SAP GRC calls the remote system via GetQueryList to get a list of queries or other data-retrieval functions on offer from the remote system for use in monitoring. This list is then displayed to the rule designer to create SAP GRC data source objects.
- **GetSignature**
  After the rule designer has selected a particular query from the list, SAP GRC calls the GetSignature method to retrieve metadata about the input parameters the query expects, and the results it returns. These are reflected in the data source attributes and become available for designers to use in defining filter criteria, deficiencies, and output formats.
- **TestQuery**
  The TestQuery method is used for ad hoc queries from data sources and business rules, although note that this method isn't always available due to technical reasons.
- **ExecuteQuery**
  The ExecuteQuery method is called to actually run the query once scheduled or executed via the planner. The key difference between TestQuery and ExecuteQuery is that TestQuery calls aren't logged or audit-trailed, while all scheduled executions are.

SAP NetWeaver PI Implementation of the Monitoring API

SAP Process Control 10.1 includes a SAP NetWeaver PI implementation of the monitoring API described previously, so customers or partners who want to create SAP NetWeaver PI-based queries (e.g., to query directly from a non-SAP database via ODBC/JDBC) can define such queries in SAP NetWeaver PI and use the SAP GRC-supplied implementation of the monitoring API to integrate those into SAP Process Control monitoring rules.

SAP NetWeaver PI rules may use asynchronous communication between SAP Process Control 10 and SAP NetWeaver PI, which requires a callback endpoint in SAP Process Control. The associated user guide describes how to configure SAP NetWeaver PI-based rules in more detail.

12.3.6 External Partner Data Sources

The external partner data sources operate via web services interfaces because they have historically been used by SAP Process Control partners to enable easier monitoring of different backend applications. In the IMG configuration screens, you'll also notice the term GL-MQT, which again reflects this history. SAP Process Control 10.1 generalizes to web services what used to be proprietary interfaces for such partners to implement. This API is the same as described earlier in Section 0, with the exception that the TEST method isn't available for partners to implement.

Implementation with External Partner Data Sources

The method implementations are, of course, the responsibility of the partner product (or custom middleware). In web services, it's usual for the implementer of a service to publish a WSDL definition of the service, to which the caller then adapts. In our case, however, SAP Process Control 10.1 has a fixed outbound proxy, and we've published the WSDL that the proxy expects the partner to implement. These are described in SAP Note 1549031.

12.3.7 ABAP Program Data Sources

Some monitoring rules might require complex processing beyond the capabilities of the query and rule engines described here. Such situations can be addressed by writing custom ABAP programs to deploy on the backend system being monitored. Such programs must conform to the overall design framework prescribed for CCM and must be registered in the SAP GRC plug-in for monitored systems. These are very similar to ABAP reports, but because they adhere to a pattern prescribed by the SAP GRC plug-in, they can be better leveraged by SAP Process Control for monitoring. To emphasize this distinction, we call them ABAP Reports for SAP GRC.

Once again, the conceptual framework is the monitoring API as described earlier in Section 0. Any ABAP report for SAP GRC must implement (extend) a defined base class, and the programmer must create an entry in a specified table with the program (class) name, parameters, and so on. The necessary classes and tables are part of the SAP GRC plug-in for SAP NetWeaver ABAP systems, which must be installed in the system to be monitored. SAP Process Control 10.1 can then look up the relevant ABAP reports for SAP GRC and their metadata, and provide SAP Process Control rule designers with the information they need.

Details about how to write such ABAP reports for SAP GRC, how to register them with the SAP GRC plug-in (RTA), and so on are found in the associated user guide.

12.4 Performance Considerations with Change Logging

Customers often comment that standard IT practice is to turn configuration table logging off globally, and turning this setting on raises concerns about performance impacts. This is addressed in more detail in SAP Note 1653464 – Enable Change Log Monitoring by Activating Table Logging (*https://service.sap.com/sap/support/notes/1653464*). SAP guidance on this matter has always been that as long as only configuration/customizing tables are being logged, and a reasonable purging/archiving strategy is used for DBTABLOG, logging should not have any discernible impact on performance or disk space consumption. SAP ERP ships with low-volume tables enabled for logging, and enabling such logging is unlikely to degrade performance.

Finally, recent customer experience suggests that purging (and, optionally, archiving) the DBTABLOG table about every 13 months provides customers the benefits of SAP Process Control 10.x change analysis without a noticeable impact on database size.

12.5 Summary

From the overview of CCM in Chapter 11, we explored in detail different data source and business rule types available to SAP Process Control customers. In particular, we spent a lot of time examining configurable data sources and rules, as a great convenience to SAP Process Control customers who want to quickly define monitoring rules without having to modify backend systems.

You saw how the change log check category of rules delivers very unique value to SAP customers. It offers something no competitor does, which is the ability to reconstruct past settings in a completely reliable way.

In the next chapter, we examine some advanced topics in monitoring. This includes the use of the powerful SAP NetWeaver rule engine, BRF+, the use of new ODP capabilities of SAP NetWeaver 7.3 to allow SAP BusinessObjects BI queries to run against application systems, and finally, SAP HANA-based monitoring.

This chapter covers some topics of interest to advanced users of continuous controls monitoring. Specifically, using ODP and SAP HANA data sources for monitoring is fairly new to SAP Process Control, with few customers and consultants having any experience in the area. Use of BRF+ to build complex rule logic is better known in the field but requires great care, as explained in this chapter.

13 Continuous Controls Monitoring: Advanced Topics

SAP Process Control Continuous Controls Monitoring (CCM) offers many different data types and business rule options. All of these variations add a great deal of complexity to the topic, but as we explained in Chapter 11, Section 11.8, approaching the topic with a clear business purpose and specific goals makes it much easier to weave through this thicket of choices. In keeping with this spirit, SAP added two new features to CCM since the release of SAP Process Control 10.0: Operational Data Provider (ODP)-based monitoring (late in the 10.0 release cycle), and SAP HANA-based monitoring (new in release 10.1). We describe ODP-based monitoring in the next section, and cover SAP HANA-based monitoring in Section 13.2.

As we mentioned in Chapter 11 and Chapter 12, CCM leverages the SAP NetWeaver Business Rules Framework Plus (BRF+) rule engine to provide great flexibility to SAP Process Control users in defining monitoring rules. BRF+ is useful because it lets SAP Process Control users define rule logic that would otherwise need to be encoded in ABAP or SQL. BRF+ rules can be configured interactively by SAP Process Control users, tested, and put into production without requiring any updates to production systems. The use of BRF+ in SAP Process Control CCM is covered in Section 13.3.

13.1 Operational Data Provider (ODP) Rules

ODP is a SAP NetWeaver feature available from SAP NetWeaver release 7.31 onward. It responds to the fact that while business intelligence and analytics topics are very popular with SAP customers, the overhead of a separate business warehouse system is often not warranted. ODP enables business intelligence tools, such as SAP Business Explorer (SAP BEx) Query Designer, SAP Visual Intelligence, SAP Crystal Reports, SAP BusinessObjects Web Intelligence (WebI), and so on, to connect directly to application systems. The old BW extractors, which previously had to literally extract data out of application databases and move it to business warehouse systems, can now be enabled to operate in-place in the SAP NetWeaver stack of application systems. Business intelligence tools can then connect to this ODP layer of SAP NetWeaver to carry out analytics.

SAP NetWeaver BW queries

SAP Process Control 10.1 (actually, starting with service pack 3 of SAP Process Control 10.0) can connect to monitored systems' ODP layers to run SAP NetWeaver BW queries for monitoring purposes. Of course, such SAP NetWeaver BW queries have to be defined first, using the same tools as described in Chapter 12. Once defined, users should create data sources of the BW QUERY type, now pointing the data source to the monitored system directly, instead of to a SAP NetWeaver BW system.

In recent years, SAP has made a strong strategic commitment to the SAP HANA database architecture. Apart from the many advantages SAP HANA offers SAP customers, there are some unique benefits CCM customers can derive from the SAP HANA platform, which we describe next.

13.2 SAP HANA

This discussion includes functional SAP ERP versions running on SAP HANA databases and also SAP ERP data replicated to SAP HANA as an analytics platform.

Given the excitement and strategic emphasis SAP has placed on SAP HANA, it's unlikely that any SAP customer is unaware of SAP HANA. Briefly, then, SAP HANA is a new database type that stores data in a hybrid form between traditional relational database forms and analytic database forms. Contents of each column of data are effectively indexed, which leads to significant compression. This enables the database server to hold large portions of all of the data in RAM, leading to an enormous speed up in processing times. It also enables processing of large amounts of data interactively.

CCM can benefit from these advances because many CCM customers have found their use of CCM limited by performance. Identifying duplicate invoice payments, for instance, is a high-value monitoring scenario for many customers. But to be effective, it needs to run against many months of data and across many organizational divisions. Many customers' use of this monitoring rule has been limited not by their ambitions but by performance constraints, and SAP HANA can help there.

Similar to SAP Query scenarios, monitoring from SAP HANA requires the customer to first build a *calculation view* on SAP HANA. At its essence, this is a query, and SAP HANA Studio is the preferred tool.

SAP HANA Studio

Figure 13.1 shows a calculation view in SAP HANA Studio. This view can be seen in the PROCESS CONTROL DATA SOURCE creation wizard, by first choosing a SAP HANA system connector, and then looking up calculation views. The steps are perfectly analogous to the ones shown in Chapter 11, Section 11.3 for SAP Query data sources, so we avoid needless repetition here, and show only the actual lookup of the SAP HANA calculation view in Figure 13.2.

As Figure 13.2 shows, wild cards can be used for looking up SAP HANA views. All other steps are exactly the same as for SAP Query data sources shown in Chapter 11.

Business rule creation based on SAP HANA

The next step in CCM content creation (see Chapter 11, Section 11.4) is creating a business rule based on the SAP HANA data source. This step diverges even less from the SAP Query business rule creation steps shown in Section 11.4, so we skip showing the details here.

The next section applies to most data source types and greatly extends the power of SAP Process Control monitoring rules by using the SAP NetWeaver standard rule engine, BRF+.

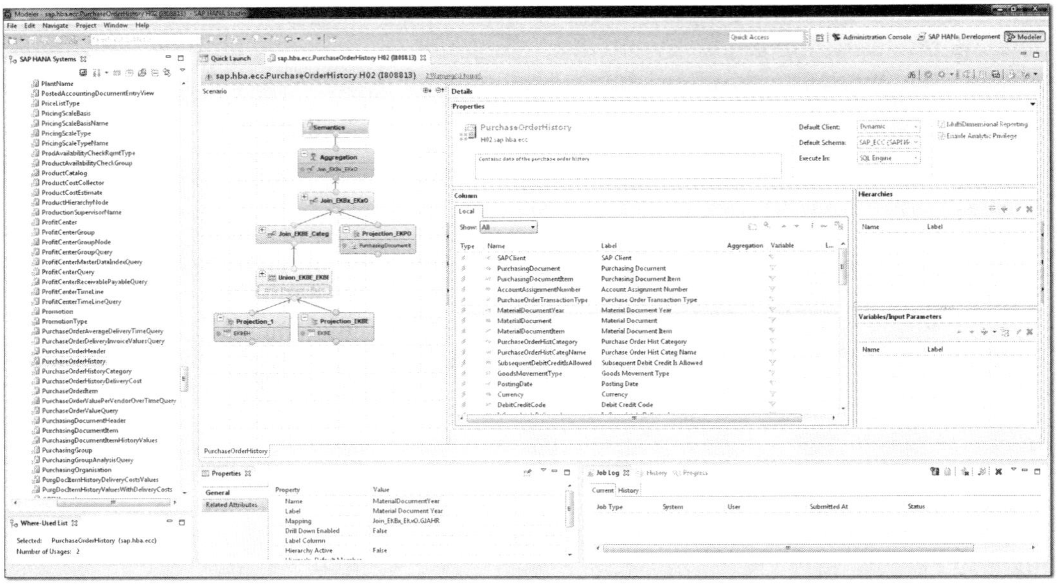

Figure 13.1 Calculation View in SAP HANA Studio

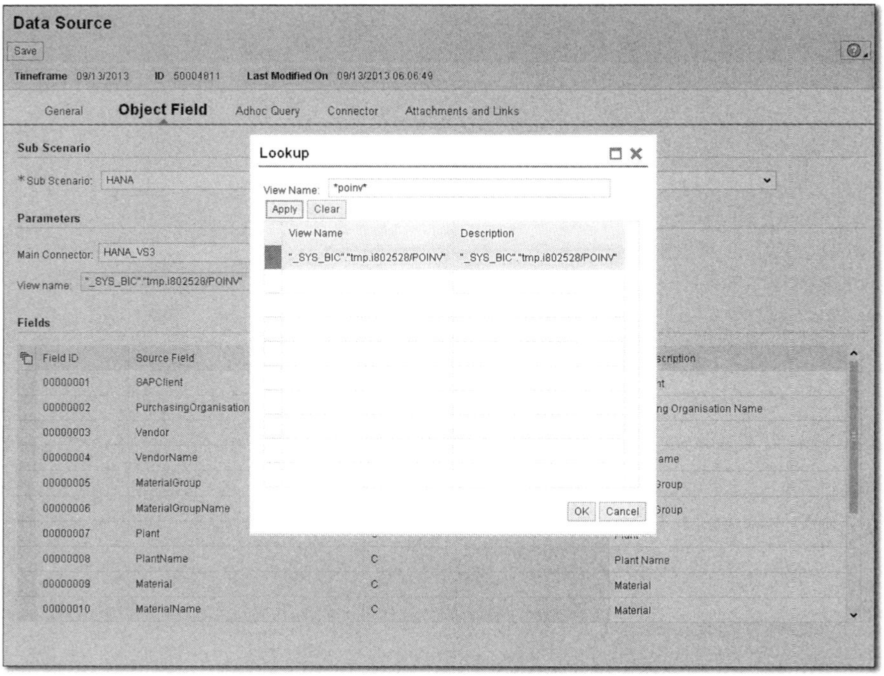

Figure 13.2 Creating a SAP HANA Data Source

13.3 Using SAP NetWeaver BRF+ to Build Advanced Rules

As mentioned before, SAP Process Control 10.1 uses the SAP NetWeaver standard rule engine, BRF+, to allow users to configure business rule logic. BRF+ itself is a very powerful rules engine, and comes with its own user interface (UI). Anticipating a few common scenarios for typical use of BRF+ in CCM, though, the SAP Process Control team created a simplified interface for it. This section first explains how to use the simple interface and then introduces the BRF+ Workbench.

13.3.1 Using BRF+ Rules in SAP Process Control Business Rules

The native SAP Process Control rule engine is very simple, in that it only supports logical expressions with a single field and only literal values with which to compare the field's values. For anything more complex—for instance, to compare the values of one field against another or to take a difference—you have to use BRF+. To illustrate the process, let's create a rule that detects when an invoice was entered before its corresponding purchase order (PO) was created.

SAP Process Control provides only one mechanism to invoke BRF+ from CCM: the CALCULATED FIELD button, as shown in Figure 13.3.

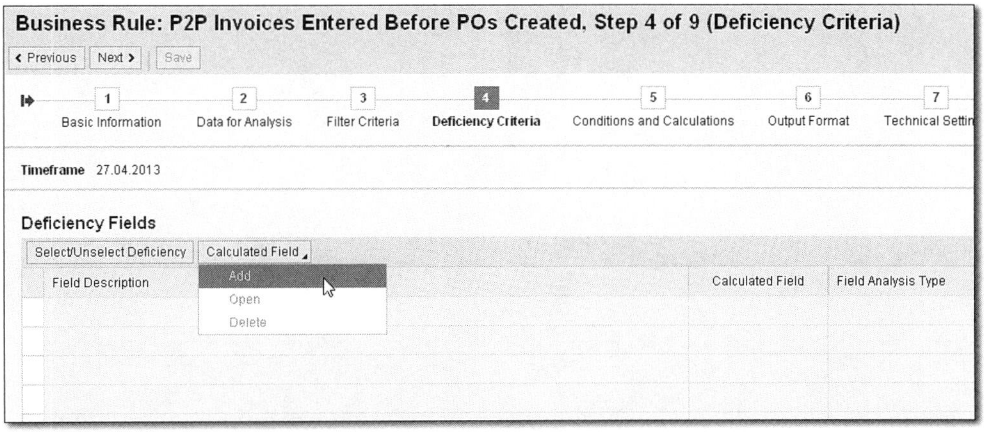

Figure 13.3 Adding Calculated Fields to Use the BRF+ Rule Engine

When you name the calculated field, keep in mind that this also becomes the name of the deficiency. In this example, choose to make it a Boolean-valued field, although other possibilities also exist: currency amounts, numbers, or text, as shown in Figure 13.4.

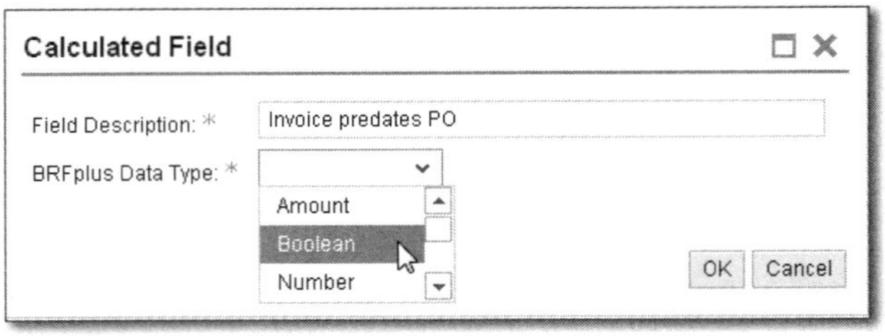

Figure 13.4 Defining the Calculated Field Name and Type

To define the calculation so that the invoice predates the PO, the calculated field takes the Boolean value "True." In ABAP, this is actually the literal X, as shown in the lower-right corner of Figure 13.5 (see arrow).

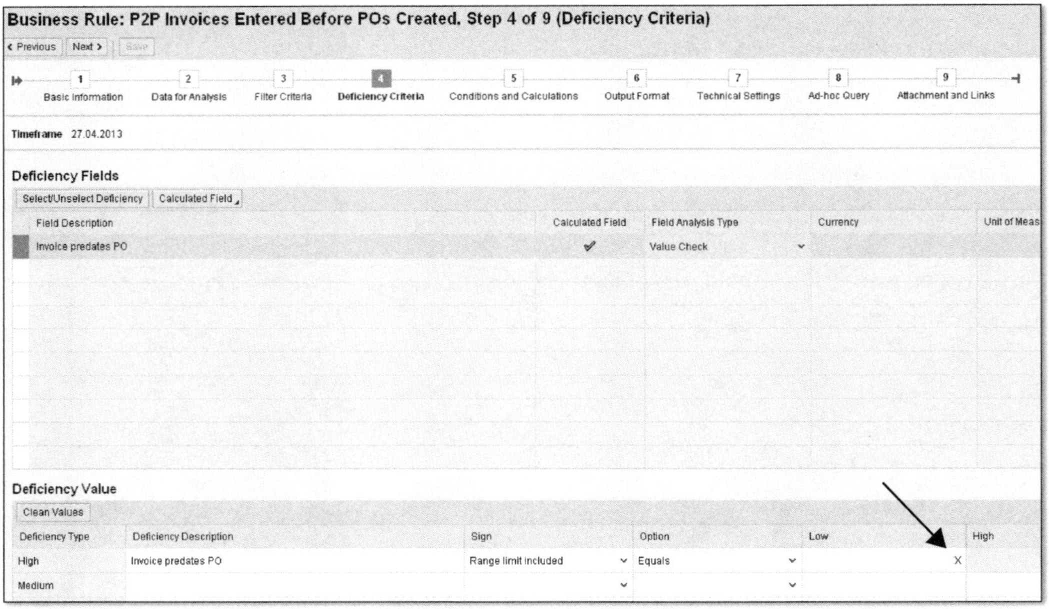

Figure 13.5 Calculated Field Deficiency Condition

Purpose of BRF+ and SAP Process Control

Of course, you still need to define the actual calculation, which you do in the next step. First, note that SAP Process Control leverages BRF+ for two purposes: to further filter the data returned by the data source, and to actually calculate the deficiency.

BRF+ filters

Additional filters defined in BRF+ might be needed (for instance) if the filter logic to be applied used conditions that the underlying data source doesn't support. Such situations can be easy to encounter because data source filtering doesn't allow conditions that compare fields to each other, for example. Figure 13.6 shows how to add additional filters, although you won't actually configure one in this example.

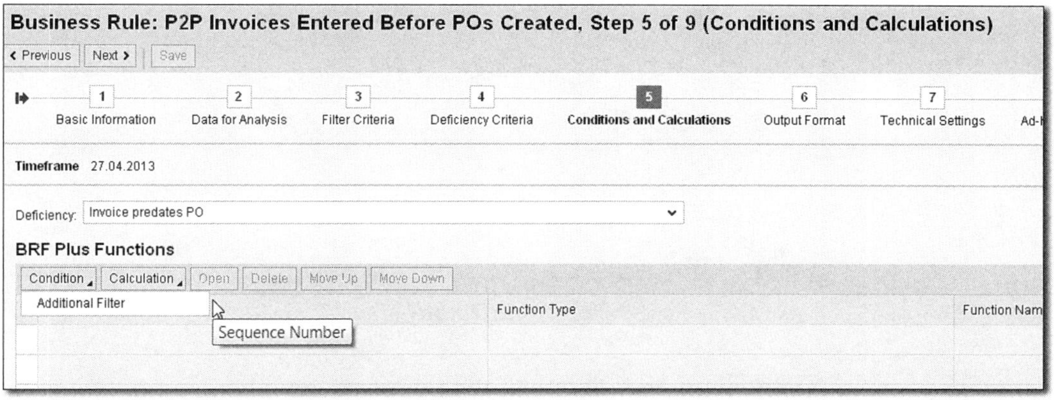

Figure 13.6 Additional BRF+ Filters

The CALCULATION button found in the BUSINESS RULE Screen, CONDITIONS AND CALCULATIONS Tab, shown in Figure 13.6, is the means of defining the actual deficiency calculation. The result of the operations defined there is assigned to the calculated field you defined earlier. Figure 13.7 shows that there are two types of calculations on offer: FIELD VALUE CALCULATION and GROUPING/AGGREGATION. We defer discussion of GROUPING/AGGREGATION to the next section, and use the current example to illustrate FIELD VALUE CALCULATION.

Choosing the FIELD VALUE CALCULATION menu option brings up the simplified SAP Process Control Expression Builder, as shown in Figure 13.8.

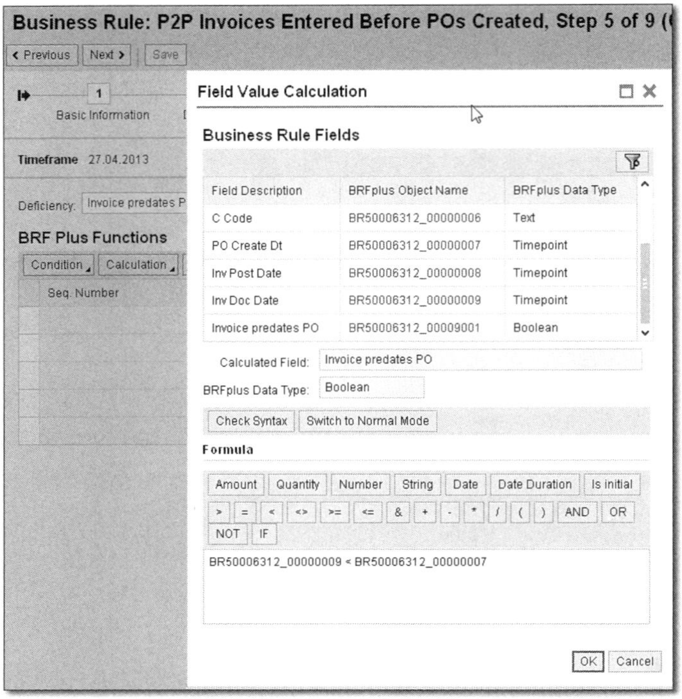

Figure 13.7 Adding Deficiency Calculation

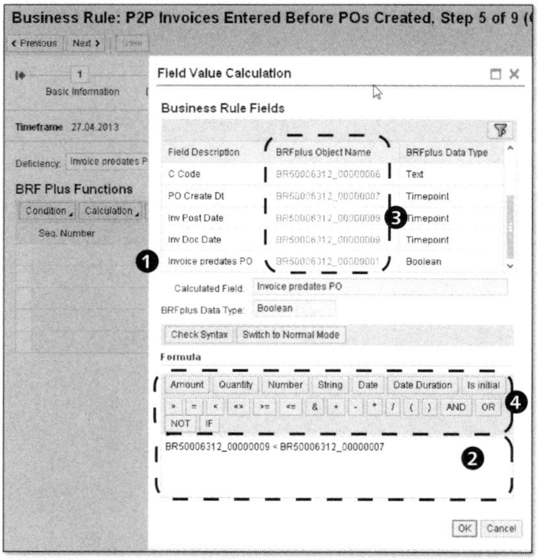

Figure 13.8 Calculated Field Expression Builder

Expression Builder key business rule fields

Each of the fields available to the rule is shown in the table display in the BUSINESS RULE FIELDS area, including the calculated deficiency field itself, INVOICE PREDATES PO ❶ (more on that later). The bottom of the figure is the expression area ❷. Although you can type into this text box, users are strongly advised to avoid this until they have gained some experience with BRF+—the expression parser is extremely sensitive to syntax, including the use of spaces. Initially, at least, it's much safer to build your expression by clicking on the BRF+ object names displayed in the second column of the table at the top ❸, and the arithmetic and Boolean operators in the ribbon above the text box ❹.

In our example, shown in Figure 13.9, the calculated field, INVOICE PREDATES PO, is now defined to evaluate to TRUE when the invoice document date is earlier than ("<") the PO create date.

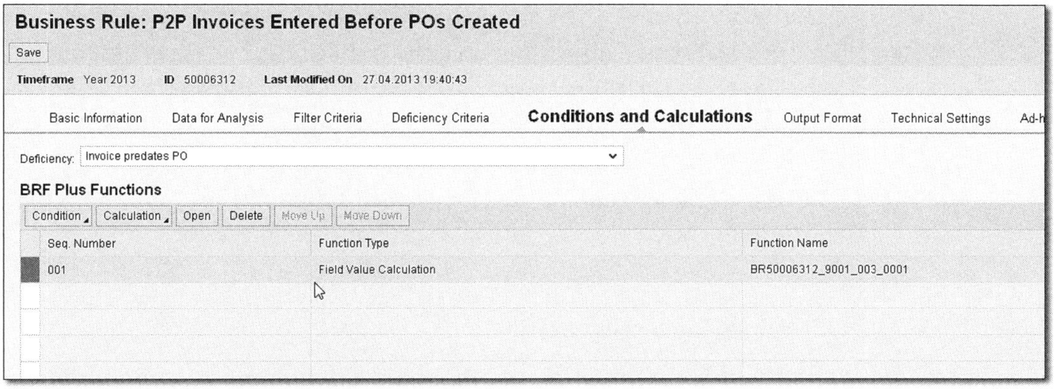

Figure 13.9 Calculated Field Fully Defined

Save the rule (a good defensive measure), and then reopen it to test it via an ad hoc query, as shown in Figure 13.10.

This completes the example of creating simple BRF+ rules. We next discuss a few additional features glimpsed along the way.

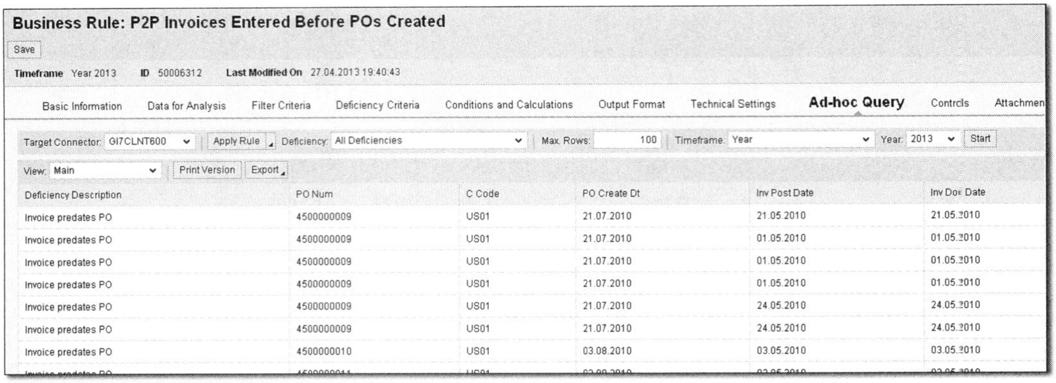

Figure 13.10 Ad Hoc Query Results for Calculated Deficiency Field

13.3.2 Additional Features of BRF+ and SAP Process Control

In the advance use of CCM and SAP Process Control, there are a few more additional features that may be of business benefit. These include the support of multiple calculation steps, SAP Expression Builder, and the system integration of Process Control Rules and the BRF+. We will look at how these additional features can improve the function of CCM but also look at some of the constraints. First, let's review the multiple calculation steps functionality.

Multiple Calculation Steps

SAP Process Control's use of BRF+ supports multiple calculation steps, as hinted at by the SEQ. NUMBER column of Figure 13.9. Additional calculation steps can be created by clicking the CALCULATION button and going through the process again. Selecting a particular step and clicking the MOVE UP/MOVE DOWN buttons will reorder the steps of the sequence.

One caveat to note here is that at every step of the sequence, the results are assigned to the calculated field (INVOICE PREDATES PO, in our example, labeled ❷ in Figure 13.8). This imposes a significant constraint because it means that the results of each step must yield an expression of the same type as the ultimate result. This is illustrated a bit later in Section 13.4.

SAP Process Control Expression Builder Limits Access to BRF+ Functionality

The SAP Process Control Expression Builder shown in Figure 13.8 only offers the usual arithmetic and logical operators, as well as the ability to type in string, date, and number literals. The BRF+ engine offers many more features, with much greater computational power. But for that, users have to use the BRF+ Workbench, as explained later in Section 13.5.

SAP Process Control Uses BRF+ in SAP Process Control System

Although not necessarily obvious, the BRF+ engine SAP Process Control uses to perform rule calculations exists in the same system as SAP Process Control. This relieves one concern but raises another. Complex BRF+ evaluations won't load the monitored system, but unnecessary reliance on BRF+ additional filters will increase the volume of data transferred over the network from the monitored system to SAP Process Control. Users are advised to use the regular SAP Process Control filters (step 3 in the rule definition process fully described in Chapter 11, Section 11.4) as much as possible to reduce network traffic.

The previous section explained how to create rules that use BRF+ to calculate deficiencies, and mentioned that BRF+ can also be used to define additional filters. We deferred discussion of grouping and aggregation, to which we turn next.

13.4 Advanced Rule Logic: Grouping, Aggregation, and Currency Conversion

Monitoring logic often requires the grouping together of related data rows; for instance, multiple payments to a vendor, sales made by a sales representative, purchases made by a single cost center, and so on might need to be assessed in their aggregate amounts, rather than individually by each instance. If you're familiar with SQL, you'll immediately understand the analogy to the "group-by" clause.

To illustrate, let's use the example of payments made to one-time vendors. SAP Purchasing allows one-time vendors to be created with minimal overhead; many customers use this feature for efficiency but impose strict limits on its use to avoid abuse.

In our example, let's create a rule to examine one-time vendor payments in two different ways: how many payments are made in a time period, and the total amount paid to a single one-time vendor. First you define the calculated deficiency field that will hold the total paid to a one-time vendor, as shown in Figure 13.11.

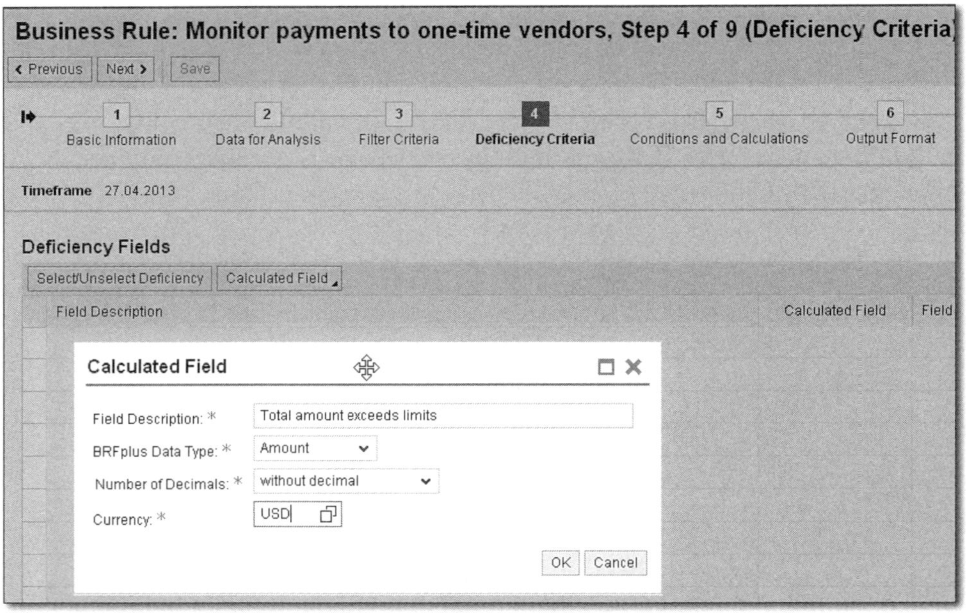

Figure 13.11 Calculated Field for Total Payment Amount

Calculated fields to hold separate payments to single vendors

Next you add another calculated field to hold the number of separate payments made to a single one-time vendor, as shown in Figure 13.12. The BRFPLUS DATA TYPE field refers to the data type of the result of the calculation (yet to be) defined. Choose NUMBER because the result of the calculation will, in fact, be a number. Other options available are AMOUNTS, BOOLEANS, and STRINGS.

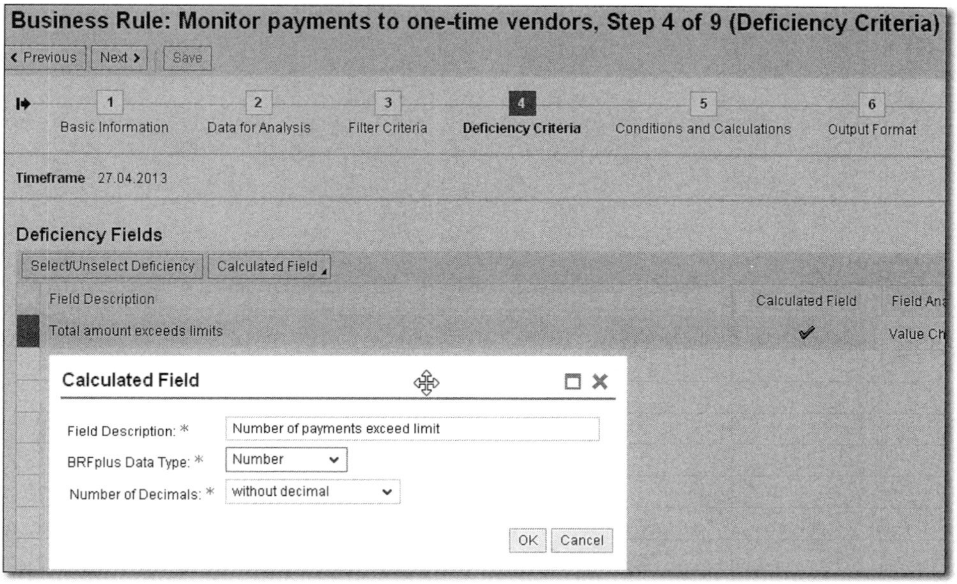

Figure 13.12 Calculated Field for Number of Payments

Currency setting and conversion

Because the first deficiency criterion involves an amount, you'll have noted that in Figure 13.11, we had to pick a particular currency, which we set to US Dollars. Because payments will, in general, occur in many currencies, it's necessary to first convert them all to one (USD, in our example), so they become comparable. Currency conversion uses Basis standard facilities and is defined in three steps. To convert a currency, follow these steps:

1. As shown in Figure 13.13, choose CURRENCY CONVERSION. This uses standard Basis currency conversion facilities, and offers you a choice of methods to decide which date to use in looking up exchange rates (see Figure 13.14).
2. Choose the original field, AMOUNT as the source of unconverted amounts.
3. Choose the clearance date from the document (CLR DT) as the reference date to use for exchange rates. Note the other choices available for dates here: BY USER INPUT DATE, BY DATE FIELD, and DETERMINED DURING EXECUTION TIME.

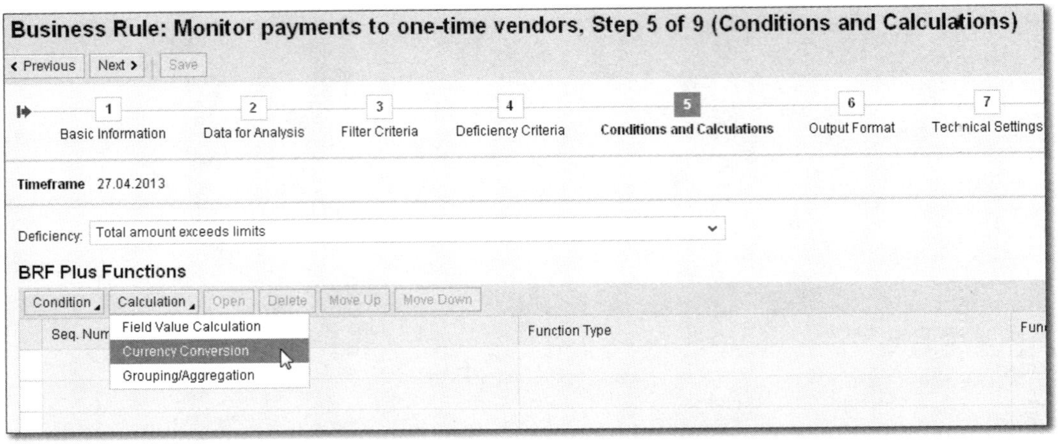

Figure 13.13 Defining Currency Conversion: Step 1

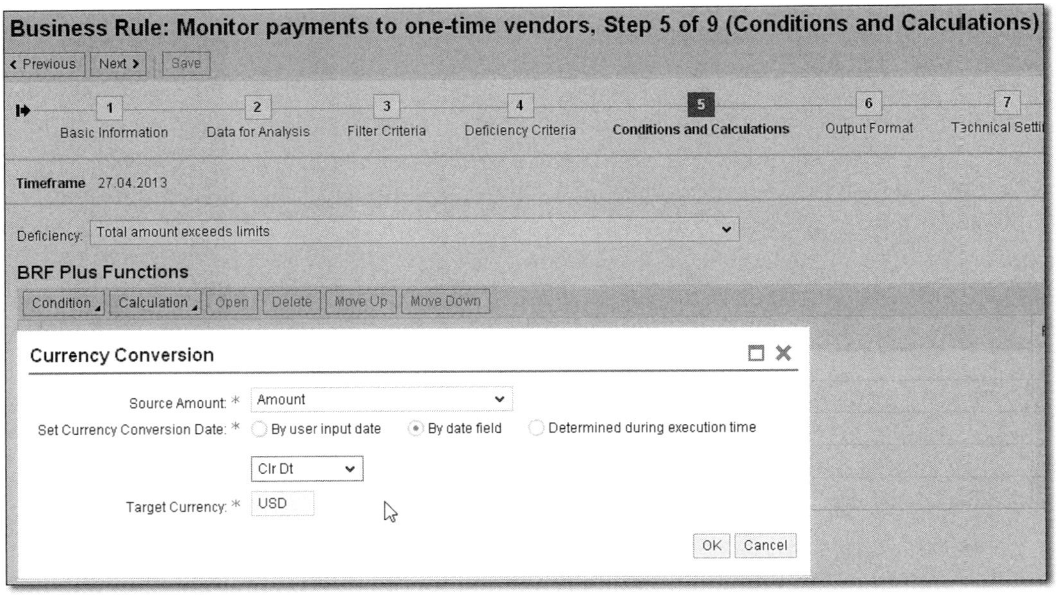

Figure 13.14 Defining Currency Conversion: Step 2

Grouping multiple currencies

Having converted amounts to a single currency, it's now meaningful to add them together. We recognize, of course, that a single vendor is unlikely to be paid in multiple currencies. But the deficiency condition defined earlier can only be expressed in a specific currency, so it's essential to convert all amounts to that reference currency.

After converting to a single currency, we next want to group by the vendor number field, summing up the payments for each vendor. Choose GROUPING/AGGREGATION as shown in Figure 13.15 to kick the process off.

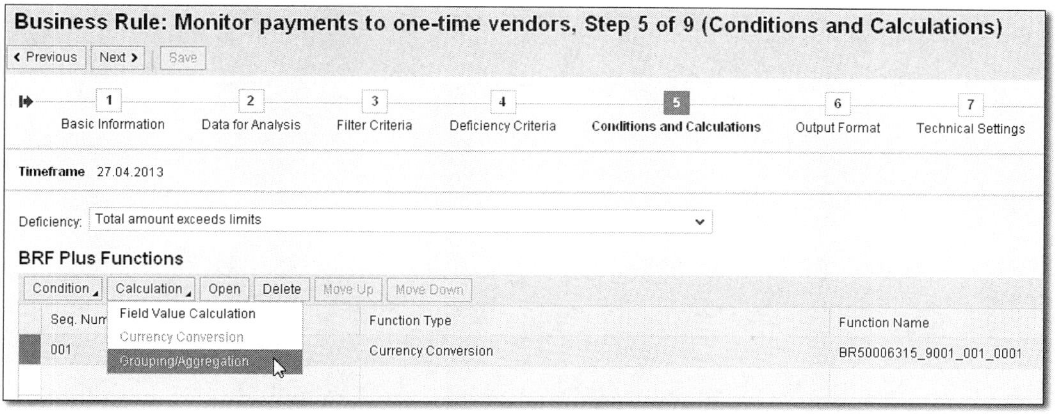

Figure 13.15 Grouping and Aggregating Amounts: Step 1

Grouping aggregation

Figure 13.16 shows the key details of the grouping aggregation. You want to collect together all data rows relevant to each one-time vendor, so use the VENDOR NUM as the field over which to group, shown in the top right of the GROUPING/AGGREGATION pop-up. The aggregation method is SUM because you want to add together the amounts.

Note

You'll note that the field to be aggregated is the deficiency field TOTAL AMOUNT EXCEEDS LIMITS, and not the original source field, AMOUNT. This is critically important to understand because this is the second step in the sequence of calculations—the first step was currency conversion. The result of that first step is stored in the calculated field, and you want to add up the converted amounts.

As noted before, SAP Process Control only allows the deficiency field in question to be the repository of BRF+ calculation results.

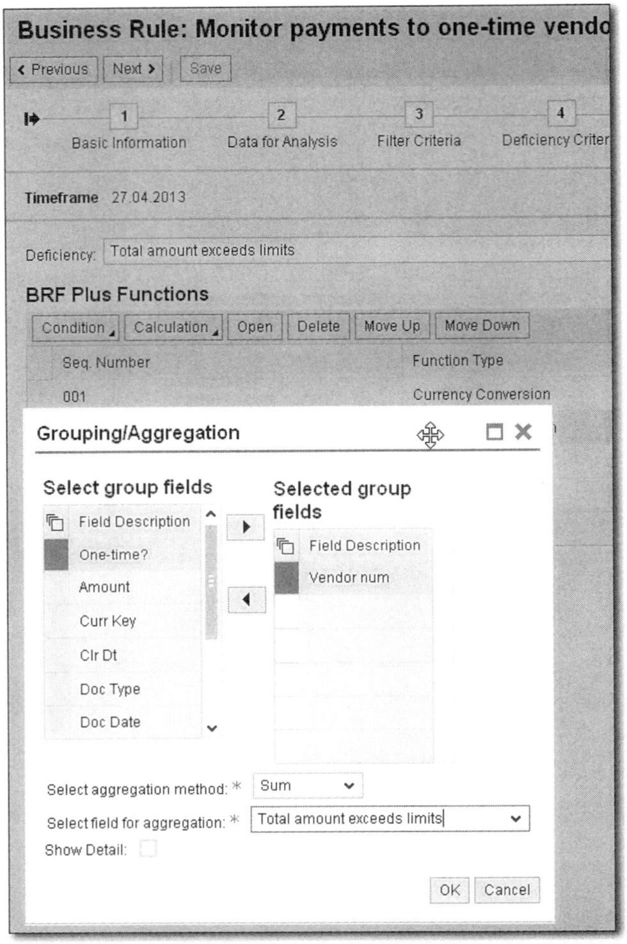

Figure 13.16 Grouping and Aggregating Amounts: Step 2

Next, you define the other calculation, for the number of separate payments made to each vendor. Figure 13.17 starts the process, by first switching to the NUMBER OF PAYMENTS EXCEEDS LIMIT deficiency.

Grouping by vendor number

Calculating the number of separate payments also requires grouping on the vendor number, but this time, the aggregation method to be used is COUNT. This aggregation method operates on the whole row, rather than on a specific field, as shown in Figure 13.18.

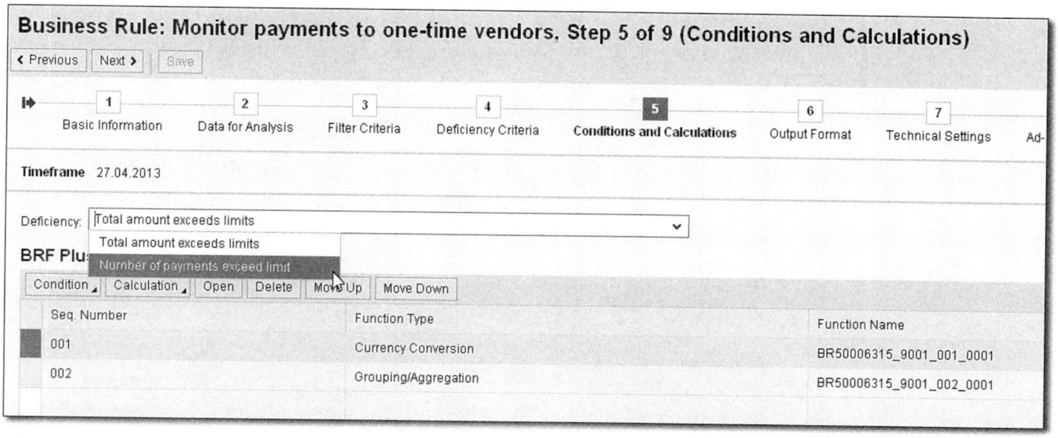

Figure 13.17 Grouping and Aggregation: Switching Deficiencies

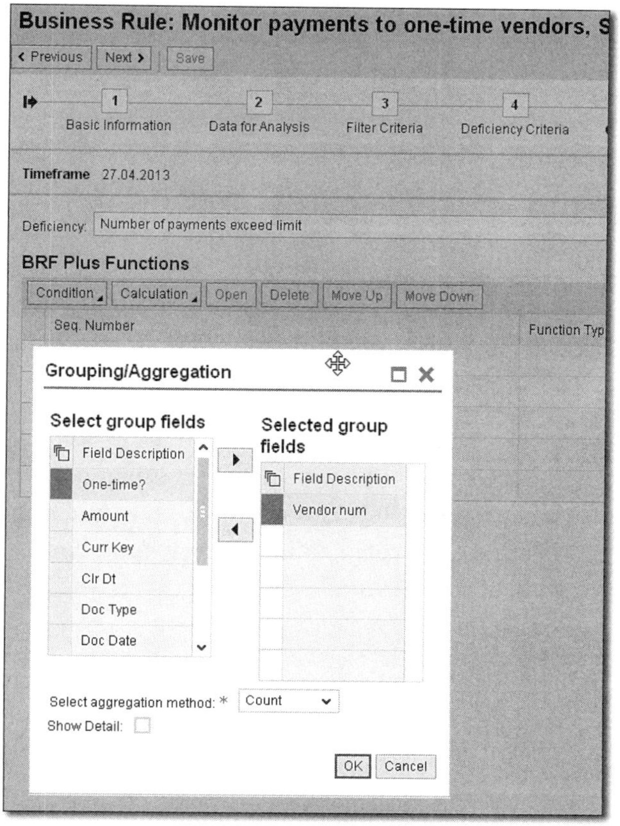

Figure 13.18 Grouping and Aggregating: Counting Number of Payments

You'll notice that Figure 13.16 and Figure 13.18 include a SHOW DETAIL checkbox, which we've left unchecked. The details this feature purports to show are the individual rows that BRF+ groups together. Because the deficiency criterion always works on an aggregated value over the entire group, it's tricky to also show the details of the grouped rows at the same time. In fact, experience has shown that showing details here can be very confusing, so you should avoid checking this box.

Note

As an aside, we recognize that this example isn't necessarily representative of how the feature is used in practice. Many customers don't create separate one-time accounts for each such vendor; instead, they create one such account, and change the vendor name and bank account to make payments to different one-time vendors. Note, however, that the concept remains the same, and you can change the data source to include bank information. You can then group data on the bank account number, for instance instead of on the vendor number.

13.5 Using the BRF+ Workbench

As mentioned earlier, BRF+ is a powerful rule engine, but SAP Process Control only presents a simplified Expression Builder natively. Nevertheless, because BRF+ is being used, you can still use that underlying power if you choose. But to do so, you have to use the *BRF+ Workbench*.

Naturally, this requires some familiarity with BRF+ itself, and it's beyond the scope of this book to describe that in any meaningful detail. But using BRF+ in the context of SAP Process Control does require some additional care, which needs to be explained here. For what follows in this section, we assume you have at least a basic familiarity with BRF+, or a willingness to explore BRF+ on your own.

BRF+ Configuration for SAP Process Control

To configure BRF+ in the Context of SAP Process Control, you'll need to follow these steps. Each of these steps will be described in detail in the following sections.

1. Create the SAP Process Control business rule, and use the CALCULATED FIELD feature to trigger the creation of a BRF+ rule.
2. Save the rule, and close the SAP Process Control UI.
3. Open the BRF+ Workbench, typically by typing "BRF+" or "BRFPlus" in the transaction code box of SAPGUI.
4. Navigate to the BRF+ rule generated by SAP Process Control for your rule from the first step. Modify the generated rule to suit your needs, and then save and activate it.
5. At all costs, ensure that SAP Process Control has generated the BRF+ rule, setting up the call mechanisms. Also make sure you don't change the parameter passing and value return mechanisms.

In more detail, the first step is to create the SAP Process Control business rule, and use the CALCULATED FIELD feature to trigger creation of a BRF+ rule. This seems a bit counter-intuitive because we've just acknowledged that with the SAP Process Control simplified Expression Builder being somewhat limited, rule designers may need to define more complex rules in the BRF+ Workbench! Nevertheless, this is a critically important first step, and the reasons are as follows.

Because CCM is a SAP Process Control-initiated action, the data source is invoked by SAP Process Control. This data is provided to BRF+ by SAP Process Control, and the mechanism of such a call is only set up if SAP Process Control knows that BRF+ is to be invoked. Again, remember that not all rules use BRF+—only those rules that create calculated fields get referred to BRF+. After BRF+ concludes its work, the results then have to be sent back to SAP Process Control, and that mechanism is also established by SAP Process Control code.

Only after SAP Process Control has set up the BRF+ invocation for each rule can users open BRF+ Workbench to use additional BRF+ features. This raises an interesting chicken-and-egg question. You only want to use the BRF+ Workbench because the SAP Process Control Expression Builder is unequal to the task, yet you have to first use SAP Process Control to create the rule!

SAP Process Control Expression Builder as way of accessing the BRF+ Workbench

The answer here is to use the SAP Process Control Expression Builder to create a simple expression temporarily. It matters very little whether the expression is even meaningful—you can simply type a literal string or number into the expression text box to first create and save the SAP Process Control rule, just to get to the BRF+ Workbench.

Process of creating a rule outside SAP Process Control

To illustrate the process, let's create a rule that is impossible to define natively in SAP Process Control. Basis security experts know that it's a recommended practice to monitor active user logins that haven't been used in a long time. The data resides in Table USR02, so you construct a data source pointing to that table. You then build a configurable rule against that data source, and add a calculated field as shown in Figure 13.19. (We're skipping the usual steps of creating a data source and then the initial steps of creating a business rule because these were well described in previous chapters.)

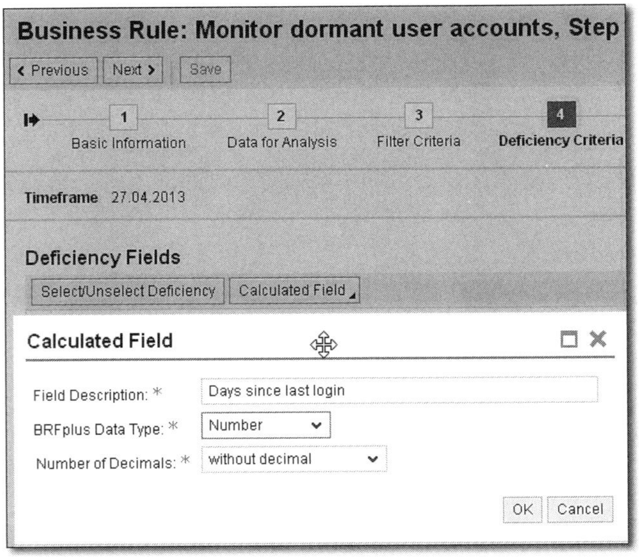

Figure 13.19 Calculated Field: Days Since Last Login

To define the calculation, bring up the SAP Process Control Expression Builder (see Figure 13.20). Notice that none of the fields are on offer for use in building the expression. This is a weakness in the SAP Process Control Expression Builder—it restricts the fields on offer depending on their type. Because the deficiency field in our example is of type NUMBER (for number of days since last login), SAP Process Control excludes dates from the available fields.

Of course, the appropriate constraint is to verify that the result of the expression matches the deficiency field type, while allowing the expression itself to include any type.

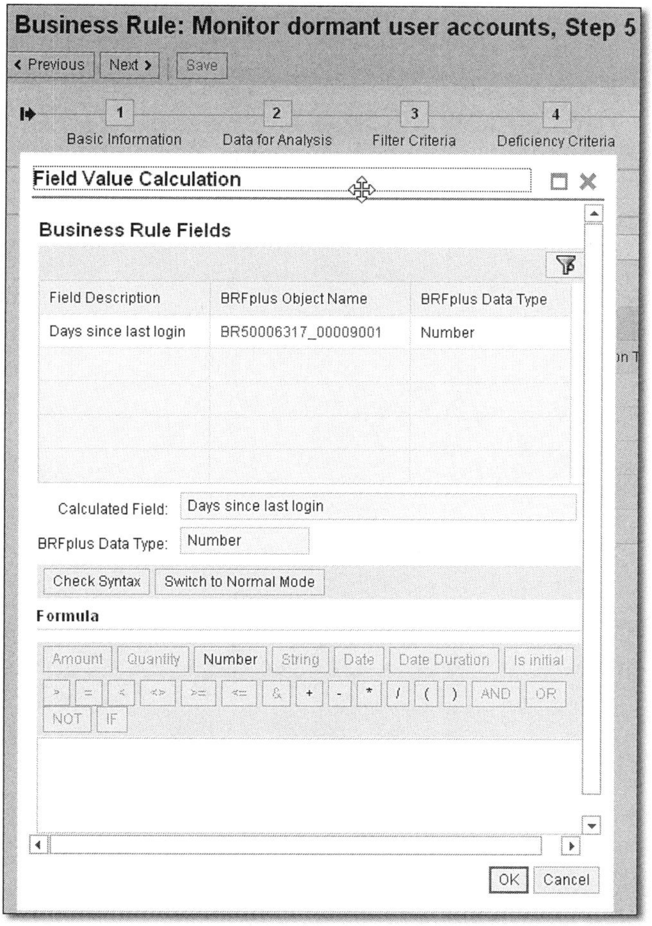

Figure 13.20 Calculated Field: Difference of Dates Can't Be Configured

The BRF+ Workbench allows you to configure this correctly. But first you have to get past this step and save the rule, so insert a temporary or placeholder value into the Expression Builder, as shown in Figure 13.21 (see the FORMULA text box, highlighted). Of course, the type of this expression must still match that of the deficiency field. In this case, it can be typed into the box; alternately, clicking the NUMBER button opens a dialog box that ensures valid numbers are entered.

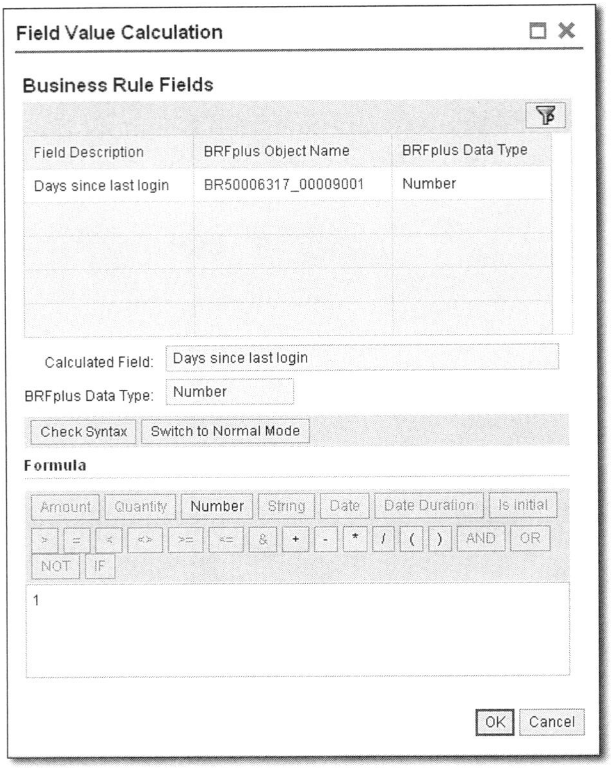

Figure 13.21 Calculated Field: Temporary Expression

Business Rule ID

Save the rule, and look for it in the BUSINESS RULE page. Note the ID of the rule, BR/50006317, as shown in Figure 13.22. This is a system-generated ID for the rule. You need to note it here because the corresponding BRF+ rule, automatically created by SAP Process Control, will have a name that includes this number.

Launching the BRF+ Workbench with your newly created business rule

Armed with this information, bring up the BRF+ Workbench. Depending on the installation, your user profile, permissions, and so on, the way to bring up BRF+ will undoubtedly vary, so keep in mind that not all of the following screens will match your experience exactly—although they should still be very close.

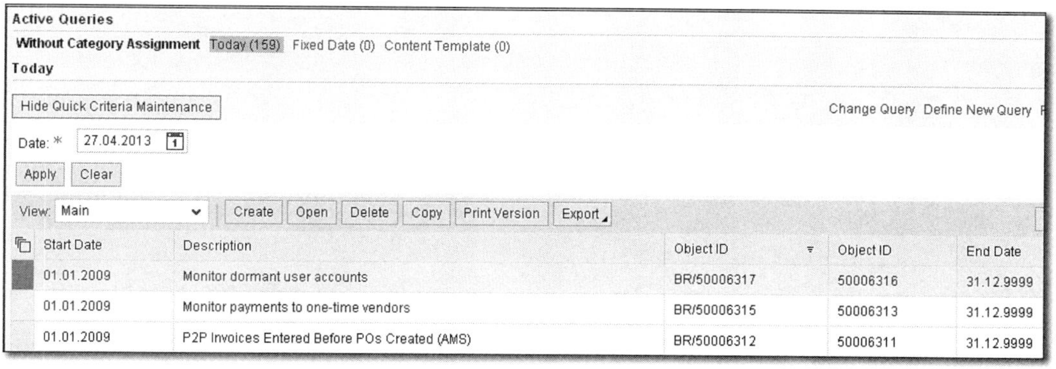

Figure 13.22 Business Rule ID

Launch the BRF+ Workbench by typing "BRF+" as the transaction code in SAPGUI, as shown in Figure 13.23.

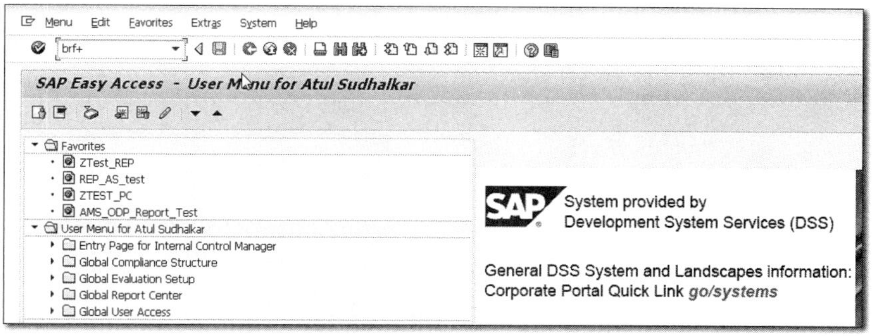

Figure 13.23 Launching BRF+ Workbench

After the workbench comes up, search for the application GRFN_AM_RUNTIME, which is the SAP Process Control runtime application into which all SAP Process Control-created rules are inserted. This is shown in Figure 13.24. Look up the list of FUNCTION objects in this application for the SAP Process Control Business Rule ID you noted previously, BR/50006317.

Open the FUNCTION (highlighted in Figure 13.24, with the name BR50006317_9001_001_001) linked to the SAP Process Control business rule (identifiable only by having the technical ID number of the rule in the function name) by clicking on the highlighted link, and then open the TOP EXPRESSION as shown in Figure 13.25.

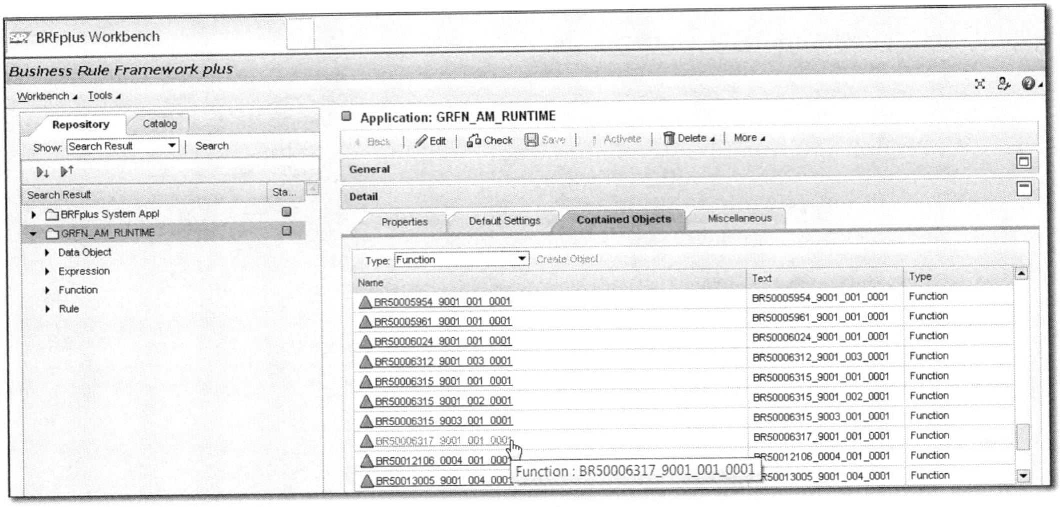

Figure 13.24 BRF+ SAP Process Control Runtime Application

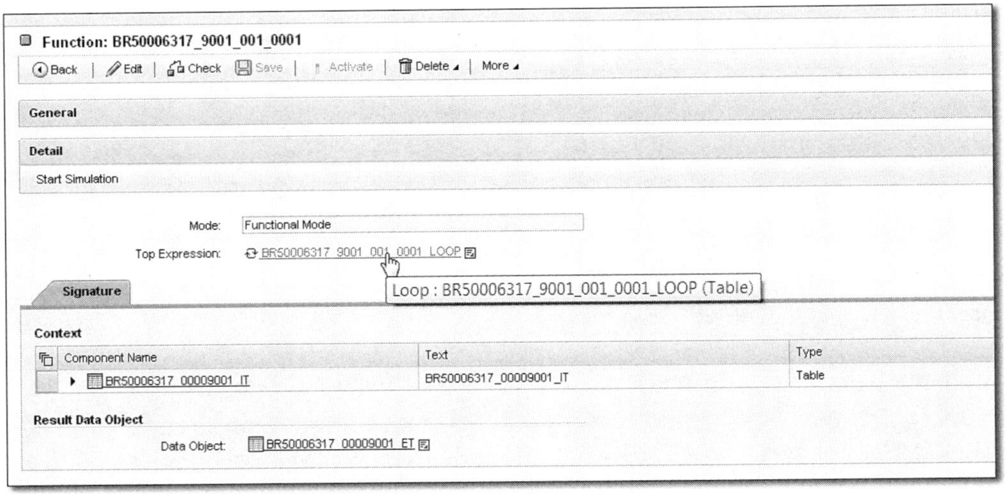

Figure 13.25 BRF+ Function

Next, open the rule referenced in the top expression by selecting the linked TOP EXPRESSION, as shown in Figure 13.25. The results are shown in Figure 13.26.

In the top expression, open the PROCESS RULE by clicking on the link under the RULES section (see bottom of Figure 13.26), which brings up the rule as shown in Figure 13.27.

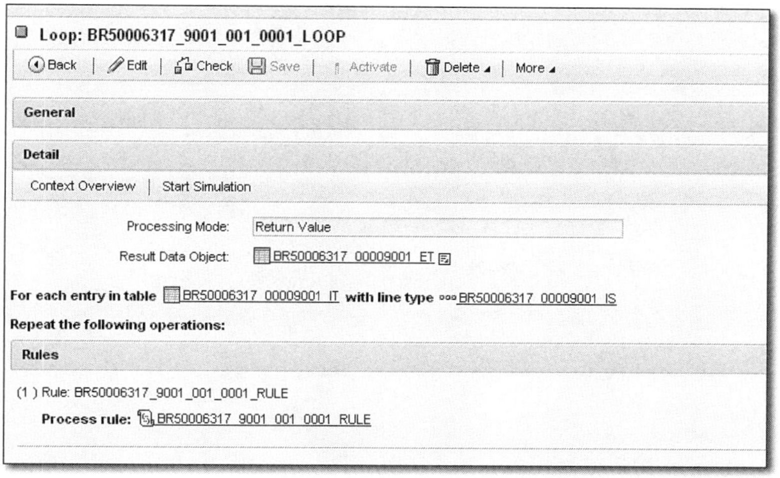

Figure 13.26 BRF+ Top Expression

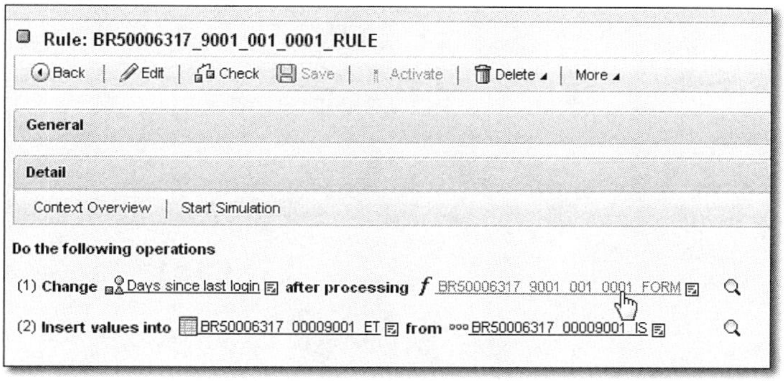

Figure 13.27 BRF+ Rule

Contained in the BRF+ RULE is the formula, which is the object you want to edit. After clicking on the formula link in Figure 13.27 (highlighted by the pointer), click the EDIT button as shown in Figure 13.28.

After you click EDIT, note that the function display expands out considerably, as shown in Figure 13.29. Also, the ACTIVATE button becomes enabled (we'll come back to this). By editing the formula in this screen, and then saving and activating the formula, you can use the full BRF+ functionality. Before proceeding with actual edits, let's discuss the components of Figure 13.29.

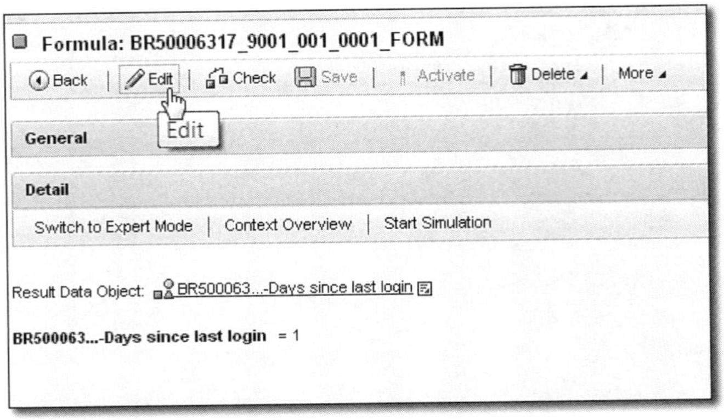

Figure 13.28 BRF+ Formula

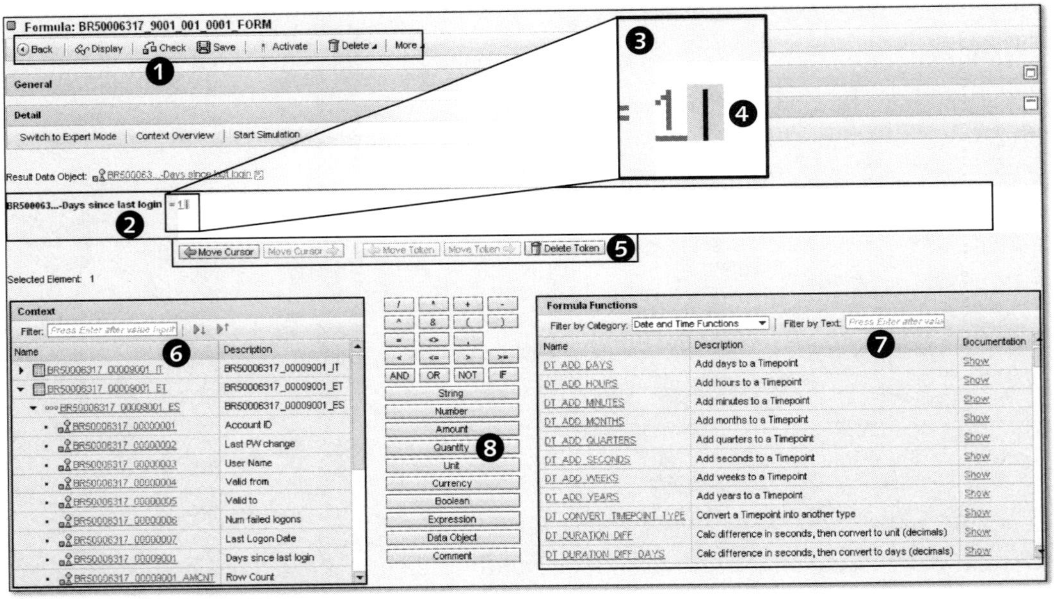

Figure 13.29 Editing BRF+ Formula

Editing a BRF+ Formula

In Figure 13.29, we've highlighted and labeled eight areas. Callout ❶ points to the control buttons ribbon at the top, which holds the EDIT, SAVE, and ACTIVATE buttons. Callout ❷ marks the actual expression being evaluated. In the screen, this is the numeral "1" shown magnified by callout ❸, as typed into the SAP Process Control business rule's simplified Expression Builder earlier in Figure 13.21. That numeral "1" ❹ in BRF+ terms is a "token" of the expression—a BRF+ expression is a sequence of tokens, literals, operators, function calls, parameters, and so on. Callout ❹ points to the BRF+ cursor—the Expression Builder is controlled by the little control buttons marked by callout ❺, the meaning of whose labels can now be understood.

Callout ❻ shows the context parameters BRF+ expects to receive from the SAP Process Control rule engine. You're restricted to using the values of these in computing your results. Callout ❼ points to the large library of BRF+ functions available. The date functions are shown here, and as the scrollbar to the right suggests, there are several screenfuls of date- and time-related functions. Finally, Callout ❽ points to the Expression Builder buttons. You can use these to build arithmetic and logical expressions of any complexity and depth, interspersing calls to BRF+ functions as desired.

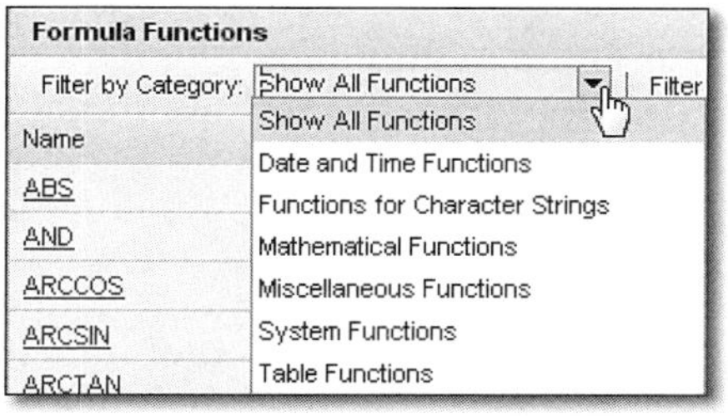

Figure 13.30 BRF+ Function Types

BRF+ Function categories

Figure 13.30 shows the many categories of functions BRF+ offers. Exploring the full capabilities is beyond the scope of this book, but Figure 13.31 shows a sample of the string-manipulation functions BRF+ offers. The EDIT_DISTANCE function is highlighted, which suggests a fuzzy-matching capability that might be of use in CCM, for instance, in finding near-duplicates in vendor or customer names, suggestive key words to search for in anti-corruption monitoring, and so on.

Two BRF+ date functions are used to define the example expression. Next, you check, save, and activate the expression. The final BRF+ expression is shown in Figure 13.32.

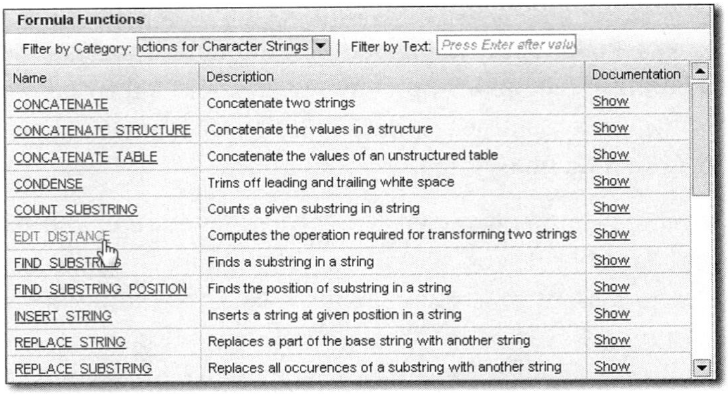

Figure 13.31 BRF+ String Functions with Edit Distance Highlighted

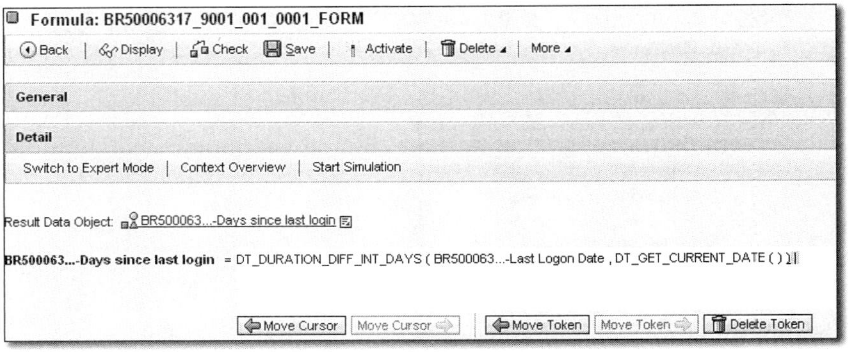

Figure 13.32 Final BRF+ Expression for Days Since Last Login

Reopen the business rule in SAP Process Control, and examine its CALCULATED FIELD definition, as shown in the SAP Process Control Expression Builder. Compare Figure 13.33 to Figure 13.21.

BRF+ rules and their interfaces

As Figure 13.21 and Figure 13.33 show, there are two interfaces to BRF+ rules, and both can be used. Traditional SAP architecture prevents simultaneous access from both interfaces, but clearly there is scope for error because of the remaining ambiguity. You should close the SAP Process Control UI before going to BRF+, and log out of BRF+ before returning to SAP Process Control. This avoids unintentional locks on the rules in both SAP Process Control and BRF+.

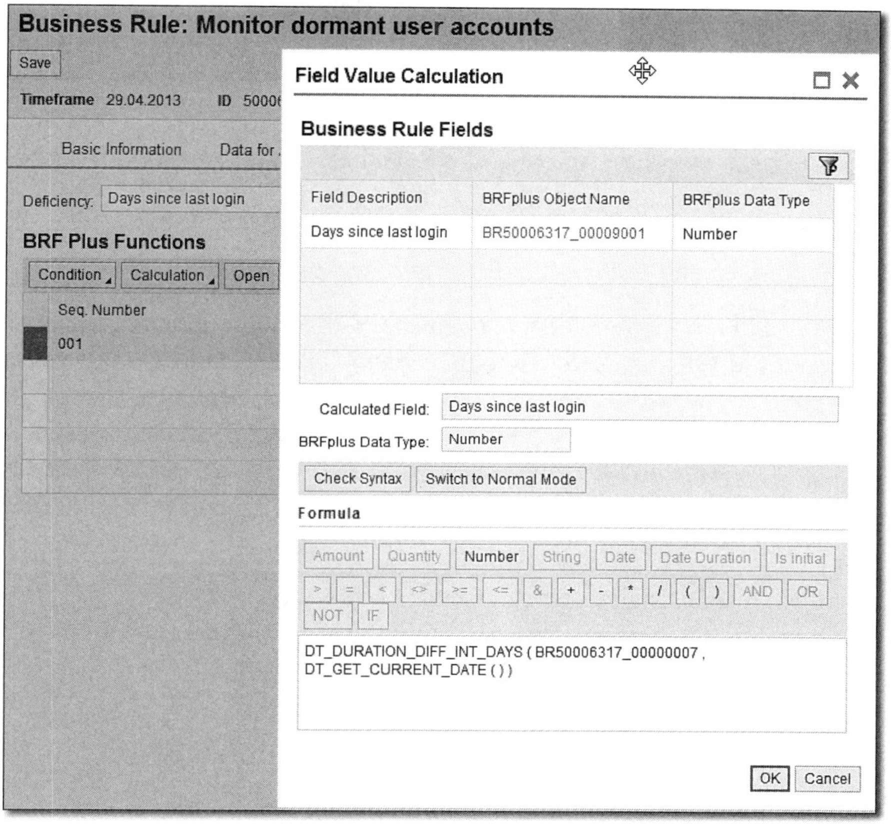

Figure 13.33 Final BRF+ Expression in SAP Process Control Expression Builder

The advantages of using BRF+ Workbench versus SAP Process Control UI for rule generation

You no doubt have noticed that using BRF+ workbench (refer to Figure 13.19 to Figure 13.24) for SAP Process Control rules is very cumbersome, so for simple expressions, the simplified SAP Process Control interface offers definite value. Unfortunately, even some simple expressions are sometimes unexpectedly difficult to build in the SAP Process Control UI. Indeed, the example we used earlier showed that a simple date difference could not be calculated in the SAP Process Control UI, for a couple of reasons. For one, when building expressions SAP Process Control restricts available data fields to those that match the type of the result; for another, the precise names and syntax of BRF+ functions may not be known to users.

When building the expression in BRF+ Workbench, we took care to stay within the framework defined by SAP Process Control. This is critically important because any changes to that framework will make at least that particular rule unusable from the SAP Process Control side. Users must never change the structure of the context variables, nor must they change any technical settings on the result type, its binding methods, and so on. They may only use the context variables on offer to build an expression and assign it to the result object in BRF+.

Still, BRF+ is a powerful rule engine, and in building SAP Process Control CCM rules, customers should certainly take advantage of the power it offers. They just need to exercise exceptional care in doing so because SAP Process Control designers assume a higher expertise bar for users of BRF+ Workbench than for the rest of SAP Process Control. So error checking and error prevention is somewhat weaker here than elsewhere in SAP Process Control.

The "pattern" analysis type of CHANGE LOG CATEGORY allows rule designers to define deficiency criteria using BRF+. In particular, this makes it possible to define deficiency conditions that span multiple fields. In lack of this, users are forced to define deficiencies using only single fields, which can be very limiting. Fortunately, the impact is mitigated by the fact that the BRF+ Workbench allows users to define any condition, across all of the fields from the underlying data source. One last advanced CCM tool that we will look at is the Content Export and Import functionality.

13.6 Continuous Control Monitoring: Content Export/Import

In Chapter 10, Section 10.6, we discussed SAP Content Lifecycle Management (CLM) and Master Data Upload Generator (MDUG), two tools available to move master data content in and out of SAP Process Control instances. But content managed by these tools has never covered all master data and specifically has never covered business rules and data sources. In release 10.0, SAP Process Control provided IMG nodes that can transport rules and data sources, but the program wasn't easy to use, and because it only transports content between SAP Process Control instances using SAP NetWeaver transports, only administrators can use it, which greatly limited its use.

With release 10.1, the SAP Process Control team made available a much easier-to-use facility to export and import CCM content. Figure 13.34 shows the SAP IMG open to the EXPORT/IMPORT DATA SOURCES AND BUSINESS RULES node, shown highlighted.

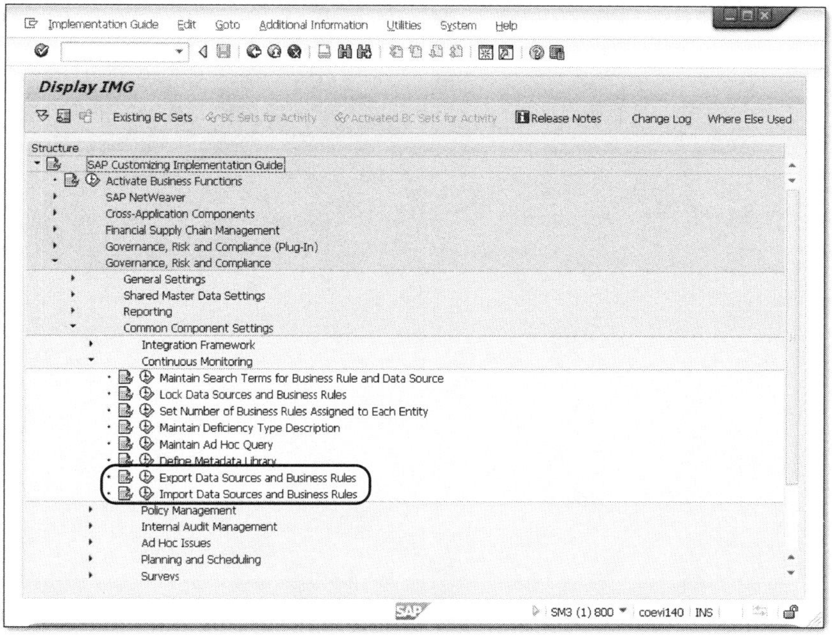

Figure 13.34 CCM Content Export and Import

Obviously, business rules depend on data sources. So exporting a business rule necessarily requires that the underlying data source also be exported with it; otherwise, the exported rule can't be guaranteed to be successfully imported into any other system.

As Figure 13.35 shows, the export facility immediately asks the user what is to be exported: business rules or data sources. Select EXPORT BUSINESS RULES WITH RELEVANT DATA SOURCES, and Figure 13.36 shows the next screen that allows you to search for content to export by multiple search criteria. Figure 13.37 and Figure 13.38 show the process completing, and Figure 13.39 shows the downloaded XML file with the exported content.

Starting the corresponding import program (the second of the highlighted nodes in Figure 13.34) brings up an import page that invites you to select a file from the local disk, as shown in Figure 13.40.

Figure 13.35 Exporting CCM Content: Business Rules and Data Sources

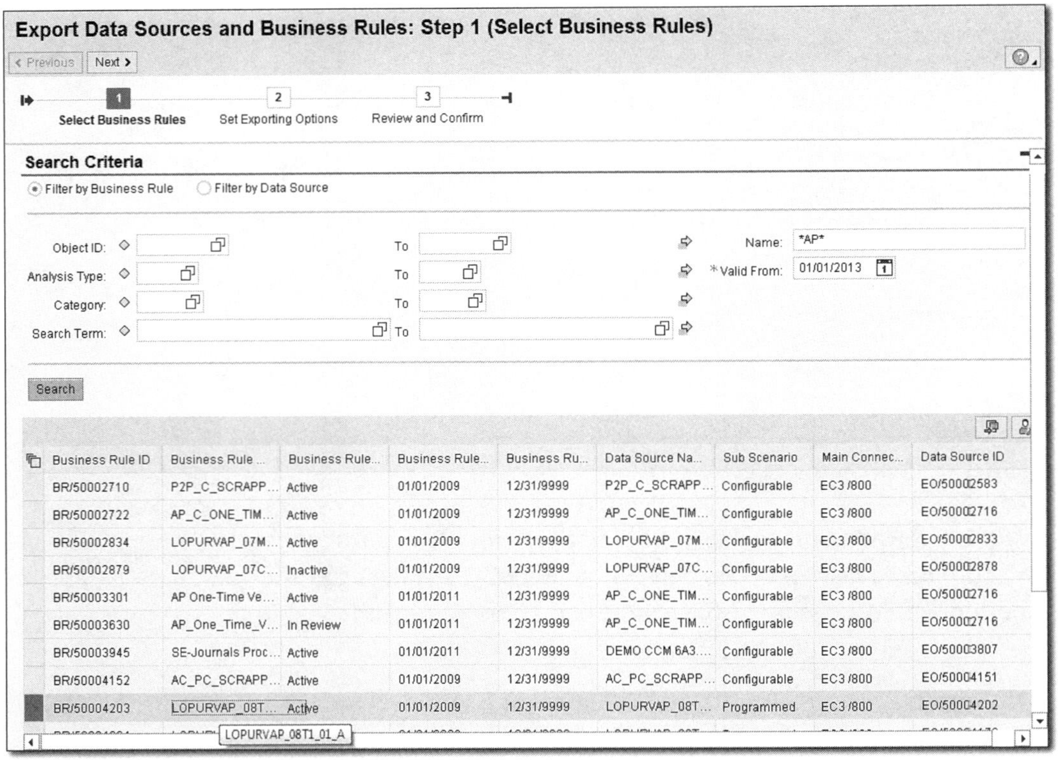

Figure 13.36 Exporting CCM Content: Search and Select

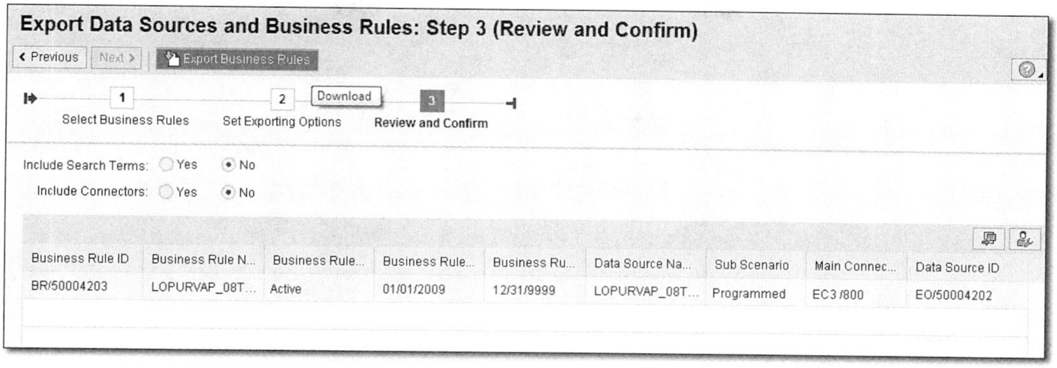

Figure 13.37 Export CCM Content: Review and Confirmation of the Export Details

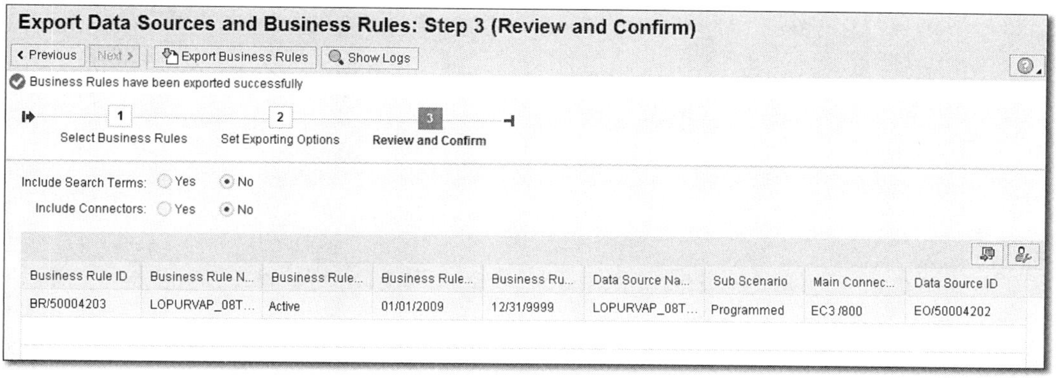

Figure 13.38 Export CCM Content: Download

Import and export considerations for SAP Process Control 10.1

There are several important points to note about the new CCM export/import in SAP Process Control 10.1:

- Only business rules, data sources, and underlying BRF+ rules can be exported and imported via this facility.
- Unlike all other methods of transporting SAP master data between systems, this CCM export/import facility relies on Globally Unique IDs (GUIDs) to keep track of CCM content across SAP Process Control instances. This makes the export/import operation safe and repeatable; that is, repeated imports won't create duplicate copies of imported content, and an inadvertent import won't lead to an unintended overwrite of a different rule with a clashing technical ID.

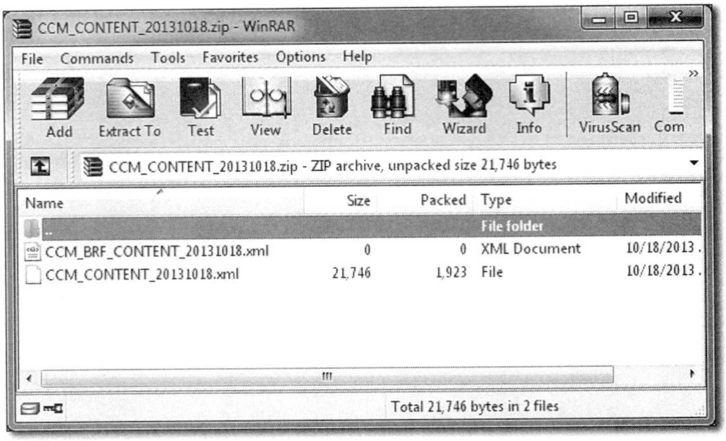

Figure 13.39 Exporting CCM Content: Downloaded XML File

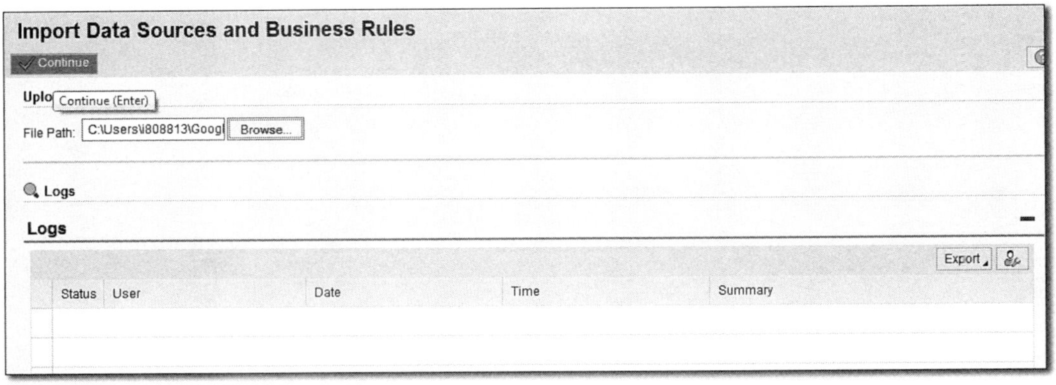

Figure 13.40 Importing CCM Content: Select XML File to Upload

- Business rules and data sources are always embedded in a host of other data: connectors, local controls, hierarchies, organization-dependent parameters (see Chapter 14), and so on. None of this related information is essential for the definition of a rule, and apart from connectors, none of it can be exported or imported. Connectors can be exported as a user-specified option. This can make sense if the source and destination SAP Process Control instance share a landscape, but otherwise not. If connectors aren't exported, then at the destination system, a new connector needs to be added to the data source. The connector being added has to be enabled for the data source type in question, but it also has to point to a compatible monitored system. In other words, a data source that originally pointed to a SAP ERP system can't suddenly now point to a SAP Customer Relationship Management (SAP CRM) system.

- Backend content isn't exported and imported. So if a data source relies on a SAP query in the backend system at which it was originally pointed, it can't after export and import now be pointed at a backend system that doesn't have that SAP query. The CCM export/import functionality only moves content on the SAP Process Control system, not necessarily content on remote (monitored) systems.

13.7 Summary

Over Chapters 11, 12, and 13, we covered all essential features of the SAP Process Control CCM framework. We covered all of the different data source types and business rule categories. We also discussed a structured approach to CCM, putting the business goals first, and then identifying the monitoring technique able to deliver results closest to those goals.

We also discussed at length the BRF+ features that SAP Process Control uses to provide some simple grouping, aggregation, currency conversion, and calculation definitions for business rules. We also showed how a skilled user can leverage the full BRF+ functionality with SAP Process Control business rules, provided some simple precautions are taken.

Finally, we discussed a new facility in SAP Process Control 10.1 to export and import business rules, related BRF+ rules, and data source definitions. This new feature was sorely needed by many customers and partners, and it should prove extremely helpful to customers in moving content across test and production systems, versioning their CCM content during implementations, and so on.

In the next chapter, we explore a few miscellaneous and advanced topics that will be of interest to customers who have a deep interest in the CCM topic and who are using CCM extensively enough to find it a challenge to manage their CCM operations efficiently.

This chapter addresses some miscellaneous topics that Continuous Controls Monitoring users will find of great interest in their planned usage of SAP Process Control for monitoring.

14 Continuous Controls Monitoring: Miscellaneous Topics

The earlier chapters introduced SAP Process Control functionality, and presented the topic of Continuous Controls Monitoring (CCM) in detail. This chapter aims to address several topics of great interest to CCM customers, although they aren't directly about CCM techniques.

Many customers get off to a quick start on their CCM practices but find that maintaining their CCM content becomes a challenge. SAP Process Control offers a few tools for better managing (reusing) common rules and data sources across many situations. Section 14.1 describes two techniques for getting the most work out of widely reusable CCM content: binding parameter values from the organizational context in which a rule executes, and binding parameter values from the date ranges for which the rule executes.

Many customers worry that wide adoption of SAP Process Control, and CCM in particular, will expose sensitive data from production systems to users of SAP Process Control, and that such exposure will be out of the oversight and control of their standard data security practices. In fact, SAP Process Control has been designed to allow customers to achieve a near-perfect match with their (backend) application's security settings for data visibility. Section 14.2 describes how customers can use SAP Process Control roles and assignments to this end.

Because we've confessed up front that this chapter discusses a miscellany of topics, we hope you'll forgive a certain lack of continuity between the major sections of this chapter.

14.1 Efficiently Managing Continuous Controls Monitoring Content

As an organization's reliance on CCM grows, so will the number of rules, the extent of their use across many organizational units and business processes, and the number of regulations and backend systems against which these are used. SAP Process Control customers quickly realize that keeping such rules updated and maintaining the monitoring schedule becomes very time-consuming and tedious.

SAP Process Control provides several means of reducing the drudgery of such maintenance, and this section provides a quick overview of these features. The main point to note is that rules, controls, and so on can and should be reused, wherever possible.

14.1.1 Data Sources

One important reason for breaking CCM content into business rules and data sources is to facilitate reuse. Data sources should be designed to be as general as possible within a functional or process area, for instance, a data source pulling in purchase order (PO) data, another for invoices as related to POs, and so on.

Data source use in business rules can be more focused because the number of fields in use can be projected down further. Then by applying suitable filters (either in the native SAP Process Control FILTER tab, or via BRF+), adding calculated fields, and using BRF+ grouping and aggregation, the business rule can implement the precise monitoring logic the customer needs.

Note that this also helps focus the more technical experts on constructing data sources, and leaves the more business-oriented process experts to craft business rules. Data source designers need to understand low-level details of SAP's Data Dictionary (DDIC), table structures, and how backend functionality maps to the underlying database persistence (i.e., which tables underlie which transactions).

Multiple Connectors for Data Sources

Where customers have more than one copy of a single SAP application (SAP ERP, SAP CRM, etc.) in production, data sources should not be copied; a single data source can be configured to run against multiple systems ("connectors" in SAP Process Control terminology), provided versions are compatible. This is illustrated in Figure 14.1.

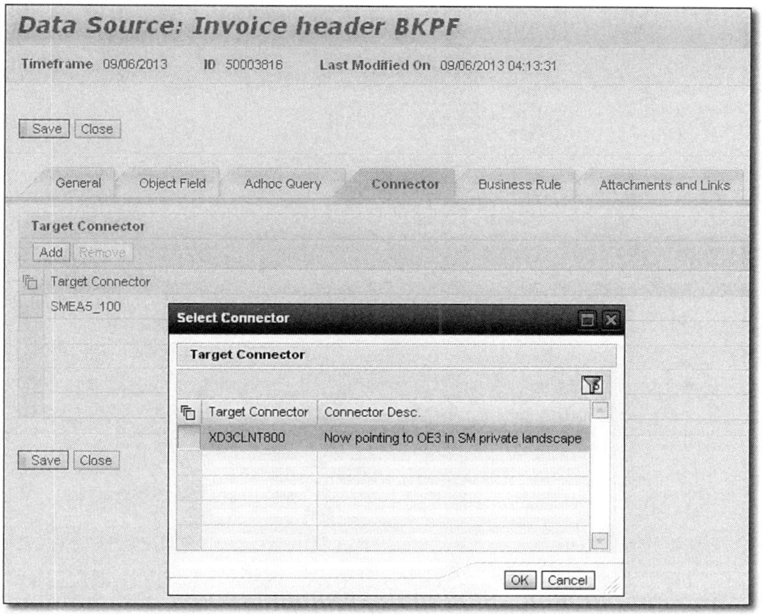

Figure 14.1 Multiple Connectors for Data Sources

In summary, remember the following when working with data sources:

- Design data sources for reuse across business rules by making them as general as possible within specific functional areas.
- Design data sources for reuse across multiple production instances of the same SAP backend application by adding additional system connectors to it, rather than make copies of the data source.

Now that we've looked at data sources, let's review business rules.

14.1.2 Business Rules

Business rules have filter and deficiency conditions (where applicable). These are obviously intended to facilitate reuse of the underlying data source in different contexts; for instance, by changing the filter condition on a company code, the same data source can be reused to monitor purchasing configuration in two different parts of the organization.

To illustrate, let's use a rule that seeks to monitor high-value payments to a vendor. The logic is simple, as shown in Figure 14.2, but the point is to create a readily understood rule that can be used to understand organizational-level system parameters (OLSP) filter conditions.

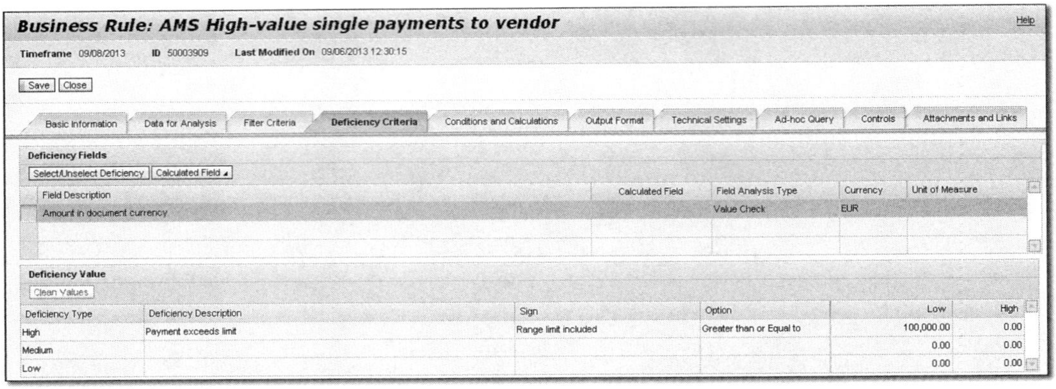

Figure 14.2 Rule Seeks High-Value Payments to Vendors

Suppose, then, that you want to apply this rule to two different organizational units; it's likely that the control owners (who will address the issues found) will be different. They may also require the rules to run on different schedules. Figure 14.3 explicitly restricts the rule to one particular company code, which suggests that you need to create copies of the rule, one for each organization.

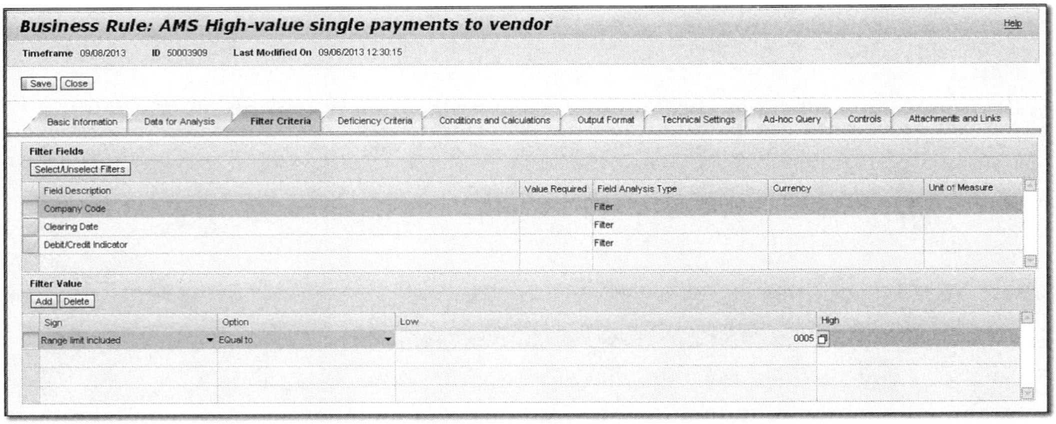

Figure 14.3 Explicit Filter Conditions in Business Rules Limiting Reuse

14.1.3 Organization-Level System Parameters (OLSP)

The OLSP page is found (somewhat unexpectedly) in the LEGACY AUTOMATED MONITORING area, on the right side of Figure 14.4. Opening that page and diving somewhat deeper shows all of the details, as captured in Figure 14.5.

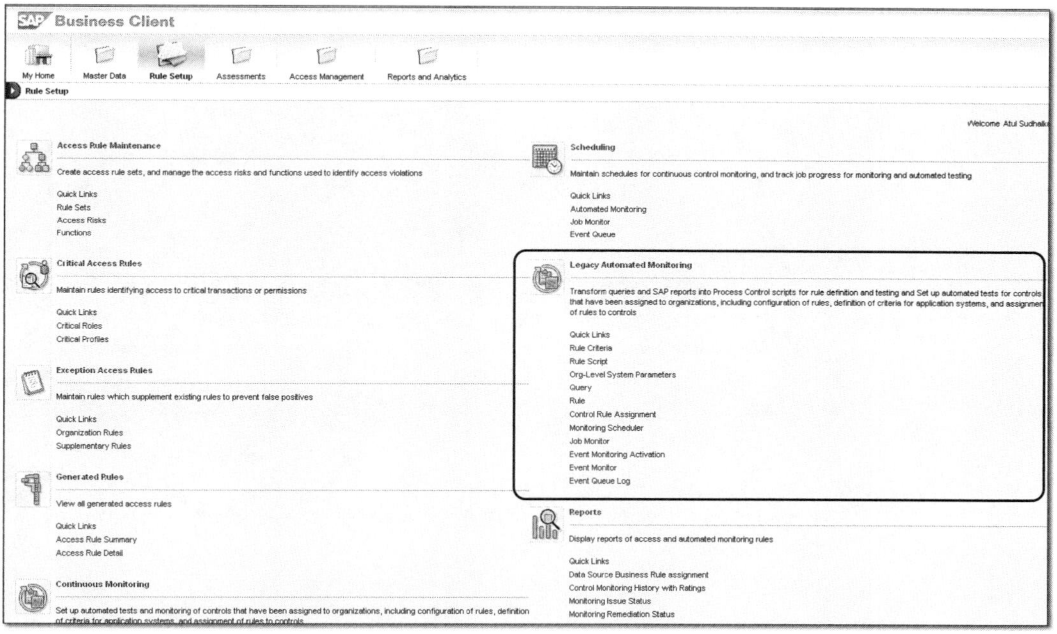

Figure 14.4 Where to Find OLSP

OLSP Conditions

Figure 14.5 shows one OLSP condition, called CRG-OLSP. Opening that set shows that OLSPs are grouped by connectors, which represent separate backend systems being monitored. For a given monitored system, SAP Process Control allows four types of rule criteria (really, filter conditions on business rules) to be defined, as shown in the figure.

In this example, we've defined the company code filter to restrict selection to company codes "between 1000 and 1001"—which suggests only two values, until you realize that, in SAP ERP, the COMPANY CODE field is actually alphanumeric, not numeric.

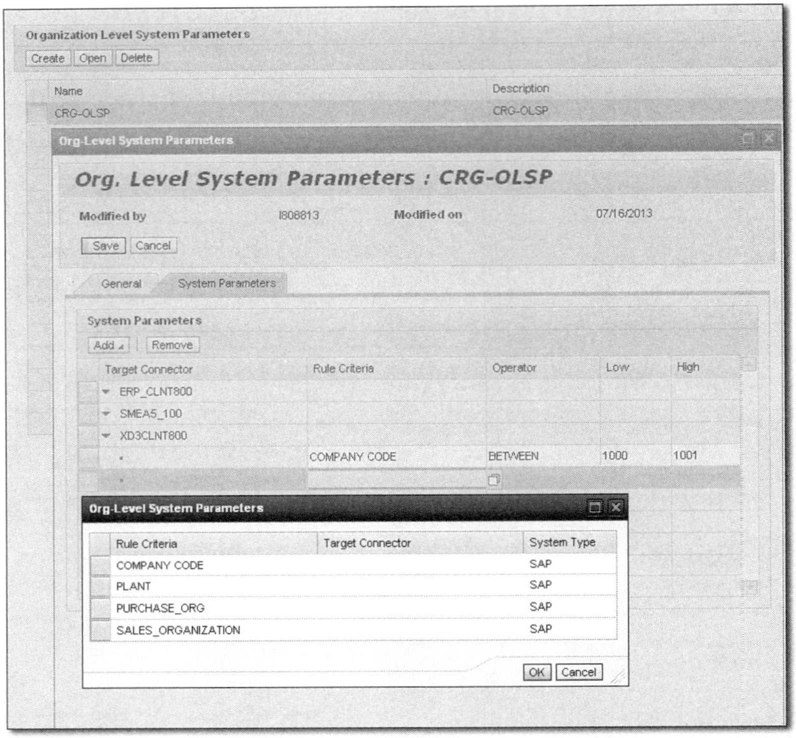

Figure 14.5 OLSP Details

Customers often ask why these particular four choices are offered, and why the list can't be expanded. The choice of company code is obviously useful and appropriate. The others were appropriate to the logistics and financial context in which SAP Process Control spent its infancy and have carried over from release to release. It certainly makes sense to allow customers to add other items as filter conditions. Equally, it would be useful to add deficiency conditions to the OLSP. In the preceding example, the threshold for considering a payment too high might vary, at least in the currency used, and very likely in the substantive limit as well. Demand for such features is growing as use of CCM grows, and SAP is committed to responding to its customers' priorities.

Binding an OLSP condition to an organizational hierarchy node

Next, we bind this OLSP condition to a specific node in the organizational hierarchy, as shown in Figure 14.6.

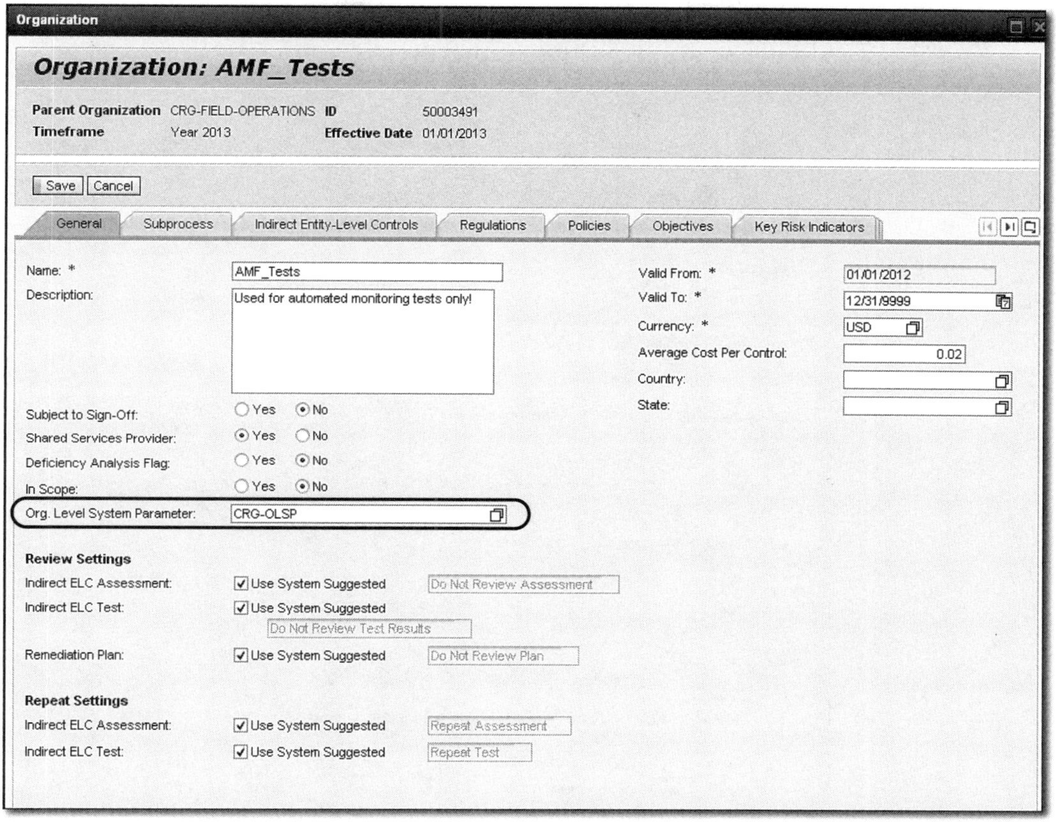

Figure 14.6 OLSP Conditions Associate with Organizational Nodes

Note that to avoid impacts to the rest of the demo system as we trace the workings of the OLSP feature, we've created a separate node reserved for CCM testing (AMF being the earlier, internal name for CCM). It pays to emphasize that OLSP conditions are separate objects, and their applicability to any particular organizational node must be explicitly specified via the OLSP attribute on the org node.

After this association is made, it then applies to every CCM rule that runs under this org unit node. We'll illustrate this by scheduling and executing the one-time vendor rule twice: once with the OLSP condition CRG-OLSP assigned to the org unit (and hence applying the company code filter), and once without.

Executing a job with an OLSP condition

Figure 14.7 shows the result of executing a job with the OLSP condition CRG-OLSP tied to the org node in question (AMF_TESTS), as shown previously.

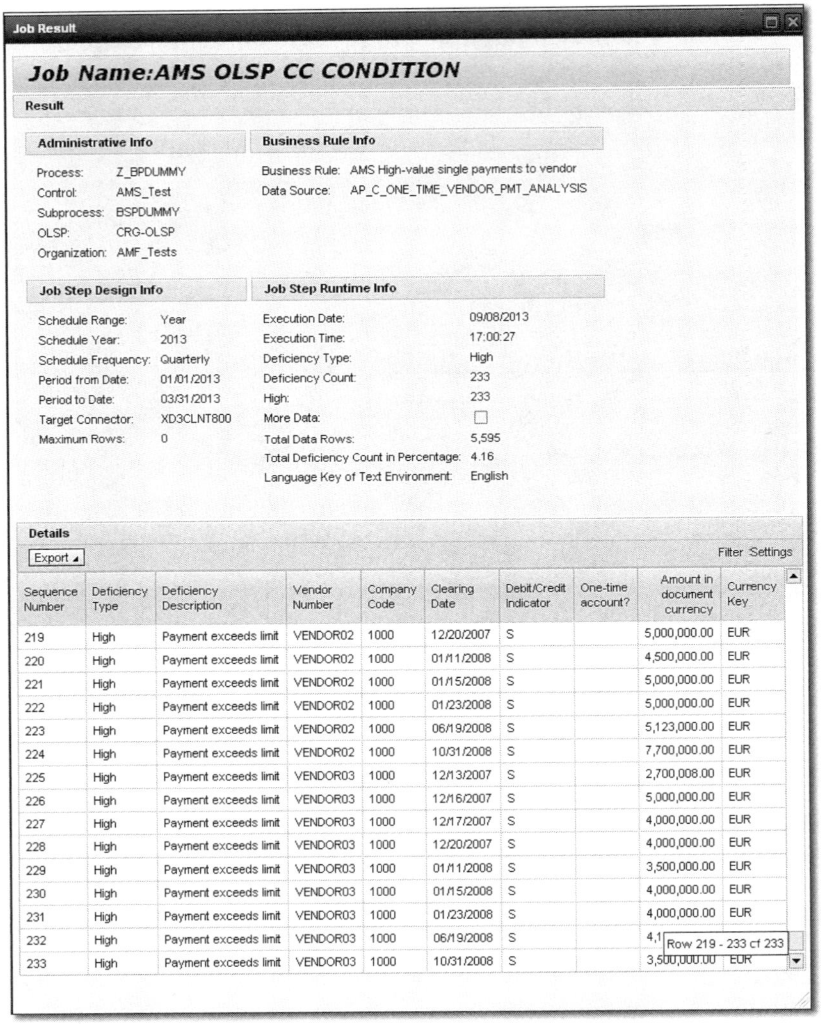

Figure 14.7 CCM Results with OLSP Conditions Applied

As can be seen, only company code 1000 has been investigated. Note that a total of 233 deficiencies are found, and although this isn't evident from the single screen shown her, all rows do correspond to a single company code, 1000.

14.1.4 OLSP and Business Rule Filter Conditions Combine

To further characterize and illustrate OLSP behavior, we configure the explicit filter condition in the business rule to be different from the OLSP condition, and then apply both. Figure 14.3 shows that we filter to select COMPANY CODE 0005 in the business rule. For clarity, we emphasize that the condition shown in Figure 14.3 wasn't in place for the rule execution whose results are shown in Figure 14.7.

Next, we again associate the OLSP condition CRG-OLSP with the org node AMF_TESTS, and then schedule and execute the rule again. The results are shown in Figure 14.8. Note that the deficiencies show that the two filter conditions are applied as a logical "OR" combination.

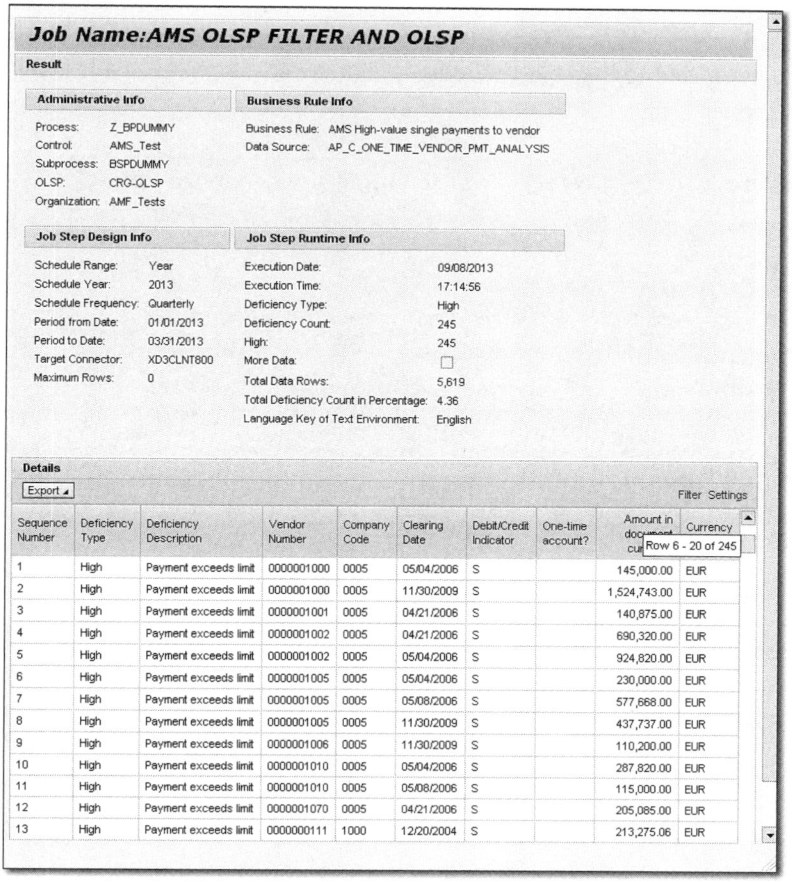

Figure 14.8 Business Rule Filter and OLSP Filter Combine in a Logical "OR"

OLSP Conditions: Not Inherited

As it happened, in conducting the tests just shown, we started with the parent organizational node of AMF_TESTS already associated with the CRG-OLSP condition. So the test results with CRG-OLSP *not* associated with AMF_TESTS shows that OLSP conditions aren't inherited from parent org node associations. As mentioned earlier in this chapter, another technique to facilitate business rule reuse is to use runtime binding of date ranges which we will review next.

14.1.5 Runtime Binding of Date Ranges

In the examples shown previously, notice that the date ranges are rather wide: Figure 14.8 shows transactions from 2004 through 2009. Obviously, it makes more sense to filter the transactions examined to those that correspond to the rule's schedule. Figure 14.9 shows that this is easily done.

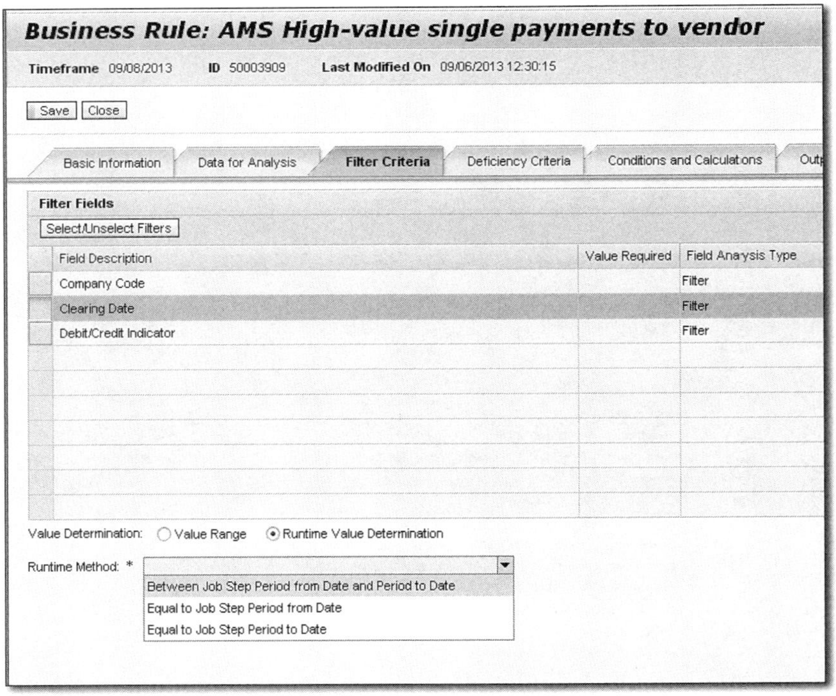

Figure 14.9 Date Fields Filtered by Runtime Binding

The choices are somewhat limited, and the limits must match either or both of the start and end of the job step period. Even so, this facilitates rule reuse because otherwise date field filters would have to be explicit in the rule definition, forcing customers to create rule copies for different period rules.

The use of date field filters

Figure 14.10 shows the Continuous Monitoring Scheduler, and we then discuss how job frequency, test period, and execution schedule interact based on the user inputs on this screen.

Continuous Monitoring Scheduler

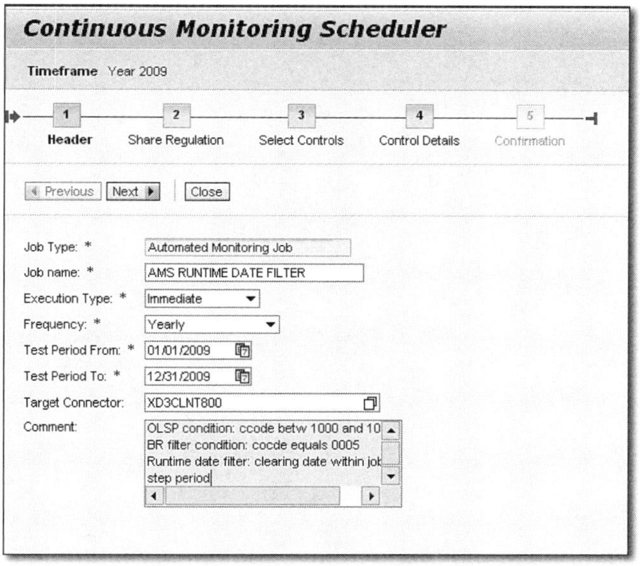

Figure 14.10 Scheduler Settings for Runtime Date Filter Binding

The settings of Figure 14.10 restrict the rule application to only those transactions whose clearing dates fall within the test period range specified.

14.1.6 Decoupling Test Schedule from Test Period

Customers ask how they can decouple the execution schedule of tests from the test period. Although this isn't, strictly speaking, a rule reuse or other CCM content management issue, the question gets raised often enough that it's worth addressing here.

In general, there are three independent variables in a CCM test schedule: test frequency, test period, and test schedule. The frequency defines how often the test runs: once a year, twice a year, every month, and so on. The test period is useful for passing date ranges to dynamically bound filter conditions, as just illustrated. Finally, the test schedule determines when each test actually runs.

For instance, a quarter-closing rule might cover the date range January 1 to March 31; but for completeness, it might be wiser to execute the rule a few days later. The scheduler can accommodate this, as shown in Figure 14.11.

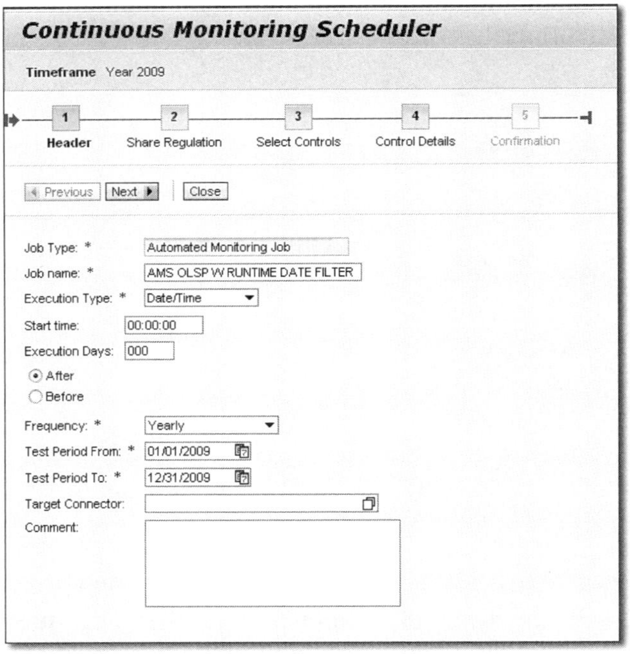

Figure 14.11 Decoupling Text Execution from Test Period

Frequency and schedule decoupling in SAP Process Control 10.x

Of the three variables, frequency, period, and schedule, SAP Process Control 10.0 and 10.1 only enable the frequency and schedule to be decoupled. The period tracks the frequency: monthly tests will have periods of a month. This is because the independent user inputs of frequency and test period are used to determine how many tests (job steps) are run. In the case of Figure 14.11, that means exactly one test will be run. If the FREQUENCY field was set to MONTHLY, 12 tests are run; furthermore, the test periods for each test correspond to the months: January 1 to January 31, February 1 to February 28 (or 29), and so on.

If, in addition, the EXECUTION DAYS field was set to 3 days after, the test is actually scheduled to run three days after the close of each test period.

Customers have also asked for the third variable to be decoupled. For instance, while running monthly tests over the whole of 2013, they might want to run each test over three months, and schedule it to run three days after the end of the period. That is, the first test of 2013 runs on February 3 and covers the time period November 1, 2012, to January 31, 2013. Similarly, the next test runs on March 3, 2013, covering transactions from December 1, 2012, to February 28, 2013.

Unfortunately, SAP Process Control 10.0 and 10.1 don't offer this additional degree of freedom. The test period and frequency are linked and can't be decoupled. This is a high-priority requirement for several customers, and the SAP Governance, Risk, and Compliance (SAP GRC) development team has already developed prototypes with the requested functionality. However, as of this writing, the decision on when to release this functionality is still pending.

14.2 CCM Data Security

SAP customers take great care in setting up authorizations in applications so that sensitive information isn't needlessly exposed. Even when employees need to see certain types of information, visibility is often restricted by organization within the company. For example, a financial officer of a regional group might not be able to see financial information for another such group. The human resources manager for one group should certainly not be able to see sensitive information about employees of another group or financial information for either group.

When SAP Process Control customers monitor backend applications, SAP Process Control can bring transactional data from such applications into itself to apply monitoring rules and present the results to SAP Process Control users. Customers rightly worry whether implementing

CCM in fact weakens data security for their company overall. SAP GRC has implemented a data security model for CCM to address this concern. In this section, we'll look at the Guiding principles that should be followed, analysis or really monitoring your system, establishing your security goals, and the implementation of a security practice. We will look at users, remote logins, and much more. First, let's review some general guiding principles that will help establish Continuous Control Monitoring data security.

14.2.1 Guiding Principles

Application conformance

The first principle of SAP Process Control CCM data security is to impose visibility constraints identical with the application setup, which is called *application conformance*.

Auditability

Another principle of the SAP Process Control security model is *auditability*. That is, SAP Process Control customers should be able to trace who can see which information by examining the role, process, organization, and user master data. Because these are all versioned (by validity date ranges), it's possible to audit the setup as of any past date. There has long been a need for a SAP Process Control report summarizing this setup.

Delegation

The final principle is *delegation*, which relaxes auditability in a sense. A control owner, who certainly can see details of issues raised by associated monitoring rules, can also delegate this visibility to other users for remediation. That is, when a remediation plan is assigned to a user for a particular issue, that user gets to see the issue details, even if the user would not otherwise be able to see the details. The presumption is that control owners who delegate to another for remediation know what they are doing and can be relied upon to mitigate any additional risks.

14.2.2 Analysis

Once you've established the guiding principles, the next step to consider for your data security is analysis. Backend conformance would be automatic if logins and roles in SAP Process Control replicated those in the monitored application. This is too simplistic, though, because SAP Process Control functionality is very different from application functionality. For instance, applications are unlikely to support a role for ensuring compliance to FCPA regulations.

Backend conformance by role replication is also impractical because SAP Process Control typically monitors many applications, and it wouldn't do to treat SAP Process Control as the dumping ground for all roles and logins to be found in all monitored applications in a company's systems landscape.

SAP Process Control is designed to operate separately from monitored applications and extracts monitoring data via remote connections. For instance, SAP Process Control communicates with SAP ERP via RFC connections. Usual principles of information security require the use of batch logins for such access, distinct from user logins. Such RFC user IDs can't be used to start interactive sessions, for instance.

Finally, note that creating and maintaining SAP Process Control monitoring job schedules can become quite a specialized activity in itself. The job scheduler needs to know the system landscape, which can become particularly detailed when multiple SAP ERP instances map to different company codes, for instance. For this reason, the role that allows scheduling a SAP Process Control monitoring job should confer no data visibility rights.

These facts require SAP Process Control to offer a unique security model. The SAP Process Control designers' goal was to make it possible for customers to perfectly align visibility constraints with the backend setup, while recognizing the specific functionality of SAP Process Control, the unique roles played by SAP Process Control users, and so on.

Note that here we refer only to the details of issues created by SAP Process Control monitoring rules. The details of whether the rule executed successfully, and whether it found problems and created an issue aren't considered sensitive, or at least not so sensitive. The job scheduler certainly needs to know if the job ran, for instance, because he needs to schedule another run if the first one fails.

Figure 14.12 summarizes the steps in the monitoring process and hence the challenge for security. SAP Process Control runs queries (or the equivalent) on monitored systems via remote connections, which require credentials. Obviously, the credentials used must have the appropriate authorization in the backend. This is really part of the security setup of the monitored system. We'll assume it exists and correctly reflects customer intent.

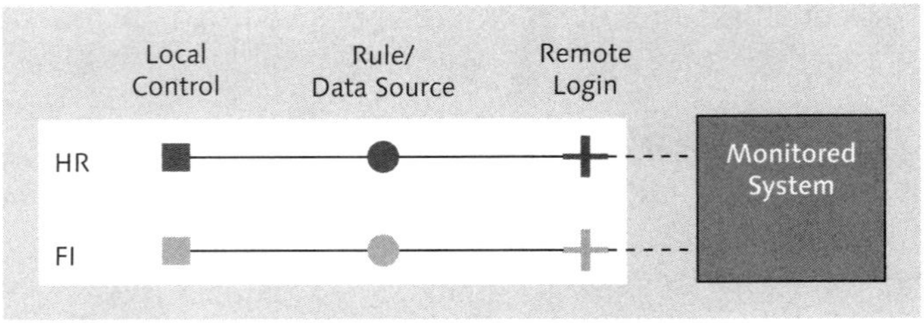

Figure 14.12 Monitored Data Traverses Many Associations

Data sources and rules have associations with specific remote destinations, which combine a remote system with a specific remote login (and hence a specific set of permissions on the remote system).

Finally, controls have associations to rules and also associations to users who are the owners of the control, and hence have access to its workings. This sets up easy visualization of problems to avoid, as shown next.

14.2.3 The Goal

The three cases in Figure 14.13 all represent crossed-wires, where you don't want data extracted from monitored systems to be visible to the control owner.

In Case 1, the HR monitoring rule (with associated login credentials to the HR backend system, with the right privileges to extract data to be monitored—again, we assume this is already correctly set up) is incorrectly assigned to a FI control. The job scheduler can execute the rule, and the results get collected. But we want to prevent the FI control owner from seeing the results because HR data isn't intended for an FI control owner's eyes.

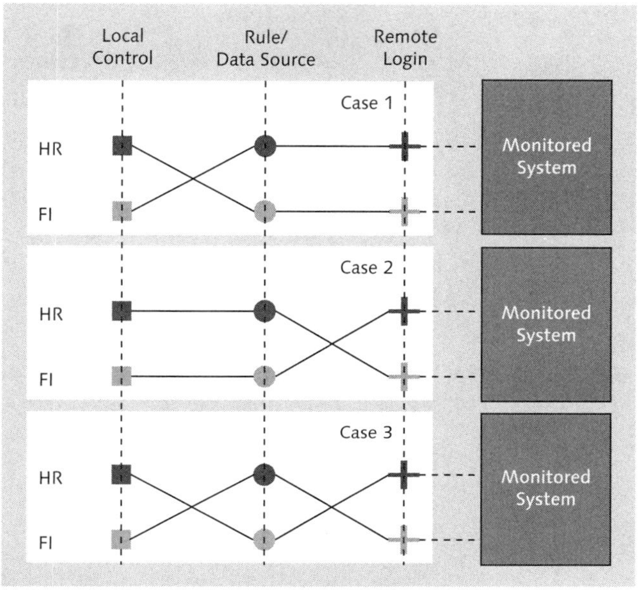

Figure 14.13 Multiple Checks Restrict Data Visibility

In Case 2, the rule-control association is correct, but by mistake the wrong remote login credentials have been supplied to the rule. The HR rule in our example has the FI remote login and vice versa. In this case, the backend system will presumably refuse to execute the query, and the SAP Process Control job will end in an error.

Case 3 combines the preceding two problems but in a way that cancels them out, at least for the limited example of the figure. That is, the remote login credentials have the right permissions for each query, and the correct control owners are assigned to field the monitoring results. However, the correctly matched triple of control owner, rule, and remote login credentials is hooked up to the wrong control. This case is shown for completeness because a careful customer will want to prevent such cases; it doesn't necessarily reflect any data security issues, however.

14.2.4 The Solution

The solution is in four parts: remote logins, association between SAP Process Control users and remote logins, association between controls and SAP Process Control users (control owners), and delegation.

Fine-Grained Remote Logins on Monitored Systems

On every monitored system, the customer should create as many remote login IDs as the granularity of access needed. In the example from the preceding figures, there should be two logins; the first should have authorization to run HR queries, and the second should be able to run FI queries.

This extends with more fine-grained visibility restrictions, should the customer need it. For instance, if there are two organizational divisions, and a central control each for HR and FI, then there are four local controls. If the HR control owner for one organizational division ought not to be able to see HR data for the other division, and so forth, this calls for four distinct logins to be created on the monitored system.

PFCG Association for Users and Remote Logins

To cover Case 1 in the preceding example, we need to prevent the FI control owner from seeing the results of an HR rule execution. To ensure this, we require that the control owner and the remote login credential used by the rule belong to the same PFCG role.

Control Ownership

Only control owners can see the result details for rules associated with that control.

Delegation for Remediation

Control owners can delegate remediation to other SAP Process Control users; such delegates obviously need to be able to see the details, and so they can. Each issue has to be explicitly delegated—there is no blanket delegation of all issues under a control.

Note this model gives SAP Process Control customers enormous leeway in how tightly they want to govern data visibility among SAP Process Control users. Some customers are very comfortable with the idea of SAP Process Control users having wide access to details of problems found by SAP Process Control monitoring rules—they consider SAP Process Control users to be privileged users, and SAP Process Control itself provides adequate audit trails of actions taken. At the other extreme, by creating many remote login IDs and role definitions, SAP Process Control customers can make it impossible for one user to see any data other than what appears in a single monitoring rule tied to a single local control.

14.2.5 CCM Data Security Model

The SAP Process Control CCM data security model shows monitored data to a user only when the following items are true:

- The remote login used to execute the monitoring rule has the appropriate authorizations in the application system.
- An issue is created—that is, the queried data failed the rule's deficiency criteria.
- The control owner has a role association with the remote login credentials used.
- The control owner or a delegate is attempting to see the details.

This security model can ensure very tight data visibility restrictions, by allowing customers to define roles with fine-grained access rights. But because such fine-grained access control is expensive to set up and maintain, SAP Process Control allows customers the flexibility of creating larger groups of users. The requirement that only control owners (or their delegates) can see issue results still caps data visibility.

14.3 Summary

After the detailed explanations of CCM functionality in the chapters before this, in this chapter, we offered some advice to regular users of CCM on how to avoid needlessly replicating effort as they use CCM more widely in their company. By reusing data sources, using business rule filters through the organization-level system parameters (OLSP) where possible, and binding date filters dynamically to test period ranges, they can reuse the same rule in many different contexts without creating multiple copies of rules and editing them.

Customers take elaborate precautions to keep data visible only to those who have a legitimate business reason to access it. They rightly worry that extracting such data to SAP Process Control for monitoring purposes defeats their data security measures because the SAP Process Control data security model seems so different from the security model of the backend systems. We explained that though SAP Process Control roles and data visibility limitations are very different from those of backend systems, the SAP Process Control data security model has been designed to make it work across many backend systems, while allowing customers to tailor its configuration to perfectly reflect backend data security. This comes at a certain cost in effort, but customers are able to trade off perfect fidelity to backend data security against convenience and ease of use.

This ends our tour of SAP Process Control functionality. The next chapter takes you through the details of SAP Risk Management.

SAP Risk Management helps organizations automate and coordinate risk management activities. Reliable and accurate risk information enables business users to make better decisions and improve performance. In this chapter, we cover the implementation process and show how customers realize business value from the solution.

15 SAP Risk Management Implementation

The number and diversity of risks grows as the business landscape become more complex, as companies expand and introduce new products, and as supply chains become more distributed. Often the capability of a business to manage these risks doesn't keep pace. To understand and manage risks, businesses must understand the risk drivers, recognize how risks impact business value, anticipate catastrophic losses, mitigate risks, and act on emerging opportunities.

The SAP Risk Management solution automates the Enterprise Risk Management (ERM) process for an organization. In addition, financial institutions can enable additional solution functionality to support their Operational Risk Management (ORM) process. In this chapter, we'll first look at an overview of Enterprise Risk Management (ERM) in Section 15.1 and then review the scenario in further detail, including business blueprints for implementation and system configuration in Section 15.2. Next we'll turn our focus to the ORM scenario with an overview in Section 15.3 followed by similar details for implementation in Section 15.4.

15.1 Enterprise Risk Management Overview

Most customers when asked about their risk management practice generally talk about a lack of transparency and unavailability of accurate risk information for decision making.

Risk management teams are in a difficult situation. They are responsible for the risk management processes but typically don't own the key risks—they are owned by the lines of business (LOBs). So they constantly struggle with follow-ups, progress, and tracking status of risks. They are also constantly wondering about risks that can blindside the organization.

Business owners and LOB managers typically aren't thinking about risks per se but only about performance. They typically get several surveys or assessments from different groups that ask similar questions (not only from the enterprise risk group but also from audit, it security, business continuity, etc.). But because risk and performance are really just two sides of the same coin, they typically come up with good solutions to address the risks they know about—but only the risks they know about—and they have absolutely no visibility into risks outside of their silo that could negatively affect them. The risk mitigation efforts that are successful are one-offs and typically never reapplied to other regions or similar business units.

Executives are mainly concerned with market expectations and delivering on strategy, and they think about risks only as an afterthought. After the strategy is developed and plans are executed, they start to ask about risks. The result is that executives are left not knowing whether any negative surprises will keep them from meeting their business objectives until it's too late.

SAP Risk Management enables the ERM process for an organization and in turn helps risk managers, business owners, and executives preserve and grow value by doing the following:

- Aligning risk management with business value drivers
- Creating continuous insight into the status of risk
- Acting on emerging risks and opportunities

Figure 15.1 shows the ERM process supported by the SAP Risk Management solution. Figure 15.1 describes the solution capabilities and closely aligns with best practice ERM frameworks such as ISO 31000 and COSO II ERM.

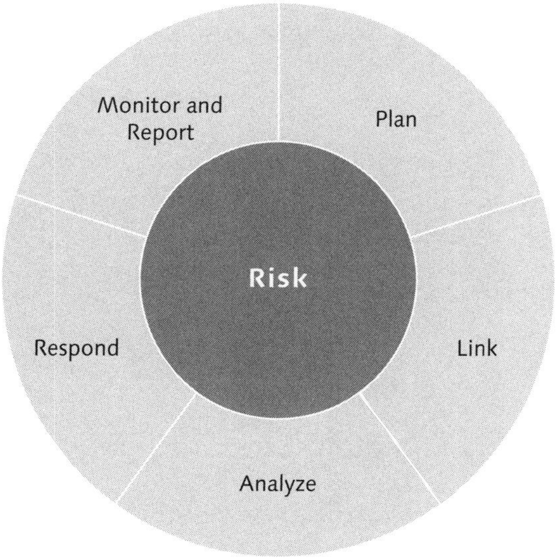

Figure 15.1 The Five Components of Enterprise Risk Management

Let's look at each of these five components shown in Figure 15.1 in a little bit more detail as it relates to ERM:

- **Plan**
  ERM begins with planning. Planning enables organizations to focus risk management implementation on what is most relevant for their business. Planning ensures that the risk management initiative starts with a complete understanding of context, business value drivers, risk appetite, threshold levels, and business objectives to be achieved.
- **Link**
  The link component is the next phase. Risks are identified, documented, and aligned with the business context—drivers/causes, impacts/consequences, organizations, risk categories, activities, and objectives.

- **Analyze**
  Next, risks are analyzed using quantitative and qualitative methods for prioritization and developing effective treatment strategies.
- **Respond**
  Risk evaluation helps select the risks (and opportunities) for treatment by balancing the costs of implementing each option against the benefits derived from it.
- **Monitor and report**
  This component covers monitoring of the effectiveness and completeness of the risk treatments, taking corrective actions, and communicating the status of risks.

Now that we have a conceptual understanding of ERM, let's explore this in further detail.

15.2 Enterprise Risk Management Scenario

The maturity of ERM practices typically varies across customers. Hence, prior to delving into the implementation process, let's review a customer adoption model. SAP Risk Management has many features and functionalities, but not all may be applicable for a particular customer. In fact, customers might prefer to adopt the solution functionality in multiple phases based on their level of risk management maturity.

SAP Risk Management adoption models

Tables 15.1 through 15.3 show a three-part solution adoption model for customers. The model aligns customer requirements with solution functionality on an increasing level of risk management maturity and expectation of business benefits. The three-part model can also be thought of as a three-phase solution implementation approach. Breaking out the implementation into multiple phases helps faster realization of business value for the customer. Note that this model is simply a recommendation, and customers can choose to ignore it and/or use a hybrid approach.

Table 15.1 describes the minimal solution adoption for customers. The goal in this phase is process automation that will help streamline risk management efforts across the organization and reduce costs.

Customer Requirements	Solution Adoption
▶ Standardize and streamline risk management activities (remove risk silos) across the organization. ▶ Automate risk management activities. ▶ Reduce the number of technologies/tools used. ▶ Real-time visibility into risk status.	▶ Set up system configuration and master data. ▶ Document risks and assign risk ownership. ▶ Perform risk assessments and surveys. ▶ Document risk responses (leverage controls and policies if using SAP Process Control). ▶ Monitor risks and responses with dashboards (risk heatmap) and reports.

Table 15.1 Phase One: Process Automation

Next, customers can leverage additional solution functionality for proactive risk prevention, as described in Table 15.2.

Customer Requirements	Solution Adoption
▶ Better understand and manage risk exposure as events occur over time. ▶ Provide warnings by measuring Key Risk Indicators (KRIs). ▶ Clearly define accountability. ▶ Model risks with Monte Carlo simulation and what-if scenarios. ▶ Document and manage risk-related issues.	▶ Expand risk ownership at the line level and enforce accountability. ▶ Evaluate need and implement KRIs for continuous risk monitoring. ▶ Document incidents and losses to improve risk assessments and identify emerging risks. ▶ Perform ad hoc issue management for risk-related remediation plans. ▶ Document ERM policies, link with risks, and perform policy certification and acknowledgement. ▶ Evaluate need and implement additional custom reporting and analytics (leverage SAP NetWeaver BW/BI Content and SAP BusinessObjects reporting tools). ▶ Perform business scenarios and simulations for critical decision making.

Table 15.2 Phase Two: Proactive Risk Prevention

Customers with highly mature risk management practices can leverage risk information for decision making and to improve performance, as described in Table 15.3.

Customer Requirements	Solution Adoption
▸ Improve decision-making ability by considering risks in the context of achieving the organization's strategic objectives. ▸ Capture opportunities for improvements. ▸ Leverage SAP investment by incorporating risk information into business processes and applications.	▸ Embed risk management activities across business processes by integrating SAP Risk Management with other SAP solutions. ▸ Leverage risk assessments for audit planning and other scoping activities. ▸ Use opportunities to capture positive events. ▸ Embed risk information into performance management processes.

Table 15.3 Phase Three: Improve Performance

Now that we've explored the customer adoption model, let's shift our focus to the solution implementation process. The ERM scenario is the standard implementation scenario for SAP Risk Management. A typical solution implementation project is described in Figure 15.2. The project follows the traditional SAP implementation process of project preparation, business blueprint, realization, final/preparations, and then go-live. Completion of each major phase of the project is marked with a milestone.

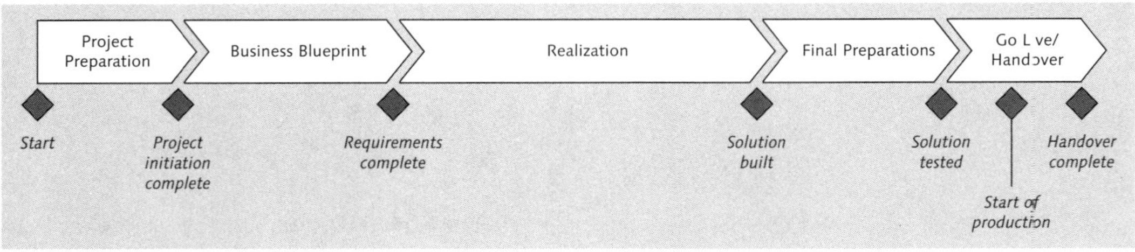

Figure 15.2 Implementation Project Plan with Milestones

Note
Complete product documentation and learning maps for SAP Risk Management are available on SAP Help Portal at *http://help.sap.com/rm*.

The business blueprint stage is the most critical phase of an implementation project. The business blueprint captures customers' requirements, project scope, and details on how to set the SAP Risk Management solution. The other stages in the project—preparation, realization, final preparations, and go-live—are standard for implementing any GRC solution and don't necessarily capture details specific to SAP Risk Management. Hence, in this chapter, we'll focus on the process of generating a business blueprint for the ERM scenario. We'll review key activities and business challenges for the blueprint stage of the implementation project.

15.2.1 Business Blueprint

The objective of this most critical phase of the project is to understand the customer's ERM process and business requirements. The business blueprint document captures the customer's business requirements, mapping the requirements to solution functionality, along with details about system configuration and data setup. The business blueprint is developed in close consultation with the business users and serves as a reference scope document for the solution implementation.

Typically, the customer's IT department proceeds in parallel to procure the servers (DEV/QAS/PRD) and install SAP NetWeaver Application Server ABAP (AS ABAP).

Blueprinting tasks for implementation projects

Next, we describe how to complete the several blueprinting tasks before launching into the realization phase of the ERM implementation. In the following sections, we'll review:

- Solution configuration
- Data conversion
- Authorizations
- Workflows
- Reporting

15.2.2 Solution Configuration

In the solution configuration task, the customer business requirements are mapped to the SAP Risk Management Customizing Implementation Guide (Transaction SPRO). The parent GOVERNANCE, RISK, AND COMPLIANCE node in the IMG specifies customizing entries for all GRC solutions. The IMG entries listed in Figure 15.3 are required to be setup for the SAP Risk Management solution. Documentation for each IMG entry is available as part of Transaction SPRO.

Start with the Risk and Opportunity Attributes IMG entries under the Shared Master Data Settings node as shown in Figure 15.3. This configuration specifies the drivers, impacts, and benefits categories.

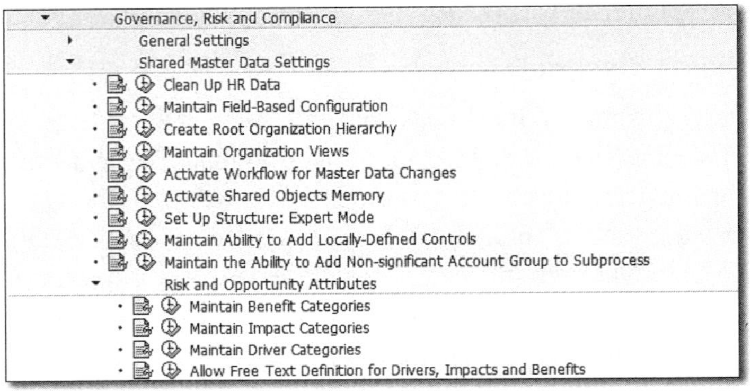

Figure 15.3 Shared Master Data IMG Entries

Next you set up the IMG entries along with all of the subentries, which are available under the Common Component Settings node as shown in Figure 15.4. The IMG entries under the Common Component Settings are applicable across all GRC solutions and need to be set up even when only implementing SAP Risk Management. Set up the following entries:

- Integration Framework
  Set up connectors for the SAP NetWeaver Portal, email, Active Directory, SAP HANA database, web services, and other data sources.
- Policy Management
  Set up the common component of SAP Policy Management.
- Ad Hoc Issues
  Set up the common component of Issue Management.
- Planning and Scheduling
  Set up the SAP Risk Management planner activities. Planner is the common SAP GRC planning and scheduling tool. These activities are described in further detail in the "Workflows" section later in this chapter.

- SURVEYS
  Set up the different types of surveys, survey questions, and valuations.

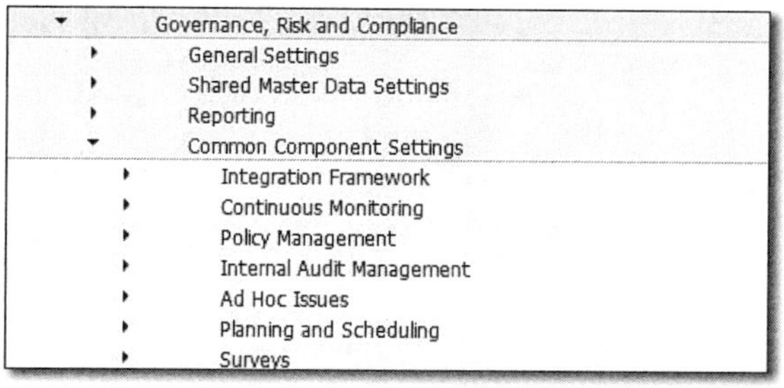

Figure 15.4 Common Component Settings IMG Entries

Finally, set up all of the IMG entries and subentries under the RISK MANAGEMENT node as shown in Figure 15.5. This node captures SAP Risk Management specific system configuration. Set up the following:

- GENERAL SETTINGS
  Set up change history and risk terminology.
- MASTER DATA SETUP
  Set up types, categories, units of measure, and other attributes of the SAP Risk Management master data entities.
- RISK AND OPPORTUNITY ANALYSIS
  Set up configuration for risk analysis and risk heatmaps (risk impact and risk probability matrix).
- RESPONSE AND ENHANCEMENT PLAN
  Set up configuration for the different types of risk responses: mitigations, controls (integration with SAP Process Control), policies, and issues.
- INCIDENT AND LOSS DATABASE
  Set up configuration for the incident and loss database in SAP Risk Management.
- KEY RISK INDICATORS
  Set up configuration for the KRIs, including connectors, data sources, and KRI classification.

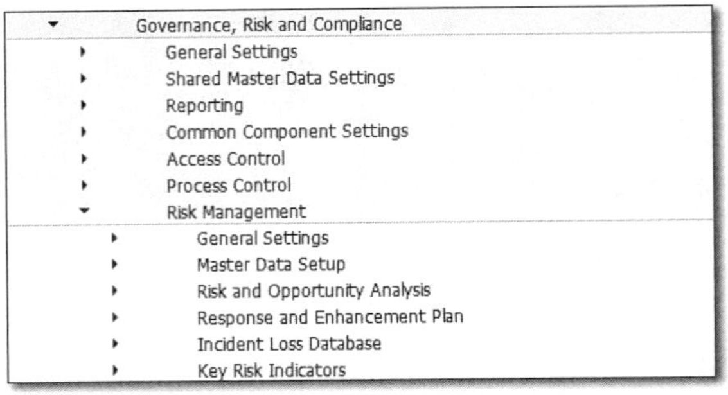

Figure 15.5 Risk Management IMG Entries

15.2.3 Data Conversion and Master Data Setup

In the data conversion task, customer business requirements are mapped to the SAP Risk Management master data elements.

Requirements are documented to set up the following master data objects available under the MASTER DATA work center as shown in Figure 15.6:

- BUSINESS OBJECTIVES
  A two-level taxonomy that defines risk strategies and objectives.
- ORGANIZATIONS
  An N-level taxonomic structure that defines the risk management organization structure. Organizations also capture additional attributes such as applicable business objectives, units of measure, risk appetite, risk threshold/impact levels, roles with user assignments, and any other additional information.
- POLICIES
  Policy categorization along with risk management policies in use.
- ACTIVITY HIERARCHY
  Multiple N-level taxonomic structures that define business activities for risk management. One or more taxonomic structures can be set up to capture the additional dimensions for risk management such as business processes, projects, products/services, and so on.
- RISK CATALOG
  An N-level taxonomic structure that defines risk category structure along with risk templates.

- **Response Catalog**
  A flat structure that defines response templates.

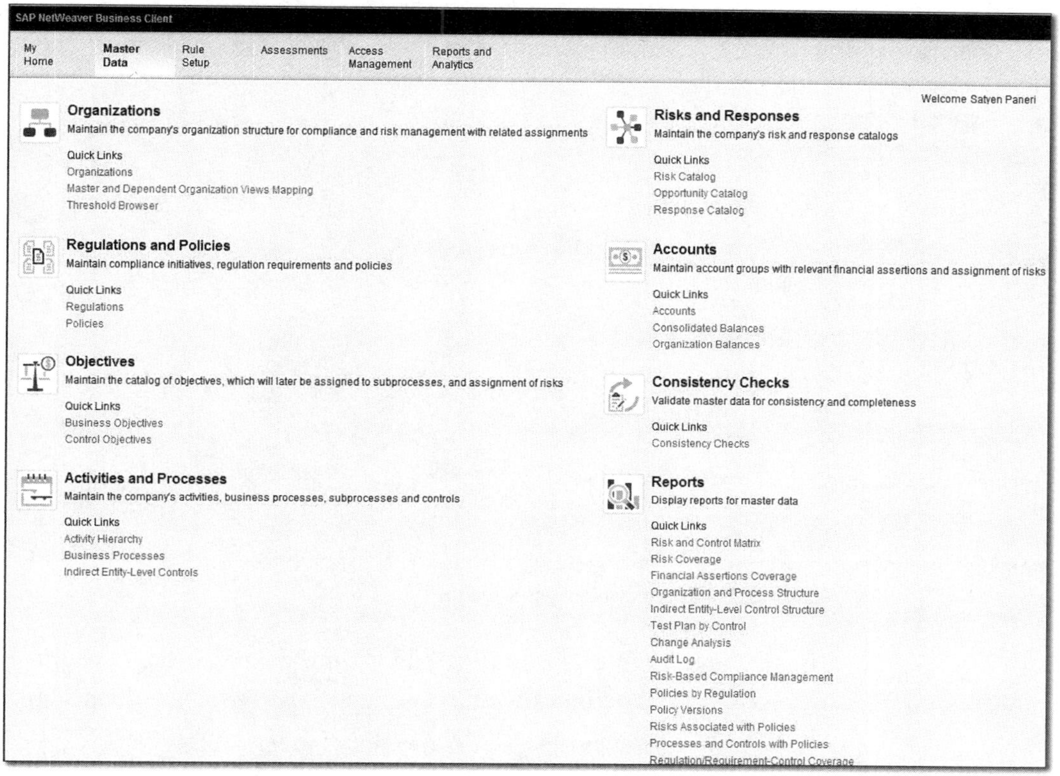

Figure 15.6 Master Data Work Center

Now let's look at each of these master data entities in further detail.

Business Objectives

The business objectives functionality can be accessed using the Business Objectives quick link in the Objectives section on the Master Data work center as shown previously in Figure 15.6. The business objectives functionality is a two-level taxonomic structure that defines risk strategies and risk objectives as shown in Figure 15.7. Use of business objectives is optional for ERM, however.

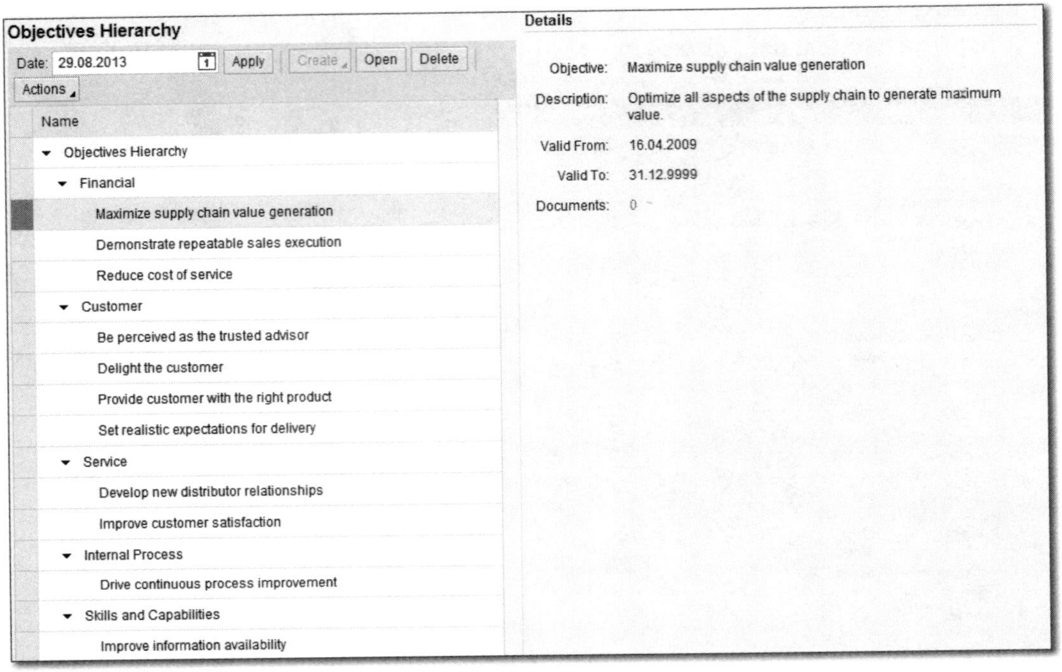

Figure 15.7 Business Objectives Structure

The first level defines the strategy and is simply a classification element. The second level defines the objective, which will be aligned with organizations. Objectives can also be categorized as shown in Figure 15.8 with the list of categories being defined in the IMG customizing.

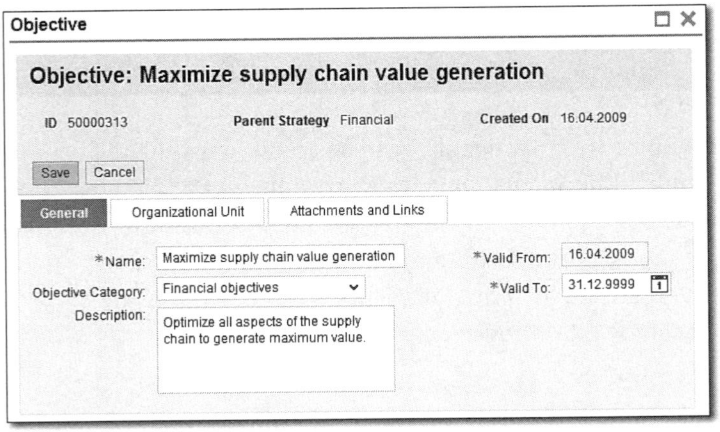

Figure 15.8 Objective Definition

Organizations

Organization structure is the central common master data entity in SAP GRC. The organization structure is a shared entity among SAP Risk Management, SAP Process Control, and SAP Access Control. The majority of SAP GRC workflows are routed based on the organization role settings.

Organizations can be accessed using the ORGANIZATIONS quick link in the ORGANIZATIONS section on the MASTER DATA work center as shown earlier in Figure 15.6. An organization is an N-level taxonomic structure that defines the SAP GRC organization structure as shown in Figure 15.9.

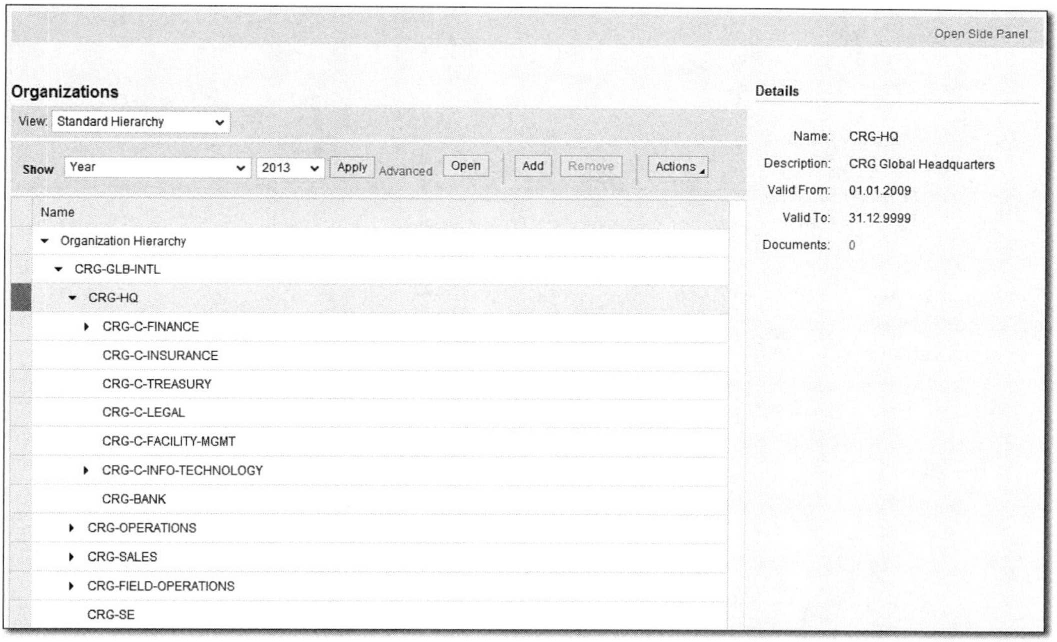

Figure 15.9 Organization Structure

Figure 15.10 shows the details for an organizational element. Because the organizations structure is a shared master data entity, it contains a lot of settings and tabs, not all of which are applicable for the ERM setup as shown in Figure 15.10.

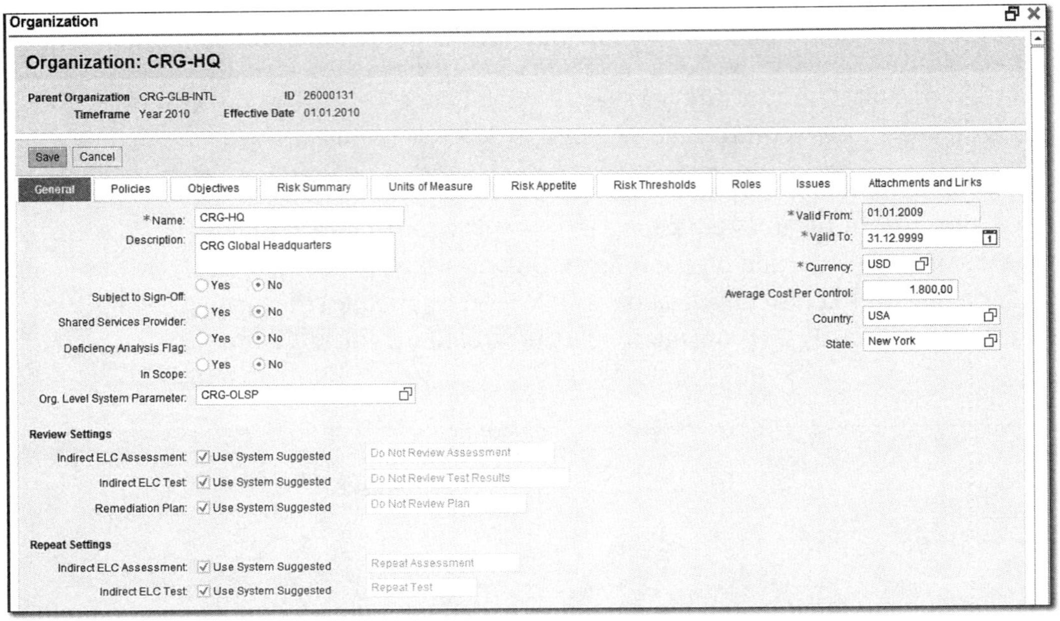

Figure 15.10 Organization Definition

Configuration and details for tabs for an organizational element

Table 15.4 describes details of the setup necessary for the various tabs for an organizational element.

Organization Tab	Description
GENERAL	Capture general attributes for an organization. Only the NAME, DESCRIPTION, VALID TO, and CURRENCY attributes are mandatory for ERM. The VALID TO attribute is used to define the validity time frame for an organization. As organization structures frequently change, so this attribute is useful to retire older organizations and hide the related information from SAP Risk Management.
POLICIES	Show the list of policies and procedures applicable for the organization. The use of this tab is optional for ERM. SAP Policy Management is a common SAP GRC component for managing policies and procedures.

Table 15.4 Organization Settings

Organization Tab	Description
Objectives	Select objectives from the Business Objectives hierarchy and link with the organization. This linkage narrows the list of objectives available for a risk that is part of the organization.
Risk Summary	Show an aggregated risk level and assessment summary for all risks defined for the organization. As users use the system, document, and analyze risks, details shown on this tab are updated.
Units of Measure	Define a unit of measure setting for each risk impact category that will convert risk analysis for the impact into a monetary amount based on the applicable currency. This setting is mandatory when using the quantitative risk analysis profile.
Risk Appetite	Define the risk appetite for the organization in quantitative and qualitative measures. This setting is mandatory for risk analysis.
Risk Thresholds	Define the quantitative lower and upper limits for each of the risk impact levels. This setting is mandatory for risk analysis.
Roles	Define the user assignments for the entity-role combinations for an organization. This process is described in the "Authorization Concept and Roles" section later in this chapter. From the available list of roles on this tab, only the following roles need to be defined for ERM: CEO/CFO, Central Risk Manager, Incident Editor, Internal Auditor, Organization Owner, System Administrator, and Unit Risk Manager.
Issues	Create and view ad hoc issues for the organization. The use of this tab is optional for ERM. Issue Management is another common SAP GRC component for logging and remediation of SAP GRC issues.
Attachments and Links	Define additional information for an organization by either attaching documents or specifying URL links. The use of this tab is optional for ERM.

Table 15.4 Organization Settings (Cont.)

Policies

SAP Policy Management is a common SAP GRC component for managing policies and procedures. Policies can be accessed using the POLICIES quick link in the REGULATIONS AND POLICIES section on the MASTER DATA work center as shown in Figure 15.6. SAP Policy Management is covered in Chapter 9 earlier and hence not described in detail here. Use of policies and procedures is optional for ERM. Customers that use policies and procedures can align risks with policies and also use procedures as risk treatment measures.

Activity Hierarchy

Enterprise risks are generally aligned with business activities. Business activities can represent any taxonomic structures such as business processes, projects/programs, products/services, assets, and so on. Use of activity hierarchy is optional for ERM, and customers that need to do so will need to use this master data entity. When using the ACTIVITY HIERARCHY, additional transaction data defined as ACTIVITIES also need to be defined prior to aligning risks with activities. The ACTIVITIES transactional element is described later in this section and assigns the ACTIVITY HIERARCHY with an organization and user-role combination.

The activity hierarchy can be accessed using the ACTIVITY HIERARCHY quick link in the ACTIVITIES AND PROCESSES section on the MASTER DATA work center as shown earlier in Figure 15.6. ACTIVITY HIERARCHY consists of multiple N-level taxonomic structures that define business activities for risk management as shown in Figure 15.11.

The SHOW dropdown shown in Figure 15.11 defines multiple taxonomic structures for different activity types. The activity types shown here are defined in IMG customizing. Note that only a single such structure is usually necessary for a customer. A single risk can only be aligned with one business activity. However, different types of risks may use different types of activities and hence, multiple structures are supported. Figure 15.12 shows the definition for an activity hierarchy element.

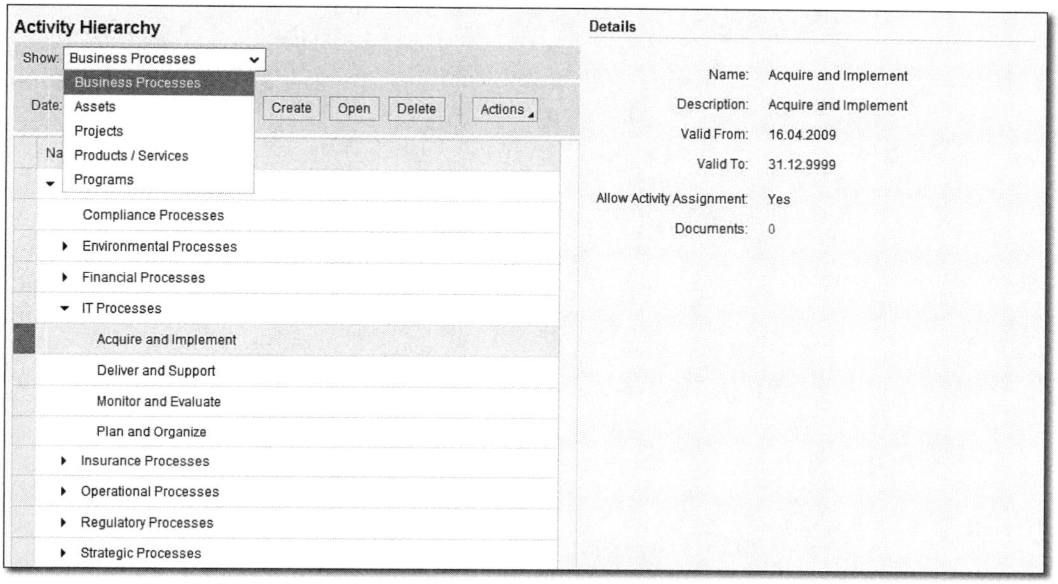

Figure 15.11 Activity Hierarchy Structure

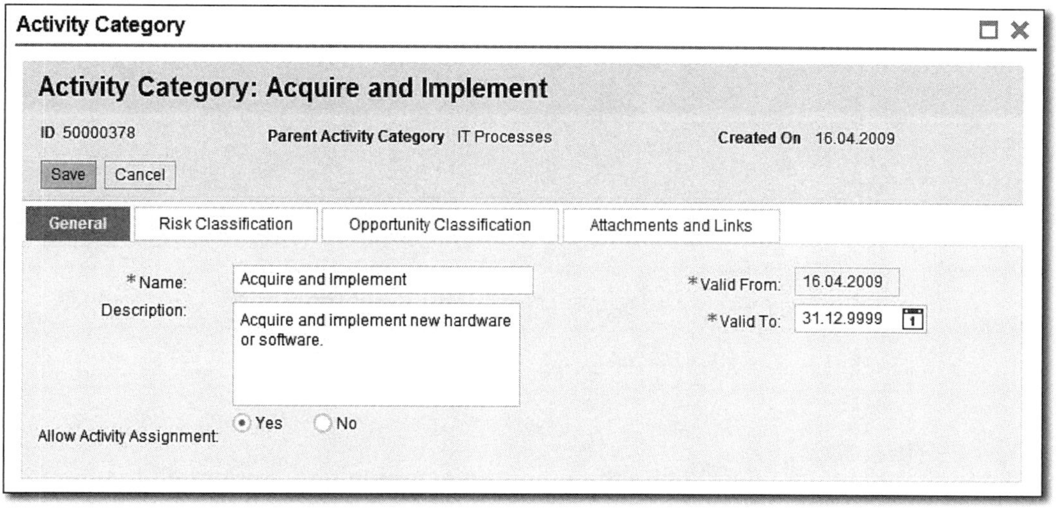

Figure 15.12 Activity Hierarchy Definition

Configuration and details for tabs in the setup of an activity hierarchy

Table 15.5 describes details of the setup necessary for the various tabs for an activity hierarchy.

Activity Hierarchy Tab	Description
GENERAL	Capture general attributes for an activity hierarchy such as NAME, DESCRIPTION, and VALID TO. The VALID TO attribute is used to define the validity time frame for an activity hierarchy. The ALLOW ACTIVITY ASSIGNMENT attribute defines whether activities can be defined for the particular activity hierarchy element.
GENERAL (Cont.)	Because these are in a taxonomic structure, activities may not be applicable for parent (or top-level) nodes, and such configuration can be controlled with this attribute.
RISK CLASSIFICATION	Certain activity hierarchy elements may only be applicable for certain risk categories. This kind of filtering is optional but when necessary can be defined using the RISK CLASSIFICATION tab.
OPPORTUNITY CLASSIFICATION	Certain activity hierarchy elements may only be applicable for certain opportunity categories. This kind of filtering is optional but when necessary can be defined using the OPPORTUNITY CLASSIFICATION tab.
ATTACHMENTS AND LINKS	Define additional information for the activity hierarchy by either attaching documents or specifying URL links. The use of this tab is optional for ERM.

Table 15.5 Activity Hierarchy Settings

Risk Catalog

The risk catalog can be accessed using the RISK CATALOG quick link in the RISKS AND RESPONSES section on the MASTER DATA work center as shown earlier in Figure 15.6. The RISK CATALOG is an N-level taxonomic structure that defines the risk category structure along with risk templates as shown in Figure 15.13. A risk classification structure is mandatory for ERM. Use of risk templates is optional, however.

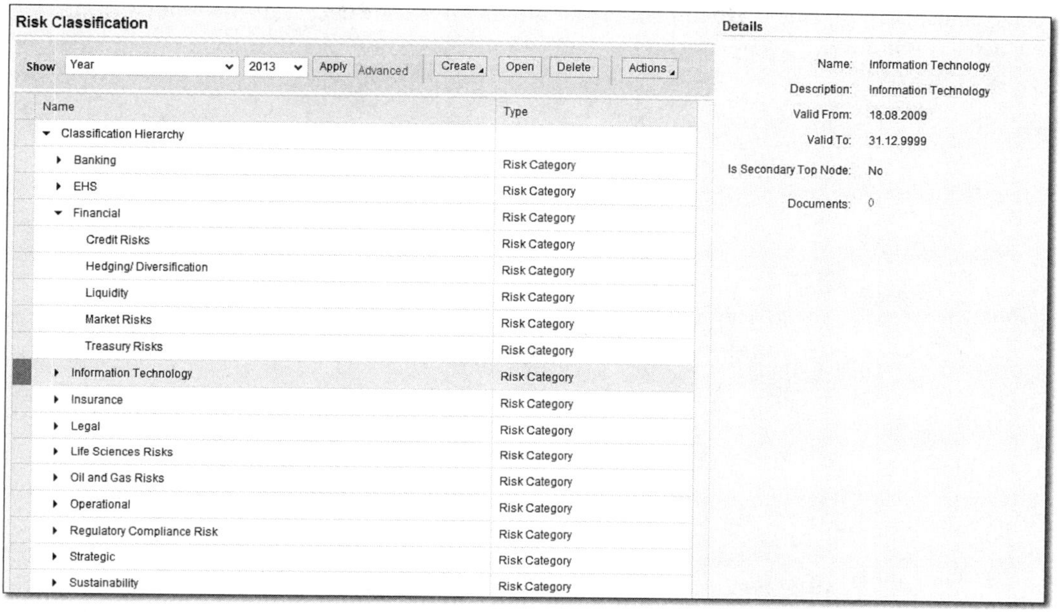

Figure 15.13 Risk Catalog Structure

Risk categorization structure

The different nodes of the risk catalog define the risk categorization structure for ERM. Details of one such risk category is shown in Figure 15.14.

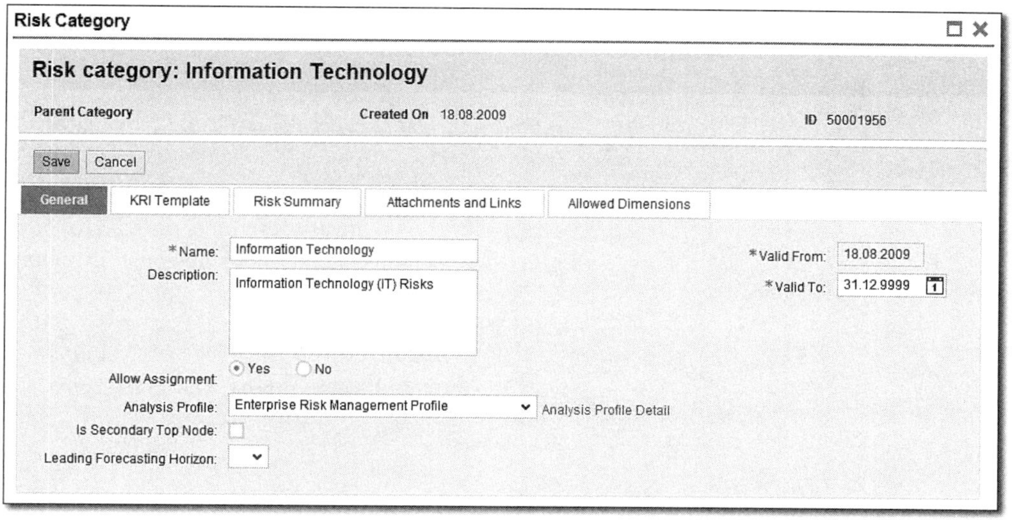

Figure 15.14 Risk Category Definition

Configuration and tab details for the setup of a risk category

Table 15.6 describes details of the setup necessary for the various tabs for a risk category.

Risk Category Tab	Description
General	Capture general attributes for a risk category such as Name, Description, and Valid To: ▸ The Valid To attribute is used to define the validity time frame for a risk category. ▸ The Allow Activity Assignment attribute defines whether risks can be defined for the particular risk category element. Because these are in a taxonomic structure, risks may not be applicable for parent (top-level) nodes, and such configuration can be controlled with this attribute. ▸ The Analysis Profile attribute defines the applicable risk analysis profile for risks belonging to risk category. The risk analysis profile is set up in IMG customizing and defines the method of risk assessment. Different types of risk assessment configurations are possible and made applicable for different risk types using this attribute. To keep things simple, customers typically use a single analysis profile to assess all enterprise risks. In such a case. a single value is available for selection in this attribute. A single risk profile for managing all enterprise risks is also recommended to make risk aggregation, consolidation, and comparison easier. ▸ The Is Secondary Top Node attribute is only applicable for the ORM scenario and is described later in this chapter. ▸ The Leading Forecasting Horizon attribute is used when risk assessment needs to be performed for one or more time frames (forecasting horizons). This type of risk assessment is only applicable for Corporate risk types and isn't covered in this chapter. Refer to SAP Note 1649904 (*https://service.sap.com/support/notes/1649904*) for more details on corporate risks.

Table 15.6 Risk Category Settings

Risk Category Tab	Description
KRI TEMPLATE	Certain KRI templates may only be applicable for certain risk categories. This kind of filtering is optional but when necessary can be defined using the KRI TEMPLATES tab.
RISK SUMMARY	Shows an aggregated risk level and assessment for all risks defined for the risk category. As users use the system, document, and analyze risks, details shown on this tab are updated.
ATTACHMENTS AND LINKS	Define additional information for the risk category by either attaching documents or specifying URL links. The use of this tab is optional for ERM.

Table 15.6 Risk Category Settings (Cont.)

The use of risk templates

Risk templates can be used to capture common risk definitions that include drivers, impacts, response templates, and central controls. A company might have multiple business units, and certain risks (such as IT risks or supply chain risks) can be common for all of the business units. Customers might want to capture a common definition of such a risk as a template and then distribute (create instances) the template for each business unit. Each such risk instance will have the basic structure of the risk template but can be further localized by risk owners and risk assessment applicable for the particular business unit. Distribution of risk templates is possible using two methods—copy and reference. Risk templates distributed with the copy method allow local risk owners to change the risk definition obtained from the template. Risk templates distributed with the reference method don't allow local risk owners to change the risk definition obtained from the template. Additional risk details that aren't obtained from the template, along with risk assessments, can always be changed for all risks.

Use of risk templates is optional and when required can be defined for any risk category. Risk templates appear as leaf nodes in the risk catalog structure. Details of one such risk template is shown in Figure 15.15.

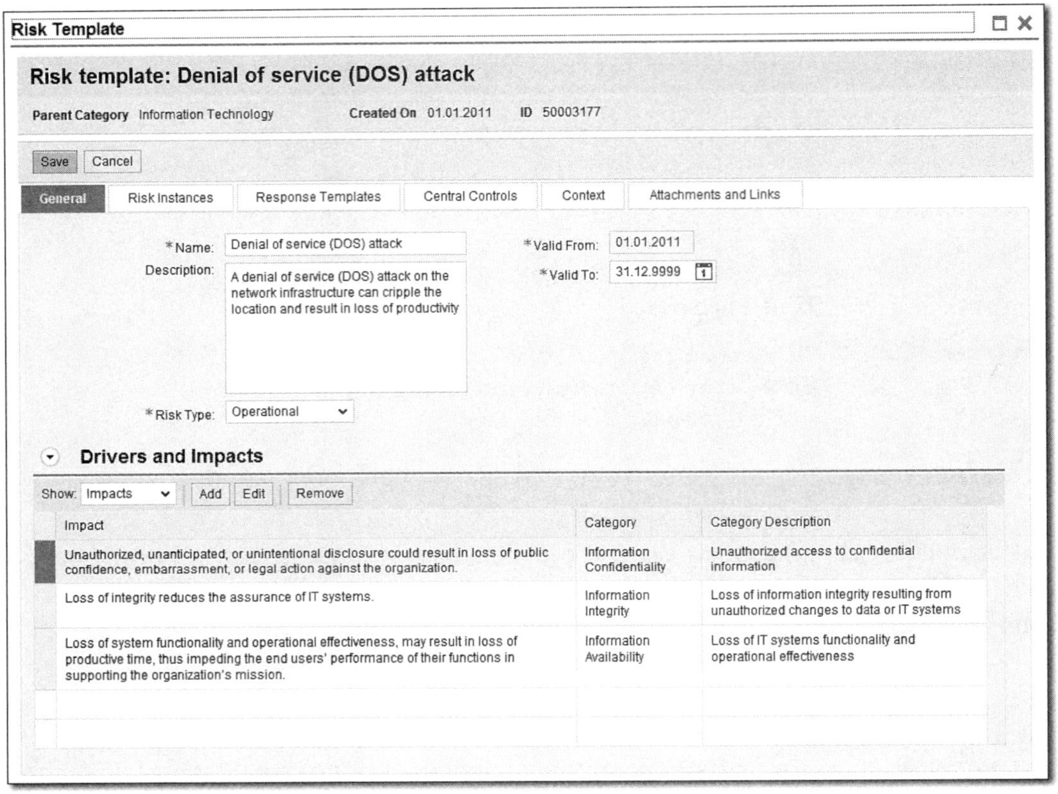

Figure 15.15 Risk Template Definition

Configuration and tab details for the setup of a Risk template

Table 15.7 describes details of the setup necessary for the various tabs for a risk template.

Risk Template Tab	Description
GENERAL	▸ Capture general attributes for a risk category such as NAME, DESCRIPTION, RISK TYPE, and VALID TO. The VALID TO attribute is used to define the valid ty time frame of a risk template. ▸ The RISK TYPE attribute can either be set as OPERATIONAL or CORPORATE. Operational risks have multiple impacts and single time frame-based assessments. This is the default risk type referred to in this chapter for both ERM and ORM scenarios.

Table 15.7 Risk Template Settings

Risk Template Tab	Description
GENERAL (Cont.)	Corporate risks support single impacts but assessments for multiple time frames (or forecasting horizons). Corporate risk types aren't covered in this chapter. Refer to SAP Note 1649904 (*https://service.sap.com/support/notes/1649904*) for more details on corporate risks. ▸ The DRIVERS AND IMPACTS section captures the drivers and impacts for a risk template.
RISK INSTANCES	Lists the instances of (local) risks that are created using this risk template.
RESPONSE TEMPLATES	Define the response templates associated with the risk template.
CENTRAL CONTROLS	Define the central controls associated with the risk template.
ATTACHMENTS AND LINKS	Define additional information for the risk template by either attaching documents or specifying URL links. The use of this tab is optional for ERM.

Table 15.7 Risk Template Settings (Cont.)

Response Catalog

The response catalog can be accessed using the RESPONSE CATALOG quick link in the RISKS AND RESPONSES section on the MASTER DATA work center as shown earlier in Figure 15.6. The response catalog is a flat structure that captures response templates as shown in Figure 15.16.

Use of the response catalog is optional for ERM. Details of one such response template are shown in Figure 15.17.

Table 15.8 describes details of the setup necessary for the various tabs for a response template.

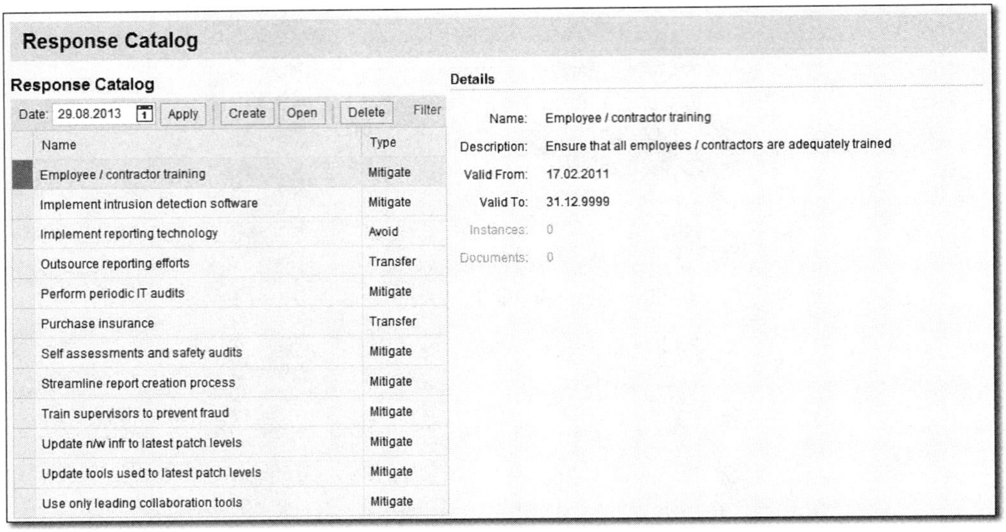

Figure 15.16 Response Catalog Structure

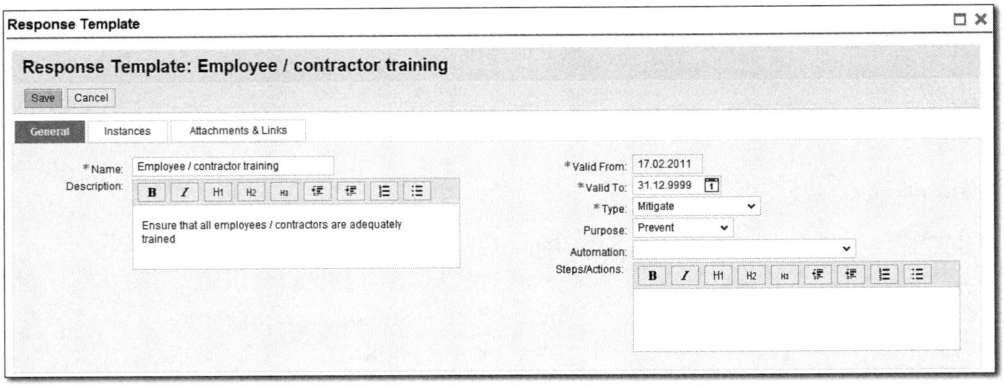

Figure 15.17 Response Template Definition

Configuration and tab details for the setup of a response template

Response Template Tab	Description
General	Capture general attributes for a response template such as Name, Description, and Valid To: ▸ The Valid To attribute is used to define the validity time frame for a response template.

Table 15.8 Response Template Settings

Response Template Tab	Description
General (Cont.)	▸ The Type and Purpose attributes classify the response template, and the available values are defined in IMG customizing. Only the Type attribute is mandatory. ▸ The Automation optional attribute specifies the type of automated actions that can follow from the response catalog. Response automation allows triggers for certain actions in SAP Business Suite and is optional with the details being configured in IMG customizing. ▸ The Steps/Actions optional attribute captures details on implementation of the response plan.
Instances	Lists the instances of (local) responses that are created using this response template.
Attachments & Links	Define additional information for the response template by either attaching documents or specifying URL links. The use of this tab is optional for ERM.

Table 15.8 Response Template Settings (Cont.)

KRI Templates

The final master data entity is the KRI templates entity that can be accessed using the KRI Templates quick link in the Key Risk Indicators section on the Rule Setup work center as shown in Figure 15.18.

KRI templates capture categorization and classification for KRIs that are used in ERM. Hence, KRI templates need not be set up if KRIs aren't being used. Figure 15.19 shows a sample list of KRI templates.

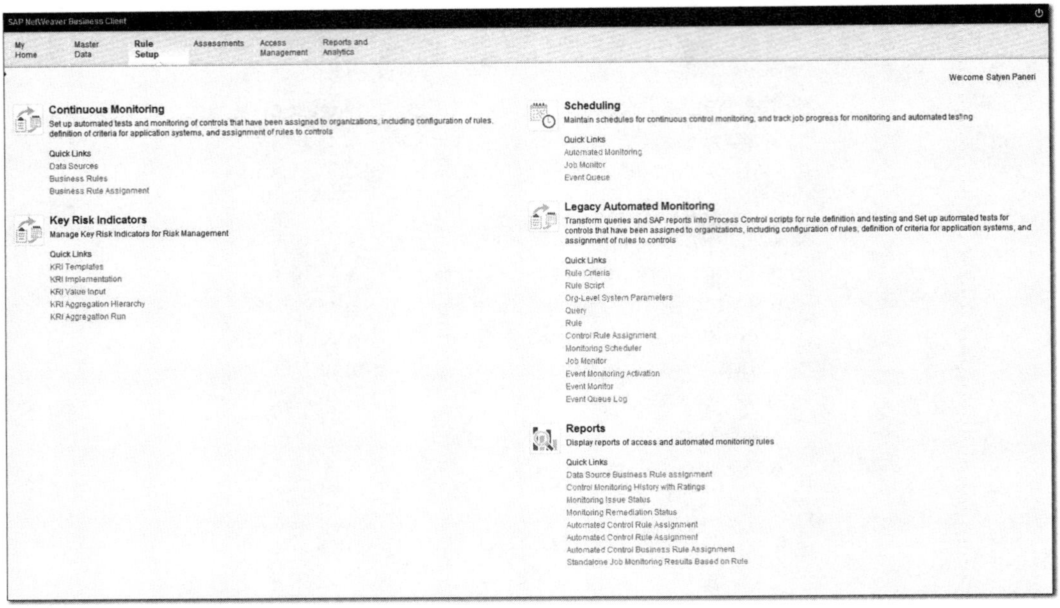

Figure 15.18 Rule Setup Work Center

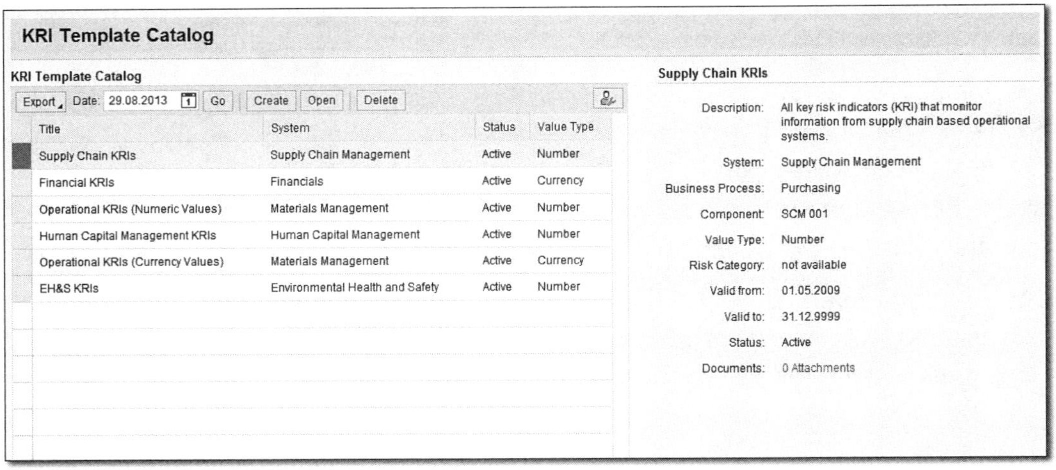

Figure 15.19 KRI Templates Structure

Details of one such KRI template is shown in Figure 15.20.

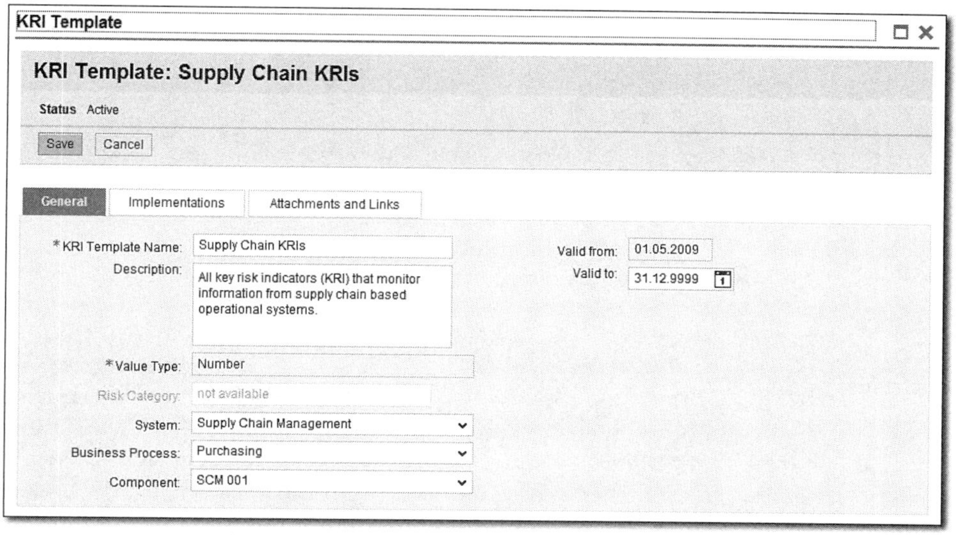

Figure 15.20 KRI Template Definition

Table 15.9 describes details of the setup necessary for the various tabs for a KRI template.

Configuration and tab details in the setup of a KRI template

KRI Template Tab	Description
GENERAL	Capture general attributes for a KRI template such as NAME, DESCRIPTION, VALID TO, and others:. ▶ The VALID TO attribute is used to define the validity time frame for a KRI template. ▶ The VALUE TYPE attribute specifies the type of KRIs (NUMBER, CURRENCY, QUANTITY, SCORE, etc.) applicable for this template. The selections available for these attributes are defined in IMG customizing. ▶ The RISK CATEGORY is a read-only attribute that shows the risk category linked with the KRI template. ▶ The SYSTEM, BUSINESS PROCESS, and COMPONENT attributes are optional and capture a three-level classification structure for KRI templates. The selections available for these attributes are defined in IMG customizing.

Table 15.9 KRI Template Settings

KRI Template Tab	Description
IMPLEMENTATIONS	Lists the KRI implementations that use the KRI template.
ATTACHMENTS AND LINKS	Define additional information for the KRI template by either attaching documents or specifying URL links. The use of this tab is optional for ERM.

Table 15.9 KRI Template Settings (Cont.)

Master Data Upload Generator and its application for SAP Risk Management

Note

The Master Data Upload Generator (MDUG) tool is currently only available for SAP Process Control. However, as the ORGANIZATIONS, POLICIES, and RISK CATALOG entities are shared between SAP Process Control and SAP Risk Management, MDUG can be used to upload them. The remaining entities (BUSINESS OBJECTIVES, ACTIVITY HIERARCHY, RESPONSE CATALOG, and KRI TEMPLATES) described previously have to be set up manually in SAP Risk Management.

Often customers manage risks using spreadsheets and other documents prior to leveraging SAP Risk Management. Hence, in addition to the master data entities described earlier, customers often have lists of activities, risks, and incidents they want to load into the solution. SAP Risk Management supports upload for such transactional data for activities, risks, and incidents. If such information needs to be set up in the SAP Risk Management system, capture the details in the blueprint document, and use the following process and screens shown to set up this data.

To upload these transactional data entities, first go to the ASSESSMENTS work center as shown in Figure 15.21.

Activities

Use the ACTIVITIES quick link under the RISK ASSESSMENTS section to upload activities. This shows the list of ACTIVITIES in the system. Use the UPLOAD menu button available on this screen (see Figure 15.22) to upload activities from a Microsoft Excel or XML document. Use the DOWNLOAD menu button to generate the upload file format document.

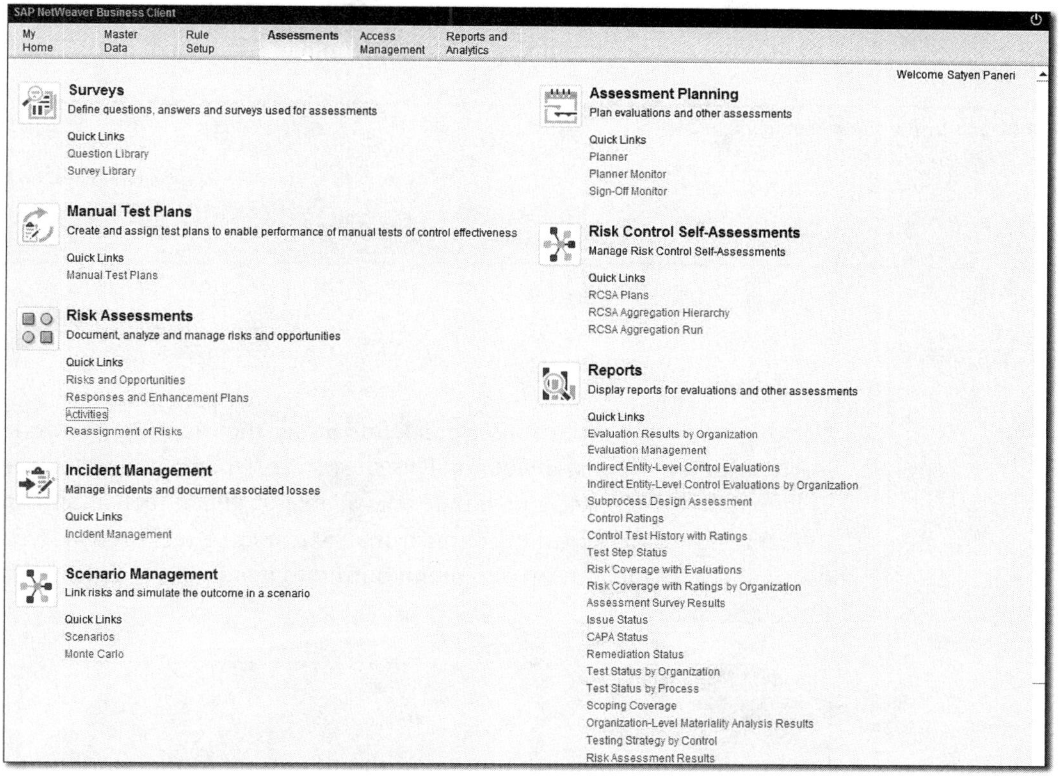

Figure 15.21 Assessments Work Center

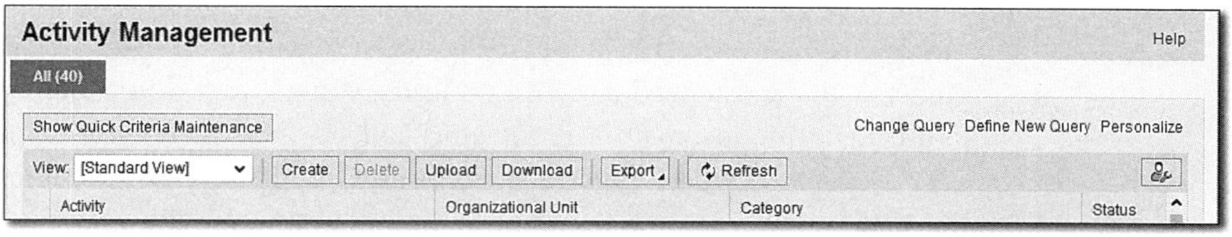

Figure 15.22 Upload for Activities

Risks

Use the RISKS AND OPPORTUNITIES quick link under the RISK ASSESSMENTS section to upload risks. This shows the list of RISKS in the system. Use the UPLOAD menu button available on this screen as shown in Figure

15.23 to upload risks from a Microsoft Excel or XML document. Use the DOWNLOAD menu button to generate the upload file format document.

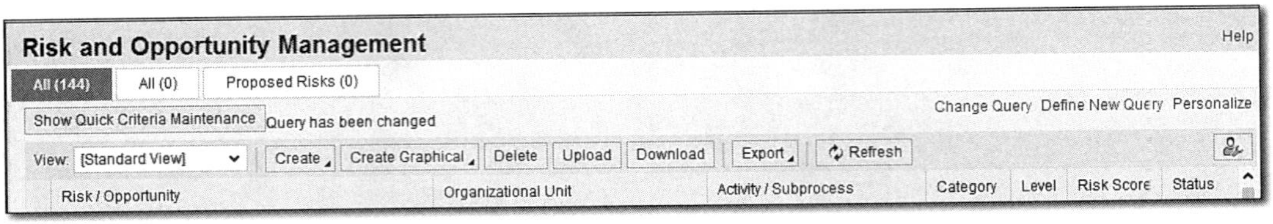

Figure 15.23 Upload for Risks

Incidents

Use the INCIDENT MANAGEMENT quick link under the INCIDENT MANAGEMENT section to upload incidents. This shows the list of INCIDENTS in the system. Use the UPLOAD menu button available on this screen as shown in Figure 15.24 to upload incidents from a Microsoft Excel or XML type document. Use the DOWNLOAD menu button to generate the upload file format document.

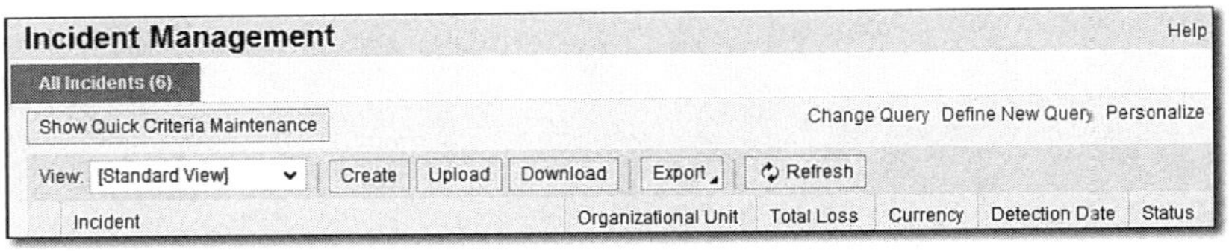

Figure 15.24 Upload for Incidents

Customers may also use surveys and questionnaires for risk assessments. If these also need to be set up in the system, capture the details in the blueprint document. Use the quick links in the SURVEYS section in the ASSESSMENTS work center as shown earlier in Figure 15.21 to set up this data.

15.2.4 Authorization Concept and Roles

The SAP Risk Management application is based on the SAP NetWeaver authorization model and assigns authorizations to users based on roles. SAP standard roles (Transaction PFCG basic roles) provide the technical standard authorizations to the ABAP server. These roles are hierarchical and provide top-down authorizations. Roles at a higher entity level have greater authorizations to perform tasks and greater access to the application than roles at a lower entity level. This hierarchy also affects task assignments, workflows, and business event processing. Furthermore, a second-level authorization allows restriction of the user selection for entity-level role assignments. So only those users who have been assigned the corresponding Transaction PFCG role in their user profile are available for an assignment.

Required role types for SAP Risk Management

To use SAP Risk Management, the following three types of roles must be set up and activated.

- **SAP NetWeaver Portal role**
  This role enables users to configure the portal navigation structures and menu tabs. This role should be assigned to all SAP Risk Management users either directly or via a group in the portal. The administrator must ensure that the portal interface can be accessed with the correct level of authorization by all other users.
- **Standard or backend roles**
  These roles define the authorizations in the backend system, where, for example, customizing is done. This kind of role should be assigned to users that require a backend user profile. The standard roles that are delivered with the SAP Risk Management application are the following:
  - **Basic role (SAP_GRC_FN_BASE)**: The basic technical role for a user who wants to use SAP Risk Management. This role contains all necessary authorizations to make the necessary customizing settings for this application. This role doesn't contain any authorizations for the portal interface.
  - **Business user (SAP_GRC_FN_BUSINESS_USER)**: A user with this role is only authorized to perform operations on assigned entities in SAP Risk Management. It's recommended that a user with this role also be assigned a portal role for SAP Risk Management to use the web interface of the application.
  - **Power user (SAP_GRC_FN_ALL)**: In addition to the authorizations of the business user, a power user also has authorization for administrative functions in customizing, such as the definition of organizational units.

- **Display user (SAP_GRC_FN_DISPLAY)**: A user with this role can display all risk data in the portal. This role is useful for external auditors.

  The portal administrator can use these standard roles directly. Administrators can also copy the delivered roles, makes any necessary adjustments to suit customer needs, and assign the modified copy of the standard roles to the end users to grant them the required access to the SAP Risk Management application. Administrators can copy and adjust these default roles in customizing (Transaction PFCG).

- **Application roles**
  These roles refine the authorizations delivered in the business user standard role (SAP_GRC_FN_BUSINESS_USER) to support application-specific operations such as create, edit, and delete for different application entities such as organizations, risks, and activities.

SAP Risk Management includes additional application roles, as detailed in Table 15.10.

Application Role Name	Business Role
SAP_GRC_RM_API_ACTIVITY_OWNER	Activity owner
SAP_GRC_RM_API_CENTRAL_RM	Central risk manager
SAP_GRC_RM_API_CEO_CFO	CEO/CFO
SAP_GRC_RM_API_INCIDENT_EDITOR	Incident editor
SAP_GRC_RM_API_INTERNAL_AUD	Internal auditor
SAP_GRC_RM_API_LIAISON	System administrator
SAP_GRC_RM_API_OPP_OWNER	Opportunity owner
SAP_GRC_RM_API_ORG_OWNER	Organization owner
SAP_GRC_RM_API_RISK_MANAGER	Unit risk manager
SAP_GRC_RM_API_RISK_OWNER	Risk owner
SAP_GRC_RM_API_RISK_EXPERT	Risk expert

Table 15.10 SAP Risk Management Application Roles

Modifying application roles

Application roles are also maintained and modified using Transaction PFCG. SAP GRC customizing (Transaction SPRO) is used to assign application roles to entities such as organizations, activities, opportunities, risks, and incidents. Users are finally assigned to the entity-role combination in the SAP Risk Management application frontend. Single or multiple users can be configured for assignment to each entity-role combination. The following three-step process is shown in Figure 15.25:

Use the standard application roles available with SAP Risk Management, or copy the role and make updates. This can be accomplished using Transaction PFCG.

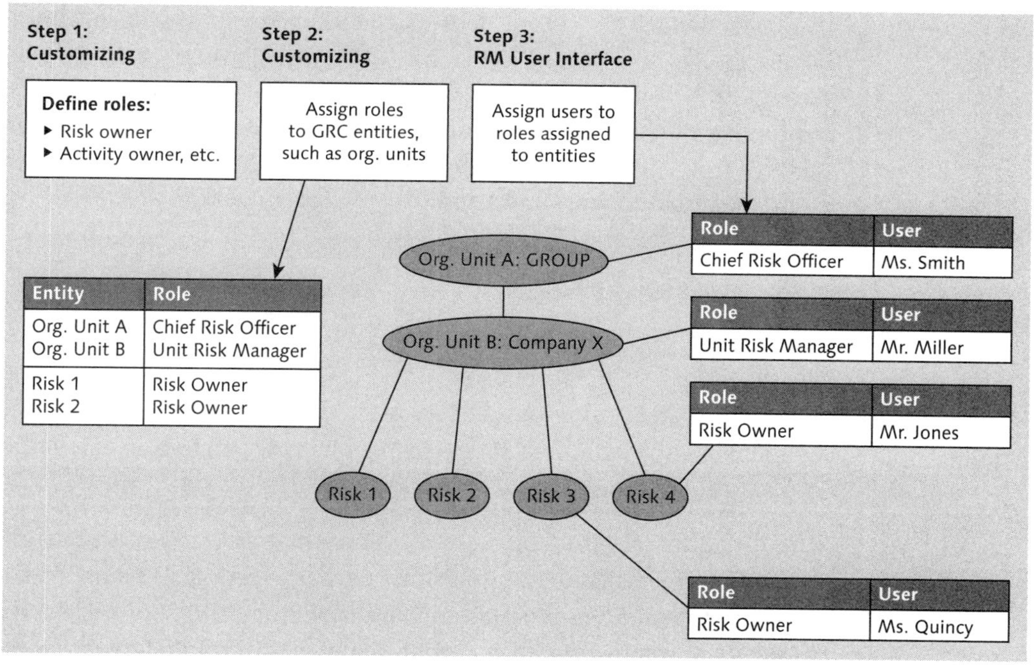

Figure 15.25 Users, Roles, and Assignments to Authorization Objects

Assign the roles to the SAP GRC entities such as organizations, activities, opportunities, risks, and incidents by using Transaction SPRO. For each entity-role combination, administrators can specify whether a single user or multiple users can be assigned.

Assign users to the entity-role combination. This is accomplished in the frontend portal. Each entity, such as organizations, activities, risks, and incidents, has a ROLES tab. Using this tab, one or more users, depending on the configuration in the preceding step 2, can be assigned to the entity-role combination.

In this part of the blueprinting exercise, users, roles, role modifications, entity-role assignments, and user to entity-role assignments are identified and documented.

15.2.5 Workflows

SAP Risk Management ships with a set of workflows that enable collaboration on risk management activities within a company by making use of the standard SAP workflow functionality. SAP workflows are based on the guided procedures that walk users through a risk management activity or process. Workflow examples include collaborative risk reassessments, validation of assessment results, or reviews of a newly documented risk. There are two types of workflows in SAP Risk Management: event-based workflows and planner-based workflows.

Event-Based Workflows

Event-based workflows are predefined end-to-end processes triggered by user actions such as proposing a risk or KRI alerts. Event-based workflows are defined using business events: A business event involves the assignment of a workflow task to a recipient, which is also known as agent determination.

Agent determination is the system process that assigns users to workflows. The entity-based authorization concept in SAP Risk Management is used for agent determination in workflow processing. For each usage of agent determination, a business event is determined. A business event is a placeholder for recipient determination in workflow-driven scenarios or surveys, and the workflow processor or survey recipient is considered the agent. For agent determination, the implementation team maps the SAP Risk Management roles to the business events in customizing (Transaction SPRO). The assignment of business events to SAP Risk Management application roles in customizing is optional. If no customizing has been defined here, the workflows route to the users defined under the ROLES tab for the relevant entity. This default system behavior might be suitable for most customers. When the workflow or survey requires the agent, it triggers the agent determination rule with the corresponding business event and object ID.

Event based workflow types for SAP Risk Management

Table 15.11 details the event-based workflows that are found in SAP Risk Management.

Workflow Name	Description	Trigger
Propose Risk	Ensures that users review a (potential) risk entered through the Propose Risk function and rework it if necessary before adding it to the risk database.	User entry through My Home • Ad Hoc Tasks • Risk Proposal
Report Incident	Ensures that users check a reported incident for completeness and accuracy before adding it to the incident database.	User entry through My Home • Ad Hoc Tasks • Incidents
KRI Implementation Request	Ensures the proper configuration and system setup for KRI-related data, which should be available for risk monitoring.	KRI implementation request
KRI Localization Request	Optional adjustment of an assigned KRI with respect to risk-specific settings.	KRI localization request
Propose Control	Allows users (e.g., risk managers) to propose a control to mitigate a risk. The control becomes part of the regular monitoring activities in SAP Process Control.	Propose • Control button on the Response Plans tab for a risk

Table 15.11 Risk Management Event-Based Workflows, Descriptions, and System Triggers

Now that we've looked at the event-based workflows and their triggers, let's look at the planner-based workflows.

Planner-Based Workflows

Planner is the common scheduling and planning tool for all SAP GRC solutions. Planner can be accessed under the Assessments work center on the SAP GRC portal. Planner-based workflows are planned and triggered through the SAP Risk Management Planner function, such as updating a risk or creating a risk survey. These workflows route to the appropriate recipients and appear as tasks in the users WORK INBOX.

Planner-based workflow types for SAP Risk Management

SAP Risk Management contains the planner-based workflows detailed in Table 15.12.

Workflow Name	Description
Activity Validation	Allows a planner (e.g., a risk manager) to obtain sign-off and confirmation for the current risk situation for an activity (such as a process, project, or company asset).
Risk Validation	Enables the risk manager to obtain sign-off and confirmation for the current risk (including the assigned responses).
Opportunity Validation	Enables the risk manager to obtain sign-off and confirmation for the current opportunity (including analysis and assigned enhancement plans).
Risk Assessment	Supports risk managers to initiate risk assessments (simple assessments, collaborative assessments, and survey-based assessments).
Opportunity Assessment	Supports opportunity managers to initiate opportunity assessments.
Response Update	Enables risk managers and risk owners to keep track of current risk responses.

Table 15.12 Planner-Based Workflows in SAP Risk Management

The workflow customizing (Transaction SPRO) activities as outlined in Table 15.13, (under GOVERNANCE, RISK AND COMPLIANCE • GENERAL SETTINGS • WORKFLOW) must be carried out to enable SAP Risk Management workflows.

Customizing Activity	Description
MAINTAIN CUSTOM AGENT DETERMINATION RULES	Specifies the agent determination rules to be used for business events in SAP Risk Management

Table 15.13 Customizing Activities in SAP Risk Management

Customizing Activity	Description
PERFORM AUTOMATIC WORKFLOW CUSTOMIZING	Assigns customer notification messages to workflow recipients
PERFORM TASK-SPECIFIC CUSTOMIZING	Makes the settings required to adapt SAP workflows to SAP Risk Management

Table 15.13 Customizing Activities in SAP Risk Management (Cont.)

Now that we've covered workflows, let's move on to reporting.

15.2.6 Reporting

As recommended when we discussed the customer adoption model, it's best to start by using the standard reports and analytics available under the REPORTS AND ANALYTICS work center as shown in Figure 15.26.

ERM reports are available through the quick links under the RISKS AND OPPORTUNITIES and the INCIDENTS AND LOSSES sections shown in Figure 15.26. The SAP Risk Management dashboards are available through the quick links under the MANAGEMENT section. The SAP Risk Management 10.0 Learning Maps on the SAP Service Marketplace provide details on all of the REPORTS AND ANALYTICS quick links shown in Figure 15.26.

However, often there is a need for custom reporting, and the requirements can be documented in the blueprint. SAP NetWeaver Business Warehouse, SAP Business Intelligence solutions, Operational Data Provider (ODP, SAP NetWeaver 7.40), and SAP HANA Live can be used for developing custom reports and analytics. SAP Risk Management includes reporting content to support all of these tools.

In Section 15.2.1, we outlined the process for generating a business blueprint document for the ERM scenario. The blueprint document is then used to configure the solution, set up master data, set up user authorizations, enable workflows, and develop custom reports if necessary. After this is complete, the implementation goes through user acceptance and integration testing. Modifications are made to the implementation based on the outcomes from the user acceptance testing. After users sign off on the readiness of system setup, the installation is replicated to the production environment use of ERM commences.

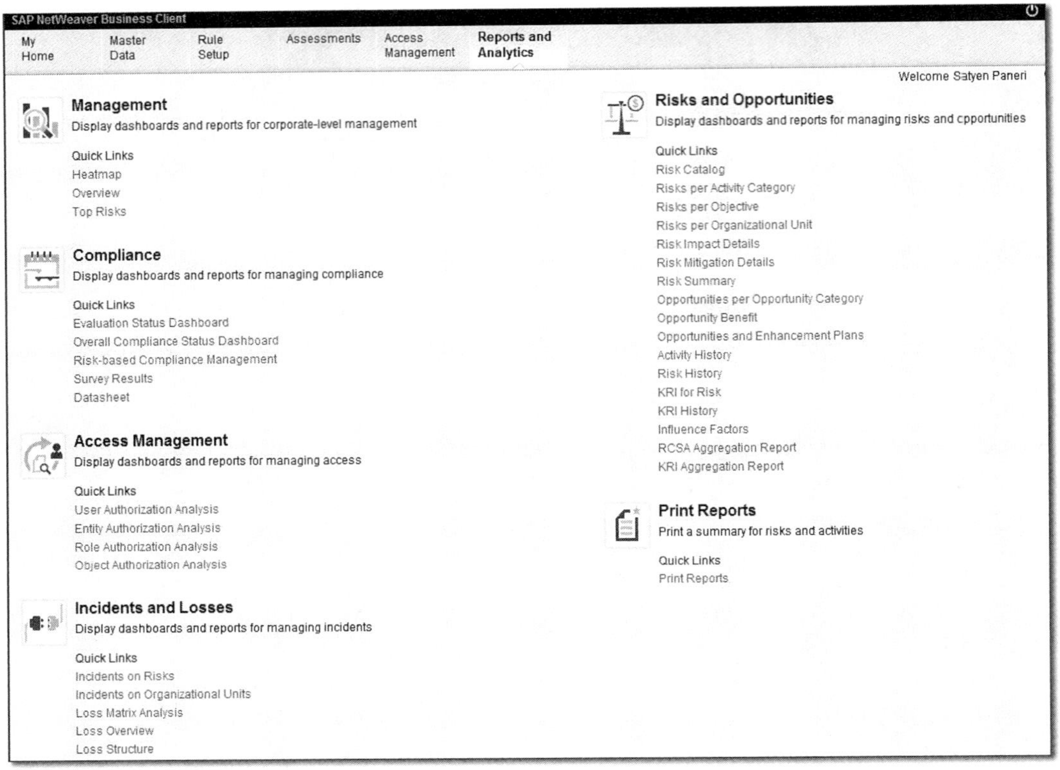

Figure 15.26 Reports and Analytics Work Center

If there are subsequent phases in ERM implementation, or the customer advances to the next stage in the adoption model outlined in the beginning, the same process should be repeated.

Now that we've fully explored ERM—the standard implementation of SAP Risk Management—from project preparation all of the way to go-live, let's look at how customers in certain industries can additionally leverage the embedded Operational Risk Management functionality.

15.3 Operational Risk Management Overview

The SAP Risk Management license includes the Operational Risk Management (ORM) functionality applicable for financial institutions—banks, insurance, automotive companies with finance divisions, as well as energy and utility companies involved in commodities trading. The default solution installation has the ORM functionality turned off. Before we discuss how to enable this additional functionality, let's define ORM, the need for financial institutions to manage operational risk along with enterprise risk, and the benefits such customers can expect from the solution.

More than ever, financial institutions are investing in IT solutions to automate and optimize GRC activities. Fraught with change, unpredictability, and risk, today's business environment demands an effective ORM strategy.

Additionally, regulatory requirements such as the Basel II Capital Accord (Basel II), the planned Basel III Capital Accord (Basel III), and Solvency II require comprehensive measurement of both internal and external risks. An organization must focus simultaneously on in-house process controls for fraud detection, employment practices, and workplace safety, as well as understand the impact of external factors on the business and have failovers in place in case of IT system failures.

In addition to obtaining reports from various LOBs, organizations must create an enterprise view of risk that reflects and measures potential threats to the institution. With the entire organization exposed to operational risk, decisions and recommendations to management must satisfy both existing and upcoming regulations and standards as well as align with the enterprise strategy.

Traditional ORM methods, where bits of information are rolled up from various LOBs, are no longer sufficient to achieve these goals. To create real value through an ORM process, an organization must evaluate the exposure of the whole institution in line with its business strategy. While meeting these business challenges, one must also understand potential exposures of IT systems. Additionally, management and regulators expect financial institutions to integrate external risk factors into a holistic picture of the risks it faces.

ORM enables customers to do the following:

- Measure, monitor, and control through KRIs.
- Improve profitability through more accurate and future-oriented risk measurement.

- Satisfy regulatory requirements such as Basel II, Basel III, and Solvency II.
- Integrate ORM processes with existing operational systems such as HR, credit processing, and transactional banking systems.
- Integrate ORM into enterprise risk reporting alongside credit risk, market, and liquidity risk management.
- Support loss and capital reduction.
- Increase rating agency confidence and profitability.
- Optimize risk mitigation through integration with the SAP Access Control application and the SAP Process Control solutions.

Customers that want to use the ORM functionality can use SAP Note 1601962 (*https://service.sap.com/support/notes/1601962*) to turn on the following additional features:

- **Static data management**
  Managing multidimensional interlinked structures to support organizational-, process-, and product-dependent views over time.
- **Loss event management**
  Categorizing and distributing losses with capital allocation embedded in flexible workflows, and grouping losses and mitigating risks to protect against recurrence of loss.
- **KRIs**
  Integrating with operative systems to automate the data collection and updating process for KRIs, and supporting calculation rules for highly flexible dynamic aggregation.
- **Risk control self-assessment**
  Creating surveys that include dynamic result aggregation, and assessment workshop with a graphical user interface that provides complete access to the data repository.
- **Scenario analysis and risk engine**
  Enabling scenario analysis through risk analysis combined with scenario loss generation, and supporting approaches for Basel II (basic indicator approach [BIA], standard approach [STA], and advanced measurement approach [AMA]) and Basel III (grouped losses).

- **Quantitative requirements**
  Obtaining high-quality calibration results based on various distributions and supporting the most prominent loss distribution approach with Monte Carlo simulations with the SAP NetWeaver certified solution OpVision (*www.opvision.es*) from SAP Partner Quantitative Risk Research (QRR, *www.qrr.es*).
- **Reporting**
  Enabling system-specific and enterprise-wide reporting that includes comprehensive analytical interactive reports and dashboards customizable for different management levels.
- **SAP Access Control and SAP Process Control**
  Enabling deeper risk mitigation through integration with SAP Access Control (access risk and SoD management) and SAP Process Control (internal control management).

Similar to our approach in the ERM sections, we'll explore an ORM implementation scenario and follow the implementation process from business blueprinting to go-live.

15.4 Operational Risk Management Scenario

Financial institutions need to manage operational risk to meet certain external regulatory requirements as well as internal requirements. Typically, the approach and functionality used for ORM varies based on the size of the institution. Hence, similar to our approach in Section 15.2, prior to delving into the implementation process, let's review a customer adoption model.

Note

Prior to using the specific ORM functionality, customers have to implement the standard ERM scenario as covered in Section 15.2. This is a prerequisite for the SAP Risk Management solution setup.

The first pillar of the Basel II Capital Accord deals with maintenance of regulatory capital calculated for three major components of risk that a financial institution faces: credit risk, operational risk, and market risk. Capital requirement refers to the standardized requirements in place for banks and other depository institutions, which determines how much capital is required to be held for a certain level of assets through regulatory agencies such as the Bank for International Settlements, Federal Deposit Insurance Corporation (FDIC), or Federal Reserve Board. These requirements are put into place to ensure that these institutions aren't participating or holding investments that increase the risk of default and that they have enough capital to sustain operating losses while still honoring withdrawals. This is also known as regulatory capital. There are three different approaches used to determine regulatory capital requirements for operational risk: basic indicator approach (BIA), standardized approach (STA), and the internal measurement approach (an advanced form of which is the advanced measurement approach [AMA]).

The model described in Tables 15.14 and 15.15 provide a recommendation for customers based on their external versus internal requirements, size of the institution, and the capital determination method being used. Note that this is simply a recommendation, and customers can choose to ignore the model and/or use a hybrid approach.

Small financial institutions implementation model

External Regulatory Requirements			Internal Requirements
Basic Indicator Approach (BIA)	Standardized Approach (STA)	Advanced Measurement Approach (AMA)	
▸ Simple static data management (organization and risk category hierarchies) ▸ Loss event management ▸ Analytics	▸ Advanced static data management (views and dependent hierarchies) ▸ Loss event management ▸ Risk control self-assessments (RCSA) and surveys ▸ Risks ▸ Analytics	▸ Usually not applicable	▸ Risk control self-assessments (RCSA) and surveys ▸ KRIs

Table 15.14 Small Financial Institution Implementation Model Comparison

Large financial institutions implementation model

External Regulatory Requirements			Internal Requirements
Basic Indicator Approach (BIA)	Standardized Approach (STA)	Advanced Measurement Approach (AMA)	
▸ Usually not applicable	▸ Advanced static data management (views and dependent hierarchies) ▸ Loss event management ▸ RCSA and surveys ▸ Risks ▸ Analytics	▸ Advanced static data management (views and dependent hierarchies) ▸ Loss event management (external losses, scenario losses, Operational Risk Exchange (ORX) integration, etc.) ▸ RCSA and surveys ▸ Risks ▸ Analytics	▸ RCSA and surveys ▸ RCSA aggregation ▸ KRIs ▸ KRI aggregation ▸ Additional static data management (product and process hierarchies) ▸ Integration with SAP Process Control and SAP Access Control

Table 15.15 Large Financial Institution Implementation Model Comparison

After you've reviewed and chosen the best implementation model, you naturally shift your focus to the solution implementation. The implementation process used is the same as shown earlier in Figure 15.2. Similar to our approach in Section 15.2, we'll only focus on the business blueprint stage that captures customer requirements for the ORM scenario.

15.4.1 Business Blueprint

The objective of this most critical phase of the project is to understand the customer's ORM process and business requirements. The business blueprint document captures the customer's business requirements, mapping the requirements to solution functionality, along with details about system configuration and data setup. The business blueprint is developed in close consultation with the business users and serves as a reference scope document for the solution implementation.

Blueprinting tasks for an Operational Risk Management implementation

Next, we describe how to complete the several blueprinting tasks before we launch into the realization phase of our implementation of ORM. In the following sections, we'll review:

- Solution configuration
- Master data setup
- Loss event management workflow and upload
- Reporting

Let's look at each of these elements of the blueprinting phase for ORM in further detail.

15.4.2 Solution Configuration

In the solution configuration task, the customer business requirements are mapped to the SAP Risk Management Customizing Implementation Guide (Transaction SPRO). The parent GOVERNANCE, RISK, AND COMPLIANCE node in the IMG specifies customizing entries for all GRC solutions. The IMG entries for the OPERATIONAL RISK MANAGEMENT FOR BANKING INDUSTRY section as shown in Figure 15.27 under the RISK MANAGEMENT node are required to be set up. These IMG entries define configuration for LOSS EVENT MANAGEMENT attributes and workflow, RISK CONTROL SELF-ASSESSMENTS setup, and AGGREGATION score and color settings. Documentation and usage details for each IMG entry is available as part of Transaction SPRO.

15.4.3 Master Data Setup

Next, let's look at the master data requirements for the customer. For ORM, the four primary master data entities are ORGANIZATIONS, RISK CATEGORIES, PROCESSES, and PRODUCTS. These entities are available in the MASTER DATA work center on the portal as shown in Figure 15.28.

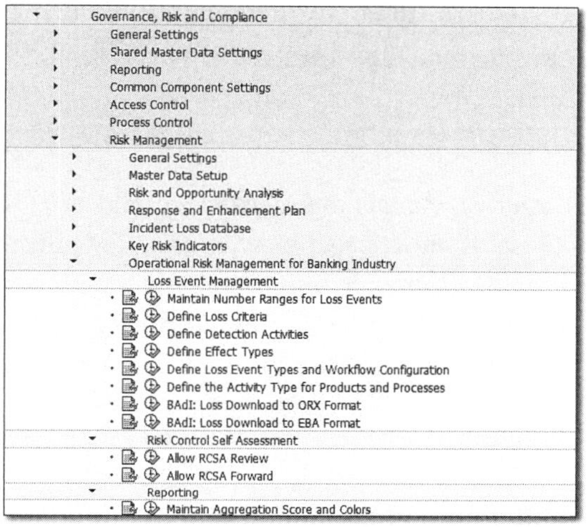

Figure 15.27 Operational Risk Management for Banking Industry IMG Entries

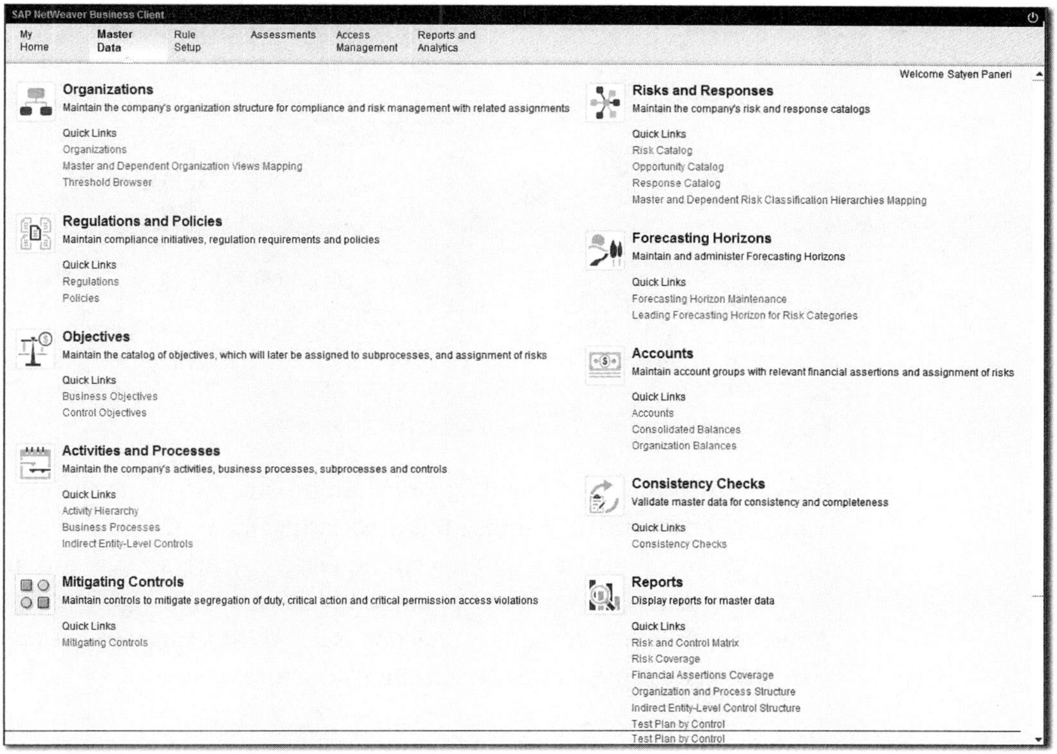

Figure 15.28 Master Data Work Center

Now let's look at each of these four entities in further detail and see how customer requirements can be captured and mapped in the solution.

Organizations

Organizations can have a master or management structure and one or more dependent structures (Basel II view, Legal view, Audit view, Business Line view, ORX view, etc.). Customer requirements for the master and dependent structures, including the mapping, are captured in the business blueprint. Figure 15.29 shows a sample of how customers may define their requirements.

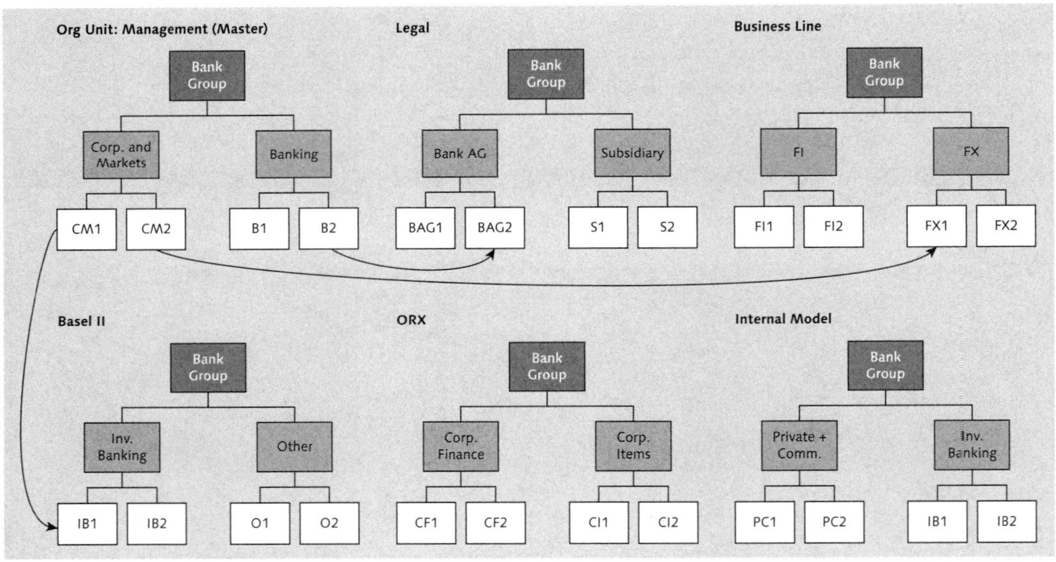

Figure 15.29 Master and Dependent Organization Structures

Both the master and dependent organization structures are captured using the ORGANIZATIONS quick link under the ORGANIZATIONS section shown earlier in Figure 15.28. Open the ORGANIZATIONS quick link to view the organizations master data. A sample is shown in Figure 15.30. At the top, the VIEW dropdown selection is set to MANAGEMENT HIERARCHY. This view is the master organization structure.

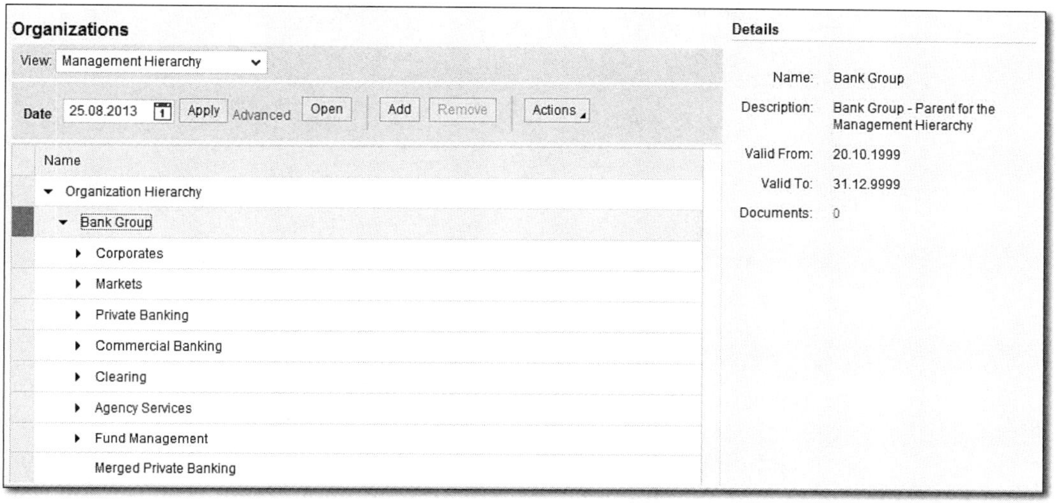

Figure 15.30 Master Organization Structure

The dependent structures are set up as organizational views. Figure 15.31 shows the ORX dependent structure view, and Figure 15.32 shows the BASEL II dependent structure view.

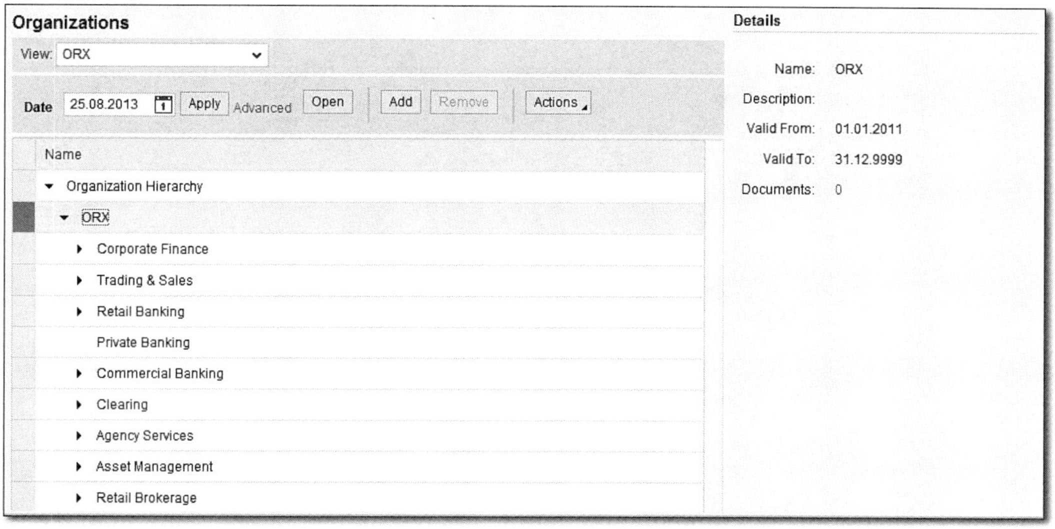

Figure 15.31 ORX Dependent Organization Structure

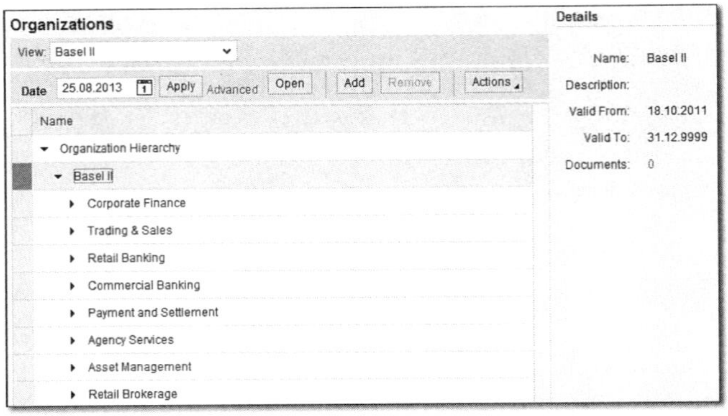

Figure 15.32 Basel II Dependent Organization Structure

In addition to capturing the master and dependent organization structures, the entities need to be mapped between these structures. The mapping enables reports and analytics to find and pull the appropriate loss and risk information for the dependent structures. This mapping is done using the MASTER AND DEPENDENT ORGANIZATION VIEWS MAPPING quick link under the ORGANIZATIONS section shown earlier in Figure 15.28. Open the MASTER AND DEPENDENT ORGANIZATION VIEWS MAPPING quick link to define this mapping as shown in Figure 15.33.

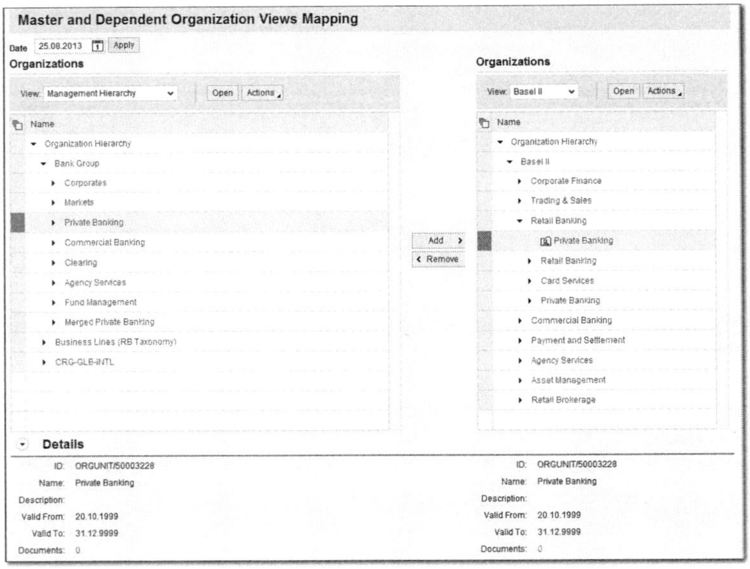

Figure 15.33 Master and Dependent Organization Views Mapping

In Figure 15.33 the Private Banking node of the master organization structure is mapped to the Retail Banking node of the Basel II dependent organization structure.

Risk Categories

Similar to organizations, risk categories can also have a master or management structure and one or more dependent structures (Basel II view, Business Line view, ORX view, etc.). Customer requirements for the master and dependent structures, including the mapping, are captured in the business blueprint. Figure 15.34 shows a sample of how customers may define their requirements.

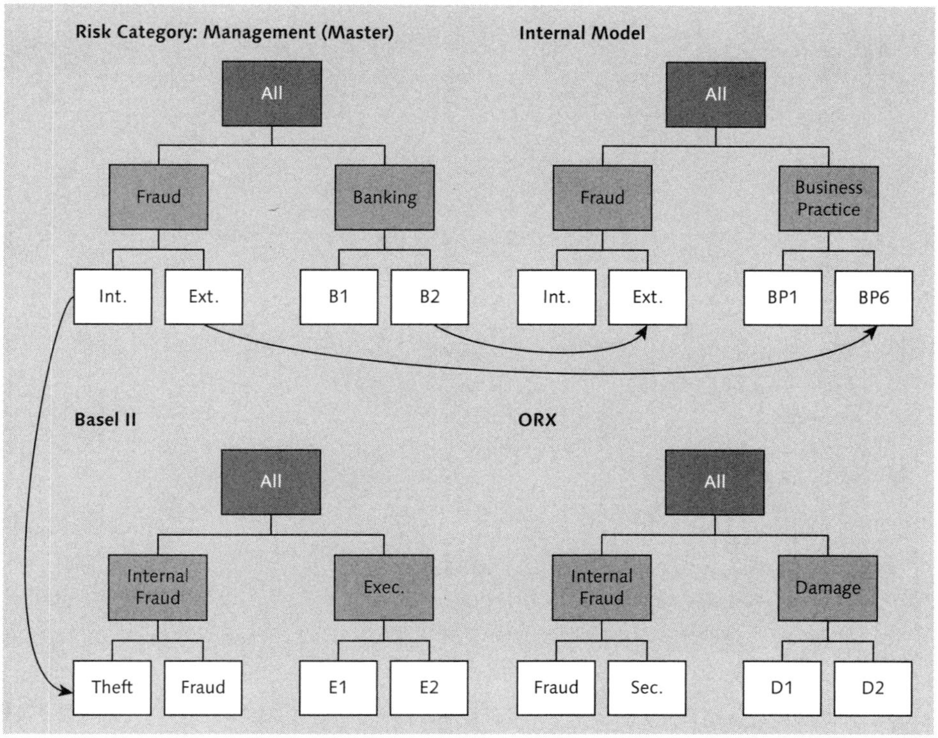

Figure 15.34 Master and Dependent Risk Category Structures

Both the master and dependent risk category structures are captured using the Risk Catalog quick link under the Risks and Responses section shown earlier in Figure 15.28. Open the Risk Catalog quick link to view the risk category master data. A sample is shown in Figure 15.35. This common master data entity captures risk categories and risk templates for the entire solution. The master and dependent structures are set up as different parent nodes under the classification hierarchy. The Is Secondary Top Node attribute of a parent node distinguishes between master and dependent structures.

The Is Secondary Top Node attribute is set as No for master structures. The Operational Risk structure as shown in Figure 15.35 is a master structure as the Is Secondary Top Node attribute is set as No. In fact, all nodes except the VOEB node in Figure 15.35 are master risk category structures. Here you see several nodes—both the ERM and the ORM scenarios in this solution—have been implemented.

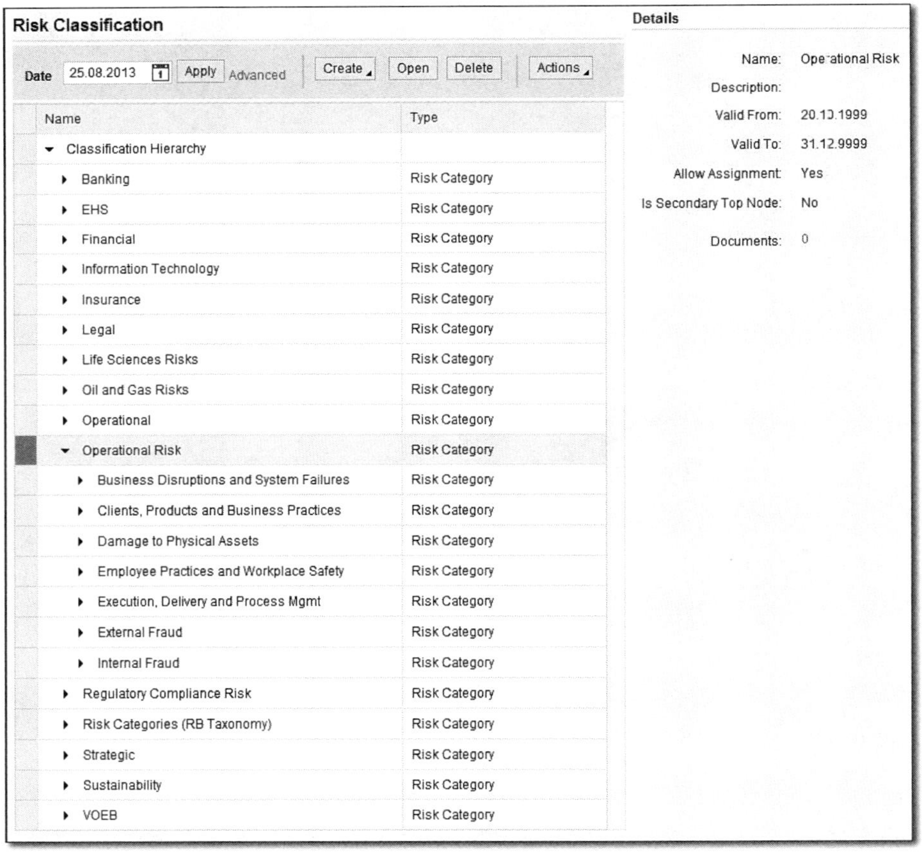

Figure 15.35 Master Risk Category Structure

Figure 15.36 shows the VOEB structure, which is a dependent risk category, as the Is Secondary Top Node attribute is set as Yes.

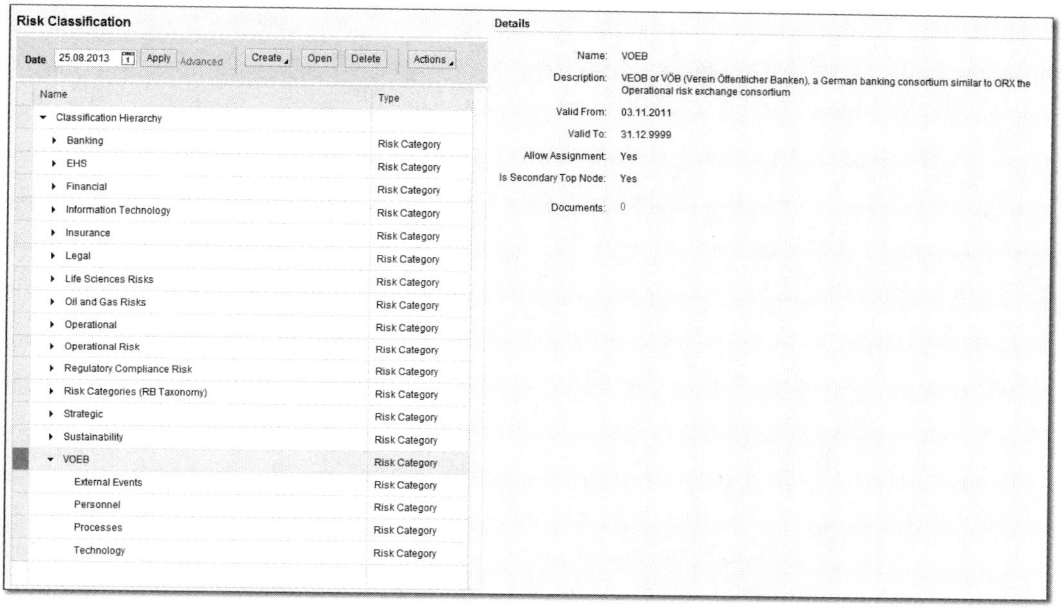

Figure 15.36 VOEB Dependent Risk Category Structure

In addition to capturing the master and dependent risk category structures, the entities need to be mapped between these structures. The mapping enables reports and analytics to find and pull the appropriate loss and risk information for the dependent structures. This mapping is done using the Master and Dependent Risk Classification Hierarchies Mapping quick link under the Risks and Responses section shown earlier in Figure 15.28. Open the Master and Dependent Risk Classification Hierarchies Mapping quick link to define this mapping as shown in Figure 15.37.

In Figure 15.37, the External Fraud node of the Operational Risk category structure is mapped to the External Events node of the VOEB dependent risk category structure.

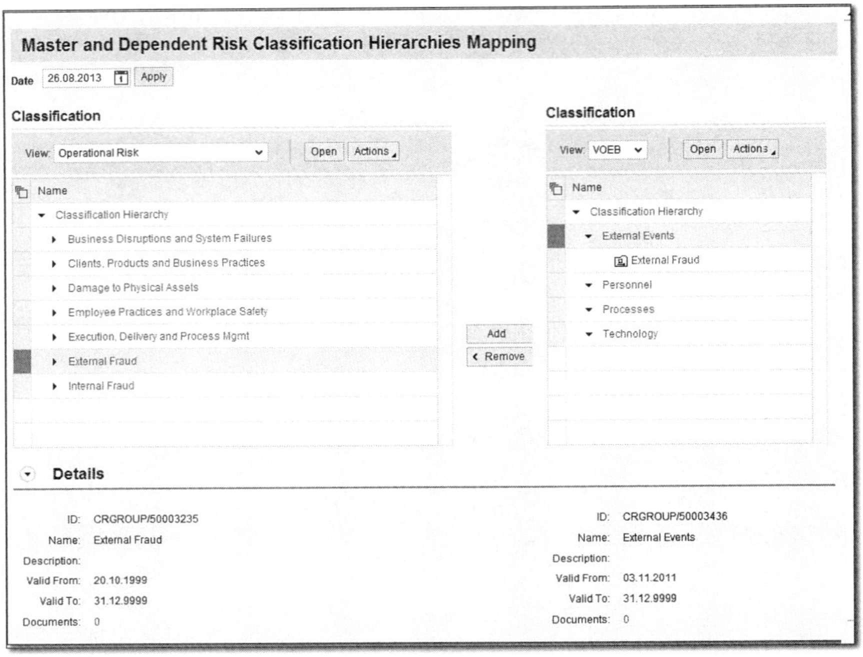

Figure 15.37 Master and Dependent Risk Classification Hierarchies Mapping

Processes and Products

Processes and products have a single master structure and don't have dependent structures customer requirements for the processes, and product structures are captured in the business blueprint. Figure 15.38 shows a sample of how customers may define their requirements.

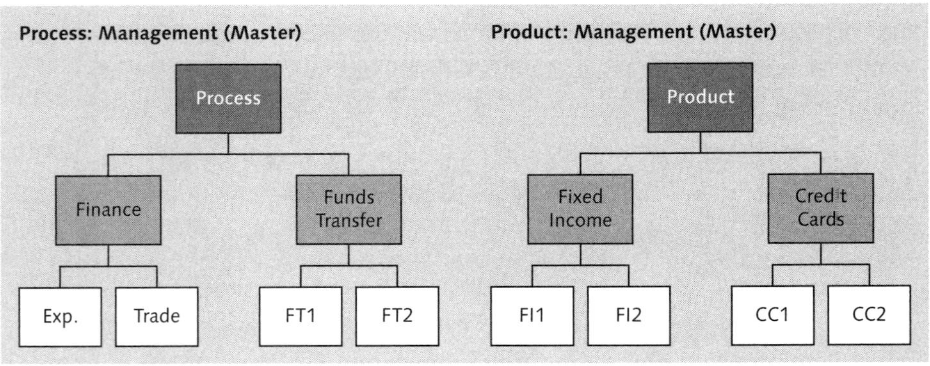

Figure 15.38 Process and Product Structures

Both the process and product structures are captured using the ACTIVITY HIERARCHY quick link under the ACTIVITIES AND PROCESSES section shown earlier in Figure 15.28. Open the ACTIVITY HIERARCHY quick link to view the activity hierarchy master data. A sample is shown in Figure 15.39. At the top, the SHOW dropdown is set to BUSINESS PROCESSES. Hence, you see the processes structure.

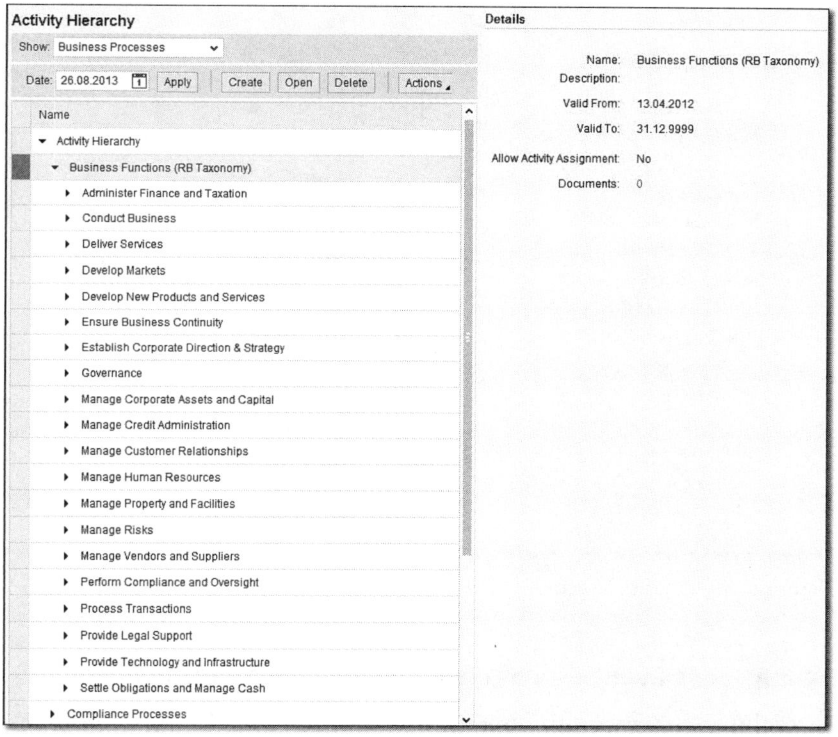

Figure 15.39 Process Structure

The product structure can be set up as another type of activity hierarchy. Figure 15.40 similarly shows the PRODUCTS/SERVICES structure.

Now that the master data business requirements are captured, let's review a few details about loss event management, which is the cornerstone of ORM. Losses are part of the transactional data, but from a blueprint perspective, a couple items need to be captured.

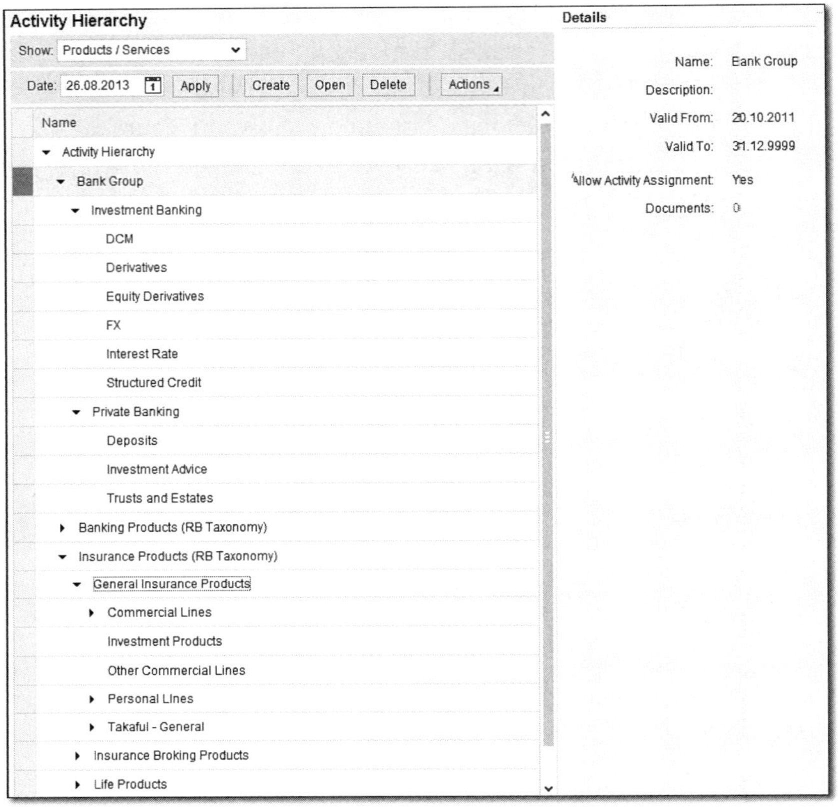

Figure 15.40 Product Structure

15.4.4 Loss Event Management Workflow and Upload

First the loss event management workflow needs to be set up. The loss event management workflow is very flexible and adaptable for all customer requirements. This workflow is set up in the IMG customizing entries (Transaction SPRO). The SOLUTION CONFIGURATION section describes the list of IMG entries to be set up. The DEFINE LOSS EVENT TYPES AND WORKFLOW CONFIGURATION, as shown earlier in Figure 15.27, captures the loss event workflow configuration.

Customers will also have historical loss information that needs to be uploaded into SAP Risk Management. Customers may also choose to periodically upload additional loss information even after go-live.

Hence, the blueprint document must capture the customer's loss information to be uploaded into the system.

Loss event management, including upload, is done using the ASSESSMENTS work center as shown in Figure 15.41. The quick links under the LOSS EVENT ASSESSMENTS section are used to manage loss events.

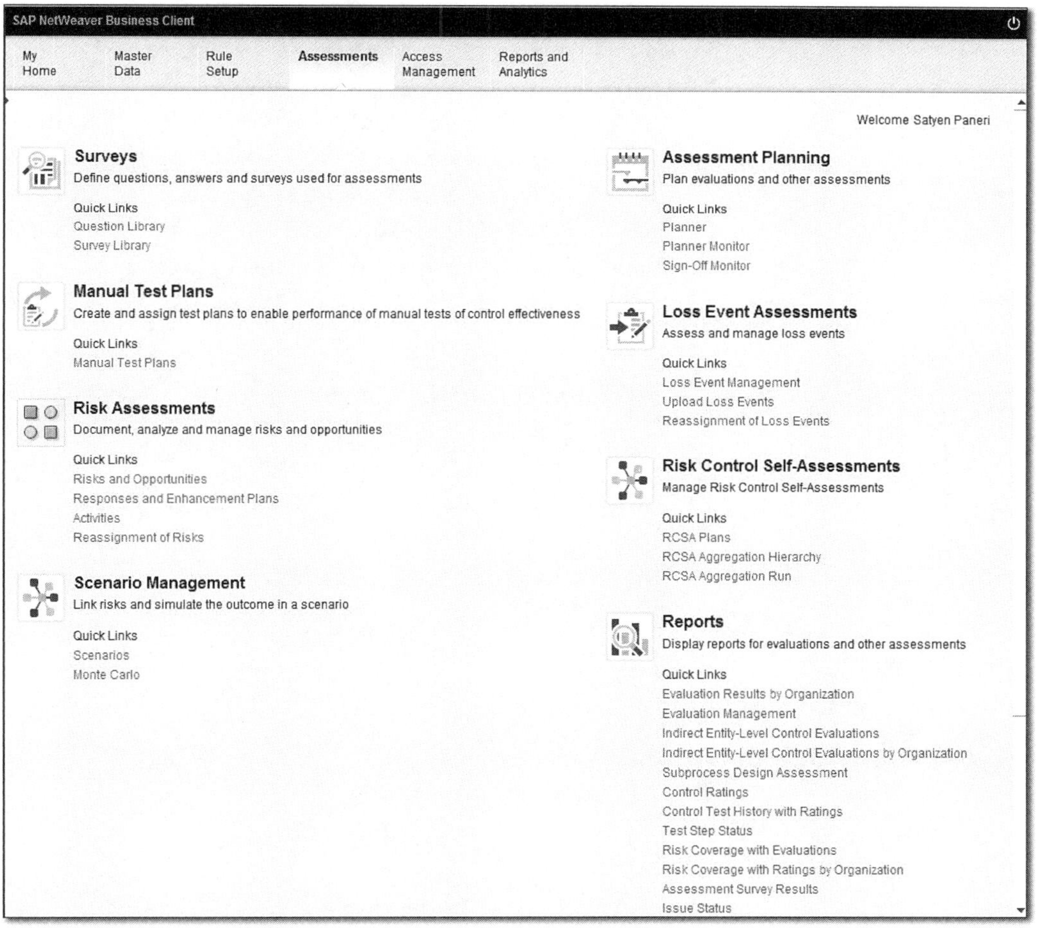

Figure 15.41 Assessments Work Center

Use the UPLOAD LOSS EVENTS quick link as shown in Figure 15.42 to upload loss events. An upload file in the Microsoft Excel or XML format needs to be used. The guided procedure checks the content, uploads the data, and confirms the results.

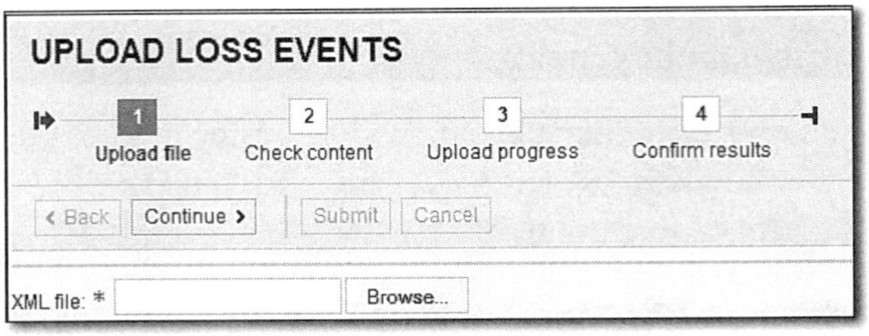

Figure 15.42 Upload Loss Events

To obtain the file format for loss event upload, use the LOSS EVENT MANAGEMENT quick link to manually enter a few loss events. Then use the DOWNLOAD button with the DOWNLOAD LOSS EVENT DATA IN QRR EXCEL option as shown in Figure 15.43. The Excel file obtained with this download operation has the format to use for uploading new loss events.

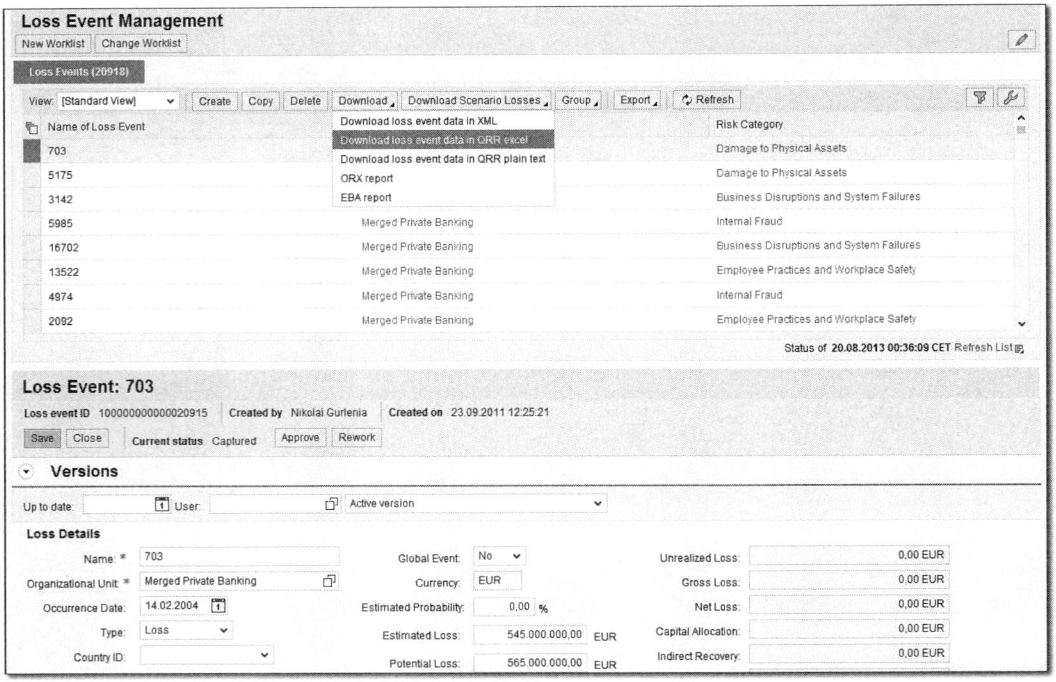

Figure 15.43 Download Loss Events

15.4.5 Reporting

Finally, let's consider the ORM reporting business requirements. As recommended when we discussed the customer adoption model, it's best to start by using the standard reports and analytics available under the Reports and Analytics work center as shown in Figure 15.44.

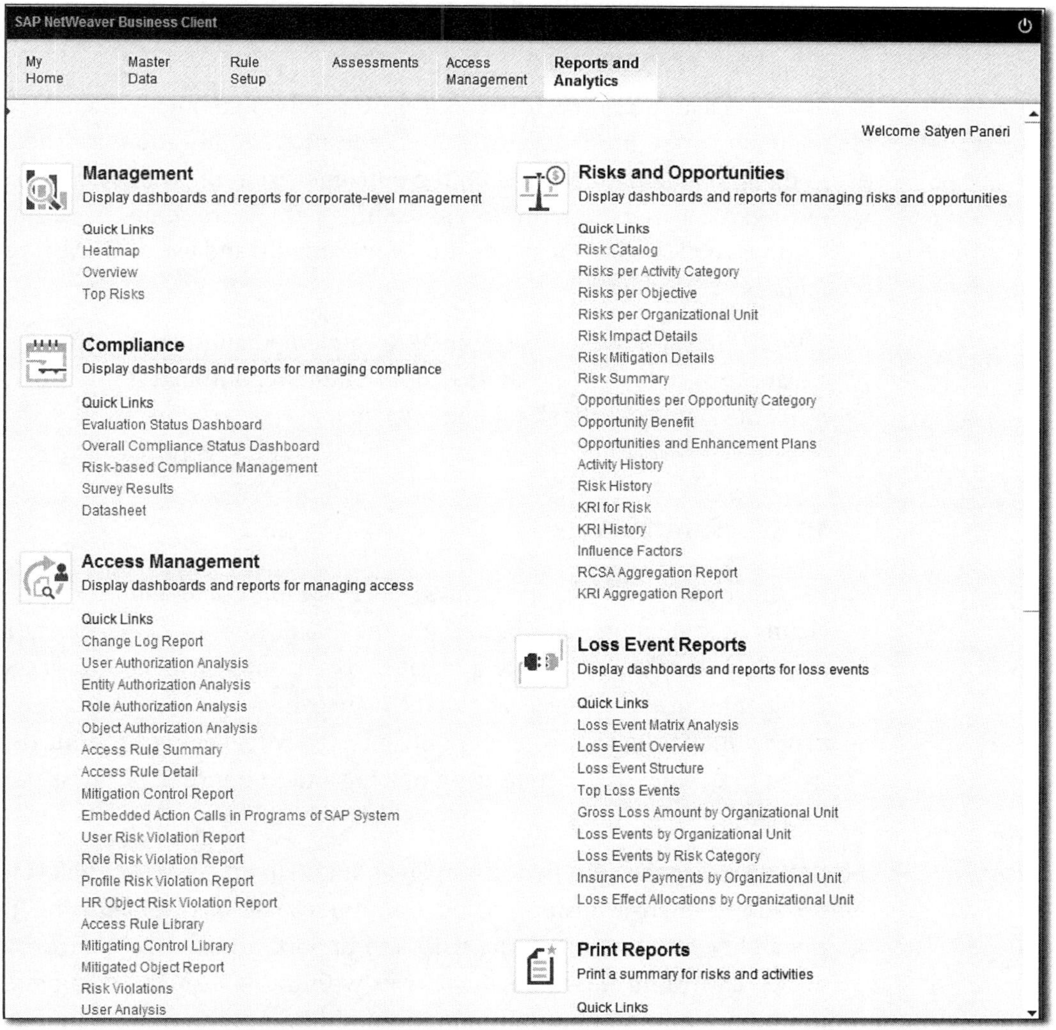

Figure 15.44 Reports and Analytics Work Center

ORM reports are available through the quick links under the LOSS EVENT REPORTS section in Figure 15.44. The first three quick links—LOSS EVENT MATRIX ANALYSIS, LOSS EVENT OVERVIEW, and LOSS EVENT STRUCTURE—are dashboards. The other links show standard reports.

In Section 15.4.1, we outlined the business blueprint process for implementing and configuring the ORM scenario. The blueprint document is then used to configure the solution, set up master data, set up loss events workflow, and upload loss events and user authorizations, and develop custom reports if necessary. After this is complete, the implementation goes through user acceptance testing. Modifications are made to the implementation based on the outcomes from the user acceptance testing. After users sign off on the readiness of system setup, the installation is replicated to the production environment and use of ORM commences.

If there are subsequent phases in ORM implementation or the customer advances to the next stage in the adoption model outlined in the beginning, the same process should be repeated.

15.5 Summary

As the business landscape grows more complex and global, supply chains become more distributed, and the practice of risk management is evolving from spreadsheets and silos to an enterprise-level process. Companies are starting to align risk management with business value drivers and in the process aren't only effectively managing risks but also using risk information in decision making and to improve business performance.

SAP Risk Management helps companies automate the process of ERM to preserve and grow business value. Continuous risk insight coupled with the ability to act on emerging risks and opportunities helps companies avoid catastrophic losses, manage risks within established risk appetite levels, and gain advantage from opportunities.

Financial institutions can leverage SAP Risk Management's operational risk capabilities in addition to ERM to reduce risk of loss resulting from inadequate or failed internal processes, people and systems, or external events. ORM enables companies to comply with external reporting requirements as well as additional internal requirements to manage and monitor performance.

In the next chapter, we'll cover trade compliance and financial risk.

SAP Global Trade Services is a standalone application that interfaces with a feeder system for master data and transactional screening. Although SAP Global Trade Services (GTS) works very closely with the logistics application and interfaces tightly with the supply chain processes, it has an effect on internal compliance in a number of ways.

16 Trade Compliance and Financial Risk

The impact of SAP Global Trade Services (SAP GTS) on daily financial activities should be indirect, yet significant. SAP GTS provides reporting features, especially for audits, that enable you to handle changing import/export requirements and controls. These audits, which are specific to import and export requirements, can use values from SAP ERP Logistics and Finance (FI) systems.

Global Trade Services and Financials

Communication from SAP GTS is one way from FI. FI sends the condition values (e.g., pricing condition) to SAP GTS. Let's say you create a sales order that you configure to send to SAP GTS. Based on the response on the order screening, if it finds any compliance issue, it might block the order and produce a legal control error. The system runs compliance checks against the transaction used for outbound (e.g., sales orders, delivery notes) and inbound (e.g., POs) deliveries with the business partner (e.g., sold to, ship to), country of destination or departure, and license requirement for the material being shipped.

Global Trade Services and Logistics

Unlike with FI, SAP GTS and Logistics have a two-way interface that indirectly affects FI. Throughout the process cycle, transactions are transferred and checked in SAP GTS for compliance and risk management. For example, when you create a sales order in SAP ERP, the system transfers information relevant to trade to SAP GTS for screening purposes, and sends results back to the SAP ERP system in real time. These checks can lead to situations such as adding customers under the boycott list. The system can then block transactions due to the lack of a license.

SAP GTS also affects FI strategically in a few ways. You can make more informed decisions to buy from duty free or countries with preferential treatment. It also helps with planning for product duty costs. For example, condition records are an indicator to the SAP GTS system for duty calculation and valuation. Billing documents are a trigger for customs shipments, which in turn generate trade documents and declarations.

Another key communication from SAP ERP is the condition record, which you use as a basis for license value decrement, duty calculation, and valuation. You use condition values of the products in the transaction (e.g., sales order, PO) for determining the license value decrement from the approved license you've created in the system. You also use the condition value for the product brought into the transaction for duty calculation for that particular shipment and valuation.

The system assesses and calculates valuation and duty when the product is shipped out or received. The valuation and the duty are based on the value, which is captured in the condition value of the product being transactioned SAP GTS generates customs declarations based on the billing document creation in SAP ERP. Billing documents are a trigger for customs shipments, which in turn generate trade documents and declarations.

Master data transfer between SAP ERP and SAP GTS use the change pointer concept.

Change Pointers and When to Run a Cleanup Program

As the change pointers are logged for every new record or changes made, it's important that you run the delete or change pointer cleanup program (RBDCPCLR). This program deletes the processed and obsolete change pointers. You can run it periodically based on the volume of the data logged in to change pointer tables.

Figure 16.1 depicts the flow of master data from SAP ERP to GTS through the change pointers. Following the initial transfer of the master data (Business Partner, Bill of Material or Material Master), you should turn on the change pointer. The change point process will capture any new records created or changed through different tables and trigger associated with the process, as explained in Figure 16.1. SAP ABAP Program – RBDMIDOC will help you transfer the records captured in the change pointer tables.

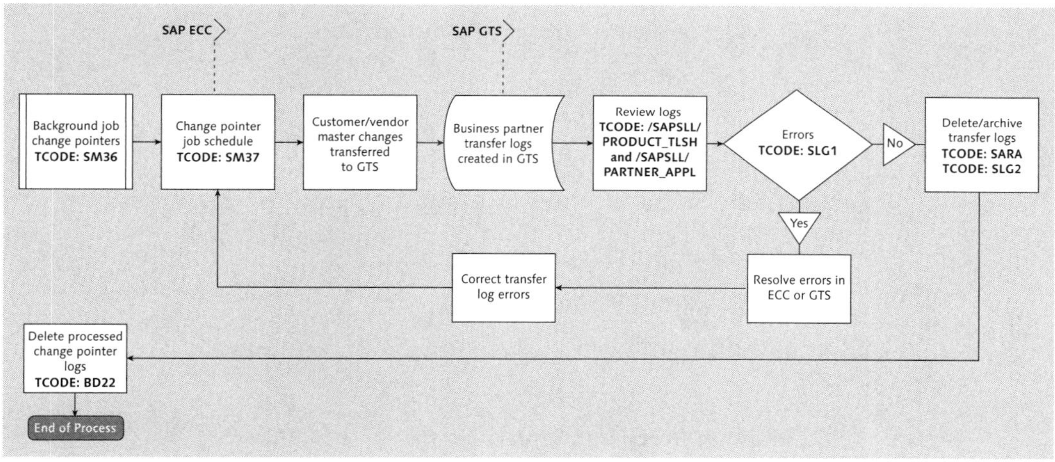

Figure 16.1 Change Pointer Data Transfer from SAP ERP to SAP GTS

Having gone through the key interfaces with SAP GTS and SAP ERP, let's review the key functions within the SAP GTS system in the next section.

16.1 Global Trade Key Functions

At a high level, SAP GTS consists of four key components: SAP Compliance Management, SAP Customs Management, SAP Risk Management, and Electronics Compliance Reporting (ECR). Figure 16.2 details the SAP Global Trade Services solution map.

Let's review each of the components within SAP GTS in detail.

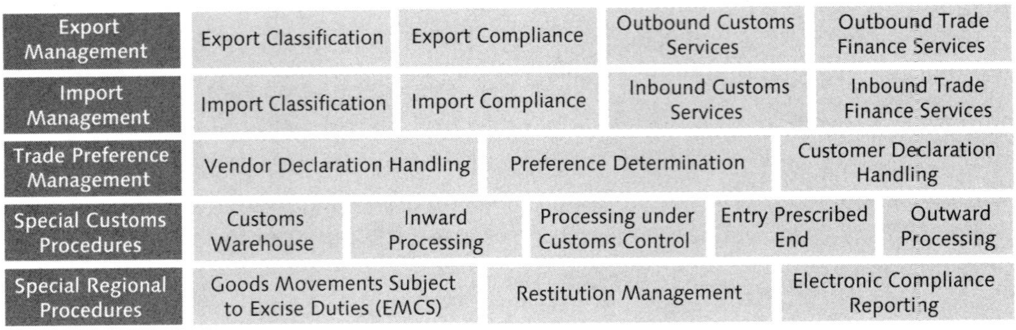

Figure 16.2 SAP Global Trade Services Solution Map

16.1.1 SAP Compliance Management

SAP Compliance Management is a component of SAP GTS that supports international trade compliance issues in three primary areas:

- Sanctioned party list (SPL) screening
- Import/export legal controlling
- Embargo checking

Sanctioned Party List Screening

The SPL screening checks your business partners against the government-provided denied party list (Figure 16.3). It's illegal to perform business transactions with listed parties, and your company could face fines or severe penalties if it does so. By streamlining the extended supply chain, SAP Compliance Management automates the complicated regulatory compliance process, which minimizes the risk of penalties and fines.

Sanctioned Part List Screening functionality

With every transaction that is exported or outbound and imported or inbound, the SPL screening can be used per the business requirement. Within an export or import, there are other compliance-related checking functions to be performed, for example, if a product requires a license or any specific exception can be applied. Every export from one country is an import for another country. Let's review the concept and functionality of import and export next.

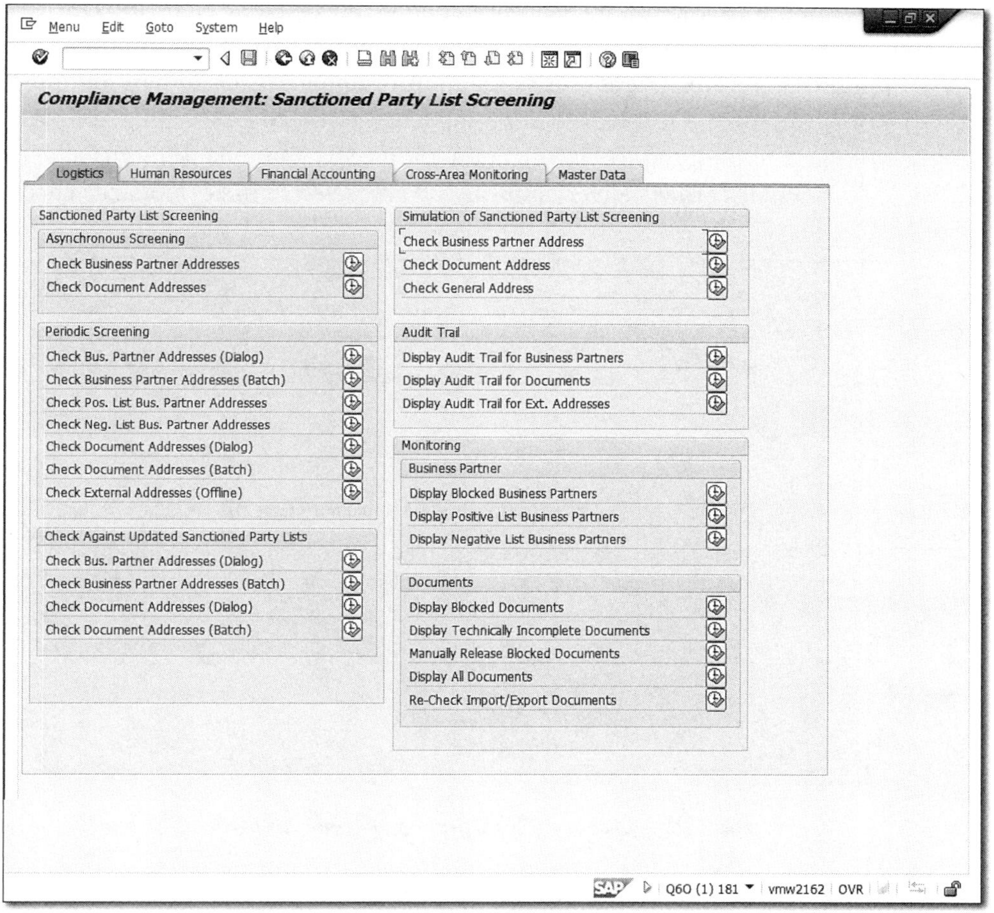

Figure 16.3 Compliance Management: Sanctioned Party List Screening Screen

Import/Export Legal Controlling

The system checks import and export legal controls against your product shipment from departure and destination country regulations. Based on these regulations, the product might need a license to export or import into a country. This functionality checks the license requirement or exemption based on the classification of the product. Some of the licenses might be value- and quantity-based, so the system uses the transaction value for the dollar value consumption.

Figure 16.4 shows the key touch point from SAP ERP Sales and Distribution (SD) and Materials Management (MM). The export process starts with the creation of master data, for example, the customers and product master. Customers can be subjected to the SPL screening and products to the product classification within SAP Compliance Management. The sales order delivery note also is subjected to the compliance check.

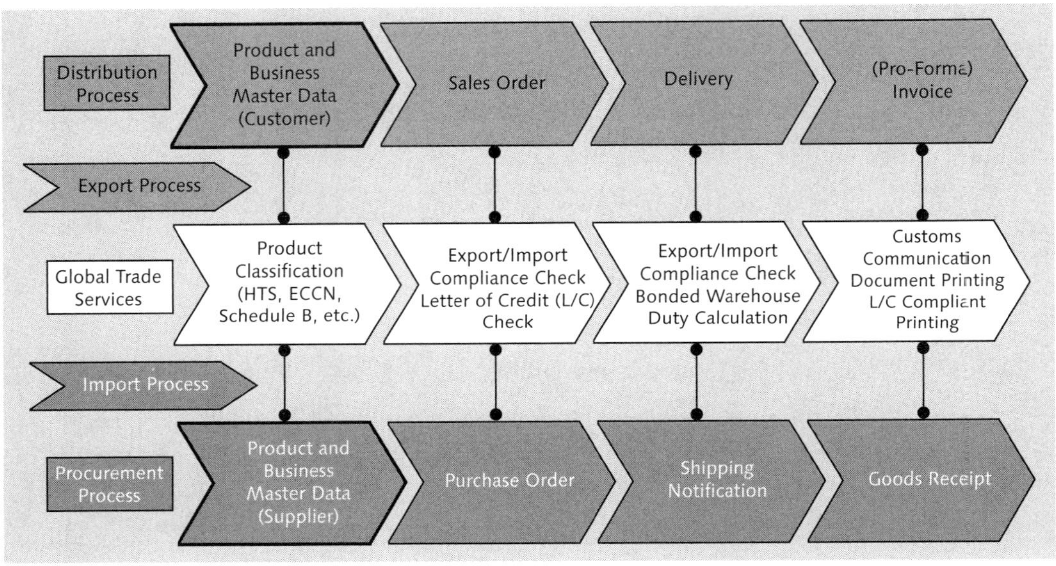

Figure 16.4 Supply Chain and Finance Integration with SAP GTS

Similar to the outbound, the inbound can be subjected to the compliance checking with the creation of a business partner, for example, vendors or suppliers, and screening of purchase orders (POs). Embargo checking is within the export and import legal control, which checks for any embargo blocking based on the embargoed countries.

Embargo is an integral part of the import and export processes. It allows you to check your business partner and transactions that are subjected to embargo.

Embargo Checking

Embargoes are based on the country of destination and departure. These are countries listed by the United Nations for embargo. You can configure to stop doing any business from these countries, and you can screen a customer before you register them into your database.

When you click on SANCTIONED PARTY LIST SCREENING under SAP COMPLIANCE MANAGEMENT, it brings up the default LOGISTICS tab on the COMPLIANCE MANAGEMENT: SANCTIONED PARTY LIST SCREENING screen (refer to Figure 16.3). Here you can view the results of your business partner screening and place them in a positive or negative list. The FINANCIAL ACCOUNTING tab brings up the similar functions and features as the LOGISTICS tab, except that here you can screen financial institutions. Similarly, you can screen employees and view the results within the HUMAN RESOURCES tab. The MASTER DATA tab allows you to upload the denied party list screening content and use the sanctioned party list control settings.

16.1.2 SAP Customs Management

SAP Customs Management is a SAP GTS component that supports cooperation with the customs authorities in the following primary areas:

- Customs communication service
- Duty calculation
- Product classification
- Trade document service

Customs Communication Service

The customs communication service helps customers set up the electronic filing for export and import declarations. With the main focus on the implementation of electronic shipping and customs procedures, SAP Customs Management facilitates imports and exports as well as communication and printing of trade documents. The customs communication service enables you to connect to customs offices and access customs IT procedures such as the New Computerized Transit System (NCTS) in Europe and the Automated Export System (AES) in North America. Online communication with the customs agency involves payment of duty as part of the clearance. The clearance of the importing or exporting goods triggers the feeder system to determine if funds are available to transfer money for duty payments. The feeder system typically is SAP ERP, but SAP GTS can also connect with non-SAP ERP systems. Because duty calculation is based on the pricing condition of the transactions, you should ensure that the calculated duty is captured in the original document for financial accounting purposes. Currently, the communication of the calculated duty in the SAP GTS customs document back to the finance document isn't available. The solution to this can be achieved through different ways; for example, you can use SAP NetWeaver Business Warehouse and do the comparison there or use an enhancement to update the value back from SAP GTS to SAP ERP.

Duty Calculation

Duty calculation supports complicated calculations of duties. The SAP GTS system derives the values of duty calculations from the master data and transaction values (e.g., material cost, product cost, document pricing). You can use a statistical value for passing this information for duty calculation if you don't want this value to post to accounting. You can use statistical conditions (type GRWR) within your pricing procedure in SAP ERP to pass it to the SAP GTS customs document.

Product Classification

Product classification is a functionality that goes across SAP Compliance Management and SAP Customs Management. The SAP GTS system gets the product details from the SAP ERP system. For international trade to recognize these parts or materials, you have to classify them for export and import purposes. From an export regulation point of view, you classify the materials to represent the control in terms of a shipment to a different destination. Legal control and license requirements are based on the export and import classification.

Trade Document Service

You can trigger the trade document service in SAP GTS with a billing document in your SAP ERP system. The billing document can be a pro forma invoice (billing document type, press [F8] or [F5]) or a final invoice to a customer. The pro forma invoice is a billing document type in

SAP ERP, not to be confused with the trade document pro forma invoice used for shipment within the European Union. The pro forma document in SAP ERP triggers a customs document in SAP GTS. This customs document in SAP GTS invokes the SAP GTS trade document service. With SAP Customs Management, you can generate different trade documents, such as a commercial invoice, pro forma invoice, shippers export declaration, or entry submission. The pro forma document that you create in SAP ERP triggers a SAP GTS customs shipment document. These have all of the relevant trade information, and you can also configure them to have messages. These messages represent the different trade documents or electronic communication that you want to generate.

Supply Chain and Financial integration with SAP GTS

SAP GTS is integrated with the Supply Chain and Financal functions within the export and import processes through master data and transactions, as shown in the Figure 16.5.

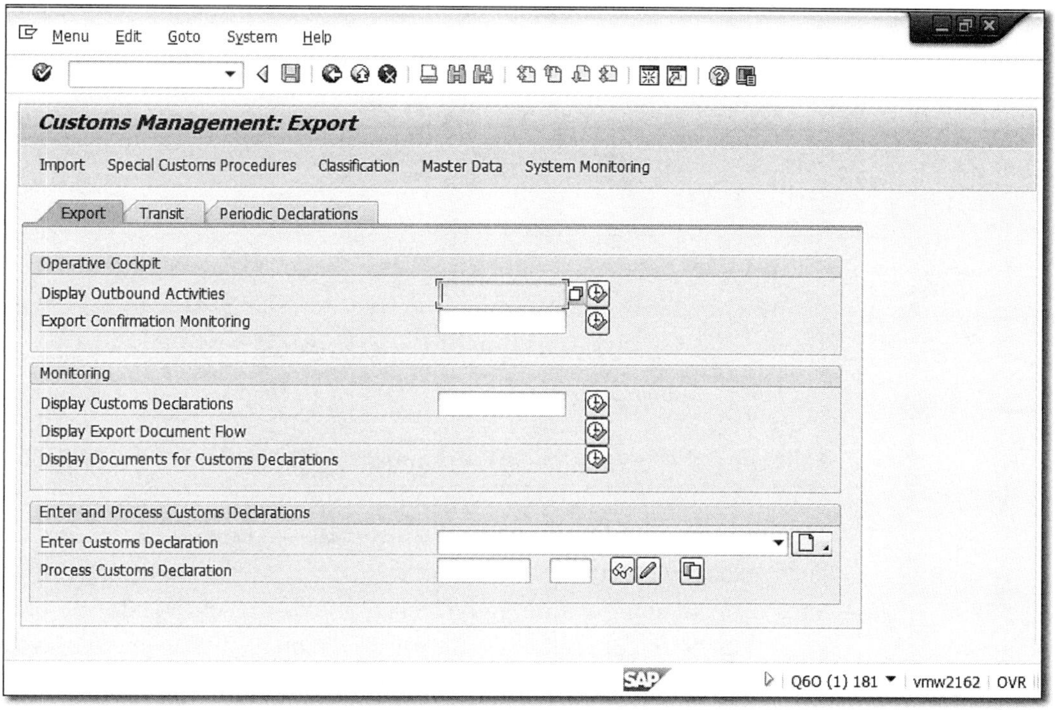

Figure 16.5 Customs Processing: Import/Export

Under the CUSTOMS PROCESSING – IMPORT/EXPORT button is the OPERATIVE COCKPIT screen shown in Figure 16.5. Here you can view all of the customs shipments created with reference to the pro forma that have been transferred to SAP GTS for trade document generation. You maintain the authorization for release of trade transactions under the AUTHORIZATIONS tab. When you import goods, in some countries, you're required to produce the securities customs authorities for release of goods.

Under CUSTOMS VALUE CALCULATION, you can click on the SIMULATE CALCULATION OF CUSTOMS DUTIES. Figure 16.6 displays a typical customs value for customs shipment line items. You can use the value of goods, transportation costs, insurance, and customs value for duty calculation.

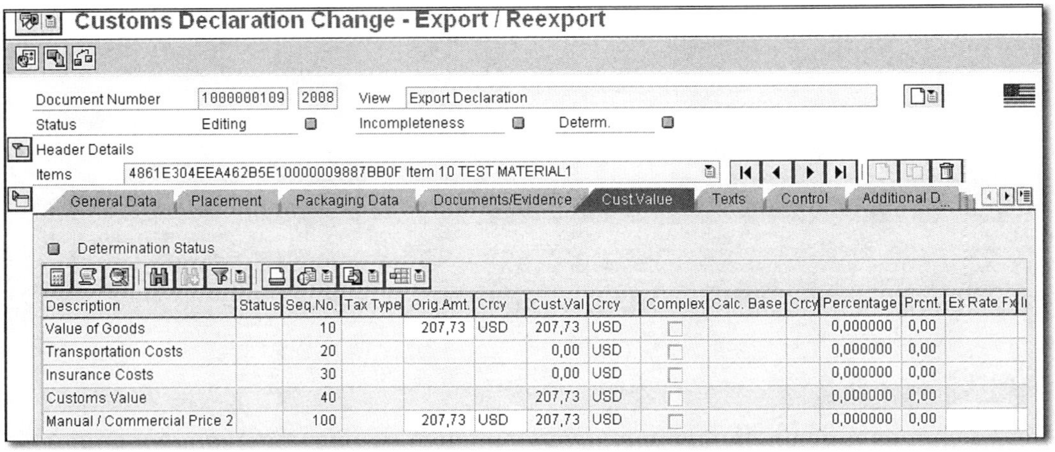

Figure 16.6 Customs Shipment Document Line Item Customs Value for Declaration

Following the review of SAP Compliance Management and SAP Customs Management, you're ready to move on to SAP Risk Management discussion. SAP Risk Management consists of two functionalities: preference management and letter of credit. We will focuses mostly on Preference management including preference processing and vendor declarations. Our letter of credit is more of a document management service provided by SAP GTS. Our coverage is solely related to SAP GRC naturally.

16.1.3 SAP Risk Management

Chapter 15 provided a comprehensive overview of SAP Risk Management. However, it is important to touch upon how SAP Risk Management can be used alongside SAP Global Trade Services. SAP Risk Management when integrated withinSAP GTS addresses the specific risks of doing business internationally from a trade point of view. It addresses the three main financial aspect of trade:

- Cost of doing business in a different country.
- Duty drawback process in which companies pay the duty while getting the goods clearance. They can follow the specific product classification, and if the duty is exempted, then they can provide the appropriate documentation to get back the duty paid.
- Financial collateral, as an assurance companies need to have in the form of a letter of credit.

Restitution addresses the duty drawback, specific to the agricultural industry, in terms of subsidies. A letter of credit provides the assurance of payment for the goods or services being delivered.

Preference Processing

Preference processing is a functionality within SAP Risk Management that supports exporters in indicating goods for preferential tariff treatment. This functionality assists exporters in determining whether you meet all of the prerequisites for preferential customs duty rates. Exporters can search for goods with preferential origin, meaning that they have reduced or zero customs duty rates. Sourcing from a foreign country has a financial element to it, not only from the logistics point of view but also from the import duties point of view. SAP Risk Management allows you to determine the costs of importing goods from various countries. Although the supplier's price quote—the exporter's Ex Works price—may be higher than a competitor's Ex Works price, you can determine the overall price of goods for customers and find the lowest rate.

Trade preference and integrations across various SAP modules

Figure 16.7 displays the key features of trade preference. You can see how these key features are integrated with the different modules within the SAP ERP, such as Purchasing, Production Planning (PP), and Sales and Distribution (SD).

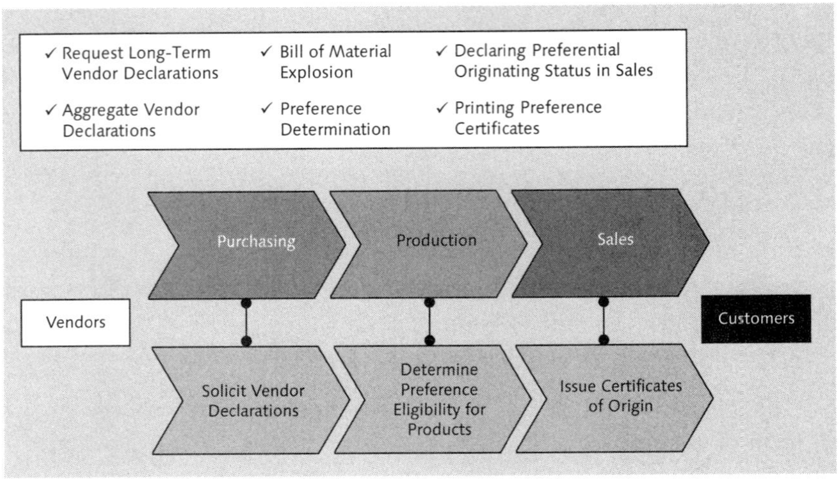

Figure 16.7 Trade Preference Integration

Figure 16.8 looks at preference processing within SAP Risk Management.

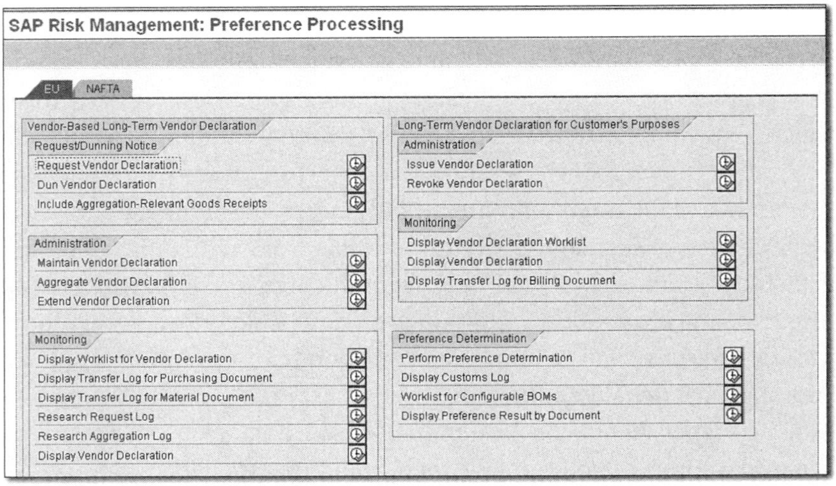

Figure 16.8 Preferential Processing within SAP Risk Management

Preference processing supports exporters in the following primary areas:

Exporter support within preference processing

- Managing vendor declarations, including requesting and sending reminders to vendors about vendor declarations and maintaining the declarations in the system
- Taking vendor declarations back from the customer if, for example, the exporter uses a different vendor as an exception, and the eligibility for preferential tariff treatment is affected
- Calculating threshold values for goods based on vendor declarations for materials
- Printing customs declaration documents based on the billing documents created in the transactional system in addition to preferential documents such as certificates of origin and vendor declarations

You can use SAP GTS to get preferential treatment. If you've paid duty initially to clear customs, now you can produce all of the relevant documents to get back the duty you paid to the government agency. The result is that customers pay less import tax for goods that are indicated for preferential tariff treatment. This has impact in terms of the cost of doing business when you can get a material at a lesser cost because you're paying less duty and import tax. Financially, you need to account for these amounts as well.

SAP Risk Management and Restitution

The restitution component within SAP Risk Management enables exporters to map the restitution process simply and efficiently to the standard export process while mitigating financial (due to international trading) and legal risks. Monitoring and controlling functions enable exporters to keep track of all of their business transactions and cooperate with the customs and legal authorities.

SAP Global Trade Services and SAP Risk Management functionalities

SAP GTS helps track consumption and reports to government agencies by managing and accounting for licenses and the quantity and value of shipped goods. Customs agencies or governments might ask for a bank guarantee or security for clearance of imported goods. You then report these financial transactions (deposits) to the government agencies as securities.

The transaction value is the value of the imported commodity based on which customs duty rates are applied. The transactional value consists of: the net value of the imported commodity, any value-adds or rebates, transportation costs (freight), and insurance costs. The transactional system passes these values through pricing procedures in the billing document and stores them in the customs document in SAP GTS.

Restitution allows exporters to manage export licenses, securities, manufacturer's recipes, and restitution calculations based on the normal export process. All of these management services required for the restitution process are part of the standard export process.

Functionality that supports EU and NAFTA agreements

Currently, SAP provides functionality for agreements within EU preferential treatment and NAFTA. These programs use complex logic to determine the country of origin for the product and the preferential treatment the companies can receive for trade based on the agreements between the trading countries. When deciding on sourcing the goods for low cost, the duty rates might be a key factor in strategic decision making and financial savings in the long run.

Duty rates

Duty and restrictions applies to goods imported into a country. Countries promote goods movement for products with countries with whom they have trade agreements. Duty rates and preference rules apply to a Harmonized Tariff Number, which comes from the *Harmonized Tariff System (HTS)*, a numbering system used by the international trade community as a common understanding for importing and exporting. A duty rate can be a percentage of the price of the part or a fixed rate, tied to the Harmonized Tariff System (Number) and the country of origin. These are also delivered as content by content providers along with corresponding HTS codes. The amount of duty rate (or not) applies to the preference rules for the specific HTS and the country of origin.

As we discussed in the previous section, Preference processing in SAP Global Trade Services and Risk Management helps exporters fulfill all of the legal requirements for customs tariff preferences and show that their goods are eligible for preferential treatment. This enables their customers to import these goods either duty free or at a reduced rate of import duty. By providing evidence of eligibility for preferential treatment, exporters gain significant competitive advantages.

To summarize, preference processing involves maintaining the following:

- Vendor declarations
- Materials or bills of material (BOMs)
- The result of the threshold value for preferential treatment
- The threshold value of the product as compared to its Ex Works price (i.e., the price quoted by the seller for delivery to the predefined location, e.g., up to the buyer's door and onward, it's the buyer's responsibility)

If you have a BOM, the preferential status is set for the main component in the product master. The system determines the results and saves them for each main component. On the sales document, you can compare the determined threshold value with the Ex Works price and determine the preference situation for the current delivery. The Ex Works price must be greater than or equal to the threshold value. If the system determines a positive preference status, it allows you to print a preferential statement.

Vendor Declarations Management

Vendor declarations management, a part of preference processing, provides functionality for requesting vendor declarations and sending reminders. You can request vendor declarations via email, XML, or supplier self-service. You need to update these vendor declarations into the system, and the system then allows you to aggregate them. The system also allows you to issue vendor declarations for the customer's purposes or revoke them.

Customs Declarations

For declaration to customs, you need to classify the goods according to a numbering schema. The numbering schema for the European Union is called combined nomenclature (CN). You declare imported and exported goods starting under which subheading of nomenclatures they fall. This determines which rate of customs duty applies and how the goods are treated for statistical purposes. SAP Risk Management provides functionality to configure for the North America Free Trade Agreement (NAFTA) and the EU Trade Agreement.

SAP GTS Implementation Consideration

Note that one of the prerequisites of a SAP Risk Management implementation is that you also need to implement the SAP Compliance Management and/or SAP Customs Management functionalities within SAP GTS. As with preferential treatment, you need to have the corresponding master transactional data from SAP Compliance Management or SAP Customs Management.

Preference processing assumes many steps are being completed in a feeder system for sales, purchasing, and so on. The next section describes the prerequisite steps in a high level, showing what must occur to make SAP GTS ready for preference processing.

16.2 SAP ERP Setup for Trade Preference Processing

You need to perform the setup in the feeder system (SAP ERP) and the receiver system (SAP GTS). In this section, we'll look at the steps necessary to set up SAP ERP. In Section 16.3, we'll review the steps necessary to setup SAP GTS as the receiver system.

Step-by-step setup of SAP ERP as a feeder system

First, let's look at the four-step process for establishing SAP ERP as a feeder system:

1. Set up communication between SAP ERP and SAP GTS.
2. Transfer documents from SAP ERP.
3. Maintain the BOM transfer settings.
4. Define a worklist for vendor-based, long-term declarations.

Now, let's look at each of these steps in further detail.

16.2.1 Set Up Communication from SAP ERP to SAP GTS

You need to set up the communication between the feeder system (e.g., SAP ERP) and SAP GTS for transferring master data types (e.g., customer, vendor, materials, and BOMs). The system communication between SAP ERP and SAP GTS uses Application Link Enabling (ALE) for master data transfer and remote function calls (RFCs) for transactions. You have to set up both SAP ERP and SAP GTS as logical systems. Then you need to set up system communication in SAP ERP and SAP GTS. To set up the communication on the SAP ERP side, use Transaction /SAPSLL/MENU_LEGALR3 to open the screen shown in Figure 16.9.

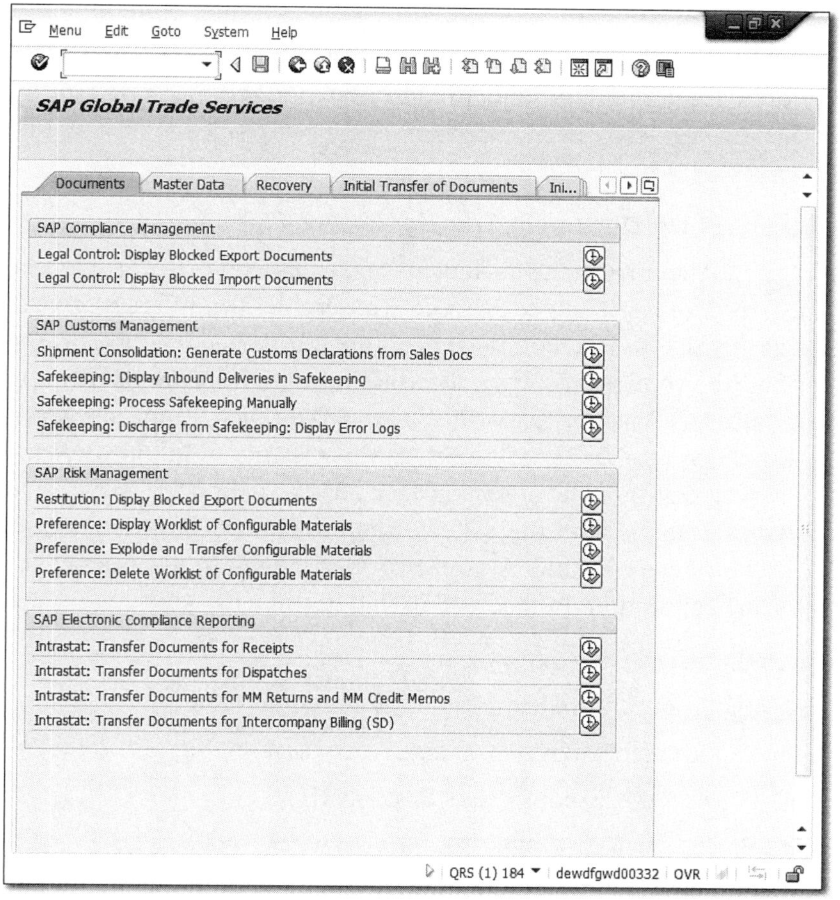

Figure 16.9 Set Up SAP ERP to Communicate with SAP GTS

Go to the Basic Settings tab and in the System Connection to SAP GTS section, you can perform all of the listed processes:

- Define Logical System
- Assign Logical System
- Maintain RFC Destination for RFC Calls
- Maintain RFC Destinations for Method Calls
- Maintain ALE Distribution Model

You need to go over these configuration steps in sequence as they are listed.

Figure 16.9 displays the configuration set up with SAP ERP for setting up the interface between SAP ERP and SAP GTS. In the following sections, we'll go over the configuration steps for document transfer in detail.

16.2.2 Set Up Document Transfer in SAP ERP

In SAP ERP, configure the documents and transactions that need to be transferred from SAP ERP to SAP GTS. This enables the different services checks in SAP GTS when the documents are transferred to SAP GTS. You can find the configuration by following menu path, SPRO • Sales and Distribution • Foreign Trade/Customs • SAP Global Trade Services – Plug-In • Control Data for Transfer to SAP Global Trade Services • Configure Control Settings for Document Transfer. Figure 16.10 shows an example with the SD0A Dispatch/Export: Sales Document application entered in the Application Level field. You can enter the following applications in that field to find documents:

- MM0A: Receipt/Import: Purchasing Document
- MM0B: Inbound / Import: Inbound Delivery Note
- MM0C: Receipt/Import: Material Document
- SD0A: Dispatch/Export: Sales Document
- SD0B: Dispatch/Export: Outbound Delivery Document
- SD0C: Dispatch/Export: Billing Document

Still in Figure 16.10, for preference processing purposes, select the Call Up SAP Risk Management Services checkbox in the Control Settings for Services section, and then select the Set Preference Indicator in

Feeder System and Check Configuration Materials checkboxes under Preference Processing in the Detail Control section.

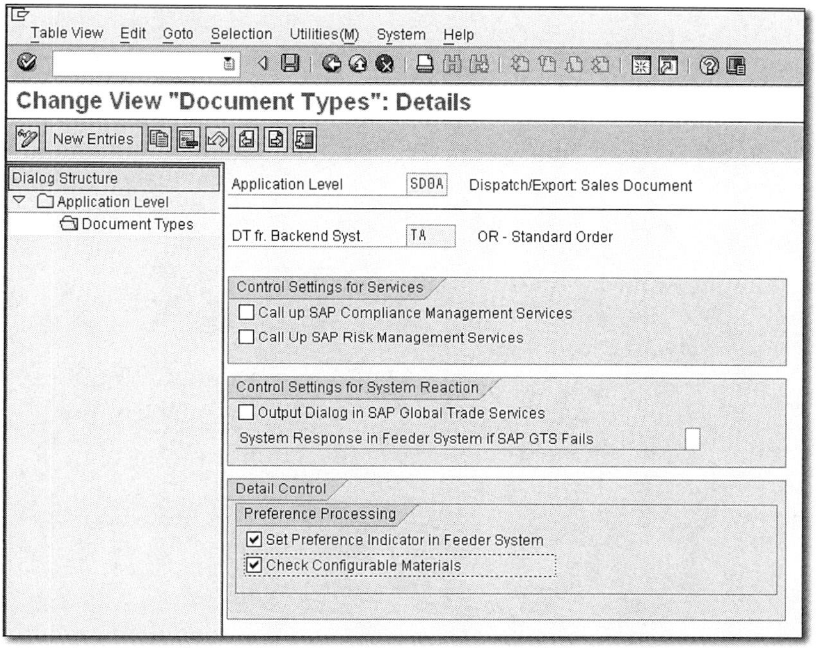

Figure 16.10 Control Settings for Document Types for Performing Service Checks in SAP GTS

Following the setup of SAP Risk Management in SAP ERP for document types within different application areas, you can next set up the BOM transfer setting.

16.2.3 Maintain BOM Transfer Settings

You maintain the settings for BOM transfer from SAP ERP at three levels: global, country, and plant. You must always begin by setting the control parameter at the global level. The system uses the data you select at the global level to propose the data at the country and plant levels. Figure 16.11 shows the configuration steps.

Levels of Bill of Materials transfer

First, select the BOM category as static or configurable. The BOM application is, for example, production or sales. You select either the cross-plant preference model or plant-specific preference model.

Then, select the rule set required for the preference agreement (e.g., EU or NAFTA). Select the type of BOM explosion you want, which is either top-down or bottom-up. Companies might use multiple versions of BOMs. If you do, in the alternative BOM, you can enter the name of any alternative BOMs you want to transfer. In the EXCLUSION OF MATERIAL TYPES section, you can select the type of materials from your feeder system that you want to exclude from the transfer if it's not part of the core product and you don't want it to be part of the preferential determination calculation (e.g., packaging materials).

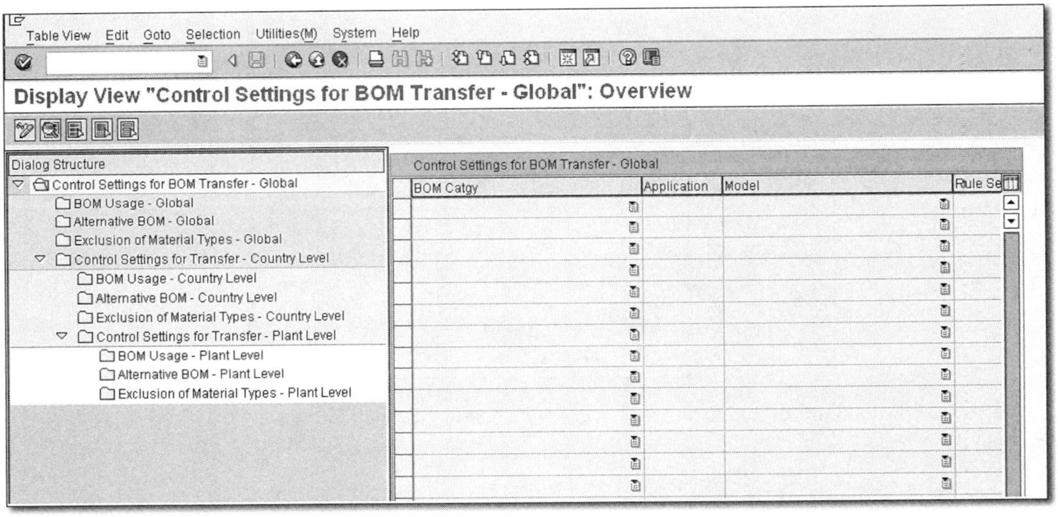

Figure 16.11 Control Setting for the BOM Transfer to SAP GTS

Now that we have established the communication between SAP ERP and SAP GTS, enabled the document transfer and maintained our BOM transfer, the final configuration that we need to make with SAP ERP, SAP Risk Management and SAP GTS is to define a worklist for Vendor declarations. These configurations enable a secure, integrated workflow for trade services.

16.2.4 Define a Worklist for Vendor-Based Long-Term Vendor Declarations

The structure of the worklist for vendor-based long-term vendor declarations in SAP GTS is based on your settings for the transfer of purchasing documents and material documents. In this IMG activity, you can filter out the documents for the worklist structure that are relevant for this process.

Vendor reminders

Requesting and sending reminders for vendor-based long-term vendor declarations only makes sense for vendors located in the same preference zone. You can record the combinations of your country and other companies in your preference zone in this activity. The system only creates entries in the worklist for vendor-based long-term vendor declarations for documents whose business partners are located in the countries you entered in this activity. The system compares your entry for the vendor country in this IMG activity with the entry from the vendor master record or from the process in MM (partner with partner role VENDOR).

If you don't configure any settings in this IMG activity for worklist for long-term vendor declarations, the system creates an entry in the worklist for every document of a document type and application level for which you've configured the preference processing service and structure of the worklist for vendor-based long-term vendor declarations.

Configuration of vendor-based long-term vendor declarations settings

To configure these settings, follow IMG menu path, SALES AND DISTRIBUTION • SAP GLOBAL TRADE SERVICES – PLUG-IN • PREFERENCE: DEFINE WORKLIST FOR VENDOR-BASED LONG-TERM VENDOR DECLARATIONS. In the COUNTRY ORGANIZATION column, enter the country where your organization is located (see Figure 16.12). In the COUNTRY ORGANIZATION column, enter the organization value and in the WORKLIST COUNTRY column, enter the country information. You need to define the countries in the COUNTRY ORGANIZATION column, the WORKLIST COUNTRY, and the NAME for the worklist for the vendors whose documents you want the system to use to structure the worklist for vendor-based long-term vendor declarations.

This is the last step in the SAP ERP portion of the procedure. Naturally, we also need to review the SAP GTS configurations to ensure optimum integration between GTS and ERP. Let's next review the setup steps in SAP GTS.

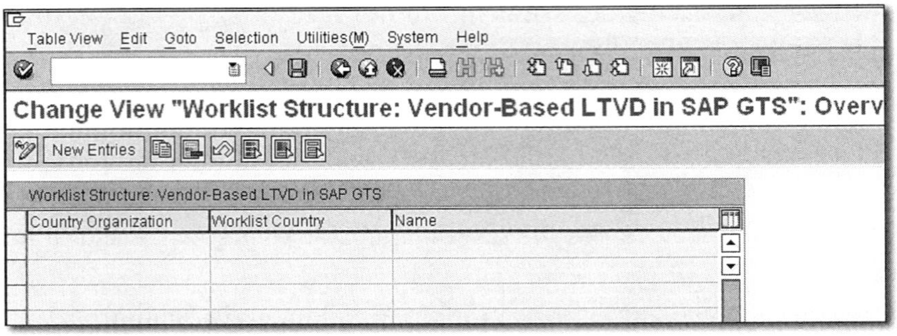

Figure 16.12 Worklist Structure Definitions for Vendor-Based Long-Term Vendor Declarations

16.3 SAP Global Trade Services Setup

Just as we setup SAP ERP as a feeder system, SAP GTS needs to be configured as a receiver system. You will note some similarities in the configuration of GTS as reviewed with SAP ERP. The following six-step process is required for establishing SAP GTS as a receiver system:

1. Define the basic settings for SAP GTS.
2. Set up the communication for SAP GTS.
3. Set up number ranges, including vendor declarations, preference models, and bills of product.
4. Define and assign organization parameters.
5. Define a country group.
6. Define a worklist for vendor-based, long-term declarations.

Now, let's look at each of these steps in further detail.

16.3.1 Define Basic Settings in SAP GTS

As we have reviewed in previous chapters, when we looked at the global GRC architecture, SAP GTS is installed in a separate client from SAP ERP. There are some basic settings that need to be reviewed. These include system time zones and units of measure. After installing SAP GTS you need to maintain system time zones. Then you synchronize settings between SAP ERP acting as the feeder system and SAP GTS, including the unit of measure, the ISO codes for the units of measure, country codes, country-specific settings, and currencies.

Unit of Measure synchronization

The units of measure play a key role in the material base unit, both when you transfer products and while using the transaction for item quantity or weight. Country-specific settings are used as part of the address with your partner in the transactions. Currencies play the role for determining the value conversion from one currency to another and the converted value for a specific transaction.

Follow IMG menu path, SAP NetWeaver • General Settings, and configure these values in the Set Countries, Currencies, and Check Units of Measurement options to adjust these settings as shown in Figure 16.13.

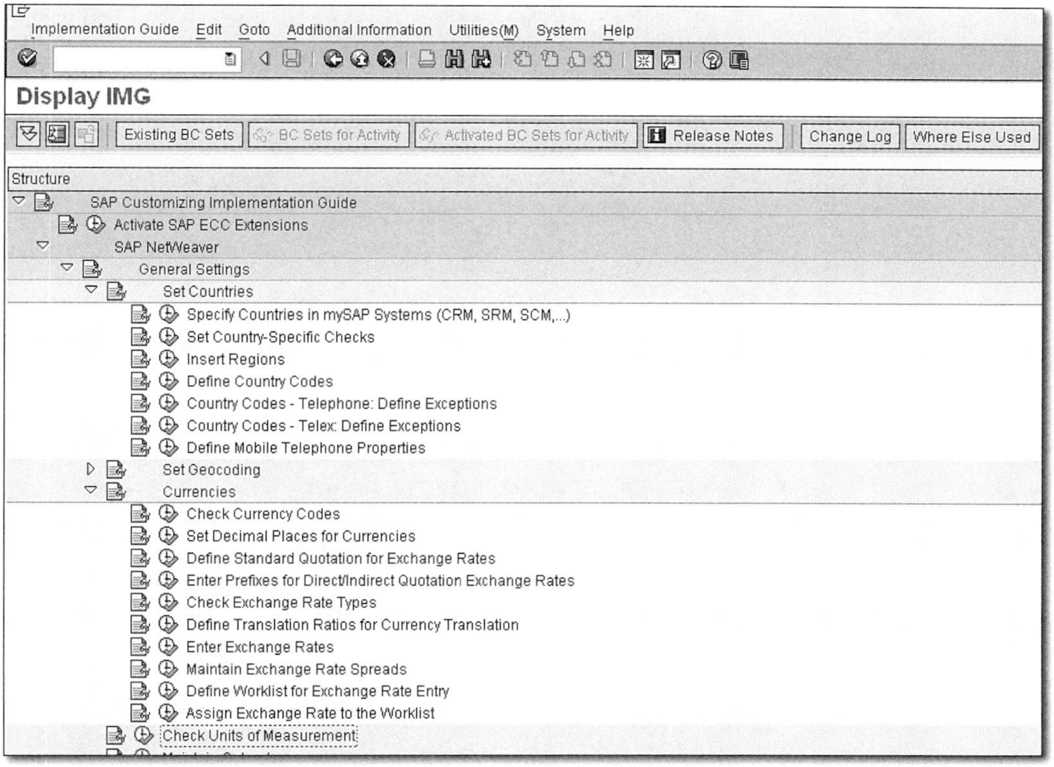

Figure 16.13 General Settings in SAP GTS to Be Synchronized with SAP ERP

16.3.2 Set Up System Communication in SAP GTS

Similar to the communication setup you did with SAP ERP, you also need to set up the communication in SAP GTS. These setups enable the connection; you can set up configurations specific to the modules later.

Communication setup process

To set up the system communication, use Transaction SPRO, and follow menu path, SAP GLOBAL TRADE SERVICES • SYSTEM COMMUNICATION • SYSTEM CONNECTION TO FEEDER SYSTEM. From there, you can perform the following functions:

1. Define a logical system for the feeder system.
2. Assign a logical system.
3. Define a group for the logical system.
4. Assign the logical system to a group of logical systems.

You need to identify SAP GTS as a logical system and assign the client to the logical system. The logical system group allows you to group the feeder system and SAP GTS so that they can share the same common data and configuration elements.

16.3.3 Number Range Configuration within SAP GTS

For master data and the transactional data that are transferred from SAP ERP to SAP GTS, SAP GTS assigns an internal number. You need to create number ranges for business partners and products as a prerequisite. Then you create both internal and external number ranges for business partners. Use internal business partner numbers for mapping the business partner that is transferred from SAP ERP. Use external number ranges for creating organizational data in SAP GTS.

Number ranges for customs documents

You also need number ranges for the customs documents, which are created for SAP Compliance Management or SAP Customs Management. Specific to preferential treatment, you need to configure the following number ranges:

- **Vendor declarations**
  You need to create three number ranges: one for vendor-based long-term vendor declarations, another for long-term vendor declarations

for the customers' purposes, and the last for the revocation of long-term vendor declarations for the customers' purposes. Note that the vendor declaration number range is year dependent and client independent.

- **Preference models**
  You need to create number ranges for different preference models, including plant-based and cross-plant models, as well as the preference model for the configuration of bills of product.
- **Bills of Material (BOM):**
  Also called bills of product, the component under the final product helps determine the preference condition. The country of origin and the tariff system influence the final product HTS number and the country of origin determination.

Because all of these number ranges are also year specific, you should create the number ranges for future years as well.

Now that we have defined our basic settings, configured our systems communications and clarified our number ranges, we need to look now to our organizational parameters and their mapping.

16.3.4 Define and Assign Organizational Parameters

You need to map SAP ERP organizational parameters in SAP GTS. For example, map the SAP ERP company code to the SAP GTS foreign trade organization and the SAP ERP plant to the SAP GTS legal unit. You can create the foreign trade organization and legal unit by using Transaction SPRO and following menu path, SAP GLOBAL TRADE SERVICES • GENERAL SETTINGS • ORGANIZATIONAL STRUCTURE. Then, select DEFINE FOREIGN TRADE ORGANIZATION, DEFINE LEGAL UNITS, and ASSIGNMENT OF ORGANIZATIONAL UNITS FROM FEEDER SYSTEM TO FOREIGN TRADE ORG. (see Figure 16.14).

Assigning a business partner role

You need to pick the right business partner role while creating the foreign trade organization or legal unit. The company code in SAP ERP represents the entity that financially owns the goods or services, and the plant represents the physical location from where the products are shipped or received.

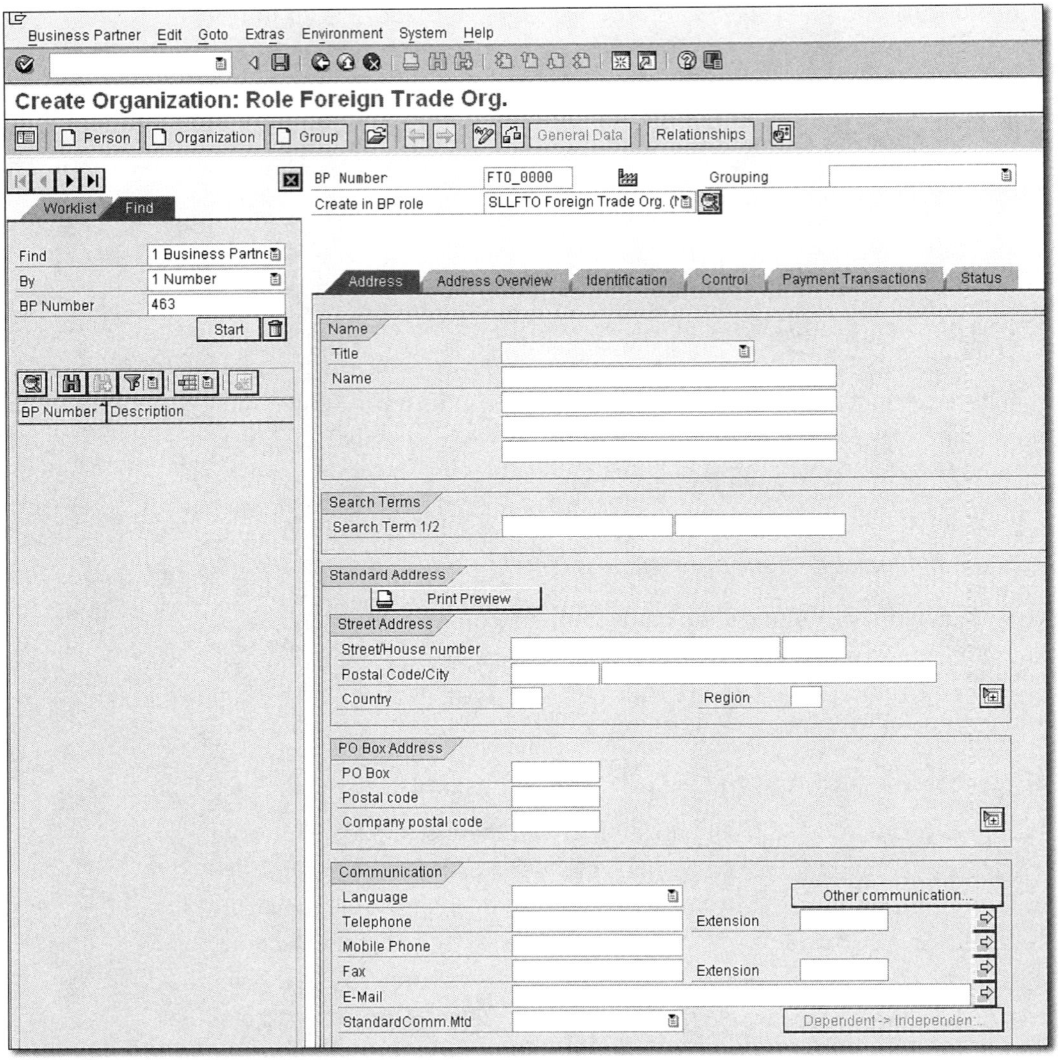

Figure 16.14 Defining a Foreign Trade Organization

Administrative units

Another important organizational unit for SAP GTS is the administrative unit. An administrative unit is responsible for all transactions within the preference program or determination. Choose the partner role SLLMGR and maintain the address data. Use Transaction SPRO, and follow menu path, SAP Risk Management • Preference Processing Services • Define Administrative Units for Vendor Declarations to perform this step.

16.3.5 Define the Country Group

Country groups simplify the process of making configuration settings. This is an option if you have countries with similar or the same legal regulations that can be grouped for the same configuration or preference rules. You can find this configuration under Transaction SPRO and then by following menu path, SAP Global Trade Services • General Settings • Legal Regulations • Define Country Group. In this step, you need to define the country group name and description (Figure 16.15).

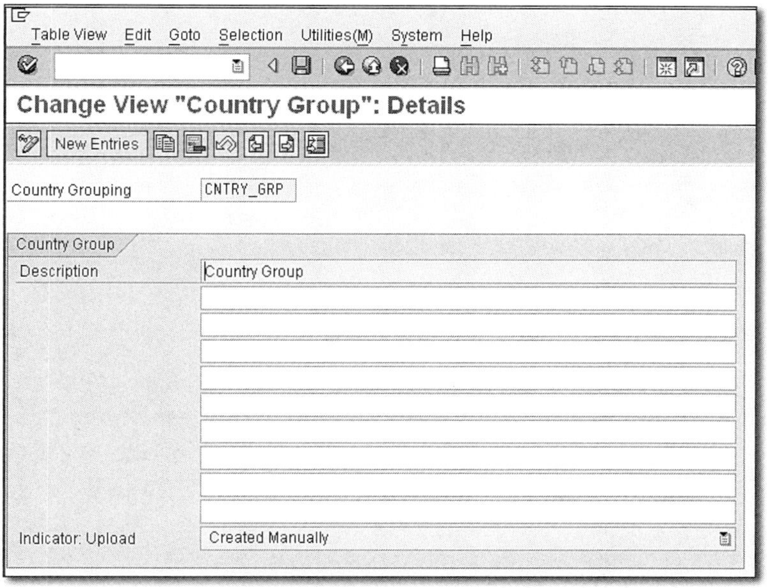

Figure 16.15 Defining the Country Group

Assigning a country to a country group

After this configuration, you can maintain or assign countries to the corresponding country group in the SAP GTS cockpit. Use Transaction /SAPSLL/MENU_LEGAL and follow menu path, GTS Area Menu: Preference Processing Service • Master Data • Preference Zones • Assign County to Country Group to open the screen shown in Figure 16.16.

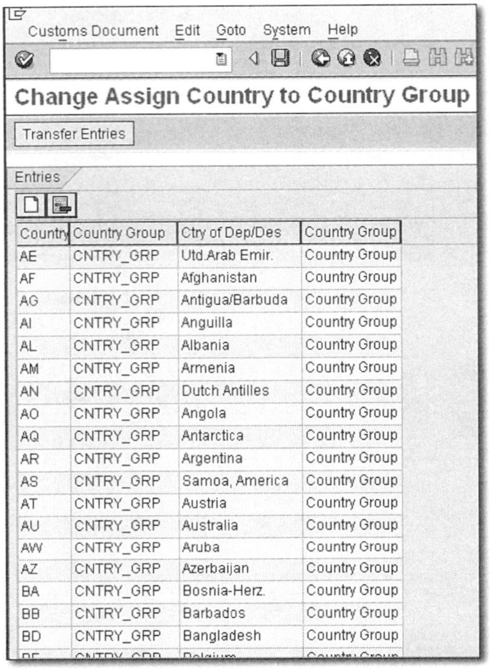

Figure 16.16 Country Assignments to the Country Group

16.3.6 Define and Activate a Legal Regulation

You define legal regulations to represent the preference law of a particular country. You assign the legal regulation to the corresponding country groups of import and export and then upload the preference rules with reference to the legal regulation. Following the definition of the regulation, you need to activate it.

Configuration of legal regulations

You can find the configuration to do this by using Transaction SPRO and then following menu path, SAP GLOBAL TRADE SERVICES • GENERAL SETTINGS • LEGAL REGULATIONS • DEFINE LEGAL REGULATION (to open the screen shown in Figure 16.17.

The type of legal code determines the kind of regulation and its functionality. You need to define if the regulation applies to both import and export or just export. Every regulation must have an original country. After you define it, you need to activate it. When you need to list the country or country group, this regulation is active.

Figure 16.17 Preferential Regulation Definitions

Figure 16.18 displays the configuration step to activate the preference by country group. Based on the country group defined, you can maintain them under the COUNTRY GROUP folder.

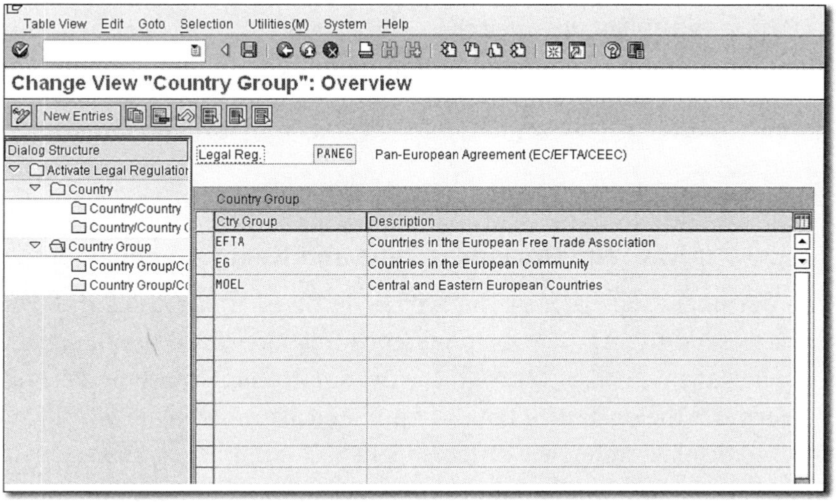

Figure 16.18 Activate Preference Regulation

The preceding setup were more of a baseline configuration, so now we'll go over specific SAP Risk Management configurations.

16.4 SAP Risk Management General Settings

In Section 1.1.5, we discuss SAP Risk Management and its key functionality. Now let's look at how we can configure the general settings to ensure that SAP Risk Management is running as part of your risk management suite alongside SAP Global Trade Services and SAP ERP. These configuration settings will differ from what we discussed in Chapter 15, as these settings specifical relate to trade monitoring.

As part of this set up, we'll review the SAP Risk Management general settings. After SAP GTS has been implemented following the steps outlined in Section 16.3, the SAP Risk Management module needs to be configured as well. To configure SAP Risk Management and the general settings, you follow these steps:

Configuration steps for SAP Risk Management general settings in support of trade services

1. Activate the document type and item category for preference processing.
2. Define an organizational structure that is either a plant-based preference or a cross-plant preference.
3. Activate a preference agreement.
4. Define and assign the rule set.
5. Set control settings and a data scope for vendor declarations.

Let's look at each of these general settings for SAP Risk Management in further detail.

16.4.1 Activate the Document Type and Item Category

The document type defines the type of business transactions that you want to send to SAP GTS for preference treatment, and the item category helps you further control the activation for preference processing. You activate the document types for preference processing in which you want to display preference statements in SAP Compliance Management or SAP Customs Management documents. You can make a provisional preference statement for a product based on order data and a binding preference statement based on sales documents, such as a billing document.

For preference processing, activate the document types for billing documents and sales documents as shown in the Figure 16.19. As mentioned earlier, the document is already activated for SAP Compliance Management or SAP Customs Management, and the services for preference determination are activated by the document type.

Configuration Settings

To perform this configuration, use Transaction SPRO, and follow menu path, SAP RISK MANAGEMENT • PREFERENCE PROCESSING SERVICE • ACTIVATION • ACTIVATE DOCUMENT TYPES.

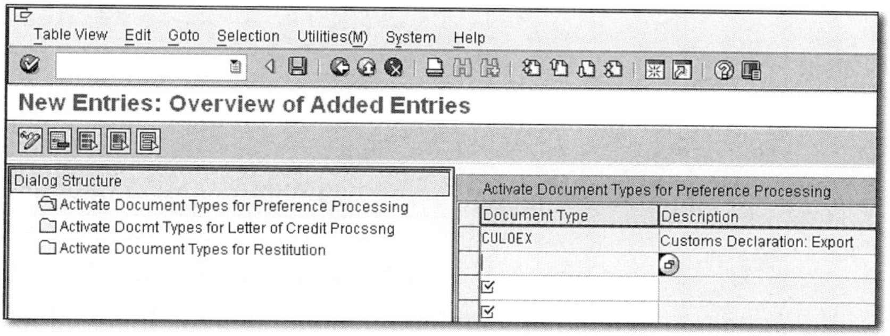

Figure 16.19 Preference Processing Activation for Document Types

Mapping ERP document types to SAP Global Trade Services

You need to map the SAP ERP document types that you defined when you established communications with SAP GTS to SAP GTS customs document types. You can do this in SAP Compliance Management by choosing GENERAL SETTINGS • DOCUMENT STRUCTURE. Here you map the feeder system document types to the SAP GTS customs document.

Similar to the order types, you also need to activate the item categories for preference processing. Use Transaction SPRO, and follow menu path, SAP RISK MANAGEMENT • PREFERENCE PROCESSING SERVICE • ACTIVATION • ACTIVATE ITEM CATEGORY.

16.4.2 Define an Organizational Structure

Administrative units are the organizations responsible for the preference rule. In Section 16.3.4, you defined the preferential-specific organizational structure. Now you need to update the attributes of the administrative unit in terms of the names and IDs. This definition depends on the model you choose for your business, either plant based or cross plant. You can also define one of two models, as described in the following subsections.

Plant-Based Preference Model

In the plant-based model, you define the parameters for aggregating vendor declarations and for regulating plant-based preference determination. These parameters include the feeder system and the plant from the feeder system for which you want to perform preference determination.

Cross-Plant Preference Model

In the cross-plant model, specify the parameters for aggregating vendor declarations and for regulating cross-plant preference determination. These parameters include the feeder system and the plant group from the feeder system for which you want to perform preference determination. If you want to aggregate the BOM as a basis for preference determination for different plants, use cross-plant preference determination.

Vendor declaration statements and Cross-Plant Preference models

If you aggregate the vendor declaration statements for goods from three different plants, and only goods from two of these plants are eligible for preferential treatment according to the vendor declarations, none of the goods are assigned the preference indicator, so they will be determined as eligible for preference. All of the plants in a plant group must belong to a group of feeder systems.

Country grouping and regulation commonalities

You can only group plants from different countries in one group if they have a common legal regulation. For example, due to the EU being a customs union, you can combine plants from different countries within the EU in one plant group. In the free trade zone of NAFTA, for example, you can only group plants from one country in a plant group.

16.4.3 Activate the Preference Agreement

The predelivered configuration has the determination procedure LEPRE as the country group activation (see Figure 16.20. You don't have to change the predelivered setting. You can see this screen by following menu path, Display IMG (SPRO) • SAP Global Trade Services • SAP Risk Management • 'Preference Processing' Service • Assign Determination Procedure for Active Preference Agreements.

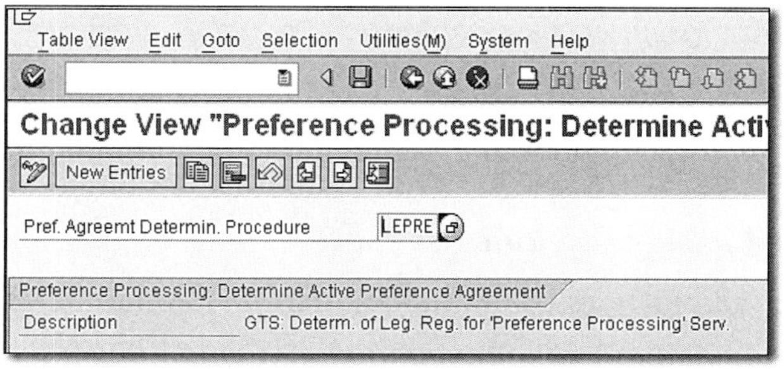

Figure 16.20 Preferential Agreement Determination Procedure

Preferential service for import and export

Under Preference Processing: Activate Legal Regulations, you can activate the preferential service for import and export. Figure 16.21 displays the preferential agreement activations for different country groups for export and import.

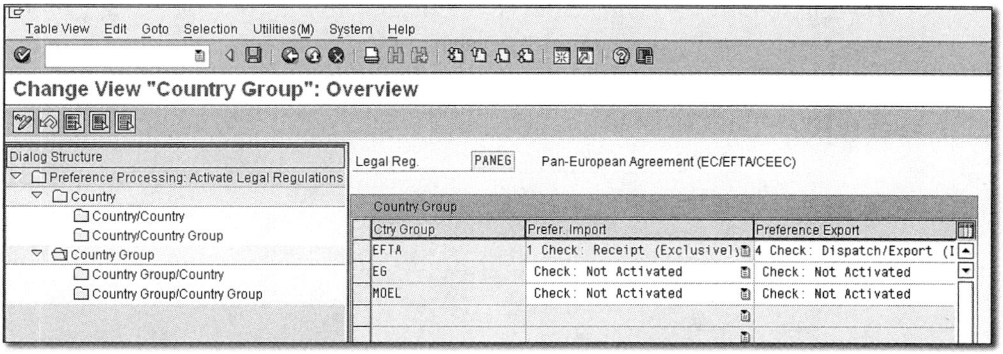

Figure 16.21 Activate Preferential Regulation

When activating these preference agreements, specify which processes in the feeder system trigger preference processing in SAP GTS. You can choose from the following processes:

- Dispatch (Exclusively)
- Export (Exclusively)

- EXPORT (EXCLUDING DOMESTIC)
- DISPATCH/EXPORT (INCLUDING DOMESTIC)
- CHECK: NOT ACTIVATED

If you want to perform preference only when it's an export, then select the EXPORT (EXCLUDING DOMESTIC), but if you want to include domestic shipments, then choose DISPATCH/EXPORT (INCLUDING DOMESTIC).

16.4.4 Define and Assign the Rule Set

These rule sets are combinations of rules of all of the preference agreements that are valid for a jurisdiction. This allows you to control the attributes that are defined for preference rules and preference agreements for each jurisdiction. To get to the rule set, use Transaction SPRO, or follow menu path, SAP GLOBAL TRADE SERVICES • SAP RISK MANAGEMENT • PREFERENCE PROCESSING SERVICE • DEFINE RULE SET.

Rule set configuration

You need to enter a RULE SET name, the RULE SET TYPE, and a NUMBER SCHEME, as shown in Figure 16.22. In a later step, you assign the various preference agreements for a jurisdiction to the corresponding rule set. By defining the numbering scheme at the rule set level, you ensure that all of the preference agreements for a jurisdiction are based on the same numbering scheme.

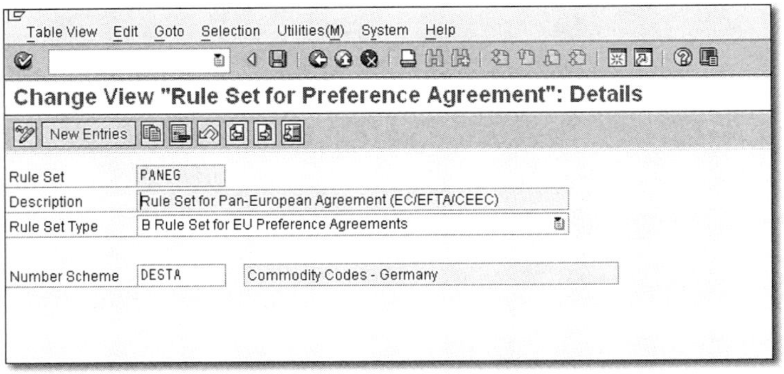

Figure 16.22 Defining a Rule Set

Trade Agreement implications for data uploads

If you're uploading data from the data provider (e.g., customs information from NAFTA), the rule sets, preference agreements, country group, and legal regulation are automatically assigned.

In the rule set, decide whether to use the rule set for NAFTA or EU preferential agreements. Enter the numbering schema for the rule set, and then assign the rule set to the preferential agreement. In a rule set, you can group all of the preference agreements that apply to a specific jurisdiction. You also need to specify a customs currency and an associated exchange rate type. Use the exchange rate type to define the type of currency translation that you're performing, such as translation between the currency of the threshold value and the document currency.

16.4.5 Set Control Settings for the Data Scope in Vendor Declarations

You can define for each administrative unit whether you can perform the following processes in relation to vendor declarations within preference processing:

- Requesting and dunning vendor-based vendor declarations
- Issuing and cancelling vendor declarations for the customer's purposes
- Issuing detailed declarations for dutiable product components

Indicator setting for vendor-based declarations within SAP Risk Management

Based on your indicator setting to activate the vendor-based declarations, the system prepares to send vendor declaration documents to your partners (e.g., vendors and customers). If you want to issue your customers with a detailed list of dutiable product components, you set the DETAILED DECLARATIONS OF DUTIABLE PRODUCTS (VENDOR DECLARATION FOR CUSTOMER PURPOSE) indicator. This configuration step can be found under SAP RISK MANAGEMENT • PREFERENCE PROCESSING SERVICE • VENDOR DECLARATION. If you don't set the indicator, the system issues a negative declaration.

Partner groups

In the partner group, you need to define the specific partner functions for which you want to issue a vendor declaration in preference processing. Based on the partner function, the system determines the relevant data from the invoice document in the feeder system to create or cancel a request or dun a vendor declaration. If you define the consignor partner function (i.e., the receiver of goods who is the importer of record) in the partner group, the system issues vendor declarations for the customer's purpose for the partners who are flagged as consignors and who are shown on the invoice documents.

Configuration steps

You can find the configuration steps by using Transaction SPRO and following menu path, SAP RISK MANAGEMENT • PREFERENCE PROCESSING SERVICE • VENDOR DECLARATION, followed by choosing the following:

- CONTROL SETTINGS FOR LONG-TERM VENDOR DECLARATIONS AND ADMINISTRATIVE UNIT (Figure 16.23)
- DEFINE STANDARD TEXTS AND LOGO FOR PRINTING DOCUMENTS
- CONTROL SETTINGS FOR VENDOR-BASED LONG-TERM VENDOR DECLARATIONS (Figure 16.24)
- CONTROL SETTINGS FOR LONG-TERM VENDOR DECLARATIONS FOR CUSTOMER'S PURPOSE (Figure 16.25)

Configuration of administrative unit settings

Figure 16.23 provides the details on the definition for the administrative unit, currency, and exchange rate type. In the PREFERENCE: CONTROL SETTINGS FOR VENDOR DECLARATION section shown in Figure 16.23, you can select the . SPECIFIC ACTIVATION OF VENDOR BASED LTVD and the SPECIFIC ACTIVATION OF LTVD F. CUST.PURPOSE checkboxes.

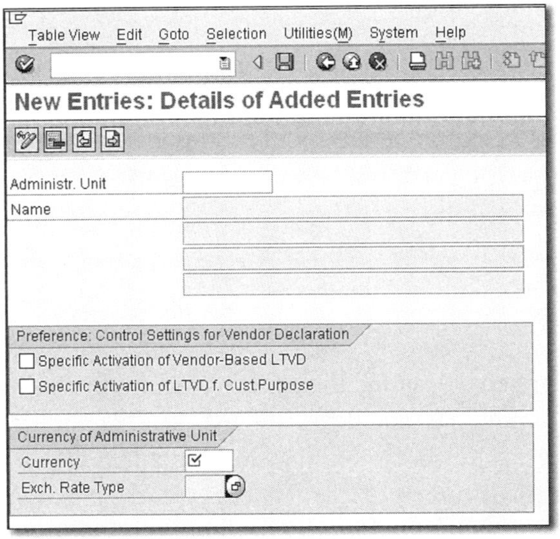

Figure 16.23 Control Settings for Long-Term Vendor Declarations and Administrative Unit

Figure 16.23 also displays the setting for the administrative unit, which is responsible for the vendor declaration. Based on the administrative unit that you create, you can define whether it's meant as vendor based or customer based, as well as the applicable currency (USD or EUR) and exchange rate.

Figure 16.24 displays the configuration for the administrative unit definition for dunning residence time, maximum dunning levels, and the forms associated with it. Figure 16.24 also displays the control settings you can apply to the administrative unit. These settings include the dunning levels which are selected from the dropdown menu (e.g., 1 – REQUEST or 2 – WARNING), residence time for retention, maximum dunning level, mode of communication (e.g., email or regulation mail), and layout of the print form (e.g., Smart Form, form text, or PDF).

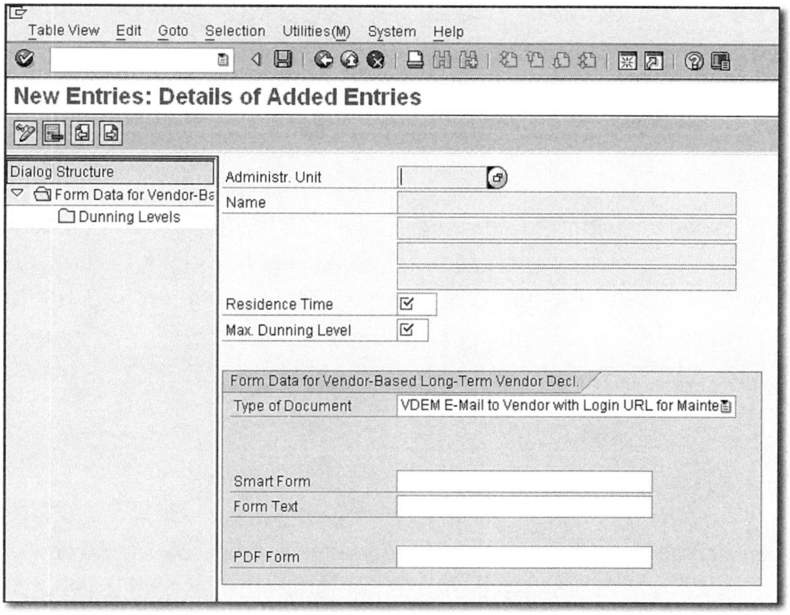

Figure 16.24 Control Settings for Vendor-Based Long-Term Vendor Declarations

Figure 16.25 displays how the settings for the administrative unit apply to the vendor declarations that are managed for the customer's purpose.

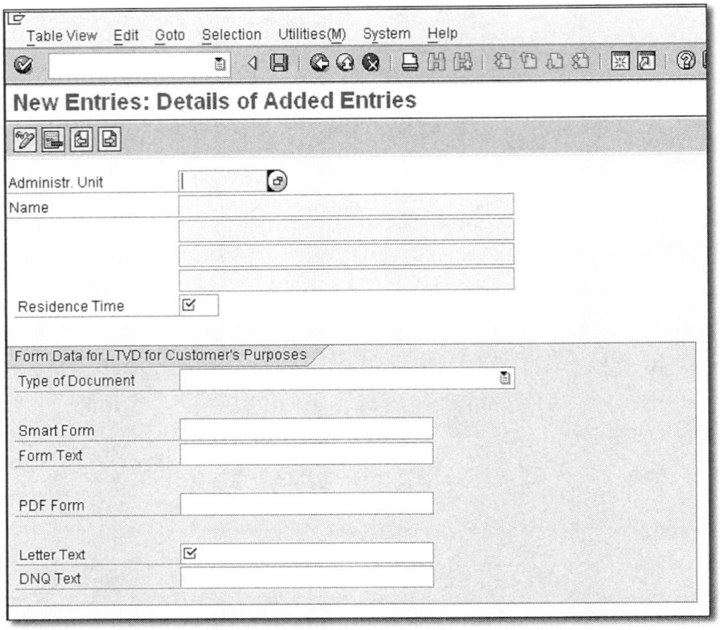

Figure 16.25 Control Settings for Long-Term Vendor Declarations for the Customer's Purpose

Now that we've explored the key functions, including SAP Customs Management, SAP Risk Management, and SAP Compliance Management, as well as the configuration and integration of SAP ERP and SAP GTS, let's review the general business benefits to an effectively integrated SAP GTS module.

16.5 SAP GTS Benefits

We've covered considerable ground in SAP GTS, SAP Risk Management, and SAP ERP. We've discussed the configuration process, reviewed how to enable SAP ERP as a feeder system and SAP GTS as a receiver system to help you effectively manage your international trade risk. In summary, let's review the benefits of SAP GTS.

Documentation support

By now, you should understand that SAP GTS supports the production of international shipping documentation, including commercial invoices, entry summaries, and pre-clearance notifications. You use a pro forma document from SAP ERP created against the outbound delivery or sales order to generate the trade documents for customs declaration. It receives the details of the transaction from the backend SAP ERP system (e.g., the material or sales price) to declare duty calculation to customs. As a standard practice, business users generate these invoices before the customer invoice because the customer has not received the goods. SAP Global Trade Services (GTS) includes a functionality called preference processing, which helps you maintain customs priorities within your system and eases your exporting operations. It allows you to separate countries with which you have trade agreements from banned countries, as well as preferred countries based on importing and exporting tax rates.

Benefits for Inbound and outbound process

SAP GTS seamlessly ties into the logistics inbound and outbound processes. The major process steps in an export scenario are creating a sales order, performing a delivery, and issuing an invoice. Classify means that official numbers and schema are assigned to all products. You might say that the goods need to speak the language of international trade. And this language is mainly the Harmonized Tariff System (HTS), an international goods nomenclature used by more than 200 customs administrations. The HTS is mainly used to determine customs tariffs, monitor controlled goods, and gather trade statistics.

Export benefits

Besides the HTS and Schedule B Number, US exporters also are required to enter an ECCN (export control classification number) on the required export documents such as the shippers export declaration (SED) if the product requires a validated license. The process of assigning these numbers to specific products is known as product classification, which is a time-consuming task that involves good knowledge of the multiple classification taxonomies and is open to a range of interpretations. Nevertheless, the process is business critical because appropriate classifications help minimize import duties.

Classification data management

SAP GTS simplifies this important task by enabling companies to upload classification data from authorized providers such as from partner FedEx Trade Networks. To classify a product, users can take advantage of powerful phonetic search capabilities, and also SAP GTS makes intelligent classification proposals. Furthermore, SAP GTS allows companies to execute mass reclassification tasks that arise when numbering systems are modified. This is especially helpful because the HTS is constantly being revised in light of developments in technology and changes in trade patterns. First of all, SAP GTS performs an export compliance precheck. This means that SAP GTS makes sure the export is in line with statutory regulations.

Business partner screening

SAP GTS automatically screens your business partners to make sure that your business partners aren't listed on one of the denied party lists. These lists are published by various governments, such as the US Commerce Department, but also by the European Union, and include some thousands of names with persons and companies you're not allowed to do business with. The official sanctioned party lists provided by external data providers can be automatically uploaded to the software, helping ensure that the customers database is complete and accurate at all times. Also SAP GTS performs an embargo check to determine whether there are restrictions on the country or countries involved. If SAP GTS identifies a problem, it automatically blocks the relevant documents and logs the reasons.

Regulation and compliance checks for exports

SAP GTS also checks whether an item or service requires an export license according to Export Administration Regulations. SAP GTS also automatically identifies export orders requiring letters of credit. And if SAP GTS identifies any issue, the transaction is automatically blocked. If everything is fine, the sales order passes through, and the export order is ready for the next step, which is the delivery.

During the delivery, SAP GTS again performs all compliance checks, and also checks if duty unpaid goods are available in a customs warehouse and updates the status of the goods in the inventory (duty paid, duty unpaid) accordingly.

SAP GTS handles all aspects associated with generating and filing export documents as well. The software identifies all documents needed for a specific export transaction to make sure customers meet the complex documentation requirements. Therefore SAP GTS includes a full set of standard forms. Also, with the help of Adobe technology, customers can easily tailor forms to changing regulatory requirements. Through its tight integration into the logistics system, SAP GTS reduces manual efforts significantly. The application automatically fills much of the required data into the appropriate forms.

If electronic filing of any document is required, SAP GTS helps to communicate with customs authorities via various platforms, including the Automated Export System in the United States and in Europe. If the export transaction has been secured with a payment guarantee, meaning a letter of credit, SAP GTS makes sure that the documents required by the issuing bank contain the right information. This helps avoid payment delays or any other issues due to incorrectly issued letter-of-credit documents.

Similar to the export scenario, SAP GTS provides several services throughout the entire import process. This includes proper classification of goods and performing all import-relevant compliance checks. Furthermore, SAP GTS creates the required import documentation and makes the appropriate forms available either in print format or in electronic format.

Through the tight integration of SAP GTS with other inbound and outbound processes, SAP GTS really helps to enhance process efficiency and provides the flexibility to add new services to meet changing business and regulatory requirements.

16.6 Summary

In this chapter, we discussed the key functions of SAP GTS, SAP Compliance, SAP Customs Management, and SAP Risk Management. We also reviewed the key integration, as we went over the detailed functionality with the key components of SAP GTS. We also took the example of the SAP GTS preference processing and covered the detailed configuration steps involved in setting up the preference processing from SAP ERP and SAP GTS.

In the next chapter we'll expand on our knowledge with the SAP GTS integration with SAP Environment, Health, and Safety Management. We'll review the integration in the configuration setup within SAP ERP and SAP GTS. We'll also go over the new user interface with the SAP GTS 10.0 release.

Environment, Health, and Safety Management is a critical part of a company's supply chain compliance. SAP Global Trade Services provides you with compliance monitoring capability to integrate with your SAP EHS Management. In this chapter, we'll explore some of the key differences in the user interface between versions 10.0 of SAP Global Trade Services and SAP Governance, Risk, and Compliance solutions, including visualization.

17 Compliance with Environment, Health, and Safety Management

You can perform hazardous substance checks in SAP Environment, Health, and Safety Management (SAP EHS Management) using SAP Global Trade Services (SAP GTS). These checks for hazardous substances help gather information from the logistics system and pass it on to the trade compliance system for early warning, reporting, and appropriate corrective actions. They also help with import and export quantity restrictions, as well as import and export restrictions for products for specific countries of origin. One piece of functionality enables you to run hazardous substance checks for the items in your SAP EHS Management logistics transactions using SAP GTS. When you create a compliance document such as a sales order or delivery note, SAP GTS creates an equivalent document in the system and performs a check for hazardous materials in SAP EHS Management.

SAP Environment, Health, and Safety components

SAP EHS Management includes several components to handle Environment, Health, and Safety (EH&S) issues:

- **Basic Data and Tools**
  Allows you to centrally manage the specifications for all other components (e.g., hazardous materials and dangerous goods).

- **Product Safety**
  Allows you to manage hazardous substances with material safety sheets and labels.
- **Hazardous Substance Management**
  Allows you to manage hazardous material and report to authorities.
- **Dangerous Goods Management**
  Allows you to manage dangerous goods within your logistics, with relevant checks and documents to go along with the shipment.
- **Waste Management**
  Allows you to manage disposal processes, transportation reporting, distribution of waste, and cost of waste management.
- **Occupational Health**
  Allows you to perform health surveillance checks with your company and manage questionnaires that employees fill out.
- **Industry Hygiene and Safety**
  Allows you to organize safety and hygiene within your enterprise, manage hazards, and report events that could cause safety issues.

In the process of manufacturing, assembly, or sourcing from a vendor, companies often deal with hazardous or dangerous goods. It's important to identify these parts or goods for tracking and to perform a compliance check for necessary trade regulatory checks for any import restrictions, export restrictions from a specific country, handling of the goods, and reporting to customs authorities. To keep track of such information, you can use SAP EHS Management, a part of SAP ERP.

17.1 Integration of SAP EHS Management and SAP Global Trade Services

When hazardous substances in logistics documents are transferred to SAP GTS, the system performs compliance checks and updates the status in the SAP GTS customs document. If the status is blocked or not okay, you can stop the next process step. For example, if you have a sales order line blocked due to a hazardous material, you can set up the system to stop the delivery note creation. If there are restrictions on the quantity, the system can check for the quantity that is allowed.

This quantity check can also be applied to imported goods through purchase order (PO) and goods receipt logistics transactions. Use Transaction SE37, and enter FUNCTION MODULE "/SAPSLL/CD_PO_EHS_CHECK_RFC_R3" to perform these EH&S checks on POs (Figure 17.1).

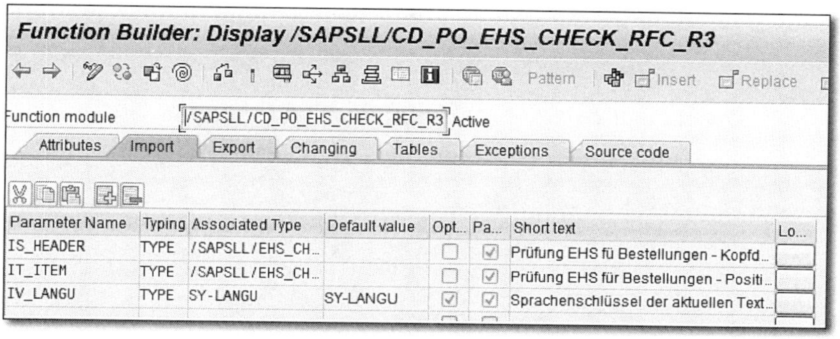

Figure 17.1 Function Module /SAPSLL/CD_PO_EHS_CHECK_RFC_R3 Checks on POs

The input parameters have header (IS_HEADER), item (IT_ITEM), and language (IV_LANGU) keys under the IMPORT tab, and the output from this function module provides the return value of okay or block (EV_BLOCK), which you can see on the EXPORT tab (Figure 17.2).

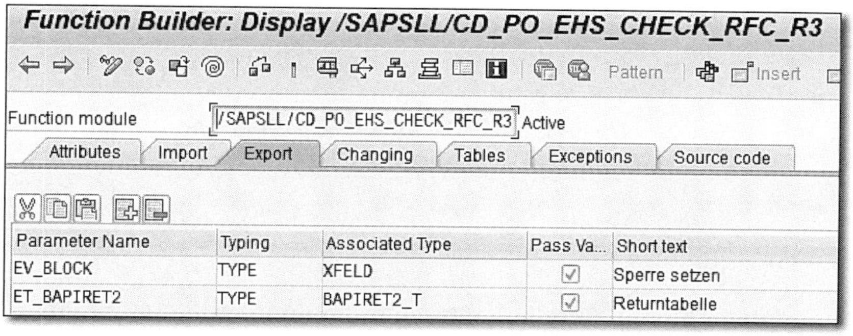

Figure 17.2 Return Value and Barrier Set as Export or Out of the Function Module

The /SAPSLL/CD_PO_EHS_CHECK_RFC_R3 function module is blocked and therefore invoked for an SAP EHS Management PO call for SAP GTS to check. Let's walk through the configuration steps that are required for a hazardous substance compliance check. There are two parts to the setup: first in the SAP EHS Management system and second within SAP GTS.

17.1.1 SAP EHS Management Configuration

Within SAP EHS Management, you need to set up configuration for hazardous substance information capture and tracking with the logistics documents. Follow these steps to enable this within SAP EHS Management:

SAP Environment, Health, and Safety configuration for logistics

1. Define a specific scenario.
2. Specify selection criteria for volume tracking.
3. Specify quantity limits and reactions on the overall status.
4. Set up online checks.
5. Specify data transfer in the property tree.
6. Specify regulatory lists.

Let's review the steps in detail.

Step 1: Define a Specific Scenario

To define the specific scenario, follow menu path, SAP Reference IMG • Environment, Health and Safety • Product Safety • Substance Volume Tracking • Specific Scenarios • Specific Data Determination per Regulation and Scenario. Here you specify the scenarios or scenario categories for this configuration step. This might apply to the specified scenarios (e.g., import or export) or scenario categories (e.g., sales order and delivery, for export; PO or purchase requisition, for import). Figure 17.3 displays the settings for import scenarios and for scenario categories, including the quantities that can be determined from purchasing, sales, or production data.

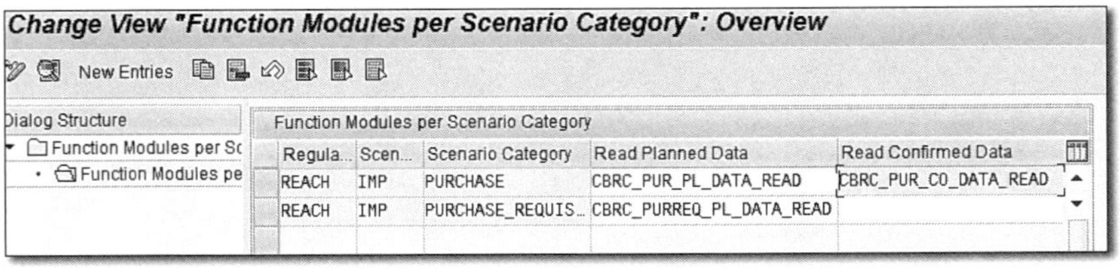

Figure 17.3 Function Modules Assignment to the Scenario Category

System data configuration In this configuration step, you define the system data determination for individual scenarios and regulations. If a function module is entered for substance determination separately for the material and for the component explosion in an entry without a specified scenario, the components are filled independently of the scenario. Otherwise, they are filled according to the scenario. The advantage is that the component and the main item are checked for hazardous substances and then reported independently.

Mapping a scenario When defining scenarios, you can delete scenarios that are not required. You should not define new scenarios or change the assignments of scenarios and scenario categories delivered with the system. If you do specify your own function modules when assigning them to the scenario category, their interfaces must match those of the standard function modules. Figure 17.4 displays the mapping of the function module (including the MATERIAL DETERMINATION and SUBSTANCE DETERMINATION) for different scenarios.

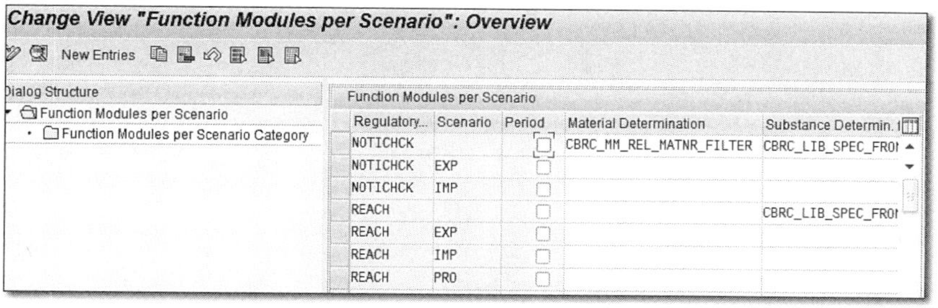

Figure 17.4 Mapping of a Function Module to Scenarios

In Figure 17.4, you can see examples of import (IMP), export (EXP), and procurement (PRO) based on the regulation REACH. Following the definition of the specific scenario, you need to specify the selection criteria for volume tracking.

Step 2: Specify Selection Criteria for Volume Tracking

You can restrict the logistics data that is monitored, and specify, for example, which documents are tracked in substance volume tracking (a configuration step in Hazardous Substance Management in SAP EHS Management). If you want to restrict substance volume tracking and monitoring to specific transactions, you can use the respective values in the TABLE and FIELD columns.

Follow menu path, SAP REFERENCE IMG • ENVIRONMENT, HEALTH AND SAFETY • PRODUCT SAFETY • SUBSTANCE VOLUME TRACKING • SPECIFIC SELECTION CRITERIA FOR VOLUME TRACKING. In the configuration shown in Figure 17.5, you specify the selection criteria for the data from SAP ERP application area tables (e.g., purchasing, sales, or delivery).

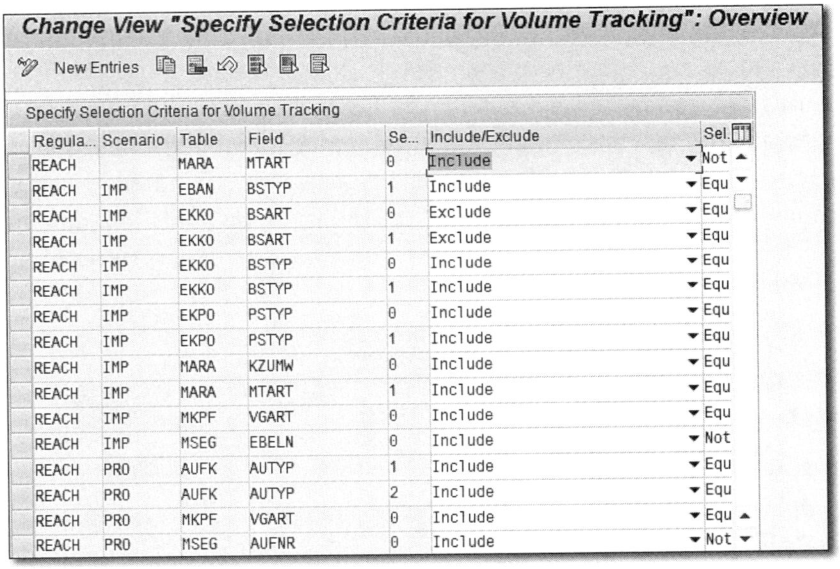
Change View "Specify Selection Criteria for Volume Tracking": Overview

New Entries

Specify Selection Criteria for Volume Tracking

Regula...	Scenario	Table	Field	Se...	Include/Exclude	Sel.
REACH		MARA	MTART	0	Include	Not
REACH	IMP	EBAN	BSTYP	1	Include	Equ
REACH	IMP	EKKO	BSART	0	Exclude	Equ
REACH	IMP	EKKO	BSART	1	Exclude	Equ
REACH	IMP	EKKO	BSTYP	0	Include	Equ
REACH	IMP	EKKO	BSTYP	1	Include	Equ
REACH	IMP	EKPO	PSTYP	0	Include	Equ
REACH	IMP	EKPO	PSTYP	1	Include	Equ
REACH	IMP	MARA	KZUMW	0	Include	Equ
REACH	IMP	MARA	MTART	1	Include	Equ
REACH	IMP	MKPF	VGART	0	Include	Equ
REACH	IMP	MSEG	EBELN	0	Include	Not
REACH	PRO	AUFK	AUTYP	1	Include	Equ
REACH	PRO	AUFK	AUTYP	2	Include	Equ
REACH	PRO	MKPF	VGART	0	Include	Equ
REACH	PRO	MSEG	AUFNR	0	Include	Not

Figure 17.5 Specification of Selection Criteria for Volume Tracking

If you want to restrict substance volume tracking and monitoring in the online checks to specific transactions, maintain the REGULATION, SCENARIO, TABLE and FIELD columns, as shown in Figure 17.5.

Volume tracking and Logistics data tables

In substance volume tracking, the system reads logistics data from the following tables, depending on the scenario: SCENARIO, SCENARIO TYPE TABLES, and DATE FOR PLANNED QUANTITIES. The date for planned quantities determines the monitoring period and the year to which the quantity is assigned. For processing of confirmed quantities, the posting date in the material document (MKPF-BUDAT) is decisive for all scenarios. For the production scenario (e.g., PRO), only the entries in the Material Documents Table (MSEG) where the order number (AUFNR field) isn't equal to zero are relevant to substance volume tracking. You can reduce the number of material documents to be evaluated by filtering the relevant valuation types (BWART field).

Use the MARA table to define selection criteria for the materials to be monitored. You can also classify materials in table MARA as relevant to substance volume tracking in the classification view of the material master. This classification is read if you click the FUNCTION MODULES PER SCENARIO CATEGORY folder shown earlier in Figure 17.4 and enter the standard function module "CBRC_MM_REL_MATNR_FILTER" under SPECIFY SCENARIOS in the MATERIAL DETERMINATION. The options just described for selectively restricting the materials for substance volume tracking affect the transfer of data from the logistics system. In addition, the data transfer program in the standard system reads selection settings for table ESTRH (specification headers) from the property tree to filter out specifications that are not relevant to material assignment. Use these filter options to limit the volume of data that is transferred from the property tree to the tables for substance volume tracking.

After you set up the selection criteria for volume tracking, you need to set up the quantity limits and reactions on the overall status.

Step 3: Specify Quantity Limits and Reactions on the Overall Status

When you specify the general quantity limit values, you need to make sure they account for every possible quantity of a substance. The upper limit value for the highest quantity threshold must contain the maximum value possible. If you specify a time period, the limit values apply for this time period, but if you don't specify a time period, the limit values apply for a calendar year. The relative quantity limit value specifies the percentage value of the general quantity limit value that must be exceeded before the system carries out an action.

Quantity limits and quantity thresholds

Follow menu path, SAP REFERENCE IMG • ENVIRONMENT, HEALTH AND SAFETY • PRODUCT SAFETY • SUBSTANCE VOLUME TRACKING • SPECIFIC QUANTITY LIMITS AND REACTIONS ON OVERALL STATUS. In this configuration step, you specify the quantity limits that apply in the individual regulations for substances that must be tracked (Figure 17.6). For each regulation, you can specify several quantity thresholds. For the quantity thresholds, you can specify limit values. The general quantity limit value contains the quantity limit values from the regulation and they can include upper and lower limit values For example, you could have the following quantity thresholds:

- Quantity threshold 1: up to 1 ton
- Quantity threshold 2: 1 to 10 tons
- Quantity threshold 3: 10 to 100 tons
- Quantity threshold 4: above 100 tons

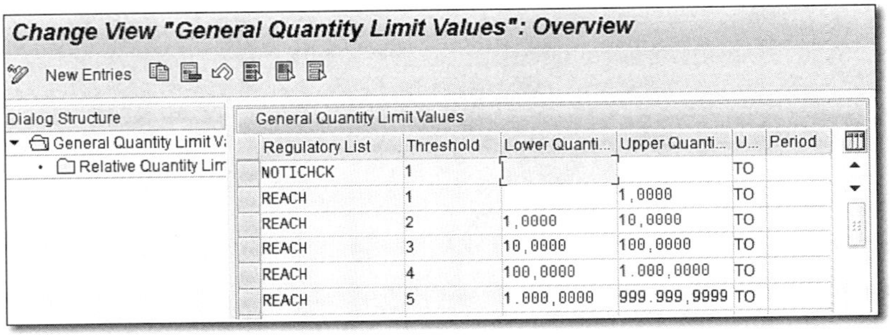

Figure 17.6 Maintain Quantity Upper and Lower Limit Values for Different Regulations

A general quantity limit value must always exist for a relative quantity limit value that is referred to by the relative limit value. There must always be at least one relative quantity limit value for each quantity threshold; otherwise, an error message appears in the application log. By specifying different relative limit values for a quantity threshold, you can determine that the system carries out actions in stages. For example, you can determine that the system notifies you when 70% is exceeded and blocks the business process when 100% is reached (Figure 17.7).

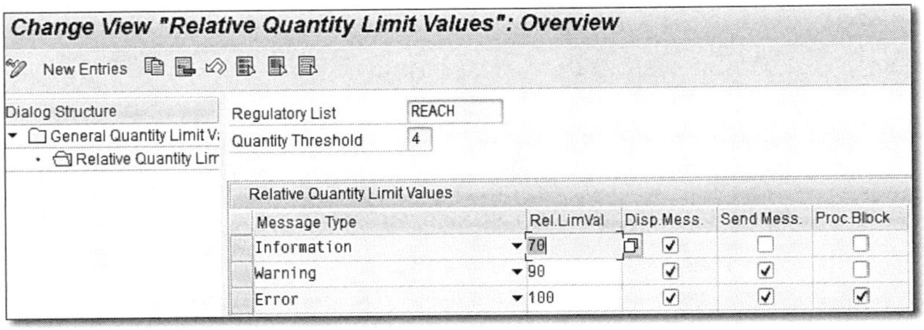

Figure 17.7 Relative Quantity Limit Values

If the property tree doesn't contain a specific quantity limit value for a substance, then quantity limit 1 applies. You can specify the quantity that was registered for the substance (registered quantity) in the substance property tree. This quantity is the quantity limit for the substance and overrides the general quantity limit from this configuration activity. Let's take an example of a chemical substance that has a statutory limit of a specific quantity volume that is safe to use, but your company has a better standard. To use your standard instead, you can use the override general quantity limit.

You can also specify a substance's relative quantity limits, which override the relative quantity limits. If you don't specify relative quantity limits for a substance, the system uses the relative quantity limits from this configuration, whose general quantity limit contains the registered quantity of the substance. The registered quantity limit can be the statutory quantity limit that you're expected to measure and monitor.

You've specified a substance's registered quantity in tons in the screen shown earlier in Figure 17.6, but you haven't defined relative quantity limits. In this configuration, you've defined the four quantity thresholds mentioned previously. Then the system uses the relative quantity limits for the substance that you entered in this configuration for quantity threshold 3 and relates the percentage values to 10 to 100 tons. When evaluating the quantity thresholds, the lower limit of an interval isn't part of the interval, but the upper limit is.

Step 4: Set Up Online Checks

In the online checks in substance volume tracking, the system checks at different places whether quantity limits are exceeded during certain actions. Follow menu path, SAP Reference IMG • Environment, Health and Safety • Product Safety • Substance Volume Tracking • Set Up Online Checks • Set up Online Checks to get to the screen shown in Figure 17.8. Thus, a quantity limit can be exceeded if, for example, you create a PO, manufacturing order, or sales document for a material to which a substance is assigned that is relevant for volume tracking.

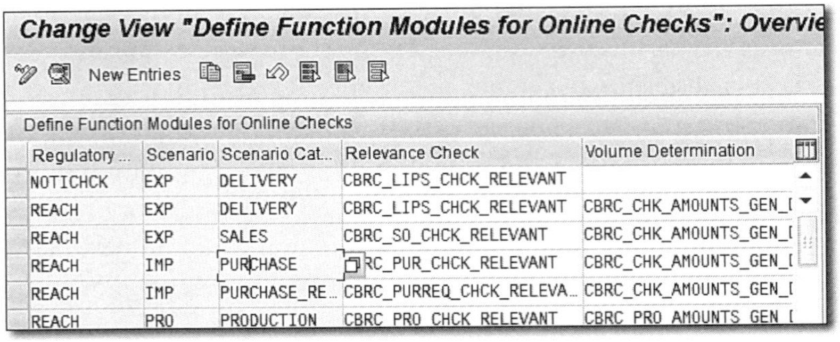

Figure 17.8 Define Function Modules for Online Checks

Online check functionality

Figure 17.8 displays the function module used for online checks. The online check can be set up to do the following:

- Specify how the system collects the orders and documents relevant to the online checks.
- Specify how the system determines the substance quantities relevant for the online checks.
- Specify how the system determines whether a quantity limit is exceeded.
- Specify how the system blocks follow-on documents and collects and outputs messages when a quantity limit is exceeded.

Handling multiple compliance regulations or multiple regulations with online checks

You might have a requirement to comply with specific regulations or multiple regulations based on the products, for example, Toxic Substance Control Act (TSCA) in the United States, and Regulation on Registration, Evaluation, Authorization and Restriction of Chemicals (REACH) in Europe, with your company operating globally. If you specify a regulation in an entry, the entry applies to that regulation only. If you don't specify a regulation in an entry, the entry applies to all regulations. If the system finds two entries (e.g., one with the relevant regulation specified and one without a regulation), it uses only the more specific entry—in this case, the one in which the regulation is specified.

Step 5: Specify Data Transfer in the Property Tree

In this specific configuration step, you specify how the system determines the substance data it requires for substance volume monitoring and tracking from the property trees and writes the data to the tables in substance volume tracking. Follow menu path, SAP REFERENCE IMG • ENVIRONMENT, HEALTH AND SAFETY • PRODUCT SAFETY • SUBSTANCE VOLUME TRACKING • SET UP ONLINE CHECKS • SPECIFY DATA TRANSFER (PROPERTY TREE) to open the screen shown in Figure 17.9. You also specify how the system transfers the condensed quantity of a substance to be tracked to the property tree for the substance. This transfer serves to archive the total substance quantity determined over a monitoring period (e.g., a calendar year).

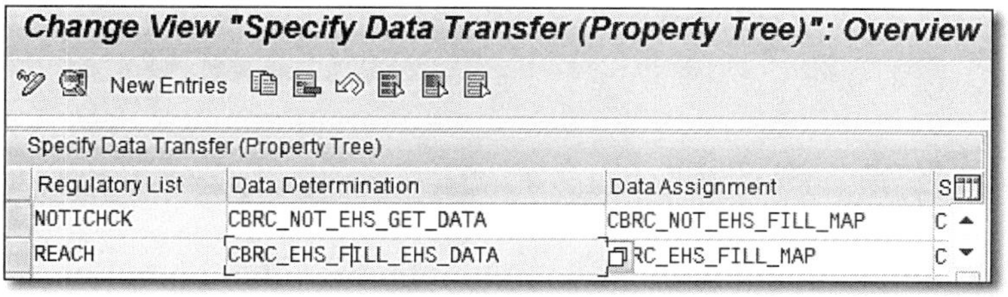

Figure 17.9 Specify Data Transfer in the Property Tree

After you set up the specific data transfer in the property tree, you need to define the regulatory lists.

Step 6: Specify Regulatory Lists

In this step, you create the regulatory lists you require, such as substance lists (see Figure 17.10 and Figure 17.11). By assigning a regulatory list to an identifier, you specify the regulatory list to which the identifier belongs or from which the identifier was taken. Follow menu path, SAP REFERENCE IMG • ENVIRONMENT, HEALTH AND SAFETY • BASIC DATA AND TOOLS • SPECIFICATION MANAGEMENT • SPECIFICATION MASTER • SPECIFY REGULATORY LISTS.

An identifier can relate to several regulatory lists. However, in a special case, one specification can occur under several different identifiers in the same regulatory list. For example, there are specifications that are entered several times in the Cost Accounting Standards (CAS) library under different CAS numbers. You need to ensure that the specification is maintained across the regulation list.

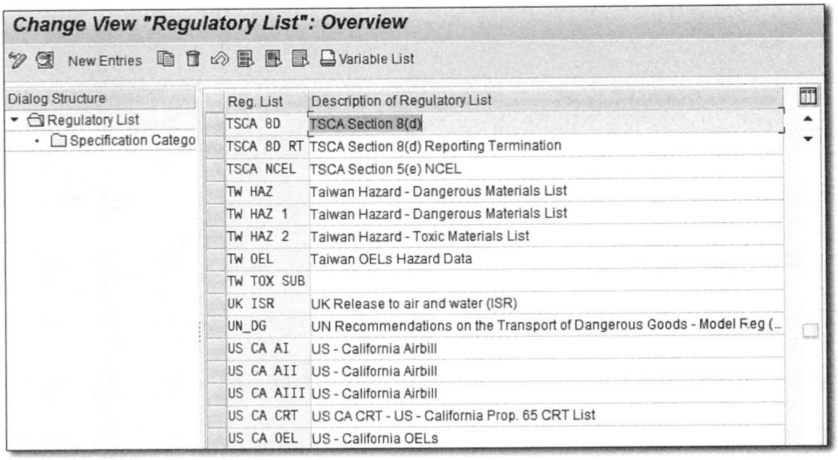

Figure 17.10 Regulatory List Definition

Entries for regulatory lists that have already been used once in the productive system must not be deleted because they are standard and might lead to inconsistency.

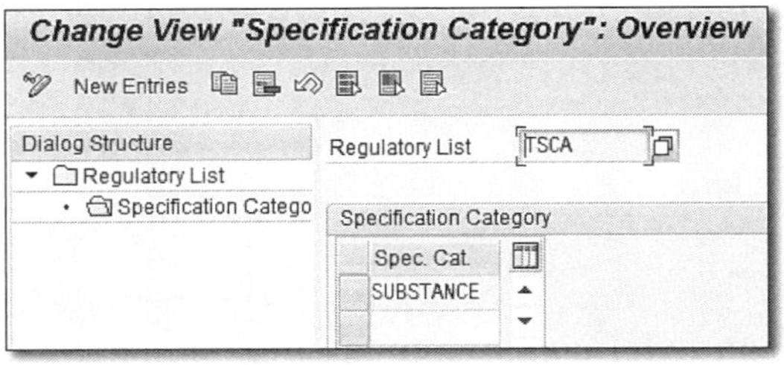

Figure 17.11 Specification Category within the Regulatory List

You can also enter regulatory lists in the Basic Data and Tools component. For more information, see the SAP Library for the Basic Data and Tools component under Regulatory List Management.

In the next section, we'll discuss the SAP GTS configuration steps that enable the compliance check for SAP EHS Management.

17.1.2 SAP Global Trade Services Configuration

To capture the compliance screening with SAP GTS, you need to perform the following steps in SAP GTS to enable the compliance check:

1. Define legal regulations.
2. Activate legal regulations at the country or country group level.
3. Define the determination procedure for active legal regulations.
4. Assign the determination procedure for active legal regulations.
5. Activate legal regulations.
6. Define control data for the hazardous substance check service.
7. (optional) Define an alternative remote function call (RFC) destination for SAP EHS Management.

Step 1: Define Legal Regulations

The first step is to define the legal unit. Follow menu path, SAP Global Trade Services • General Settings • Legal Regulations • Define Legal Regulations. You're defining the legal regulation for the hazardous substance check (Figure 17.12). In the Type of Legal Code field, select Prohibitions and Restrictions from the dropdown list, and select Import/Arrival and Export/Dispatch from the Import/Export field. Enter the country in Original Ctry of LR (e.g., "US").

Figure 17.12 Defining Legal Regulations

After you define the legal unit, you need to activate the legal regulation.

Step 2: Activate Legal Regulations at the Country or Country Group Level

Activation of the legal regulation is based on the outbound or the inbound country of the transaction in use. Follow menu path, SAP Global

Trade Services • General Settings • Legal Regulations • Activate Legal Regulations at Country/Country Group Level. In this configuration step, you need to list all of the countries from which you export and to which you import (Figure 17.13). This country information is included in the logistics documents (e.g., sales order or PO), which will be used to perform the hazardous substance check.

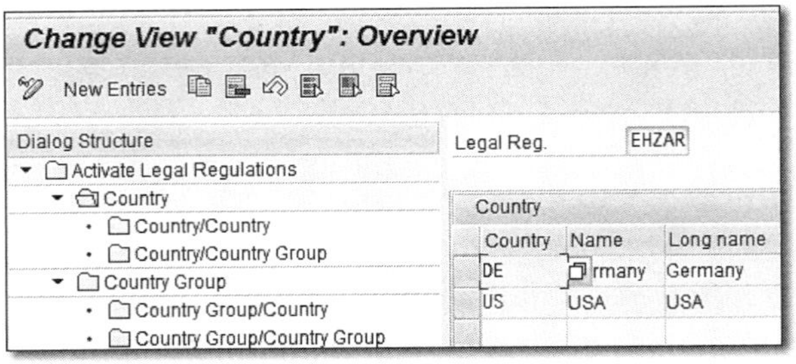

Figure 17.13 Activate Legal Regulations

Step 3: Define the Determination Procedure for Active Legal Regulations

The determination procedure contains the rules that the system uses to determine the active legal regulation (Figure 17.14).

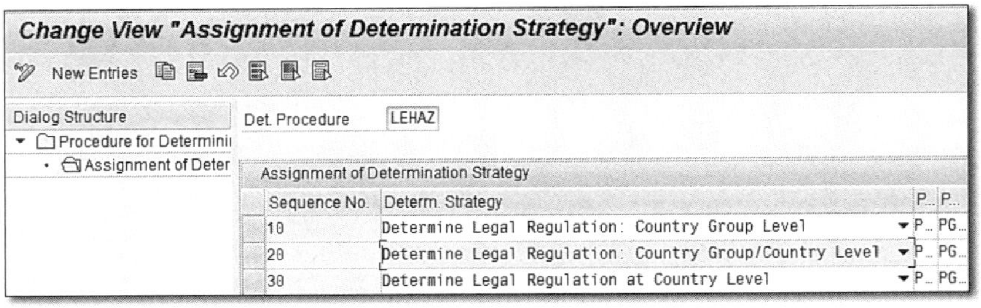

Figure 17.14 Assignment of Determination Procedure for Legal Regulation Determination

Follow menu path, SAP Global Trade Services • General Settings • Legal Regulations • Activate Legal Regulations at Country/Country Group Level. In this configuration step, you specify which determination procedure the system should use to determine the active legal regulation in the hazardous substance check service. While you're in this configuration, select the determination strategy for legal regulation determination. SAP GTS has the sequence number 10 for legal regulation at the country level and 20 for the legal regulation at the country group/country level. You can delete the 20 if you want to perform the determination against the country level.

Step 4: Assign Determination Procedure for Active Legal Regulations

Following the definition of the determination procedure, you need to assign it to the hazardous substance check for determination of active legal regulation. This helps the system determine the legal regulation based on the procedure defined in the earlier step. Follow menu path, SAP Global Trade Services • SAP Compliance Management • "Hazardous Substance Check" Service • Assign Determination Procedure for Active Legal Regulation. You can select the determination procedure from the Det. Proc: Legal Reg dropdown list (e.g., "ZHAZD") as shown in Figure 17.15.

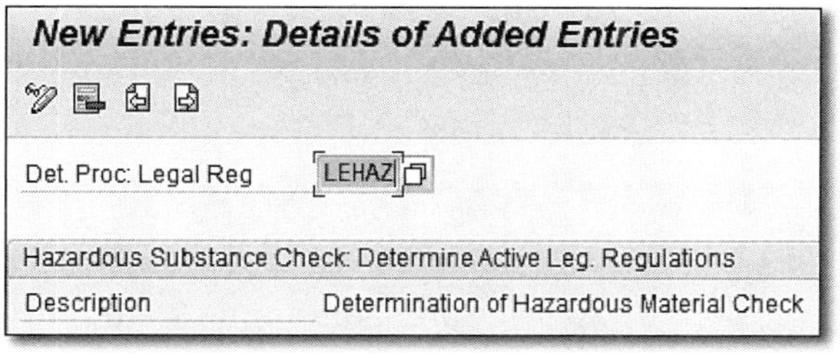

Figure 17.15 Assignment of the Hazardous Substance Check Determination Procedure

Step 5: Activate Legal Regulations

Based on the countries you defined in Step 2, you need to activate the import or export check for the hazardous substance check service. Follow menu path, SAP Global Trade Services • SAP Compliance Management • Hazardous Substance Check Service • Activate Legal Regulation. Select Check: Dispatch/Export (Including Domestic) to check for export transactions and domestic transactions (Figure 17.16).

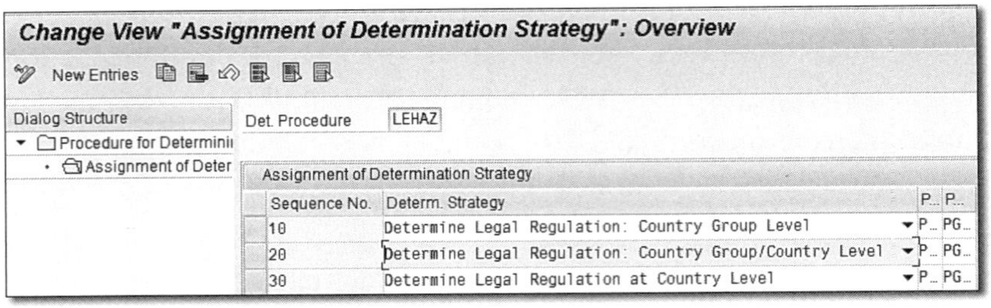

Figure 17.16 Legal Regulation Activation for Import and Export Services

Step 6: Define Control Data for the Hazardous Substance Check Service

Define the hazardous substance check for the legal regulation (defined in Step 1) by checking the Haz. Subst. Check Active box (Figure 17.17). Follow menu path, SAP Global Trade Services • SAP Compliance Management • Hazardous Substance Check Service • Control Data for Hazardous Substance Check Service. Then you need to define partner functions for exporting within the Partner Group to Determine Country of Dest. (destination) and for importing within Partner Group to Determine Country of Depart. (departure) dropdown lists (e.g., PGLDT1 and PGLDT2, respectively).

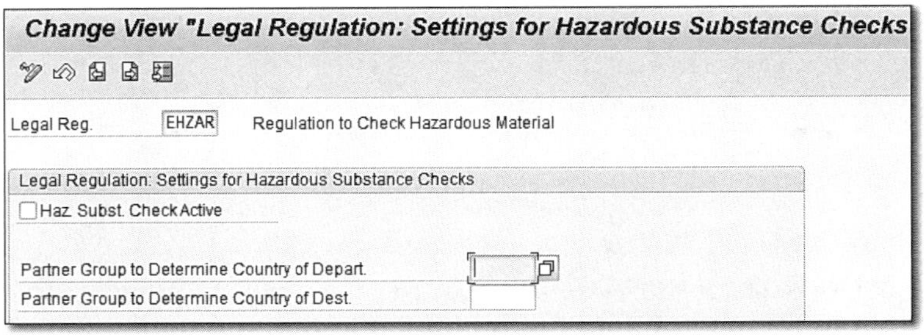

Figure 17.17 Control Settings for the Hazardous Substance Check

Step 7: Define Alternative RFC Destinations for SAP EHS Management

This step is optional. The hazardous substance check uses functions in SAP EHS Management to perform the checks of business transactions in SAP GTS. If you've installed your SAP EHS Management on a system other than your feeder system, configure an IMG activity to specify the RFC destination from which SAP GTS can call the hazardous substance check in SAP EHS Management. This is especially necessary in situations in which a company has multiple SAP R/3 or SAP ERP systems, where a dedicated SAP EHS Management system differs from the logistics or financial system.

Configuration of Alternative RFC Destinations

Follow menu path, SAP Global Trade Services • SAP Compliance Management • Hazardous Substance Check Service • Define Alternative RFC Destination for SAP ERP EH&S. Choose the logical system from which you want to transfer the logistics documents, and assign it to the RFC destination for SAP EHS Management (Figure 17.18).

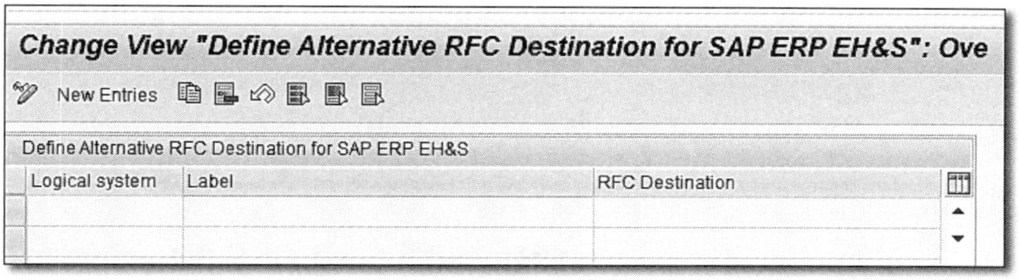

Figure 17.18 Define RFC Destination for Alternative SAP ERP System

Hazardous service checks against sales orders or purchase orders

When you create a sales order, delivery note, or PO after completing the configuration steps, SAP GTS creates a customs document within its SAP Compliance Management component and performs the hazardous service check. If a hazard is found, then the system produces a block (or red light). Figure 17.19 shows an example report in SAP GTS via menu path, SAP GTS Area Menu • SAP Compliance Management • SAP Legal Control Export • Display Blocked Document. The document went through the hazardous service check, and there were no issues. (The two red lights are for legal control license determination, so they don't indicate issues with a hazardous substance.)

Following the review of SAP EHS Management configuration, let's go over the new visualization features with the SAP GTS 10.0 and SAP GRC 10.1n the next section.

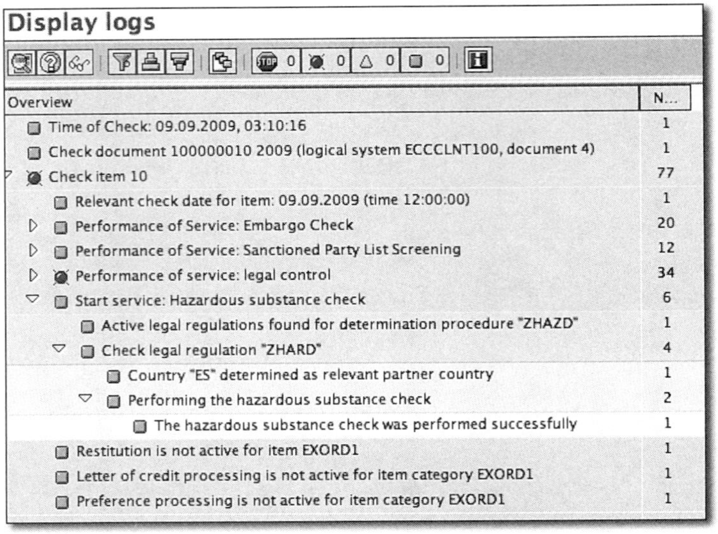

Figure 17.19 Hazardous Compliance Check in SAP Global Trade Services

17.2 Visualization Features with SAP GTS 10

In this section, we will review the latest visualization features for GTS 10. These visualizations are connected to SAP Environment, Health, and Safety in the broadest of ways. Visualization is one of the common features between version 10.0 of SAP GRC solutions, including Environment, Health, and Safety, and version 10.0 of SAP GTS. The visualization is the new user interface (UI) that uses SAP NetWeaver Business Client (NWBC) or SAP NetWeaver Portal with the main objective of user productivity and ease of use. These are defined with the business users' experience in mind and provide them with work centers that are configurable and applicable to their business case. SAP GTS 10.0 version was also major introduction; SAP GTS 10.0 is part of SAP GRC 10.0 solutions.

In addition to visualization, SAP GRC version 10.0 solutions also offer the following common features and functions that are introduced across applications including SAP Environment, Health, and Safety

- **Technical platform**
  Unifies SAP Risk Management, SAP Access Control, and SAP Process Control within a common ABAP platform along with SAP GTS 10.0.
- **Configurable UI**
  A customizable display component through configuration.
- **Reporting**
  Use of business objects for reporting and analytics.
- **SAP Content Lifecycle Management (CLM)**
  Supporting version control, packaging, import and export of content, and updates.

The prior releases of SAP GTS (8.0 and lower) had an ABAP GUI. In version 10.0, however, this new UI has been introduced specifically to the SAP GTS sanctioned party list (SPL) screening function. This new UI is part of the new visualization feature introduced with SAP GRC 10. 0 solutions. It's targeted at the business users, with a UI that is configurable and allows each user to select the information that is important to him. The visualization is also based on the SAP NetWeaver Portal or the SAP NetWeaver Business Client, so the look and feel is similar to the web interfaces. SAP GTS 10.0 allows you to configure the new UI and also work with the traditional ABAP GUI to help you migrate from an old version to the newer version.

17.2.1 Accessing the New User Interface

There are two methods for accessing the new UI of SAP GTS 10.0:

- Through the SAP NetWeaver Business Client view (GUI) from the SAP NetWeaver Business Client installed on your PC
- Through the SAP NetWeaver Business Client view from a link saved in Windows Explorer

These are different links based on the transactions. You can find the link by using Transaction NWBC in SAP GTS.

Figure 17.20 displays the screen that appears after you use Transaction NWBC. Figure 17.21 displays the individual transaction accessed with the NWBC installed on your PC. When you log on to the SAP GTS system, it brings up the SAP Easy Access screen. As shown in Figure 17.20, you enter the transaction code "NWBC" within the command window. After you've entered the transaction code, the screen shown in Figure 17.21 appears.

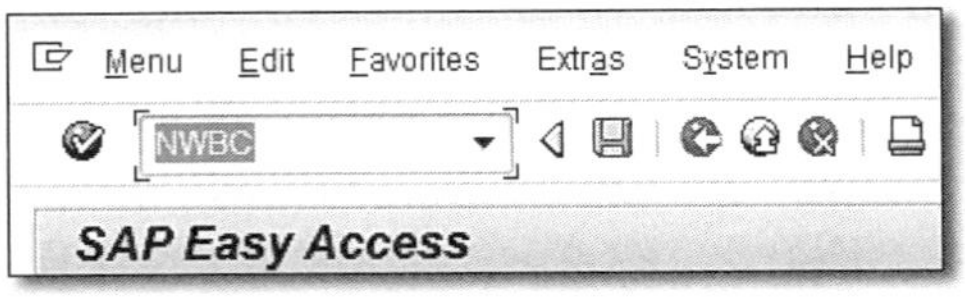

Figure 17.20 SAP Global Trade Services Easy Access GUI Transaction Window

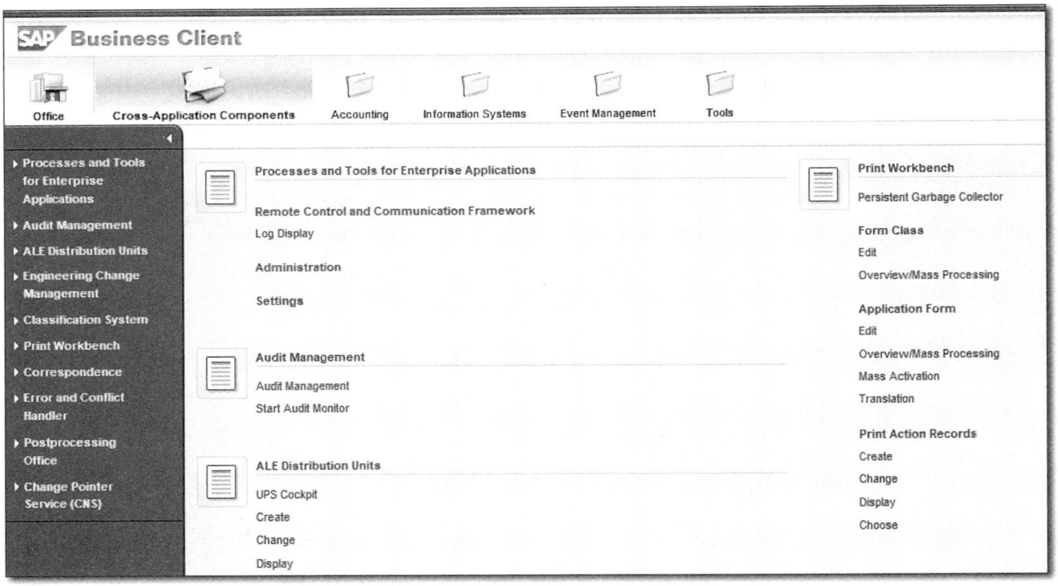

Figure 17.21 Link to SAP NetWeaver Business Client for SAP Global Trade Services: Specific Transactions

17.2.2 SAP NetWeaver Business Client (NWBC)

In this section, we'll review the two ways to access the SAP NetWeaver Business Client. The screen shown previously in Figure 17.20 appears when you log on to the SAP GTS GUI or the SAP Easy Access menu. The screen shown in Figure 17.22 displays the SAP NETWEAVER BUSINESS

CLIENT view of an SAP GTS transaction or report, with the SANCTIONED PARTY LIST SCREENING overview. As you can see, this screen is organized with different tabs or folders, with REPORTS FOR GLOBAL TRADE SERVICES displayed and with two other selection folders: SANCTIONED PARTNER LIST SCREENING and SANCTIONED PARTY LIST SCREENING: MASTER DATA. This view provides the user with a work area with one window and three selection folders, organized by different functions and transactions within.

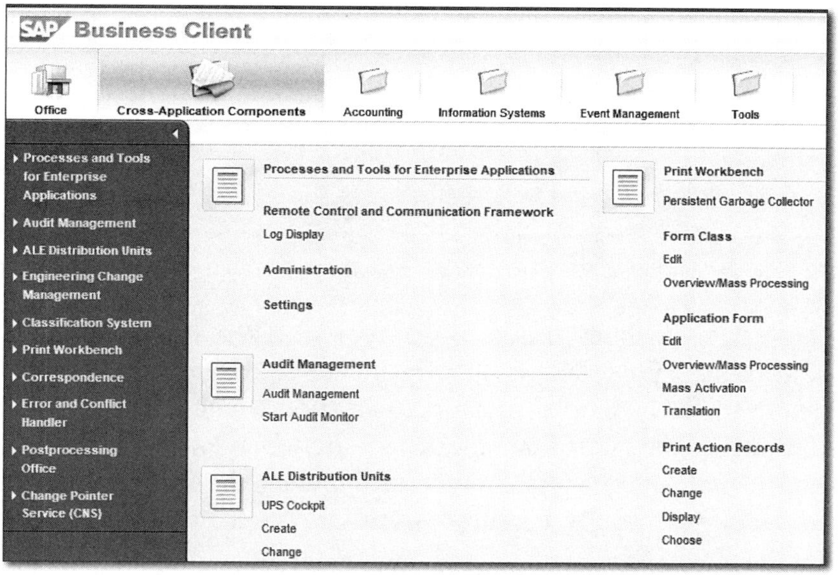

Figure 17.22 The SAP NetWeaver Business Client UI

Now that we've reviewed how to access the new UI, in the next section, we'll review the configuration settings requirement to enable this new UI.

17.3 Sanctioned Party List Screening Configuration

Now let's review the configuration with SAP GTS 10.0 Sanctioned Party List screening specific to the new UI that needs to be set up. Figure 17.23 displays the SAP GTS SANCTIONED PARTY LIST SCREENING configurations.

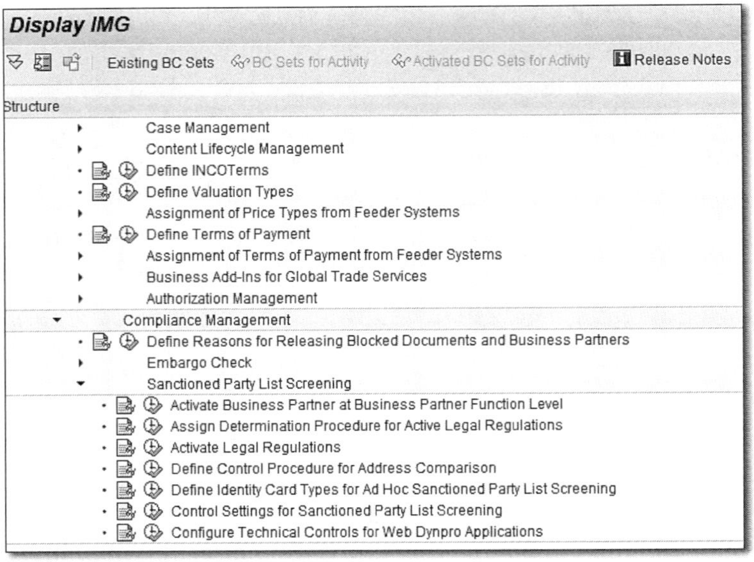

Figure 17.23 Sanctioned Party List Configuration in SAP GTS 10.0 and Higher

Access the CONFIGURE TECHNICAL CONTROLS FOR WEB DYNPRO APPLICATIONS configuration step by using Transaction SPRO and following IMG menu path, SAP CUSTOMIZING IMPLEMENTATION GUIDE • GLOBAL TRADE SERVICES • COMPLIANCE MANAGEMENT • SANCTIONED PARTY LIST SCREENING. The new UI configuration is enabled through the CONFIGURE TECHNICAL CONTROLS FOR WEB DYNPRO APPLICATIONS option.

You can enable the Web Dynpro setup configuration only when you have the SAP NetWeaver Business Client installed. So, as part of the prerequisite, when you're installing version 10.0 of SAP GTS, you need to install of the SAP NetWeaver Business Client in addition to the SAP NetWeaver 7.0 Enhancement Pack. You can access the Web Dynpro configuration by clicking the execute button to the left of CONFIGURE TECHNICAL CONTROLS FOR WEB DYNPRO APPLICATIONS under Transaction SPRO (refer to Figure 17.23). This brings you to the screen shown in Figure 17.24.

Technical parameters for Sanction Party List screening

Define the technical parameters that you need to control the SPL screening in Web Dynpro applications in one central function. You can select DISPLAY DETAILED RESULTS OF LIST SCREENING from the possible two options, DATA FORMATTING FOR RESULTS DISPLAY, NUMBER RANGE

NUMBER TO OPEN CASE, and GROUP OF LOG. SYSTEMS FOR SCREENING. You'll see two options for DATA FORMATTING FOR RESULTS DISPLAY, the other option available is the summary. In terms of the number range, this information is meant for capturing the screening results and assigning an internal number for the display results.

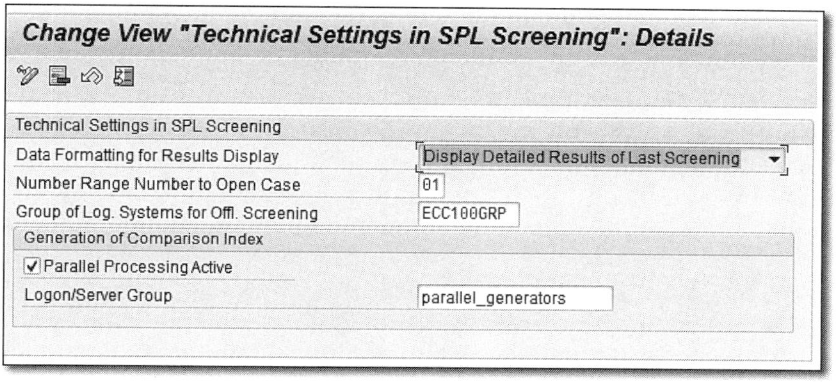

Figure 17.24 The Configuration Setup for the Sanctioned Party List Screening with Web Dynpro

The logical system group is defined based on the feeder system that is connected to for sending the data for screening. Following the installation, this setup is done by the functional team to enable the SAP NetWeaver Business Client. These technical parameters include the entries for data formatting and offline SPL screening. With the review of the new UI and SAP NetWeaver Business Client complete, in the next section, let's review the key architecture component.

17.4 SAP Global Trade Services Deployment and Reporting

This section will cover key architectural components of GTS 10.0 which informs the architecture of SAP Environment, Health, and Safety. The components of the technical architecture are SAP SLL (Legal and Logistics) 900, SAP AP 700, SAP NetWeaver 7.02, and Java Stack for Adobe Document Services (ADS). Let's review the new UI with the SAP NetWeaver Business Client.

Accessing Governance, Risk, and Compliance solutions through NetWeaver Business Client

There are three different ways to access SAP GRC solutions and, in this specific example, SAP GTS:

- By logging on to SAPGUI 6.40 onward
- By accessing SAP NetWeaver Business Client 3.0+ (see the example in Figure 17.25)
- By accessing the SAP NetWeaver Portal

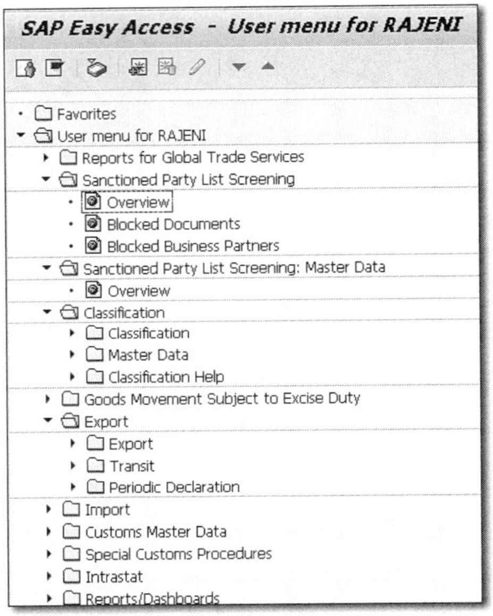

Figure 17.25 User Menu with Applications Built Using SAP NetWeaver Business Client

SAP Easy Access menu

Figure 17.25 shows the SAP Easy Access menu for the user with access to the transactions or functions, within which the NWBC transactions are defined, for example, within the User menu • Sanctioned Party List screening • Overview.

17.4.1 Deployment Options

In terms of the deployment options, you have the option to deploy SAP NetWeaver Portal, SAP NetWeaver Business Client, or the SAP NetWeaver browser, which resembles a web link (also called NWBC lite). The underlying architecture of SAP GTS 10.0 has been supplemented with a new User Interface Object (UIO) layer that enables the new SPL UI. You can also use the UIO as a basis for customer project-specific UI extensions and development of a new UI, using any frontend technology.

17.4.2 Reporting

Building upon the architecture discussion, let's briefly review the reporting options available for Environment, Health, and Safety, Global Trade Services, and the entire GRC suite. Let's first start with the Sanctioned Party list report. When you click the OVERVIEW icon under the SANCTIONED PARTY LIST SCREENING folder, the screen shown in Figure 17.26 appears.

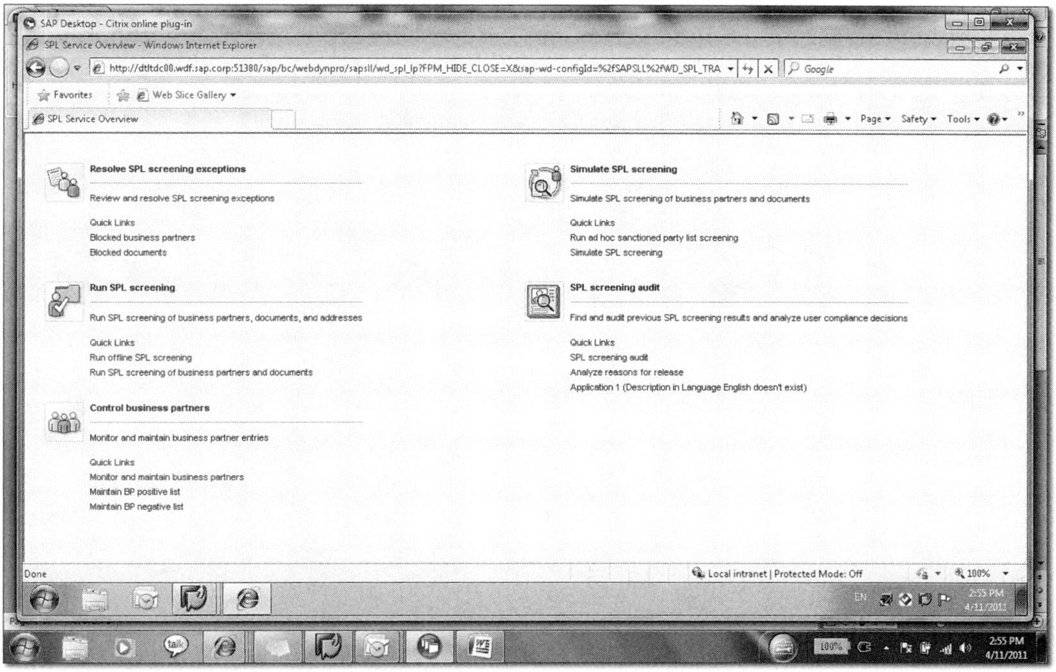

Figure 17.26 The SAP SPL Service Overview Screen

In Figure 17.26, the UI looks different from the SAP GTS traditional cockpit. As in Figure 17.22 shown earlier, the screen in Figure 17.26 is a display of certain functions grouped together called work centers. The different functions are shown within the SPL SERVICE OVERVIEW tab, and key functions are displayed with links. When you click the SIMULATE SPL SCREENING link, the screen shown in Figure 17.27 appears.

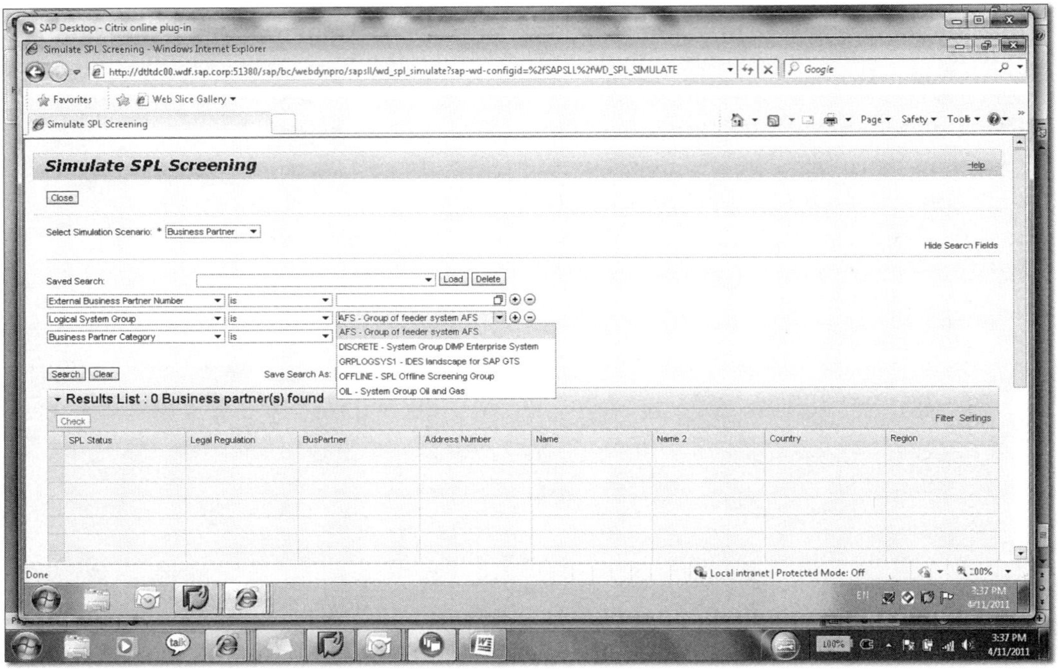

Figure 17.27 Simulate SPL Screening with Different Options

You can execute the SPL SCREENING report shown in Figure 17.27 with saved values. It can help having the data within your variant for this report. This report provides you with more selection options with a configurable view. The searches within the selection fields are available in the dropdown menu (Figure 17.27). The report is an example of a transaction that provides you with one window with the selection of data at the top section, and the results of your selection—the SPL screening of the parameter selected—displayed at the bottom. This makes reviewing and analyzing the results against your preselected data easier.

While working on this SIMULATE SPL SCREENING screen, you can also open another transaction with a different window tab, or they can be grouped as folders, as you saw previously in Figure 17.22. This provides the user with a web-like UI with tabs. Users can toggle between windows for access to the different reports. These windows are also organized by work center for the information or business user's ease of use.

You might need to change the selection data and the output of a report based on your requirement. Here's another option that allows you to define a new query and allows you to personalize your query and reports.

Blocked business partner reporting

In Figure 17.26, let's take the example of the blocked business partner, where you can create a query for the report. Click BLOCKED BUSINESS PARTNERS to bring up the screen shown in Figure 17.28.

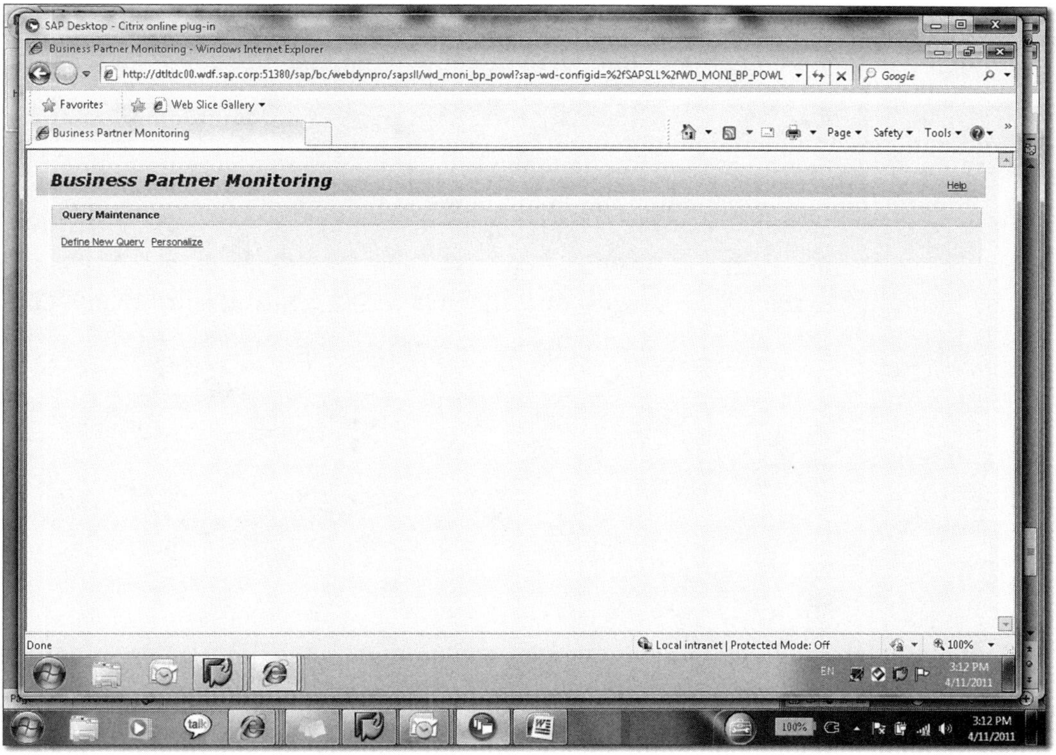

Figure 17.28 Business Partner Monitoring Screen

The blocked business partner report brings up the option of creating a new query or personalizing it. When you click DEFINE NEW QUERY, it brings up the screen shown in Figure 17.29.

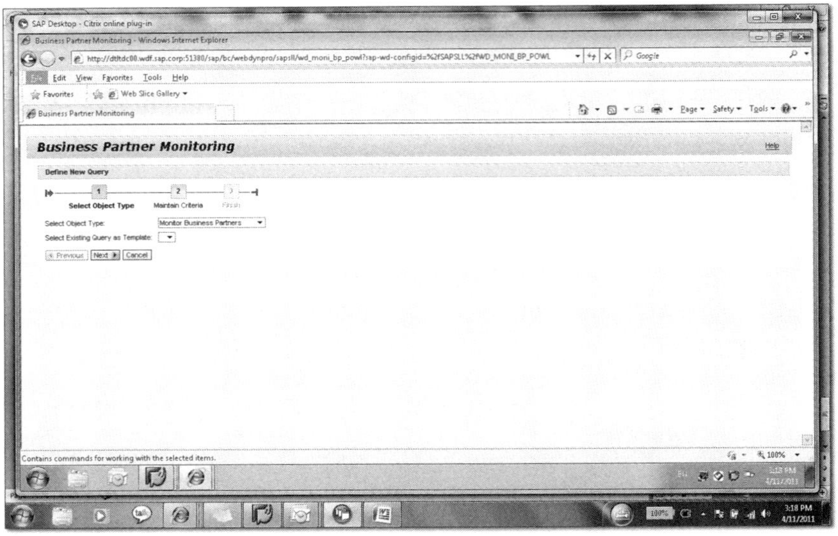

Figure 17.29 Defining a New Query in Business Partner Monitoring

Now you select the criteria in the SELECT OBJECT TYPE and SELECT EXISTING QUERY AS TEMPLATE options, from the dropdown menu. For this example, let's say it's MONITOR BUSINESS PARTNERS (Figure 17.29). Click the NEXT button, and the screen in Figure 17.30 appears.

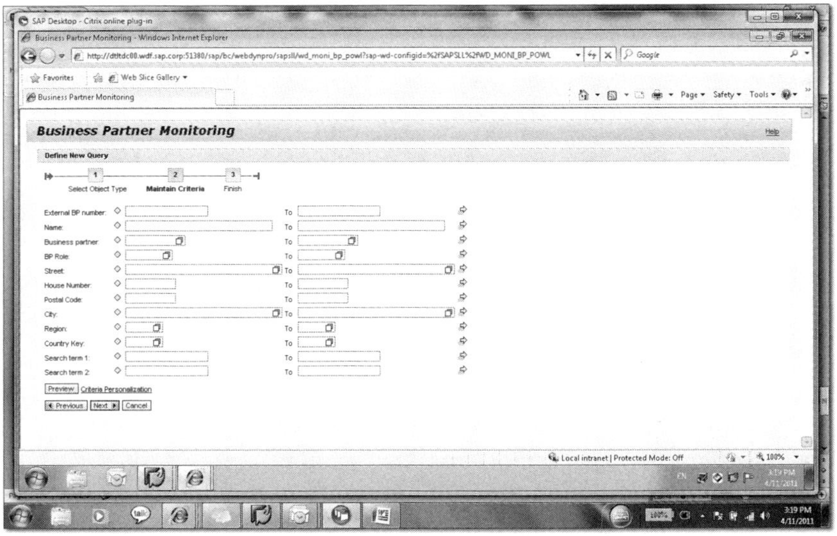

Figure 17.30 Key Selected Criteria in Business Partner Monitoring

Figure 17.30 displays the key selection criteria. Execute the report by clicking the NEXT button to go to the finish step. Executing the final step displays the blocked business partner report (Figure 17.31).

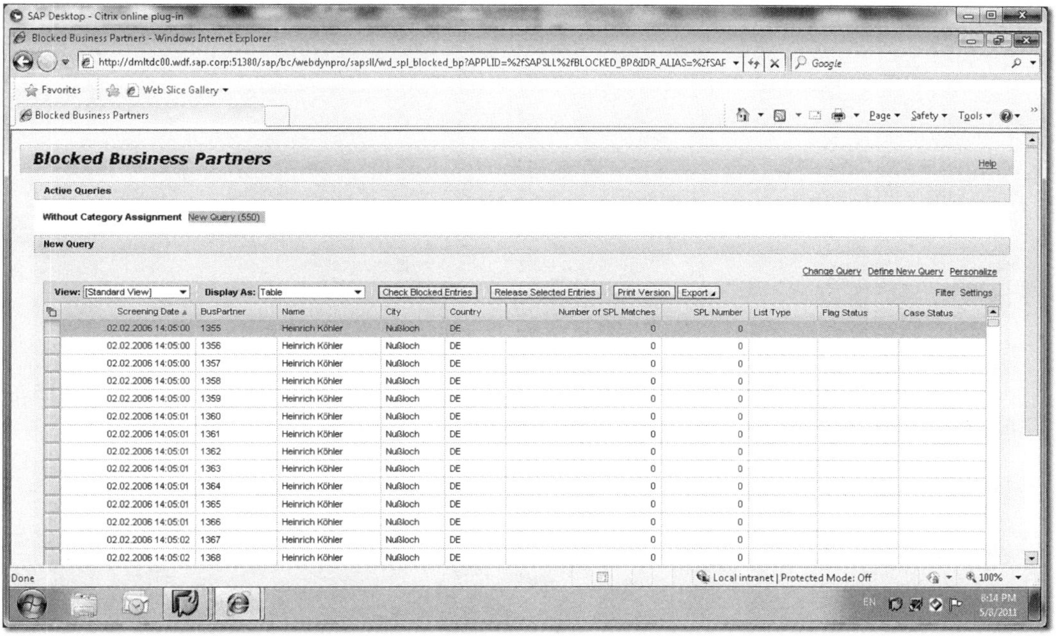

Figure 17.31 A Blocked Business Report with Fields of Interest to the Business User Displayed

The report shown in Figure 17.31 displays the output of the saved query (refer to Figure 17.30). Within this report, you can personalize the view and create custom-specific views.

Blocked business partner report

To demonstrate the SPL screening results of the business partner, here's an example of another report that helps explain some functional analysis of the SPL screening results: the ad hoc SPL screening report.

You can run the ad hoc screening while you're in the SPL SERVICE OVERVIEW screen, as shown earlier in Figure 17.26 under the SIMULATE SPL SCREENING section. When you click on RUN AD HOC SANCTIONED PARTY LIST SCREENING, the screen shown in Figure 17.32 appears. To run the ad hoc SPL screening, enter the NAME (e.g., "Dawood") and other address details, and click the CHECK button. This brings up the screen shown in Figure 17.33 as output.

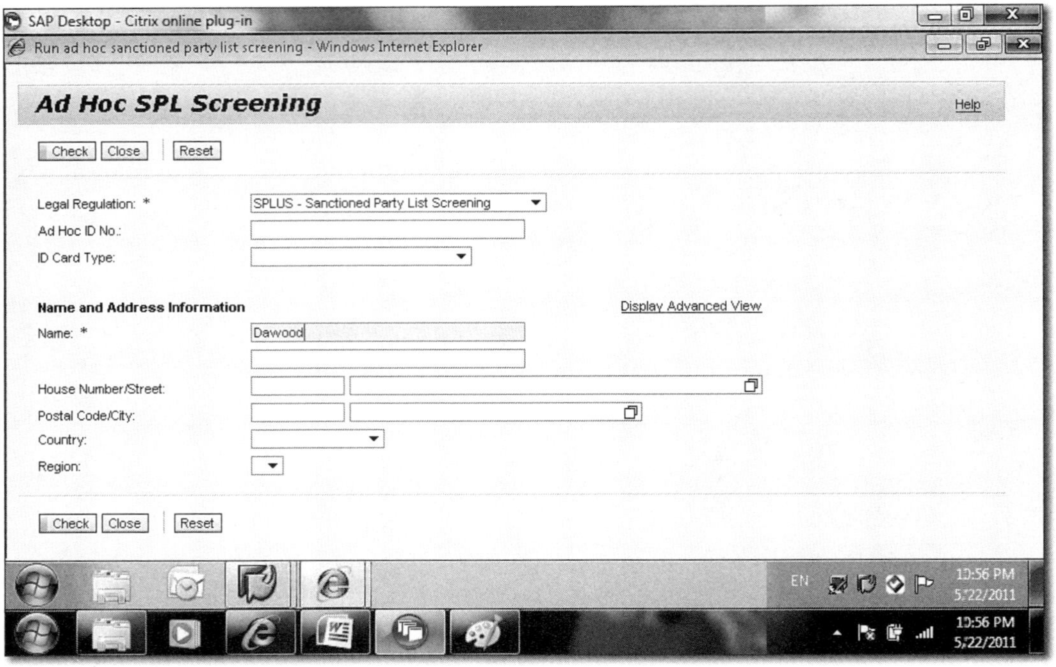

Figure 17.32 The Ad Hoc SPL Screening Input Screen

The screening results provide the display of the names that are matched with the SPL content you've maintained within the system with the names and addresses. The same report exists with the earlier version of SAP GTS; now you run a quick comparison with the same data and compare the view of the outputs.

Figure 17.34 is the traditional SAP GUI display with the SPL entry. It shows the hit details on the bottom of the screen. This information is more background information for further research and isn't needed for the initial review; the detail information has now been eliminated and simplified.

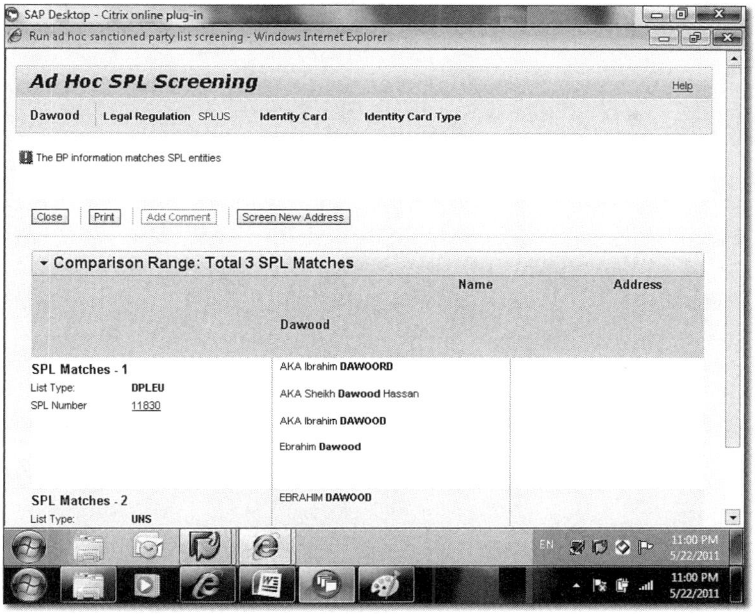

Figure 17.33 Ad Hoc SPL Screening of the Name Results

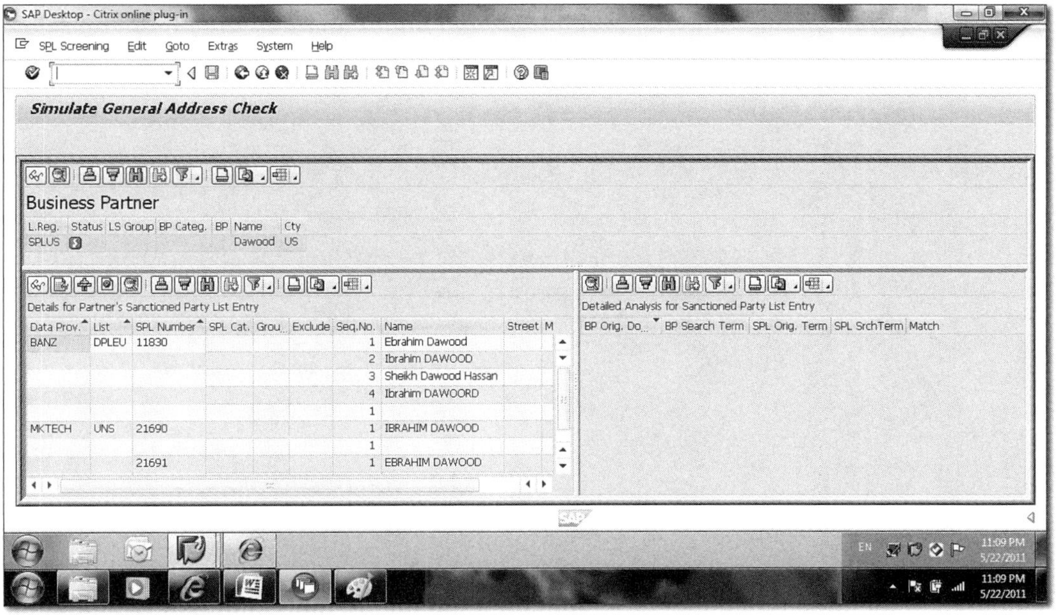

Figure 17.34 Simulating SPL Screening Results

17.5 Summary

In this chapter, we discussed how to perform hazardous substance checks in SAP EHS Management using SAP GTS. We also went over how these checks for hazardous substances help gather information from the logistics system and pass it on to the trade compliance system for early warning, reporting, and appropriate corrective actions. They also help with import and export quantity restrictions, as well as import and export restrictions for products for specific countries of origin. When you create a compliance document such as a sales order or delivery note, SAP GTS creates an equivalent document in the system and performs a check for hazardous materials in SAP EHS Management.

With SAP GTS 10.0 and higher, we have the new feature of visualization. The visualization is the new UI that uses NWBC or SAP NetWeaver Portal with the main objective of user productivity and ease of use. These are defined with the business users' experience in mind and provide them with work centers that are configurable and applicable to their business case. We went over the new look and feel of the SAP GTS 10.x visualization features.

In the next chapter, we'll look at the import filing and declarations that can help reduce the compliance cost. We'll also look at how to improve on efficiency, reduce costs in your compliance process, and avoid delays in customs clearance; you can automate your import declarations using functionality in SAP GTS.

We'll discuss the import processes setup using SAP ERP and SAP GTS, as well as the key configuration setup for building a robust solution, data, and process to support the requirement. We'll also provide details on building an automated interface with your brokers for import declarations. We'll go over the logistics integration and the process overview of the import management.

In this chapter, we will review the benefit of import filing to reduce compliance costs, SAP Global Trade Services import declarations, the Customs import process and configuration settings.

18 Supply Chain Compliance

Supply chain compliance entails not only monitoring your business partner and transactions with outbound processes but also the goods coming into the country through imports. Import filing to customs is performed in different stages, such as cargo manifest, entry summary, automated clearing house (ACH) authorization for duty payment, and finally the daily and monthly statement.

A bonded warehouse is a warehouse in which goods on which the duties are unpaid are stored under bond and in the joint custody of the importer, or his agent, and the customs officers. It may be managed by the state or by private enterprise. In the latter case a customs bond must be posted with the government. Companies sometimes pay the duty for imported goods and later submit documents for duty drawback. They do this if they want the goods to be released immediately and they don't have the relevant document for claiming they are duty free or to prove that they are not meant for consumption.

SAP Global Trade Services allows you to manage both the paid and unpaid duty within the bonded warehouse. Products that are meant for bonded warehouse tracking are identified within the SAP Global Trade Services product master data maintenance. From an importing point of view, companies use different approaches to meet the requirement. We'll discuss the import processes setup using SAP ERP and SAP GTS and the key configuration setup for building a robust solution, data, and process to support the requirement. We'll also provide details on building an automated interface with your brokers for import declarations.

18.1 Import Filing to Reduce Compliance Costs

Companies have to deal with the import of goods into their country and the declarations that go along with importing. To improve efficiency, reduce costs in your compliance process, and avoid delays in customs clearance, you can automate your import declarations using the functionality in SAP Global Trade Services (SAP GTS).

For shipments that are sent through vessels, US Customs and Border Protection (CBP) has mandated to send the notification 24 hours prior to cargo being set aboard. These are called 10 plus 2 critical data elements. Upon the arrival or prior to the arrival of the goods, the products are declared to the customs authorities in two formats: CF 3461 (entry or immediate delivery) and CF 7501 (entry summary). With CF 3461, you're notifying customs of the goods that are arriving, and with CF 7501, you're declaring the goods with values for appropriate duty and other fee payments.

US Customs and Border Protection import and non-compliance example

CBP may issue liquidation of $5,000 per violation for the submission of an inaccurate, incomplete, or untimely filing. If goods for which an Importer Security Filing (ISF) hasn't been filed arrive in the United States, the CBP may withhold the release or transfer of the cargo, refuse the unloading of the merchandise, or seize it if it's illegally unloaded. Additional noncompliant cargo can be subject to "do not load" orders at origin or further inspection on arrival.

We'll go over the logistics integration and the process overview of the import management.

18.2 Import Processes within SAP ERP

Import processes are triggered based on your incoming schedule, which can trigger based on the vendor purchase order (PO). Let's take the example of a PO logged in an SAP ERP system with the United States as the country of destination. Follow menu path, User Menu • Logistics • Materials Management • Purchasing • Create/Change/Display Purchase Orders to see a PO with product 11361 (Figure 18.1).

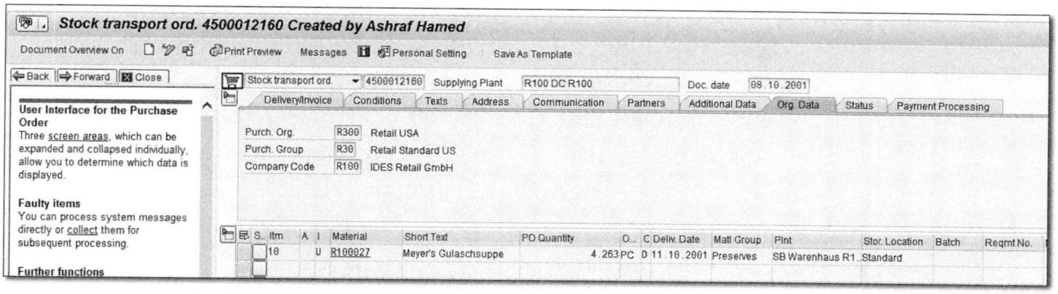

Figure 18.1 Purchase Order with Product 11361

From the Display/Change Purchase Order screen, click the Conditions tab to see the screen shown in Figure 18.2, and click the Partners tab to see the screen shown in Figure 18.3. These screens provide the document data details that trigger the document in SAP GTS for customs declarations, the PO, net value, and the statistical value.

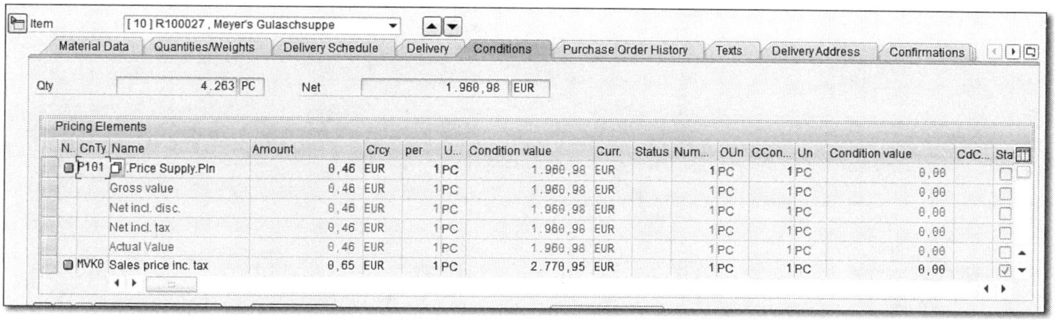

Figure 18.2 Purchase Conditions

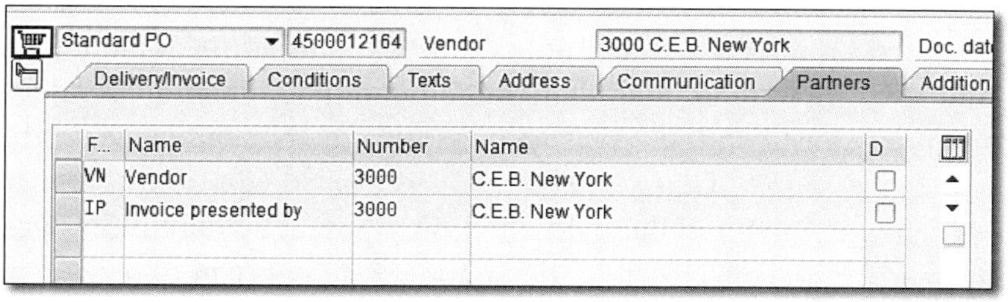

Figure 18.3 Partners in the Purchase Order

Following the review of the SAP ERP purchasing document, let's review the SAP GTS functions that enable the import declarations.

18.3 SAP Global Trade Services Declarations

As the PO is saved in SAP ERP, this information is automatically transferred to SAP GTS, and an equivalent customs declaration document is created in that system. Figure 18.4 displays the report in SAP GTS, which shows the customs declaration worklist. This can be found under SAP Global Trade Service Area Menu • Customs Management • Import. Select the Pre-Declarations tab.

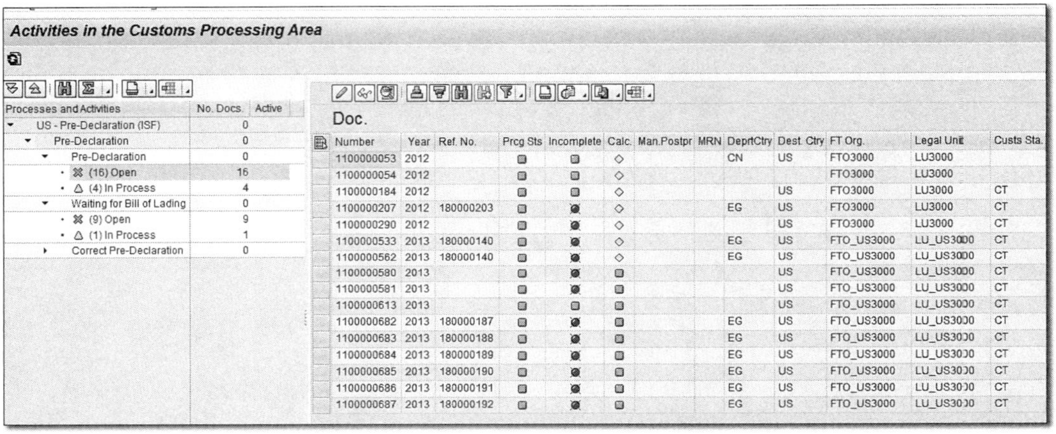

Figure 18.4 Predeclarations Worklist

Pre-Declarations worklist

Click on Display Inbound Activities to bring up the report shown in Figure 18.4, the Predeclarations Worklist. The Inbound activities report displays all of the POs that have been logged in SAP ERP, for which there are equivalent SAP GTS customs.

The predeclarations worklist provides the details of the vendor, PO, item number, any inbound delivery, open quantity, unit of measure, product number, and the declared quantity. The inbound delivery triggers confirmation of the goods arrival (also called advanced shipment notification, ASN), and these documents are identified for customs preclearance. Prior to the customs declaration, it's important to review the document for key data elements.

In the next section, we'll review the customs document in SAP GTS.

18.3.1 Customs Document Review

In this section, we'll go over the different data elements in the customs document that is transferred from SAP ERP to SAP GTS. We will review the following tabs found within the Customs Declaration screen:

- ITEM OVERVIEW Tab
- TRANSPORTATION Tab
- DOCUMENTS/EVIDENCE Tab
- PACKAGING DATA Tab
- ADDITIONAL DATA Tab
- COMMUNICATIONS Tab

Let's look at each of these tabs in further detail

Item Overview Tab

Within the ITEM OVERVIEW tab of the default screen of the Customs Declaration that comes up when customs declaration is displayed, you can see the status of the item. If the item is complete, you see a green square in the INCOMPLETE column; it's red if it isn't complete (Figure 18.5).

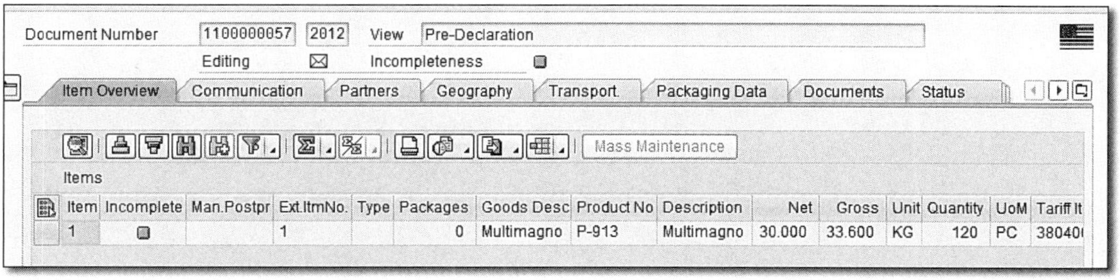

Figure 18.5 Purchase Item Data

Partner data, also called partner functions within the document, is important information in reporting the data to customs. This includes the declaring party, consignee, seller, and other functions shown in Figure 18.6.

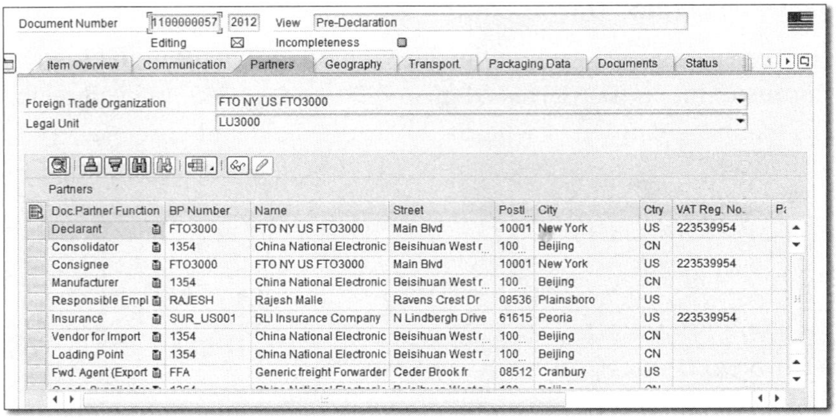

Figure 18.6 Partner Details

Transportation Tab

The TRANSPORTATION tab provides the key dates for declaration date, import date, mode of transport, and Incoterms (Figure 18.7). The key dates can be found under the DATES AND TIMES section.

Figure 18.7 The Transportation Tab

Documents/Evidence Tab

In the DOCUMENTS/EVIDENCE tab, you can store the reference number against which the import customs declaration is stored (Figure 18.8).

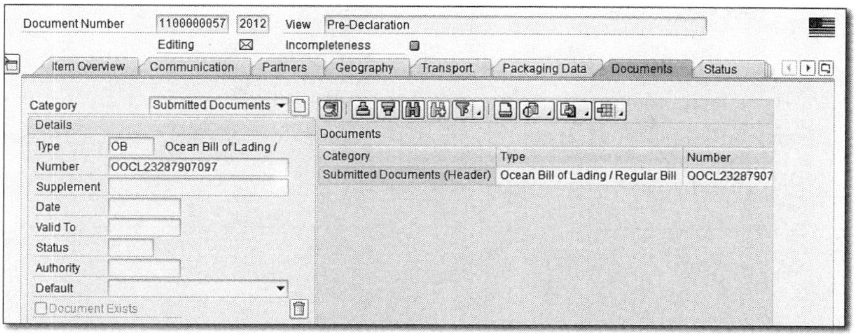

Figure 18.8 Storing the Reference Number

Following the review of the header data, let's review some critical item data. In the DEFAULT view of the customs declaration item overview, click the DOCUMENT EVIDENCE tab. So far, you've been reviewing the header data, but you can click the ITEM DATA to view item-related information. The GENERAL DATA view provides the overview of the item with the product number, description, tariff number (Harmonized Tariff Number), other governmental agency (OGA) codes, item quantities, and weight (Figure 18.9). Users should review this information prior to submitting it to customs because if it's incorrect, they will get an error message.

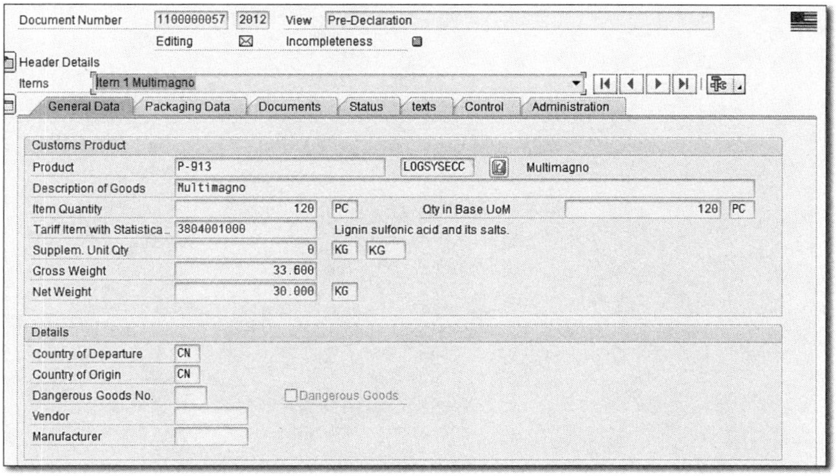

Figure 18.9 The General Data Tab

Packaging Data Tab

Next, click the PACKAGING DATA tab. In this view, the packaging data is stored by type, displaying the container number. This is a critical piece of information that is transferred to customs for declaration purposes (Figure 18.10).

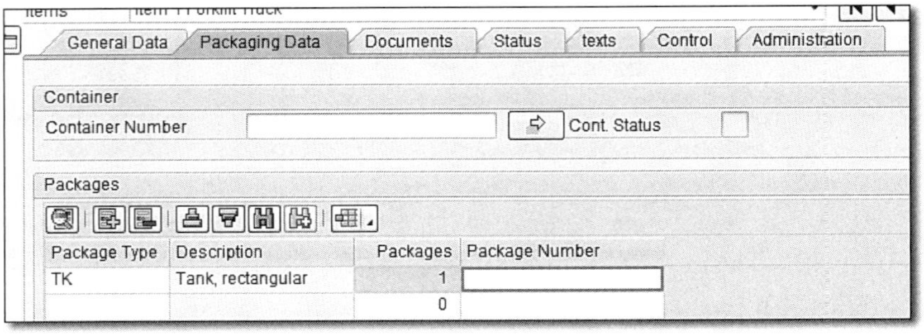

Figure 18.10 Customs Declaration Document with Packaging Data View

In the same view, click the CUST.VALUE tab to view the customs values with duties details (Figure 18.11).

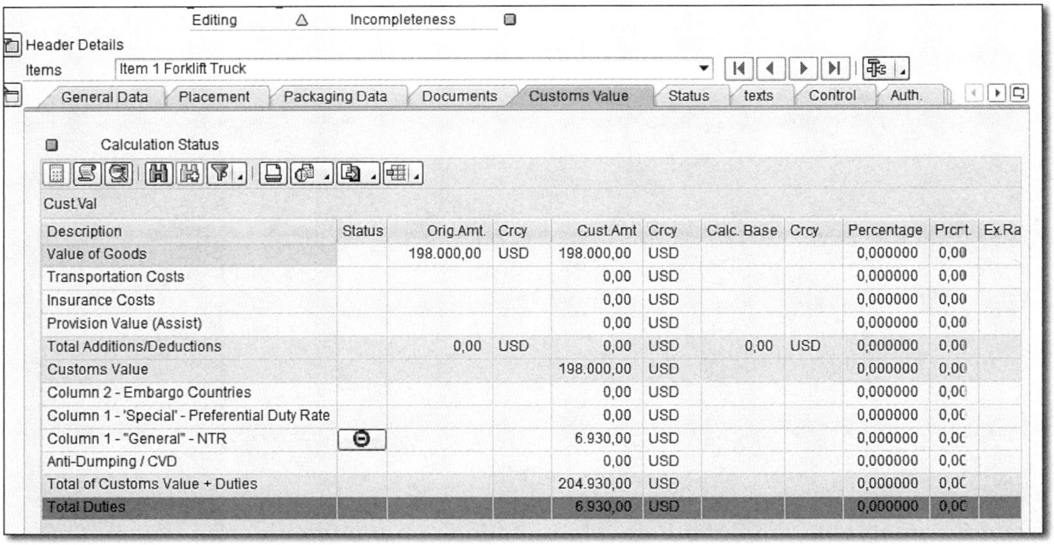

Figure 18.11 Customs Declarations Document: Item Customs Value Details

The CUST.VALUE view provides you with the details on the particular line item, including goods value, any insurance cost, assist, and duties for preferential country, merchandise processing fee, and harbor maintenance fee. The customs values, also called duty types, are used for calculating the customs value and the duties that need to be paid to customs.

While in the CUSTOMS DECLARATIONS: CUSTOMS VALUE view, click the TEXTS view to review details captured within the texts (Figure 18.12). In our example, we've created a text item called SEAL NUMBERS to capture the identification number of the seal used in the vessel shipments.

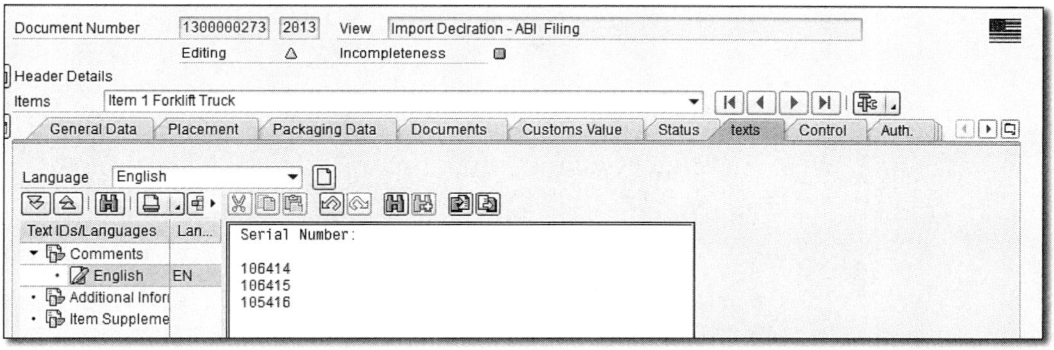

Figure 18.12 Customs Document Item Text with Customized Item IDs

Additional Data Field

Similar to the use of item text to capture vessel seal numbers, you can use the ADDITIONAL DATA field to capture certain additional critical data, such as whether the customs document has a placeholder for, for example, the HAZARDOUS MATERIAL indicator. With customs declaration, hazardous materials are identified, handled, and declared appropriate. While you're in the customs declaration item, click the ADDITIONAL DATA tab (Figure 18.13). Three fields are available for use. In this example, the ADDL DATA 1 has already been configured as HAZARDOUS GOODS (H) and ADDITIONAL DATA 3 as REFERENCE NUMBERS; ADDNL DATA 2 remains as is.

So far, we've reviewed the critical data required for generating the declarations documents. This doesn't enable you to generate trade declaration documents. This case demonstrates where the customer is using the service of a broker for declarations. The two important documents that are generated are the broker manifest and the import master. These two documents are passed on to the broker, and the broker in turns uses this information to declare the shipment for imports. These documents are defined as messages, and the communication is sent to broker to file ISF and entry for consumption shown in Figure 18.14.

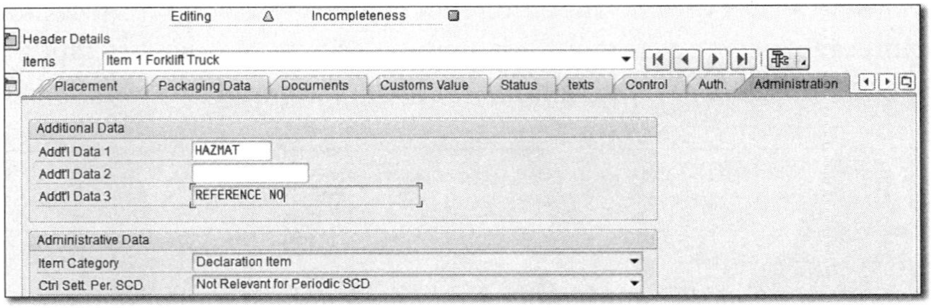

Figure 18.13 The Additional Data Tab: Customs Declaration Document Item View

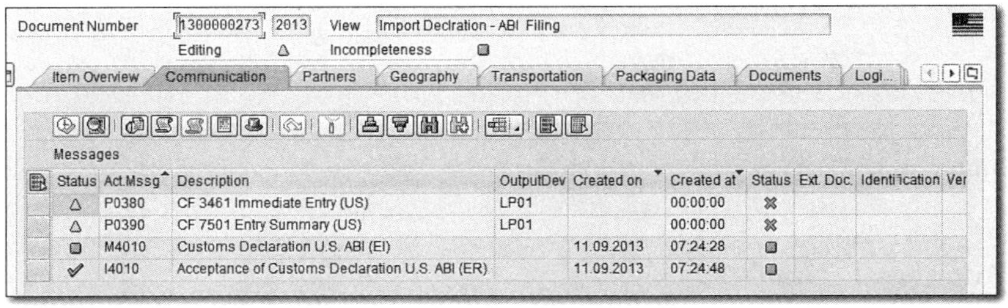

Figure 18.14 Customs Document Communication with Messages Display and Print

Communication Tab

In the Communication tab, select the Message, and click Print Preview to view the document details. Figure 18.15 shows the broker manifest document, which includes the data that we've configured in SAP GTS and SAP ERP (Figure 18.15).

After the goods arrive, you'll have to provide a more detailed document to allow the broker to import the goods. This can be achieved through the import master declaration document. Message type P0380 displays the import master declaration document, as shown in Figure 18.16.

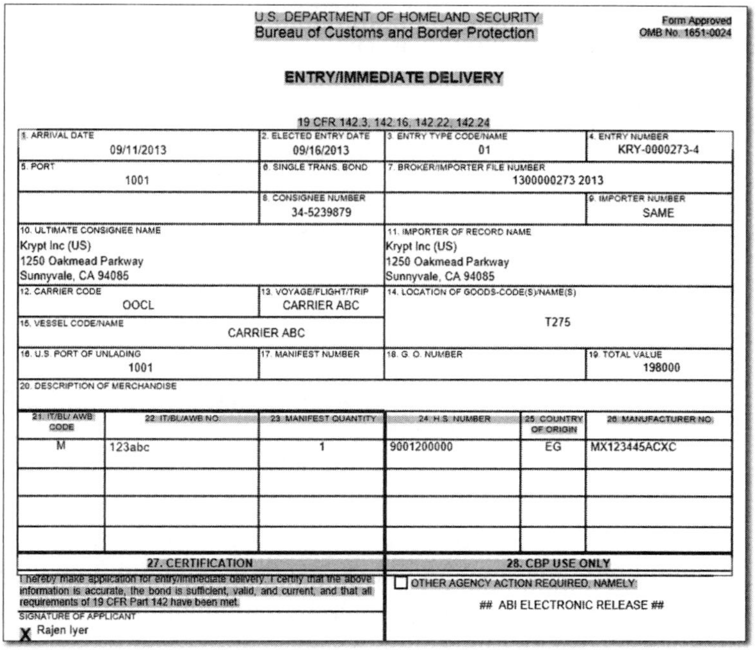

U.S. DEPARTMENT OF HOMELAND SECURITY
Bureau of Customs and Border Protection

Form Approved
OMB No. 1651-0024

ENTRY/IMMEDIATE DELIVERY

19 CFR 142.3, 142.16, 142.22, 142.24

1. ARRIVAL DATE 09/11/2013	2. ELECTED ENTRY DATE 09/16/2013	3. ENTRY TYPE CODE/NAME 01	4. ENTRY NUMBER KRY-0000273-4
5. PORT 1001	6. SINGLE TRANS. BOND	7. BROKER/IMPORTER FILE NUMBER 1300000273 2013	
	8. CONSIGNEE NUMBER 34-5239879		9. IMPORTER NUMBER SAME
10. ULTIMATE CONSIGNEE NAME Krypt Inc (US) 1250 Oakmead Parkway Sunnyvale, CA 94085		11. IMPORTER OF RECORD NAME Krypt Inc (US) 1250 Oakmead Parkway Sunnyvale, CA 94085	
12. CARRIER CODE OOCL	13. VOYAGE/FLIGHT/TRIP CARRIER ABC	14. LOCATION OF GOODS-CODE(S)/NAME(S) T275	
15. VESSEL CODE/NAME CARRIER ABC			
16. U.S. PORT OF UNLADING 1001	17. MANIFEST NUMBER	18. G. O. NUMBER	19. TOTAL VALUE 198000
20. DESCRIPTION OF MERCHANDISE			

21. IT/BL/AWB CODE	22. IT/BL/AWB NO.	23. MANIFEST QUANTITY	24. H.S. NUMBER	25. COUNTRY OF ORIGIN	26. MANUFACTURER NO.
M	123abc	1	9001200000	EG	MX123445ACXC

27. CERTIFICATION

I hereby make application for entry/immediate delivery. I certify that the above information is accurate, the bond is sufficient, valid, and current, and that all requirements of 19 CFR Part 142 have been met.

SIGNATURE OF APPLICANT
X Rajen Iyer

28. CBP USE ONLY

☐ OTHER AGENCY ACTION REQUIRED, NAMELY:

ABI ELECTRONIC RELEASE

Figure 18.15 Display of Broker Manifest Document

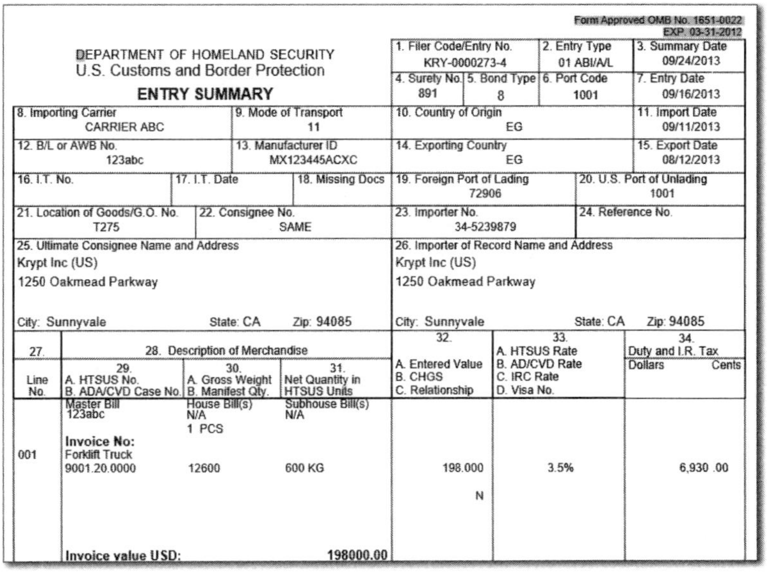

Form Approved OMB No. 1651-0022
EXP. 03-31-2012

DEPARTMENT OF HOMELAND SECURITY
U.S. Customs and Border Protection
ENTRY SUMMARY

1. Filer Code/Entry No. KRY-0000273-4	2. Entry Type 01 ABI/A/L	3. Summary Date 09/24/2013	
4. Surety No. 891	5. Bond Type 8	6. Port Code 1001	7. Entry Date 09/16/2013

8. Importing Carrier CARRIER ABC	9. Mode of Transport 11	10. Country of Origin EG	11. Import Date 09/11/2013
12. B/L or AWB No. 123abc	13. Manufacturer ID MX123445ACXC	14. Exporting Country EG	15. Export Date 08/12/2013
16. I.T. No.	17. I.T. Date	18. Missing Docs	19. Foreign Port of Lading 72906
20. U.S. Port of Unlading 1001			
21. Location of Goods/G.O. No. T275	22. Consignee No. SAME	23. Importer No. 34-5239879	24. Reference No.

25. Ultimate Consignee Name and Address Krypt Inc (US) 1250 Oakmead Parkway City: Sunnyvale State: CA Zip: 94085	26. Importer of Record Name and Address Krypt Inc (US) 1250 Oakmead Parkway City: Sunnyvale State: CA Zip: 94085

27. Line No.	28. Description of Merchandise — 29. A. HTSUS No. B. ADA/CVD Case No.	30. A. Gross Weight B. Manifest Qty.	31. Net Quantity in HTSUS Units	32. A. Entered Value B. CHGS C. Relationship	33. A. HTSUS Rate B. AD/CVD Rate C. IRC Rate D. Visa No.	34. Duty and I.R. Tax Dollars Cents
	Master Bill 123abc	House Bill(s) N/A 1 PCS	Subhouse Bill(s) N/A			
001	Invoice No: Forklift Truck 9001.20.0000	12600	600 KG	198.000 N	3.5%	6,930 .00
	Invoice value USD:		198000.00			

Figure 18.16 Import Master Declaration Document Display

Import master declaration as master file

The import master declaration acts as a master file for broker for import filing. Global companies need to deal with export and import. US Customs and Border Protection (CBP) has introduced the mandatory Importer Security Filing (ISF). As we review in this chapter, the system allows you to declare before any goods arrive by vessel into the United States. The ISF needs to be submitted by the importer or the agent (licensed customs broker) electronically in advance to the CBP. This requirement only applies to cargo arriving in the United States by ocean vessel, not to other modes of transportation.

The customs authorities for many countries allow you to defer or eliminate duty payment if the goods imported into the country are meant for re-export after value addition rather than for consumption. We discussed how you can make use of SAP GTS to provide these accurate and timely declarations. For example, a company can subcontract some finishing work or testing on a particular good to a company in another country and then import it back. Another example involves a company receiving semi-finished parts and after assembly exporting the finished product back to a company in another country. The assembly, in this case, is the value addition. We went over the process and system flow with the import process, and in the next section, we'll review the configuration steps for the customs import process.

18.4 Customs Import Process Configuration with SAP ERP

We've reviewed the overall customs declaration process steps, let's now go over the configuration steps to set up this process. First, we'll start with an overview of the general process, and then we'll explore each step in further detail. The configuration of the customs import process consists of the following:

Configuration steps

1. Perform the feeder systems settings.
2. Set the PO type FBN and schedule agreement types LLP and LZP as active.Set the inbound delivery documents EL, ZELN, and ZELT to active for customs processing.
3. Configure the goods receipt or materials document.

Now that you know the overall steps, follow the detailed steps here:

1. Perform feeder system settings for MMOA, MMOB, and MMOC (Figure 18.17). The first step in the configuration starts with setting up the feeder system documents that are identified for transfer to SAP GTS and are used for customs declarations. In SAP ERP, follow IMG menu path, SALES AND DISTRIBUTION • FOREIGN TRADE/CUSTOMS • SAP GLOBAL TRADE SERVICES – PLUG IN • CONTROL DATA FOR TRANSFER TO SAP GLOBAL TRADE SERVICES • CONFIGURE CONTROL SETTINGS FOR DOCUMENT TRANSFER.

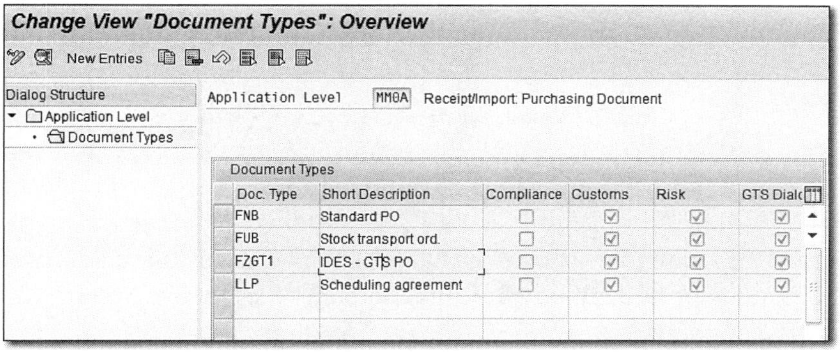

Figure 18.17 Document Transfer Configuration Setup with SAP ERP

2. Make PO type FBN and schedule agreement type LLP and LZP active for the compliance, customs, and risk components of SAP GTS. While you're in step 1, select the APPLICATION LEVEL MMOA, and click the DOCUMENT TYPES folder, which brings up the list of document types shown in Figure 18.17.

3. Select the appropriate services. For import customs declarations, select the relevant document type (in this example, PO type FNB), and then select the CALL UP SAP CUSTOMS MANAGEMENT SERVICES (see Figure 18.18). Check the OUTPUT DIALOG IN SAP GLOBAL TRADE SERVICES option if you want the system to prompt you with a pop-up window of the compliance screening results before the document is saved in SAP ERP. If you plan to activate SAP Risk Management in SAP GTS, you need to check the GENERATE WORKLIST OF VENDOR-BASED LONG-TERM VENDOR DECLARATIONS.

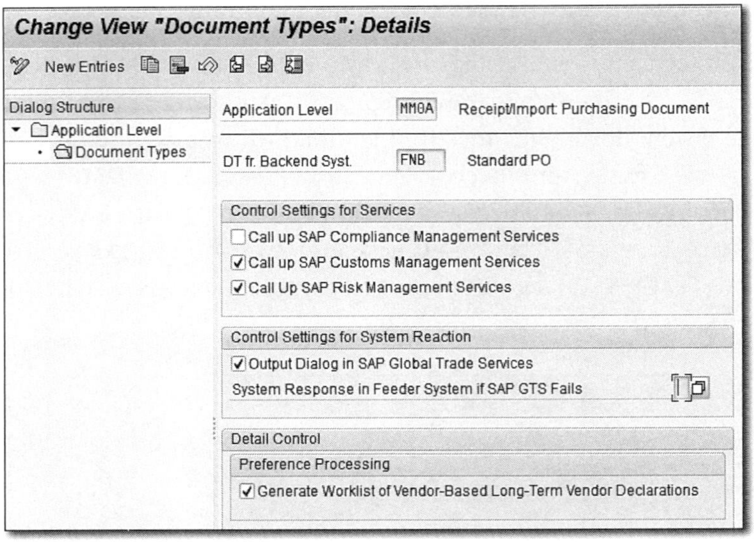

Figure 18.18 Document Types Details Setup for Control Settings

4. Set the inbound delivery documents EL, ZELN, and ZELT to active for customs processing. In configuration step 1, select the APPLICATION LEVEL MMOB (Figure 18.19).

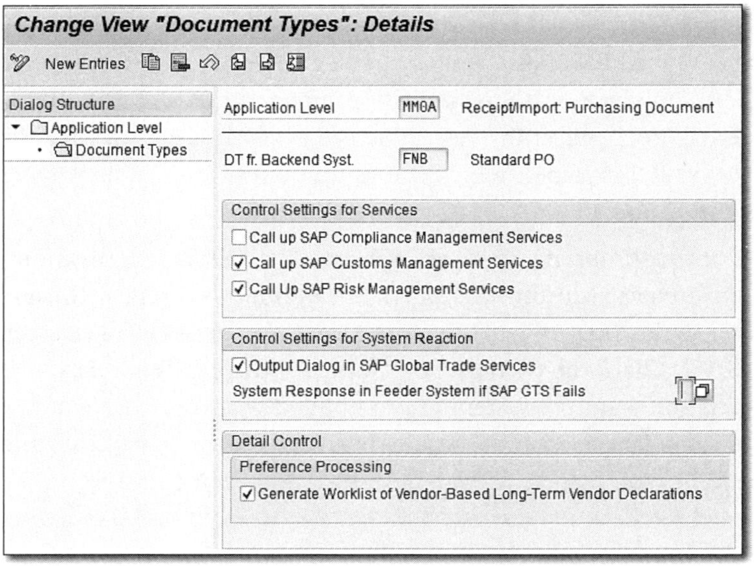

Figure 18.19 Configuration Setup for Inbound Delivery

Here you configure the inbound deliveries that are transferred to SAP GTS import declarations (Figure 18.20). Click the New Entries button and maintain the entry for the inbound delivery document. In the details screen, select the Call up SAP Customs Management Services checkbox. If you plan to identify the customs status as bonded, you need to check the Place into Customs Status Before GR checkbox; however, if you identify it as in transit, you should select the Hold Goods Receipt if Unloading Permission is Missing option.

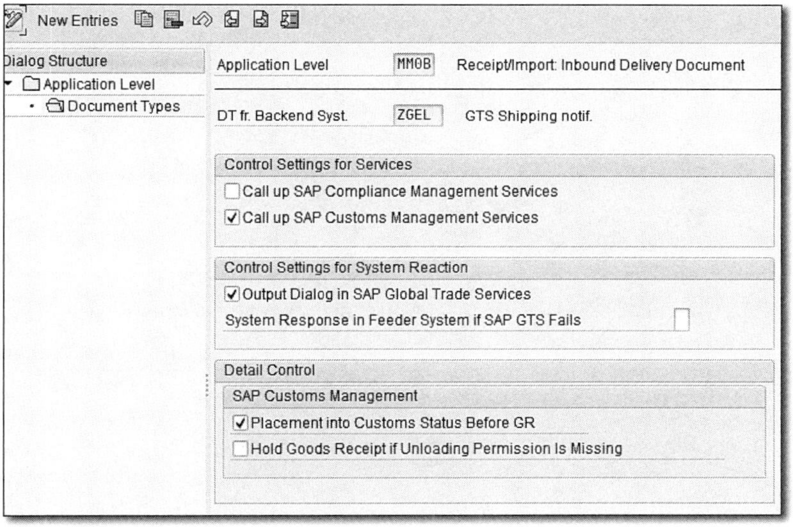

Figure 18.20 Document Type Configurations Details for Inbound Delivery

5. Configure the goods receipt or materials document. Set the indicator for document transfer for goods movements. Goods movement documents are generated when you post goods issue to the inbound delivery. From the configuration in step 1, select the Application Level MMOC (Figure 18.21). The documents are predefined.
6. Click the New Entries button to maintain a new entry, for example, GR document type 101B (Figure 18.22). Then check the Call up SAP Customs Management Services checkbox. All of the material movements are selected to monitor customs service. As shown in Figure 18.22, don't check the Generate Worklist of Vendor-Based Long-Term Vendor Declarations under Preference Processing because it's only needed if you want to perform a preference determination.

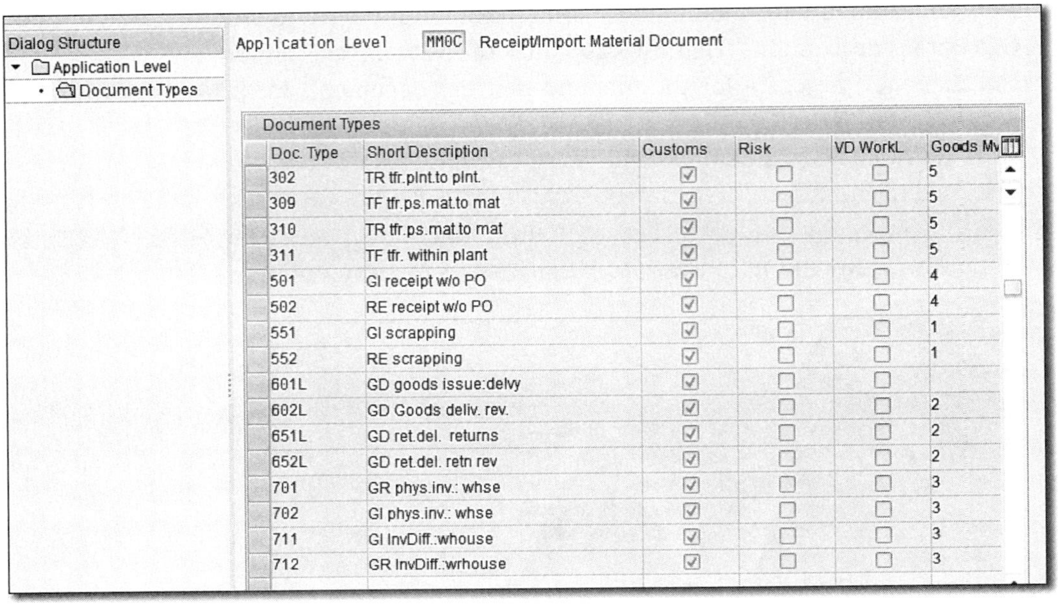

Figure 18.21 Document Transfer Setup for Goods Receipt Material Document

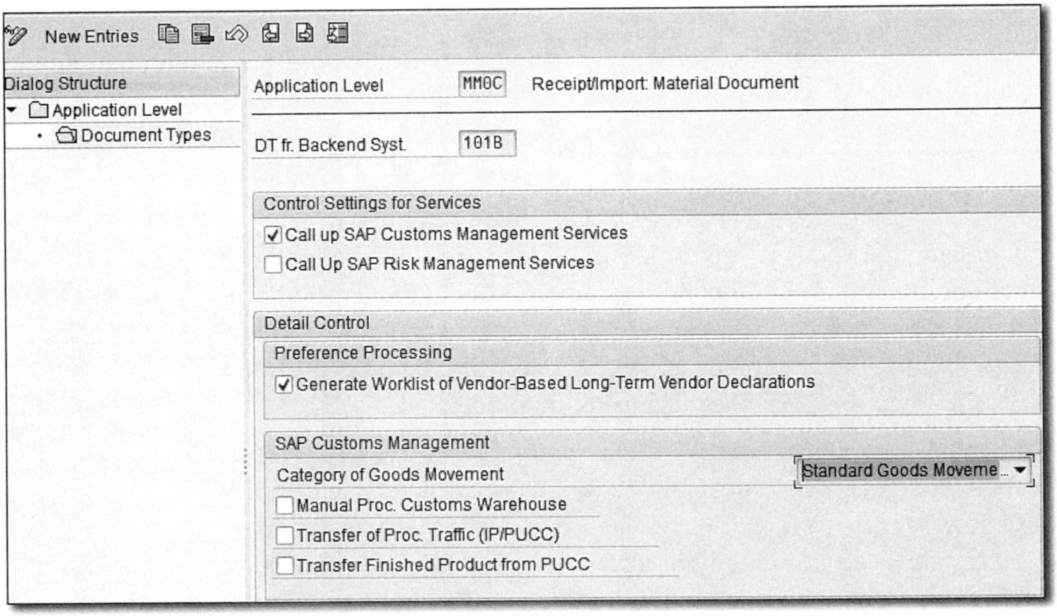

Figure 18.22 Details Configuration Setup

We reviewed the SAP ERP configurations. Now we need to go over the SAP GTS-related configurations in the next section.

18.5 SAP Global Trade Services Configuration

Now we'll go over the step that needs to be done in SAP GTS. First, we'll start with an overview of the general process and then we'll explore each step in further detail. The configuration of the customs import process consists of the following:

Customs Import Process configuration steps in SAP Global Trade Services

1. Define partner functions that are in use within the customs declarations.
2. Set partner grouping.
3. Map the partner type to the logical system group.
4. Define the legal regulation.
5. Assign the country or country group.
6. Set the determination procedure.
7. Define the harmonized tariff number structure.
8. Assign the numbering scheme to the legal regulation.
9. Assign a foreign trade organization (FTO) and legal units.

Let's look at each step in further detail.

Define partner functions that are in use within the customs declarations

1. Define partner functions that are in use within the customs declarations. Follow IMG menu path, SAP Global Trade Services • General Settings • Partner Structure • Define Partner Functions (Figure 18.23). Review the partner functions that are predefined in the system, and, if needed, you can define your own custom partner function by selecting one of the predelivered ones and clicking the Copy with Reference Function.

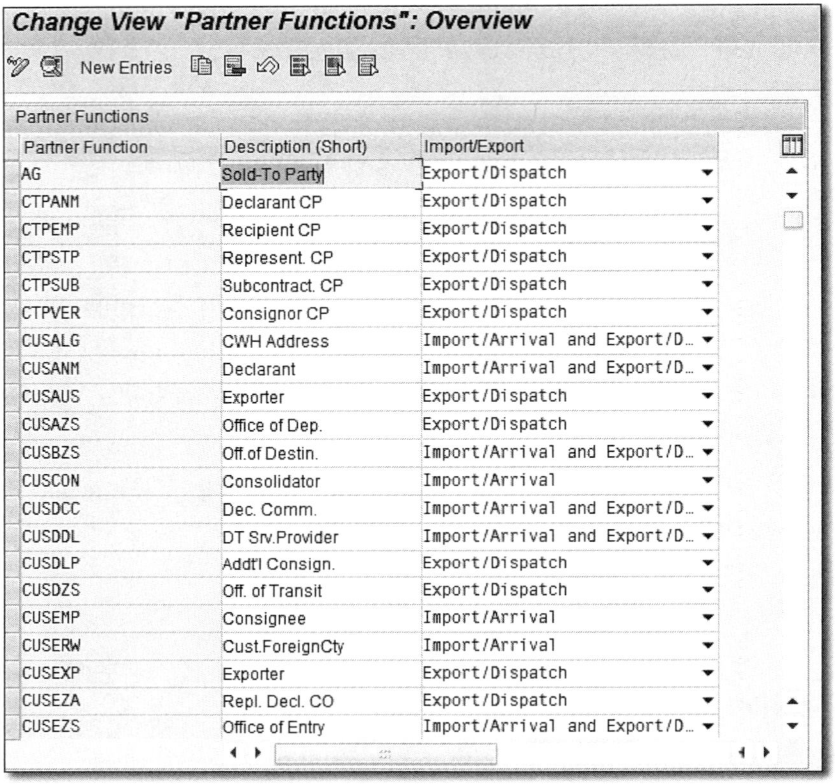

Partner Function	Description (Short)	Import/Export
AG	Sold-To Party	Export/Dispatch
CTPANM	Declarant CP	Export/Dispatch
CTPEMP	Recipient CP	Export/Dispatch
CTPSTP	Represent. CP	Export/Dispatch
CTPSUB	Subcontract. CP	Export/Dispatch
CTPVER	Consignor CP	Export/Dispatch
CUSALG	CWH Address	Import/Arrival and Export/D...
CUSANM	Declarant	Import/Arrival and Export/D...
CUSAUS	Exporter	Export/Dispatch
CUSAZS	Office of Dep.	Export/Dispatch
CUSBZS	Off.of Destin.	Import/Arrival and Export/D...
CUSCON	Consolidator	Import/Arrival
CUSDCC	Dec. Comm.	Import/Arrival and Export/D...
CUSDDL	DT Srv.Provider	Import/Arrival and Export/D...
CUSDLP	Addt'l Consign.	Export/Dispatch
CUSDZS	Off. of Transit	Export/Dispatch
CUSEMP	Consignee	Import/Arrival
CUSERW	Cust.ForeignCty	Import/Arrival
CUSEXP	Exporter	Export/Dispatch
CUSEZA	Repl. Decl. CO	Export/Dispatch
CUSEZS	Office of Entry	Import/Arrival and Export/D...

Figure 18.23 Define Partner Functions for Customs Declarations

Set partner grouping

2. After defining the partner functions, you need to assign the partner types to the group (Figure 18.24). Follow IMG menu path, SAP Global Trade Services • General Settings • Partner Structure • Define Groups of Partner Functions. There are predefined partner groupings delivered by SAP GTS. The one for importing in SAP Customs Management is PSCCUI. Select it and click the Assign Partner Function folder to see the partner functions that have been assigned. If you want to add a new one, click the New Entries button, and add a new one as defined in step 1 of the configuration process. Figure 18.25 displays the partner functions that are assigned to the partner group.

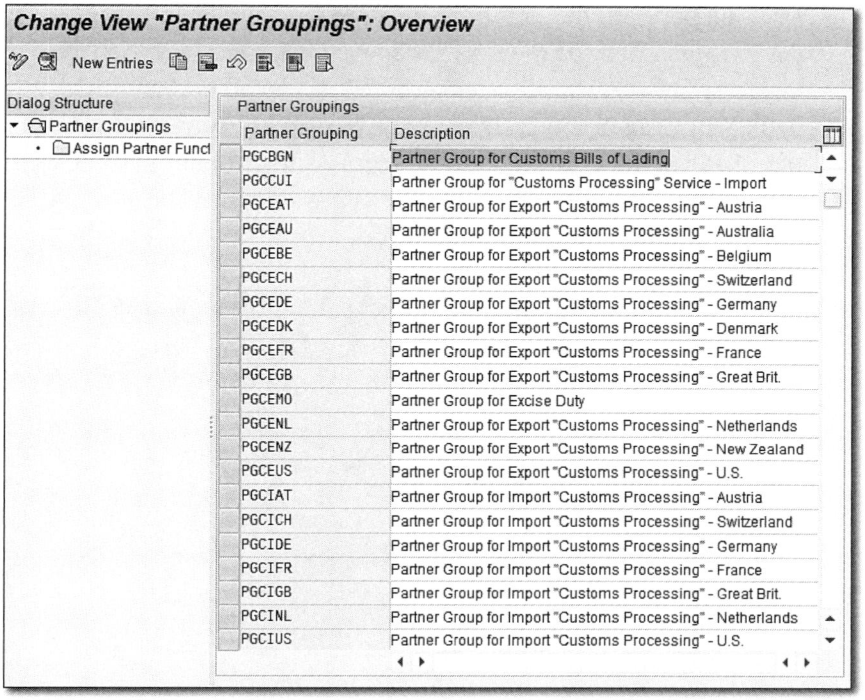

Partner Grouping	Description
PGCBGN	Partner Group for Customs Bills of Lading
PGCCUI	Partner Group for "Customs Processing" Service - Import
PGCEAT	Partner Group for Export "Customs Processing" - Austria
PGCEAU	Partner Group for Export "Customs Processing" - Australia
PGCEBE	Partner Group for Export "Customs Processing" - Belgium
PGCECH	Partner Group for Export "Customs Processing" - Switzerland
PGCEDE	Partner Group for Export "Customs Processing" - Germany
PGCEDK	Partner Group for Export "Customs Processing" - Denmark
PGCEFR	Partner Group for Export "Customs Processing" - France
PGCEGB	Partner Group for Export "Customs Processing" - Great Brit.
PGCEMO	Partner Group for Excise Duty
PGCENL	Partner Group for Export "Customs Processing" - Netherlands
PGCENZ	Partner Group for Export "Customs Processing" - New Zealand
PGCEUS	Partner Group for Export "Customs Processing" - U.S.
PGCIAT	Partner Group for Import "Customs Processing" - Austria
PGCICH	Partner Group for Import "Customs Processing" - Switzerland
PGCIDE	Partner Group for Import "Customs Processing" - Germany
PGCIFR	Partner Group for Import "Customs Processing" - France
PGCIGB	Partner Group for Import "Customs Processing" - Great Brit.
PGCINL	Partner Group for Import "Customs Processing" - Netherlands
PGCIUS	Partner Group for Import "Customs Processing" - U.S.

Figure 18.24 Partner Grouping Definitions

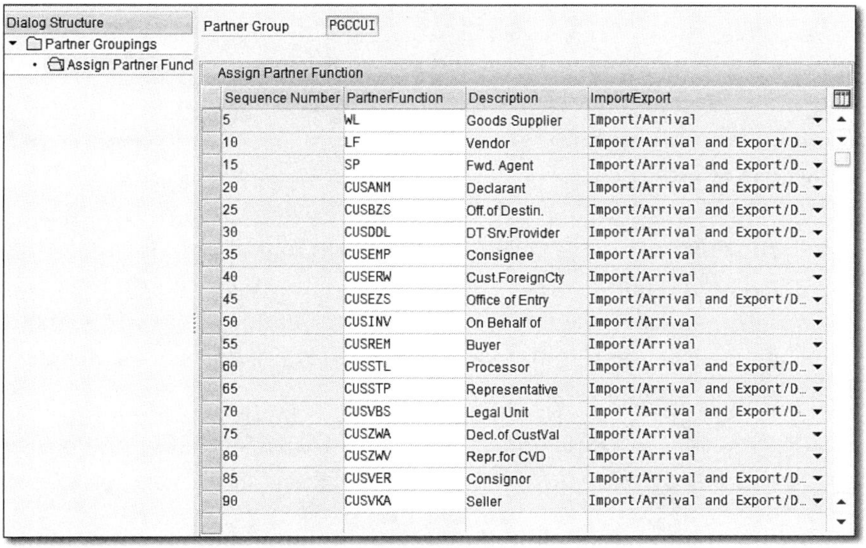

Sequence Number	PartnerFunction	Description	Import/Export
5	WL	Goods Supplier	Import/Arrival
10	LF	Vendor	Import/Arrival and Export/D...
15	SP	Fwd. Agent	Import/Arrival and Export/D...
20	CUSANM	Declarant	Import/Arrival and Export/D...
25	CUSBZS	Off.of Destin.	Import/Arrival and Export/D...
30	CUSDDL	DT Srv.Provider	Import/Arrival and Export/D...
35	CUSEMP	Consignee	Import/Arrival
40	CUSERW	Cust.ForeignCty	Import/Arrival
45	CUSEZS	Office of Entry	Import/Arrival and Export/D...
50	CUSINV	On Behalf of	Import/Arrival
55	CUSREM	Buyer	Import/Arrival
60	CUSSTL	Processor	Import/Arrival and Export/D...
65	CUSSTP	Representative	Import/Arrival and Export/D...
70	CUSVBS	Legal Unit	Import/Arrival and Export/D...
75	CUSZWA	Decl.of CustVal	Import/Arrival
80	CUSZWV	Repr.for CVD	Import/Arrival
85	CUSVER	Consignor	Import/Arrival and Export/D...
90	CUSVKA	Seller	Import/Arrival and Export/D...

Figure 18.25 Assignment of Partner Function to the Partner Groupings

Map the partner type to the logical system group

3. Map the partner type to the logical system group (Figure 18.26). The partner types defined in step 1 are to be mapped to the feeder system logical system or logical system group. You can do this via IMG menu path, SAP GLOBAL TRADE SERVICES • GENERAL SETTINGS • ASSIGN PARTNER TYPE TO THE LOGICAL SYSTEM GROUP. The different partner types that might be part of your supply chain documents include sold to, ship to, third party, vendor, and so on.

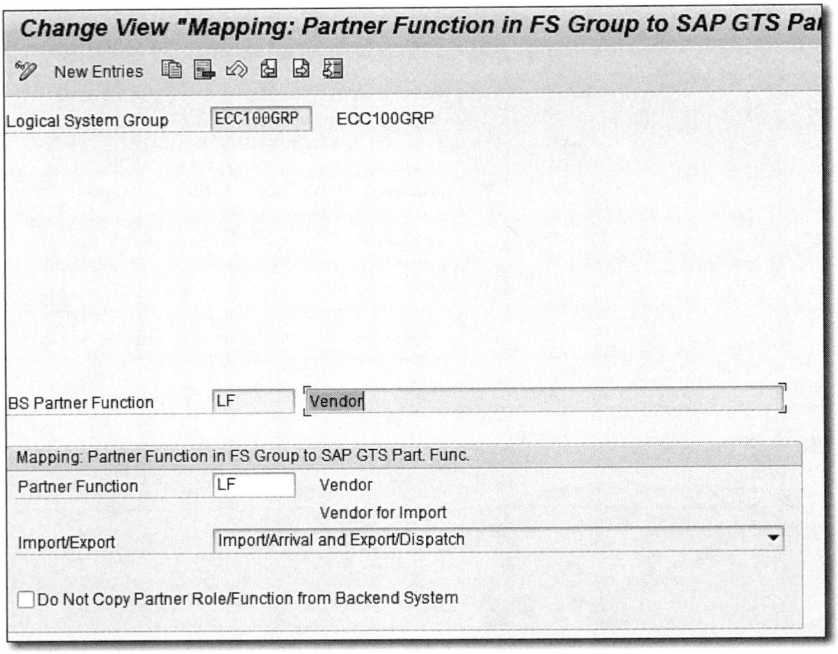

Figure 18.26 Mapping of Partner Type to the Feeder System Logical Group

Define the legal regulation

4. Define the customs regulations in SAP GTS to represent the importing regulation (Figure 18.27). Here you can define the customs procedure against which the key determinations are defined. Follow IMG menu path, SAP GLOBAL TRADE SERVICES • GENERAL SETTINGS • LEGAL REGULATIONS • DEFINE LEGAL REGULATIONS.

Review the predefined legal regulation

5. Review the predefined legal regulation (CUSUS for US), and ensure the TYPE OF LEGAL CODE (CUSTOMS PROCESSING), IMPORT/EXPORT (IMPORT/ARRIVAL), and ORIGINAL CITY OF LR (US) are correct.

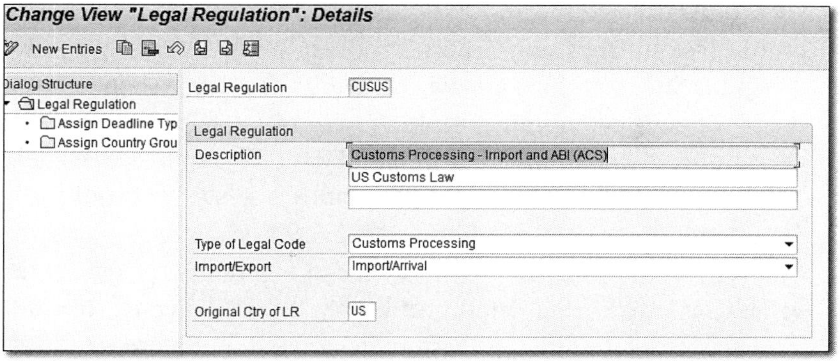

Figure 18.27 Define Legal Regulations

Assign the country or country group

6. Assign the country or country group (Figure 18.28). In this case, let's consider the example of a country group. You can choose to use a country group for legal regulation. Follow IMG menu path, SAP GLOBAL TRADE SERVICES • GENERAL SETTINGS • LEGAL REGULATIONS • DEFINE LEGAL REGULATION. Select the LEGAL REGULATION, and click the ASSIGN COUNTRY GROUP folder.

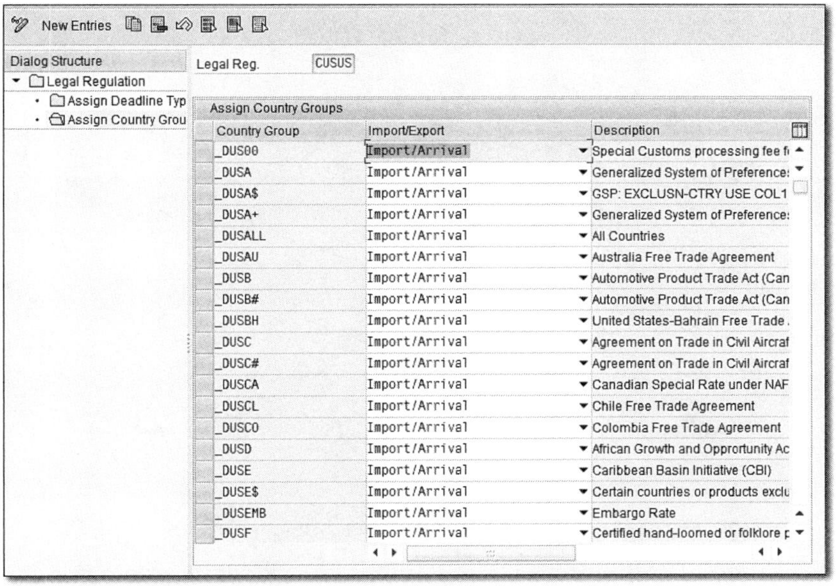

Figure 18.28 Assign the Country Group to the Legal Regulation

Set the determination procedure

7. Set the determination procedure. SAP GTS has a default determination procedure that you can use or make changes to as required. When the documents are transferred to SAP GTS, the system refers to the procedure to determine if a country or country group is used for legal regulation determination. Follow IMG menu path, SAP GLOBAL TRADE SERVICES • CUSTOM MANAGEMENT • DEFINE PROCEDURE FOR ACTIVE LEGAL REGULATIONS (Figure 18.29). Click the ASSIGNMENT OF DETERMINATION folder to see the screen in Figure 18.30. Review the default settings for the determination procedure delivered. In some implementations, define the custom determination procedures.

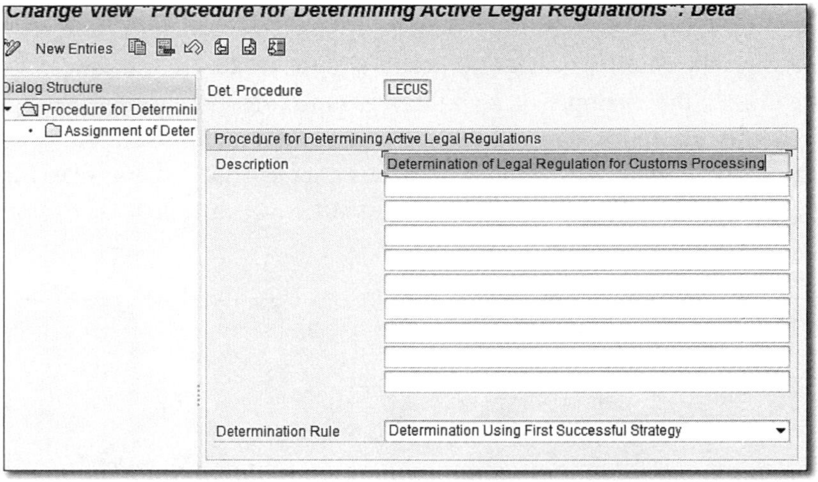

Figure 18.29 Define Determination Procedure for Active Legal Regulations

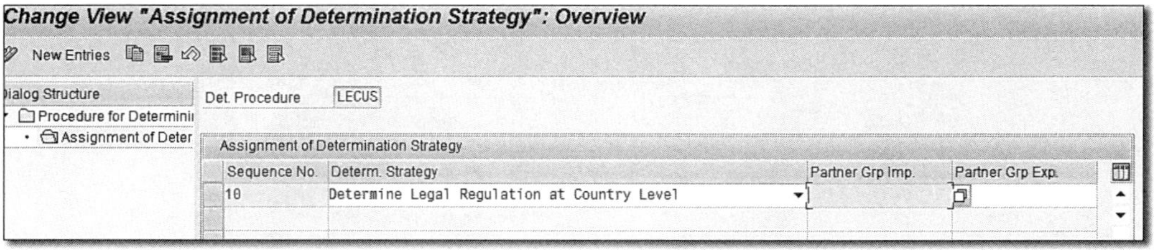

Figure 18.30 Define the Strategy within the Determination Procedure

Activate the legal regulation

8. Activate the legal regulation by following IMG menu path, SAP GLOBAL TRADE SERVICES • GENERAL SETTINGS • LEGAL REGULATION • ACTIVATE LEGAL REGULATIONS (Figure 18.31).

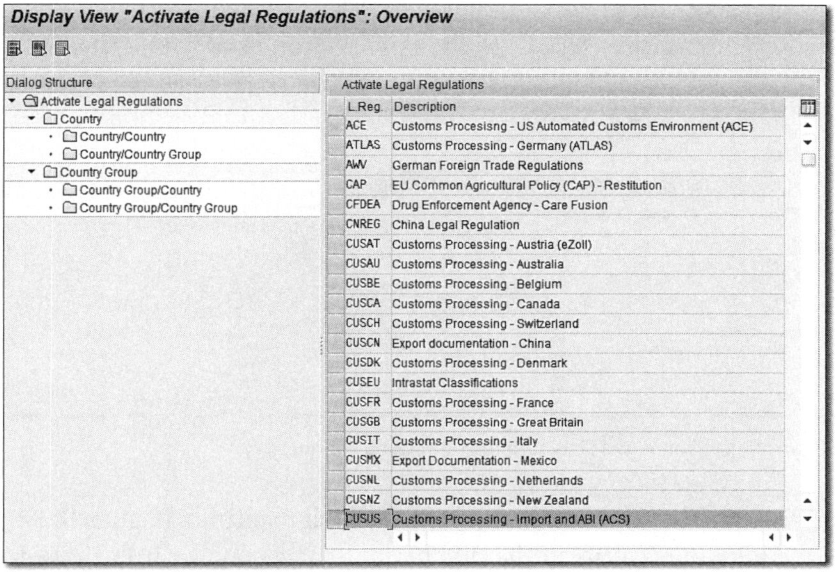

Figure 18.31 Activate Legal Regulations

Choose the Country or Country Group folder

9. You can choose between the COUNTRY and COUNTRY GROUP folder. If you select the COUNTRY folder, then you activate it at the country level (Figure 18.32). You can add entries by clicking the NEW ENTRIES button, which brings up the countries that are active for importing.

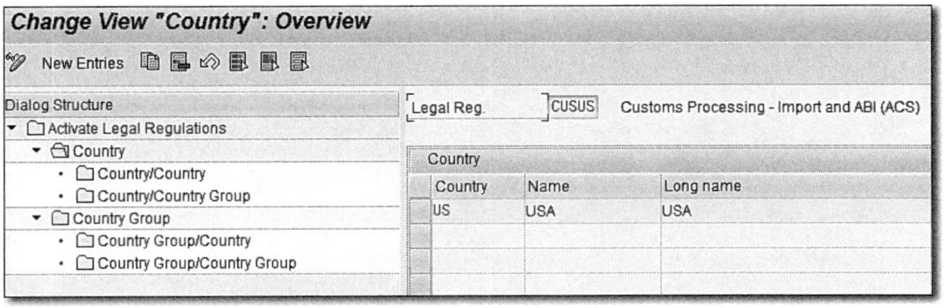

Figure 18.32 Country Activation for Legal Regulation

Define the harmonized tariff number structure

10. Define the harmonized tariff number structure (Figure 18.33). A harmonized tariff schedule is used for classifying your product and for import declaration of the products being imported. Follow IMG menu path, SAP GLOBAL TRADE SERVICES • GENERAL SETTINGS • NUMBERING SCHEME • DEFINE NUMBERING SCHEME OF TARIFF CODE

NUMBER. There are some predelivered numbering schemes from which you can select. Click the COPY AS icon to copy to a new numbering scheme. You can define a structure similar to what is shown in Figure 18.33.

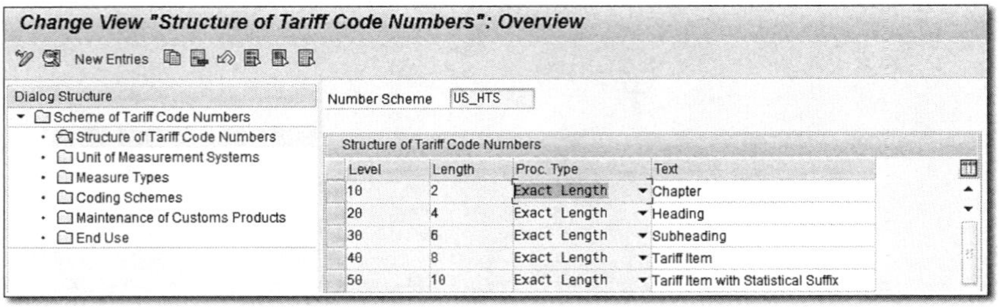

Figure 18.33 Define the Structure for Tariff Code Numbers

Assign the numbering scheme to the legal regulation

11. Assign the numbering scheme to the legal regulation (Figure 18.34). After you've defined the numbering scheme, assign it to the legal regulation for use with product classifications. Follow IMG menu path, SAP GLOBAL TRADE SERVICES • GENERAL SETTINGS • NUMBERING SCHEME • ASSIGN NUMBERING SCHEME OF TARIFF CODE NUMBER FOR CUSTOMS PROCESSING. Assign the IMPORT CTS TO THE EXPORT CTS for the legal regulation CUSUS.

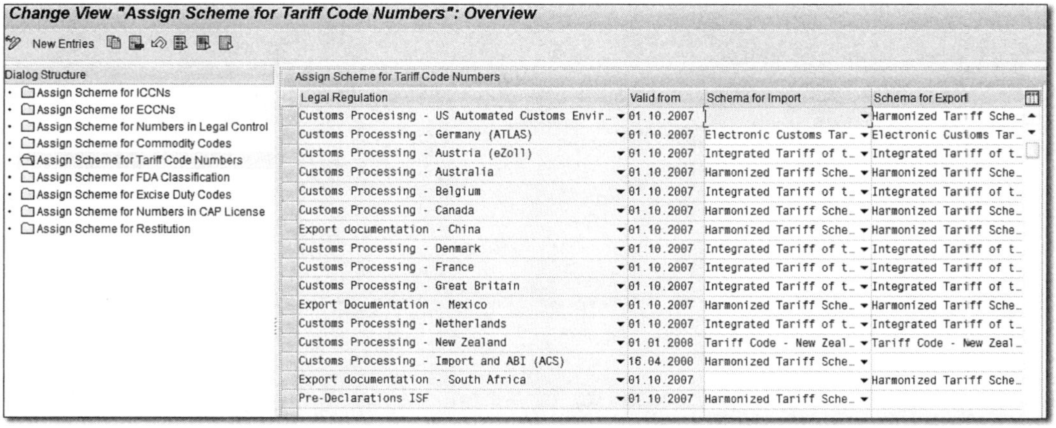

Figure 18.34 Assign a Numbering Scheme of Tariff Code Number for Customs Processing

12. Assign a foreign trade organization (FTO) and legal units (Figure 18.35). An FTO is the entity financially responsible for the shipment imported, and the legal unit represents the SAP ERP plant where the shipments are received. Follow IMG menu path, SAP GLOBAL TRADE SERVICES • GENERAL SETTINGS • ORGANIZATION STRUCTURE. DEFINE FOREIGN TRADE ORGANIZATION/LEGAL UNIT.

Assign a foreign trade organization (FTO) and legal units

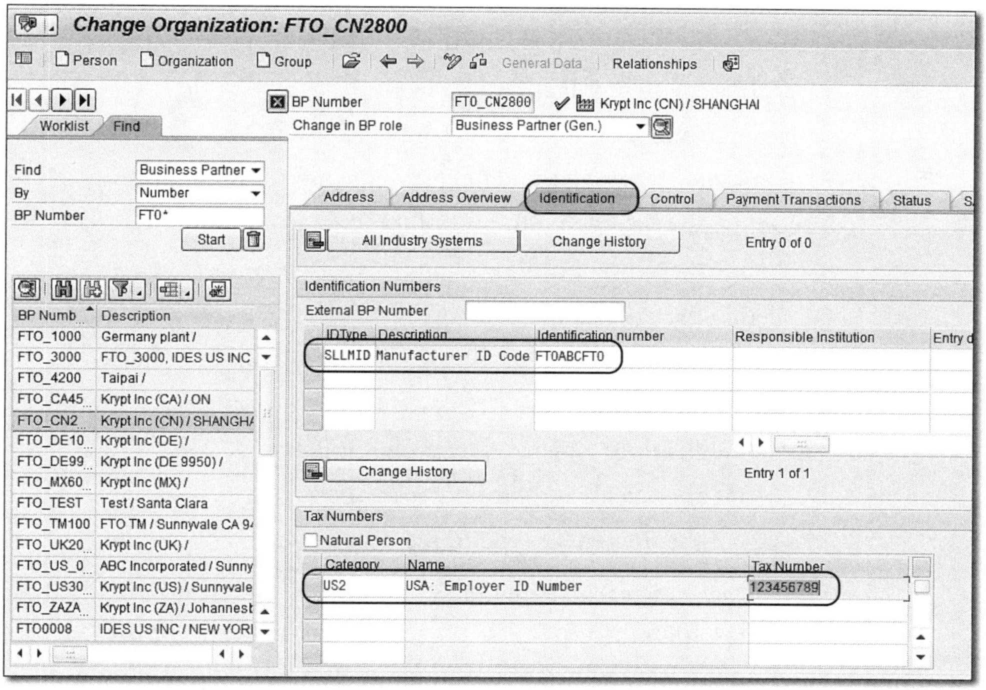

Figure 18.35 Define the FTO

That concludes the configuration of SAP GTS; however, there are SAP Customs Management settings within SAP GTS that need to be defined as described next.

18.6 Configuration Settings for SAP Customs Management

Continuing on the SAP GTS configuration setup, we're now moving on to the SAP Customs Management module. Similar to the previous sections, we'll start with an overview of the general process, and then we'll explore each step in further detail. The configuration of the customs management consists of the following

Customs Management configuration steps

1. Define the document types.
2. Activate the document type.
3. Map the customs declaration with the legal regulation.
4. Perform control settings for the document type.
5. Define the item category.
6. Map document type to the feeder system.
7. Map the item category defined.
8. Define the incompletion procedure.
9. Define the action profile.
10. Define the process template.
11. Define the custom status for the import process.
12. Map the package type to the logical feeder system.
13. Define the duty type for the custom declaration.
14. Define the calculation profile for the import.
15. Assign the document type to the duty profile.

Now let's look at each configuration steps in further detail. Follow these detailed steps:

Define document types

1. Define document types. Document types in SAP GTS define the processes that are carried out in the system for export or import declarations (Figure 18.36). Follow IMG menu path, SAP Global Trade Services • SAP Customs Management • Document Structure • Define Document Type. Click the Details (magnifying glass) icon to see the information shown in Figure 18.37. Ensure that there is a number range defined. Assign Document Type/Legal Regulation as the Access Control, and maintain the Partner Grouping from the predefined options in the dropdown menu.

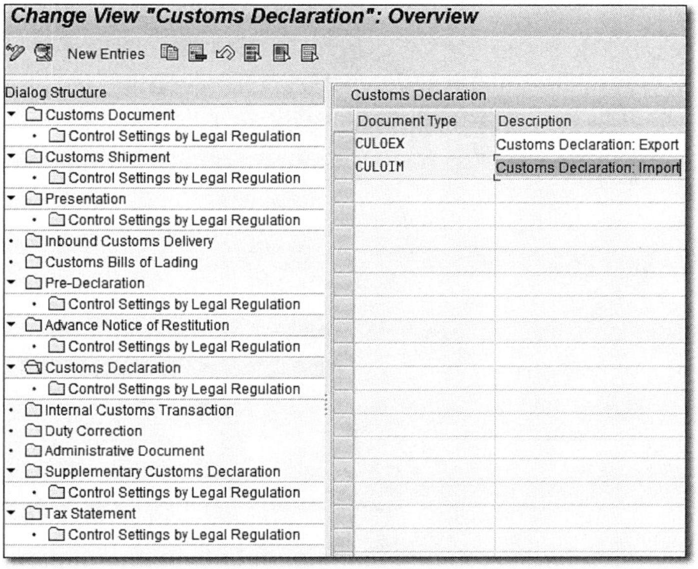

Figure 18.36 Define the Customs Document Type for Importing

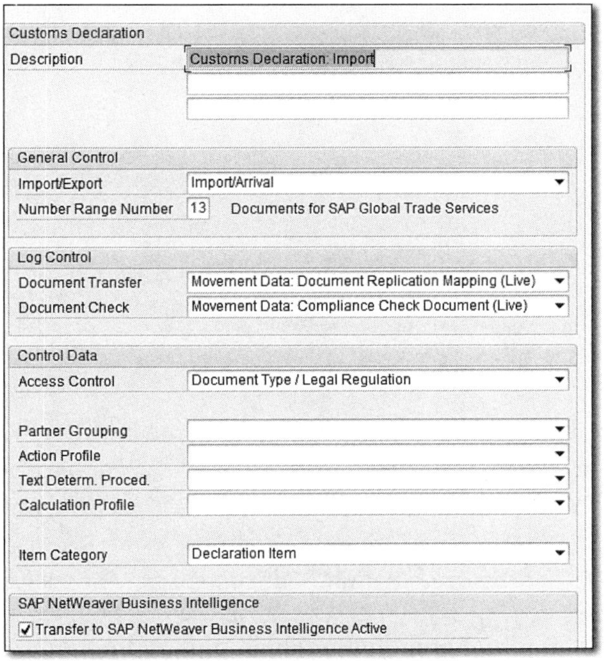

Figure 18.37 Detailed Configuration for the Import Declaration Document Type

Activate the document type

2. Document types are activated for different services: customs or transit. In this example, we just define customs. You need to activate the import declaration document types defined in the earlier step for import customs processing. Follow IMG menu path, SAP GLOBAL TRADE SERVICES • GENERAL SETTINGS • DOCUMENT STRUCTURE • ACTIVATE DOCUMENT TYPE (Figure 18.38).

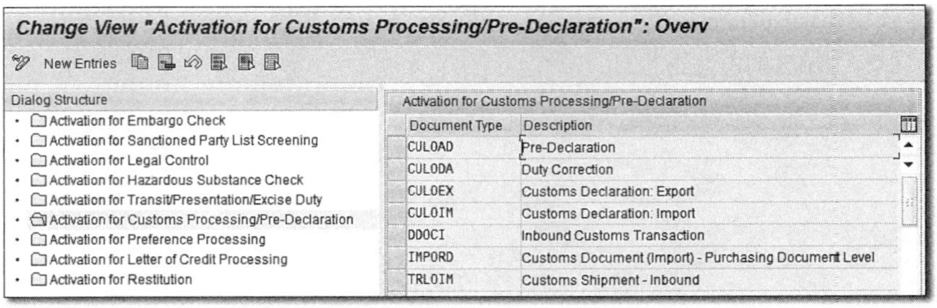

Figure 18.38 Activate the Document Type for Customs Processing

Map customs declaration with the legal regulation

3. Following the activation, the document types are mapped for determination (Figure 18.39). Follow IMG menu path, SAP GLOBAL TRADE SERVICES • GENERAL SETTINGS • DOCUMENT STRUCTURE • DEFINE CONTROL SETTINGS AT DOC TYPE LEVEL AND LEGAL REG. LEVEL FOR CD/CS.

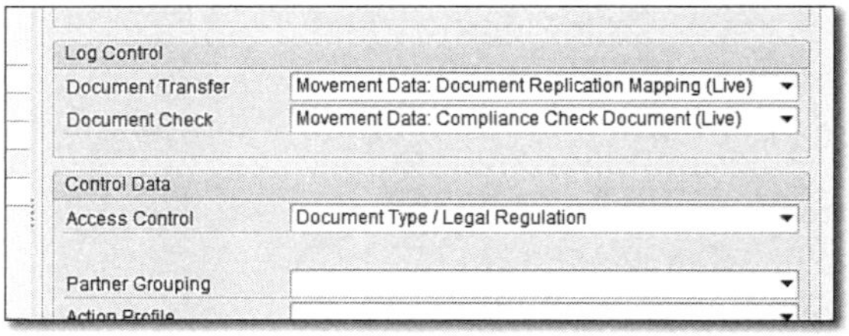

Figure 18.39 Control Data for Document Type or Legal Regulations

Perform control settings for the document type

4. Set up the control data based on the mapping with the document type and legal regulation. Follow IMG menu path, SAP GLOBAL TRADE SERVICES • GENERAL SETTINGS • DOCUMENT STRUCTURE • DEFINE CONTROL SETTINGS AT DOC TYPE LEVEL FOR CUSTOMS DOC AND LEGAL REGULATION (Figure 18.40). For the combination of document type and legal regulation, assign the ACTION PROFILE, PARTNER GROUP, TEXT DETERMINATION PROCEDURE, and CALCULATION PROFILE (Figure 18.41).

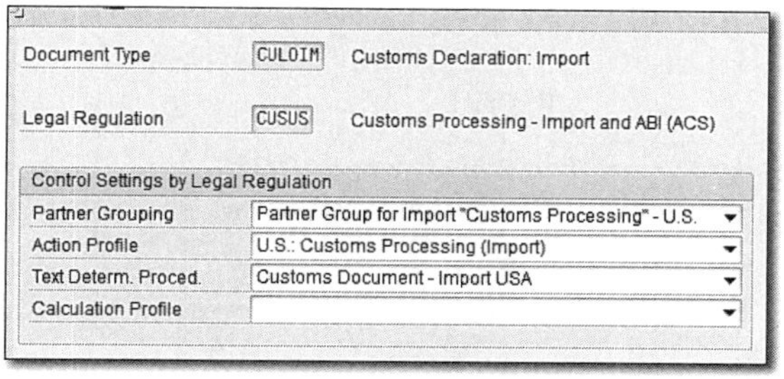

Figure 18.40 Control Data for Document Type or Legal Regulation

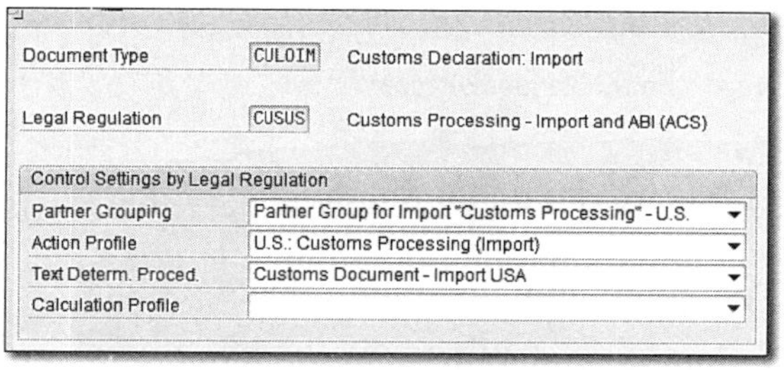

Figure 18.41 Define the Item Category

Define the item category

5. Follow IMG menu path, SAP GLOBAL TRADE SERVICES • GENERAL SETTINGS • DOCUMENT STRUCTURE • DEFINE ITEM CATEGORY. The settings are predelivered, but you need to ensure that the TRANSFER TO SAP NETWEAVER BUSINESS INTELLIGENCE ACTIVE checkbox is checked to make sure that the data is extracted to SAP NetWeaver BW for reporting purposes.

Map the document type to the feeder system document type

6. The document type defined in an earlier step is mapped to the feeder system. Follow IMG menu path, SAP GLOBAL TRADE SERVICES • GENERAL SETTINGS • DOCUMENT STRUCTURE • ASSIGNMENT OF THE DOCUMENT TYPE FROM FEEDER SYSTEMS.

Map the item category

7. Similar to the document type, you need to map the item category defined earlier to the feeder logical system group. Follow IMG menu path, SAP GLOBAL TRADE SERVICES • GENERAL SETTINGS • DOCUMENT STRUCTURE • ASSIGNMENT OF THE ITEM CATEGORY TYPE FROM FEEDER SYSTEMS (Figure 18.42). The screen shown in Figure 18.43 allows you to map the APPLICATION LEVEL (IMPORT FOR INBOUND DELIVERY) to the LOGICAL SYSTEM GROUP from the feeder system to the ITEM CATEGORY.

Assign the feeder system or SAP ERP item category to the SAP GTS item category that is defined.

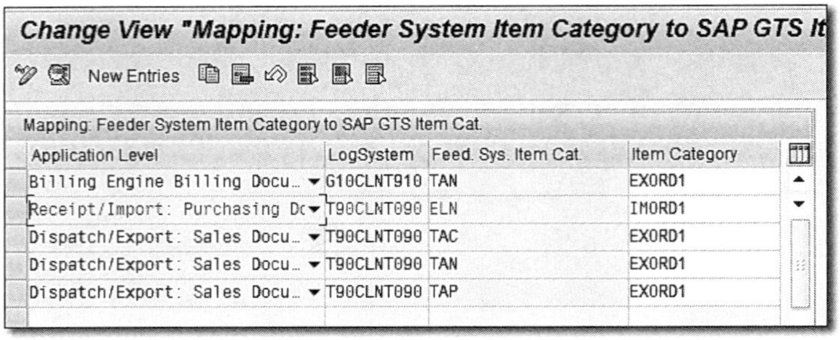

Figure 18.42 Map the Item Category to the Feeder System

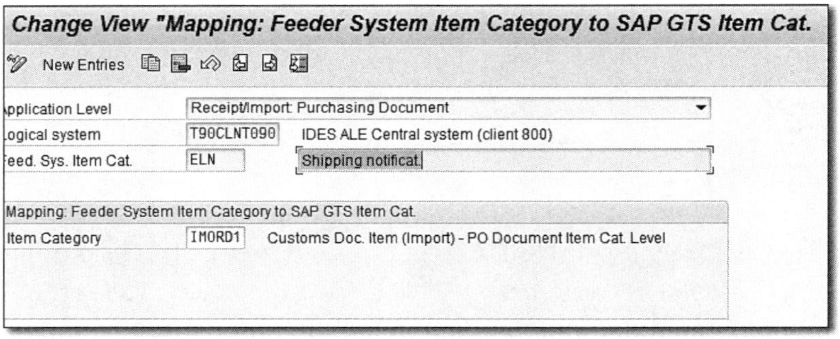

Figure 18.43 Details of the Configuration Mapping of the Item Category to the Feeder System

Define the incompletion procedure

8. Define the incompletion procedure (Figure 18.44). You use the incompletion procedure to check the completeness of the data before preparing it for import declaration. Follow IMG menu path, SAP GLOBAL TRADE SERVICES • GENERAL SETTINGS • DOCUMENT STRUCTURE • CONTROL INCOMPLETENESS CHECKS IN CUSTOMS SHIPMENTS AND CUSTOMS DECLARATIONS. This shows the fields that are checked for completeness. If you want to add any fields, you can do so via the NEW ENTRIES button.

Define the action profile

9. Under the action profile, you also can set action definitions (Figure 18.45). Follow IMG menu path, SAP GLOBAL TRADE SERVICES • GENERAL SETTINGS • COMMUNICATION PROCESSES • DEFINE TECHN. MEDIUM FOR MSGS (PPF ACTION) F. CUSTOMS SHIPMENT AND CUST. DECL. The

action profile consists of action definitions, and each action definition captures the details of the communication in terms of a print form or Intermediate Document (IDoc). It shows the associated OBJECT TYPE associated and the CLASS. Click the ACTION DEFINITION folder to see a list of action definitions assigned to the action profile (Figure 18.46).

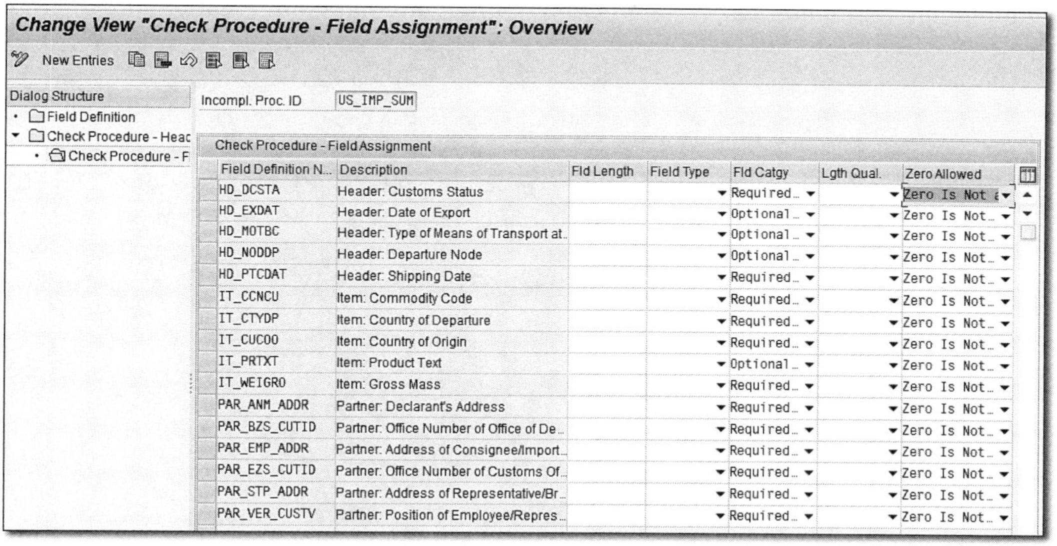

Figure 18.44 Field Assignment to the Incompletion Procedure

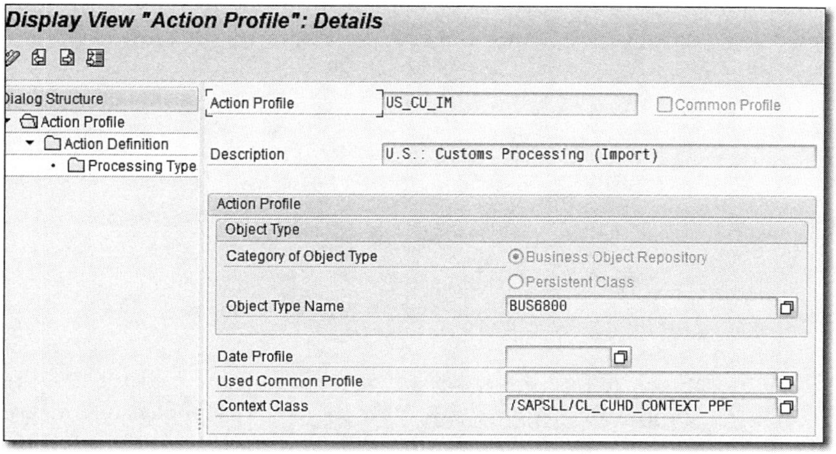

Figure 18.45 Define the Action Profile

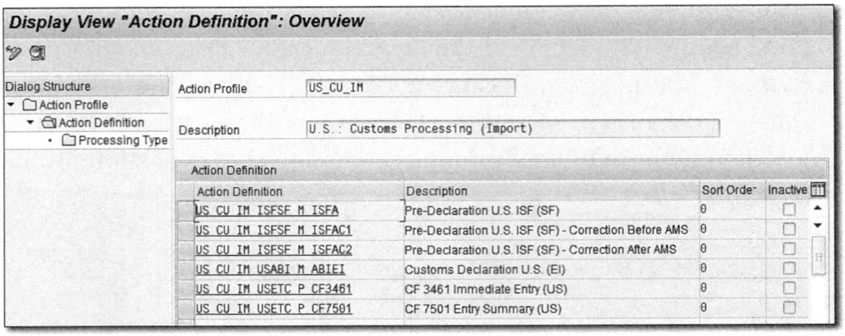

Figure 18.46 Action Definitions Defined within the Action Profile

In this example, we've defined several action definitions: CF 3461 FOR IMMEDIATE ENTRY and CF 7501 FOR ENTRY SUMMARY. You can select one of the action definitions and click the PROCESSING TYPE folder to see the details behind each action definition (Figure 18.47).

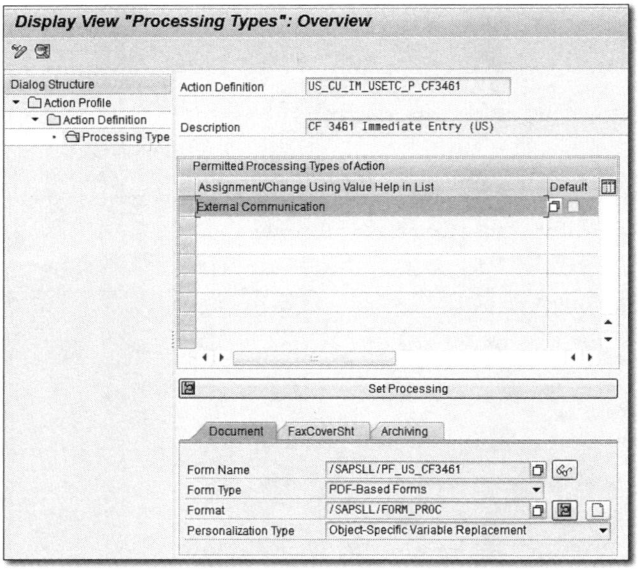

Figure 18.47 Processing Type Details Behind the Action Definitions

Define the process template

10. Here you can define the message type and output message (Figure 18.48). Follow IMG menu path, SAP GLOBAL TRADE SERVICES • GENERAL SETTINGS • COMMUNICATION PROCESSES • DEFINE CONTROL SETTINGS FOR COMMUNICATION PROCESSES.

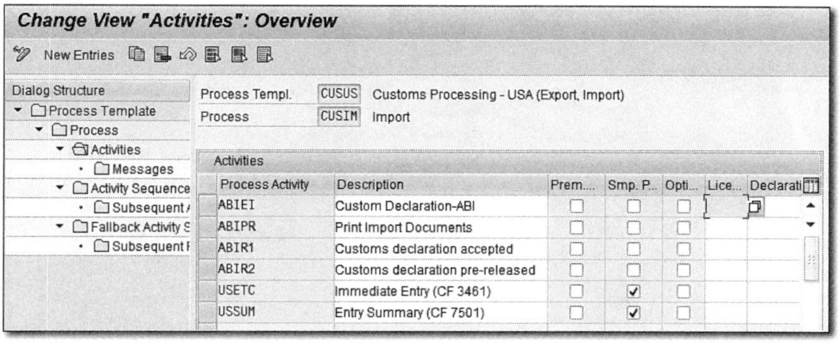

Figure 18.48 Process Overview of a Process Template for Customs Declarations

The Process Type CUSIM' captures the details of activities and messages defined for importing. While in the preceding configuration, select the process CUSIM and click Activities to bring up the screen in Figure 18.49. This shows the process activity within the process CUSIM (import). Select USETC, and click Messages to bring up the screen in Figure 18.50.

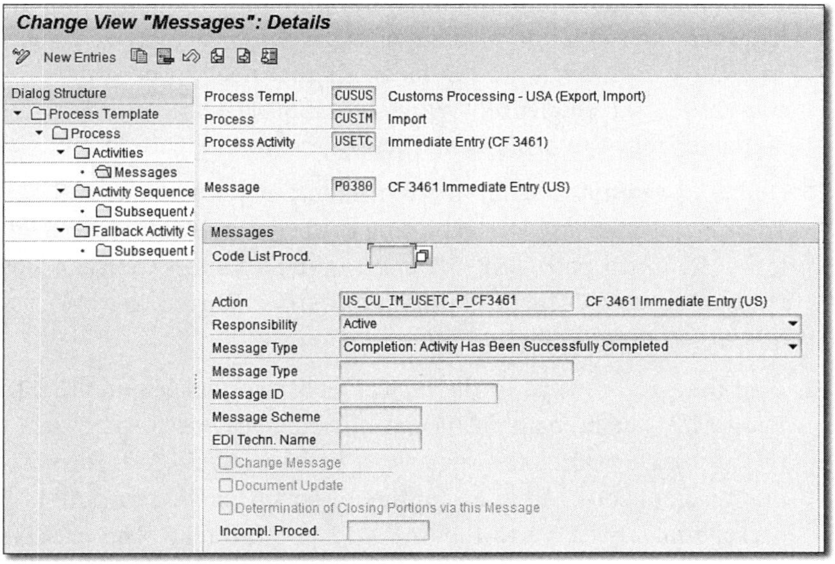

Figure 18.49 Activities Defined under Process CUSIM

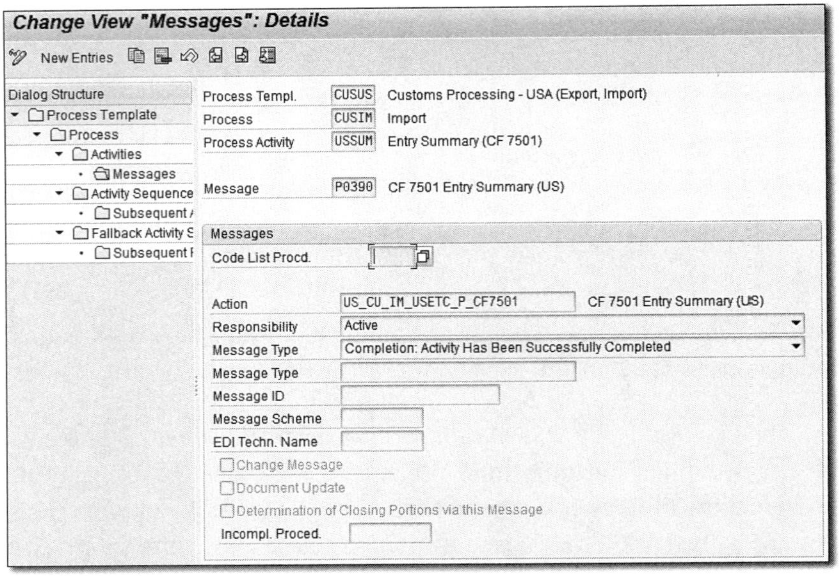

Figure 18.50 Message Definition under Process and Process Activity

Figure 18.50 shows the messages that are part of the process activity. These messages can be defined as part of the activity sequence. In other words, what are the messages that need to be printed or transmitted in sequence. While in CUSIM, click the ACTIVITY SEQUENCE folder to bring up the screen shown in Figure 18.51.

Define the customs status for the import process

11. Define the customs status for the import process (Figure 18.52). These statuses are used for reporting to the customs authorities. Follow IMG menu path, SAP GLOBAL TRADE SERVICES • GENERAL SETTINGS • CUSTOMS CODE LISTS • ASSIGN CUSTOMS STATUS TO A PROCESS AND LEGAL REGULATION.

Map the package type to the logical feeder system

12. Map the package type to the logical feeder system (Figure 18.53). Follow IMG menu path, SAP GLOBAL TRADE SERVICES • ASSIGNMENT OF PACKAGING MATERIALS TYPES FROM FEEDER SYSTEM. In this configuration step, you need to assign the feeder system or your SAP ERP package material type to the SAP GTS package type. The package type from SAP ERP can be a drum, cylinder, or carton, and you need to map it to a similar package type in SAP GTS.

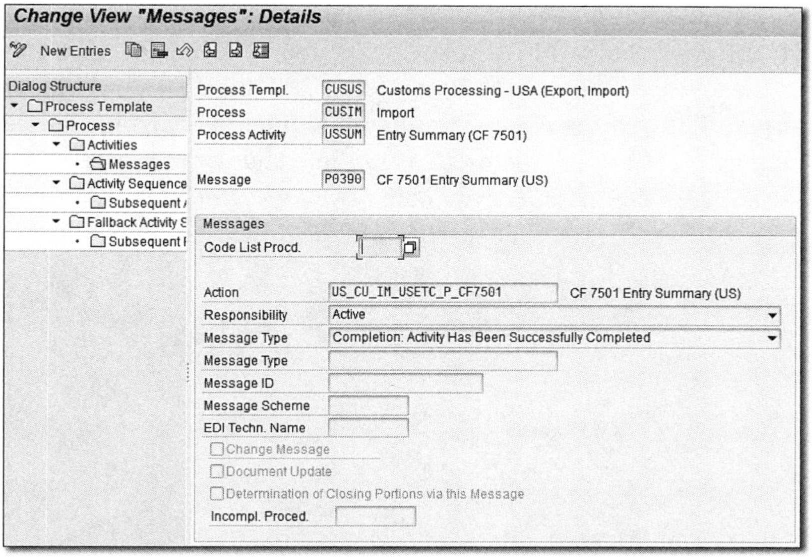

Figure 18.51 Activity Sequence Definition under Process Template and Process

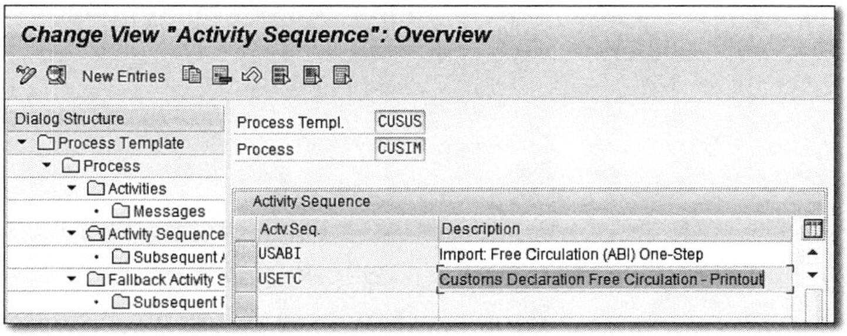

Figure 18.52 Assign the Custom Status to the Import Customs Process

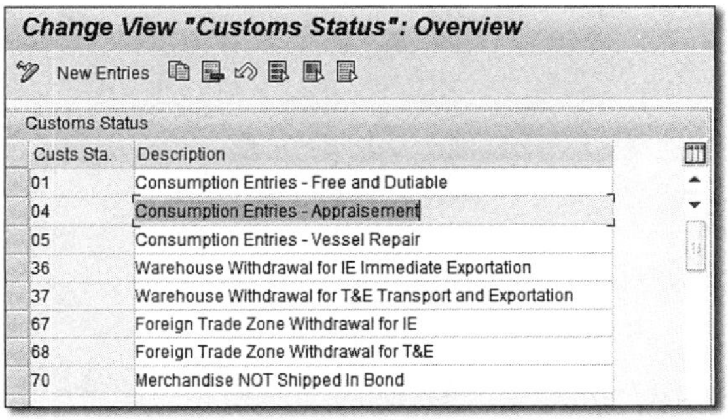

Figure 18.53 Assign the Packaging Type Material to the Feeder System

Define the duty type for the customs declaration

13. Define the duty type for the customs declaration (Figure 18.54). Follow IMG menu path, SAP Global Trade Services • SAP Customs Management • "Customs Processing" Services • Define Type of Customs Duty. The duty types shown are predelivered, but you can ensure the ones that are needed are there and the ones that aren't needed are not there. For example, if you don't need Preferential Customs Duty, you can delete it from the duty structure.

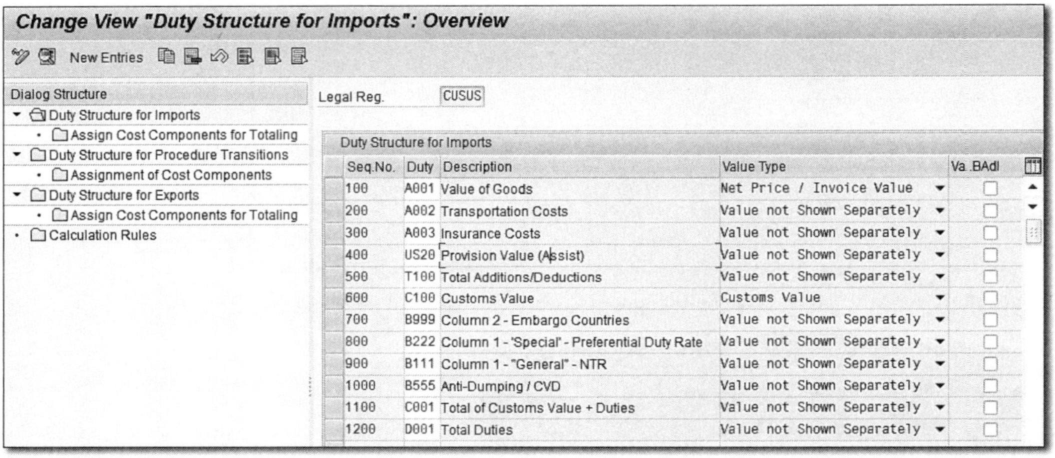

Figure 18.54 Define a Duty Structure for Import

Define the calculation profile for the import

14. Define the calculation profile for the import (Figure 18.55). Follow IMG menu path, SAP Global Trade Services • SAP Customs Management • "Customs Processing" Services • Configure Control Setting for Customs Duty Calculations. Assign a calculation profile in the Calc. Prof column, such as the custom one that we assigned called IMP_02.

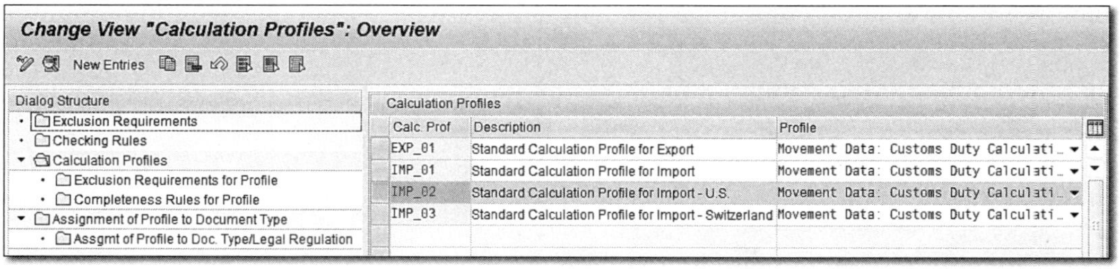

Figure 18.55 Define the Customs Duty Framework

Click the COMPLETENESS RULES folder to see the standard calculation profile for importing (Figure 18.56). Review the check rules that are predelivered within SAP GTS along with the type of duty associated.

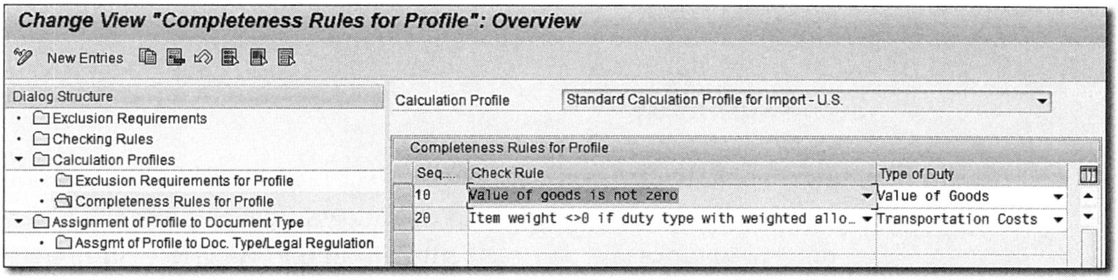

Figure 18.56 Calculation Profile Completeness Check for Profile

Assign the document type to the calculation profile.

15. Click the ASSIGNMENT OF PROFILE TO DOCUMENT TYPE folder in Figure 18.56 to get to this screen. Click on the ASSIGNMENT OF PROFILE TO DOCUMENT TYPE subfolder while you're in the screen shown in Figure 18.56. Assign the DUTY TYPE to the legal regulation for duty determination in the customs declaration document.

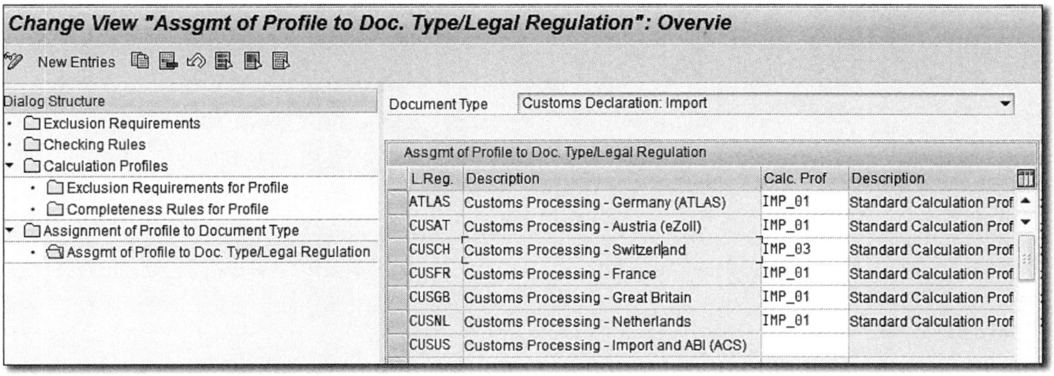

Figure 18.57 Assignment of Duty Type to the Customs Regulation

We reviewed the configuration setup for import declaration. As part of the ISF, there are 12 data elements that need to be sent to the customs authority: seller, buyer, importer of record number, consignee number, manufacturer (or supplier), ship-to party, country of origin, and the commodity's Harmonized Tariff Schedule of the United States (HTSUS) number. Two additional data elements—container stuffing location and consolidator—must be submitted as early as possible but no later than 24 hours prior to the ship's arrival at a US port. We've reviewed the configuration setup to enable these data elements that can be brought into the SAP GTS customs document for ISF.

18.7 Summary

In this chapter, we reviewed the import declarations and documentation requirement for goods coming into a country. We went over the different documentations and data elements within the SAP GTS customs declaration document. We looked at how to configure them and the important data that are required for different import filings. This importer filing is mandated and also important for compliance. We reviewed the integration requirement from SAP ERP to SAP GTS.

The next chapter provides a conclusion of this book and reviews what we've covered as a whole.

In our concluding chapter, we'll review our coverage of implementing SAP Governance, Risk and Compliance with a look at the GRC suite in total, review what we have discussed, the business benefits of an properly implemented GRC system and take a glimps at the future outlook of the suite.

19 Conclusion

An enterprise-wide, proactive, and systematic approach to risk management that is embedded into mainstream processes not only helps you make better decisions but also helps preserve and grow enterprise value. SAP Governance, Risk, and Compliance provides a unified platform across SAP Process Control, SAP Access Control, SAP Risk Management, and SAP Global Trade Services. SAP GTS is an integrated part of the supply chain compliance.

SAP GRC release 10 has provided the harmonization of the platform across all of the SAP GRC applications: SAP GTS, SAP Access Control, SAP Process Control, and SAP Risk Management. SAP GTS functionality is getting richer and stronger with the supply chain compliance, by integrating within your logistics or internal manufacturing. With SAP GTS 10.0, the integration with the SAP Transportation Management for outbound transportation was available out of the box. The integration of the supply chain from the inbound transaction is strengthened with the import self-filing for inbound transactions. This helps companies provide automated broker interfaces and supply chain compliance. As you've seen, every compliance aspect of your supply chain is very tightly integrated with your operation; for example, the screening of vendors impacts your inbound transactions and procurement, and the capture of your manufacturing in house or external sourcing impacts how the preference determination of a product. This integration helps accelerate the cross-border transactions with reduction in the cycle time using seamless integration and expedited inbound and outbound customs clearance.

Naturally, we would be remiss if we did not reflect upon the content coverage that we are covered in the book. Let's review what we have discussed in each chapter and some of the take-aways for our readers.

19.1 Chapter Review

- Chapter 1 provided an overview of the unified SAP GRC suite and foundation elements, such as shared master data and Content Lifecycle Management (CLM), that you needed to understand the concepts outlined throughout the book.
- Chapter 2 explains the core business to build an effective policy with a review of regulations and policies and the data structures that are in place to manage the compliance.
- Chapter 3 offered an in-depth look at SAP Access Control, including concepts, general assumptions made during implementation, and configurations.
- Chapter 4 addressed the tool set for Emergency Access Management that mitigates risk with workflows.
- Chapter 5 provided an overview of Access Risk Analysis to monitor risk associated with user roles.
  Chapter 6 described the business role manager, which helps manage the approval and creation of role types within SAP Access Control.
- Chapter 7 discussed User Access Management to manage requests through SAP Access Control, such as workflow approvals, custom fields, templates, and audits.
- Chapter 8 covered SAP Access Control advanced topics on integration with Emergency Access Management, Access Risk Analysis, and non-standard business roles.
- Chapter 9 started with the overview of SAP Process Control and business rule setup and assessment.

- Chapter 10 covered the SAP Process Control master data with policies, regulations, organization, business processes, and role assignments.
- Chapter 11 discussed continuous controls monitoring (CCM) with creating business rules, data source types, and related rules; assigning controls; and scheduling monitoring rules.
- Chapter 12 covered the advanced topics related to CCM of using advanced rule logic, using SAP NetWeaver BRF+, and performance consideration with change logging.
- Chapter 13 discussed SAP Process Control and SAP HANA with the SAP HANA virtual data model and SAP HANA Studio.
- Chapter 14 addressed some miscellaneous CCM topics that CCM users will find of great interest in their planned usage of SAP Process Control for monitoring.
- Chapter 15 explained the SAP Risk Management implementation process and how you can realize the value from the solution.
- Chapter 16 covered the SAP GTS with supply chain interfaces and preference setup.
- Chapter 17 covered the Environment, Health, and Safety (EH&S) setup from SAP Compliance Management.
- Chapter 18 covered the supply chain compliance with import filing.

19.2 Business Benefits of the GRC Suite

It is our ultimate hope that this title has clearly explore the benefits of a well-executed and configured GRC suite. Executives realize the importance of risk management for their companies but find it difficult to bring disparate pieces of data together to gain a clear view of the risks on an enterprise-wide basis. Risk management today is siloed with different departments or business units managing different types of risks: operational risks, financial risks, market risks, IT risks, human capital risks, EH&S risks, supply chain risks, and so on. Moreover, the risk management approach is project/program based, reactive in nature, and separate from mainstream processes and decision making. Very often, risk management methods are tactical, control/compliance focused with high costs, and low value added. As a result, risk management practitioners struggle to measure success or define return on investments. Lack of a standardized methodology with fragmented technologies worsens the situation.

19.3 GRC Suite and their Value

We've written an implementation guide for leveraging the full potential of the SAP GRC suite. As you've seen, each module has its advantages and disadvantages for an overall governance, risk, and compliance solution. As we conclude our implementation of the SAP GRC suite, let's revisit the modules themselves and their value.

SAP Risk Management helps organizations automate and coordinate their enterprise risk management activities. Risk ownership, risk assessments, surveys, simulations, incident management, and reporting and analytics provide reliable and accurate risk information that enables business users to make better decisions.

SAP Process Control delivers a control assessment and monitoring solution with strong underlying compliance themes. Organizations that have a strong motivation to achieve, track, and demonstrate compliance to regulations and policies greatly benefit from unifying the establishment and monitoring of their practices via SAP Process Control. In particular, the powerful CCM capabilities of SAP Process Control differentiate SAP Process Control from documentation and audit tools.

SAP Access Control helps companies meet their unique compliance requirements (e.g., documentation) and mitigate business process risks by monitoring access to critical business functions, by mitigating SoD risks with automated or manual controls defined in SAP Process Control, or performing standalone SoD risk remediation from the SAP Access Control perspective.

SAP Global Trade Services allows you to enable standardized, enterprise-wide compliance processes and mitigate financial risk. You can manage your screening of business partners, and streamline exports, import licenses, and embargo checks throughout your supply chain. You can seamlessly integrate with your supply chain and gain visibility with inbound and outbound transactions. You can exploit the trade preference agreements by determining the eligibility of products. SAP Risk Management also helps board members and C-suite executives answer simple questions and assist in their risk oversight role. Integration with SAP Process Control and SAP Access Control helps better mitigate enterprise risks. A strategic, objectives-based approach to enterprise risk management can also help improve business performance. Customers should be better served by considering an implementation plan for all of the three SAP GRC solutions together.

19.4 SAP GRC Future Outlook

There have been steady SAP advancements in the GRC space, with innovations in Global Trade Services, Environment, Health, and Safety, Continuous Control Monitoring and more. SAP has recognized the business need for a more comprehensive and responsive GRC suite. SAP Process Control has opened a great vista of opportunities for SAP customers and partners. One is the ability to monitor SAP HANA because this sets SAP Process Control customers up to take advantage of the enormous investment being made in SAP HANA by SAP, partners, and even other customers. As analytic and other content gets built for SAP ERP applications on SAP HANA, SAP Process Control customers can start consuming such content for monitoring.

The other recent advance is the ability to monitor SAP applications via Operational Data Provider (ODP). This eliminates the overhead of maintaining SAP NetWeaver BW servers, yet enables business intelligence tools such as Query Designer, Visual Analyzer, and so on to be used to craft custom queries. Such queries can now be used in SAP Process Control for monitoring.

Building on these advances, many SAP partners and even SAP itself is likely to deliver and update a lot of content suitable—either directly or with small tweaks—for monitoring.Reporting, long a customer pain point with earlier releases, is becoming ever more flexible and integrated. Improved integration between SAP GRC products will also enhance reporting because cross-SAP GRC reporting has always proven challenging.

In SAP GRC 10.0, SAP Access Control, SAP Process Control, SAP Risk Management, and SAP GTS are integrated, which allows the organization pervasive risk management across business processes and user access provisioning activities via risk reporting capabilities and by improving key automated monitoring . This product suite helps risk and compliance teams improve their ability to work with the business by managing risks and controls pervasively and within a single platform by leveraging the shared processes, data, and user interface across the SAP GRC 10.0 suite. Although each solution is run independently, the control catalog only needs to be created once and then shared across the suite. This simplifies and reduces the maintenance activities of SAP GRC systems.

In today's current dynamic and challenging heterogeneous environment of enterprises, the SAP GRC initiative can be handled more efficiently and effectively by newly harmonized SAP GRC 10.0 with increased scalability and integration between SAP and non-SAP products.

The Authors

Asokkumar Christian is currently leading the GRC practice of Krypt, Inc. With refined expertise, he continues to lead and successfully implement SAP GRC projects. He also guides various business and technical teams, including SAP EHS Management, SAP GTS, SAP Access Control/SAP Process Control, and SAP Risk Management.

Asok started his career in the service industry. Working alongside business teams, his cross-industry and cross-system experience in various core SAP ERP and SAP GRC solutions as technical and functional consultant exceeded expectations in delivering custom-built solutions. Asok honed his skills at SAP LABS in Palo Alto, California, as Regional Implementation Group Sr. Consultant by delivering and coordinating ramp-up activities with clients and the internal SAP team for SAP GRC solutions in SAP Process Control.

D. Rajen Iyer is a founder of product company, Kryaa, and co-founder of a fast growing supply chain solutions company, Krypt, Inc. He is recognized in the industry and by his peers as a supply chain and compliance solutions expert, an entrepreneur for innovative products and services, and a thought leader, with several patents and trademarks to his credit. He is the author of several SAP PRESS titles on supply chain, trade, and logistics. He is also an invited speaker at industry conferences. Rajen can be reached via email at *Rajen@kryptinc.com* or *Rajen@kryaa.com*.

Atul Sudhalkar is a product manager for SAP's Governance, Risk, and Compliance group at SAP's Palo Alto, California, offices. Before SAP, Atul worked as an architect and development manager at PeopleSoft. Atul holds engineering degrees from the Indian Institute of Technology and the University of Massachusetts at Amherst. He obtained a doctorate in engineering from Carnegie Mellon University, where his thesis research focused on computational geometry and geometric solid modeling. Atul holds several patents on product ideas he has developed and has several more patents pending in the United States and abroad.

The Contributor

Satyen Paneri is Senior Director for Solutions go-to-market at SAP. In this role, he is responsible for revenue growth, customer success, and portfolio effectiveness for the SAP Governance, Risk, and Compliance (SAP GRC) solutions. Over his five years at SAP, Satyen has been successful at formulating and driving key initiatives for revenue target achievement; planning and executing solutions in GTM; driving product innovation across numerous SAP technologies; and supporting product strategy and roadmaps with new market requirements.

In a career spanning more than 15 years in technology, Satyen is a seasoned professional with extensive large company and entrepreneurial enterprise software experience in product management, product marketing, and go-to-market. Satyen is a strategic and conceptual thinker with a proven ability to deliver innovative solutions for customers. Satyen holds an MBA from Santa Clara University and a bachelor's degree in computer science.

Index

A

B

S